KU-471-662

ELEMENTARY LEARNER'S

最新汉英初阶辞典

(第4版)

THE NEW CHINESE-ENGLISH DICTIONARY

胜友编辑部 编著
王竞波 修订

DANIEL OZORIO

世界图书出版公司
广州·上海·西安·北京

图书在版编目(CIP)数据

最新汉英初阶辞典/胜友编辑部编.—4版.—广州:广东世界图书出版公司,1999.12

ISBN 7-5062-2887-4

Ⅰ.最…　Ⅱ.胜…　Ⅲ.①英语-词典　②词典-汉、英　Ⅳ.H316

中国版本图书馆CIP数据核字(1999)第56439号

最新汉英初阶辞典

(第4版)

胜友编辑部 编著

王竞波 修订

广东世界图书出版公司 出版

广东世界图书出版公司发行

各地新华书店经销

广州大一印刷有限公司印刷

2005年2月第4版 开本:880×1280　1/64

2005年2月第8次印刷 12印张

ISBN 7-5062-2887-4/H·0024

版权贸易合同登记号:19-2001-168

出版社注册号:粤014

定价:15.90元

服务热线:020-84469182/84451969

前　言

一、这本辞典选收词、词组、成语等共一万八千余条，以日常生活常用词语为主。

二、辞典正文按汉语拼音方案的字母次序排列，同音同调的按汉字笔画多少排列，少的在前，多的在后。辞典附录共五个。(详见目录)

三、这本辞典采用笔画查字法。具体查字方法另见“笔画查字表”。

四、从学习中文的实际需要出发，我们对部分词条标注了常用量词；对一些词头、词尾标注了“头”或“尾”字样，对大部分词条标注了词性，所标词性，仅供参考。但由于语言的不同，少量词条的英译文词性与汉语词性不尽相符。

编者

目　录
Contents

词类简称表
Abbreviations of Parts of Speech

(名)	míng	名词	noun
(代)	dài	代词	pronoun
(动)	dòng	动词	verb
(助动)	zhùdòng	助动词	aux. verb
(形)	xíng	形容词	adjective
(数)	shù	数词	numeral
(量)	liàng	量词	measure word
(副)	fù	副词	adverb
(介)	jiè	介词	preposition
(连)	lián	连词	conjunction
(助)	zhù	助词	particle
(叹)	tàn	叹词	interjection
(象声)	xiàngshēng	象声词	onomatopoeia
(头)	tóu	词头	prefix
(尾)	wěi	词尾	suffix

笔画查字表

Character Stroke Index

〔说明〕

Notes on the use of the index

一、本表所列汉字按笔画多少排列；笔画少的在前，多的在后。同笔画的字，则按第一笔横（一）、竖（丨）、撇（丿）、点（丶）、横折（乛）、竖折（乚）先后排列。

Chinese characters in this index are arranged according to the number of strokes. Those with fewer strokes come first, followed by those with more strokes. Characters with the same number of strokes are arranged according to the order of the first stroke of the character. The order is：（一），（丨），（丿），（丶），（乛），（乚）

二、"一丨丿丶乛乚"以外的笔形按下面的办法处理：

Apart from the "一丨丿丶乛乚", all the other strokes are arranged as follows：

1.（㇀ ㇀）are taken as （一）

2.（亅 ㇁）are taken as （丨）

3.（㇒ ㇒ ㇒）are taken as （丿）

4.（㇏ ㇏ ㇏）are taken as （丶）

5.（㇖ ㇆ ㇌ ㇋ ㇇ ㇂ ㇅ ㇉）are taken as （乛）

6.（ㄐ ㄟ ㄑ ㄥ ㄣ）are taken as （ㄥ）

三、有些字的笔画容易数错，为方便使用者查阅起见，本辞典采用两开门的办法。如："马"在三画和四画、"母"在五画和六画、"好"在六画和七画、"那"在六画和七画、"这"在七画和八画里都可以查到。

Certain strokes of Chinese characters are liable to be miscounted. Therefore, for the convenience of the user, the method of double entry is adopted, e.g. "马" is placed under three strokes and also under four strokes, "母" under five and six strokes, "好" under six and seven strokes, "那" under six and seven strokes, "这" under seven and eight strokes, and so on.

五画

5 strokes

六画
6 strokes

七 画
7 strokes

八　画
8 strokes

[ㄱ]

[ㄴ]

九 画
9 strokes

[一]

十画
10 strokes

十一画
11 strokes

十二画
12 strokes

十三画
13 strokes

十五画
15 strokes

十六画 16 strokes

十七画 17 strokes

十八画
18 strokes

十九画
19 strokes

二十画
20 strokes

二十一画
21 strokes

二十二画
22 strokes

二十三画
23 strokes

二十四画
24 strokes

A

ā

阿[ā]

另见 ē

〖阿斗〗(名)[ādǒu]

a weak-minded person; fool

〖阿飞〗(名)[āfēi]

hooligan; young rowdy

〖阿訇〗(名)[āhōng]

ahung; imam

〖阿拉伯数字〗(名)[ālābóshùzì]

Arabic numerals

〖阿姨〗(名)[āyí]

① auntie (a child's form of address for any woman about his mother's age) ② nurse (in a family)

啊(叹)[ā]

int. exclamation of surprise or admiration (e.g. ah; eh; oh; oho)

另见 a

a

啊(助)[a]

a modal particle

另见 ā

āi

哎(叹)[āi]

int. exclamation of surprise or regret

〖哎呀〗(叹)[āiyā]

int. exclamation of surprise (e.g. Aah! Ho! Dear me! Oh my!)

〖哎哟〗(叹)[āiyō]

int. exclamation of surprise or cry of pain or misery (e.g. Good gracious! Goodness me! Oh dear! Ouch!)

哀[āi]

〖哀悼〗(动)[āidào]

mourn for (the dead); lament or grieve over (sb.'s death); express condolences (on the death

A

of ...)
〖哀求〗(动)[āiqiú]
beg; implore; beseech
〖哀思〗(名)[āisī]
grief; sad memories (of the dead)
〖哀叹〗(动)[āitàn]
sigh in sorrow; lament; bewail
〖哀乐〗(名)[āiyuè]
funeral music; dirge

唉(叹)[āi]
① *int.* used as an answer to sb.'s call (e.g. Right! Yes!) ② *int.* used in the form of sigh (e.g. Alas!)
另见 ài
〖唉声叹气〗[āishēngtànqì]
heavy deep sighs; moan and groan; sigh in despair

挨(动)[āi] ① be close to; approach ② from (house) to (house)
另见 ái
〖挨次〗(副)[āicì]
(do sth.) in sequence or one after the other; by turns; in succession
〖挨个儿〗(副)[āigèr]
one by one; one after another
〖挨近〗(动)[āijìn]
be close by; come close to (person)
〖挨门挨户〗[āiménāihù]
go from door to door

ái

呆[ái]
另见 dāi
〖呆板〗(形)[áibǎn]
inflexible (tactics); wooden (face); mechanical (interpretation, etc.); rigid; fixed

挨(动)[ái]
suffer; undergo; come in for
另见 āi
〖挨打〗(动)[áidǎ]
suffer a beating; be trounced and beaten
〖挨饿〗(动)[áiè]
suffer from hunger; driven by hunger
〖挨骂〗(动)[áimà]
get a good scolding

癌(名)[ái] cancer
〖癌扩散〗(名)[áikuòsàn]
proliferation of cancer
〖癌细胞〗(名)[áixìbāo]
cancer cell

ǎi

矮(形)[ǎi]
short (person); low (stool, house, etc.)
〖矮小〗(形)[ǎixiǎo]
short and small
〖矮子〗(名)[ǎizi]
a short person; dwarf

ài

艾(名)[ài]
argy wormwood

〖艾滋病〗(名)[àizībìng]
Aids, AIDS (Acquired Immune Deficiency Symptoms)

唉(叹)[ài]
exclamation of pity or distress
另见 āi

爱(动)[ài]
① love; be in love ② like; be in the habit of; be fond of ③ be prone to
〖爱不释手〗[àibùshìshǒu]
fondle admiringly
〖爱财如命〗[àicáirúmìng]
love money like one's very life
〖爱称〗(名)[àichēng]
a pet or affectionate name
〖爱戴〗(动)[àidài]
(win) genuine affection; love and support; love with profound respect; revere
〖爱抚〗(动)[àifǔ] caress
〖爱国〗[ài guó]
be patriotic; love one's country
〖爱国人士〗(名)[àiguórénshì]
patriotic personage
〖爱国卫生运动〗(名)
[àiguówèi shēngyùndòng]
patriotic public health campaign
〖爱国者〗(名)[àiguózhě]
patriot
〖爱国主义〗(名)[àiguózhǔyì]
patriotism
〖爱好〗(动、名)[àihào]
〖爱好〗(动、名)[àihào]
① love for; cherish (justice, etc.) ② be fond of; take a liking to; hobby; taste; liking
〖爱好者〗(名)[àihàozhě]
amateur; enthusiast; fan; lover (of art, sports, etc.)
〖爱护〗(动)[àihù]
show genuine affection for; cherish; concern for; look after well; take loving care of
〖爱理不理〗[àilǐbùlǐ]
look cold and indifferent; be standoffish
〖爱面子〗[àimiànzi]
keep up appearances; keen on facesaving
〖爱莫能助〗[àimònéngzhù]
willing to help but unable to do so
〖爱慕〗(动)[àimù]
love; adore
〖爱情〗(名)[àiqíng]
love
〖爱人〗(名)[àiren]
① husband; wife ② sweetheart
〖爱屋及乌〗[àiwūjíwū]
love for a person extends even to the crows on his roof; love me, love my dog
〖爱惜〗(动)[àixī]
① hold ... dear; well care for ② use ... sparingly; treasure; cherish
〖爱憎分明〗[àizēngfēnmíng]
unequivocal love and hatred; recognise whom to love and whom to hate; be clear about what to

A

love and what to hate

碍 (动)[ài]
hinder; stand in the way of
〖碍事〗[ài shì]
detrimental; highly inconvenient
〖碍于情面〗[àiyúqíngmiàn]
for fear of hurting sb.'s feelings; just to spare sb.'s feelings

暧 [ài]
〖暧昧〗(形)[àimèi]
① vague; ambiguous (meaning, attitude) ② equivocal; shady (behaviour)

ān

安 (动)[ān]
fix; install
〖安插〗(动)[ānchā]
place in a certain position; assign to a job (e.g. put one's trusted followers in key positions)
〖安定〗(形、动)[āndìng]
① stable;stabilize;settle down to ② be reassured
〖安定人心〗[āndìngrénxīn]
reassure the public; set people's minds at rest
〖安定团结〗[āndìngtuánjié]
stability and unity
〖安分守己〗[ānfènshǒujǐ]
① law abiding; abide by the law and behave oneself ② be contented with one's lot
〖安家落户〗[ānjiāluòhù]
settle down in; make one's home
〖安静〗(形)[ānjìng]
peaceful and serene; quiet; tranquil (conditions)
〖安居乐业〗[ānjūlèyè]
live and work in peace and contentment
〖安乐死〗(名)[ānlèsǐ]
euthanasia
〖安乐窝〗(名)[ānlèwō]
cosy nest; bed of roses; place of ease and comfort; an easy, comfortable life
〖安乐椅〗(名)[ānlèyǐ]
easy chair
〖安眠药〗(名)[ānmiányào]
sleeping-pill
〖安民告示〗(名)[ān mín gàoshì]
notice to reassure the public
〖安宁〗(形)[ānníng]
① peaceful; free from troubles ② free from worries; (be) easy in mind
〖安排〗(动)[ānpái]
arrange
〖安培〗(量)[ānpéi]
ampere
〖安全〗(形)[ānquán]
safe; secure
〖安全带〗(名)[ānquándài]
seat belt; safety belt
〖安全岛〗(名)[ānquándǎo]
safety island; pedestrian island
〖安全理事会〗(名)

[ānquán lǐshìhuì]
Security Council (of the United Nations)
〖安全帽〗(名)[ānquánmào]
helmet; protective cap
〖安全门〗(名)[ānquánmén]
emergency exit
〖安全系数〗(名)[ānquánxìshù]
safety coefficient
〖安危〗(名)[ānwēi]
security and danger
〖安慰〗(动)[ānwèi]
comfort; console
〖安稳〗(形)[ānwěn]
calm; steady; safe and secure
〖安息〗(动)[ānxī]
rest in peace (R.I.P.)
〖安详〗(形)[ānxiáng]
serene; leisurely; unhurried
〖安心〗(形)[ānxīn]
feel at ease; set one's mind at rest; be free from worries
〖安逸〗(形)[ānyì]
leisurely and comfortable
〖安营扎寨〗[ānyíngzhāzhài]
make camp; encamp
〖安置〗(动)[ānzhì]
place ... in certain post; arrange; make arrangement for
〖安置费〗(名)[ānzhìfèi]
settlement allowance (e.g. settlement allowance to be determined by a worker's length of service)
〖安装〗(动)[ānzhuāng]
install; fix; erect; mount; assemble

鞍(名)[ān]
saddle
〖鞍部〗(名)[ānbù]
saddle (of a hill or mountain)
〖鞍马〗(名)[ānmǎ]
pommelled horse; side horse (gymnastics)
〖鞍马劳顿〗[ānmǎláodùn]
travel-worn

鹌[ān]
〖鹌鹑〗(名)[ānchún]
quail

àn

岸[àn]
bank (of a river); shore; coast; beach

按[àn]
① press (e.g. button) ② hold something back ③ press something down ④ according to
〖按比例〗[ànbǐlì]
pro rata; in proportion
〖按兵不动〗[ànbīngbùdòng]
① keep troops entrenched ② bide one's time; take no action
〖按部就班〗[ànbùjiùbān]
follow the prescribed order; keep to conventional ways of doing things
〖按键〗(名)[ànjiàn]
button (e.g. push-button for selecting wavebands)
〖按揭〗(名)[ànjiē]

loan; mortgage (e.g. purchase an apartment with a loan from the bank or from the collective housing funds; the bank to provide a 50% mortgage)
〖按劳分配〗[ànláofēnpèi]
to each according to his work; distribution according to labour
〖按脉〗[ànmài]
feel the pulse; take the pulse
〖按摩〗(动、名)[ànmó]
massage
〖按期〗(片)[àn qī]
according to the agreed dates
〖按时〗(片)[àn shí]
according to scheduled or prescribed time; (fulfil ... plan) on schedule
〖按说〗(连)[ànshuō]
by rights or logically; according to reason
〖按图索骥〗[àntúsuǒjì]
look for a steed with the aid of its picture; try to locate sth. by following up a clue
〖按下葫芦浮起瓢〗
[ànxiàhúlufúqǐpiáo]
hardly has one gourd been pushed under water when another bobs up; (fig.) solve one problem only to find another cropping up
〖按需分配〗[ànxūfēnpèi]
to each according to his needs
〖按语〗(名)[ànyǔ]
comment; (editor's, author's) note or remarks
〖按照〗(介)[ànzhào]
in accordance with (the circumstances); taking (each case) on its merits

案(名)[àn]
① legal case ② a big table
〖案件〗(名)[ànjiàn]
legal case; court case
〖案卷〗(名)[ànjuàn]
records; archives; dossier; files
〖案例〗(名)[ànlì]
case; example of case
〖案情〗(名)[ànqíng]
the facts of a legal case
〖案子〗(名)[ànzi]
① a case at court ② a big table

暗(形)[àn]
① dark ② secret
〖暗藏〗(动)[àncáng]
hide; conceal
〖暗淡〗(形)[àndàn]
①dim; dull (of colour); dismal (picture) ② bleak (future)
〖暗地里〗(副)[àndìli]
secretly; behind sb.'s back
〖暗害〗(动)[ànhài]
① murder or injure secretly; sabotage ② stab sb. in the back
〖暗号〗(名)[ànhào]
secret sign; password
〖暗盒〗(名)[ànhé]
magazine; cassette (for placing film in a camera)
〖暗箭伤人〗[ànjiànshāngrén]

stab sb. in the back; injure sb. by underhand means; slander sb. behind his back
〖暗礁〗(名)[ànjiāo]
hidden rock; submerged reef
〖暗流〗(名)[ànliú]
undercurrent
〖暗杀〗(动)[àn shā]
assassinate
〖暗示〗(动)[ànshì]
hint; imply
〖暗送秋波〗[ànsòngqiūbō]
make eyes at sb.; make secret overtures to sb.
〖暗算〗[ànsuàn]
plot against
〖暗无天日〗[ànwútiānrì]
complete darkness; total absence of justice
〖暗笑〗[ànxiào]
laugh in one's sleeve; snigger
〖暗指〗(动)[ànzhǐ]
hint at; imply
〖暗中〗(名、副)[ànzhōng]
in secret; secretly; furtively

āng

肮[āng]
〖肮脏〗(形)[āngzāng]
dirty; filthy

áng

昂[áng]
〖昂贵〗(形)[ángguì]
very expensive; dear
〖昂首阔步〗[ángshǒukuòbù]
march forward with head high

āo

凹(形)[āo]
concave; hollow
〖凹透镜〗(名)[āotòujìng]
concave lens
〖凹凸不平〗[āotūbùpíng]
full of bumps and holes; uneven
〖凹陷〗(形)[āoxiàn]
hollow; sunken; depressed

熬(动)[āo]
boil (vegetables); cook in water
另见 áo

áo

熬[áo]
① stew ② decoct (medicinal herbs) ③ endure; pull through
另见 āo
〖熬夜〗[áo yè]
stay up all night; (work) far into the night

遨[áo]
〖遨游〗(动)[áoyóu]
roam; stroll; travel

翱[áo]
〖翱翔〗(动)[áoxiáng]
soar; sail; wheel in the air

ǎo

袄(名)[ǎo]〔件 jiàn〕
lined jacket

A

ào

傲[ào]

〖傲骨〗(名)[àogǔ]
lofty and unyielding character

〖傲慢〗(形)[àomàn]
haughty; impudent; arrogant

〖傲气〗(名、形)[àoqì]
overbearing pride; arrogant

奥[ào]

〖奥妙〗(形)[àomiào]
mysterious; wonderful

懊[ào]

〖懊悔〗(形)[àohuǐ]
regretful; repentant; remorseful

〖懊恼〗(形)[àonǎo]
annoyed; vexed; displeased

〖懊丧〗(形)[àosàng]
dismayed; dispirited; downcast

拗[ào]

〖拗口〗(形)[àokǒu]
另见 niù
hard to pronounce; awkward-sounding

bā

八(数)[bā]
eight
〖八宝饭〗(名)[bābǎofàn]
eight-treasure rice pudding
〖八成〗(副)[bāchéng]
①eighty per cent ②most probably; most likely
〖八角形〗(名)[bājiǎoxíng]
octagon
〖八九不离十〗[bājiǔbùlíshí]
pretty close; very near; about right
〖八开〗(名)[bākāi]
octavo; 8vo
〖八路军〗(名)[Bālùjūn]
the Eighth Route Army
〖八面玲珑〗[bāmiànlínglóng]
be smooth and slick (in establishing social relations)
〖八仙过海,各显神通〗
[bāxiānguòhǎigèxiǎnshéntōng]
like the Eight Immortals crossing the sea, each one showing his or her special prowess
〖八小时工作制〗
[bāxiǎoshí gōngzuòzhì]
eight-hour day
〖八一建军节〗(名)
[bā yī jiàn jūnjié]
August 1st Army Day (of the Chinese People's Liberation Army)
〖八月〗(名)[bāyuè]
August
〖八字没(见)一撇〗
[bāzìméi (jiàn)yīpiě]
there's not the slightest sign of anything happening yet

巴(动)[bā]
① hope earnestly; wait anxiously ② cling to; stick to
〖巴不得〗(副)[bābude]
only too glad to; earnestly hope
〖巴结〗(动)[bājie]
toady; curry favour with; fawn

B

on

〖巴望〗(动)[bāwàng]
look forward to

〖巴掌〗(名)[bāzhǎng]
① palm ② a slap with the open palm

扒 (动)[bā]
① take hold of ② pull down; tear down (house) ③ peel; strip off
另见 pá

芭 [bā]

〖芭蕉扇〗(名)[bājiāoshàn]
palm-leaf fan

〖芭蕾舞〗(名)[bālěiwǔ]
ballet

疤 (名)[bā]
scar

bá

拔 (动)[bá]
pull out; pluck; extract (a tooth)

〖拔除〗(动)[báchú]
uproot; eradicate

〖拔河〗(名)[báhé]
tug of war

〖拔尖儿〗[bá jiānr]
① out-standing; top-notch ② self-glorification

〖拔苗助长〗[bámiáozhùzhǎng]
(lit.) try to make rice shoots grow by pulling or stretching; (fig.) spoil things by being too impatient and subjective

跋 (名)[bá]
postscript (in a book)

〖跋扈〗(形)[báhù]
domineering; bullying; bossy

〖跋山涉水〗[báshānshèshuǐ]
(lit.) scale mountains and ford streams; (fig.) make an arduous journey

〖跋涉〗(动)[báshè]
cross land and water (a difficult journey); trek; trudge

bǎ

把 (动、名、量、介)[bǎ]
① hold; grip ② guard ③ handlebar ④ a measure word (for things usually with handles, e.g. scissors, spade, knife) ⑤ used to transpose the object in front of the verb
另见 bà

〖把柄〗(名)[bǎbǐng]
(lit.) handle; (fig.) sth. that can be used as a hold over sb.

〖把持〗(动)[bǎchí]
keep ... under control; keep a tight grip

〖把关〗(动)[bǎ guān]
① guard the passes ② make the final check

〖把势〗(名)[bǎshi]
skilled person in a certain job (farming, carting, gardening, etc.)

〖把守〗(动)[bǎshǒu]
guard(an entrance,a pass, etc.); defend; hold on
〖把手〗(名)[bǎshou]
handle; knob; hand grip
〖把握〗(动、名)[bǎwò]
① have a thorough grasp of; be sure of sth. ② assurance; certainty
〖把戏〗(名)[bǎxì]
① jugglery ② trick; game

靶(名)[bǎ]
target
〖靶场〗(名)[bǎchǎng]
shooting range
〖靶心〗(名)[bǎxīn]
bull's-eye
〖靶子〗(名)[bǎzi]
target; butt

bà

坝(名)[bà]
dam; dike; embankment

把(名)[bà]
handle
另见 bǎ

爸(名)[bà]
pa; dad; father
〖爸爸〗(名)[bàba]
papa; dad; father

罢(动)[bà]
① stop; cease ② dismiss ③ finish
〖罢工〗[bàgōng]
go on strike
〖罢官〗[bàguān]
dismiss officials from their posts
〖罢课〗[bàkè]
student strike
〖罢了〗[bàle]
a modal particle placed at the end of a declarative sentence meaning "that's all", "only", etc.
〖罢免〗(动)[bàmiǎn]
remove from office; dismiss sb. from his (her) post; recall
〖罢市〗[bàshì]
close up shops in going on strike; shopkeeper strike
〖罢休〗[bàxiū]
give up; stop; let the matter drop

霸[bà]
〖霸道〗[bàdào]
despotism; tyranny; overbearing; high-handed
〖霸权〗[bàquán]
hegemony
〖霸权主义〗[bàquánzhǔyì]
hegemonism
〖霸占〗[bàzhàn]
forcibly occupy; usurp
〖霸主〗[bàzhǔ]
① powerful chief of the feudal princes of the Spring and Autumn period in Chinese history

②overlord; hegemony

ba

B

吧(助)[ba]
① expressing request ② expressing agreement ③ expressing uncertainty ④ expressing supposition tinged with dilemma

bāi

掰(动)[bāi]
tear sth. apart or off with both hands; break off with the fingers and thumb
〖掰腕子〗[bāiwànzi]
handwrestling

bái

白(形、副)[bái]
① white ② blank; plain ③ in vain ④ for nothing; free of charge
〖白菜〗(名)[báicài]〔棵 kē〕
Chinese cabbage
〖白痴〗(名)[báichī]
idiot; mentally subnormal
〖白搭〗[báidā]
no use; no good
〖白费〗(动)[báifèi]
waste; in vain
〖白果〗(名)[báiguǒ]
ginkgo; gingko
〖白话〗(名)[báihuà]
vernacular; the vernacular language
〖白金〗(名)[báijīn]
platinum
〖白酒〗(名)[báijiǔ]
white spirit (usu. distilled from sorghum or maize)
〖白开水〗(名)[báikāishuǐ]
plain boiled water
〖白茫茫〗(形)[báimángmáng]
in an endless whiteness (snow, cloud, fog)
〖白描〗(名)[báimiáo]
① line drawing in trditional ink and brush style ②simple, straightforward style of writing
〖白内障〗(名)[báinèizhàng]
cataract
〖白热化〗(动)[báirèhuà]
get into a state of white heat
〖白日做梦〗[báirìzuòmèng]
daydream; indulge in wishful thinking
〖白色〗(名)[báisè]
① white colour ② reactionary; counter-revolutionary
〖白色恐怖〗(名)[báisèkǒngbù]
white terror
〖白色人种〗(名)[báisèrénzhǒng]
the white race
〖白手起家〗[báishǒuqǐjiā]
start from scratch; build up from nothing
〖白薯〗(名)[báishǔ]
sweet potato
〖白糖〗(名)[báitáng]
white sugar
〖白天〗(名)[báitiān]
daytime
〖白铁皮〗(名)[baitiěpí]
galvanized iron sheet

〖白头偕老〗[baitóuxiélǎo]
live to ripe old age in conjugal bliss; remain a devoted couple to the end of their lives
〖白血病〗(名)[báixuèbìng]
leukemia
〖白血球〗(名)[báixuèqiú]
white blood cell; white corpuscle
〖白眼〗(名)[báiyǎn]
supercilious look
〖白衣战士〗(名)[báiyīzhànshì]
warrior in white; medical worker
〖白蚁〗(名)[báiyǐ]
termite; white ant
〖白银〗(名)[báiyín]〔两 liǎng〕
silver
〖白字〗(名)[báizì]
wrongly written or mispronounced character

bǎi

百(数)[bǎi]
①hundred ②many
〖百般〗(副)[bǎibān]
all manner of; in a hundred and one ways; in every possible way; by all means
〖百发百中〗[bǎifābǎizhòng]
hit the bull's eye every time; shoot with great accuracy
〖百尺竿头,更进一步〗
[bǎichǐgāntóu, gèngjìnyībù]
make still futher progress
〖百川归海〗[bǎichuānguīhǎi]
all rivers flow to the sea; all things tend in one direction
〖百分比〗(名)[bǎifēnbǐ]
percent; percentage
〖百分率〗(名)[bǎifēnlǜ]
percentage
〖百分之百〗(数、副)
[bǎifēnzhībǎi]
a hundred percent; absolutely; out and out
〖百分制〗(名)[bǎifēnzhì]
hundred-mark system
〖百感交集〗[bǎigǎnjiāojí]
all sorts of feelings well up in one's heart; a multitude of feelings surges up
〖百合〗(名)[bǎihé]
lily
〖百花齐放,百家争鸣〗[bǎihuā qífàng, bǎijiāzhēngmíng]
let a hundred flowers blossom and a hundred schools of thought contend
〖百花齐放,推陈出新〗
[bǎi huāqífàng, tuīchénchūxīn]
let a hundred flowers blossom, weed through the old to bring forth the new
〖百货公司〗(名)[bǎihuògōngsī]
department store; emporium
〖百科全书〗(名)[bǎikēquánshū]
encyclopaedia
〖百里挑一〗[bǎilitiāoyī]
one in a hundred; cream of the crop
〖百炼成钢〗[bǎiliànchénggāng]
tempered in repeated struggles; toughened and hardened
〖百灵〗(名)[bǎilíng]
lark

B

〖百忙(之)中〗
[bǎimáng(zhī)zhōng]
in the midst of pressing affairs; despite many claims on one's time; while fully engaged
〖百年大计〗(名)[bǎiniándàjì]
fundamental task crucial for generations to come; matter of vital and lasting importance
〖百万〗(数)[bǎiwàn]
million
〖百闻不如一见〗
[bǎiwénbù rúyījiàn]
(lit.)better to see once than hear a hundred times; seeing for oneself is a hundred times better than hearing from others; seeing is believing
〖百无禁忌〗[bǎiwújìnjì]
no prohibitions of any kind; nothing is under taboo
〖百无聊赖〗[bǎiwúliáolài]
bored to death; overcome with boredom
〖百姓〗(名)[bǎixìng]
common people
〖百页窗〗(名)[bǎiyèchuāng]
shutter; louver window
〖百战百胜〗[bǎizhànbǎishèng]
a hundred battles, a hundred victories; come out victorious in every battle; invincible
〖百折不挠〗[bǎizhébùnáo]
undaunted by repeated set-backs; keep forging ahead in spite of all setbacks; long and persistent effort

柏(名)[bǎi]
cypress
〖柏树〗(名)[bǎishù]〔棵 kē〕
cypress
〖柏油〗(名)[bǎiyóu]
pitch; asphalt; tar

摆(动、名)[bǎi]
① put; place; display ② oscillate; swing ③ make manifest; show; exhibit ④ pendulum
〖摆布〗(动)[bǎibù]
order ... about; manhandle at will
〖摆地摊〗[bǎidìtān]
set up a temporary stall (on a sidewalk to sell wares); lay out various items to sell (on a cloth etc. or simply on the ground)
〖摆动〗(动)[bǎidòng]
oscillate; swing
〖摆渡〗(动)[bǎidù]
ferry
〖摆架子〗[bǎi jiàzi]
put on airs; assume airs
〖摆阔气〗[bǎikuòqi]
show off one's wealth; parade one's wealth; be ostentatious and extravagant
〖摆老资格〗[bǎilǎozīgé]
flaunt one's seniority
〖摆擂台〗[bǎilèitái]
give an open challenge; invite an emulation
〖摆龙门阵〗[bǎilóngménzhèn]
chat; gossip; spin a yarn
〖摆弄〗(动)[bǎinòng]

①play about with ②fiddle about with
〖摆设〗(动、名)[bǎishè]
furnish and decorate (a room); furnishings; decoration; decor
〖摆事实,讲道理〗
[bǎi shìshí, jiǎng dàolǐ]
present the facts and reason things out
〖摆脱〗(动)[bǎituō]
get rid of; throw off; break away from; extricate oneself from
〖摆样子〗[bǎi yàngzi]
do sth. for show

bài

败(动)[bài]
① suffer defeat ② spoil; ruin ③wither away
〖败笔〗(名)[bàibǐ]
①a faulty stroke in calligraphy or painting ②a faulty expression in writing
〖败坏〗(动)[bàihuài]
ruin; corrupt
〖败家子〗(名)[bàijiāzǐ]
spendthrift; wastrel; prodigal
〖败类〗(名)[bàilèi]
dregs (of society); scum
〖败露〗(动)[bàilù]
(of a plot) be exposed; be uncovered
〖败落〗(动)[bàiluò]
decline (in wealth and position)
〖败诉〗(动)[bàisù]
lose a lawsuit
〖败退〗(动)[bàituì]
retreat in defeat
〖败仗〗(名)[bàizhàng]
①a lost battle ②a defeat

拜(动)[bài]
①visit ②pay one's respects to
〖拜倒〗(动)[bàidǎo]
bow before; prostrate oneself before sb.; bow and scrape
〖拜访〗(动)[bàifǎng]
pay a visit to; call to pay respects
〖拜会〗(动)[bàihuì]
make an official visit; pay a courtesy call
〖拜金主义〗(名)[bàijīnzhǔyì]
money worship; mammonism
〖拜年〗(动)[bàinián]
pay a New Year call; wish sb. a Happy New Year
〖拜师〗(动)[bàishī]
formally acknowledge sb. as one's master; take sb. as one's teacher
〖拜寿〗(动)[bàishòu]
congratulate an elderly person on his or her birthday; offer birthday felicitations
〖拜托〗(动)[bàituō]
①entrust ②make a request

稗[bài]
〖稗子〗(名)[bàizi]
barnyard grass; barnyard millet

bān

扳(动)[bān]

B

pull; turn (bar, switch, shift gears)
〖扳成平局〗[bānchéngpíngjú]
equalize the score
〖扳手〗(名)[bānshǒu]〔把 bǎ〕
wrench; spanner

班(名)[bān]
①squad ②class; team ③shift; duty ④a measure word (e.g. number of flight or bus)
〖班车〗(名)[bānchē]
bus on regular schedule
〖班房〗(名)[bānfáng]
jail
〖班机〗(名)[bānjī]
scheduled flight
〖班级〗(名)[bānjí]
class or grade in a school
〖班轮〗(名)[bānlún]
regular passenger or cargo ship
〖班门弄斧〗[Bānménnòngfǔ]
(lit.) wield an axe at the door of the master carpenter Lu Pan; (fig.) show off in the presence of an expert
〖班委会〗(名)[bānwěihuì]
class committee
〖班长〗(名)[bānzhǎng]
①monitor (class) ②squad leader
〖班主任〗(名)[bānzhǔrèn]
a teacher in charge of a class
〖班子〗(名)[bānzi]
a set-up (organisation)

颁[bān]
〖颁布〗(动)[bānbù]
promulgate; issue
〖颁发〗(动)[bānfā]
①promulgate ②award; confer

斑[bān]
〖斑白〗(形)[bānbái]
(of hair) grizzled; grey
〖斑点〗(名)[bāndiǎn]
stains; spots
〖斑马〗(名)[bānmǎ]
zebra
〖斑纹〗(名)[bānwén]
stripe; streak

搬(动)[bān]
remove; move
〖搬家〗[bānjiā]
move house
〖搬弄是非〗[bānnòngshìfēi]
tell tales; make mischief; sow discord
〖搬起石头打自己的脚〗[bānqǐshítoudǎzìjǐdejiǎo]
lift a rock only to drop it on one's own toes
〖搬迁〗(动)[bānqiān]
move
〖搬运〗(动)[bānyùn]
carry; convey; transport
〖搬运工〗(名)[bānyùngōng]
porter; docker

bǎn

板(名)[bǎn]
board; plank
〖板壁〗(名)[bǎnbì]

wooden partition
〖板擦儿〗(名)[bǎncār]〔个 gè〕
(blackboard) duster
〖板凳〗(名)[bǎndèng]〔条 tiáo〕
wooden bench
〖板结〗(形)[bǎnjié]
(of soil) hard-packed
〖板栗〗(名)[bǎnlì]
Chinese chestnut
〖板面孔〗[bǎnmiànkǒng]
put on a stern expression; keep a straight face
〖板鸭〗(名)[bǎnyā]
pressed salted duck
〖板眼〗(名)[bǎnyǎn]
① measure in traditional Chinese music ② orderliness; methodicalness
〖板子〗(名)[bǎnzi]〔块 kuài〕
board; plank

版(名)[bǎn]
① plate; printing block ② edition; print ③ page (of a newspaper)
〖版本〗(名)[bǎnběn]
edition (of books)
〖版画〗(名)[bǎnhuà]〔张 zhāng〕
print; block print; engraving
〖版面〗(名)[bǎnmiàn]
layout or make-up of a printed sheet
〖版权〗(名)[bǎnquán]
copyright
〖版权所有〗[bǎnquánsuǒyǒu]
all rights reserved
〖版税〗(名)[bǎnshuì]
royalty (on books)
〖版图〗(名)[bǎntú]
domain; territory

bàn

办(动)[bàn]
① do; handle; take; manage; go about ② found; set up; start; run ③ punish; bring to justice
〖办不到〗[bànbudào]
① unfeasible; impossible ② impermissible; Never!
〖办得到〗[bàndedào]
can be done; feasible; possible
〖办法〗(名)[bànfǎ]
way; means; measures
〖办公〗[bàngōng]
do office work; work in an office
〖办公室〗(名)[bàngōngshì]
office
〖办公桌〗(名)[bàngōngzhuō]
desk; bureau
〖办理〗(动)[bànlǐ]
do; undertake; handle; conduct
〖办事〗[bàn shì]
run affairs
〖办事处〗(名)[bànshìchù]
local office; office; (liaison) office
〖办手续〗[bànshǒuxù]
go through the formalities; go through procedure
〖办喜事〗[bànxǐshì]
manage a wedding; prepare for a happy occasion

半(数)[bàn]

B

①half; semi- ②mid- ③partly
〖半百〗[bànbǎi]
fifty (years of age) (e.g. getting on for fifty; over/above fifty)
〖半壁江山〗[bànbìjiāngshān]
half of the country
〖半边天〗(名)[bànbiāntiān]
half the sky (e.g. women hold up half the sky)
〖半成品〗(名)[bànchéngpǐn]
semi-finished product; semi-manufactured product
〖半导体〗(名)[bàndǎotǐ]
transistor; semiconductor
〖半岛〗(名)[bàndǎo]
peninsula
〖半封建〗[bàn fēngjiàn]
semi-feudal
〖半工半读〗[bàngōngbàndú]
part-work and part-study
〖半截〗(名)[bànjié]
half
〖半斤八两〗[bànjīnbāliǎng]
six of one and half a dozen of the other; there is not much to choose between the two
〖半径〗(名)[bànjìng]
radius
〖半决赛〗(名)[bànjuésài]
semifinals
〖半路〗(名)[bànlù]
midway; half-way
〖半路出家〗[bànlùchūjiā]
(lit.) become a monk or nun late in life; (fig.) switch to a job one was not trained for
〖半瓶醋〗(名)[bànpíngcù]
dabbler; smatterer
〖半球〗(名)[bànqiú]
hemisphere
〖半日制学校〗(名)[bànrìzhìxuéxiào]
half-day school; double-shift school
〖半身像〗(名)[bànshēnxiàng]
①half-length photo or portrait ②bust
〖半生〗(名)[bànshēng]
half of one's life-time
〖半生不熟〗[bànshēngbùshú]
half cooked
〖半死不活〗[bànsǐbùhuó]
half-dead; more dead than alive
〖半天〗(名)[bàntiān]
①half a day ②(for) a long time
〖半途而废〗[bàntú'érfèi]
abandon half way; give up half way; be left off unfinished
〖半脱产〗[bàntuōchǎn]
partly released from productive labour; partly released from one's regular work
〖半信半疑〗[bànxìnbànyí]
half-believing and half doubting; not quite convinced
〖半夜〗(名)[bànyè]
midnight; in the middle of the night
〖半元音〗(名)[bànyuányīn]
semi-vowel
〖半圆〗(名)[bànyuán]
semicircle
〖半月刊〗(名)[bànyuèkān]
semimonthly; fortnightly
〖半殖民地〗(名)[bànzhímíndì]

semi-colony
〚半自动化〛[bànzìdònghuà]
semi-automatization

扮(动)[bàn]
dress up as
〚扮鬼脸〛[bànguǐliǎn]
make grimaces; make faces
〚扮相〛(名)[bànxiàng]
the appearance of an actor or actress in costume and makeup
〚扮演〛(动)[bànyǎn]
play the part of; have a role (in a play, etc.)

伴(动)[bàn]
accompany
〚伴唱〛(动)[bànchàng]
accompany (a singer)
〚伴侣〛(名)[bànlǚ]
companion; mate; partner
〚伴随〛(动)[bànsuí]
follow; be in the wake of; simultaneously
〚伴舞〛[bànwǔ]
be a dancing partner
〚伴音〛(名)[bànyīn]
audio
〚伴奏〛(动)[bànzòu]
accompany; play to the accompaniment of

拌(动)[bàn]
mix; mix in
〚拌面〛(名)[bànmiàn]
noodles served with soy sauce, sesame butter, etc.
〚拌嘴〛[bànzuǐ]
bicker; squabble; quarrel

绊(动)[bàn]
hamper; hinder; catch (one's foot on sth. and fall); trip over
〚绊倒〛(动)[bàndǎo]
stumble and fall
〚绊脚石〛(名)[bànjiǎoshí]
stumbling-block; obstruction

瓣(名)[bàn]
petal; segment; section

bāng

邦[bāng]
〚邦交〛(名)[bāngjiāo]
diplomatic relations between sovereign states

帮(动)[bāng]
help; assist
〚帮倒忙〛[bāngdàománg]
be more of a hindrance than a help
〚帮工〛(名)[bānggōng]
helper
〚帮会〛(名)[bānghuì]
secret society; underworld gang
〚帮忙〛[bāngmáng]
help; lend a (helping) hand
〚帮派〛(名)[bāngpài]
faction
〚帮腔〛[bāngqiāng]
① choral accompaniment ② back

B

(sb. up); chime in with
〖帮手〗(名)[bāngshou]
helper; assistant; accomplice
〖帮凶〗(名)[bāngxiōng]
accomplice; accessory
〖帮助〗(动、名)[bāngzhù]
help; aid; assist; assistance; aid; help

bǎng

绑(动)[bǎng]
tie; bind; fasten
〖绑架〗(动)[bǎngjià]
kidnap

榜(名)[bǎng]
list of names posted on a notice-board or wall (e.g. candidates)
〖榜样〗(名)[bǎngyàng]
example; model; pattern

bàng

棒(名、形)[bàng]
① stick; cudgel ② (colloq.) capable; competent; intelligent; excellent
〖棒球〗(名)[bàngqiú]
baseball
〖棒子〗(名)[bàngzi]
cudgel; stick; club

傍[bàng]
〖傍晚〗(名)[bàngwǎn]
evening; nightfall; dusk

磅(量)[bàng]
a measure word (pound)
另见 páng
〖磅秤〗(名)[bàngchèng]
platform scale; platform balance

bāo

包(动、名、量)[bāo]
① wrap ② be responsible for ③ hire; charter ④ parcel; package ⑤ a measure word (bundle, sack, bale)
〖包办〗(动)[bāobàn]
take everything on oneself; run the whole show; keep everything in one's own hand
〖包庇〗(动)[bāobì]
shield; harbour
〖包藏祸心〗[bāocánghuòxīn]
harbour evil intentions
〖包产〗[bāochǎn]
make a production contract; take full responsibility for output quotas
〖包产到户〗[bāochǎndàohù]
fix farm output quotas on a household basis; fix farm quotas to the household
〖包袱〗(名)[bāofu]
① cloth wrapper; bundle ② load; encumbrance; (mental) burden
〖包干儿〗[bāogānr]
be solely responsible for an assigned task until it is fulfilled
〖包工〗(名)[bāogōng]
contract for a job; contract wo-

rker

〖包工头〗(名)[bāogōngtóu]
job contractor; labour contractor

〖包裹〗(名)[bāoguǒ]
parcel; package

〖包含〗(动)[bāohán]
contain; embody; imply (of speech, etc.)

〖包涵〗(动)[bāohan]
excuse (e.g. excuse me for my poor pronunciation)

〖包伙〗[bāohuǒ]
get or supply all meals at a fixed rate (e.g. by week or month); table board

〖包括〗(动)[bāokuò]
include; contain; cover

〖包罗万象〗
[bāoluówànxiàng]
all-embracing; cover and contain everything; all-inclusive

〖包退包换〗[bāotuìbāohuàn]
Merchandise will be exchanged if found unsatisfactory.

〖包围〗(动)[bāowéi]
surround; encircle; besiege

〖包销〗(动)[bāoxiāo]
have exclusive selling rights; be the sole agent for a firm or a production unit

〖包扎〗(动)[bāozā]
① dress (a wound) ② wrap up; pack up

〖包装〗(动)[bāozhuāng]
wrap up; pack

〖包子〗(名)[bāozi]
steamed stuffed buns

剥(动)[bāo]
peel; skin
另见 bō

褒[bāo]

〖褒贬〗(动)[bāobiǎn]
① pass critical judgement on; appraise ② blame; speak ill of; cry down

〖褒义词〗(名)[bāoyìcí]
laudatory word; word of praise

báo

雹[báo]

〖雹子〗(名)[báozi]
hailstone

薄(形)[báo]
① thin ② poor (soil); flimsy
另见 bó

bǎo

饱(形)[bǎo]
full; well-filled (with food); having eaten one's fill

〖饱和〗(形)[bǎohé]
saturated

〖饱经风霜〗
[bǎojīngfēngshuāng]
having gone through the hardships of life; weather-beaten

〖饱满〗(形)[bǎomǎn]
full; flush; filled

〖饱食终日,无所用心〗
[bǎoshízhōngrì, wúsuǒyòngxīn]
eat three square meals a day and

think of nothing else; be well-fed and care about nothing else

B

宝(名)[bǎo]
treasure
〖宝贝〗(名)[bǎobèi]
① treasure; treasured object ② little darling (of child)
〖宝贵〗(形)[bǎoguì]
valuable; precious
〖宝剑〗(名)[bǎojiàn]〔把 bǎ〕
double-edged sword
〖宝库〗(名)[bǎokù]
treasurehouse
〖宝石〗(名)[bǎoshí]
precious stone; gem
〖宝塔〗(名)[bǎotǎ]
pagoda
〖宝藏〗(名)[bǎozàng]
treasure-trove; buried treasure (usually national resources)
〖宝座〗(名)[bǎozuò]
throne; seat of power

保(动)[bǎo]
① defend; protect ② guarantee; insure ③ keep
〖保安人员〗(名)
[bǎo'ānrényuán]
security personnel
〖保镖〗(名)[bǎobiāo]
bodyguard
〖保藏〗(动)[bǎocáng]
preserve; keep
〖保持〗(动)[bǎochí]
keep; remain; maintain; preserve; hold
〖保存〗(动)[bǎocún]
keep; preserve; conserve; take care of
〖保管〗(动、名)[bǎoguǎn]
keep (in safe place); conserve; preserve; safekeeping; care
〖保护〗(动)[bǎohù]
protect; safeguard
〖保护伞〗(名)[bǎohùsǎn]
protective umbrella
〖保护色〗(名)[bǎohùsè]
① protective colouring (of animal or insects) ② (metaphor) disguise; camouflage
〖保护主义〗(名)[bǎohùzhǔyì]
protectionism
〖保健〗[bǎojiàn](名)
health protection; health care
〖保健操〗(名)[bǎojiàncāo]
setting-up exercises
〖保健箱〗(名)[bǎojiànxiāng]
medical kit
〖保龄球〗(名)[bǎolíngqiú]
bowling
〖保留〗(动)[bǎoliú]
reserve; retain; maintain (one's different views); keep back
〖保密〗[bǎomì]
keep secret; maintain secrecy
〖保密文件〗(名)
[bǎomì wénjiàn]
classified document
〖保姆〗(名)[bǎomǔ]
(children's) nurse; baby-sitter
〖保全〗(动)[bǎoquán]
save; preserve; keep (sth.) int-

act
〖保释〗[bǎoshì]
release on bail; bail
〖保守〗(形、动)[bǎoshǒu]
① conservative ② guard; keep; hold on
〖保税区〗(名)[bǎoshuìqū]
bonded area
〖保送〗(动)[bǎosòng]
send on recommendation (e.g. to college)
〖保卫〗(动)[bǎowèi]
defend; safeguard
〖保温〗[bǎowēn]
heat preservation
〖保温瓶〗(名)[bǎowēnpíng]
vacuum flask; vacuum bottle; thermos
〖保险〗(形、名)[bǎoxiǎn]
① safe and sound; secure ② be sure; security; insurance
〖保险单〗(名)[bǎoxiǎndān]
insurance policy
〖保险费〗(名)[bǎoxiǎnfèi]
insurance premium
〖保险公司〗(名)[bǎoxiǎngōngsī]
insurance company; insurer
〖保险丝〗(名)[bǎoxiǎnsī]
fuse; fuse-wire
〖保险箱〗(名)[bǎoxiǎnxiāng]
safe
〖保修〗(动)[bǎoxiū]
guarantee to keep sth. in good repair; guarantee on sth. (e.g. the watch is guaranteed for one year)
〖保养〗(动)[bǎoyǎng]
keep fit; maintain
〖保育员〗(名)[bǎoyùyuán]
kindergarten nurse; childcare worker
〖保障〗(动、名)[bǎozhàng]
ensure; guarantee; safeguard
〖保证〗(动、名)[bǎozhèng]
pledge; guarantee; assure; assurance
〖保值〗[bǎozhí]
be inflation proof in value; value-guaranteed
〖保值储蓄〗(名)[bǎozhíchǔxù]
inflation-proof savings deposit; value-guaranteed savings
〖保质保量〗[bǎozhìbǎoliàng]
guarantee both quality and quantity
〖保重〗(动)[bǎozhòng]
look after oneself

堡[bǎo]
〖堡垒〗(名)[bǎolěi]
fortification; fortress; fort; stronghold

bào

报(动、名)[bào]〔张 zhāng〕
① report; announce; declare; inform ② newspaper
〖报案〗[bào'àn]
report a case to the security authorities
〖报表〗[bàobiǎo]
forms for reporting statistics, etc.; report forms
〖报仇〗[bàochóu]

B

revenge; avenge; redress a grievance
〖报仇雪恨〗[bàochóuxuěhèn]
redress a wrong; have one's revenge
〖报酬〗(名)[bàochóu]
reward; remuneration
〖报答〗(动)[bàodá]
requite; repay
〖报到〗[bào dào]
report for duty; report on one's arrival
〖报道〗(动、名)[bàodào]
report on (news); report; cover
〖报废〗(动)[bàofèi]
be declared or classified worthless (of old car, machine, etc.); write off
〖报复〗(动)[bàofù]
retaliate; get even with someone; pay sb. back
〖报告〗(动、名)[bàogào]
give a report, speech or talk; report; speech
〖报告文学〗(名)[bàogàowénxué]
reportage
〖报户口〗[bàohùkǒu]
apply for a residence permit; register one's residence
〖报话机〗(名)[bàohuàjī]
walkie-talkie
〖报刊〗(名)[bàokān]
newspapers and periodicals; the press
〖报名〗[bàomíng]
enter one's name (for sth.)
〖报幕〗[bàomù]
announce (e.g. items in a programme, performance)
〖报批〗[bàopī]
submit (a plan, etc.) for approval
〖报社〗(名)[bàoshè]
a newspaper office
〖报摊〗(名)[bàotān]
news-stand; news stall
〖报头〗(名)[bàotóu]
masthead
〖报喜〗[bào xǐ]
announce good news; report success
〖报销〗(动)[bàoxiāo]
① put in an expense account ② be destroyed; be finished off
〖报纸〗(名)[bàozhǐ]〔张 zhāng〕
newspaper; the press

刨(动)[bào]
plane (sth. smooth)
另见 páo
〖刨床〗(名)[bàochuáng]〔台 tái〕planing machine
〖刨子〗(名)[bàozi]〔把 bǎ〕
(carpenter's) plane

抱(动)[bào]
① hold or carry in one's arm(s) ② embrace ③ cherish
〖抱不平〗[bàobùpíng]
be out-raged by an injustice done to another person; champion the cause of a wronged person
〖抱残守缺〗[bàocánshǒuquē]
cherish the outmoded and pres-

erve the outworn; be conservative

〖抱佛脚〗[bàofójiǎo]
clasp Buddha's feet; profess devotion only when in trouble; make a hasty last-minute effort; do nothing until the last minute(e.g. never burn incense when all is well but clasp Buddha's feet when in distress)

〖抱负〗(名)[bàofù]
lofty aim; ideal

〖抱歉〗[bàoqiàn]
be sorry; feel apologetic

〖抱头鼠窜〗[bàotóushǔcuàn]
cover the head and sneak away like a rat back to its hole; scurry away or scamper off like frightened rats

〖抱怨〗(动)[bàoyuàn]
complain; grumble

豹 (名)[bào][只 zhī]
leopard

暴 (形)[bào]
① sudden and violent; furious
② cruel; fierce

〖暴跌〗(动)[bàodiē]
steep fall(in price); slump

〖暴动〗(动)[bàodòng]
resort to insurrection

〖暴发户〗(名)[bàofāhù]
upstart

〖暴风雨〗(名)[bàofēngyǔ]
storm

〖暴风骤雨〗[bàofēngzhòuyǔ]
mighty storm; (furious or violent) storm; hurricane (usu. fig.)

〖暴君〗(名)[bàojūn]
tyrant; despot

〖暴力〗(名)[bàolì]
violence; force

〖暴力革命〗[bàolì gémìng]
violent revolution

〖暴利〗(名)[bàolì]
fabulous profits; extravagant profits; sudden wealth acquired by profiteering

〖暴露〗(动)[bàolù]
expose; unmask; reveal; lay bare

〖暴露文学〗(名)[bàolùwénxué]
literature of exposure

〖暴露无遗〗[bàolùwúyí]
be completely exposed; completely unmasked

〖暴乱〗(名)[bàoluàn]
insurrection; riot

〖暴跳如雷〗[bàotiàorúléi]
stamp with rage; stamp about in a frenzy

〖暴徒〗(名)[bàotú]
ruffians; hoodlums; delinquents; hooligans

〖暴行〗(名)[bàoxíng]
atrocity; savage act; outrages

〖暴雨〗(名)[bàoyǔ]
rainstorm; torrential rain

〖暴躁〗(形)[bàozào]
short-tempered; irascible

〖暴涨〗(动)[bàozhǎng]
rise suddenly and sharply (riv-

er); soar; skyrocket (price)
〖暴政〗(名)[bàozhèng]
tyranny

B

爆 (动)[bào]
explode; burst
〖爆发〗(动)[bàofā]
break out; burst out; erupt
〖爆米花〗(名)[bàomǐhuā]
puffed rice
〖爆破〗(动)[bàopò]
blow up; explode
〖爆破音〗(名)[bàopòyīn]
plosive
〖爆玉米花〗(名)[bàoyùmǐhuā]
popcorn
〖爆炸〗(动)[bàozhà]
explode
〖爆竹〗(名)[bàozhú]
firecracker

bēi

杯 (名)[bēi]
cup
〖杯弓蛇影〗[bēigōngshéyǐng]
mistaking the reflection of a bow in the cup for a snake; extremely suspicious
〖杯水车薪〗[bēishuǐchēxīn]
trying to put out a burning cartload of faggots with a cup of water; an utterly inadequate measure
〖杯子〗(名)[bēizi]〔个 gè〕
cup

卑 (形)[bēi]
low; lowly; mean
〖卑鄙〗(形)[bēibǐ]
despicable; contemptible; mean; base
〖卑鄙无耻〗[bēibǐwúchǐ]
utterly shameless; unscrupulous; base and shameless
〖卑躬屈膝〗[bēigōngqūxī]
servile; cringing; subservient
〖卑贱〗(形)[bēijiàn]
lowly; mean
〖卑劣〗(形)[bēiliè]
sordid; abject; base; mean; vulgar; despicable and unscrupulous

背 (动)[bēi]
① carry on one's back ② be burdened
另见 bèi
〖背包〗(名)[bēibāo]
knapsack; rucksack
〖背带〗(名)[bēidài]
① braces; suspenders ② sling ③ straps
〖背黑锅〗[bēihēiguō]
be made a scapegoat; be unjustly blamed
〖背债〗[bēizhài]
be in debt; be saddled with debts

悲 (形)[bēi]
sad; grieved
〖悲哀〗(形)[bēi'āi]
sorrowful; grieved; grievous
〖悲惨〗(形)[bēicǎn]miserable;

tragic
〖悲愤〗(形)[bēifèn]
grievous and indignant; grief-stricken and enraged; incensed with grief
〖悲观〗(形)[bēiguān]
pessimistic
〖悲观主义〗(名)[bēiguān zhǔyì]
pessimism
〖悲欢离合〗[bēihuānlíhé]
joys and sorrows, partings and reunions; vicissitudes of life
〖悲剧〗(名)[bēijù]
tragedy
〖悲伤〗(形)[bēishāng]
sad; sorrowful
〖悲痛〗(形)[bēitòng]
grievous; deeply grieved over; distressing; sorrowful
〖悲壮〗(形)[bēizhuàng]
solemn and stirring; tragic and moving

碑(名)[bēi]
stone tablet; stele; monument
〖碑文〗(名)[bēiwén]
inscription on a memorial tablet

běi

北(名)[běi]
north
〖北半球〗(名)[běibànqiú]
the Northern Hemisphere
〖北冰洋〗(名)[Běibīngyáng]
the Arctic Ocean
〖北大荒〗(名)[běidàhuāng]
the Great Northern Wilderness (in northeast China)
〖北斗星〗(名)[běidǒuxīng]
the Dipper; the Plough
〖北伐战争〗(名)
[Běifá Zhànzhēng]
the Northern Expedition (1926—1927)
〖北方〗(名)[běifāng]
the northern part of; the north
〖北国〗(名)[běiguó]
the northern part of the country; the North
〖北回归线〗(名)[běihuíguīxiàn]
the Tropic of Cancer
〖北极〗(名)[běijí]
North Pole
〖北极星〗(名)[běijíxīng]
Polaris; the North Star; the polestar
〖北极熊〗(名)[běijíxióng]
polar bear
〖北京〗(名)[Běijīng]
Beijing
〖北京猿人〗(名)
[Běijīng Yuánrén]
Peking Man (anthropology)
〖北美洲〗(名)[Běiměizhōu]
North America
〖北洋军阀〗(名)[Běiyáng Jūnfá]
Northern warlords (1912—1927)
〖北约〗(名)[běiyuē]
NATO (the North Atlantic Treaty Organization)

bèi

备(动)[bèi]

①prepare;get ready ②provide; fit out; be equipped with
〖备耕〗(动)[bèi gēng]
prepare for ploughing and planting
〖备荒〗(名)[bèi huāng]
preparedness against natural calamities
〖备考〗(名)[bèikǎo]
remarks; appendix for reference
〖备课〗(动)[bèi kè]
prepare lessons
〖备受欢迎〗[bèishòuhuānyíng]
enjoy great popularity; be very popular
〖备忘录〗(名)[bèiwànglù]
memorandum; a written reminder
〖备战〗[bèi zhàn]
①prepare for war;war preparations ②be prepared against war
〖备至〗(副)[bèizhì]
to the utmost; in every possible way
〖备用〗(动)[bèiyòng]
reserve; spare; alternate
〖备注〗(名)[bèizhù]
remarks; appendix

背(名、动)[bèi]
①back; reverse side ②with the back towards;behind one's back ③recite; learn by heart ④abandon; renounce
另见 bēi
〖背道而驰〗[bèidào'érchí]
run in the opposite direction; run counter to
〖背光〗[bèiguāng]
be in a poor light; do sth. with one's back to the light
〖背后〗(副)[bèihòu]
behind; behind one's back; behind the scene
〖背景〗(名)[bèijǐng]
①background; setting ②backdrop
〖背离〗(动)[bèilí]
turn one's back on; deviate from
〖背面〗(名)[bèimiàn]
back; wrong side; reverse side
〖背叛〗(动)[bèipàn] betray
〖背诵〗(动)[bèisòng]
recite; say by heart
〖背心〗(名)[bèixīn]〔件 jiàn〕
① waistcoat ② vest; (sleeveless) undershirt ③ sleeveless sweater
〖背信弃义〗[bèixìnqìyì]
breach of faith; perfidy; treachery; perfidious
〖背影〗(名)[bèiyǐng]
a view of sb.'s back; a figure viewed from behind

倍(量)[bèi]
...-times; ...-fold
〖倍加〗(副)[bèijiā]
doubly
〖倍数〗(名)[bèishù]
multiple
〖倍增〗(动)[bèizēng]
double; increase

被(名、介)[bèi]〔床 chuáng〕

①blanket; cotton-padded quilt② by (a preposition indicating the passive voice)
〖被乘数〗(名)[bèichéngshù]
multiplicand (a number to be multiplied)
〖被除数〗(名)[bèichúshù]
dividend (a number to be divided)
〖被动〗(形)[bèidòng]
passive
〖被动式〗(名)[bèidòngshì]
passive form; passive voice
〖被告〗(名)[bèigào]
the accused; defendant
〖被告席〗(名)[bèigàoxí]
defendant's seat; dock
〖被害人〗(名)[bèihàirén]
the injured party; the victim
〖被减数〗(名)[bèijiǎnshù]
minuend (a number from which another number is to be subtracted)
〖被迫〗[bèipò]
be forced; be compelled; be coerced; under compulsion
〖被子〗(名)[bèizi]〔床 chuáng〕
cotton-padded quilt

辈(名)[bèi]
①generation ②life; lifetime
〖辈分〗(名)[bèifèn]
seniority in the family or clan; position in the family hierarchy

bei

呗(助)[bei]
a modal particle, placed at the end of a sentence to imply that the reason or fact is obvious

bēn

奔(动)[bēn]
① run quickly ② hurry; rush; hasten
〖奔波〗(动)[bēnbō]
be on the go; be busy running about
〖奔驰〗(动)[bēnchí]
gallop; speed on
〖奔放〗(形)[bēnfàng]
bold and unrestrained
〖奔赴〗(动)[bēnfù]
rush to; hasten to
〖奔流〗(动)[bēnliú]
flow on at a great speed; pour
〖奔跑〗(动)[bēnpǎo]
run; hasten
〖奔腾〗(动)[bēnténg]
①gallop ②surge forward
〖奔走〗(动)[bēnzǒu]
①hasten; run ②rush about (on business); busy running around

běn

本(名、量)[běn]
① root or stem of a plant ② foundation; basis; origin ③ a measure word (for books, pictorials, etc.)
〖本本主义〗(名)[běnběnzhǔyì]
book worship
〖本地〗(名)[běndì]
local; native

B

〖本分〗(名)[běnfèn]
one's duty
〖本国〗(名)[běnguó]
one's own country
〖本行〗(名)[běnháng]
one's own profession; in one's line
〖本届〗(名)[běnjiè]
current; this year's (e.g. this year's graduates; the current session of the U.N. General Assembly)
〖本科〗(名)[běnkē]
undergraduate course; ordinary course
〖本科生〗(名)[běnkēshēng]
undergraduate
〖本来〗(形、副)[běnlái]
original; originally
〖本领〗(名)[běnlǐng]
skill; ability; capability; know-how
〖本末倒置〗[běnmòdàozhì]
put the cart before the horse; confuse cause and effect
〖本能〗(名)[běnnéng]
instinct
〖本钱〗(名)[běnqián]
capital
〖本人〗(代)[běnrén]
the person himself
〖本色〗(名)[běnsè]
intrinsic character; true qualities; natural colour (of cloth, etc.)
〖本身〗(名)[běnshēn]
oneself; itself
〖本事〗(名)[běnshi]
ability; skill
〖本性〗(名)[běnxìng]
nature; natural instincts (character, disposition)
〖本义〗(名)[běnyì]
original meaning; literal sense
〖本意〗(名)[běnyì]
original meaning; original intention
〖本质〗(名)[běnzhì]
nature; innate character; intrinsic quality
〖本子〗(名)[běnzi]〔本 běn〕
note-book; exercise book

bèn

笨(形)[bèn]
unintelligent; slow-witted
〖笨蛋〗(名)[bèndàn]
fool; stupid fellow
〖笨鸟先飞〗[bènniǎoxiānfēi]
clumsy birds have to start flying early; the slow need to start early
〖笨手笨脚〗[bènshǒubènjiǎo]
clumsy
〖笨重〗(形)[bènzhòng]
clumsy; heavy; cumbersome
〖笨拙〗(形)[bènzhuō]
clumsy; stupid

bēng

崩(动)[bēng]
① collapse; fall in ruins ② break down ③ fail to reach agreement

〖崩溃〗(动)[bēngkuì]
collapse; crumble
〖崩裂〗(动)[bēngliè]
crack; burst apart
〖崩塌〗(动)[bēngtā]
cave in; crumble; collapse

bèng

迸(动)[bèng]
burst forth; spurt
〖迸发〗(动)[bèngfā]
burst out; burst forth
〖迸裂〗(动)[bèngliè]
burst; split; burst open

蹦(动)[bèng]
bounce; jump; hop

bī

逼(动)[bī]
① force; compel; press ② press for; extort
〖逼近〗(动)[bījìn]
approach; draw near; press forward; gain on; close in on (sb.)
〖逼迫〗(动)[bīpò]
force; compel; coerce; constrain
〖逼上梁山〗[bīshàngliángshān]
be driven to join the rebels on Liangshan; be compelled to revolt
〖逼真〗(形)[bīzhēn]
life-like; true to life; vivid

bí

鼻(名)[bí]
nose
〖鼻孔〗(名)[bíkǒng]
nostrils
〖鼻腔〗(名)[bíqiāng]
① nasal cavity ② nasal twang
〖鼻涕〗(名)[bítì]
snivel; nasal mucus; snot
〖鼻音〗(名)[bíyīn]
nasal sound; nasal
〖鼻子〗(名)[bízi]
nose
〖鼻祖〗(名)[bízǔ]
the earliest ancestor; originator (of a tradition, school of thought, etc.)

bǐ

匕[bǐ]
〖匕首〗(名)[bǐshǒu][把 bǎ]
dagger

比(动、名、介)[bǐ]
① compare; contrast; comparison ② gesture (with hands) ③ ratio; proportion ④ more than, better than, longer than, etc.
〖比比皆是〗[bǐbǐjiēshì]
such is found everywhere; (such a person, thing or case) can be found everywhere
〖比不上〗[bǐ bu shàng]
cannot compare with; no match for
〖比得上〗[bǐ de shàng]
comparable
〖比方〗(名)[bǐfang]
analogy; example

B

〖比分〗(名)[bǐfēn]
score
〖比价〗(名)[bǐjià]
price relations; parity; rate of exchange (e.g. between the RMB yuan and the U.S. dollar)
〖比较〗(动、副)[bǐjiào]
compare; comparatively
〖比例〗(名)[bǐlì]
①proportion ②ratio ③scale
〖比例尺〗(名)[bǐlìchǐ]
scale(e.g. on a map)
〖比拟〗(动)[bǐnǐ]
compare;draw a parallel ②metaphor
〖比如〗(副)[bǐrú]
① for example; for instance; such as ②if; suppose; say
〖比赛〗(动、名)[bǐsài]
contest; compete; match; race; competition
〖比上不足,比下有余〗
[bǐshàngbùzú, bǐxiàyǒuyú]
fall short of the best but be better than the worst; can pass muster
〖比喻〗(动、名)[bǐyù]
metaphor; analogy; parable
〖比重〗(名)[bǐzhòng]
specific gravity

彼(代)[bǐ]
① that; those; the other; another ② one's opposite
〖彼岸〗(名)[bǐ'àn]
①the other shore ②nirvana
〖彼此〗[bǐcǐ]
① this and that ② each other; one another
〖彼一时,此一时〗
[bǐyīshí, cǐyīshí]
times have changed; that was one time, and this is another

笔(名、量)[bǐ]〔枝 zhī〕
① pen; pencil; writing brush ② stroke of a Chinese character ③ a measure word (a stroke, a sum of money, etc.)
〖笔调〗(名)[bǐdiào]
(of writing) tone; style
〖笔杆〗(名)[bǐgǎn]
holder of a writing brush
〖笔杆子〗(名)[bǐgǎnzi]
an effective writer
〖笔画〗(名)[bǐhuà]
stroke of a Chinese character
〖笔迹〗(名)[bǐjī]
handwriting
〖笔记〗(名)[bǐjì]
notes; memorandum
〖笔记本〗(名)[bǐjìběn]
notebook
〖笔尖〗(名)[bǐjiān]
pen nib
〖笔名〗(名)[bǐmíng]
pen name; pseudonym
〖笔墨〗(名)[bǐmò]
pen and ink; (fig.) writing; words; articles
〖笔墨官司〗(名)[bǐmòguānsi]
written polemics; written controversy; a battle of words
〖笔试〗(名、动)[bǐshì]

(take) written examination
〖笔顺〗(名)[bǐshùn]
order of strokes in writing a Chinese character
〖笔误〗(名)[bǐwù]
slip of the pen
〖笔译〗(名、动)[bǐyì]
written translation
〖笔直〗(形)[bǐzhí]
perfectly straight; upright

鄙[bǐ]

〖鄙薄〗(动)[bǐbó]
despise; scorn
〖鄙视〗(动)[bǐshì]
despise; disdain; look down upon

bì

币[bì]

〖币值〗(名)[bìzhí]
currency value
〖币制〗(名)[bìzhì]
currency system; monetary system

必[bì]

〖必不可免〗[bìbùkěmiǎn]
unavoidable
〖必不可少〗[bìbùkěshǎo]
absolutely necessary; indispensable; essential
〖必定〗(副)[bìdìng]
① be bound to; undoubtedly ② will certainly; be sure to
〖必将〗(副)[bìjiāng]
surely will
〖必然〗(形、副)[bìrán]
be bound to; inevitable; necessarily; certainly
〖必然王国〗(名)[bìránwángguó]
realm of necessity
〖必然性〗(名)[bìránxìng]
necessity; inevitability; certainty
〖必修课〗(名)[bìxiūkè]
compulsory subject; required course
〖必须〗(助动)[bìxū]
must; have to; necessary
〖必需〗(形、动)[bìxū]
essential; indispensable
〖必需品〗(名)[bìxūpǐn]
(daily) necessities
〖必要〗(形)[bìyào]
necessary; essential; indispensable
〖必要性〗(名)[bìyàoxìng]
necessity
〖必由之路〗[bìyóuzhīlù]
road one must follow or take; the only road to; the only way
〖必争之地〗[bìzhēngzhīdì]
hotly contested spot (e.g. in a battle)

毕[bì]

〖毕恭毕敬〗[bìgōngbìjìng]
reverent and respectful; extremely deferential
〖毕竟〗(副)[bìjìng]
after all; all in all; all said and done; in the final analysis

B

〖毕生〗(名)[bìshēng]
all one's life; life-long; lifetime
〖毕业〗(动)[bìyè]
finish school; graduate
〖毕业班〗(名)[bìyèbān]
graduating class
〖毕业分配〗(名)[bìyèfēnpèi]
job assignment on graduation
〖毕业生〗(名)[bìyèsheng]
graduate
〖毕业证书〗(名)[bìyèzhèngshū]
(graduation) certificate; diploma

闭(动)[bì]
① shut; close ② stop up; obstruct
〖闭关政策〗(名)[bìguānzhèngcè]
closed-door policy
〖闭关自守〗[bìguānzìshǒu]
close the country to international intercourse
〖闭路电视〗(名)[bìlùdiànshì]
closed-circuit television
〖闭门羹〗(名)[bìméngēng]
refusal of entrance; cold shoulder treatment
〖闭门造车〗[bìménzàochē]
make a cart behind closed doors; work behind closed doors; draw up a plan without considering the actual conditions
〖闭目塞听〗[bìmùsètīng]
shut one's eyes and stop up one's ears; have a closed mind
〖闭幕〗[bìmù]
① the curtain falls; lower the curtain ② (of meetings) close; conclude ③ closing (e.g. closing address; closing ceremony)
〖闭塞〗(动、形)[bìsè]
close up; stop up; cut off from the world; out of touch
〖闭音节〗(名)[bìyīnjié]
closed syllable

庇[bì]
〖庇护〗(动)[bìhù]
shelter; shield; put under one's protection
〖庇护所〗(名)[bìhùsuǒ]
sanctuary; asylum

毙(动)[bì]
die; be killed
〖毙命〗[bì mìng]
(derog.) be done for; lose one's life

蓖[bì]
〖蓖麻〗(名)[bìmá]
castor oil plant

碧(形)[bì]
emerald colour; green and blue; green or blue
〖碧空〗(名)[bìkōng]
a clear blue sky; an azure sky
〖碧绿〗(形)[bìlǜ]
jade green
〖碧血〗(名)[bìxuè]

blood shed in a just cause
〖碧血丹心〗[bìxuèdānxīn]
righteous blood and loyal heart

弊(名)[bì]
①malpractice ②defect
〖弊病〗(名)[bìbìng]
①abuse; corrupt practices; malpractices ②evil; malady

壁(名)[bì]
wall; something wall-like
〖壁报〗(名)[bìbào]
wall newspaper
〖壁橱〗(名)[bìchú]
built-in wardrobe or cupboard
〖壁画〗(名)[bìhuà]
wall painting; fresco; mural
〖壁垒〗(名)[bìlěi]
①strongly fortified; barrier ②rival camps confronting each other; two sharply opposed sides
〖壁炉〗(名)[bìlú]
fireplace
〖壁毯〗(名)[bìtǎn]
tapestry; wall hanging

避(动)[bì]
①avoid; evade; shun; eschew ②prevent; keep away
〖避而不谈〗[bì'érbùtán]
evade the question; keep silent about the matter
〖避风头〗[bìfēngtou]
lie low; stay away from trouble
〖避讳〗(动、名)[bìhuì]
①evade the issue; dodge ②a word or phrase to be avoided as taboo; taboo
〖避开〗(动)[bìkāi]
evade; dodge; steer clear of; keep away from
〖避雷器〗(名)[bìléiqì]
lightning arrester; lightning conductor
〖避雷针〗(名)[bìléizhēn]
lightning rod;
〖避免〗(动)[bìmiǎn]
avoid; avert; refrain from
〖避难〗[bì nàn]
take refuge; seek asylum
〖避暑〗[bì shǔ]
avoid the summer heat; take a summer holiday; go away for the summer holidays
〖避孕〗[bì yùn]
contraception; birth control
〖避孕套〗(名)[bìyùntào]
condom
〖避重就轻〗[bìzhòngjiùqīng]
avoid the important and dwell on the trivial; take up the minor issue to evade the major one

biān

边(名)[biān]
①side ②margin; border; edge; rim ③border; frontier; boundary
〖边防〗(名)[biānfáng]
frontier defence
〖边防部队〗(名)[biānfángbùduì]
frontier guards

B

〖边锋〗(名)[biānfēng]
wing; wing forward
〖边际〗(名)[biānjì]
limit; bound; boundary
〖边际效用论〗(名)
[biānjìxiàoyònglùn]
the theory of marginal utility
〖边疆〗(名)[biānjiāng]
border area; frontier; frontier region
〖边角料〗(名)[biānjiǎoliào]
leftover bits and pieces (of industrial material)
〖边界〗(名)[biānjiè]
border; boundary; boundary line; borderline
〖边境〗(名)[biānjìng]
border; frontier
〖边贸〗(名)[biānmào]
frontier trade
〖边门〗(名)[biānmén]
side door; wicket door
〖边卡〗(名)[biānqiǎ]
border checkpoint
〖边区〗(名)[biānqū]
border area
〖边音〗(名)[biānyīn]
a lateral sound; lateral (phonet.)
〖边缘〗(名)[biānyuán]
brink; verge; edge
〖边缘科学〗(名)[biānyuánkēxué]
borderline science
〖边远〗(形)[biānyuǎn]
distant; remote

编(动)[biān]
① weave; plait ② form; organize; arrange ③ edit; compile ④ write; compose
〖编号〗(名)[biān hào]
① number ② serial number
〖编辑〗(动、名)[biānjí]
edit; compile; editor; compiler
〖编辑部〗(名)[biānjíbù]
editor's office; editorial department
〖编剧〗(名)[biān jù]
playwright; scriptwriter; scenario-writer
〖编码〗[biānmǎ]
coding
〖编目〗[biān mù]
① make a catalogue of ② catalogue; list
〖编年史〗(名)[biānniánshǐ]
annals; chronicle
〖编排〗(动、名)[biānpái]
arrange; lay out; layout
〖编入〗(动)[biānrù]
enroll; put in; classify
〖编审〗(动、名)[biānshěn]
read and edit; copy editor
〖编外人员〗(名)
[biānwàirényuán]
non-permanent staff; unofficial personnel
〖编写〗(动)[biānxiě]
compile
〖编造〗(动)[biānzào]
① make; prepare; work out ② invent; fabricate; frame up; concoct ③ create out of imagination

〖编者〗(名)[biānzhě]
editor; compiler
〖编者按〗(名)[biānzhě àn]
editor's note; comment
〖编织〗(动)[biānzhī]
weave; braid; plait; knit
〖编制〗(动、名)[biānzhì]
①weave; plait; braid ②make; work out; draw up (rules and regulations) ③ fixed number of personnel of a unit; authorized strength of a unit; establishment
〖编著〗(动)[biānzhù]
compile; write
〖编纂〗(动)[biānzuǎn]
compile

鞭 (名)[biān]
whip; lash
〖鞭策〗(动)[biāncè]
spur on; urge on
〖鞭长莫及〗[biānchángmòjí]
beyond the reach of one's power; too far away for one to be able to help
〖鞭笞〗(动)[biānchī]
whip; flog; castigate
〖鞭炮〗(名)[biānpào]
firecrackers; strings of firecrackers
〖鞭子〗(名)[biānzi]
whip

biǎn

贬(动)[biǎn]
① demote; reduce; devaluate② censure; depreciate
〖贬低〗(动)[biǎndī]
disparage; belittle; play down
〖贬义〗(名)[biǎnyì]
derogatory sense
〖贬义词〗(名)[biǎnyìcí]
derogatory word
〖贬值〗[biǎn zhí]
devaluate; depreciate

扁(形)[biǎn]
flat
〖扁担〗(名)[biǎndan]〔条 tiáo〕
carrying-pole; shoulder pole
〖扁桃体〗(名)[biǎntáotǐ]
tonsil

biàn

变 (动)[biàn] change
〖变本加厉〗[biànběnjiālì]
become aggravated; with ever-increasing intensity; go even further
〖变成〗(动)[biànchéng]
change into; become
〖变动〗(动)[biàndòng]
change; rearrange
〖变革〗(动、名)[biàngé]
transform; reform; transformation; reformation; change reality
〖变更〗(动)[biàngēng]
alter; change; modify
〖变故〗(名)[biàngù]
an unforeseen event; accident; misfortune
〖变卦〗[biàn guà]

B

change one's mind; change one's tune
〖变化〗(动、名)[biànhuà]
change; changeable
〖变幻莫测〗[biànhuànmòcè]
unpredictable; erratic
〖变换〗(动)[biànhuàn]
change; substitute
〖变焦镜头〗(名)
[biànjiāojìngtóu]
zoom lens
〖变节〗[biàn jié]
change of loyalty; betray a (cause); turn one's coat
〖变迁〗(动、名)[biànqiān]
change in trend or conditions
〖变色〗[biàn sè]
① change colour ② change countenance; become angry
〖变色龙〗(名)[biànsèlóng]
chameleon
〖变速〗[biànsù]
variable velocity; speed change; gearshift
〖变态〗(名、形)[biàntài]
① metamorphosis; change of character or attitude ② abnormal; sick
〖变天〗[biàn tiān]
① weather change for the worse; (weather) turn overcast ② stage a come-back (by the reactionaries)
〖变通〗(动)[biàntōng]
accommodate; fall in with; change method; do sth. in another way
〖变相〗[biàn xiàng]
disguised form of; in disguised form
〖变形〗[biànxíng]
be out of shape; become deformed
〖变压器〗(名)[biànyāqì]
(electr.) transformer
〖变质〗[biànzhì]
go bad; degenerate; deteriorate
〖变种〗(名)[biànzhǒng]
variation; mutation
〖变奏〗(名)[biànzòu]
variation

便(副)[biàn]
then; no sooner than ...; thereupon
另见 pián
〖便秘〗(名)[biànbì]
constipation
〖便当〗(形)[biàndang]
convenient; handy; easy
〖便道〗(名)[biàndào]
① sidewalk; pavement ② shortcut; makeshift road
〖便饭〗(名)[biànfàn]〔顿 dùn〕
informal meal; potluck
〖便服〗(名)[biànfú]
informal dress; plain clothes; civilian clothes
〖便笺〗(名)[biànjiān]
notepaper; memo; memo pad
〖便览〗(名)[biànlǎn]
brief guide (e.g. a road-book)
〖便利〗(形、动)[biànlì]
convenient; facilitate

〖便条〗(名)[biàntiáo]
short note (written on a slip of paper)
〖便携式〗(形、名)[biànxiéshì]
portable
〖便衣〗(名)[biànyī]
informal dress; plain-clothes (man)
〖便宜行事〗[biànyíxíngshì]
act at one's discretion; act as one sees fit
〖便于〗(动)[biànyú]
be convenient to
〖便中〗[biànzhōng]
at one's convenience;when it's convenient

遍(形、动、量)[biàn]
① all over② spread; reach③ a verbal measure word (time in repetition)
〖遍布〗(动)[biànbù]
be found everywhere; spread all over
〖遍地〗(副)[biàndì]
everywhere
〖遍及〗(动)[biànjí]
reach as far as; reach every place
〖遍体鳞伤〗[biàntǐlínshāng]
the body is covered with wounds all over

辨(动)[biàn]
distinguish; recognize
〖辨别〗(动)[biànbié]
distinguish; differentiate
〖辨明〗(动)[biànmíng]
distinguish; discriminate
〖辨认〗(动)[biànrèn]
recognize; make out
〖辨证论治〗[biànzhènglùnzhì]
(traditional Chinese medicine) diagnosis and treatment based on an overall analysis of the illness and the patient's condition

辩(动)[biàn]
argue; discuss; dispute
〖辩白〗(动)[biànbái]
try to justify (oneself for one's behaviour, etc.)
〖辩驳〗(动)[biànbó]
argue and refute
〖辩护〗(动)[biànhù]
come out in defence of; defend
〖辩护人〗(名)[biànhùrén]
defender; counsel
〖辩护士〗(名)[biànhùshì]
apologist
〖辩解〗(动)[biànjiě]
argue; justify; explain away
〖辩论〗(动)[biànlùn]
debate; argue
〖辩证〗(形)[biànzhèng]
dialectical
〖辩证法〗(名)[biànzhèngfǎ]
dialectics
〖辩证唯物主义〗(名)[biànzhèngwéiwùzhǔyì]
dialectical materialism

辫[biàn]

〖辫子〗(名)[biànzi]〔条 tiáo〕
braid; queue; a hold(over sb.)

B

biāo

标(动、名)[biāo]
label; mark; tender; bid; prize
〖标榜〗(动)[biāobǎng]
brag about; give favourable publicity to; style or present (oneself as)
〖标本〗(名)[biāoběn]
specimen
〖标兵〗(名)[biāobīng]
pacesetter
〖标尺〗(名)[biāochǐ]
surveyor's rod; staff gauge
〖标点〗(名、动)[biāodiǎn]
punctuation; punctuate
〖标点符号〗(名)[biāodiǎnfúhào]
punctuation marks
〖标号〗(名)[biāohào]
grade(e.g. high-grade cement)
〖标记〗(名)[biāojì]
mark; sign; symbol
〖标价〗[biāojià]
mark a price on(sth.); marked price
〖标明〗(动)[biāomíng]
mark; indicate
〖标签〗(名)[biāoqiān]
label; tag
〖标枪〗(名)[biāoqiāng]
javelin
〖标题〗(名)[biāotí]
heading; title; headline
〖标题音乐〗(名)[biāotíyīnyuè]
programme music
〖标新立异〗[biāoxīnlìyì]
create what is new and original
〖标语〗(名)[biāoyǔ]〔条 tiáo〕
slogan; poster
〖标志〗(动、名)[biāozhì]
make; show; symbolize; symbol; distinguishing mark
〖标致〗(形)[biāozhi]
beautiful; handsome
〖标准〗(名、形)[biāozhǔn]
standard; criterion; standardized

biǎo

表(名、动)[biǎo]
① watch ② metre ③ surface ④ table; form; chart ⑤ express; show
〖表白〗(动)[biǎobái]
vindicate; justify oneself; profess
〖表层〗(名)[biǎocéng]
top layer
〖表达〗(动)[biǎodá]
express; voice(one's opinion)
〖表弟〗(名)[biǎodì]
male cousin who is younger than oneself(son of father's sister or mother's brother or sister)
〖表格〗(名)[biǎogé]
form; table; chart
〖表姐〗(名)[biǎojiě]
femal cousin who is older than

oneself (daughter of father's sister or mother's brother or sister)
〖表决〗(动)[biǎojué]
decide by vote; put to the vote; vote
〖表里不一〗[biǎolǐbùyī]
not being what one professes to be
〖表里如一〗[biǎolǐrúyī]
one's appearance tallies with one's inner mind; integrity
〖表露〗(动)[biǎolù]
show; demonstrate; reveal
〖表妹〗(名)[biǎomèi]
female cousin who is younger than oneself (daughter of father's sister or mother's brother or sister)
〖表面〗(名、形)[biǎomiàn]
surface; superficial; ostensible
〖表面化〗(动)[biǎomiànhuà]
become overt; come out into the open; be only the first open signs of
〖表面文章〗(名)[biǎomiànwénzhāng]
specious writing; pretence; cover-up
〖表明〗(动)[biǎomíng]
make clear; demonstrate; indicate
〖表盘〗(名)[biǎopán]
dial plate; dial
〖表皮〗(名)[biǎopí]
(biol.)epidermis; (bot.)bark
〖表情〗(名)[biǎoqíng]
facial expression
〖表示〗(动)[biǎoshì]
indicate; express; mean
〖表叔〗(名)[biǎoshū]
uncle(son of grandmother's brother)
〖表率〗(名)[biǎoshuài]
good example
〖表态〗[biǎotài]
make public one's stand on; clarify one's position
〖表现〗(动、名)[biǎoxiàn]
show; behave; behaviour
〖表兄〗(名)[biǎoxiōng]
male cousin who is older than oneself(son of father's sister or mother's brother or sister)
〖表演〗(动)[biǎoyǎn]
perform; act
〖表扬〗(动)[biǎoyáng]
praise; commend
〖表意文字〗(名)[biǎoyìwénzì]
ideograph
〖表语〗(名)[biǎoyǔ]
predicative
〖表彰〗(动)[biǎozhāng]
cite; commend

biē

憋(动)[biē]
① choke; stifle ② hold back; restrain
〖憋闷〗(形)[biēmen]
bored; depressed
〖憋气〗(形)[biēqì]
short of breath; suffocated

B

bié

别(动、形、副)[bié]
① leave; depart ② clip things together ③ other; another; some other ④ do not; must not
另见 biè
〖别出心裁〗[biéchūxīncái]
have an unconventional idea; an unusual idea
〖别处〗(名)[biéchù]
elsewhere; other place
〖别的〗(代)[biéde]
other
〖别管〗(连)[biéguǎn]
no matter; however; whatever
〖别开生面〗[biékāishēngmiàn]
in a novel way
〖别名〗(名)[biémíng]
another name
〖别人〗(名)[biérén]
others
〖别墅〗(名)[biéshù]
villa
〖别有用心〗[biéyǒuyòngxīn]
with ulterior motives or purpose
〖别针〗(名)[biézhēn]
pin
〖别致〗(形)[biézhì]
new and unusual; interesting and novel
〖别字〗(名)[biézì]
wrongly written or mispronounced character

蹩[bié]
〖蹩脚〗(形)[biéjiǎo]
inferior in skill or quality; poor and incompetent

biě

瘪(形)[biě]
shrivelled up; drab (language)

biè

别[biè]
另见 bié
〖别扭〗(形)[bièniu]
① frustrating; bungling; out of place ② hard to get along with

bīn

宾(名)[bīn]
guest
〖宾馆〗(名)[bīnguǎn]
guest house
〖宾语〗(名)[bīnyǔ]
(gram.) object
〖宾至如归〗[bīnzhìrúguī]
guests feel at home; a home from home
〖宾主〗(名)[bīnzhǔ]
guest and host

濒[bīn]
〖濒临〗(动)[bīnlín]
be close to; border on
〖濒危〗[bīnwēi]
be in imminent danger; be critically ill
〖濒于〗(动)[bīnyú]
be on the verge of

bīng

冰(名)[bīng]
ice
〖冰雹〗(名)[bīngbáo]
hailstones
〖冰川〗(名)[bīngchuān]
glacier
〖冰点〗(名)[bīngdiǎn]
freezing point
〖冰冻三尺,非一日之寒〗[bīngdòngsānchǐ, fēiyīrìzhīhán]
(lit.)It takes more than one cold day for the river to freeze three feet deep; (fig.)The trouble has been brewing for quite some time
〖冰棍儿〗(名)[bīnggùnr]
[根 gēn]ice-sticks (of different flavours); ice lolly
〖冰块〗(名)[bīngkuài]
ice cube; lump of ice
〖冰冷〗(形)[bīnglěng]
icecold; very cold
〖冰凉〗(形)[bīngliáng]
(of things)very cool; very cold
〖冰淇淋〗(名)[bīngqílín]
ice-cream
〖冰球〗(名)[bīngqiú]
ice hockey
〖冰山〗(名)[bīngshān]
iceberg
〖冰糖〗(名)[bīngtáng]
crystallized sugar
〖冰天雪地〗[bīngtiānxuědì]
icy and snowy field;all covered with ice and snow
〖冰箱〗(名)[bīngxiāng]
ice box; refrigerator
〖冰鞋〗(名)[bīngxié]
skating boots; skates
〖冰雪〗(名)[bīngxuě]
ice and snow
〖冰镇〗(动)[bīngzhèn]
ice; iced (e.g. ice beer; iced coke)

兵(名)[bīng]
soldier, fighter; army; weapons; military affairs
〖兵变〗(名)[bīngbiàn]
mutiny
〖兵法〗(名)[bīngfǎ]
art of war; military strategy and tactics
〖兵工厂〗(名)[bīnggōngchǎng]
munitions factory; arsenal
〖兵荒马乱〗[bīnghuāngmǎluàn]
turmoil and chaos of war
〖兵力〗(名)[bīnglì]
force; military strength
〖兵马俑〗(名)[bīngmǎyǒng]
wood or clay figures of warriors and horses buried with the dead
〖兵器〗(名)[bīngqì]
weaponry; weapons; arms
〖兵戎相见〗[bīngróngxiāngjiàn]
resort to arms; appeal to arms
〖兵团〗(名)[bīngtuán]
army corps
〖兵役〗(名)[bīngyì]
military service
〖兵役法〗(名)[bīngyìfǎ]
law of military service

B

〖兵营〗(名)[bīngyíng]
military camp; barracks
〖兵种〗(名)[bīngzhǒng]
different branches of the military service

bǐng

丙(名)[bǐng]
the third of the ten Heavenly Stems; number three; third
〖丙纶〗(名)[bǐnglún]
poly-propylene fibre
〖丙酮〗(名)[bǐngtóng]
acetone
〖丙种球蛋白〗(名)[bǐngzhǒngqiúdànbái]
gamma globulin

饼(名)[bǐng]〔张 zhāng〕
cake; pastry; any of various pastries
〖饼干〗(名)[bǐnggān]〔块 kuài〕
biscuit

bìng

并(连、副)[bìng]
① and ② placed before a negative word to show not as might be expected(e.g. by no means)
〖并存〗(动)[bìngcún]
coexist
〖并发症〗(名)[bìngfāzhèng]
complication
〖并驾齐驱〗[bìngjiàqíqū]
run neck and neck; can well stand side by side with
〖并肩〗(副)[bìngjiān]
shoulder to shoulder; side by side
〖并举〗(动)[bìngjǔ]
promote or work simultaneously;simultaneous employment(of modern and indigenous methods of production); simultaneous development of ...
〖并联〗(名)[bìnglián]
parallel connection
〖并列〗(动)[bìngliè]
put ... on a par with ...; parallel
〖并列句〗(名)[bìnglièjù]
(gram.)compound sentence
〖并排〗(副)[bìngpái]
keep abreast of; be side by side; lie alongside
〖并且〗(连)[bìngqiě]
moreover; and also
〖并吞〗(动)[bìngtūn]
annex; gobble up
〖并行〗(动)[bìngxíng]
go side by side
〖并重〗(动)[bìngzhòng]
regard both as equally important; attach equal importance to

病(名、动)[bìng]
illness; fall ill
〖病虫害〗(名)[bìngchónghài]
plant diseases and insect pests
〖病床〗(名)[bìngchuáng]
sickbed

〖病从口入〗[bìngcóngkǒurù]
illness finds its way in by the mouth
〖病毒〗(名)[bìngdú]
virus
〖病房〗(名)[bìngfáng]
sickroom; ward
〖病根〗(名)[bìnggēn]
(lit.)cause of disease; (fig.) root of trouble
〖病故〗(动)[bìnggù]
die of illness
〖病号〗(名)[bìnghào]
sick person
〖病急乱投医〗[bìngjíluàntóuyī]
(lit.)turn to any doctor one can find when critically ill; (fig.)try anything when in a desperate situation
〖病假〗(名)[bìngjià]
sick leave
〖病菌〗(名)[bìngjūn]
harmful germ
〖病理〗(名)[bìnglǐ]
pathology
〖病历〗(名)[bìnglì]
medical record; case history
〖病情〗(名)[bìngqíng]
state of an illness; patient's condition; symptom
〖病人〗(名)[bìngrén]
sick person; patient
〖病入膏肓〗[bìngrùgāohuāng]
(lit.)fatal disease; mortally ill; (fig.)past all hope
〖病态〗(名)[bìngtài]
physiologically or psychologically abnormal; morbid (state)

bō

拨(动)[bō]
stir or poke with hand or stick
〖拨款〗[bō kuǎn]
allot or appropriate funds
〖拨乱反正〗[bōluànfǎnzhèng]
bring order out of chaos; set wrong things right
〖拨弄〗(动)[bōnòng]
① stir up; fiddle with ② provoke; stir up; sow dissension ③ manipulate

波(名)[bō]
wave
〖波长〗(名)[bōcháng]
wavelength
〖波动〗(动)[bōdòng]
undulate; fluctuate; unsettle; rise and fall
〖波及〗(动)[bōjí]
affect; involve
〖波澜壮阔〗[bōlánzhuàngkuò]
on a magnificent scale; surge forward with tremendous momentum
〖波浪〗(名)[bōlàng]
wave (water)
〖波涛〗(名)[bōtāo]
huge waves; billows
〖波涛汹涌〗[bōtāo xiōngyǒng]
billowy waves
〖波折〗(名)[bōzhé]
setbacks

B

玻[bō]

〖玻璃〗(名)[bōlí]〔块 kuài〕
glass; pane
〖玻璃杯〗(名)[bōlibēi]
glass; tumbler
〖玻璃纸〗(名)[bōlizhǐ]
cellophane; glassine

剥(动)[bō]
peel; skin
另见 bāo
〖剥夺〗(动)[bōduó]
deprive; expropriate
〖剥削〗(动)[bōxuē]
exploit
〖剥削阶级〗(名)[bōxuē jiējí]
exploiting class
〖剥削者〗(名)[bōxuēzhě]
exploiter

菠[bō]
〖菠菜〗(名)[bōcài]
spinach
〖菠萝〗(名)[bōluó]
pineapple

播(动)[bō]
① sow ② broadcast
〖播送〗(动)[bōsòng]
broadcast
〖播音〗[bō yīn]
broadcast
〖播种〗[bō zhǒng]
seed planting
〖播种机〗(名)[bōzhǒngjī]
seeder; seed planting machine
〖播种〗(动)[bōzhòng]
sow

bó

伯(名)[bó]
① uncle ② earl
〖伯父〗(名)[bófù]
① uncle (father's elder brother) ② a term of respectful address to elderly people (male)
〖伯母〗(名)[bómǔ]
① aunt (wife of father's elder brother) ② a term of respectful address to elderly people (female)

驳(动)[bó]
refute; repudiate
〖驳斥〗(动)[bóchì]
repudiate; refute
〖驳船〗(名)[bóchuán]
barge
〖驳倒〗(动)[bódǎo]
refute; overcome (sb.) by argument
〖驳回〗(动)[bóhuí]
reject (with comment)

勃[bó]
〖勃然〗(副)[bórán]
① prosperously (in a vigorous and flourishing state) ② suddenly (burst into)
〖勃然大怒〗[bórándànù]
fly into a rage

脖[bó]

〖脖子〗(名)[bózi]
neck

博[bó]
〖博大精深〗[bódàjīngshēn]
broad and profound
〖博得〗(动)[bódé]
win(praise, applause, etc.)
〖博古通今〗[bógǔtōngjīn]
conversant with things past and present; erudite and informed
〖博览会〗(名)[bólǎnhuì]
fair; exposition
〖博士〗(名)[bóshì]
doctor (of medicine, philosophy, etc.)
〖博物馆〗(名)[bówùguǎn]
museum
〖博学〗[bóxué]
well-learned

搏[bó]
〖搏动〗(动)[bódòng]
(heart, etc.)beat rhythmically; throb
〖搏斗〗(动)[bódòu]
wrestle; fight

薄(形)[bó]
thin
另见 báo
〖薄利多销〗[bólìduōxiāo]
small profits but quick turnover
〖薄膜〗(名)[bómó]
membrane; film
〖薄弱〗(形)[bóruò]
weak; vulnerable
〖薄雾〗(名)[bówù]
mist; haze

bò

簸[bò]
〖簸箕〗(名)[bòji]
a basket or a winnowing pan (for grain); a dustpan(for dust)

bǔ

补(动)[bǔ]
① mend; patch ② nourish
〖补偿〗(动)[bǔcháng]
compensate
〖补充〗(动)[bǔchōng]
make up(to a required number); supplement; add to
〖补丁〗(名)[bǔding]
patch
〖补给〗(动)[bǔjǐ]
supply; material supply
〖补角〗(名)[bǔjiǎo]
supplementary angle
〖补救〗(动)[bǔjiù]
remedy; rectify(error)
〖补考〗(名)[bǔkǎo]
make-up examination
〖补课〗[bǔ kè]
make up for missed lessons
〖补贴〗(名)[bǔtiē]
subsidy; allowance
〖补习〗(动)[bǔxí]
take supplementary classes

B

〖补药〗(名)[bǔyào]
tonic
〖补语〗(名)[bǔyǔ]
(gram.) complement
〖补助〗(动)[bǔzhù]
subsidize; help; supply needs
〖补足〗(动)[bǔzú]
supply what is lacking; make up a deficiency

捕(动)[bǔ]
catch
〖捕风捉影〗[bǔfēngzhuōyǐng]
catch at shadows; beat the air; (make accusations) on hearsay
〖捕获〗(动)[bǔhuò]
succeed in catching; capture
〖捕捉〗(动)[bǔzhuō]
catch

哺[bǔ]
〖哺乳动物〗(名)[bǔrǔ dòngwù]
mammal
〖哺育〗(动)[bǔyù]
nurture

bù

不(副)[bù]
not; no
〖不安〗(形)[bù'ān]
uneasy; perturbed; worried
〖不卑不亢〗[bùbēibùkàng]
neither humble nor pert; neither obsequious nor arrogant
〖不比〗[bù bǐ]
different from
〖不必〗(副)[bùbì]
not necessary; need not
〖不便〗(形)[bùbiàn]
inconvenient
〖不曾〗(副)[bùcéng]
never in the past
〖不成文法〗(名)[bùchéngwénfǎ]
unwritten law
〖不辞而别〗[bùcí'érbié]
leave without saying good-bye
〖不辞劳苦〗[bùcíláokǔ]
spare no pains; take pains
〖不错〗(形)[bùcuò]
pretty good; not bad
〖不打自招〗[bùdǎzìzhāo]
(lit.) confess without duress; (fig.) in voluntary or unintentional confession; let the cat out of the bag without being pressed
〖不大〗(副)[bùdà]
① not often; seldom ② not very; not quite
〖不但〗(连)[bùdàn]
not only
〖不到黄河心不死〗
[bùdàohuánghéxīnbùsǐ]
not stop until one reaches the Huanghe River; not stop until one reaches one's goal; refuse to give up until all hope is gone
〖不得不〗[bùdébù]
have no choice but
〖不得了〗[bùdéliǎo]
① terrible; be in a bad way ② extremely
〖不得已〗[bùdéyǐ]
have no choice but

〖不等式〗(名)[bùděngshì]
inequality
〖不定〗(副)[bùdìng]
① may or may not ② indefinitely
〖不动产〗(名)[bùdòngchǎn]
real estate; immovable property
〖不断〗(副)[bùduàn]
unceasingly; ceaselessly; incessantly
〖不对〗[bù duì]
wrong; not so
〖不法〗(形)[bùfǎ]
unlawful
〖不妨〗(副)[bùfáng]
it would be well if ...; no harm; may as well
〖不服水土〗[bùfúshuǐtǔ]
not accustomed to the climate of a new place; not acclimatized
〖不甘〗(动)[bùgān]
be unwilling to; will not be reconciled to; will not take it lying down
〖不敢当〗[bùgǎndāng]
I really don't deserve this; you flatter me
〖不攻自破〗[bùgōngzìpò]
self collapse;self discrediting
〖不共戴天〗[bùgòngdàitiān]
not live under the same sky (with one's enemy); sworn (enemy)
〖不顾〗[bù gù]
disregard; turn a deaf ear to ...; regardless; in defiance of ...
〖不管〗(连)[bùguǎn]
no matter (how, what ...); despite; however
〖不过〗(连)[bùguò]
① only; merely ② but
〖不寒而栗〗[bùhán'érlì]
shudder with extreme fear; shudder at the thought of
〖不好意思〗[bù hǎoyìsi]
shy; embarrassed; reluctant to; be diffident
〖不和〗[bù hé]
not on good terms with; in discord; at odds; at variance; discord
〖不慌不忙〗[bùhuāngbùmáng]
no hurry; unhurriedly
〖不及格〗[bùjígé]
fail; flunk (in an exam)
〖不假思索〗[bùjiǎsīsuǒ]
without thinking
〖不见得〗[bùjiàndé]
not necessarily
〖不解〗(动)[bù jiě]
puzzled; do not understand
〖不禁〗(副)[bùjīn]
cannot help (doing something)
〖不仅〗(连)[bùjǐn]
not only ...
〖不久〗(名、副)[bùjiǔ]
soon; before long
〖不咎既往〗[bùjiùjìwǎng]
forgive past misdeeds; irrespective of one's past
〖不堪〗(形)[bùkān]
unendurable; unbearable
〖不堪设想〗[bùkānshèxiǎng]

B

inconceivable;unimaginable (referring to grave consequences)
〖不可避免〗[bùkěbìmiǎn]
unavoidable; inevitable; inescapable
〖不可多得〗[bùkěduōdé]
rare; hard to come by
〖不可告人〗[bùkěgàorén]
ulterior motives that cannot bear the light of day
〖不可救药〗[bùkějiùyào]
incorrigible; incurable; beyond help or remedy; be beyond cure
〖不可开交〗[bùkěkāijiāo]
① unmanageable ② be terribly (busy) ③ ineradicable
〖不可磨灭〗[bùkěmómiè]
indelible
〖不可偏废〗[bùkěpiānfèi]
do not over-emphasize one thing to the neglect of the other
〖不可思议〗[bùkěsīyì]
unimaginable; inconceivable
〖不可调和〗[bùkětiáohé]
irreconcilable; implacable
〖不可一世〗[bùkěyīshì]
overbearing; swagger like a conquering hero
〖不可知论〗(名)[bùkězhīlùn]
agnosticism
〖不可终日〗[bùkězhōngrì]
be on tenterhooks all the time; in a desperate situation
〖不可阻挡〗[bùkězǔdǎng]
irresistible
〖不客气〗[bù kèqi]
① don't mention it② impolite
〖不愧〗(动)[bùkuì]
be worthy of; live up to
〖不劳动者不得食〗
[bù láodòngzhě bùdé shí]
he who does not work, neither shall he eat
〖不劳而获〗[bùláo'érhuò]
reap without sowing; be idle and profit by other's toil
〖不力〗(形)[bùlì]
①half-hearted(prosecution)
②impotent; inefficient
〖不利〗(形)[bùlì]
disadvantageous; unfavourable
〖不良〗(形)[bùliáng]
bad; unhealthy; undesirable
〖不了了之〗[bùliǎoliǎozhī]
settle a thing by leaving it unsettled; end up in nothing definite
〖不料〗(副)[bùliào]
unexpectedly
〖不伦不类〗[bùlúnbùlèi]
neither fish nor fowl; nondescript
〖不论〗(连)[bùlùn]
no matter(how, what, etc.)
〖不满〗(动、形)[bùmǎn]
pass censure on; be discontented; dissatisfied; discontent
〖不免〗(副)[bùmiǎn]
bound to; have to; unavoidably
〖不明飞行物〗
[bùmíngfēixíngwù]
unidentified flying objects; UFO
〖不谋而合〗[bùmóu'érhé]

happen to coincide with
〖不偏不倚〗[bùpiānbùyǐ]
without bias or favour; impartial; avoid leaning to either side
〖不平〗(形)[bùpíng]
unjust; unfair
〖不平等条约〗(名)
[bùpíngděngtiáoyuē]
unequal treaty
〖不求甚解〗[bùqiúshènjiě]
do not seek to understand things thoroughly
〖不求有功,但求无过〗
[bùqiúyǒugōng, dànqiúwúguò]
seek not to be meritorious, but only to avoid blame
〖不屈〗(动)[bùqū]
undaunted
〖不屈不挠〗[bùqūbùnáo]
unswerving; unyielding
〖不然〗(连)[bùrán]
otherwise; or else; but for this
〖不忍〗(形)[bùrěn]
cannot bear (to do sth.).
〖不如〗(动、连)[bùrú]
① be not as good as ② had better; would rather
〖不入虎穴,焉得虎子〗
[bùrùhǔxué, yāndéhǔzǐ]
how can you catch tiger cubs without entering the tiger's lair; No pains, no gains.
〖不三不四〗[bùsānbùsì]
① neither one thing nor the other ② dubious (character)
〖不声不响〗[bùshēngbùxiǎng]
quiet; on the quiet
〖不胜枚举〗[bùshèngméijǔ]
too numerous to mention; defy enumeration
〖不时〗(副)[bùshí]
frequently; from time to time
〖不是…而是…〗(连)
[bùshì…érshì…]
not ... but ...
〖不是…就是…〗(连)
[bùshì…jiùshì…]
either ... or ...
〖不速之客〗[bùsùzhīkè]
casual visitor; uninvited guest; chance comer
〖不同〗(形)[bù tóng]
different
〖不外〗(动)[bùwài]
not beyond; nothing more than
〖不闻不问〗[bùwénbùwèn]
shut one's eyes to; indifferent
〖不惜〗(动)[bù xī]
have no scruples about; spare no (expense, effort, etc.)
〖不相干〗[bù xiānggān]
have nothing to do with
〖不相上下〗[bùxiāngshàngxià]
on a par (with); match; without much difference; be roughly the same
〖不像话〗[bù xiànghuà]
absurd; ridiculous; improper; unpresentable
〖不屑〗(动)[bùxiè]
disdain to; will not condescend to
〖不行〗[bù xíng]

① won't do; not up to standard ② cannot; not allowed
〖不幸〗(形)[bùxìng]
unfortunate
〖不朽〗(动)[bùxiǔ]
immortal
〖不锈钢〗(名)[bùxiùgāng]
stainless steel
〖不许〗[bù xǔ]
not allowed; do not permit
〖不言而喻〗[bùyán'éryù]
matter of course; it goes without saying
〖不要紧〗[bùyàojǐn]
unimportant; nothing serious; No matter!
〖不一而足〗[bùyī'érzú]
a lot of (same kind of things)
〖不遗余力〗[bùyíyúlì]
spare no efforts; never relax in
〖不翼而飞〗[bùyì'érfēi]
(lit.) fly without wings; (fig.) disappear suddenly; ... have grown wings
〖不用〗[bù yòng]
there is no need to
〖不由得〗[bùyóude]
involuntarily; could not help doing
〖不由自主〗[bùyóuzìzhǔ]
involuntarily; cannot restrain oneself
〖不约而同〗[bùyuē'értóng]
coincidence; do sth. in concert without previous arrangement; agree without previous consultation
〖不在乎〗[bù zàihu]
do not care about; do not mind
〖不在话下〗[bùzàihuàxià]
be nothing difficult; be a cinch
〖不择手段〗[bùzéshǒuduàn]
by hook or by crook; by fair means or foul; unscrupulously
〖不折不扣〗[bùzhébùkòu]
out and out; pure and simple
〖不知不觉〗[bùzhībùjué]
without one's knowing it; unawares
〖不知所措〗[bùzhīsuǒcuò]
at a loss; do not know what to do
〖不止〗(动)[bùzhǐ]
① not to stop at; keep on ② exceed
〖不只〗(连)[bùzhǐ]
not only
〖不致〗(副)[bùzhì]
not likely to
〖不置可否〗[bùzhìkěfǒu]
avoid saying yes or no; prevaricate
〖不至于〗[bù zhìyú]
not so ... as to ...
〖不着边际〗[bùzhuóbiānjì]
off the point; irrelevant
〖不自量力〗[bùzìliànglì]
overreach oneself; not to take a proper measure of oneself; go beyond one's depth
〖不足〗(动)[bùzú]
① insufficient; not enough ② not worth
〖不足道〗[bùzúdào]
not worth mentioning; not up to

the mark
〖不足为奇〗[bùzúwéiqí]
not at all surprising; entirely to be expected

布(名、动)[bù]
① cloth made of cotton or flax ② spread ③ arrange; deploy
〖布告〗(名)[bùgào]
notice
〖布景〗(名)[bùjǐng]
built-up scenery; setting
〖布局〗(名)[bùjú]
overall arrangement; lay-out
〖布匹〗(名)[bùpǐ]
(general term) cloth
〖布鞋〗(名)[bùxié]〔双 shuāng〕
cloth-shoes
〖布置〗(动)[bùzhì]
arrange; dispose

步(名、量)[bù]
① step ② a measure word (e.g. move in chess, etc.)
〖步兵〗(名)[bùbīng]
infantry
〖步步为营〗[bùbùwéiyíng]
make a stand at every step; advance gradually and entrench at every step
〖步调〗(名)[bùdiào]
① pace or speed (in walking or running) ② way, procedure or speed (in doing sth.)
〖步伐〗(名)[bùfá]
pace
〖步枪〗(名)[bùqiāng]〔枝 zhī〕
rifle
〖步人后尘〗[bùrénhòuchén]
follow in someone's footsteps; follow in the wake of
〖步行〗(动)[bùxíng]
be on foot
〖步骤〗(名)[bùzhòu]
steps; procedure

部(名、量)[bù]
① ministry ② a measure word (set of books)
〖部队〗(名)[bùduì]
unit; army; armed forces
〖部分〗(名)[bùfen]
part; section
〖部件〗(名)[bùjiàn]
parts or component parts
〖部落〗(名)[bùluò]
tribe
〖部门〗(名)[bùmén]
department
〖部首〗(名)[bùshǒu]
radicals by which characters are arranged in traditional Chinese dictionaries
〖部署〗(动)[bùshǔ]
arrange; deploy
〖部位〗(名)[bùwèi]
position; place; location
〖部下〗(名)[bùxià]
troops or officers under a commander
〖部优产品〗[bùyōuchǎnpǐn]
quality products designated by a ministry
〖部长〗(名)[bùzhǎng]
minister

B

C

cā

擦 (动)[cā]
① scrub; polish; rub; wipe ② rub... on; apply(ointment) ③ brush past
〖擦边球〗(名)[cābiānqiú]
touch ball
〖擦拭〗(动)[cāshì]
clean
〖擦音〗(名)[cāyīn]
fricative(consonants)

cāi

猜 (动)[cāi]
guess
〖猜测〗(动)[cāicè]
guess
〖猜忌〗(动)[cāijì]
suspicion and jealousy
〖猜谜〗[cāimí]
solve a riddle
〖猜想〗(动)[cāixiǎng]
guess; conjecture
〖猜疑〗(动)[cāiyí]
suspect

cái

才 (名、副)[cái]
① talent; ability ② just now; only; only just; only then
〖才干〗(名)[cáigàn]
practical ability
〖才华〗(名)[cáihuá]
rich talent; brilliance of mi-nd
〖才能〗(名)[cáinéng]
ability; talent
〖才子〗(名)[cáizǐ]
gifted scholar

材 [cái]
〖材料〗(名)[cáiliào]
materials

财 (名)[cái]
wealth

〖财产〗(名)[cáichǎn]
property; fortunes
〖财大气粗〗[cáidàqìcū]
rich and self-assured; He speaks louder who has wealth; with abundant financial resources
〖财富〗(名)[cáifù]
wealth; fortunes; riches
〖财力〗(名)[cáilì]
financial resources; financial capacity
〖财贸〗(名)[cáimào]
finance and trade
〖财迷〗(名、形)[cáimí]
money-mad; person obsessed by lust for money
〖财团〗(名)[cáituán]
consortium; financial group
〖财务〗(名)[cáiwù]
financial affairs; treasure
〖财物〗(名)[cáiwù]
money and property
〖财源〗(名)[cáiyuán]
source of revenue
〖财政〗(名)[cáizhèng]
finance

裁(动)[cái]
① cut ② reduce; cut down
〖裁缝〗(名)[cáiféng]
tailor; dressmaker
〖裁减〗(动)[cáijiǎn]
cut down; dismiss
〖裁剪〗(动)[cáijiǎn]
cut (a dress)
〖裁决〗(动)[cáijué]
make a ruling; judge; decide; verdict
〖裁军〗[cái jūn]
disarmament
〖裁判〗(动、名)[cáipàn]
① judge; decide; judgement ② referee
〖裁员〗[cáiyuán]
reduce the staff; cut down the number of persons employed

cǎi

采(动)[cǎi]
gather; select; pluck
〖采伐〗(动)[cǎifá]
fell timber
〖采访〗(动)[cǎifǎng]
cover news; be on a reporting assignment; interview sb.
〖采购〗(动)[cǎigòu]
purchase
〖采集〗(动)[cǎijí]
gather; collect
〖采矿〗[cǎi kuàng]
mine; obtain (coal, etc.) from a mine
〖采纳〗(动)[cǎinà]
adopt; take (sb.'s advice)
〖采取〗(动)[cǎiqǔ]
adopt; take (action); follow (a policy)
〖采用〗(动)[cǎiyòng]
employ; adopt; put to use
〖采摘〗(动)[cǎizhāi]
pluck; pick

彩(名)[cǎi]

C

① colour ② (of soldiers) be wounded in action
〖彩车〗(名)[cǎichē]
float (in a parade)
〖彩绘〗(名)[cǎihuì]
coloured drawing or pattern
〖彩礼〗(名)[cǎilǐ]
betrothal gifts (from the bridegroom to the bride's family); bride-price
〖彩排〗(动)[cǎipái]
dress rehearsal
〖彩票〗(名)[cǎipiào]
lottery ticket
〖彩旗〗(名)[cǎiqí]〔面 miàn〕
coloured flags; streamers
〖彩色〗(名)[cǎisè]
colour
〖彩色片〗(名)[cǎisèpiàn]〔部 bù〕
colour film
〖彩霞〗(名)[cǎixiá]
roseate clouds

踩(动)[cǎi]
stamp; tread; step on

cài

菜(名)[cài]
① vegetable ② a dish (either meat or vegetable)
〖菜单〗(名)[càidān]
menu
〖菜刀〗(名)[càidāo]
kitchen knife
〖菜花〗(名)[càihuā]
① cauliflower ② rape flower
〖菜篮子工程〗(名)
[càilánzigōngchéng]
vegetable basket project; non-staple food supply project
〖菜牛〗(名)[càiniú]
beef cattle
〖菜农〗(名)[càinóng]
vegetable grower
〖菜谱〗(名)[càipǔ]
① cookbook ② recipe
〖菜色〗(名)[càisè]
famished look; emaciated look
〖菜市场〗(名)[càishìchǎng]
market
〖菜园〗(名)[càiyuán]
vegetable garden
〖菜子儿〗(名)[càizǐr]
① vegetable seeds ② rapeseed

cān

参(动)[cān]
join; take part in
另见 cēn
〖参股〗[cāngǔ]
mutual purchasing of shares in enterprises
〖参观〗(动)[cānguān]
visit
〖参加〗(动)[cānjiā]
participate in; take part in; join
〖参见〗(动)[cānjiàn]
① see also; cf. ② pay respects to; make a formal visit to
〖参军〗[cānjūn]
join the army
〖参考〗(动)[cānkǎo]
be for reference (materials);

consult (reference materials, etc.); refer to
〖参谋〗(名、动)[cānmóu]
① staff officer ② give advice
〖参谋长〗(名)[cānmóuzhǎng]
chief of staff
〖参与〗(动)[cānyù]
take part in; join; be a party to
〖参阅〗(动)[cānyuè]
read for reference; consult (reference materials)
〖参赞〗(名)[cānzàn]
councillor
〖参展〗[cānzhǎn]
take part in an exhibition; participate in a commodities fair
〖参战〗[cān zhàn]
participate in war
〖参照〗(动)[cānzhào]
① confer; refer to; see; consult ② in the light of
〖参政〗[cānzhèng]
participate in government and political affairs

餐 (名、动、量)[cān]
① meal; eat ② a measure word for meals
〖餐车〗(名)[cānchē]
dining car
〖餐巾〗(名)[cānjīn]
table napkin
〖餐具〗(名)[cānjù]
dinnerset; table-ware
〖餐厅〗(名)[cāntīng]
① large dining room; large dining hall ② restaurant

cán

残 (形)[cán]
① cruel; ruthless ② broken (house, utensil); defective; incomplete; crippled ③ remnant
〖残暴〗(形)[cánbào]
tyrannical; brutal; merciless
〖残兵败将〗[cánbīngbàijiàng]
a routed army and a beaten general; a completely defeated army
〖残存〗(动)[cáncún]
survive; remnant
〖残废〗(名、动)[cánfèi]
physically disabled; deformed; crippled
〖残骸〗(名)[cánhái]
remains; wreckage
〖残害〗(动)[cánhài]
① damage; do harm to ② murder; slaughter
〖残疾〗(名)[cánji]
physical deformity
〖残局〗(名)[cánjú]
① the last stages (e.g. of a chess game) ② a lost situation
〖残酷〗(形)[cánkù]
cruel; ruthless; brutal; merciless
〖残缺不全〗[cánquēbùquán]
incomplete; deficient
〖残忍〗(形)[cánrěn]
brutal; cruel; merciless
〖残杀〗(动)[cánshā]
slaughter; kill brutally; mas-

sacre

〖残余〗(名)[cányú]
remnants; survivals

蚕(名)[cán]
silkworm

〖蚕豆〗(名)[cándòu]
broad beans

〖蚕茧〗(名)[cánjiǎn]
silkworm cocoon

〖蚕农〗(名)[cánnóng]
silkworm raiser; sericulturist

〖蚕食〗(动)[cánshí]
nibble up

〖蚕丝〗(名)[cánsī]
silk

惭[cán]

〖惭愧〗(形)[cánkuì]
ashamed; abashed

cǎn

惨(形)[cǎn]
miserable; wretched

〖惨案〗(名)[cǎn'àn]
massacre; tragedy

〖惨白〗(形)[cǎnbái]
① ghostly pale ② dim; vague; hazy

〖惨淡经营〗[cǎndànjīngyíng]
keep (an enterprise, etc.) going by painstaking effort; take great pains to carry on one's work under difficult circumstances

〖惨剧〗(名)[cǎnjù]
a tragic event

〖惨痛〗(形)[cǎntòng]
bitter; grievous

〖惨无人道〗[cǎnwúréndào]
brutal and callous; inhuman; cruel and inhuman

〖惨重〗(形)[cǎnzhòng]
grievous and heavy (loss)

càn

灿[càn]

〖灿烂〗(形)[cànlàn]
glorious; bright; magnificent; splendid

cāng

仓(名)[cāng]
granary; store-house

〖仓促〗(形)[cāngcù]
hasty; hurried; on the spur of the moment

〖仓皇〗(形)[cānghuáng]
scared and hasty; hastily

〖仓库〗(名)[cāngkù]
warehouse; store

苍[cāng]

〖苍白〗(形)[cāngbái]
①pale (complexion) ②(of hair) grey

〖苍翠〗(形)[cāngcuì]
dark green (emerald)

〖苍劲〗(形)[cāngjìng]
①(of trees) vigorous and upright ② (of handwriting) vigorous and bold

〖苍老〗(形)[cānglǎo]

ravaged by age; age-worn
〖苍茫〗(形)[cāngmáng]
boundless and indistinct; vast and hazy; growing shades of ...
〖苍天〗(名)[cāngtiān]
① the blue sky ② Heaven
〖苍蝇〗(名)[cāngying]
a fly

沧[cāng]
〖沧海一粟〗[cānghǎiyīsù]
one grain afloat on a vast ocean; a drop in the ocean; (fig.) very small portion of sth. ...
〖沧桑〗(名)[cāngsāng]
(lit.) seas change into mulberry fields; (fig.) the world is changing all the time

cáng

藏(动)[cáng]
hide
〖藏龙卧虎〗[cánglóngwòhǔ]
"hidden dragons and crouching tigers"; (fig.) talented men still remained in concealment
〖藏身〗[cángshēn]
hide oneself; go into hiding
〖藏书〗(名)[cángshū]
collection of books
〖藏污纳垢〗[cángwū nàgòu]
a sewer in which all that is evil finds a home; a vehicle for filth; (fig.) shelter evil people or things

cāo

操(动、名)[cāo]
drill; train; exercise; training
〖操场〗(名)[cāochǎng]
sportsground; playground
〖操持〗(动)[cāochí]
① manage ② prepare
〖操劳〗(动)[cāoláo]
labour painstakingly; do sth. industriously
〖操练〗(动)[cāoliàn]
drill
〖操心〗[cāo xīn]
worry about; be concerned over
〖操之过急〗[cāozhīguòjí]
act with undue haste; too hasty
〖操纵〗(动)[cāozòng]
control; manipulate
〖操作〗(动)[cāozuò]
operate; practise

cáo

嘈[cáo]
〖嘈杂〗(形)[cáozá]
noisy

槽(名)[cáo]
① trough; manger ② groove

cǎo

草(名、形)[cǎo]〔棵 kē、株 zhū〕
① grass ② slipshod (writing); careless; rough
〖草案〗(名)[cǎo'àn]
a draft (of plan, resolution,

proposal, etc.)
〖草包〗(名)[cǎobāo]
① straw bag or sack; packing mat ② a sack loaded with straw ③(fig.)an incapable person; a mindless person
〖草草〗(副)[cǎocǎo]
in a great hurry; rashly(done)
〖草地〗(名)[cǎodì]
lawn; grassland
〖草稿〗(名)[cǎogǎo]
manuscript; a draft (of an article, drawing, etc.)
〖草绿〗(形)[cǎolǜ]
green (the colour of growing grass)
〖草帽〗(名)[cǎomào]〔顶 dǐng〕
straw hat
〖草莓〗(名)[cǎoméi]
strawberry
〖草木皆兵〗[cǎomùjiēbīng]
(lit.)see every bush and tree as an enemy soldier; (fig.)state of imaginary fears
〖草拟〗(动)[cǎonǐ]
draft
〖草坪〗(名)[cǎopíng]
lawn
〖草签〗(动)[cǎoqiān]
initial(eg.an agreement,a treaty,etc.)
〖草书〗(名)[cǎoshū]
rapid cursive style of writing; a running hand
〖草率〗(形)[cǎoshuài]
rash; careless
〖草图〗(名)[cǎotú]
sketch(drawing, designing)
〖草鞋〗(名)[cǎoxié]〔双 shuāng〕
straw sandal
〖草药〗(名)[cǎoyào]
medicinal herbs
〖草原〗(名)[cǎoyuán]
grassland; steppe; prairie

cè

册 (名、量)[cè]
① a thin pamphlet or booklet ② a measure word(for book)
〖册子〗(名)[cèzi]〔本 běn〕
a thin pamphlet or booklet

厕 [cè]
〖厕所〗(名)[cèsuǒ]
toilet; lavatory

侧 (名、动)[cè]
① side ② incline towards
〖侧面〗(名)[cèmiàn]
① side view; side dimension; profile ② indirect
〖侧翼〗(名)[cèyì]
flank
〖侧影〗(名)[cèyǐng]
silhouette; profile
〖侧重〗(动)[cèzhòng]
lay emphasis on

测 (动)[cè]
survey
〖测绘〗(动)[cèhuì]
survey and make map
〖测量〗(动)[cèliáng]
survey

〖测验〗(动)[cèyàn]
check; test

策 (名、动)[cè]
① plan; method ② policy ③ cause(sb.)to do sth.
〖策动〗(动)[cèdòng]
incite; instigate; engineer
〖策反〗[cè fǎn]
instigate rebellion within the enemy camp
〖策划〗(动)[cèhuà]
hatch plot
〖策略〗(名)[cèlüè]
tactics
〖策源地〗(名)[cèyuándì]
hotbed; source; cradle; place of origin

cēn

参 [cēn]
另见 cān
〖参差不齐〗[cēncībùqí]
untrimmed; uneven; not uniform

céng

层 (量)[céng]
a measure word(for layer)
〖层出不穷〗[céngchūbùqióng]
emerge in an endless stream
〖层次〗(名)[céngcì]
series; orderly arrangement; level; layer; tier

曾 (副)[céng]
at some time in the past
〖曾几何时〗[céngjǐhéshí]
before long; not long after
〖曾经〗(副)[céngjīng]
at some time in the past

cèng

蹭 (动)[cèng]
rub; scrape

chā

叉 (名、动)[chā]
①fork; prong; cross ② spear(a fish); pick (with a fork or spear)
〖叉腰〗[chāyāo]
(with arms)akimbo
〖叉子〗(名)[chāzi]〔把 bǎ〕
fork

差 (名)[chā]
difference
另见 chà chāi
〖差别〗(名)[chābié]
difference
〖差错〗(名)[chācuò]
① mistake; mishap; error ② untoward accident
〖差额〗(名)[chā'é]
deficit
〖差价〗(名)[chājià]
price differences
〖差距〗(名)[chājù]
① gap (lagging behind) ② leeway
〖差异〗(名)[chāyì]
difference; diversity
〖差之毫厘,谬以千里〗

[chā zhīháolí, miùyǐqiānlǐ]
an error the breadth of a single hair can lead you a thousand li astray; a small discrepancy leads to a great error

插 (动)[chā]
① insert; stick in ② interrupt (in speech)
〖插班〗[chābān]
join a class in the middle of the course
〖插翅难飞〗[chāchìnánfēi]
even with wings (he) couldn't escape
〖插管〗(动)[chāguǎn]
intubate
〖插话〗[chā huà]
interrupt in speech; cut in
〖插曲〗(名)[chāqǔ]
interlude; a song from a film or a play
〖插手〗[chā shǒu]
meddle; have a hand in
〖插头〗(名)[chātóu]
plug
〖插图〗(名)[chātú]
illustration in a book
〖插销〗(名)[chāxiāo]
① bolt ② plug
〖插叙〗(名)[chāxù]
narration interspersed with flashbacks
〖插秧〗[chā yāng]
transplant rice shoots
〖插秧机〗(名)[chāyāngjī]
rice-transplanter
〖插嘴〗[chā zuǐ]
put in a word; interrupt speech
〖插座〗(名)[chāzuò]
socket

chá

茬 (量)[chá]
a measure word, for crop (e.g. ...yields four crops a year)

茶 (名)[chá]
tea
〖茶杯〗(名)[chábēi]〔个 gè〕
tea cup
〖茶点〗(名)[chádiǎn]
tea served with pastry; refreshments
〖茶馆〗(名)[cháguǎn]
teahouse
〖茶壶〗(名)[cháhú]〔把 bǎ〕
tea pot
〖茶花〗(名)[cháhuā]
camellia
〖茶会〗(名)[cháhuì]
tea party
〖茶几〗(名)[chájī]
tea table; teapoy; side table
〖茶具〗(名)[chájù]
tea-set
〖茶水〗(名)[cháshuǐ]
drink (e.g. tea, water, etc.)
〖茶叶〗(名)[cháyè]
tea leaf
〖茶叶罐〗(名)[cháyèguàn]
tea caddy; cannister

查 (动)[chá]

① check ② investigate
〖查办〗(动)[chábàn]
investigate and prosecute (case, person, etc.)
〖查点〗(动)[chádiǎn]
check item by item
〖查对〗(动)[cháduì]
check up
〖查封〗(动)[cháfēng]
confiscate and seal up
〖查获〗(动)[cháhuò]
hunt down; ferret out
〖查禁〗(动)[chájìn]
ban; prohibit
〖查看〗(动)[chákàn]
look into; inspect
〖查问〗(动)[cháwèn]
enquire
〖查询〗(动)[cháxún]
investigate; make inquiry
〖查阅〗(动)[cháyuè]
read for information; consult (books)

察 (动)[chá]
① observe; notice; see ② look over; inspect; examine; detect
〖察访〗(动)[cháfǎng]
go about finding out; fact-finding
〖察觉〗(动)[chájué]
realize; sense
〖察看〗(动)[chákàn]
look over; examine
〖察言观色〗[cháyánguānsè]
examine a man's words and observe his countenance

chà

岔 [chà]
〖岔路〗(名)[chàlù]
① a fork (in a road) ② a branch road
〖岔子〗(名)[chàzi]
unexpected and undesirable turn of events

刹 [chà]
另见 shā
〖刹那〗(名)[chànà]
the twinkling of an eye; in a flash

诧 [chà]
〖诧异〗(形)[chàyì]
be struck with surprise

差 (动、形)[chà]
① lack; short of ② not up to standard ③ different
另见 chā chāi
〖差不多〗[chà bu duō]
more or less; not too much difference
〖差点儿〗(副)[chàdiǎnr]
almost; narrowly; nearly
〖差劲儿〗(形)[chàjìnr]
① poor in quality ② worthless ③ hard (condition, etc.)

chāi

拆 (动)[chāi]
① tear apart ② tear down
〖拆除〗(动)[chāichú]

dismantle; demolish
〖拆穿〗(动)[chāichuān]
expose; reveal
〖拆股〗[chāigǔ]
dissolve a partnership
〖拆毁〗(动)[chāihuǐ]
destroy; break down; tear sth. down
〖拆迁〗(动)[chāiqiān]
demolish a dwelling and relocate the residents; pull down dilapidated houses and persuadethe residents to remove
〖拆迁户〗(名)[chāiqiānhù]
residents who have to remove from their original living area where new buildings will be constructed; households having to move to a new address because their dwellings are to be demolished
〖拆散〗(动)[chāisǎn]
break up
〖拆台〗[chāi tái]
undermine; disrupt
〖拆卸〗(动)[chāixiè]
take apart; dismantle; disassemble

差(名、动)[chāi]
① a mission ② send (sb. to do sth.); dispatch
另见 chā chà
〖差遣〗(动)[chāiqiǎn]
send(sb.); dispatch
〖差事〗(名)[chāishi]
assigned duty

chái

柴(名)[chái]
firewood
〖柴火〗(名)[cháihuo]
kindling; firewood
〖柴油〗(名)[cháiyóu]
diesel oil
〖柴油机〗(名)[cháiyóujī]
diesel engine

豺(名)[chái]
ravenous beast, akin to jackal
〖豺狼〗(名)[cháiláng]
jackals(ravenous beasts); (fig.)evil men

chān

搀(动)[chān]
① support(sb. with one's arm)
② mix; add
〖搀扶〗(动)[chānfú]
give one's arm to (an aged or invalid person)
〖搀和〗(动)[chānhuo]
mix; blend
〖搀杂〗(动)[chānzá]
mix into other things

chán

馋(形)[chán]
greedy; gluttonous

缠(动)[chán]
wind; coil
〖缠绵〗(形)[chánmián]
sentimental

〖缠绕〗(动)[chánrǎo]
bind round; entangle

潺 [chán]
〖潺潺〗(象声)[chánchán]
onomatopoeia, gurgling and babbling; purling

chǎn

产 (动、名)[chǎn]
① produce; product ② property
〖产地〗(名)[chǎndì]
place of production; place of origin; producing area
〖产量〗(名)[chǎnliàng]
volume of production; output
〖产品〗(名)[chǎnpǐn]
product
〖产权〗(名)[chǎnquán]
equity; property right
〖产生〗(动)[chǎnshēng]
① produce ② give rise to; result from; originate in
〖产物〗(名)[chǎnwù]
products; outcome; results
〖产销〗(名)[chǎnxiāo]
production and marketing
〖产业〗(名)[chǎnyè]
① property; estate ② industry
〖产业工人〗[chǎnyègōngrén]
industrial workers
〖产值〗(名)[chǎnzhí]
value of output

铲 (名、动)[chǎn]
spade
〖铲车〗(名)[chǎnchē]
forklift; carry-scraper
〖铲除〗(动)[chǎnchú]
uproot; eradicate; exterminate
〖铲子〗(名)[chǎnzi]〔把 bǎ〕
spade

阐 [chǎn]
〖阐明〗(动)[chǎnmíng]
explain; expound

chàn

忏 [chàn]
〖忏悔〗(动)[chànhuǐ]
show repentance; repent

颤 (动)[chàn]
quiver; vibrate
〖颤动〗(动)[chàndòng]
quiver; vibrate
〖颤抖〗(动)[chàndǒu]
tremble

chāng

昌 [chāng]
〖昌盛〗(形)[chāngshèng]
prosperous and strong; flourish

猖 [chāng]
〖猖獗〗(形)[chāngjué]
rampant
〖猖狂〗(形)[chāngkuáng]
frantic; on the rampage

cháng

长 (形)[cháng]

long
另见 zhǎng
〖长波〗(名)[chángbō]
long wave(in a radio, etc.)
〖长城〗(名)[Chángchéng]
the Great Wall
〖长处〗(名)[chángchù]
merit; strong point
〖长此以往〗[chángcǐyǐwǎng]
if things go on like this; if things continue this way
〖长度〗(名)[chángdù]
length
〖长短〗(名)[chángduǎn]
① length ② long and short; right and wrong; gossip
〖长方形〗(名)[chángfāngxíng]
rectangle
〖长工〗(名)[chánggōng]
farm labourers hired by the year
〖长话短说〗
[chánghuàduǎnshuō]
make a long story short
〖长久〗(形)[chángjiǔ]
for long; lasting; permanent
〖长年累月〗[chángniánlěiyuè]
all the year round; year after year
〖长跑〗(名)[chángpǎo]
long distance running
〖长篇大论〗[chángpiāndàlùn]
long-winded tirade; lengthy (writing, speech, argument)
〖长篇小说〗
[chángpiān xiǎo shuō]
novel
〖长期〗(名)[chángqī]
longterm
〖长驱直入〗[chángqūzhírù]
drive straight in
〖长寿〗(动)[chángshòu]
longevity; long life
〖长途〗(名)[chángtú]
long distance
〖长线产品〗[chángxiànchǎnpǐn]
overstocked goods;over-supplied goods; goods in excessive supply
〖长远〗(形)[chángyuǎn]
long-range
〖长征〗(名、动)[chángzhēng]
① go on an expedition ② the Long March (1934—1935)—the 25,000 li Long March of the Chinese Workers' and Peasants' Red Army under the leadership of the Communist Party of China and Chairman Mao

场(名、量)[cháng]
① open space ② threshing floor ③ a measure word (for snow, performance, war, etc.)
另见 chǎng
〖场院〗(名)[chángyuàn]
threshing floor; threshing ground

肠(名)[cháng]
intestines
〖肠胃病〗(名)[chángwèibìng]
stomach trouble
〖肠炎〗(名)[chángyán]

enteritis
〖肠子〗(名)[chángzi]
intestine

尝 (动)[cháng]
taste; feel
〖尝试〗(动)[chángshì]
try; attempt

常 (形、副)[cháng]
frequent; often; always
〖常备不懈〗[chángbèibùxiè]
all-time preparedness (against war); be always vigilant; maintain constant vigilance
〖常备军〗(名)[chángbèijūn]
regular army; standing army
〖常常〗(副)[chángcháng]
often; frequently
〖常规〗(名)[chángguī]
convention; regular; conventional
〖常见病〗(名)[chángjiànbìng]
commonly encountered disease
〖常年〗(名)[chángnián]
all the year round
〖常设〗(名)[chángshè]
permanent; standing
〖常识〗(名)[chángshí]
① common sense ②general knowledge
〖常态〗(名)[chángtài]
normal state
〖常务委员〗[chángwùwěiyuán]
member of a standing committee
〖常务委员会〗
[chángwù wěi yuánhuì]
standing committee

偿 (动)[cháng]
make up; compensate; pay back
〖偿还〗(动)[chánghuán]
compensate; pay back
〖偿清〗(动)[chángqīng]
clear off

chǎng

厂 (名)[chǎng]
factory
〖厂矿〗(名)[chǎngkuàng]
factories and mines
〖厂校挂钩〗[chǎngxiàoguàgōu]
establish direct contact between factories and schools
〖厂长〗(名)[chǎngzhǎng]
director of a factory
〖厂长责任制〗
[chǎngzhǎng zérènzhì]
factory director responsibility system; system of overall responsibility by the factory manager

场 (名、量)[chǎng]
① ground ② a measure word (for sports and recreation, etc.)
另见 cháng
〖场地〗(名)[chǎngdì]
an area of level ground
〖场合〗(名)[chǎnghé]
occasion
〖场面〗(名)[chǎngmiàn]
scene; occasion; a stage
〖场所〗(名)[chǎngsuǒ]

place; location

敞 (动、形)[chǎng]
① open ② spacious
〖敞开〗(动)[chǎngkāi]
be widely open
〖敞亮〗(形)[chǎngliàng]
spacious and bright
〖敞篷车〗(名)[chǎngpéngchē]
open car

chàng

怅 [chàng]
〖怅惘〗(形)[chàngwǎng]
depressed; dispirited

畅 [chàng]
〖畅快〗(形)[chàngkuài]
delightful; pleased
〖畅所欲言〗[chàngsuǒyùyán]
speak one's mind freely
〖畅谈〗(动)[chàngtán]
talk freely and contentedly
〖畅通〗(动)[chàngtōng]
unimpeded
〖畅想〗(动)[chàngxiǎng]
give rein to one's imagination (as when one thinks about a bright future)
〖畅销〗(动)[chàngxiāo]
sell well; have a ready market; be in great demand; marketable
〖畅行〗(动)[chàngxíng]
advance unimpeded
〖畅游〗(动)[chàngyóu]
① swim to one's heart's content ② enjoy a sightseeing tour

倡 [chàng]
〖倡导〗(动)[chàngdǎo]
advocate; initiate; introduce; promote
〖倡议〗(动、名)[chàngyì]
initiate; initiative; proposal
〖倡议书〗(名)[chàngyìshū]
written proposal

唱 (动)[chàng]
sing
〖唱白脸〗[chàngbáiliǎn]
wear the white make up of the stage villain; play the villain; pretend to be harsh and severe
〖唱段〗(名)[chàngduàn]
arias; singing passage
〖唱对台戏〗[chàng duìtáixì]
put on a rival show; set oneself up against
〖唱反调〗[chàngfǎndiào]
harp on a discordant tune
〖唱高调〗[chàng gāodiào]
chant bombastic words
〖唱歌〗[chàng gē]
sing (a song)
〖唱红脸〗[chànghóngliǎn]
wear the red make up of the stage hero; play the hero; pretend to be generous and kind
〖唱片〗(名)[chàngpiàn]
〔张 zhāng〕
gramophone record

〖唱腔〗(名)[chàngqiāng]
aria

chāo

抄(动)[chāo]
① copy; transcribe ② take (a shortcut) ③ search and confiscate
〖抄获〗(动)[chāohuò]
search and capture
〖抄录〗(动)[chāolù]
copy
〖抄袭〗(动)[chāoxí]
copy; plagiarize; follow (sb.'s footsteps)
〖抄写〗(动)[chāoxiě]
copy; transcribe

钞[chāo]
〖钞票〗(名)[chāopiào]
banknote

超(动)[chāo]
overtake; surpass; exceed; transcend
〖超产〗[chāo chǎn]
overfulfil the planned figure
〖超出〗(动)[chāochū]
exceed
〖超短波〗(名)[chāoduǎnbō]
ultrashort wave
〖超短裙〗(名)[chāoduǎnqún]
miniskirt
〖超额〗[chāo'é]
overfulfil
〖超过〗(动)[chāoguò]
surpass; overtake; surmount
〖超级〗(形)[chāojí]
extrahigh (quality); super
〖超级大国〗[chāojí dàguó]
super-power
〖超龄〗[chāo líng]
over-age
〖超然〗(形)[chāorán]
stand aloof; transcendent
〖超声波〗(名)[chāoshēngbō]
ultrasonic waves; supersonics
〖超生〗[chāoshēng]
exceed the targeted birth rate; have more children than what the plan allows
〖超市〗(名)[chāoshì]
supermarket
〖超音速〗(名)[chāoyīnsù]
supersonic
〖超越〗(动)[chāoyuè]
transcend; excel; surmount
〖超支〗[chāo zhī]
over-expenditure
〖超重〗[chāo zhòng]
over weight

cháo

巢(名)[cháo]
nest; den
〖巢穴〗(名)[cháoxué]
den

朝(名、介)[cháo]
① dynasty ② toward; facing; direct
另见 zhāo
〖朝代〗(名)[cháodài]
dynasty

C

〖朝圣〗(动、名)[cháoshèng]
pilgrimage; hadji
〖朝廷〗(名)[cháotíng]
royal or imperial court

嘲[cháo]
〖嘲弄〗(动)[cháonòng]
mock; ridicule
〖嘲笑〗(动)[cháoxiào]
ridicule; jeer

潮(名、形)[cháo]
tide; damp
〖潮流〗(名)[cháoliú]
trend; current; the tide
〖潮湿〗(形)[cháoshī]
damp
〖潮水〗(名)[cháoshuǐ]
tide

chǎo

吵(动、形)[chǎo]
① quarrel ② noisy
〖吵架〗[chǎo jià]
quarrel
〖吵闹〗(动)[chǎonào]
① make a great noise ② kick up a fuss; wrangle

炒(动)[chǎo]
fry
〖炒更〗[chǎogēng]
be engaged in a second occupation in one's spare time; take on a second job for added cash.
〖炒股〗[chǎogǔ]
speculate in stocks
〖炒面〗(名)[chǎomiàn]
fried flour; fried noodles
〖炒鱿鱼〗[chǎoyóuyú]
fire; sack; dismiss; give the sack

chē

车(名、动)[chē]〔辆 liàng〕
① vehicle ② shape (things) on a lathe
〖车床〗(名)[chēchuáng]
lathe
〖车次〗(名)[chēcì]
number (of train journey)
〖车到山前必有路〗
[chēdàoshānqiánbìyǒulù]
the cart will find its way round the hill when it gets there; (fig.) things will eventually sort themselves out
〖车工〗(名)[chēgōng]
lathe turner
〖车间〗(名)[chējiān]
workshop
〖车轮〗(名)[chēlún]
wheel
〖车票〗(名)[chēpiào]
(train or bus) ticket
〖车水马龙〗[chēshuǐmǎlóng]
heavy traffic
〖车胎〗(名)[chētāi]
tyre
〖车厢〗(名)[chēxiāng]
railway carriage; coach (of a train)
〖车站〗(名)[chēzhàn]

① railway station ② a bus stop

chě

扯(动)[chě]
① tear off or apart ② pull apart or off
〖扯后腿〗[chěhòutuǐ]
be a drag on an enterprise; be a hindrance to production; hold sb. back (from action)
〖扯皮〗(动)[chěpí]
haggle over trifles

chè

彻[chè]
〖彻底〗(形)[chèdǐ]
thorough; thoroughgoing; completely; thoroughly
〖彻头彻尾〗[chètóuchèwěi]
from head to foot; out-and-out
〖彻夜〗(名)[chèyè]
all night

撤(动)[chè]
withdraw
〖撤换〗(动)[chèhuàn]
dismiss and replace
〖撤回〗(动)[chèhuí]
withdraw; draw back; pull back
〖撤军〗[chè jūn]
withdraw troops
〖撤离〗(动)[chèlí]
withdraw
〖撤退〗(动)[chètuì]
withdraw; evacuate; retreat
〖撤销〗(动)[chèxiāo]
annul; abolish; dismiss
〖撤职〗[chè zhí]
remove... from office; dismiss sb. from his post; dismissal

chén

尘[chén]
〖尘土〗(名)[chéntǔ]
dust

沉(动、形)[chén]
① sink ② heavy
〖沉淀〗(动、名)[chéndiàn]
precipitate; precipitation
〖沉寂〗(形)[chénjì]
dead silent
〖沉浸〗(动)[chénjìn]
be absorbed in
〖沉静〗(形)[chénjìng]
quiet; poised
〖沉闷〗(形)[chénmèn]
boring; dull; tedious
〖沉没〗(动)[chénmò]
submerge
〖沉默〗(形)[chénmò]
silent
〖沉默寡言〗[chénmòguǎyán]
habitually silent; taciturn
〖沉溺〗(动)[chénnì]
drown oneself (in pleasures, etc.); indulge in; be infatuated with
〖沉睡〗(动)[chénshuì]
sleep soundly
〖沉思〗(动)[chénsī]
ponder; contemplate; think deeply

C

〖沉痛〗(形)[chéntòng]
grievous; extremely painful; deep in sorrow; deep grief
〖沉重〗(形)[chénzhòng]
heavy
〖沉着〗(形)[chénzhuó]
cool; composed
〖沉醉〗(动)[chénzuì]
heavily drunk; be intoxicated with

陈 (形)[chén]
old
〖陈词滥调〗[chéncílàndiào]
platitude; senseless prate; cliche; often-repeated rubbish
〖陈腐〗(形)[chénfǔ]
stale; antiquated; outworn (views, opinions)
〖陈旧〗(形)[chénjiù]
out of date; stale (ideas); outmoded
〖陈列〗(动)[chénliè]
exhibit; display
〖陈列馆〗(名)[chénlièguǎn]
exhibition hall
〖陈设〗(动、名)[chénshè]
display; arrange; arrangement
〖陈述〗(动)[chénshù]
state; explain; recount
〖陈述句〗(名)[chénshùjù]
declarative sentence

chèn

衬 (动)[chèn]
serve for contrast or as background
〖衬衫〗(名)[chènshān]
shirt
〖衬托〗(动)[chèntuō]
serve for contrast or as background
〖衬衣〗(名)[chènyī]
shirt

称 (动)[chèn]
suit; correspond; fit; match; be worthy of
另见 chēng
〖称心〗[chènxīn]
to one's liking; just as one wishes
〖称职〗[chèn zhí]
be competent for one's work

趁 (动)[chèn]
take advantage of (opportunity, time, etc.)
〖趁火打劫〗[chènhuǒdǎjié]
take advantage of a bad situation to loot; fish in troubled waters
〖趁机〗[chèn jī]
take advantage of
〖趁热打铁〗[chènrèdǎtiě]
strike while the iron is hot
〖趁早〗(副)[chènzǎo]
while there's yet time; before it is too late

chēng

称 (动)[chēng]
① call; address; say ② weigh

另见 chèn
〖称霸〗[chēng bà]
dominate; play the tyrant; seek hegemony
〖称号〗(名)[chēnghào]
name; title
〖称呼〗(动、名)[chēnghu]
call; address; style; name; title; a form of address
〖称颂〗(动)[chēngsòng]
pay tribute to; praise
〖称王称霸〗
[chēngwángchēngbà]
rule supreme; lord it over others
〖称赞〗(动)[chēngzàn]
praise
〖称作〗(动)[chēngzuò]
call; style

撑(动)[chēng]
① prop(up); hold ② hold sth. widely open ③ overeat; overfill
〖撑竿跳〗(名)[chēnggāntiào]
pole-vault
〖撑腰〗[chēng yāo]
support; back up

chéng

成(动)[chéng]
① succeed ② become; turn into
〖成败〗(名)[chéngbài]
success or failure
〖成倍〗(副)[chéngbèi]
(increase) several times; (an increase of)-fold
〖成本〗(名)[chéngběn]
production costs
〖成分〗(名)[chéngfèn]
① ingredient ② element ③ composition(soil)
〖成风〗[chéngfēng]
become a common practice
〖成功〗(动)[chénggōng]
succeed
〖成果〗(名)[chéngguǒ]
result; accomplishment
〖成绩〗(名)[chéngjì]
achievement
〖成绩单〗(名)[chéngjìdān]
school report card; academic record
〖成见〗(名)[chéngjiàn]
prejudice
〖成交〗(动)[chéngjiāo]
strike a deal; close a business deal
〖成就〗(名、动)[chéngjiù]
achievements; make progress; achieve success
〖成立〗(动)[chénglì]
① found; establish; set up
②(argument) hold water
〖成龙配套〗[chénglóngpèitào]
fitting together of parts
〖成名成家〗
[chéngmíngchéngjiā]
pursuit of personal fame and career
〖成年〗(名、副)[chéngnián]
① adult ② all year round
〖成批〗(副)[chéngpī]
in groups; in large number
〖成品〗(名)[chéngpǐn]

finished products
〖成千上万〗[chéngqiānshàngwàn]
hundreds of thousands
〖成人〗(名)[chéngrén]
adult; grown-up
〖成人教育〗[chéngrénjiàoyù]
adult education
〖成人高校〗[chéngréngāoxiào]
institution of higher education for adults
〖成熟〗(动、形)[chéngshú]
ripe; mature
〖成套〗[chéngtào]
complete set (of machinery or equipment)
〖成天〗(副)[chéngtiān]
all day long
〖成为〗(动)[chéngwéi]
become; turn into; grow into
〖成效〗(名)[chéngxiào]
effect
〖成心〗(形)[chéngxīn]
purposely; intentionally
〖成语〗(名)[chéngyǔ]
idiom; idiomatic phrase
〖成员〗(名)[chéngyuán]
member
〖成长〗(动)[chéngzhǎng]
grow up

呈(动)[chéng]
present; offer
〖呈报〗(动)[chéngbào]
submit a report; present a report
〖呈递〗(动)[chéngdì]
present to; submit
〖呈现〗(动)[chéngxiàn]
loom; emerge; present; exhibit; show

诚[chéng]
〖诚恳〗(形)[chéngkěn]
hearty; cordial
〖诚然〗(副)[chéngrán]
indeed
〖诚实〗(形)[chéngshí]
honest
〖诚心〗(名)[chéngxīn]
sincerity
〖诚意〗(名)[chéngyì]
sincerity; cordiality; earnest
〖诚挚〗(形)[chéngzhì]
sincere

承[chéng]
〖承办〗(动)[chéngbàn]
undertake
〖承包〗(动)[chéngbāo]
contract to do sth.; contract for sth.
〖承担〗(动)[chéngdān]
assume; bear; accept; undertake (task, responsibility)
〖承当〗(动)[chéngdāng]
be responsible for
〖承认〗(动)[chéngrèn]
recognize; admit; acknowledge
〖承上启下〗[chéngshàngqǐxià]
continue; carry forward (what goes before)
〖承受〗(动)[chéngshòu]
bear; stand; withstand; sus-

tain
〖承袭〗(动)[chéngxí]
inherit

城(名)[chéng]
① city wall ② city; town
〖城堡〗(名)[chéngbǎo]
castle
〖城郊〗(名)[chéngjiāo]
outskirts; suburbs
〖城楼〗(名)[chénglóu]
tower
〖城市〗(名)[chéngshì]
city
〖城乡〗(名)[chéngxiāng]
city and countryside
〖城乡差别〗
[chéngxiāngchābié]
difference between town and country
〖城乡结合部〗
[chéngxiāng jiéhébù]
town-country bordering areas
〖城镇〗(名)[chéngzhèn]
city and town

乘(动)[chéng]
① ride (in vehicle, ship, aeroplane) ② multiply
〖乘法〗(名)[chéngfǎ]
multiplication
〖乘方〗(名)[chéngfāng]
(math.) square
〖乘风破浪〗[chéngfēngpòlàng]
brave the winds and waves
〖乘机〗[chéng jī]
seize opportunity
〖乘客〗(名)[chéngkè]
passenger
〖乘凉〗[chéng liáng]
enjoy cool air
〖乘人之危〗[chéngrénzhīwēi]
take advantage of other's disasters
〖乘胜前进〗[chéngshèngqiánjìn]
go forward in triumph; continue to march forward from victory already won
〖乘数〗(名)[chéngshù]
multiplier
〖乘务员〗(名)[chéngwùyuán]
crew
〖乘虚而入〗[chéngxū'érrù]
seize the opportunity to step in

盛(动)[chéng]
① contain ② hold; fill with
另见 shèng

程[chéng]
〖程度〗(名)[chéngdù]
degree; extent
〖程式〗(名)[chéngshì]
(chem., math.) formula; equation
〖程序〗(名)[chéngxù]
procedure; sequence; order

惩(动)[chéng]
punish; discipline
〖惩办〗(动)[chéngbàn]
punish; punishment
〖惩罚〗(动)[chéngfá]

C

punish
〖惩前毖后〗[chéngqiánbìhòu]
learn from past mistakes to avoid future ones

澄 [chéng]
另见 dèng
〖澄清〗(动、形)[chéngqīng]
clarify; clear
另见 dèngqīng

chěng

逞 (动)[chěng]
① boast (of one's ability); be boastful ② succeed in; accomplish one's aim
〖逞能〗[chěng néng]
cut a dash; boast of one's ability
〖逞强〗[chěng qiáng]
display one's ability or courage; demonstrate one's strength

chèng

秤 (名)[chèng]
steelyard; scales

chī

吃 (动)[chī]
eat
〖吃不开〗[chī bu kāi]
unpopular
〖吃不消〗[chī bu xiāo]
cannot bear; cannot stand
〖吃醋〗[chīcù]
be jealous (usu. of a rival in love)
〖吃大锅饭〗[chīdàguōfàn]
eat from a big common pot; everyone receiving the same pay regardless of his performance on the job and actual contribution
〖吃得开〗[chī de kāi]
popular; in current demand
〖吃得消〗[chī de xiāo]
can bear
〖吃饭〗[chī fàn]
take a meal
〖吃喝风〗[chīhēfēng]
practice of eating and drinking on public funds; be spendthrift in feasting
〖吃皇粮〗[chīhuángliáng]
live on the salaries paid by the government
〖吃惊〗[chī jīng]
startle; get a fright; get a shock
〖吃苦〗[chī kǔ]
suffer hardships
〖吃苦耐劳〗[chīkǔnàiláo]
endure hardships
〖吃亏〗[chī kuī]
get the worst of; suffer losses; suffer reverses
〖吃老本〗[chī lǎoběn]
live off one's past glory; rest on one's laurels
〖吃力〗(形)[chīlì]
painstaking; strenuous
〖吃哑巴亏〗[chīyǎbakuī]

be unable to speak out one's grievances; be forced to keep one's grievances to himself despite the losses he has suffered
〖吃一堑,长一智〗
[chīyīqiàn, zhǎngyīzhì]
a fall in a pit, a gain in wit; a fall into the pit, a gain in your wit

嗤 (象声)[chī]
onomatopeia, titter
〖嗤之以鼻〗[chīzhīyǐbí]
turn up one's nose at; be contemptuous

痴 (形)[chī]
silly; foolish; stupid; dull
〖痴呆〗(形、名)[chīdāi]
① dull-witted; stupid ②(senile) dementia
〖痴心妄想〗[chīxīnwàngxiǎng]
wishful thinking; hope vainly for

chí

池 (名)[chí]
pool
〖池塘〗(名)[chítáng]
pond

驰 [chí]
〖驰骋〗(动)[chíchěng]
gallop
〖驰名〗(动)[chímíng]
become famous; become celebrated

迟 (形)[chí]
late
〖迟到〗(动)[chídào]
arrive late
〖迟钝〗(形)[chídùn]
slow-witted
〖迟缓〗(形)[chíhuǎn]
slow
〖迟误〗(动)[chíwù]
miss... by delay
〖迟延〗(动)[chíyán]
postpone; drag on
〖迟疑〗(动)[chíyí]
hesitate

持 (动)[chí]
hold
〖持家有方〗[chíjiāyǒufāng]
manage the affairs of the family methodically
〖持久〗(形)[chíjiǔ]
① hold out long ② persistent; protracted
〖持久战〗(名)[chíjiǔzhàn]
protracted war
〖持续〗(动)[chíxù]
carry on; sustain; continue
〖持之以恒〗[chízhīyǐhéng]
in a persistent way

踟 [chí]
〖踟蹰〗(动)[chíchú]
hesitate

C

C

chǐ

尺(名、量)[chǐ]〔把 bǎ〕
ruler; a foot (measurement)
〖尺寸〗(名)[chǐcùn]
size; dimension; measurements
〖尺度〗(名)[chǐdù]
dimension

齿(名)[chǐ]
tooth
〖齿轮〗(名)[chǐlún]
cogwheel; gear

侈[chǐ]
〖侈谈〗(动)[chǐtán]
engage in glib talk

耻(名)[chǐ]
shame; disgrace
〖耻辱〗(名)[chǐrǔ]
shame
〖耻笑〗(动)[chǐxiào]
scoff at; sneer at

chì

斥(动)[chì]
scold; blame
〖斥责〗(动)[chìzé]
rebuke; denounce

赤(形)[chì]
red;bare
〖赤膊上阵〗[chìbóshàngzhèn]
step forward in person; come out without any disguise; come out into the open
〖赤胆忠心〗[chìdǎnzhōngxīn]
a red heart with complete dedication
〖赤道〗(名)[chìdào]
the equator
〖赤裸裸〗(形)[chìluǒluǒ]
naked
〖赤贫〗(名)[chìpín]
extreme poverty; destitution
〖赤手空拳〗[chìshǒukōngquán]
unarmed; with naked fist
〖赤卫队〗(名)[chìwèiduì]
the Red Guards
〖赤字〗(名)[chìzì]
financial deficit

炽[chì]
〖炽热〗(形)[chìrè]
scorching hot

翅(名)[chì]
wing
〖翅膀〗(名)[chìbǎng]
wing

chōng

充(动)[chōng]
fill
〖充斥〗(动)[chōngchì]
fill up
〖充当〗(动)[chōngdāng]
act as; pose as
〖充电〗[chōng diàn]
charge with electricity
〖充耳不闻〗[chōng'ěrbùwén]
turn a deaf ear to
〖充分〗(形)[chōngfèn]

full; completely; thoroughly
〖充公〗[chōng gōng]
confiscate
〖充满〗(动)[chōngmǎn]
fill up; be filled up with
〖充沛〗(形)[chōngpèi]
full of (energy)
〖充其量〗(副)[chōngqíliàng]
at most
〖充实〗(形、动)[chōngshí]
solid; replenish and enrich; reinforce; fill... with (new content); substantiate
〖充数〗[chōng shù]
merely take a part; nominally make up the number
〖充裕〗(形)[chōngyù]
well off; ample
〖充足〗(形)[chōngzú]
abundant

冲(动)[chōng]
rush; dash; charge
另见 chòng
〖冲淡〗(动)[chōngdàn]
dilute
〖冲动〗(形)[chōngdòng]
excited
〖冲锋〗(动)[chōngfēng]
charge forward
〖冲锋陷阵〗
[chōngfēngxiànzhèn]
storm and shatter the enemy's position
〖冲昏头脑〗[chōnghūntóunǎo]
be carried away (by success); get dizzy with (success)
〖冲击〗(动)[chōngjī]
batter
〖冲击波〗(名)[chōngjībō]
blast wave; shock wave
〖冲破〗(动)[chōngpò]
break through; breach
〖冲刷〗(动)[chōngshuā]
wash and brush clean
〖冲天〗(形)[chōngtiān]
soaring; boundless (enthusiasm)
〖冲突〗(动)[chōngtū]
conflict
〖冲洗〗(动)[chōngxǐ]
① flush; wash sth. down ② develop (film)

憧[chōng]
〖憧憬〗(动)[chōngjǐng]
long for

chóng

虫(名)[chóng]〔条 tiáo〕
insect
〖虫害〗(名)[chónghài]
insect pest

重(量、副)[chóng]
① a measure word, piled one on another ② reiterated; repeatedly; again
另见 zhòng
〖重操旧业〗[chóngcāojiùyè]
return to one's old trade
〖重重〗(形)[chóngchóng]
circle upon circle; ring upon ring; heavily

〖重蹈覆辙〗[chóngdǎofùzhé]
repeat the same mistake
〖重叠〗(动)[chóngdié]
reduplicate; overlap
〖重复〗(动)[chóngfù]
repeat; reiterate
〖重建〗(动)[chóngjiàn]
rebuild
〖重申〗(动)[chóngshēn]
reiterate; reaffirm; restate
〖重围〗(名)[chóngwéi]
be encircled ring upon ring; under heavy besiegement
〖重新〗(副)[chóngxīn]
anew
〖重整旗鼓〗[chóngzhěngqígǔ]
begin all over again; rally forces again

崇 [chóng]
〖崇拜〗(动)[chóngbài]
worship
〖崇高〗(形)[chónggāo]
lofty; noble
〖崇敬〗(动)[chóngjìng]
respect; respect and admire
〖崇山峻岭〗[chóngshānjùnlǐng]
high mountains and lofty hills

chǒng

宠 (动)[chǒng]
treat with care and affection
〖宠爱〗(动)[chǒng'ài]
treat as a favourite
〖宠儿〗(名)[chǒng'ér]
a favourite person; a pet

chòng

冲 (形、动)[chòng]
forceful; dynamic
另见 chōng

chōu

抽 (动)[chōu] draw; pump
〖抽查〗(动)[chōuchá]
make sample check
〖抽调〗(动)[chōudiào]
transfer
〖抽空〗[chōu kòng]
take advantage of any free time
〖抽泣〗(动)[chōuqì]
sob
〖抽身〗[chōu shēn]
leave a place
〖抽水机〗(名)[chōushuǐjī]
〔台 tái〕water pump
〖抽屉〗(名)[chōuti]〔个 gè〕
drawer (in desk or table)
〖抽象〗(形)[chōuxiàng]
abstract
〖抽烟〗[chōu yān]
smoke (cig.)
〖抽样调查〗[chōuyàngdiàochá]
sampling survey

chóu

仇 (名)[chóu]
hatred; enmity; animosity
〖仇敌〗(名)[chóudí]
enemy; foe
〖仇恨〗(动)[chóuhèn]
hate
〖仇人〗(名)[chóurén]

enemy

〖仇视〗(动)[chóushì]

hate; be hostile to

惆 [chóu]

〖惆怅〗(形)[chóuchàng]

sad; depressive; disconsolate

绸 (名)[chóu]

silk

〖绸缎〗(名)[chóuduàn]

silks and satins

〖绸子〗(名)[chóuzi]

silk fabric

酬 [chóu]

〖酬宾〗[chóubīn]

sell at a discount; sell at a preferential price (eg. sell with 10% discount from the original price)

〖酬劳〗(动)[chóuláo]

remunerate

稠 (形)[chóu]

dense

〖稠密〗(形)[chóumì]

dense

愁 (动)[chóu]

worry

〖愁苦〗(形)[chóukǔ]

distressed

〖愁眉苦脸〗[chóuméikǔliǎn]

knit one's brows in despair; distressed looks

筹 [chóu]

〖筹办〗(动)[chóubàn]

sponsor; make preparations

〖筹备〗(动)[chóubèi]

prepare

〖筹划〗(动)[chóuhuà]

plan

〖筹集〗(动)[chóují]

collect and prepare (funds)

〖筹资〗[chóuzī]

raise funds

踌 [chóu]

〖踌躇〗(动)[chóuchú]

hesitate

chǒu

丑 (形)[chǒu]

ugly

〖丑恶〗(形)[chǒu'è]

loathsome; despicable

〖丑化〗(动)[chǒuhuà]

defame; disfigure

〖丑剧〗(名)[chǒujù]

farce; foul performance

〖丑陋〗(形)[chǒulòu]

ugly

〖丑态〗(名)[chǒutài]

disgusting manner

〖丑态百出〗[chǒutàibǎichū]

act like a buffoon; utterly ridiculous; cut a ludicrous figure

〖丑媳妇总要见公婆〗[chǒuxífù zǒngyàojiàngōngpó]

People may hide the worst side of their nature from casual

friends, but they cannot hide it from those with whom they live

chòu

臭 (形)[chòu]
smelly; stink
〖臭架子〗[chòu jiàzi]
the ugly mantle of pretentiousness
〖臭名远扬〗
[chòumíngyuǎnyáng]
notorious; infamous
〖臭名昭著〗[chòumíngzhāozhù]
infamous; notorious
〖臭味〗(名)[chòuwèi]
① discredited ② foul smell; ill smell
〖臭味相投〗[chòuwèixiāngtóu]
(derog.)like attracts like;be two of a kind

chū

出 (动、量)[chū]
① come out; go out ② take place; happen; occur ③ produce; manufacture; issue ④ offer; give; contribute ⑤ crop up; come up; emanate ⑥ a measure word(for performance, etc.)
〖出版〗(动)[chūbǎn]
publish
〖出版社〗(名)[chūbǎnshè]
publishing house
〖出兵〗[chū bīng]
march army for battle
〖出岔子〗[chū chàzi]
run into trouble
〖出差〗[chū chāi]
be out on duty; be out on an official mission
〖出产〗(动)[chūchǎn]
produce; make; manufacture
〖出超〗(动)[chūchāo]
export surplus; balance of trade surplus
〖出丑〗[chū chǒu]
expose one's weak points; be disgraced; cut a poor or foolish figure
〖出处〗(名)[chūchù]
source
〖出动〗(动)[chūdòng]
start out
〖出尔反尔〗[chū'ěrfǎn'ěr]
inconsistent; promise and then deny in succession; go back on one's words
〖出发〗(动)[chūfā]
set out; start off
〖出发点〗(名)[chūfādiǎn]
starting point; point of departure
〖出风头〗[chū fēngtou]
cut a figure; show off; seek limelight
〖出乎意料〗[chūhūyìliào]
unforeseen; beyond expectations
〖出工〗[chūgōng]
go to work
〖出海〗[chū hǎi]
put to sea
〖出击〗(动)[chūjī]
launch attack

〖出嫁〗(动)[chūjià]
be married(of girls)
〖出界〗[chū jiè]
outside(hit wide; be out of bounds)
〖出境〗[chū jìng]
leave a country; exit (visa)
〖出口〗(动、名)[chūkǒu]
export; exit
〖出口转内销〗
[chūkǒuzhuǎnnèixiāo]
exportoriented commodities sold on the home market; rejected export commodities domestically marketed
〖出来〗[chū lái]
come out
〖出类拔萃〗[chūlèibácuì]
stand out among others;far above the average; eminent above all others
〖出力〗[chū lì]
do one's best; contribute one's strength
〖出笼〗(动)[chūlóng]
come out into the open; turn out; emerge(usu. derog.)
〖出路〗(名)[chūlù]
outlet; way out
〖出卖〗(动)[chūmài]
① offer for sale ② betray
〖出面〗[chū miàn]
(do sth.)in the name of...; in person
〖出名〗[chū míng]
become famous
〖出没〗(动)[chūmò]
infest;haunt;swarm around;appear and disappear(without regularity)
〖出谋划策〗[chūmóuhuàcè]
(derog.)offer advice;give advice and suggestions
〖出纳〗(名)[chūnà]
① cashier ② the work of receiving and paying out money
〖出品〗(动、名)[chūpǐn]
artistic or manufactured product; produce; manufacture; make
〖出其不意〗[chūqíbùyì]
catch one unawares;take by surprise
〖出奇制胜〗[chūqízhìshèng]
defeat... by surprise attack
〖出勤〗(动)[chūqín]
attend work; attendance(rate)
〖出去〗[chū qù]
go out
〖出人头地〗[chūréntóudì]
stand above others
〖出入〗(动、名)[chūrù]
① come in and go out ② difference; in conformity with (the fact,etc.)
〖出色〗(形)[chūsè]
outstanding; remarkable; distinguished
〖出身〗(动、名)[chūshēn]
come from (...family); class origin; family background
〖出神〗[chū shén]
appear occupied in thought; deep in thought
〖出生〗(动)[chūshēng]
be born

〖出生入死〗[chūshēngrùsǐ]
brave countless dangers; go through thick and thin
〖出世〗(动)[chūshì]
be born
〖出售〗(动)[chūshòu]
offer for sale
〖出台〗(动)[chūtái]
introduce; come out
〖出头〗[chūtóu]
raise (their) heads (the day had come for them to raise their heads)
〖出头露面〗[chūtóulùmiàn]
① appear publicly; appear in public ② (figure) prominent
〖出土〗[chū tǔ]
unearth; be excavated
〖出息〗(名)[chūxi]
promising
〖出席〗(动)[chūxí]
be present (at meeting)
〖出现〗(动)[chūxiàn]
appear; emerge; arise
〖出以公心〗[chūyǐgōngxīn]
without any selfish considerations; from intentions for the public
〖出诊〗(动)[chūzhěn]
make a house call (of doctor)
〖出租〗(动)[chūzū]
for hire; rent
〖出租汽车〗[chūzūqìchē]
taxi; taxicab; cab

初 (形、头)[chū]
① beginning; at first; early (spring) ② first ③ junior
〖初步〗(形)[chūbù]
preliminary; initial
〖初出茅庐〗[chūchūmáolú]
a debut; a beginner
〖初等〗(形)[chūděng]
elementary; preliminary
〖初稿〗(名)[chūgǎo]
draft
〖初级〗(形)[chūjí]
elementary
〖初见成效〗[chūjiànchéngxiào]
begin to take shape; achieve an initial success
〖初期〗(名)[chūqī]
initial stage
〖初中〗(名)[chūzhōng]
junior middle school

chú

除 (动)[chú]
divide
〖除法〗(名)[chúfǎ]
(math.) division
〖除非〗(连)[chúfēi]
unless
〖除开〗(连)[chúkāi]
except; besides; with the exception of
〖除了…以外〗[chúle…yǐwài]
except; besides
〖除数〗(名)[chúshù]
(math.) divider
〖除外〗(动)[chúwài]
except; apart from
〖除夕〗(名)[chúxī]
New Year's Eve

厨 [chú]
〖厨房〗(名)[chúfáng]
kitchen
〖厨师〗(名)[chúshī]
cook

锄 (名、动)[chú]
hoe
〖锄头〗(名)[chútou]〔把 bǎ〕
hoe

雏 [chú]
〖雏形〗(名)[chúxíng]
embryonic form

橱 (名)[chú]
cabinet; wardrobe
〖橱窗〗(名)[chúchuāng]
show window; display case

chǔ

处 (动)[chǔ]
① get along with ② be in a position ③ manage; handle; deal with
另见 chù
〖处罚〗(动)[chǔfá]
punish
〖处分〗(动)[chǔfèn]
be disciplined
〖处境〗(名)[chǔjìng]
circumstances; conditions
〖处决〗(动)[chǔjué]
execute (criminals)
〖处理〗(动)[chǔlǐ]
treat; deal with; handle; run affairs
〖处世〗(动)[chǔshì]
deal with people and affairs
〖处事〗(动)[chǔshì]
deal with affairs; handle
〖处死〗(动)[chǔsǐ]
sentence to death
〖处心积虑〗[chǔxīnjīlǜ]
have all along nurtured schemes to ...
〖处于〗(动)[chǔyú]
find oneself in; stand in
〖处置〗(动)[chǔzhì]
handle; dispose

储 [chǔ]
〖储备〗(动)[chǔbèi]
reserve
〖储备粮〗(名)[chǔbèiliáng]
grain reserves
〖储藏〗(动)[chǔcáng]
store
〖储存〗(动)[chǔcún]
accumulate; store
〖储蓄〗(动)[chǔxù]
have a deposit; save

chù

处 (名)[chù]
① place; spot ② department
另见 chǔ
〖处处〗(名)[chùchù]
everywhere
〖处所〗(名)[chùsuǒ]
place; location

畜 [chù]
另见 xù
〖畜力〗(名)[chùlì]
animal power

触 (动)[chù]
touch
〖触电〗[chù diàn]
get an electric shock
〖触动〗(动)[chùdòng]
touch; touch on
〖触犯〗(动)[chùfàn]
violate
〖触及〗(动)[chùjí]
touch
〖触及灵魂〗[chùjílínghún]
touch the people to their very souls
〖触角〗(名)[chùjiǎo]
antenna; feelers of insects
〖触景生情〗[chùjǐngshēngqíng]
see sth. which arouses one's deep feelings
〖触觉〗(名)[chùjué]
sense of touch
〖触目惊心〗[chùmùjīngxīn]
a startling fact; a ghastly sight; shocking
〖触怒〗(动)[chùnù]
provoke; offend; arouse wrath

矗 [chù]
〖矗立〗(动)[chùlì]
tower; erect; rise

chuāi

揣 (动)[chuāi]
① put into ② estimate; calculate; figure
另见 chuǎi

chuǎi

揣 [chuǎi]
另见 chuāi
〖揣测〗(动)[chuǎicè]
give a guess; reckon
〖揣度〗(动)[chuǎiduó]
reckon; conjecture
〖揣摩〗(动)[chuǎimó]
weigh and consider

chuài

踹 (动)[chuài]
trample; tread heavily

chuān

川 (名)[chuān]
① river; stream ② an area of level country
〖川流不息〗[chuānliúbùxī]
a continuous flow of

穿 (动)[chuān]
① wear; put on ② perforate; penetrate; pass through
〖穿插〗(动)[chuānchā]
do alternately
〖穿戴〗(名)[chuāndài]
what one wears (hat, hair, decorations and dress)
〖穿孔〗[chuān kǒng]
perforate
〖穿梭〗[chuān suō]

shuttle
〖穿针引线〗[chuānzhēnyǐnxiàn]
act as a go-between
〖穿着〗(名)[chuānzhuó]
what one wears

chuán

传(动)[chuán]
pass from... to...; circulate; pass on to
另见 zhuàn
〖传播〗(动)[chuánbō]
spread over; propagate
〖传布〗(动)[chuánbù]
spread
〖传达〗(动)[chuándá]
transmit; convey; communicate
〖传达室〗(名)[chuándáshì]
reception office
〖传单〗(名)[chuándān]
a handbill; leaflet
〖传导〗(动)[chuándǎo]
conduct (heat, electricity)
〖传递〗(动)[chuándì]
hand round; pass on
〖传呼〗(动)[chuánhū]
communicate; inform; send for (e.g. sb. to take a phone call)
〖传呼电话〗[chuánhūdiànhuà]
neighbourhood telephone service
〖传家宝〗(名)[chuánjiābǎo]
hereditary treasure
〖传奇〗(名)[chuánqí]
① short stories (Tang and Sung dynasties); long plays (Ming and Ching dynasties) ② legendary; legendary story
〖传染〗(动)[chuánrǎn]
infect; communicate (disease)
〖传神〗(形)[chuánshén]
vivid; graphic; expressive (of creative work)
〖传声筒〗(名)[chuánshēngtǒng]
① microphone ② mouthpiece
〖传授〗(动)[chuánshòu]
teach; hand down
〖传说〗(动、名)[chuánshuō]
story that goes around; legend
〖传送〗(动)[chuánsòng]
deliver (message, news)
〖传颂〗(动)[chuánsòng]
praises are being sung everywhere
〖传统〗(名)[chuántǒng]
tradition; conventions
〖传统观念〗[chuántǒngguānniàn]
traditional concepts
〖传闻〗(名)[chuánwén]
hearsay
〖传阅〗(动)[chuányuè]
circulate; pass around (e.g. circular)
〖传真〗(名)[chuánzhēn]
fax; facsimile
〖传真机〗(名)[chuánzhēnjī]
fax machine; facsimile equipment

船(名)[chuán]
〔只 zhī、条 tiáo〕 boat; ship; vessel
〖船舶〗(名)[chuánbó]

ship; boat; vessel
〖船舱〗(名)[chuáncāng]
cabin(of ship)
〖船帆〗(名)[chuánfān]
sail
〖船坞〗(名)[chuánwù]
dock; dockyard

C

chuǎn

喘(动)[chuǎn]
gasp; pant
〖喘气〗[chuǎn qì]
① gasp; pant; short of breath
② take a break
〖喘息〗(动)[chuǎnxī]
gain a respite; pause for breath

chuàn

串(动、量)[chuàn]
① string up ② a measure word, strain, string, bunch, etc.
〖串联〗(动)[chuànlián]
establish ties with; contact
〖串通〗(动)[chuàntōng]
collude with; conspire with (sb.); work hand in glove with

chuāng

创[chuāng]
另见 chuàng
〖创伤〗(名)[chuāngshāng]
wound; injury; trauma

疮(名)[chuāng]
a sore; fester
〖疮疤〗(名)[chuāngbā]
a scab; wound scars

窗(名)[chuāng]
window
〖窗户〗(名)[chuānghu]
window
〖窗口〗(名)[chuāngkǒu]
window opening
〖窗帘〗(名)[chuānglián]
window curtains; window screen
〖窗台〗(名)[chuāngtái]
window sill

chuáng

床(名)[chuáng]〔张 zhāng〕
bed
〖床单〗(名)[chuángdān]
bed sheet
〖床铺〗(名)[chuángpù]
bed (with bedding); a general term for bed
〖床位〗(名)[chuángwèi]
bed or berth (in hospital, hotel, ship, train, etc.)

chuǎng

闯(动)[chuǎng]
① force one's way in or out ② come successfully through the ordeal
〖闯祸〗[chuǎng huò]
precipitate a disaster; lead to trouble
〖闯将〗(名)[chuǎngjiàng]

pathbreakers
〖闯劲儿〗(名)[chuǎngjìnr]
spirit of a pathbreaker

chuàng

创 (动)[chuàng]
initiate; inaugurate
另见 chuāng
〖创办〗(动)[chuàngbàn]
found; sponsor
〖创汇〗(动)[chuànghuì]
earn foreign exchange
〖创见〗(名)[chuàngjiàn]
a new idea or viewpoint
〖创建〗(动)[chuàngjiàn]
found; create; establish
〖创举〗(名)[chuàngjǔ]
new creation; initiative; pioneering undertaking
〖创刊〗(动)[chuàngkān]
initial issue (of a magazine); first issue
〖创立〗(动)[chuànglì]
set up; originate; establish
〖创设〗(动)[chuàngshè]
found; open
〖创始〗(动)[chuàngshǐ]
begin; beginning; initiative
〖创收〗(动)[chuàngshōu]
make economic income earning; increase income by providing paid services
〖创新〗(动)[chuàngxīn]
create something new
〖创业〗(动)[chuàngyè]
pioneer; start an enterprise; start a project
〖创造〗(动)[chuàngzào]
create
〖创造性〗(名)[chuàngzàoxìng]
creativeness
〖创作〗(动、名)[chuàngzuò]
create; creation; creative work

chuī

吹 (动)[chuī]
① blow ②brag; boast ③ end up in failure
〖吹风〗[chuīfēng]
① dry one's hair;dry hair with a blower ② let sb.in on sth. in advance; give a cue
〖吹风会〗(名)[chuīfēnghuì]
briefing; background briefing
〖吹鼓手〗(名)[chuīgǔshǒu]
trumpeter; bugler
〖吹灰之力〗[chuīhuīzhīlì]
as easy as blowing away dust
〖吹毛求疵〗[chuīmáoqiúcī]
blow upon the hair trying to discover a mole; hair-splitting; fault-finding; find fault with
〖吹牛〗[chuī niú]
boast; brag
〖吹捧〗(动)[chuīpěng]
lavish praise on; laud; flatter and tout
〖吹嘘〗(动)[chuīxū]
brag; glibly profess; boost up; crack oneself up

炊 [chuī]

〖炊事员〗(名)[chuīshìyuán]
member of the kitchen staff; cook

chuí

垂(动)[chuí]
① hang; droop; dangle; bend downward ② be on the verge of
〖垂死挣扎〗[chuísǐzhēngzhá]
give dying kicks; death-bed struggle; desperate struggle
〖垂头丧气〗[chuítóusàngqì]
crestfallen; in low spirit; become dejected and despondent
〖垂危〗(形)[chuíwēi]
close to death as a result of serious illness
〖垂涎〗[chuí xián]
cannot hide one's greed; the mouth watering coveteously for
〖垂涎三尺〗[chuíxiánsānchǐ]
with mouth watering copiously for(hankering after sth.)
〖垂直〗(动)[chuízhí]
perpendicular

锤(名、动)[chuí]
hammer; knock with hammer
〖锤炼〗(动)[chuíliàn]
steel and temper; temper
〖锤子〗(名)[chuízi]〔把 bǎ〕
hammer

chūn

春(名)[chūn]
Spring
〖春播〗(名)[chūnbō]
Spring sowing
〖春风满面〗
[chūnfēngmǎnmiàn]
face radiates happiness; face beaming with smiles
〖春耕〗(名)[chūngēng]
Spring ploughing
〖春光〗(名)[chūnguāng]
the splendour of Spring
〖春季〗(名)[chūnjì]
Spring season
〖春节〗(名)[chūnjié]
Spring Festival
〖春雷〗(名)[chūnléi]
thunder-clap
〖春联〗(名)[chūnlián]〔副 fù〕
New Year couplets
〖春色〗(名)[chūnsè]
the beautiful scenery of Spring
〖春天〗(名)[chūntiān]
Springtime

chún

纯(形)[chún]
pure
〖纯粹〗(形)[chúncuì]
pure; complete; sheer
〖纯洁〗(形)[chúnjié]
pure
〖纯洁性〗(名)[chúnjiéxìng]
purity
〖纯熟〗(形)[chúnshú]
skillful; fluent
〖纯正〗(形)[chúnzhèng]

① upright; honest ② pure

唇 (名)[chún]
lips
〖唇齿相依〗[chúnchǐxiāngyī]
as closely related as the lips and the teeth; interdependent as lips and teeth
〖唇齿音〗(名)[chúnchǐyīn]
labio-dental
〖唇舌〗(名)[chúnshé]
lips and tongue; plausible speech; words; language
〖唇亡齿寒〗[chúnwángchǐhán]
when the lips are gone the teeth will be exposed to the cold; be on intimate terms with each other

淳 [chún]
〖淳厚〗(形)[chúnhòu]
honest; devoted
〖淳朴〗(形)[chúnpǔ]
simple and honest

chǔn

蠢 (形)[chǔn]
stupid
〖蠢蠢欲动〗[chǔnchǔnyùdòng]
(derog.) (of person) restless and about to start some move; itch for action
〖蠢动〗(动)[chǔndòng]
insidious move (on the part of the enemy or bad elements)

chuō

戳 (动)[chuō]
poke (a hole in); thrust
〖戳穿〗(动)[chuōchuān]
lay bare; expose

chuò

绰 [chuò]
〖绰号〗(名)[chuòhào]
nickname

cí

词 (名)[cí]
① words; phrases ② a poem of classical Chinese verse
〖词典〗(名)[cídiǎn]
〔本 běn、部 bù〕
a dictionary of words and phrases
〖词汇〗(名)[cíhuì]
vocabulary
〖词句〗(名)[cíjù]
words and phrases
〖词类〗(名)[cílèi]
part of speech
〖词头〗(名)[cítóu]
prefix
〖词尾〗(名)[cíwěi]
suffix
〖词性〗(名)[cíxìng]
part of speech
〖词序〗(名)[cíxù]
word order
〖词语〗(名)[cíyǔ]
word; phrase
〖词藻〗(名)[cízǎo]
ornate phraseology (in pedan-

C

tic writing)
〖词组〗(名)[cízǔ]
word group

祠 [cí]

〖祠堂〗(名)[cítáng]
the ancestral temple

瓷 (名)[cí]

porcelain
〖瓷器〗(名)[cíqì]
porcelain ware

辞 (名、动)[cí]

①word; phrase ② a poem of classical Chinese verse ③ take leave ④ resign
〖辞别〗(动)[cíbié]
say goodbye; bid farewell
〖辞行〗(动)[cíxíng]
say goodbye (before going on a long journey)
〖辞职〗[cí zhí]
resign

慈 [cí]

〖慈爱〗(形)[cí'ài]
kindly; gentle
〖慈悲〗(形)[cíbēi]
merciful
〖慈善〗(形)[císhàn]
charitable
〖慈祥〗(形)[cíxiáng]
amiable; kindly

磁 (名)[cí]

magnet
〖磁场〗(名)[cíchǎng]
magnetic field
〖磁带〗(名)[cídài]〔盘 pán〕
magnetic tape
〖磁石〗(名)[císhí]
loadstone
〖磁铁〗(名)[cítiě]
magnetic iron; magnet
〖磁性〗(名)[cíxìng]
magnetic; of a magnetic nature

雌 (形)[cí]

female(e.g. flower, dog, etc.)

cǐ

此 (代)[cǐ]

this
〖此地无银三百两〗
[cǐdìwúyínsānbǎiliǎng]
a thief posts a marker saying: "the missing treasure is not buried here" (self-exposing)
〖此后〗(连)[cǐhòu]
henceforth; hereafter
〖此刻〗(名)[cǐkè]
now; this moment
〖此起彼伏〗[cǐqǐbǐfú]
ebb and flow; rising here and subsiding there
〖此外〗(连)[cǐwài]
besides; in addition

cì

次 (量、形)[cì]

① a measure word(e.g.first time, many times) ② the second;

the next; second-rate
〖次品〗(名)[cìpǐn]
shoddy products; products not up to the required standard
〖次数〗(名)[cìshù]
number of times
〖次序〗(名)[cìxù]
order of sequence
〖次要〗(形)[cìyào]
next in importance

刺 (动、名)[cì]
① stab; prick ② thorns; small fish bones
〖刺刀〗(名)[cìdāo]〔把 bǎ〕
bayonet
〖刺耳〗(形)[cì'ěr]
irritating or unpleasant to the ear
〖刺骨〗(形)[cìgǔ]
piercing to the bones;biting
〖刺激〗(动)[cìjī]
irritate; stimulate; excite; be provoked
〖刺杀〗(名、动)[cìshā]
① assassination ② assassinate ③ bayonet fighting
〖刺探〗(动)[cìtàn]
detect
〖刺绣〗(名)[cìxiù]
embroidery
〖刺眼〗(形)[cìyǎn]
① dazzling ② unpleasant to the eye

赐 [cì]
〖赐予〗(动)[cìyǔ]
bestow... on

cōng

从 [cōng]
另见 cóng
〖从容〗(形)[cōngróng]
confident and without haste
〖从容不迫〗[cōngróngbùpò]
take one's time in doing...

匆 [cōng]
〖匆匆〗(形)[cōngcōng]
hurriedly
〖匆促〗(形)[cōngcù]
hurriedly; in a rush
〖匆忙〗(形)[cōngmáng]
hurriedly; in a hurry

葱 (名)[cōng]
onions
〖葱葱〗(形)[cōngcōng]
green
〖葱绿〗(形)[cōnglǜ]
pale yellowish green
〖葱郁〗(形)[cōngyù]
luxuriantly green

聪 [cōng]
〖聪明〗(形)[cōngmíng]
intelligent; clever; bright; wise

cóng

从 (介)[cóng]
from
另见 cōng

〖从长计议〗[cóngchángjìyì]
talk over at length; take time to consider it
〖从此〗(连)[cóngcǐ]
from now on
〖从…到…〗[cóng…dào…]
from...to...
〖从而〗(连)[cóng'ér]
therefore
〖从…看来〗[cóng…kànlái]
judging from; in view of
〖从来〗(副)[cónglái]
at all times; always
〖从略〗(动)[cónglüè]
① omit ② in brief
〖从…起〗[cóng…qǐ]
from...on
〖从前〗(名)[cóngqián]
formerly; before
〖从事〗(动)[cóngshì]
engage in; be taken up with
〖从属〗(动)[cóngshǔ]
be subordinated to
〖从头〗(副)[cóngtóu]
from the beginning; once again
〖从中〗(副)[cóngzhōng]
thereby; therefrom

丛 (名)[cóng]
bush; shrubbery
〖丛刊〗(名)[cóngkān]
a collection of periodicals
〖丛林〗(名)[cónglín]
the jungle; woods; forest
〖丛生〗(动)[cóngshēng]
grow up in great variety and profusion
〖丛书〗(名)[cóngshū]
a collection of books

còu

凑 (动)[còu]
① assemble; put together ② press near
〖凑合〗(动)[còuhe]
have to make do with; fair to middling; make shift
〖凑巧〗(形)[còuqiǎo]
happen to; by chance; accidentally
〖凑热闹〗[còu rè nào]
take part in and join the fun
〖凑数〗[còu shù]
make up a number without active work; some incompetent person has been assigned simply to fill the post

cū

粗 (形)[cū]
rough; not thorough; bulky
〖粗暴〗(形)[cūbào]
coarse; rude; outrageous
〖粗笨〗(形)[cūbèn]
heavy; awkward; clumsy
〖粗糙〗(形)[cūcāo]
rough; crude
〖粗放〗(形)[cūfàng]
forthright
〖粗放经营〗[cūfàngjīngyíng]
extensive management; low technology production of cheap products
〖粗犷〗(形)[cūguǎng]

rash and boorish
〖粗粮〗(名)[cūliáng]
coarse grain
〖粗鲁〗(形)[cūlǔ]
crude
〖粗略〗(形)[cūlüè]
not detailed
〖粗浅〗(形)[cūqiǎn]
superficial
〖粗细〗(名)[cūxì]
roughness and polish; coarse and fine
〖粗心〗(形)[cūxīn]
careless
〖粗野〗(形)[cūyě]
rude
〖粗枝大叶〗[cūzhīdàyè]
be crude and careless; crude and perfunctory
〖粗制滥造〗[cūzhìlànzào]
roughly made
〖粗壮〗(形)[cūzhuàng]
stout; robust; strong

cù

促(动)[cù]
① hurry to do ② promote; spur; urge
〖促成〗(动)[cùchéng]
help materialize; cause (sb. to do sth.)
〖促进〗(动)[cùjìn]
promote
〖促进派〗(名)[cùjìnpài]
promoters of progress; those who promote progress
〖促使〗(动)[cùshǐ]
precipitate; cause
〖促膝谈心〗[cùxītánxīn]
have a heart-to-heart talk

醋(名)[cù]
vinegar

簇(量)[cù]
a measure word, a bunch (flowers)
〖簇新〗(形)[cùxīn]
brand-new
〖簇拥〗(动)[cùyōng]
escort

cuàn

窜(动)[cuàn]
flee
〖窜犯〗(动)[cuànfàn]
raid; make an inroad
〖窜扰〗(动)[cuànrǎo]
harass
〖窜逃〗(动)[cuàntáo]
flee and hide

篡(动)[cuàn]
usurp; arrogate
〖篡夺〗(动)[cuànduó]
usurp; arrogate
〖篡改〗(动)[cuàngǎi]
(derog.) tamper with; alter; revise

cuī

催(动)[cuī]
urge

〖催促〗(动)[cuīcù]
press for
〖催化剂〗(名)[cuīhuàjì]
a catalyst
〖催泪弹〗(名)[cuīlèidàn]
tear-gas bomb
〖催眠〗(动)[cuīmián]
hypnotize

摧(动)[cuī]
destroy; devastate; ravage
〖摧残〗(动)[cuīcán]
trample down; tread under foot
〖摧毁〗(动)[cuīhuǐ]
smash to pieces; completely destroy; shatter
〖摧枯拉朽〗[cuīkūlāxiǔ]
smash easily like breaking dry branches; easily overcome

cuì

脆(形)[cuì]
① crisp ② clear; well enunciated
〖脆弱〗(形)[cuìruò]
weak; fragile

啐(动)[cuì]
spit

翠[cuì]
〖翠绿〗(形)[cuìlǜ]
jade-green

cūn

村(名)[cūn]
village
〖村落〗(名)[cūnluò]
hamlet; village
〖村镇〗(名)[cūnzhèn]
villages and small towns
〖村庄〗(名)[cūnzhuāng]
village
〖村子〗(名)[cūnzi]〔个 gè〕
village

cún

存(动)[cún]
exist; keep; preserve
〖存车处〗(名)[cúnchēchù]
parking place (for bicycles)
〖存放〗(动)[cúnfàng]
put aside for safe-keeping
〖存货〗(名)[cúnhuò]
goods in stock or in storage
〖存款〗(名)[cúnkuǎn]
deposit; savings
〖存亡〗(名)[cúnwáng]
survival or extinction
〖存心〗[cún xīn]
bent on; purposely; intentionally
〖存衣处〗(名)[cúnyīchù]
cloakroom; a place where clothes are kept
〖存在〗(动)[cúnzài]
exist
〖存折〗(名)[cúnzhé]
pass book

cùn

寸(量)[cùn]
a measure word, inch

〖寸步不离〗[cùnbùbùlí]
stay without leaving a step
〖寸步难行〗[cùnbùnánxíng]
difficult even to move one step
〖寸土必争〗[cùntǔbìzhēng]
fight for every inch of land

cuō

搓(动)[cuō]
rub or roll with hand

蹉[cuō]
〖蹉商〗(动)[cuōshāng]
discuss; consult

撮(动)[cuō]
hold between fingers
〖撮合〗(动)[cuōhé]
bring(two parties)together

cuò

挫(动)[cuò]
balk; baffle
〖挫败〗(动)[cuòbài]
thwart; frustrate; foil
〖挫伤〗(动)[cuòshāng]
frustrate; deflate
〖挫折〗(名)[cuòzhé]
setbacks

措[cuò]
〖措辞〗[cuò cí]
wording; phrasing; terms
〖措施〗(名)[cuòshī]
measure; steps
〖措手不及〗[cuòshǒubùjí]
too late to do anything about; attack and take them before they know what is happening

锉(名、动)[cuò]〔把 bǎ〕
a file(tool); file
〖锉刀〗(名)[cuòdāo]〔把 bǎ〕
file(tool)

错(形、名)[cuò]
mistaken; wrong; mistake; error
〖错别字〗(名)[cuòbiézì]
wrongly written or pronounced characters; wrong character
〖错处〗(名)[cuòchù]
mistake; error in conduct
〖错怪〗(动)[cuòguài]
blame wrongly
〖错过〗(动)[cuòguò]
miss(opportunity)
〖错觉〗(名)[cuòjué]
an illusion
〖错误〗(名)[cuòwù]
an error
〖错综复杂〗[cuòzōngfùzá]
complicated

C

dā

搭(动)[dā]

① put up; erect; ② place (sth.) on...

〖搭伴〗 [dā bàn]

travel with others; accompany another

〖搭档〗(名)[dādàng]

partner; work-mate

〖搭救〗(动)[dājiù]

rescue

〖搭配〗(动)[dāpèi]

match (e.g. find sth. that matches sth. else); be a partner with; go together

答[dā]

另见 dá

〖答应〗(动)[dāying]

① answer ② consent; promise

dá

打(量)[dá]

dozen

另见 dǎ

达(动)[dá]

reach; accomplish

〖达成〗(动)[dáchéng]

reach (an agreement); conclude

〖达到〗(动)[dádào]

reach (goal); attain (unity); achieve

答(动)[dá]

answer; reply

另见 dā

〖答案〗(名)[dá'àn]

answer to question; solution (of mathematical problem, etc.)

〖答辩〗(动)[dábiàn]

① defend ② reply in argument

〖答词〗(名)[dácí]

speech in reply; response (e.g. to an address of congratu-

lation, etc.)
〖答复〗(动)[dáfù]
reply; answer; in response
〖答谢〗(动)[dáxiè]
reciprocate (e.g. reciprocal banquet)

dǎ

打(动)[dǎ]
① strike;beat ② knit ③ make (mark); draw (line) ④ drill ⑤ hoist ⑥ buy (e.g. sauce) ⑦ fetch (water) ⑧ play (e.g. basketball)
另见 dá
〖打靶〗[dǎ bǎ]
target practice
〖打败〗(动)[dǎbài]
defeat
〖打扮〗(动、名)[dǎban]
① dress...up as; deck...up; ② dressing (of clothes)
〖打抱不平〗[dǎbàobùpíng]
lend a helping hand to right a wrong
〖打草惊蛇〗[dǎcǎojīngshé]
beat the grass and startle the snakes
〖打岔〗[dǎ chà]
lead the talk astray; interrupt a conversation
〖打场〗[dǎ cháng]
thresh (grain)
〖打成一片〗[dǎchéngyīpiàn]
become integrated with; become one with; merge with; be fused with; be at one with
〖打倒〗(动)[dǎdǎo]
overthrow; down with
〖打电报〗[dǎ diànbào]
send a telegram
〖打电话〗[dǎ diànhuà]
make a telephone call
〖打动〗(动)[dǎdòng]
arouse
〖打断〗(动)[dǎduàn]
cut short; interrupt
〖打哆嗦〗[dǎ duōsuo]
tremble; shiver
〖打官腔〗[dǎ guānqiāng]
assume official airs in speech and action; put person off by talking formalities as an excuse
〖打官司〗[dǎ guānsi]
go to law (against sb.)
〖打火机〗(名)[dǎhuǒjī]
cigarette lighter
〖打击〗(动)[dǎjī]
strike; knock
〖打击乐〗(名)[dǎjīyuè]
percussion music
〖打假〗[dǎjiǎ]
mount an attack on producers of counterfeit products; make an attack on counterfeiters
〖打架〗[dǎjià]
fight; engage in a broil
〖打江山〗[dǎ jiāngshān]
seize political power by force
〖打交道〗[dǎ jiāodao]
deal with; negotiate
〖打搅〗(动)[dǎjiǎo]
disturb; interrupt

〖打井〗[dǎ jǐng]
sink wells
〖打开〗(动)[dǎkāi]
① open up ② break(a deadlock); make a beginning
〖打垮〗(动)[dǎkuǎ]
crush; be completely defeated
〖打雷〗[dǎ léi]
a crash of thunder; thunderclap

D

〖打量〗(动)[dǎliang]
size up; measure (sb.) with one's eyes
〖打猎〗[dǎ liè]
go hunting
〖打埋伏〗[dǎ máifu]
lie in ambush; keep under cover
〖打喷嚏〗[dǎ pēntì]
sneeze
〖打破〗(动)[dǎpò]
break; smash
〖打破常规〗[dǎpò chángguī]
break away from convention
〖打破记录〗[dǎpò jìlù]
break record
〖打破砂锅问到底〗
[dǎpòshā guōwèndàodǐ]
probe a matter to the bottom; keep asking questions till one gets to the bottom of the matter
〖打气〗[dǎ qì]
inflate (tire); (fig.)bolster up
〖打球〗[dǎ qiú]
play a ball game
〖打趣〗(动)[dǎqù]
make fun
〖打入冷宫〗[dǎrùlěnggōng]
be out of favour; relegate; consign to the back
〖打扫〗(动)[dǎsǎo]
clean up
〖打闪〗[dǎshǎn]
lightning flashes
〖打手〗(名)[dǎshǒu]
bully; hatchetman
〖打水〗[dǎ shuǐ]
fetch water
〖打算〗(动、名)[dǎsuàn]
intend; plan; propose; intent; intention
〖打听〗(动)[dǎting]
inquire; ask
〖打通〗(动)[dǎtōng]
① break through; open up ② convince
〖打退堂鼓〗[dǎtuìtánggǔ]
beat a retreat; draw in one's horns
〖打响〗(动)[dǎxiǎng]
①open fire ②achieve preliminary success (in certain undertaking); make a good start
〖打消〗(动)[dǎxiāo]
dispel; withdraw; get rid of
〖打掩护〗[dǎ yǎnhù]
provide cover for; shield
〖打仗〗[dǎ zhàng]
fight (war)
〖打针〗[dǎ zhēn]
have an injection
〖打字〗[dǎ zì]
type; typewrite
〖打字机〗(名)[dǎzìjī]
type-writer

dà

大(形)[dà]
① big;large ② the eldest ③ honoured ④ important ⑤ large (scale, number, amount, quantity, etc.)
另见 dài
〖大半〗(副)[dàbàn]
more than half; largely
〖大本营〗(名)[dàběnyíng]
① headquarters ② nerve centre
〖大便〗(名、动)[dàbiàn]
defecation; stools; move the bowels; go to stool
〖大不了〗[dàbuliǎo]
the worst that could happen is...
〖大不相同〗[dàbùxiāngtóng]
great difference; quite unlike
〖大材小用〗[dàcáixiǎoyòng]
waste or misuse of materials or talents; great talent employed in small capacity
〖大车〗(名)[dàchē]〔辆 liàng〕
cart
〖大吃大喝〗[dàchīdàhē]
extravagant eating and drinking; indulge in excessive eating and drinking
〖大吃一惊〗[dàchīyījīng]
be startled; greatly shocked; be astounded
〖大吹大擂〗[dàchuīdàléi]
boast of; talk big; brag; trumpeting loudly
〖大胆〗(形)[dàdǎn]
bold; brave; daring
〖大刀阔斧〗[dàdāokuòfǔ]
make snap decisions; cut the Gordian knot
〖大道〗(名)[dàdào]〔条 tiáo〕
main road; avenue; the main lines of communication
〖大地〗(名)[dàdì]
the earth
〖大豆〗(名)[dàdòu]
soybean
〖大都〗(副)[dàdū]
mostly
〖大多〗(副)[dàduō]
mostly; most
〖大多数〗(名)[dàduōshù]
the majority
〖大发雷霆〗[dàfāléitíng]
flare up
〖大方〗(形)[dàfang]
generous; large-minded
〖大放厥词〗[dàfàngjuécí]
say something utterly wrong
〖大风大浪〗[dàfēngdàlàng]
great storms and waves
〖大概〗(副)[dàgài]
generally; most probably; probably
〖大纲〗(名)[dàgāng]
outline; compendium
〖大哥大〗(名)[dàgēdà]
walkable phone; cellular phone; walkie-talkie
〖大功告成〗[dàgōnggàochéng]
the task is accomplished
〖大公无私〗[dàgōngwúsī]
selfless; selflessness
〖大规模〗[dà guīmó]

on a large scale; large-scale
〖大国沙文主义〗
[dàguóshāwénzhǔyì]
great-power chauvinism
〖大国主义〗(名)[dàguózhǔyì]
big-nation chauvinism; great-power chauvinism
〖大海〗(名)[dàhǎi]
the sea
〖大海捞针〗[dàhǎilāozhēn]
look for a needle in a haystack
〖大好〗(形)[dàhǎo]
excellent; beautiful
〖大会〗(名)[dàhuì]
assembly; conference; meeting; rally; congress
〖大伙儿〗(代)[dàhuǒr]
all; everybody
〖大计〗(名)[dàjì]
a question of fundamental importance; major point
〖大家〗(代)[dàjiā]
all (people)
〖大街〗(名)[dàjiē]〔条 tiáo〕
streets
〖大节〗(名)[dàjié]
matter of principle
〖大捷〗(名)[dàjié]
great victory
〖大惊小怪〗[dàjīngxiǎoguài]
make a fuss (over sth.)
〖大局〗(名)[dàjú]
general situation;overall situation; large interest; general prospect
〖大军〗(名)[dàjūn]
a huge army; large force
〖大快人心〗[dàkuàirénxīn]
to the satisfaction of the masses
〖大款〗(名)[dàkuǎn]
nouveau riche; upstart; substantial individuals
〖大理石〗(名)[dàlǐshí]
marble
〖大力〗(副)[dàlì]
all-out; energetically
〖大力士〗(名)[dàlìshì]
a person of great physical strength
〖大量〗(形)[dàliàng]
in great quantities; a great deal; big scale
〖大路货〗(名)[dàlùhuò]
popular goods of dependable quality; run-of-the-mill goods
〖大陆〗(名)[dàlù]
① continent② mainland
〖大陆架〗(名)[dàlùjià]
continental shelf
〖大陆性气候〗[dàlùxìngqìhòu]
continental climate
〖大乱〗(形)[dàluàn]
disorder; upheaval
〖大米〗(名)[dàmǐ]
rice
〖大名鼎鼎〗[dàmíngdǐngdǐng]
famous; well-known; celebrated; celebrity
〖大拇指〗(名)[dàmǔzhǐ]
thumb
〖大难临头〗[dànànlíntóu]
a disaster has befallen (sb.)
〖大脑〗(名)[dànǎo]
cerebrum; brain

〖大娘〗(名)[dàniáng]
auntie; aunt
〖大炮〗(名)[dàpào]〔门 mén〕
artillery; cannon
〖大批〗(形)[dàpī]
in great number
〖大气层〗(名)[dàqìcéng]
atmospheric layer; atmosphere
〖大气压〗(名)[dàqìyā]
atmospheric pressure
〖大秋〗(名)[dàqiū]
in the prime of autumn (during September and October when corn and sorghum are harvested)
〖大人〗(名)[dàren]
grown-ups; adults
〖大厦〗(名)[dàshà]
great hall; vast edifice
〖大赦〗(动)[dàshè]
amnesty; general pardon
〖大声〗(名)[dàshēng]
loud voice
〖大声疾呼〗[dàshēngjíhū]
shout at the top of one's voice (so as to draw the attention of others)
〖大失所望〗[dàshīsuǒwàng]
greatly disappointed
〖大使〗(名)[dàshǐ]
ambassador
〖大使馆〗(名)[dàshǐguǎn]
embassy
〖大势所趋〗[dàshìsuǒqū]
irresistible trend of events; the general trend
〖大是大非〗[dàshìdàfēi]
question of principle
〖大手大脚〗[dàshǒudàjiǎo]
spend extravagantly
〖大肆〗(副)[dàsì]
(derog.)violently; recklessly; defiantly
〖大肆吹嘘〗[dàsì chuīxū]
boast of
〖大肆宣扬〗[dàsì xuānyáng]
(derog.)widely advertise;give wide publicity
〖大踏步〗[dàtàbù]
great strides
〖大体〗(名、副)[dàtǐ]
① on the whole; in general; in the main② main principle
〖大庭广众〗
[dàtíngguǎng zhòng]
in broad daylight; in front of everybody
〖大同小异〗[dàtóngxiǎoyì]
more or less the same
〖大腕〗(名)[dàwàn]
① star (usu. referring to actors, singer, etc.)② past master; master-hand
〖大无畏〗(形)[dàwúwèi]
utterly fearless; dauntless
〖大西洋〗(名)[Dàxīyáng]
the Atlantic Ocean
〖大显身手〗[dàxiǎnshēnshǒu]
show one's best; fully display one's skill
〖大写〗(名、动)[dàxiě]
capital (letter); capitalize
〖大型〗(名)[dàxíng]
big size; grand
〖大选〗(名)[dàxuǎn]
general election
〖大学〗(名)[dàxué]〔所 suǒ〕

university
〖大言不惭〗[dàyánbùcán]
boast without shame
〖大洋〗(名)[dàyáng]
the ocean
〖大洋洲〗(名)[Dàyángzhōu]
Oceania
〖大爷〗(名)[dàye]
uncle; term of respectful address to an elderly person
〖大衣〗(名)[dàyī]〔件 jiàn〕
overcoat
〖大义凛然〗[dàyìlǐnrán]
fearless of death for a just cause
〖大意〗(名)[dàyì]
gist of idea; gist
〖大意〗(形)[dàyi]
rough (estimate); careless
〖大有可为〗[dàyǒukěwéi]
there is plenty of room for development
〖大有文章〗[dàyǒuwénzhāng]
there is much more to it than appears
〖大有作为〗[dàyǒuzuòwéi]
there is plenty of room for development
〖大约〗(副)[dàyuē]
about; approximately
〖大跃进〗(名)[dàyuèjìn]
The Great Leap Forward
〖大洲〗(名)[dàzhōu]
continent
〖大张旗鼓〗[dàzhāngqígǔ]
on a grand scale
〖大致〗(副)[dàzhì]
on the whole; with a few exceptions
〖大篆〗(名)[dàzhuàn]
Chinese script in the time of Chou Dynasty
〖大众〗(名)[dàzhòng]
the masses; the people
〖大众化〗(动)[dàzhònghuà]
popularize; a mass style
〖大专院校〗[dàzhuānyuànxiào]
universities and colleges; institutions of higher education
〖大自然〗(名)[dàzìrán]
the world of nature

dāi

呆(动、形)[dāi]
① stay② stupid; foolish
另见 ái
〖呆头呆脑〗[dāitóudāinǎo]
idiotic
〖呆滞〗(形)[dāizhì]
dull; slack; sluggish; stagnant
〖呆子〗(名)[dāizi]
idiot

dǎi

歹(形)[dǎi]
bad; evil

逮(动)[dǎi]
catch
另见 dài

dài

大[dài]

另见 dà
〖大夫〗(名)[dàifu]
doctor

代(名、动)[dài]
① age; period② generation③ dynasty④ act or do for others; act on behalf of
〖代办〗(名、动)[dàibàn]
① charge d'affaires; agent ② act or do for others
〖代表〗(名、动)[dàibiǎo]
representative; represent
〖代表团〗(名)[dàibiǎotuán]
delegation; mission
〖代表性〗(名)[dàibiǎoxìng]
typical; representative
〖代词〗(名)[dàicí]
pronoun
〖代管〗(动)[dàiguǎn]
take care of... for others
〖代号〗(名)[dàihào]
code name, number or letter (which symbolise sth. else)
〖代价〗(名)[dàijià]
price (e.g. at the price of...); cost
〖代劳〗(动)[dàiláo]
do for another
〖代理〗(动)[dàilǐ]
act for; act as; take (sb.'s) place
〖代理人〗(名)[dàilǐrén]
agent
〖代数〗(名)[dàishù]
algebra
〖代替〗(动)[dàitì]
replace; displace; substitute
〖代销〗(动)[dàixiāo]
act as commission agents; distribute for the state on a commission basis
〖代言人〗(名)[dàiyánrén]
spokesman
〖代用〗(动)[dàiyòng]
substitute
〖代用品〗(名)[dàiyòngpǐn]
substitution

带(动、名)[dài]
① take or bring with② a belt; a girdle
〖带动〗(动)[dàidòng]
lead in action; be spurred by...
〖带劲〗(形)[dàijìn]
with great energy and efforts
〖带领〗(动)[dàilǐng]
lead; give...guidance
〖带路〗[dàilù]
lead the way; serve as a guide
〖带头〗[dài tóu]
take the lead
〖带子〗(名)[dàizi]〔条 tiáo〕
belt; girdle; strap

贷(动)[dài]
loan
〖贷款〗(名)[dàikuǎn]〔笔 bǐ〕
financial loan

待(动)[dài]
① treat ② await; hang around
〖待命〗(动)[dàimìng]

pending further orders; ready for orders
〖待业〗(动)[dàiyè]
job-waiting; waiting for employment
〖待遇〗(名)[dàiyù]
treatment; pay; salary; wages

怠[dài]
〖怠工〗(动)[dàigōng]
① go slow at work; slacking at work ② slow down
〖怠慢〗(动)[dàimàn]
slight; suffer slights; receive (sb.) without due attention; leave (sb.) in the cold

袋(名)[dài]
bag
〖袋鼠〗(名)[dàishǔ]
kangaroo
〖袋子〗(名)[dàizi]
bag

逮[dài]
另见 dǎi
〖逮捕〗(动)[dàibǔ]
arrest

戴(动)[dài]
wear; put on

dān

担(动)[dān]
① carry on a pole ② bear; shoulder; assume (responsibility)
另见 dàn
〖担保〗(动)[dānbǎo]
assure; guarantee; vouch for
〖担当〗(动)[dāndāng]
take up the responsibility; undertake
〖担风险〗[dānfēngxiǎn]
take the risk of
〖担负〗(动)[dānfù]
carry (burden,responsibility); shoulder; undertake
〖担架〗(名)[dānjià]〔副 fù〕
stretcher
〖担任〗(动)[dānrèn]
fill (post); take charge of (responsibility); hold; do its duty
〖担心〗[dān xīn]
worry; be worried; anxious; be perturbed
〖担忧〗[dān yōu]
be worried

单(形、副)[dān]
① single ② thin (of clothing) ③ alone; only; merely
〖单薄〗(形)[dānbó]
weak; meagre; thin
〖单产〗(名)[dānchǎn]
per unit yield
〖单程〗(名)[dānchéng]
oneway trip
〖单纯〗(形)[dānchún]
simple; pure
〖单纯词〗(名)[dānchúncí]
simple word
〖单刀直入〗[dāndāozhírù]

be outspoken; speak up without beating about the bush

〖单调〗(形)[dāndiào]
monotonous; dull

〖单独〗(形)[dāndú]
alone; single-handed; purely; isolated

〖单方面〗[dān fāngmiàn]
one-sided; unilateral

〖单干〗(动)[dāngàn]
go it alone; work on one's own

〖单杠〗(名)[dāngàng]
horizontal bar

〖单价〗(名)[dānjià]
unit price

〖单晶硅〗(名)[dānjīngguī]
single crystal silicon

〖单据〗(名)[dānjù]〔张 zhāng〕
receipt; invoice; bill

〖单枪匹马〗[dānqiāngpǐmǎ]
(go) single-handed

〖单身〗(名)[dānshēn]
person, unmarried or away from home

〖单数〗(名)[dānshù]
odd number

〖单位〗(名)[dānwèi]
unit (of organization, measurement)

〖单位面积〗[dānwèimiànjī]
unit of area

〖单行本〗(名)[dānxíngběn]
an article in pamphlet form

〖单衣〗(名)[dānyī]〔件 jiàn〕
light clothing; unlined jacket; thin clothing

〖单元〗(名)[dānyuán]
① flat (suite of rooms) ② unit (e.g. teaching)

耽 [dān]

〖耽搁〗(动)[dānge]
delay; stop over (at) place

〖耽误〗(动)[dānwu]
delay

dǎn

胆 (名)[dǎn]

① gall bladder ② courage

〖胆敢〗(副)[dǎngǎn]
dare

〖胆量〗(名)[dǎnliàng]
courage; boldness

〖胆略〗(名)[dǎnlüè]
mettle

〖胆怯〗(形)[dǎnqiè]
timid; cowardly; faint-hearted; chicken-hearted

〖胆小如鼠〗[dǎnxiǎorúshǔ]
very timid; timid as a mouse

〖胆战心惊〗[dǎnzhànxīnjīng]
tremble with fear; in constant dread

〖胆子〗(名)[dǎnzi]
courage; bravery

掸 (动)[dǎn]

dust; wipe off

〖掸子〗(名)[dǎnzi]〔把 bǎ〕
duster

dàn

石 (量)[dàn]

a dry measure for grain (approx. 2.8 bushels)

另见 shí

旦[dàn]
〖旦夕〗(名)[dànxī]
a short moment; any moment

但(连)[dàn]
but
〖但是〗(连)[dànshì]
but; nevertheless

担(名)[dàn]
a load to be carried
另见 dān
〖担子〗(名)[dànzi]〔副 fù〕
burden

诞[dàn]
〖诞辰〗(名)[dànchén]
birthday; birth
〖诞生〗(动)[dànshēng]
be born; give birth to

淡(形)[dàn]
① insipid (food) ② light (colour) ③ cold; indifferent
〖淡薄〗(形)[dànbó]
thin; weak
〖淡季〗(名)[dànjì]
slack season
〖淡漠〗(形)[dànmò]
indifferent; apathetic
〖淡水〗(名)[dànshuǐ]
fresh water
〖淡雅〗(形)[dànyǎ]
simple elegance

弹(名)[dàn]
bullets
另见 tán
〖弹坑〗(名)[dànkēng]
crater
〖弹片〗(名)[dànpiàn]
shrapnel
〖弹药〗(名)[dànyào]
ammunition

蛋(名)[dàn]
egg
〖蛋白〗(名)[dànbái]
egg white
〖蛋白质〗(名)[dànbáizhì]
protein; albumin
〖蛋糕〗(名)[dàngāo]〔块 kuài〕
cake
〖蛋黄〗(名)[dànhuáng]
yolk

氮(名)[dàn]
nitrogen
〖氮肥〗(名)[dànféi]
nitrogenous fertilizer

dāng

当(动、介、象声)[dāng]
① fill an office; carry out duty ② regard as; take as... ③ ought to; should be ④ in front of; facing ⑤ onomatopoeia (the tinkle of a bell)
另见 dàng
〖当场〗(副)[dāngchǎng]
on the spot

〖当初〗(名)[dāngchū]
at the beginning; in days past
〖当代〗(名)[dāngdài]
present age; contemporary world
〖当地〗(名)[dāngdì]
at the given place; local (e.g. time)
〖当…的时候〗[dāng…deshíhòu]
when; at the time of
〖当机立断〗[dāngjīlìduàn]
prompt decision at the right moment
〖当家作主〗[dāngjiāzuòzhǔ]
be the master of one's own country; be the master of one's own affairs
〖当局〗(名)[dāngjú]
authorities
〖当面〗[dāng miàn]
to a person's face; in the face of; face to face
〖当年〗(名)[dāngnián]
in that year
另见 dàngnián
〖当前〗(名)[dāngqián]
present; now; for the time being; nowadays
〖当权〗[dāng quán]
in power
〖当然〗(形、副)[dāngrán]
of course; certainly; naturally
〖当仁不让〗[dāngrénbùràng]
take something as one's obligation
〖当时〗(名)[dāngshí]
at that time; then
另见 dàngshí
〖当事人〗(名)[dāngshìrén]
the person concerned
〖当头一棒〗[dāngtóuyībàng]
a blow on the head
〖当务之急〗[dāngwùzhījí]
pressing obligation
〖当心〗(动)[dāngxīn]
take care! look out!
〖当选〗(动)[dāngxuǎn]
be elected
〖当之无愧〗[dāngzhīwúkuì]
deserve; merit the reward
〖当中〗(名)[dāngzhōng]
middle; in the middle
〖当众〗(副)[dāngzhòng]
in front of everybody

dǎng

挡(动)[dǎng]
block off; hold back
〖挡箭牌〗(名)[dǎngjiànpái]
shield; excuse; pretext

党(名)[dǎng]
political party
〖党八股〗(名)[dǎngbāgǔ]
stereotyped party writing
〖党阀〗(名)[dǎngfá]
party tyrants
〖党纲〗(名)[dǎnggāng]
programme of the party
〖党籍〗(名)[dǎngjí]
party membership
〖党纪〗(名)[dǎngjì]
party discipline
〖党龄〗(名)[dǎnglíng]

party standing
〚党派〛(名)[dǎngpài]
party groupings; political parties and groups; factions
〚党旗〛(名)[dǎngqí]〔面 miàn〕
party flag
〚党群关系〛[dǎng qún guānxi]
the relation between the party and the masses
〚党徒〛(名)[dǎngtú]
gangsters; gang
〚党外人士〛[dǎngwài rénshì]
non-Party people;persons outside the Party
〚党委〛(名)[dǎngwěi]
party committee
〚党性〛(名)[dǎngxìng]
party spirit
〚党羽〛(名)[dǎngyǔ]
hangerson; member of gang; gangsters
〚党员〛(名)[dǎngyuán]
party member
〚党章〛(名)[dǎngzhāng]
party's constitution
〚党中央〛(名)[dǎngzhōng yāng]
the central committee of the party

dàng

当(动)[dàng]
① regard (sth.) as...; take... for ② pawn
另见 dāng
〚当年〛(名)[dàngnián]
in that year; in the same year
另见 dāngnián
〚当时〛(名)[dàngshí]
at that time; immediately, at once
另见 dāngshí
〚当天〛(名)[dàngtiān]
that day
〚当真〛(形、副)[dàngzhēn]
① take it as true ② really; true
〚当做〛(动)[dàngzuò]
take something as...

荡(动)[dàng]
drift
〚荡涤〛(动)[dàngdí]
clean up
〚荡漾〛(动)[dàngyàng]
afloat; float

档[dàng]
〚档案〛(名)[dàng'àn]
archives; records; files
〚档次〛(名)[dàngcì]
grade; class; differential

dāo

刀(名)[dāo]〔把 bǎ〕
knife
〚刀片〛(名)[dāopiàn]〔片 piàn〕
razor blade
〚刀枪〛(名)[dāoqiāng]
swords and spears;weapons
〚刀刃〛(名)[dāorèn]
the cutting edge of a knife of sword
〚刀山火海〛[dāoshānhuǒhǎi]
(lit.)a mountain of swords and a sea of flames; (go through)

immense dangers and difficulties
〖刀子〗(名)[dāozi]〔把 bǎ〕
knife

dǎo

导(动)[dǎo]
① guide; show the way② conduct
〖导弹〗(名)[dǎodàn]〔枚 méi〕
missile
〖导电〗[dǎo diàn]
conduct (electricity)
〖导航〗(动)[dǎoháng]
pilot; guide
〖导火线〗(名)[dǎohuǒxiàn]
fuse
〖导论〗(名)[dǎolùn]
introduction (to book)
〖导热〗[dǎo rè]
conduct
〖导师〗(名)[dǎoshī]
teacher; tutor
〖导线〗(名)[dǎoxiàn]
(elect.)guideline; conductor
〖导言〗(名)[dǎoyán]
foreword; introduction
〖导演〗(动、名)[dǎoyǎn]
direct (to do sth.); director (for film, etc.)
〖导致〗(动)[dǎozhì]
bring about; cause; lead to

岛(名)[dǎo]〔个 gè〕
island
〖岛国〗(名)[dǎoguó]
island country
〖岛屿〗(名)[dǎoyǔ]
islands

捣(动)[dǎo]
① pound;beat;pummel② make trouble
〖捣鬼〗[dǎo guǐ]
create disturbances; play tricks
〖捣毁〗(动)[dǎohuǐ]
crush; destroy
〖捣乱〗[dǎo luàn]
make trouble; create disturbance; stir up a riot

倒(动)[dǎo]
fall down; lie down; crumble; collapse
另见 dào
〖倒闭〗(动)[dǎobì]
close down; go bankrupt
〖倒车〗[dǎo chē]
change train, bus, etc.
〖倒伏〗(动)[dǎofú]
fall down (of rice, millet); flop down to the ground
〖倒买倒卖〗[dǎomǎidǎomài]
fraudulent buying and selling; engage in profiteering
〖倒霉〗[dǎo méi]
out of luck; bad luck; get into trouble
〖倒塌〗(动)[dǎotā]
collapse; downfall
〖倒爷〗(名)[dǎoyé]
pedlar; dealer

祷 [dǎo]
〖祷告〗(动)[dǎogào]
pray

dào

到 (动) [dào]
arrive; go to
〖到处〗(名)[dàochù]
everywhere
〖到达〗(动)[dàodá]
reach
〖到底〗(副)[dàodǐ]
after all; to the end; undoubtedly
〖到手〗[dào shǒu]
succeed in getting
〖到头〗[dào tóu]
to the end
〖到头来〗(副)[dàotóulái]
in the end
〖到…为止〗[dào…wéizhǐ]
till

倒 (动、副) [dào]
fall; pour; reverse; in reverse order or wrong direction
另见 dǎo
〖倒打一耙〗[dàodǎyīpá]
make unfounded counter-charges; blame others when one is at fault
〖倒退〗(动)[dàotuì]
reverse; go backwards; slip back; retrogression
〖倒行逆施〗[dàoxíngnìshī]
act in a perverse manner; go against the historical trend; turn back the wheel of history
〖倒置〗(动)[dàozhì]
put upside down

悼 [dào]
〖悼词〗(名)[dàocí]
memorial speech
〖悼念〗(动)[dàoniàn]
mourn; grieve over; pay last respects to

盗(名、动)[dào]
rob; steal; thief; burglar
〖盗匪〗(名)[dàofěi]
bandits
〖盗卖〗(动)[dàomài]
illegally sell public property
〖盗窃〗(动)[dàoqiè]
steal
〖盗用〗(动)[dàoyòng]
usurp

道(名、动、量) [dào]
① way; path ② speak; say ③ a measure word (for river, door, etc.)
〖道白〗(名)[dàobái]
spoken part of dialogue in opera
〖道德〗(名)[dàodé]
morality; moral integrity; ethics
〖道具〗(名)[dàojù]
prop for stage
〖道理〗(名)[dàolǐ]
reason; the whys and wherefo-

res
〖道路〗(名)[dàolù]
road; way
〖道貌岸然〗[dàomào'ànrán]
assume the appearance of a man of integrity
〖道歉〗[dào qiàn]
apologize
〖道听途说〗[dàotīngtúshuō]
hearsay
〖道义〗(名)[dàoyì]
moral principle

稻(名)[dào]
paddy; (unhusked) rice
〖稻草〗(名)[dàocǎo]〔根 gēn〕
rice straw
〖稻谷〗(名)[dàogǔ]
paddy; (unhusked) rice
〖稻田〗(名)[dàotián]
paddy field
〖稻种〗(名)[dàozhǒng]
rice seed
〖稻子〗(名)[dàozi]
rice

dé

得(动)[dé]
get; obtain; acquire
另见 de děi
〖得不偿失〗[débùchángshī]
lose more than gain
〖得逞〗(动)[déchěng]
accomplish or succeed in (an evil purpose)
〖得寸进尺〗[décùnjìnchǐ]
give him an inch and he will take a mile; insatiable; ever greater demands
〖得当〗(形)[dédàng]
proper; fitting; right
〖得到〗(动)[dédào]
get; gain; win; obtain; score
〖得道多助,失道寡助〗[dédàoduōzhù, shīdàoguǎzhù]
a just cause enjoys abundant support while unjust cause finds little support
〖得法〗(形)[défǎ]
in proper method
〖得力〗(形)[délì]
strong; efficient; most capable
〖得胜〗[dé shèng]
win victory
〖得失〗(名)[déshī]
advantages and disadvantages; gains and losses
〖得势〗[dé shì]
be in power; be in favour
〖得体〗(形)[détǐ]
in proper form or correct style
〖得心应手〗[déxīnyìngshǒu]
be easy to handle and work with great efficiency
〖得以〗(动)[déyǐ]
manage; be able to; have the opportunity to
〖得意〗(形)[déyì]
① elated; exulting ② be proud of
〖得意忘形〗[déyìwàngxíng]
be beside oneself with glee; go wild with joy; gleefully

〖得意扬扬〗[déyìyángyáng]
very proud and satisfied; have one's tail in the air
〖得罪〗(动)[dézuì]
offend

德(名)[dé]
moral character
〖德才兼备〗[décáijiānbèi]
combine ability with political integrity
〖德行〗(名)[déxíng]
moral conduct
〖德育〗(名)[déyù]
an education to develop morally

de

地(助)[de]
modal particle for adverbial adjuncts
另见 dì

的(助)[de]
modal particle for attributives
另见 dí
〖…的话〗[…dehuà]
if; suppose; in case
〖…的时候〗[…deshíhòu]
at the time when...

得(助)[de]
① used after a verb to show possibility ② used between a verb and its complement to show possibility ③ used after a verb or adjective to connect a complement of result or a complement of degree to it
另见 dé děi
〖…得慌〗[…dehuāng]
(gram.)a complement of degree—very; awfully; extremely

děi

得(助动、动)[děi]
① must; have to; need; should ② acquire
另见 dé de

dēng

灯(名)[dēng]〔盏 zhǎn〕
light; lamp; lantern
〖灯光〗(名)[dēngguāng]
light
〖灯火〗(名)[dēnghuǒ]
lights in general
〖灯火辉煌〗[dēnghuǒhuīhuáng]
very bright with lights
〖灯笼〗(名)[dēnglong]
lantern
〖灯泡〗(名)[dēngpào]
bulb
〖灯塔〗(名)[dēngtǎ]
lighthouse; beacon
〖灯头〗(名)[dēngtóu]
socket for electric light; burning part of wick in oil lamp
〖灯罩〗(名)[dēngzhào]
lamp shade

登(动)[dēng]

① climb; mount; ascend; scale ② publish (in newspaper)
〖登报〗[dēng bào]
publish in newspaper
〖登场〗[dēng chǎng]
go on the stage (to give one's performance)
〖登峰造极〗[dēngfēngzàojí]
reach the peak
〖登记〗(动)[dēngjì]
enrol; register
〖登陆〗[dēng lù]
landing
〖登山〗[dēng shān]
climb mountain; ascend (of mountains)
〖登载〗(动)[dēngzǎi]
be carried in the papers

蹬(动)[dēng]
① step; tread ② pedal

děng

等(名、动、代)[děng]
① class; grade ② wait; await ③ and such like; and so forth
〖等次〗(名)[děngcì]
sequence
〖等待〗(动)[děngdài]
wait; await
〖等到〗(动)[děngdào]
wait till
〖等份〗(名)[děngfèn]
division; halving
〖等号〗(名)[děnghào]
sign of equality
〖等候〗(动)[děnghòu]
wait; await
〖等级〗(名)[děngjí]
grade; rank; level; degree
〖等价〗(名)[děngjià]
equal value
〖等价物〗(名)[děngjiàwù]
objects of equal value
〖等量〗(名)[děngliàng]
equal quantity
〖等量齐观〗[děngliàngqíguān]
be regarded as equal (in value, merit)
〖等式〗(名)[děngshì]
equality; equation
〖等同〗(动)[děngtóng]
equal to
〖等闲〗(形)[děngxián]
(regard it) casually; lightly; idly
〖等于〗(动)[děngyú]
be equal to; tantamount to

dèng

凳(名)[dèng]
stool
〖凳子〗(名)[dèngzi]〔个 gè〕
stool; bench

澄(动)[dèng]
clarify water by letting it stand
另见 chéng
〖澄清〗(动)[dèngqīng]
clarify
另见 chéngqīng

瞪(动)[dèng]

stare

dī

低(形、动)[dī]
① low ② lower; bend; bow
〖低产〗(名)[dīchǎn]
low-yielding
〖低潮〗(名)[dīcháo]
low tide; ebb
〖低沉〗(形)[dīchén]
deep and low
〖低估〗(动)[dīgū]
underestimate
〖低级〗(形)[dījí]
① low-grade; primary; elementary; on a low level ② vulgar
〖低落〗(动)[dīluò]
lower; on the ebb
〖低三下四〗[dīsānxiàsì]
servile; submissive; degrading; crawling; fawning
〖低声下气〗[dīshēngxiàqì]
meek and submissive; servile; cringing
〖低头〗[dī tóu]
bend one's head
〖低温〗(名)[dīwēn]
low temperature
〖低下〗(形)[dīxià]
low; lowly; humble
〖低压〗(名)[dīyā]
low pressure; depression

堤(名)[dī]
dam; dike
〖堤岸〗(名)[dī'àn]
bank; embankment
〖堤坝〗(名)[dībà]
dam; dike

提[dī]
另见 tí
〖提防〗(动)[dīfang]
guard against

滴(动、量)[dī]
① drip by drops ② a measure word, drop (e.g. water, oil)
〖滴滴涕〗(名)[dīdītì]
D. D. T.
〖滴水成冰〗[dīshuǐchéngbīng]
the dripping water forms into ice—the cold is intense

dí

的[dí]
另见 de
〖的确〗(形)[díquè]
indeed; sure; really

敌(名、动)[dí]
① enemy; foe ② rival; match in strength
〖敌对〗(形)[díduì]
hostile adverse; stand against; antagonistic
〖敌后〗(名)[díhòu]
behind the enemy lines
〖敌寇〗(名)[díkòu]
enemy
〖敌情〗(名)[díqíng]
the enemy's situation; the state of the enemy

〖敌人〗(名)[dírén]
enemy
〖敌视〗(动)[díshì]
be hostile to; regard as enemy
〖敌手〗(名)[díshǒu]
rival
〖敌我矛盾〗[dí wǒ máodùn]
contradiction between the enemy and ourselves
〖敌意〗(名)[díyì]
hostile at titude

涤[dí]
〖涤荡〗(动)[dídàng]
wipe out; clean up
〖涤纶〗(名)[dílún]
dacron; terylene

笛(名)[dí]
flute
〖笛子〗(名)[dízi]〔枝 zhī〕
flute

嘀[dí]
〖嘀咕〗(动)[dígu]
① talk in a low voice ② hesitate

嫡[dí]
〖嫡系〗(名)[díxì]
① lineal (relatives); lineage ②closest ties of relationship (e.g. one's own troops)

dǐ

诋[dǐ]
〖诋毁〗(动)[dǐhuǐ]
vilify; discredit; slander; smear

抵(动)[dǐ]
① resist② deny③ serve as compensation ④ reach; arrive at
〖抵偿〗(动)[dǐcháng]
compensate for loss; make amends; offset; make good
〖抵触〗(动)[dǐchù]
conflict with; contradict
〖抵达〗(动)[dǐdá]
reach; arrive
〖抵挡〗(动)[dǐdǎng]
stem; stand up against; resist; keep off
〖抵抗〗(动)[dǐkàng]
resist; oppose; stand up against; withstand
〖抵赖〗(动)[dǐlài]
refuse to admit (guilt); deny facts
〖抵消〗(动)[dǐxiāo]
offset; cancel out each other; counterbalance
〖抵押〗(动、名)[dǐyā]
offer as collateral; security
〖抵御〗(动)[dǐyù]
resist; withstand; stand up against
〖抵制〗(动)[dǐzhì]
boycott; reject; counteract; combat

底(名)[dǐ]
① bottom ② end of period

〖底稿〗(名)[dǐgǎo]
original of manuscript; draft
〖底片〗(名)[dǐpiàn]〔张 zhāng〕
negative (of photograph)
〖底细〗(名)[dǐxì]
the inside details; the ins and outs of
〖底下〗(名)[dǐxià]
① underneath; under ② afterwards; after that
〖底子〗(名)[dǐzi]
background; foundation

dì

地(名)[dì]
① the earth;land;ground ② place; locality; site
另见 de
〖地板〗(名)[dìbǎn]
(wooden) floor
〖地步〗(名)[dìbù]
situation; state
〖地大物博〗[dìdàwùbó]
vast territory and rich resources
〖地带〗(名)[dìdài]
district; region; zone
〖地道〗(名)[dìdào]
tunnel
〖地道〗(形)[dìdao]
① out-and-out; through and through; pure; real ② fine; up to standard
〖地道战〗(名)[dìdàozhàn]
tunnel warfare
〖地点〗(名)[dìdiǎn]
locality; place
〖地洞〗(名)[dìdòng]
tunnel; cave
〖地方〗(名)[dìfāng]
local; locality
〖地方〗(名)[dìfang]
a place
〖地方保护主义〗
[dìfāng bǎohùzhǔyì]
local protectionism
〖地方戏〗(名)[dìfāngxì]
local opera
〖地窖〗(名)[dìjiào]
cellar
〖地雷〗(名)[dìléi]
a mine (explosive)
〖地理〗(名)[dìlǐ]
geography
〖地面〗(名)[dìmiàn]
the earth's surface
〖地盘〗(名)[dìpán]
room; territory; sphere of action; domain
〖地平线〗(名)[dìpíngxiàn]
horizon
〖地壳〗(名)[dìqiào]
the earth's crust
〖地勤〗(名)[dìqín]
ground duty (in the air force)
〖地球〗(名)[dìqiú]
the earth
〖地球仪〗(名)[dìqiúyí]
globe model
〖地区〗(名)[dìqū]
district; area; zone
〖地势〗(名)[dìshì]
physical features of the earth; topography of the land; terrain

〖地毯〗(名)[dìtǎn]〔块 kuài〕
carpet
〖地头〗(名)[dìtóu]
field
〖地头蛇〗(名)[dìtóushé]
local tyrant
〖地图〗(名)[dìtú]〔张 zhāng〕
map
〖地委〗(名)[dìwěi]
prefectural party committee
〖地位〗(名)[dìwèi]
social position; rank; status
〖地下〗(名)[dìxià]
underground
〖地下室〗(名)[dìxiàshì]
basement
〖地下水〗(名)[dìxiàshuǐ]
subsoil waters
〖地下铁道〗[dìxià tiědào]
underground railway
〖地线〗(名)[dìxiàn]
(elec.)earth wire
〖地形〗(名)[dìxíng]
terrain; topography
〖地狱〗(名)[dìyù]
hell
〖地域〗(名)[dìyù]
territory; place; area
〖地震〗(名、动)[dìzhèn]
earthquake; have an earthquake
〖地址〗(名)[dìzhǐ]
address
〖地质〗(名)[dìzhì]
geology
〖地主〗(名)[dìzhǔ]
landlord
〖地主阶级〗[dìzhǔ jiējí]
landlord class
〖地租〗(名)[dìzū]
land rent

弟(名)[dì]
younger brother
〖弟弟〗(名)[dìdi]
younger brother
〖弟媳〗(名)[dìxí]
younger brother's wife
〖弟兄〗(名)[dìxiong]
brothers

帝(名)[dì]
emperor
〖帝国〗(名)[dìguó]
empire
〖帝国主义〗(名)[dìguózhǔyì]
imperialism
〖帝制〗(名)[dìzhì]
imperial system; monarchy

递(动)[dì]
hand over; deliver by hand
〖递减〗(动)[dìjiǎn]
decrease by degrees
〖递交〗(动)[dìjiāo]
present; deliver
〖递进〗(动)[dìjìn]
rising
〖递送〗(动)[dìsòng]
send; deliver by messenger
〖递增〗(动)[dìzēng]
increasing

第(头)[dì]
prefix for ordinal numbers

D

〖第二次世界大战〗
[Dì'èr Cì Shìjiè Dàzhàn]
The Second World War
〖第二国际〗[Dì'èr Guójì]
The Second International
〖第二世界〗[Dì'èr Shìjiè]
The Second World
〖第二信号系统〗
[dì'èr xìnhào xìtǒng]
(physiology) second signal system
〖第三国际〗[Dìsān Guójì]
The Third International
〖第三世界〗[Dìsān Shìjiè]
The Third World
〖第一〗[dìyī]
first
〖第一把手〗[dìyī bǎ shǒu]
those who are in primary responsibility
〖第一次世界大战〗
[Dìyī Cì Shìjiè Dàzhàn]
The First World War
〖第一国际〗[Dìyī Guójì]
The First International
〖第一流〗[dìyī liú]
first class
〖第一世界〗[Dìyī Shìjiè]
The First World
〖第一手材料〗
[dìyīshǒucáiliào]
first-hand material
〖第一线〗[dìyī xiàn]
at the front
〖第一信号系统〗
[dìyī xìnhào xìtǒng]
(physiology) first signal system

缔 [dì]
〖缔结〗(动)[dìjié]
conclude
〖缔约〗[dì yuē]
sign a treaty
〖缔造〗(动)[dìzào]
create

diān

掂(动) [diān]
weigh in the hand
〖掂量〗(动)[diānliáng]
weigh in the hand; estimate

颠 (动) [diān]
totter; fall; tumble
〖颠簸〗(形、动)[diānbǒ]
bumping; bump; rock; reel; swing
〖颠倒〗(动)[diāndǎo]
reverse; turn sth. upside down; confound (right and wrong)
〖颠倒黑白〗[diāndǎohēibái]
call white black and black white; stand truth on its head
〖颠倒是非〗[diāndǎoshìfēi]
turn right and wrong upside down; confuse truth and falsehood
〖颠覆〗(动)[diānfù]
subvert; overthrow
〖颠来倒去〗[diānláidǎoqù]
all in confusion; change story frequently; merely rings the changes
〖颠扑不破〗[diānpūbùpò]
irrefutable; unbreakable

〖颠三倒四〗[diānsāndǎosì]
all in confusion

diǎn

典 [diǎn]

〖典范〗(名)[diǎnfàn]
model to be followed

〖典故〗(名)[diǎngù]
classical reference or allusion

〖典礼〗(名)[diǎnlǐ]
ceremony

〖典型〗(名、形)[diǎnxíng]
model; typical example; typical

点(动、名、量)[diǎn]
① touch lightly ② count ③ kindle; light ④ dribble ⑤ nod ⑥ a drop ⑦ o'clock; fixed time ⑧ dot; point ⑨ a measure word (a little, a few)

〖点滴〗(形)[diǎndī]
droplet

〖点火〗[diǎn huǒ]
kindle the flames; set fire; igniting

〖点名〗[diǎn míng]
roll call; by name

〖点破〗(动)[diǎnpò]
point out

〖点燃〗(动)[diǎnrán]
kindle

〖点头〗[diǎn tóu]
give a nod

〖点心〗(名)[diǎnxin]
cakes; pastry

〖点缀〗(动)[diǎnzhuì]
decorate; make elegant

〖点子〗(名)[diǎnzi]
droplet

碘(名)[diǎn]
iodine

〖碘酒〗(名)[diǎnjiǔ]
tincture of iodine

diàn

电(名、动)[diàn]
electricity; be electrocuted; be electrified

〖电报〗(名)[diànbào]〔份 fèn〕
telegram; cable

〖电表〗(名)[diànbiǎo]
electric meter

〖电冰箱〗(名)
[diànbīngxiāng]〔个 gè〕
refrigerator

〖电波〗(名)[diànbō]
electric waves

〖电唱机〗(名)[diànchàngjī]
a record player

〖电车〗(名)[diànchē]〔辆 liàng〕
tramcar; trolley bus

〖电池〗(名)[diànchí]
(elec.) battery

〖电灯〗(名)[diàndēng]〔盏 zhǎn〕
electric light

〖电动机〗(名)[diàndòngjī]
electric motor

〖电镀〗(动、名)[diàndù]
galvanize; electroplating; galvanization

〖电工〗(名)[diàngōng]

electrician
〖电焊〗(动、名)[diànhàn]
electric welding;be done by electric welding
〖电荷〗(名)[diànhè]
electric charge
〖电话〗(名)[diànhuà]
telephone
〖电话簿〗(名)[diànhuàbù]
telephone book; directory
〖电化教育〗[diànhuàjiàoyù]
education with electrical audiovisual aids
〖电机〗(名)[diànjī]
generator; motor
〖电极〗(名)[diànjí]
electrode
〖电解〗(动)[diànjiě]
electrolysis
〖电老虎〗(名)[diànlǎohǔ]
big power consumer
〖电力〗(名)[diànlì]
electric force
〖电量〗(名)[diànliàng]
〔库仑 kùlún〕
quantity of electric charge; quantity of electricity
〖电疗〗(动)[diànliáo]
electrotherapy
〖电流〗(名)[diànliú]〔安培 ānpéi〕
electric current
〖电炉〗(名)[diànlú]
electric furnace
〖电路〗(名)[diànlù]
electric circuit
〖电脑〗(名)[diànnǎo]
computer
〖电脑磁盘〗[diànnǎo cípán]
computer disc
〖电钮〗(名)[diànniǔ]
power switch button
〖电气化〗(动)[diànqìhuà]
electrify
〖电容〗(名)[diànróng]
electric capacity
〖电扇〗(名)[diànshàn]
electric fan
〖电视〗(名)[diànshì]
television; T.V.
〖电视机〗(名)[diànshìjī]〔台 tái〕
T.V. set
〖电视台〗(名)[diànshìtái]
television station
〖电台〗(名)[diàntái]
radio station
〖电梯〗(名)[diàntī]
elevator
〖电文〗(名)[diànwén]
content of telegram
〖电线〗(名)[diànxiàn]
wire; cable
〖电讯〗(名)[diànxùn]
telephone or telegraphic message
〖电压〗(名)[diànyā]〔伏特 fútè〕
electric pressure; voltage
〖电唁〗(动)[diànyàn]
send a message of condolence by telegram
〖电影〗(名)[diànyǐng]
film; motion picture
〖电影放映机〗
[diànyǐngfàngyìngjī]
projector
〖电影摄影机〗
[diànyǐngshèyǐngjī]

cine-camera
〖电影院〗(名)[diànyǐngyuàn]
cinema; (film) theatre
〖电源〗(名)[diànyuán]
(electr.) the mains
〖电子〗(名)[diànzǐ]
electron
〖电子管〗(名)[diànzǐguǎn]
electron tube
〖电子计算机〗[diànzǐjìsuànjī]
electronic computer
〖电阻〗(名)[diànzǔ]〔欧姆 ōumǔ〕
electric resistance

佃 [diàn]
〖佃户〗(名)[diànhù]
tenant peasants
〖佃农〗(名)[diànnóng]
tenant peasants
〖佃租〗(名)[diànzū]
rent

店(名)[diàn]
shop; store
〖店员〗(名)[diànyuán]
shop assistant; counter clerk

玷 [diàn]
〖玷辱〗(动)[diànrǔ]
humiliate; sully
〖玷污〗(动)[diànwū]
humiliate; smear

垫 (动、名)[diàn]
① make even higher or thicker by putting sth. under... ② pay for sb. for the time being ③ cushion
〖垫子〗(名)[diànzi]
cushion

惦 (动)[diàn]
remember; think of
〖惦记〗(动)[diànjì]
remember; have constantly in mind
〖惦念〗(动)[diànniàn]
remember; have constantly in mind; miss

淀 [diàn]
〖淀粉〗(名)[diànfěn]
starch; glucose

奠 (动)[diàn]
① lay foundation ② sacrifice (offerings)
〖奠定〗(动)[diàndìng]
make firm; establish; lay (foundation); set up; form
〖奠基〗[diànjī]
lay foundation

殿 (名)[diàn]
hall; temple; palace

diāo

刁(形)[diāo]
artful; knavish; rascally; sly
〖刁滑〗(形)[diāohuá]
deceitful
〖刁难〗(动)[diāonàn]
purposely make difficulties

for; deliberately set up obstruction for

凋 [diāo]

〖凋零〗(形)[diāolíng]
dwindling; fading
〖凋落〗(动)[diāoluò]
dwindle; fade
〖凋谢〗(动)[diāoxiè]
wither away; fade

碉 [diāo]

〖碉堡〗(名)[diāobǎo]
pillbox; fortification

雕 (动) [diāo]

carve
〖雕刻〗(动、名)[diāokè]
carve; sculpture; inscribe; engraving
〖雕漆〗(名)[diāoqī]
carved and lacquered objects
〖雕塑〗(动、名)[diāosù]
carve and mould; sculpture; engraving
〖雕琢〗(动)[diāozhuó]
chisel and embellish

diào

吊 (动) [diào]

hang
〖吊车〗(名)[diàochē]
crane
〖吊儿郎当〗[diào'erlángdāng]
behave haphazardly; take a careless and casual attitude in everything
〖吊环〗(名)[diàohuán]
swinging rings
〖吊唁〗(动)[diàoyàn]
offer condolence; pay last respects to

钓 (动) [diào]

fish
〖钓饵〗(名)[diào'ěr]
bait; lure
〖钓钩〗(名)[diàogōu]
fishing hook; (fig.) wiles

调 (动、名) [diào]

① allot; transfer; dispatch; change ② a melody; tune
另见 tiáo
〖调兵遣将〗[diàobīngqiǎnjiàng]
deploy forces
〖调拨〗(动)[diàobō]
allot and deliver
〖调查〗(动)[diàochá]
investigate; fact-finding
〖调动〗(动)[diàodòng]
transfer; move
〖调度〗(动、名)[diàodù]
dispatch; regulate; reorganize; alignment
〖调号〗(名)[diàohào]
tone marks (for Chinese characters)
〖调虎离山〗[diàohǔlíshān]
lure the tiger out of the mountains; lure the enemy away from its base
〖调换〗(动)[diàohuàn]

change; interchange
〖调集〗(动)[diàojí]
concentrate; assemble; mass
〖调配〗(动)[diàopèi]
allot; distribute
〖调遣〗(动)[diàoqiǎn]
send to different places
〖调演〗(动)[diàoyǎn]
theatrical festival
〖调值〗(名)[diàozhí]
articulation of a tone
〖调子〗(名)[diàozi]
tune; tone; air; melody

掉(动)[diào]
① drop down ② lose
〖掉队〗[diào duì]
drop off; fall out
〖掉头〗[diào tóu]
turn one's head; change direction
〖掉以轻心〗[diàoyǐqīngxīn]
let down one's guard;casual attitude

diē

爹(名)[diē]
father; dad

跌(动)[diē]
fall down; tumble
〖跌倒〗(动)[diēdǎo]
fall down; tumble
〖跌价〗[diē jià]
fall in price
〖跌跤〗[diē jiāo]
fall down
〖跌落〗(动)[diē luò]
drop

dié

喋[dié]
〖喋喋不休〗[diédiébùxiū]
keep on clamouring; an endless stream of words

叠(动)[dié]
fold; pile

碟(名)[dié]
plate; dish
〖碟子〗(名)[diézi]〔个 gè〕
plate; dish

蝶[dié]
〖蝶泳〗(名)[diéyǒng]
butterfly stroke

dīng

丁(名)[dīng]
① the fourth of the ten stems; number four;fourth ② small cubes of meat or vegetables
〖丁当〗(象声)[dīngdāng]
(onomatopoeia)tinkle; jingle
〖丁香〗(名)[dīngxiāng]
lilac

叮(动)[dīng]
(insect) bite
〖叮咛〗(动)[dīngníng]
give repeated, earnest instruction; admonish

〖叮嘱〗(动)[dīngzhǔ]
repeated advice on departure

盯(动)[dīng]
stare; keep an eye on

钉(名、动)[dīng]
① nail② follow; trail; pursue closely and persistently
〖钉梢〗[dīng shāo]
follow closely and persitently; be on (sb.'s) trail
〖钉子〗(名)[dīngzi]〔根 gēn〕
nail

dǐng

顶(名、动)[dǐng]
① top; peak; summit ② carry on head ③ set against ④ substitute
〖顶点〗(名)[dǐngdiǎn]
peak; top
〖顶风〗[dǐngfēng]
go against the wind
〖顶峰〗(名)[dǐngfēng]
peak; top
〖顶替〗(动)[dǐngtì]
substitute
〖顶天立地〗[dǐngtiānlìdì]
(lit.)towering from earth to sky; (fig.) unright and high-minded; heroic and absolutely fearless
〖顶用〗(形)[dǐngyòng]
be of use; useful
〖顶住〗(动)[dǐngzhù]
hold on; stand up against; stand one's ground
〖顶撞〗(动)[dǐngzhuàng]
① charge; knock against ② offend by rude remarks

鼎(名)[dǐng]
tripod
〖鼎鼎大名〗[dǐngdǐngdàmíng]
great reputation; illustrious
〖鼎立〗(动)[dǐnglì]
a situation dominated by three powerful rivals

dìng

订(动)[dìng]
① make (e.g. agreement); conclude ② subscribe to; place an order for (periodicals)
〖订户〗(名)[dìnghù]
subscriber (to newspaper, periodical)
〖订婚〗[dìng hūn]
engagement (agree to marry)
〖订立〗(动)[dìnglì]
conclude; complete; enter into; reach (e.g. agreement)
〖订阅〗(动)[dìngyuè]
subscribe to (newspaper, etc.)
〖订正〗(动)[dìngzhèng]
correct; revise; amend

定(动)[dìng]
set; settle; fix
〖定案〗[dìng àn]
judgment; decision in a case
〖定额〗(名)[dìng'é]
quota; allotment

〚定购〛(动)[dìnggòu]
order (request to supply goods)
〚定规〛(名)[dìngguī]
rules and regulations
〚定价〛(名)[dìngjià]
fixed price
〚定居〛(动)[dìngjū]
settle down
〚定局〛(名、动)[dìngjú]
foregone conclusion; make final decision
〚定理〛(名)[dìnglǐ]〔条 tiáo〕
law of physical universe
〚定量〛(名)[dìngliàng]
ration; allowance; quota
〚定律〛(名)[dìnglǜ]〔条 tiáo〕
law (of nature)
〚定论〛(名)[dìnglùn]
conclusion; final verdict
〚定名〛[dìng míng]
choose name for; be called
〚定期〛[dìng qī]
fixed term
〚定时〛(形)[dìngshí]
regular; fixed time
〚定时炸弹〛[dìngshí zhàdàn]
time bomb
〚定息〛(名)[dìngxī]
fixed interest
〚定型〛[dìng xíng]
fixed; rigid
〚定义〛(名)[dìngyì]
definition
〚定语〛(名)[dìngyǔ]
(gram.) attribute
〚定员〛(名)[dìngyuán]
fixed number of staff

diū

丢(动)[diū]
① throw; cast ② lose
〚丢掉〛(动)[diūdiào]
throw away
〚丢盔卸甲〛[diūkuīxièjiǎ]
throw away one's shield and armour; fly pell-mell
〚丢脸〛[diū liǎn]
lose face; disgrace
〚丢人〛[diū rén]
lose face; disgrace; shame
〚丢三落四〛[diūsānlàsì]
always losing this and forgetting that; miss this and that; forgetful
〚丢失〛(动)[diūshī]
lose; miss

dōng

东(名)[dōng]
the east
〚东边〛(名)[dōngbian]
the east side
〚东道国〛(名)[dōngdàoguó]
host country
〚东道主〛(名)[dōngdàozhǔ]
host or hostess; the one who stands a treat
〚东方〛(名)[dōngfāng]
the east
〚东山再起〛[dōngshānzàiqǐ]
stage a come-back
〚东西〛(名)[dōngxi]
things

冬(名)[dōng]

winter
〖冬瓜〗(名)[dōngguā]〔个 gè〕
white gourd
〖冬季〗(名)[dōngjì]
winter season
〖冬眠〗(名、动)[dōngmián]
hibernation
〖冬天〗(名)[dōngtiān]
winter
〖冬装〗(名)[dōngzhuāng] winter clothes

D

dǒng

董[dǒng]
〖董事〗(名)[dǒngshì]
director
〖董事会〗(名)[dǒngshìhuì]
board of directors
〖董事长〗(名)[dǒngshìzhǎng]
chairman(president)of the board

懂(动)[dǒng]
understand
〖懂得〗(动)[dǒngde]
understand
〖懂事〗(形)[dǒngshì]
with good understanding

dòng

动(动)[dòng]
① move ② arouse; excite
〖动宾结构〗[dòng bīn jiégòu]
verb-object construction
〖动补结构〗[dòng bǔ jiégòu]
verb-complement construction
〖动不动〗(副)[dòngbudòng]
at every move; on every occasion; easily; at the slightest provocation
〖动产〗(名)[dòngchǎn]
movable property
〖动词〗(名)[dòngcí]
verb
〖动荡〗(动)[dòngdàng]
being shaky and unstable; in flux
〖动工〗[dòng gōng]
begin the construction
〖动画片〗(名)[dònghuàpiàn]
cartoon film
〖动机〗(名)[dòngjī]
motive; intention
〖动静〗(名)[dòngjing]
① happenings; events ② stir; noise
〖动力〗(名)[dònglì]
motive force
〖动乱〗(名)[dòngluàn]
turmoil
〖动脉〗(名)[dòngmài]
artery
〖动能〗(名)[dòngnéng]
energy of motion
〖动人〗(形)[dòngrén]
very moving
〖动身〗[dòng shēn]
begin journey; set out
〖动手〗[dòng shǒu]
① start work; get going ② use one's own hands
〖动态〗(名)[dòngtài]
tendencies; general trend of affairs; probable cause of action

〖动弹〗(动)[dòngtan]
move
〖动听〗(形)[dòngtīng]
moving; persuasive; interesting
〖动物〗(名)[dòngwù]
animals
〖动物园〗(名)[dòngwùyuán]
zoo
〖动向〗(名)[dòngxiàng]
the trends of; the direction; moving direction
〖动心〗[dòng xīn]
touched; moved
〖动摇〗(动)[dòngyáo]
waver; shake; vacillate; wave and falter
〖动用〗(动)[dòngyòng]
① draw upon ② resort to (force)
〖动员〗(动)[dòngyuán]
mobilize
〖动作〗(名)[dòngzuò]
action; movement

冻(动)[dòng]
freeze
〖冻疮〗(名)[dòngchuāng]
frostbite; chilblains
〖冻结〗(动)[dòngjié]
freeze
〖冻伤〗(名、动)[dòngshāng]
frostbite

栋(量)[dòng]
a measure word (for building)
〖栋梁〗(名)[dòngliáng]
pillars of the state (fig.)

恫[dòng]
〖恫吓〗(动)[dònghè]
frighten; scare

洞(名)[dòng]
cave; a hole; leak; tunnel
〖洞察〗(动)[dòngchá]
see through clearly; have penetrating insight
〖洞口〗(名)[dòngkǒu]
entrance to cave
〖洞穴〗(名)[dòngxué]
cave

dōu

都(副)[dōu]
① all ② even ③ already
另见 dū

兜(名、动)[dōu]
① pocket ② wrap up
〖兜揽〗(动)[dōulǎn]
find customers for trade
〖兜售〗(动)[dōushòu]
make a sale of; peddle; hawk
〖兜子〗(名)[dōuzi]
pocket

dǒu

斗(名、量)[dǒu]
① a peck ② a measure word (a dry or liquid measure)
另见 dòu
〖斗笠〗(名)[dǒulì]〔顶 dǐng〕

large (bamboo) rain hat
〖斗篷〗(名)[dǒupeng]〔件 jiàn〕
cloak

抖 (动)[dǒu]
give a shake
〖抖动〗(动)[dǒudòng]
tremble; shake
〖抖擞〗(动)[dǒusǒu]
pluck up; be in high spirits

D

陡 (形)[dǒu]
steep
〖陡坡〗(名)[dǒupō]
steep slope
〖陡峭〗(形)[dǒuqiào]
steep; abrupt (slope)

dòu

斗 (动)[dòu]
struggle; fight
另见 dǒu
〖斗鸡〗(名)[dòujī]
① gamecock ② cock-fighting
〖斗气〗(动)[dòuqì]
quarrel or contend with sb. on account of a personal grudge
〖斗争〗(动、名)[dòuzhēng]
struggle; fight
〖斗争性〗(名)[dòuzhēngxìng]
fighting spirit
〖斗志〗(名)[dòuzhì]
fighting will
〖斗志昂扬〗[dòuzhì'ángyáng]
strong fighting will; militant and daring

豆 (名)[dòu]〔粒 lì〕
(various kinds of) beans
〖豆腐〗(名)[dòufu]
bean curd
〖豆浆〗(名)[dòujiāng]
soya-bean milk
〖豆角儿〗(名)[dòujiǎor]
bean or pea pod
〖豆子〗(名)[dòuzi]
beans

逗 (动)[dòu]
① tease (for fun) ② tarry; stop
〖逗号〗(名)[dòuhào]
comma
〖逗留〗(动)[dòuliú]
tarry; stop over for a time

dū

都 [dū]
另见 dōu
〖都城〗(名)[dūchéng]
capital
〖都会〗(名)[dūhuì]
metropolis; large city
〖都市〗(名)[dūshì]
city

督 [dū]
〖督促〗(动)[dūcù]
urge; press; push forward

dú

毒 (形)[dú]
① poisonous ② malicious; cruel; vicious

〖毒草〗(名)[dúcǎo]
poisonous weeds
〖毒害〗(动)[dúhài]
poison; infect
〖毒化〗(动)[dúhuà]
poison; infect
〖毒计〗(名)[dújì]
insidious scheme; deadly trap; venomous plot
〖毒辣〗(形)[dúlà]
treacherous; vicious; murderous; devilish
〖毒品〗(名)[dúpǐn]
harmful drugs
〖毒气〗(名)[dúqì]
poison gas
〖毒气弹〗(名)[dúqìdàn]
gas bomb
〖毒蛇〗(名)[dúshé]〔条 tiáo〕
poisonous snake; venomous snake
〖毒手〗(名)[dúshǒu]
murderous means
〖毒素〗(名)[dúsù]
poisonous element; poison
〖毒刑〗(名)[dúxíng]
cruel punishment; torture
〖毒药〗(名)[dúyào]
poisons

独(形)[dú]
alone; only
〖独霸〗(动)[dúbà]
dominate exclusively; monopolize
〖独白〗(名)[dúbái]
monologue; soliloquy
〖独裁〗(动、名)[dúcái]
exercise dictatorship; dictatorship
〖独裁者〗(名)[dúcáizhě]
dictator
〖独唱〗(名、动)[dúchàng]
solo; sing a solo
〖独出心裁〗[dúchūxīncái]
be original; create new styles
〖独词句〗(名)[dúcíjù]
single word sentence
〖独当一面〗[dúdāngyīmiàn]
be solely responsible (for some work)
〖独断独行〗[dúduàndúxíng]
decide and act arbitrarily
〖独家〗(形)[dújiā]
sole; exclusive
〖独立〗(动)[dúlì]
① stand alone ② win independence; be independent ③ be on one's own
〖独立经营,自负盈亏〗
[dúlìjīngyíng, zìfùyíngkuī]
engage in independent management and assume sole responsibility for profits and losses
〖独立王国〗[dúlì wángguó]
"independent kingdom"
〖独立性〗(名)[dúlìxìng]
in a state of independence
〖独立自主〗[dúlìzìzhǔ]
independence and initiative; maintain independence and keep the initiative in one's own hands
〖独幕剧〗(名)[dúmùjù]
one-act play

D

〖独树一帜〗[dúshùyīzhì]
fly one's own colours; create a separate school
〖独特〗(形)[dútè]
special; original
〖独一无二〗[dúyīwú'èr]
unique; unmatched; unrivalled
〖独自〗(代)[dúzì]
oneself (e.g. all by oneself)
〖独奏〗(名、动)[dúzòu]
solo;recital(e.g. a piano solo); play a solo

读(动)[dú]
read
〖读本〗(名)[dúběn]
reader; school textbook
〖读书〗(动)[dúshū]
read(a book);study(e.g. lessons)
〖读物〗(名)[dúwù]
reading material
〖读者〗(名)[dúzhě]
reader

dǔ

堵(动、量)[dǔ]
① block up; stop up; shut up ② a measure word (for wall)
〖堵塞〗(动)[dǔsè]
block; jam; stop up; choke; gag

赌(动)[dǔ]
gamble; bet
〖赌博〗(名)[dǔbó]
gambling
〖赌气〗[dǔ qì]
for spite; get in a rage (often insist on doing something regardless of the consequences)
〖赌徒〗(名)[dǔtú]
gambler
〖赌咒〗[dǔ zhòu]
swear; an oath; a swear-word
〖赌注〗(名)[dǔzhù]
a counter for gambling; stake

dù

杜[dù]
〖杜鹃〗(名)[dùjuān]
the cuckoo
〖杜绝〗(动)[dùjué]
completely eradicate; put an end to
〖杜撰〗(动)[dùzhuàn]
fabricate (story)

肚(名)[dù]
the belly; stomach
〖肚子〗(名)[dùzi]
the belly;

度(动、名、量)[dù]
① pass; spend (of time) ② degree;limit ③ a measure word, degree
〖度过〗(动)[dùguò]
spend; pass (of time)
〖度量〗(名)[dùliàng]
tolerance (e.g. broad-minded or narrow-minded)
〖度量衡〗(名)[dùliànghéng]
measurements of length,area and weight

〖度数〗(名)[dùshù]
degree (e.g. at 20℃.)

渡 (动) [dù]
cross over
〖渡船〗(名)[dùchuán]
ferry boat
〖渡口〗(名)[dùkǒu]
ferry station

镀 (动) [dù]
plate
〖镀金〗[dù jīn]
gold-plated; gilded

duān

端(动、名) [duān]
① hold with hand (esp. with both hands) ②end (e.g. both ends)
〖端午节〗(名)[Duānwǔjié]
Dragon Boat Festival (the fifth day of fifth lunar month)
〖端详〗(动)[duānxiang]
scrutinize; examine
〖端正〗(形、动)[duānzhèng]
① upright; right ② straighten
〖端庄〗(形)[duānzhuāng]
demure; dignified

duǎn

短 (形) [duǎn]
short; brief
〖短兵相接〗[duǎnbīngxiāngjiē]
close-quarters fighting; fight hand to hand
〖短波〗(名)[duǎnbō]
short wave
〖短处〗(名)[duǎnchù]
shortcomings; weak point; defect
〖短促〗(形)[duǎncù]
pressed for time; of short duration; short; swift
〖短工〗(名)[duǎngōng]
seasonal labourer (short term)
〖短命〗[duǎnmìng]
short-lived
〖短跑〗(名)[duǎnpǎo]
short distance running
〖短篇小说〗[duǎnpiānxiǎoshuō]
short story
〖短评〗(名)[duǎnpíng]
short review
〖短期〗(名)[duǎnqī]
short term; short period
〖短期行为〗[duǎnqīxíngwéi]
short-sighted behaviour
〖短少〗(动)[duǎnshǎo]
be short of; lack
〖短途〗(名)[duǎntú]
short distance
〖短线产品〗[duǎnxiànchǎnpǐn]
short line products
〖短小精悍〗[duǎnxiǎojīnghàn]
small but effective; small but capable (of a person); short but forceful (of a play, writing, etc.)
〖短语〗(名)[duǎnyǔ]
phrase
〖短暂〗(形)[duǎnzàn]
momentary; mere instant; twinkling; flash

duàn

段(量)[duàn]
a measure word, section, period, segment
〖段落〗(名)[duànluò]
paragraph; section

断(动)[duàn]
cut; break off; snap; discontinue
〖断定〗(动)[duàndìng]
decide; form a judgement
〖断断续续〗(形)[duànduànxùxù]
interrupted; intermittent
〖断绝〗(动)[duànjué]
cut off definitely; sever
〖断然〗(副)[duànrán]
flatly; categorically; absolutely
〖断送〗(动)[duànsòng]
forfeit; ruin
〖断言〗(动)[duànyán]
say with certainty
〖断章取义〗[duànzhāngqǔyì]
a garbled quotation; garble a statement
〖断肢再植〗[duànzhī zàizhí]
rejoin the severed limb

锻(动)[duàn]
forge
〖锻工〗(名)[duàngōng]
forge worker
〖锻件〗(名)[duànjiàn]
forging
〖锻炼〗(动)[duànliàn]
toughen; steel; temper
〖锻压〗(动)[duànyā]
forging and pressing
〖锻造〗(动)[duànzào]
forge

duī

堆(动、名)[duī]
① pile up ② a measure word, e.g. heap, pile
〖堆积〗(动)[duījī]
pile up;accumulate
〖堆砌〗(动)[duīqì]
pile

duì

队(名、量)[duì]
① a group; team; corps; line; rank ② a measure word, group, team, corps
〖队伍〗(名)[duìwu]
troops; rank; contingent
〖队形〗(名)[duìxíng]
form of rank; line
〖队员〗(名)[duìyuán]
members of teams
〖队长〗(名)[duìzhǎng]
group leader; team leader

对(动、形、量、介)[duì]
① answer② check③ agree④ deal with; cope with ⑤ add (water) ⑥ correct ⑦ facing; opposite ⑧ a measure word, pair,couple ⑨ at; for; toward; to; in; regard to
〖对比〗(动)[duìbǐ]

compare; show by contrast
〖对不起〗[duì bu qǐ]
let (sb.) down; do disservice to; (I'm) sorry!
〖对策〗(名)[duìcè]
counter-measure
〖对称〗(形)[duìchèn]
symmetric
〖对待〗(动)[duìdài]
treat; deal; with regard to
〖对得起〗[duì de qǐ]
live up to;be worthy of;act worthily of
〖对等〗(形)[duìděng]
on an equal footing; equal to; reciprocal
〖对方〗(名)[duìfāng]
opposite side
〖对付〗(动)[duìfu]
cope with; deal with; tackle; manage
〖对话〗(动、名)[duìhuà]
have dialogue; dialogue
〖对角〗(名)[duìjiǎo]
(geom.) vertical angles
〖对角线〗(名)[duìjiǎoxiàn]〔条 tiáo〕
diagonal line
〖对抗〗(动)[duìkàng]
oppose; resist; counter; antagonise; antagonism
〖对抗性〗(名)[duìkàngxìng]
antagonism; antagonistic
〖对口〗(动)[duìkǒu]
fit in with; be suited to (e.g. a job suited to one's special training)
〖对立〗(动)[duìlì]
stand opposed to; set oneself against; oppose; counterpose
〖对立面〗(名)[duìlìmiàn]
opposite sides
〖对立统一规律〗[duìlìtǒngyīguīlǜ]
the law of the unity of opposites
〖对联〗(名)[duìlián]〔副 fù〕
couplets
〖对流〗(动)[duìliú]
convection of heat or electrified particles
〖对门〗(名)[duìmén]
opposite the gate; across the road (of houses); facing each other
〖对面〗(名)[duìmiàn]
opposite
〖对牛弹琴〗[duìniútánqín]
(lit.) play the lute to a cow; (fig.) preach to deaf ears
〖对手〗(名)[duìshǒu]
opponent in contest
〖对台戏〗(名)[duìtáixì]
put up a rival show;vigorously oppose each other
〖对头〗(形)[duìtóu]
true; correct
〖对头〗(名)[duìtou]
adversary
〖对外开放〗[duìwàikāifàng]
opening to the outside world
〖对外贸易〗[duì wài màoyì]
foreign trade
〖对虾〗(名)[duìxiā]
prawn
〖对象〗(名)[duìxiàng]

① object; target ② the other party in love

〖对于〗(介)[duìyú]
at; to; for; in regard to; toward

〖对照〗(动)[duìzhào]
contrast with; compare with

〖对证〗(动)[duìzhèng]
check; verify

D

〖对症下药〗[duìzhèngxiàyào]
prescribe for a complaint

〖对峙〗(动)[duìzhì]
face each other; stand opposite each other; stalemate

兑(动)[duì]
cash

〖兑换〗(动)[duìhuàn]
exchange

〖兑现〗(动)[duìxiàn]
① pay-cash② realize; make good; fulfill the promise; make real

dūn

吨(量)[dūn]
a measure word, a ton

〖吨位〗(名、量)[dūnwèi]
tonnage

敦[dūn]

〖敦促〗(动)[dūncù]
urge

〖敦厚〗(形)[dūnhòu]
honest and simple

〖敦实〗(形)[dūnshi]
solid

蹲(动)[dūn]
squat

〖蹲点〗[dūn diǎn]
work at selected place; choose some place for gaining experience

dùn

囤(名)[dùn]
grain receptacle; bin
另见 tún

炖(动)[dùn]
simmer; boil in water over slow fire

盾(名)[dùn]
shield

〖盾牌〗(名)[dùnpái]
shield

钝(形)[dùn]
① blunt ② mentally slow; stupid

〖钝角〗(名)[dùnjiǎo]
obtuse angle

顿(动、量)[dùn]
① pause; make a meaningful pause as in calligraphy② a measure word, times (e.g. a meal, beating, etc.)

〖顿号〗(名)[dùnhào]
punctuation mark

〖顿时〗(副)[dùnshí]

at once; immediately; in a short space

遁 [dùn]
〖遁词〗(名)[dùncí] subterfuge

duō

多 (形、动、数、副) [duō]
many; much; more; exceed; multi-; more than; poly-
〖多半〗(副)[duōbàn]
mostly; probably
〖多边〗(名)[duōbiān]
multilateral
〖多边形〗(名)[duōbiānxíng]
polygon
〖多此一举〗[duōcǐyījǔ]
superfluous action
〖多多益善〗[duōduōyìshàn]
the more the better
〖多发病〗(名)[duōfābìng]
common disease; diseases with a high incidence of occurence
〖多方〗(副)[duōfāng]
on many occasions; in many ways; with various devices
〖多快好省〗[duōkuàihǎoshěng]
with greater, faster, better and more economical results
〖多亏〗(动、副)[duōkuī]
thanks to; owing to; fortunately
〖多劳多得〗[duōláoduōdé]
more pay for more work
〖多么〗(副)[duōme]
how
〖多少〗(代)[duōshao]
① how much; how many ② a certain amount, number, etc.
〖多数〗(名)[duōshù]
most; greater part or number; majority
〖多思〗[duōsī]
think more
〖多谢〗(动)[duōxiè]
many thanks
〖多心〗[duō xīn]
distrustful; prone to suspect
〖多样〗(形)[duōyàng]
various
〖多余〗(形)[duōyú]
surplus; uncalled for; not necessary
〖多种经营〗[duōzhǒngjīngyíng]
diversified economy

咄 [duō]
〖咄咄逼人〗[duōduōbīrén]
overbearing; aggressive; arrogant; insolent
〖咄咄怪事〗[duōduōguàishì]
absurd; extraordinary; out of the ordinary

哆 [duō]
〖哆嗦〗(动)[duōsuo]
tremble

duó

夺 (动) [duó]
rob; take by force; seize
〖夺得〗(动)[duódé]
capture

〖夺目〗(形)[duómù]
dazzling
〖夺取〗(动)[duóqǔ]
seize; take by force

duǒ

朵 (量)[duǒ]
a measure word (for flower or cloud)

D

躲 (动)[duǒ]
hide
〖躲避〗(动)[duǒbì]
avoid (meeting); evade
〖躲藏〗(动)[duǒcáng]
hide away
〖躲躲闪闪〗[duǒduǒshǎnshǎn]
evasive
〖躲开〗(动)[duǒkāi]
avoid; stay away

duò

剁 (动)[duò]
chop; hack

垛 (动、名)[duò]
① pile up ② stack

舵 (名)[duò]
rudder
〖舵手〗(名)[duòshǒu]
helmsman

堕 [duò]
〖堕落〗(动)[duòluò]
go downhill; degenerate
〖堕入〗(动)[duòrù]
fall into; be carried away

惰 [duò]
〖惰性〗(名)[duòxìng]
laziness; inertia

跺 (动)[duò]
stamp (about)
〖跺脚〗[duò jiǎo]
stamp one's feet

E

ē

阿 [ē]
另见 ā
〖阿谀奉承〗[ēyúfèngchéng]
curry favour with; flatter and fawn on

é

讹 (动) [é]
extort; blackmail
〖讹诈〗(动)[ézhà]
blackmail; extort

蛾 (名) [é]
a moth
〖蛾子〗(名)[ézi]
a moth

鹅 (名) [é]〔只 zhī〕
goose

额 (名) [é]
① the forehead ② quota; a fixed number or amount ③ a signboard (on the top of a hall, etc.)
〖额外〗(形)[éwài]
extra

ě

恶 [ě]
另见 è
〖恶心〗(形)[ě xin]
① nauseous ② disgust

è

扼 [è]
〖扼杀〗(动)[èshā]
smother; strangle; suffocate; stifle
〖扼要〗(形)[èyào]
concise; to the point

恶 (形) [è]
evil; vice; wicked
另见 ě

〖恶霸〗(名)[èbà]
local tyrant; local despot
〖恶毒〗(形)[èdú]
vicious; malicious
〖恶感〗(名)[ègǎn]
deep resentment; hostility; detest
〖恶贯满盈〗[èguànmǎnyíng]
full of iniquities; a person with towering crimes is heading for his doom
〖恶棍〗(名)[ègùn]
a roughneck; rascal; scoundrel
〖恶果〗(名)[èguǒ]
evil results of evil doing
〖恶狠狠〗(形)[èhěnhěn]
very fierce
〖恶化〗(动)[èhuà]
deteriorate
〖恶劣〗(形)[èliè]
evil; bad; ill; most unfavourable (condition)
〖恶习〗(名)[èxí]
evil habits; evil practice
〖恶性〗(名)[èxìng]
malignant
〖恶意〗(名)[èyì]
malice
〖恶作剧〗(名)[èzuòjù]
mischievous tricks; a practical joke

饿(动、形)[è]
feel hungry; starve

愕[è]
〖愕然〗(形)[èrán]
startled

遏[è]
〖遏止〗(动)[èzhǐ]
stop
〖遏制〗(动)[èzhì]
restrain; contain (e.g.the imperialist policy of containing...)

噩[è]
〖噩耗〗(名)[èhào]
news of death
〖噩梦〗(名)[èmèng]
terrible dreams; nightmares

鳄[è]
〖鳄鱼〗(名)[èyú]〔条 tiáo〕
crocodile

ēi

诶(叹)[ēi]
an interjection, expressing a reply or consent

ēn

恩(名)[ēn]
a favour or kindness from above
〖恩赐〗(动)[ēncì]
bestow (sth. on sb.) as a favour
〖恩赐观点〗[ēncì guāndiǎn]
the attitude of bestowing (sth. on sb.) as a favour; paternalistic attitude

〖恩惠〗(名)[ēnhuì]
special girt or kindness; special favour
〖恩将仇报〗[ēnjiāngchóubào]
return evil for good
〖恩情〗(名)[ēnqíng]
great goodness; kindness
〖恩人〗(名)[ēnrén]
benefactor
〖恩怨〗(名) [ēnyuàn]
kindness and grudge (usu. referring to grudge)

ér

儿(名、尾)[ér]
① son; child ② a suffix
〖儿歌〗(名)[érgē]
song for children
〖儿化〗(动)[érhuà]
the suffixing of a non-syllabic "r" to nouns and sometimes verbs; causing a retroflexion of the preceding vowel, a typical feature of Pekingnese and some other Chinese dialects
〖儿女〗(名)[érnǚ]
sons and daughters
〖儿童〗(名)[értóng]
children
〖儿童节〗(名)[Értóngjié]
Children's Day
〖儿童团〗(名)[Értóngtuán]
Children's Corps
〖儿童文学〗[értóng wénxué]
literature for children
〖儿媳妇〗(名)[érxífu]
daughter-in-law
〖儿戏〗(名)[érxì]
trifling matter
〖儿子〗(名)[érzi]
son

而(连)[ér]
and; but; till; if
〖而后〗(副)[érhòu]
and then; after that
〖而今〗(名)[érjīn]
now; now then; at present; nowadays
〖而且〗(连)[érqiě]
moreover; besides; furthermore; and; (not only...) ...but also
〖而已〗(助)[éryǐ]
only

ěr

尔(代)[ěr]
① you; your ②(archaic)thus
〖尔虞我诈〗[ěryúwǒzhà]
mutual suspicion and deception; each trying to cheat and outwit the other

耳(名)[ěr]
the ear
〖耳朵〗(名)[ěrduo]
ears
〖耳光〗(名)[ěrguāng]
a slap in the face
〖耳机〗(名)[ěrjī]
earphones
〖耳鸣〗(名)[ěrmíng]
buzzing in the ears; tinnitus

〖耳目〗(名)[ěrmù]
① what a person sees and hears ② a person who watches and reports on doings for others ③ eyes and ears

〖耳目一新〗[ěrmùyīxīn]
a pleasant change of atmosphere or appearance of a place

〖耳旁风〗(名)[ěrpángfēng]
go in one ear and out of the other; something to be disregarded; turn a deaf ear to

〖耳濡目染〗[ěrrúmùrǎn]
influence of surroundings; what one hears and sees

〖耳闻目睹〗[ěrwénmùdǔ]
what one hears and sees

〖耳语〗(动)[ěryǔ]
whisper

èr

二(数)[èr]
two

〖二把手〗(名)[èrbǎshǒu]
number two man; cadre who is second in command

〖二重性〗(名)[èrchóngxìng]
dual character

〖二七大罢工〗[Èrqī Dàbàgōng]
The Great February 7th Strike (1923)

〖二线〗(名)[èrxiàn]
second line; positions without direct responsibility for decision making

〖二氧化碳〗(名)[èryǎnghuàtàn]
carbon dioxide

〖二元论〗(名)[èryuánlùn]
dualism

〖二月〗(名)[èryuè]
February

〖二者必居其一〗[èrzhěbìjūqíyī]
either one or the other

F

fā

发(动、量)[fā]
①send out; issue; give out; dispatch ② a measure word, volley, burst
〖发报机〗(名)[fābàojī][台 tái]
telegraph-transmitter
〖发表〗(动)[fābiǎo]
publish; issue; voice; announce
〖发布〗(动)[fābù]
issue; publish; announce
〖发财〗[fā cái]
get rich; make a fortune; make a pile
〖发愁〗[fā chóu]
become sad; sullen; worried
〖发出〗(动)[fāchū]
① send out; dispatch; issue ② shine out
〖发达〗(形)[fādá]
developed; advanced; prosperous
〖发呆〗[fā dāi]
stunned
〖发电〗[fā diàn]
power-generating
〖发电厂〗(名)[fādiànchǎng]
power plant
〖发电机〗(名)[fādiànjī]
generator
〖发电站〗(名)[fādiànzhàn]
power station
〖发动〗(动)[fādòng]
launch; wage; stimulate; mobilise
〖发动机〗(名)[fādòngjī]
motor
〖发抖〗(动)[fādǒu]
tremble; shiver; shake; quiver
〖发放〗(动)[fāfàng]
issue; give out
〖发奋〗(动)[fāfèn]
work hard; work energetically
〖发愤图强〗[fāfèntúqiáng]
work hard and aim high; work energetically
〖发疯〗[fā fēng]

lose one's senses; frantic; be out of one's mind
〖发号施令〗[fāhàoshīlìng]
issue orders; order people about
〖发慌〗[fā huāng]
be flurried;panic-stricken; be perturbed
〖发挥〗(动)[fāhuī]
give scope to; bring into full play; exert
〖发火〗[fā huǒ]
① become angry; enrage ② start the fire;ignite;ignition③burst; explode
〖发酵〗[fā jiào]
ferment; leaven
〖发觉〗(动)[fājué]
discover; find out; realize
〖发掘〗(动)[fājué]
unearth; excavate
〖发刊词〗(名)[fākāncí]
introduction to a magazine; inaugural statement on first issue of periodical
〖发愣〗[fā lèng]
be stunned
〖发霉〗[fā méi]
mould
〖发明〗(动、名)[fāmíng]
invent; invention
〖发难〗(动)[fānàn]
be the first to start revolt
〖发怒〗[fā nù]
flare up; fly into rage
〖发脾气〗[fā píqi]
fly into a rage
〖发票〗(名)[fāpiào]〔张 zhāng〕
commercial invoice; receipt
〖发起〗(动)[fāqǐ]
initiate; start; cause to happen
〖发起人〗(名)[fāqǐrén]
sponsor; initiator
〖发球〗[fā qiú]
serve the ball
〖发人深省〗[fārénshēnxǐng]
something to think deeply about; make one wide awake
〖发烧〗[fā shāo]
have a fever; have a temperature
〖发烧友〗(名)[fāshāoyǒu]
fan; fancier; audiophile
〖发射〗(动)[fāshè]
shoot; fire; launch (e.g. launch a man-made satellite)
〖发生〗(动)[fāshēng]
arise; happen; take place
〖发誓〗[fā shì]
take an oath; swear; pledge
〖发现〗(动)[fāxiàn]
discover; find out
〖发泄〗(动)[fāxiè]
give free vent to; let off steam
〖发行〗(动)[fāxíng]
①distribute②publish
〖发芽〗[fā yá]
sprout
〖发言〗[fā yán]
give a speech; speak
〖发言权〗(名)[fāyánquán]
the right to speak
〖发言人〗(名)[fāyánrén]
spokesman
〖发炎〗[fā yán]
inflame

〖发扬〗(动)[fāyáng]
promote; bring into full play
〖发扬光大〗[fāyángguāngdà]
carry forward; give full play to; foster and enhance
〖发音〗[fā yīn]
pronounce; pronunciation
〖发育〗(动)[fāyù]
grow; develop
〖发源〗(动)[fāyuán]
originate
〖发展〗(动)[fāzhǎn]
develop; promote; give scope to
〖发展中国家〗
[fāzhǎnzhōngguójiā]
developing countries
〖发作〗(动)[fāzuò]
burst out (with violent emotion); emerge or take effect suddenly

fá

乏 (形)[fá]
①lack②tired③dull
〖乏味〗(形)[fáwèi]
dull; lacking in flavour or interest

罚 (动)[fá]
punish
〖罚不当罪〗[fábùdāngzuì]
the punishment exceeds the crime; unduly punished; punishment not in keeping with the crime
〖罚款〗[fá kuǎn]
fine; impose fine
〖罚球〗[fá qiú]
penalty kick (e.g. football)

fǎ

法 (名)[fǎ]
①method; way; means ②law
〖法办〗(动)[fǎbàn]
be dealt with according to law
〖法宝〗(名)[fǎbǎo]
wonder-working magic; treasured tricks; effective weapon; magic weapon
〖法官〗(名)[fǎguān]
judge; justice
〖法家〗(名)[Fǎjiā]
the Legalist School
〖法令〗(名)[fǎlìng]
order; law; statutes; orders and decrees
〖法律〗(名)[fǎlǜ]
laws
〖法盲〗(名)[fǎmáng]
legal illiterate; person ignorant of the law
〖法权〗(名)[fǎquán]
right privilege
〖法人〗(名)[fǎrén]
legal person; legal entity; juridical person
〖法庭〗(名)[fǎtíng]
law court
〖法网〗(名)[fǎwǎng]
legal system
〖法西斯〗(名)[fǎxīsī]
fascist
〖法西斯主义〗(名)
[fǎxīsīzhǔyì]

fascism
〖法院〗(名)[fǎyuàn]
court of law
〖法则〗(名)[fǎzé]
rules; principle
〖法治〗(名)[fǎzhì]
the rule of law
〖法制〗(名)[fǎzhì]
legality; legal system
〖法子〗(名)[fǎzi]
method; way; means

砝[fǎ]
〖砝码〗(名)[fǎmǎ]
brass or lead weights (used in old style scales)

F

fān
帆(名)[fān]
sail
〖帆布〗(名)[fānbù] canvas
〖帆船〗(名)[fānchuán]〔只 zhī〕
sail boat

番(量)[fān]
a measure word(a course, a turn)
〖番号〗(名)[fānhào]
unit designation

蕃[fān]
〖蕃茄〗(名)[fānqié]
tomato

翻(动)[fān]
turn over; turn around; reverse
〖翻案〗[fān àn]
reverse the previous verdict; reverse a case; reverse a correct decision
〖翻版〗(名)[fānbǎn]
reproduce; reprint
〖翻滚〗(动)[fāngǔn]
roll over and over
〖翻江倒海〗[fānjiāngdǎohǎi]
(lit.) turn the river and sea upside down; (fig.) world-shaking; epoch-making
〖翻来覆去〗[fānláifùqù]
toss and turn
〖翻脸〗[fān liǎn]
fall out; suddenly turn hostile
〖翻然悔悟〗[fānránhuǐwù]
be determined to make a clean break with their past
〖翻砂〗(名)[fānshā]
metal castings
〖翻身〗[fān shēn]
① turn oneself over ② be liberated; throw off the oppressor
〖翻腾〗(动)[fānténg]
upset; overturn everything; toss over
〖翻天覆地〗[fāntiānfùdì]
earth-shaking; epoch-making; the world is being turned upside down
〖翻箱倒柜〗[fānxiāngdǎoguì]
(fig.) turn over things in thorough search; (lit.) rummage through chests and cupboards
〖翻新〗(动)[fānxīn]
rehash; renew; make anew
〖翻修〗(动)[fānxiū]
repair
〖翻译〗(动、名)[fānyì]

translate; interpret; translator; translation; interpreter; interpretation
〖翻印〗(动)[fānyìn]
reprint
〖翻阅〗(动)[fānyuè]
glance through; read over

fán

凡(代)[fán]
any; all; anybody; anytime; everything
〖凡士林〗(名)[fánshìlín]
vaseline
〖凡是〗[fánshì]
every thing which; all that

矾(名)[fán]
alum

烦(形、动)[fán]
① vexed; unrest; upset ② request; trouble
〖烦闷〗(形)[fánmèn]
out of sorts; vexed; worried; upset; unrest
〖烦恼〗(形)[fánnǎo]
feel worried; confusing; vexing; annoyed
〖烦扰〗(动)[fánrǎo]
confuse; bother; incommode
〖烦琐〗(形)[fánsuǒ]
trivial; trifling
〖烦琐哲学〗[fánsuǒ zhéxué]
scholasticism; scholastic research
〖烦躁〗(形)[fánzào]
irritable

繁(形)[fán]
① complicated ② numerous
〖繁多〗(形)[fánduō]
numerous
〖繁华〗(形)[fánhuá]
flourishing; prosperous
〖繁忙〗(形)[fánmáng]
busily engaged
〖繁荣〗(形、动)[fánróng]
prosperous; flourishing and thriving
〖繁荣昌盛〗
[fánróngchāngshèng]
thriving and prospering
〖繁体字〗(名)[fántǐzì]
characters which have simplified equivalents (e.g. 體 is the 繁体字 of the simplified character 体)
〖繁星〗(名)[fánxīng]
an array of stars
〖繁杂〗(形)[fánzá]
detailed and complicated; complicated and overloaded
〖繁殖〗(动)[fánzhí]
breed; multiply
〖繁重〗(形)[fánzhòng]
heavy; difficult; hard; innumerable and crushing

fǎn

反(形、动)[fǎn]
① contrary; opposite; anti-; counter ② revolt; oppose ③ turn over; reverse

F

〖反霸〗[fǎn bà]
anti-hegemony
〖反比〗(名)[fǎnbǐ]
inverse ratio
〖反驳〗(动)[fǎnbó]
confute; rebut; refute
〖反常〗(形)[fǎncháng]
abnormal; unusual
〖反倒〗(副)[fǎndào]
on the contrary
〖反帝〗[fǎn dì]
anti-imperialism; against imperialism
〖反动〗(形)[fǎndòng]
reactionary
〖反动派〗(名)[fǎndòngpài]
reactionary
〖反对〗(动)[fǎnduì]
oppose; object to; reject
〖反而〗(副)[fǎn'ér]
on the contrary; instead of; but
〖反腐蚀〗[fǎn fǔshí]
struggle against the corrosive influence (of the bourgeoisie)
〖反复〗(动)[fǎnfù]
① repeat; repeatedly; time and again ② change constantly
〖反复无常〗[fǎnfùwúcháng]
changeable; inconsistent; play fast and loose; capricious
〖反感〗(形)[fǎngǎn]
distasteful; repugnant; resentful
〖反戈一击〗[fǎngēyījī]
turn round and hit back
〖反革命〗(名)[fǎngémìng]
counter-revolutionary
〖反攻〗(动)[fǎngōng]
counter-attack; counter-offensive
〖反攻倒算〗[fǎngōngdàosuàn]
launch a vindictive counter-attack
〖反光镜〗(名)[fǎnguāngjìng]
reflector
〖反话〗(名)[fǎnhuà]
irony; ironical
〖反悔〗(动)[fǎnhuǐ]
repent
〖反击〗(动)[fǎnjī]
launch counter-attacks
〖反骄破满〗[fǎnjiāopòmǎn]
oppose arrogance and do away with complacency
〖反抗〗(动)[fǎnkàng]
resist; revolt against
〖反馈〗(名)[fǎnkuì]
feedback
〖反面〗(名)[fǎnmiàn]
the opposite; negative side
〖反面教材〗[fǎnmiàn jiàocái]
lesson by negative example; serve in a negative way to teach
〖反面教员〗[fǎnmiànjiàoyuán]
teacher by negative example
〖反面人物〗[fǎnmiàn rénwù]
negative character
〖反扑〗(动)[fǎnpū]
(of a cornered enemy or animal) counter-attack; pounce back
〖反其道而行之〗
[fǎnqídào'érxíngzhī]
act in opposition to; do exactly the opposite
〖反射〗(动)[fǎnshè]
reflect

F

〖反问〗(动)[fǎnwèn]
interrogate
〖反问句〗(名)[fǎnwènjù]
interrogative question
〖反响〗(名)[fǎnxiǎng]
echo; repercussions
〖反省〗(动)[fǎnxǐng]
examine one's own errors
〖反修〗[fǎn xiū]
oppose revisionism
〖反义词〗(名)[fǎnyìcí]
antonym
〖反应〗(名、动)[fǎnyìng]
repercussion; reaction; make response
〖反映〗(动)[fǎnyìng]
mirror; reflect
〖反映论〗(名)[fǎnyìnglùn]
the theory of reflection
〖反正〗(副)[fǎnzhèng]
anyway; anyhow; all the same
〖反证〗(动、名)[fǎnzhèng]
furnish counter-evidence; counter-evidence
〖反之〗(连)[fǎnzhī]
conversely
〖反殖〗[fǎn zhí]
anti-colonialism
〖反作用〗(名)[fǎnzuòyòng]
reaction
〖反作用力〗(名)[fǎnzuòyòng lì]
reaction; the force of reaction

返(动)[fǎn]

return
〖返工〗[fǎn gōng]
do (poor work) over again
〖返航〗(动)[fǎnháng]
return from a voyage
〖返回〗(动)[fǎnhuí]
return; go back
〖返青〗(动)[fǎnqīng]
reawakening (plants)

fàn

犯(动)[fàn]

violate; infringe; commit
〖犯病〗[fàn bìng]
have an attack of an illness
〖犯不上〗[fàn bu shàng]
it won't pay; it is not worthwhile
〖犯不着〗[fàn bu zháo]
it won't pay; it is not worthwhile
〖犯得上〗[fàn de shàng]
it is worth while (doing)
〖犯得着〗[fàn de zháo]
it is worth while (doing)
〖犯法〗[fàn fǎ]
break the law
〖犯规〗[fàn guī]
foul
〖犯人〗(名)[fànrén]
criminal; convict; prisoner; the guilty
〖犯罪〗[fàn zuì]
commit a crime; commit an offence
〖犯罪分子〗(名)[fàn zuì fènzǐ]
offender; criminal

饭(名)[fàn]

rice; meal

〖饭店〗(名)[fàndiàn]
hotel; restaurant
〖饭馆〗(名)[fànguǎn]
restaurant
〖饭厅〗(名)[fàntīng]
dining hall
〖饭碗〗(名)[fànwǎn]
①bowl②means of living

泛[fàn]

〖泛泛〗(形)[fànfàn]
general
〖泛滥〗(动)[fànlàn]
flood; spread unchecked
〖泛指〗(动)[fànzhǐ]
refer to something in general

F

范[fàn]

〖范畴〗(名)[fànchóu]
categories; scope
〖范例〗(名)[fànlì]
model; example; pattern
〖范围〗(名)[fànwéi]
scope; range; boundary; extent; confines

贩(动)[fàn]

peddle; sell
〖贩卖〗(动)[fànmài]
deal in some traffic; peddle; marketing
〖贩运〗(动)[fànyùn]
(of merchant's goods) transport for trade

fāng

方(名、形、量、副)[fāng]

①party; side(e.g. party A) ② square ③ a measure word (for square, cubic) ④just now; just then
〖方案〗(名)[fāng'àn]
plan; project; outline
〖方便〗(形、动)[fāngbiàn]
convenient; handy; facilitate
〖方才〗(副)[fāngcái]
just now; only then
〖方程〗(名)[fāngchéng]
equation
〖方程式〗(名)[fāngchéngshì]
equation
〖方法〗(名)[fāngfǎ]
method; way; means
〖方法论〗(名)[fāngfǎlùn]
methodology
〖方面〗(名)[fāngmiàn]
aspect; direction; sphere
〖方式〗(名)[fāngshì][种 zhǒng]
fashion; form; way; manner
〖方位〗(名)[fāngwèi]
locality
〖方位词〗(名)[fāngwèicí]
word of locality
〖方向〗(名)[fāngxiàng]
direction; orientation; trend
〖方向盘〗(名)[fāngxiàngpán]
steering gear; steering wheel
〖方兴未艾〗[fāngxīngwèi'ài]
rising; in the ascendant
〖方言〗(名)[fāngyán]
dialect
〖方圆〗(名)[fāngyuán]
surroundings (area)
〖方针〗(名)[fāngzhēn]
guiding principles; orienta-

tion; guiding line

芳[fāng]
〖芳香〗(形)[fāngxiāng]
fragrant

fáng

防(动)[fáng]
defend; prevent
〖防备〗(动)[fángbèi]
be on guard; take precaution
〖防毒〗[fáng dú]
take measures against poisoning
〖防范〗(动)[fángfàn]
guard against
〖防腐〗[fáng fǔ]
anti-corrosion
〖防腐蚀〗[fáng fǔshí]
① antiseptic; anti-corrosion
② guard against corruption
〖防洪〗[fáng hóng]
flood control
〖防护林〗(名)[fánghùlín]
sand-break and wind-break; shelter belt
〖防患未然〗[fánghuànwèirán]
nip sth. in the bud; take precaution beforehand
〖防火〗[fáng huǒ]
① fire prevention ② fireproof
〖防空〗[fáng kōng]
air-raid precaution; anti-aircraft; various devices against air raids
〖防涝〗[fáng lào]
flood control
〖防守〗(动)[fángshǒu]
guard; defend; hold
〖防水〗[fáng shuǐ]
waterproof
〖防微杜渐〗[fángwēidùjiàn]
nip sth. in the bud
〖防卫〗(动)[fángwèi]
defend; guard against
〖防线〗(名)[fángxiàn]
defence line
〖防修〗[fáng xiū]
guard against revisionism
〖防汛〗[fáng xùn]
flood-prevention
〖防疫〗[fáng yì]
anti-epidemic
〖防御〗(动)[fángyù]
guard against; defend
〖防震〗[fáng zhèn]
shock-proof; shock-resistant; make preparations against earth-quake
〖防止〗(动)[fángzhǐ]
prevent; guard against
〖防治〗(动)[fángzhì]
prevention and cure

妨[fáng]
〖妨碍〗(动)[fáng'ài]
interfere with; hinder; stand in the way; obstruct

房(名)[fáng]〔间 jiān〕
house
〖房地产〗(名)[fángdìchǎn]
real estate; property
〖房东〗(名)[fángdōng]

F

house-owner; landlord or landlady (of a house)
〖房间〗(名)[fángjiān]
room
〖房屋〗(名)[fángwū]
house; building
〖房子〗(名)[fángzi]〔间 jiān〕
house; building
〖房租〗(名)[fángzū]
house rent

fǎng

仿 (动)[fǎng]
imitate; copy; pattern after
〖仿佛〗(动)[fǎngfú]
it seems like
〖仿宋体〗(名)[fǎngsòngtǐ]
copy of Sung Dynasty (style of lettering)
〖仿效〗(动)[fǎngxiào]
imitate; copy; follow suit
〖仿造〗(动)[fǎngzào]
made from other model
〖仿照〗(动)[fǎngzhào]
follow; in accordance with
〖仿制〗(动)[fǎngzhì]
made from other model

访 (动)[fǎng]
interview; visit
〖访贫问苦〗[fǎngpínwènkǔ]
go to see the poor and ask about their past bitterness
〖访问〗(动)[fǎngwèn]
visit

纺 (动)[fǎng]
reel; spin
〖纺织〗(动)[fǎngzhī]
spin and weave; textile
〖纺织品〗(名)[fǎngzhīpǐn]
textile fabrics; textiles

fàng

放 (动)[fàng]
① put; place ② let go; release ③ blossom
〖放大〗(动)[fàngdà]
enlarge
〖放大镜〗(名)[fàngdàjìng]
magnifying glass
〖放荡〗(形)[fàngdàng]
dissolute
〖放虎归山〗[fànghǔguīshān]
(lit.) let tiger back to mountain; (fig.) cause future trouble
〖放火〗[fàng huǒ]
commit arson; set on fire
〖放假〗[fàng jià]
have holiday
〖放空炮〗[fàngkōngpào]
empty talk; talk big; boast
〖放牧〗(动)[fàngmù]
graze; grazing
〖放弃〗(动)[fàngqì]
give up; abandon; forsake
〖放任〗(动)[fàngrèn]
do nothing about it; let things take their course
〖放任自流〗[fàngrènzìliú]
let things slide; let things take their own course (e.g. give up due guidance)
〖放哨〗[fàng shào]

set up patrol; stand sentinel

〖放射〗(动)[fàngshè]

give off; emit; radiate

〖放射性〗(名)[fàngshèxìng]

radiation

〖放手〗[fàng shǒu]

① let go ② give one a free hand to do something; boldly and freely

〖放肆〗(形)[fàngsì]

unbridled; rampant; unserupulous; wanton

〖放松〗(动)[fàngsōng]

loosen up; relax

〖放下包袱〗[fàngxià bāofu]

get rid of the baggage; cast off mental burdens

〖放心〗[fàng xīn]

make one's mind easy; set one's heart at ease

〖放行〗(动)[fàngxíng]

let pass (of customs, sentry)

〖放学〗[fàng xué]

let out ((of school); dismiss

〖放眼世界〗[fàngyǎnshìjiè]

keep the whole world in view

〖放映〗(动)[fàngyìng]

(of film) exhibit; show; project

〖放债〗[fàng zhài]

lend money for interest

〖放之四海而皆准〗

[fàngzhīsì hǎi 'érjiēzhǔn]

valid everywhere; be universally applicable

〖放纵〗(动)[fàngzòng]

give the reins to; allow to run wild; give freedom to

fēi

飞(动)[fēi]

fly

〖飞驰〗(动)[fēichí]

move or run very fast; gallop

〖飞船〗(名)[fēichuán]

space ship

〖飞黄腾达〗[fēihuángténgdá]

rise high; climb up the social ladder rapidly

〖飞机〗(名)[fēijī]〔架 jià〕

airplane

〖飞机场〗(名)[fēijīchǎng]

airport

〖飞快〗(形)[fēikuài]

very fast

〖飞轮〗(名)[fēilún]

fly wheel

〖飞速〗(副)[fēisù]

very fast

〖飞舞〗(动)[fēiwǔ]

fly about; flutter

〖飞翔〗(动)[fēixiáng]

fly

〖飞行〗(动)[fēixíng]

fly

〖飞行员〗(名)[fēixíngyuán]

pilot; airman

〖飞扬〗(动)[fēiyáng]

float; sail; flutter

〖飞扬跋扈〗[fēiyángbáhù]

throw one's weight around; arrogant

〖飞跃〗(动)[fēiyuè]

increase by leaps and bounds; leap; fly; jump into the air and fly away

非(名、形、副)[fēi]
①wrongdoing; mistake; not right ②non-; un-; not; be not ③only; must
〖非…不可〗[fēi…bùkě]
must; it is absolutely necessary that; have to
〖非…才…〗[fēi…cái…]
only; on condition that; unless
〖非常〗(形、副)[fēicháng]
extraordinary; special; very; extremely; exceedingly; highly
〖非但〗(连)[fēidàn]
not only; far from being
〖非得〗(助动)[fēiděi]
must; it is necessary that
〖非法〗(形)[fēifǎ]
illegal
〖非凡〗(形)[fēifán]
outstanding; unusual
〖非驴非马〗[fēilǘfēimǎ]
neither hay nor grass; neither fish, flesh, nor fowl
〖非难〗(动)[fēinàn]
censure; blame; reprehend
〖非人待遇〗[fēi rén dàiyù]
inhuman treatment
〖非同小可〗[fēitóngxiǎokě]
no trivial matter
〖非洲〗(名)[Fēizhōu]
Africa

扉[fēi]
〖扉页〗(名)[fēiyè]
flyleaf

féi

肥(形)[féi]
fat; greasy
〖肥料〗(名)[féiliào]
fertilizer; manure
〖肥瘦〗(名)[féishòu]
①width of clothes ②half lean (e.g. pork)
〖肥沃〗(形)[féiwò]
fertile; rich
〖肥皂〗(名)[féizào]〔块 kuài〕
soap
〖肥壮〗(形)[féizhuàng]
stout; portly

fěi

匪(名)[fěi]
bandit
〖匪帮〗(名)[fěibāng]
bandit gang; bandit clique; bandit
〖匪巢〗(名)[fěicháo]
bandits' lair
〖匪军〗(名)[fěijūn]
bandit; bandit army
〖匪徒〗(名)[fěitú]
bandits

诽[fěi]
〖诽谤〗(动)[fěibàng]
vilify; slander; smear; defame; calumniate

fèi

废(形、动)[fèi]
abandoned; neglected; abandon;

give up (halfway); abolish

〖废除〗(动)[fèichú]

abolish; cancel; cast aside; renounce

〖废黜〗(动)[fèichù]

depose

〖废话〗(名)[fèihuà]

nonsense; empty phrase

〖废料〗(名)[fèiliào]

rubbish; cast-off things; waste matters

〖废品〗(名)[fèipǐn]

rejects

〖废弃〗(动)[fèiqì]

throw off; cast aside; abandon; neglect; abolish

〖废寝忘食〗[fèiqǐnwàngshí]

neglect one's sleep and meals

〖废物〗(名)[fèiwù]

rubbish; cast-off things; discards

〖废墟〗(名)[fèixū]

debris; ruins

〖废止〗(动)[fèizhǐ]

abolish

沸[fèi]

〖沸点〗(名)[fèidiǎn]

boiling point

〖沸腾〗(动)[fèiténg]

boil over; seethe

肺(名)[fèi]

lung

〖肺腑〗(名)[fèifǔ]

the bottom of one's heart

〖肺结核〗(名)[fèijiéhé]

T.B.

〖肺炎〗(名)[fèiyán]

pneumonia

费(动、名)[fèi]

cost; waste; fees; expense

〖费解〗[fèi jiě]

difficult to understand

〖费尽心机〗[fèijìnxīnjī]

pain-stakingly; rack one's brains

〖费力〗[fèi lì]

hard to tackle; take pains; waste energy; strenuous

〖费事〗[fèi shì]

troublesome

〖费心〗[fèi xīn]

take great pains to; take the trouble to; rack one's brains

〖费用〗(名)[fèiyòng]〔笔 bǐ〕

expenses; cost; expenditure

fēn

分(动、名、量)[fēn]

① separate; divide ② give; distribute; get (a share) ③ distinguish; differentiate ④ branch; sub- ⑤ minute ⑥ points; marks; ten percent ⑦ cent (hundredth of a yuan); hundredth of an ounce

另见 fèn

〖分崩离析〗[fēnbēnglíxī]

disintegrate; fall apart; collapsing; disunite

〖分辨〗(动)[fēnbiàn]

compare and see the difference;

distinguish
〖分辩〗(动)[fēnbiàn]
give explanation in defense
〖分别〗(动、副)[fēnbié]
①depart; separate ②differentiate; distinguish ③separately; respectively; according to (it's own merits)
〖分布〗(动)[fēnbù]
distribute; spread; scatter
〖分寸〗(名)[fēncùn]
① very small amount ② proper restraint
〖分担〗(动)[fēndān]
shoulder burden separately; share responsibility
〖分道扬镳〗[fēndàoyángbiāo]
go by different roads
〖分封制〗(名)[fēnfēngzhì]
vassalage — the system of installing hereditary nobles to rule domains
〖分割〗(动)[fēngē]
cut up; divide up
〖分隔〗(动)[fēngé]
separate
〖分工〗[fēn gōng]
division of labour
〖分号〗(名)[fēnhào]
semicolon
〖分红〗[fēn hóng]
share out bonus; distribute dividends
〖分化〗(动)[fēnhuà]
①disintegrate ②sow dissension; differentiation
〖分解〗(动)[fēnjiě]
①dissolve; disintegrate; dissociate; break up into separate elements ②be explained
〖分界〗[fēn jiè]
demarcation of boundary; dividing line
〖分界线〗(名)[fēnjièxiàn]
[条 tiáo]
demarcation line
〖分句〗(名)[fēnjù]
clause
〖分开〗(动)[fēnkāi]
set apart; separate
〖分类〗[fēn lèi]
classify
〖分离〗(动)[fēnlí]
part; leave; separate
〖分裂〗(动)[fēnliè]
split up; crack up; create splits
〖分门别类〗[fēnménbiélèi]
sort out into categories
〖分泌〗(动)[fēnmì]
secrete; act of secretion
〖分娩〗(动)[fēnmiǎn]
give birth to child
〖分秒必争〗[fēnmiǎobìzhēng]
every minute counts; race against time; not a second is to be lost
〖分明〗(形)[fēnmíng]
clear
〖分母〗(名)[fēnmǔ]
denominator of fraction
〖分蘖〗(动)[fēnniè]
offshoot; tiller
〖分配〗(动)[fēnpèi]
assign; distribute; allot
〖分批〗[fēn pī]

F

group by group; in batches
〖分期〗[fēn qī]
① stage by stage; at different times ② in instalments
〖分歧〗(名、形)[fēnqí]
difference; (of opinion) discord; divergence; divergent; different
〖分散〗(动)[fēnsàn]
disperse; scatter
〖分数〗(名)[fēnshù]
① fraction ② marks; points
〖分水岭〗(名)[fēnshuǐlǐng]
watershed; demarcation line
〖分庭抗礼〗[fēntíngkànglǐ]
meet as an equal; stand up to; defy
〖分析〗(动)[fēnxī]
analyze; differentiate
〖分享〗(动)[fēnxiǎng]
have a share in
〖分心〗[fēn xīn]
distract one's attention; divert one's attention to
〖分赃〗[fēn zāng]
share the spoils
〖…分之…〗[…fēn zhī…]
part e.g. 五分之四 4/5; fraction e.g. 五分之四 4/5
〖分子〗(名)[fēnzǐ]
numerator of fraction; molecule; element

芬 [fēn]
〖芬芳〗(形、名)[fēnfāng]
fragrant

吩 [fēn]
〖吩咐〗(动)[fēnfù]
tell; order; instruct; give orders

纷 [fēn]
〖纷繁〗(形)[fēnfán]
profuse and confusing
〖纷飞〗(动)[fēnfēi]
flutter about
〖纷纷〗(形)[fēnfēn]
profuse; one after another
〖纷乱〗(形)[fēnluàn]
disorderly; topsy-turvy; confused

F

fén

坟 (名)[fén]
grave
〖坟墓〗(名)[fénmù]
grave

焚 (动)[fén]
burn
〖焚毁〗(动)[fénhuǐ]
destroy by fire; burn down
〖焚烧〗(动)[fénshāo]
burn

fěn

粉 (名、形)[fěn]
① powder ② pink
〖粉笔〗(名)[fěnbǐ]〔根儿 gēnr〕
chalk
〖粉红〗(形)[fěnhóng]
pink; rosy

〖粉末〗(名)[fěnmò]
powder
〖粉墨登场〗[fěnmòdēngchǎng]
① mount the stage in full regalia ② go on political stage (contempt)
〖粉身碎骨〗[fěnshēnsuìgǔ]
utterly crush; be ground to dust
〖粉饰〗(动)[fěnshì]
present pleasant appearance; cover up faults; whitewash (fig.); camouflage
〖粉刷〗(动)[fěnshuā]
whitewash
〖粉丝〗(名)[fěnsī]
a food resembling vermicelli made from beans

〖粉碎〗(动)[fěnsuì]
smash; shatter; crush
〖粉条〗(名)[fěntiáo]
a food resembling vermicelli (larger) made from beans

fèn

分[fèn]
另见 fēn
〖分量〗(名)[fènliàng]
weight; amount
〖分内〗(名)[fènnèi]
part of one's duty; included in one's duties
〖分外〗(名、副)[fènwài]
① other than one's duty ② very; exceedingly
〖分子〗(名)[fènzǐ]
element

份(量)[fèn]
a measure word, share, portion, part, a copy

奋[fèn]
〖奋不顾身〗[fènbùgùshēn]
regardless of personal danger
〖奋斗〗(动)[fèndòu]
fight hard; struggle dauntlessly; strive
〖奋发〗(动)[fènfā]
make resolve to succeed; work hard and aim high
〖奋发图强〗[fènfātúqiáng]
rise in great vigour; work with stamina and diligence
〖奋起〗(动)[fènqǐ]
make a vigorous start
〖奋勇〗(形)[fènyǒng]
heroic; vigorous; courageous
〖奋勇当先〗[fènyǒngdāngxiān]
take vigorous lead in advancing
〖奋战〗(动)[fènzhàn]
fight vigorously; struggle

愤[fèn]
〖愤愤〗(形)[fènfèn]
angry
〖愤恨〗(形)[fènhèn]
angry; indignant
〖愤慨〗(形)[fènkǎi]
indignant
〖愤懑〗(形)[fènmèn]
resentful
〖愤怒〗(形)[fènnù]
angry

粪(名)[fèn]
manure; dung; night soil
〖粪便〗(名)[fènbiàn]
excrement; night soil
〖粪肥〗(名)[fènféi]
manure
〖粪土〗(名)[fèntǔ]
dirt; filth

fēng

丰[fēng]
〖丰产〗(形)[fēngchǎn]
high-yield
〖丰产田〗(名)[fēngchǎntián]
high-yield land
〖丰富〗(形、动)[fēngfù]
rich; abundant; plentiful; inexhaustible; enrich; be abundant
〖丰功伟绩〗[fēnggōngwěijī]
gigantic contribution; heroic deeds
〖丰满〗(形)[fēngmǎn]
plump; full and round
〖丰年〗(名)[fēngnián]
year of good harvest
〖丰盛〗(形)[fēngshèng]
sumptuous; splendid
〖丰收〗(动、名)[fēngshōu]
have bumper harvest; rich harvest
〖丰硕〗(形)[fēngshuò]
rich; abundant
〖丰衣足食〗[fēngyīzúshí]
ample clothing and sufficient food

风(名)[fēng]〔阵 zhèn〕
wind
〖风暴〗(名)[fēngbào]
storm
〖风波〗(名)[fēngbō]〔场 chǎng〕
disturbances; crisis
〖风餐露宿〗[fēngcānlùsù]
(lit.) feed on the wind and drink the dew; (fig.) undergo the hardships of roughing it on a trek
〖风潮〗(名)[fēngcháo]
campaign; storm and stress
〖风车〗(名)[fēngchē]
windmill
〖风尘〗(名)[fēngchén]
hardships of journey
〖风尘仆仆〗[fēngchénpúpú]
hard journey
〖风驰电掣〗[fēngchídiànchè]
go by like the wind
〖风吹草动〗[fēngchuīcǎodòng]
grass bends as the wind blows; slight stir
〖风度〗(名)[fēngdù]
manner
〖风格〗(名)[fēnggé]
style
〖风光〗(名)[fēngguāng]
landscape; special atmosphere
〖风化〗(动)[fēnghuà]
weathering of rocks
〖风景〗(名)[fēngjǐng]
scenery; scene
〖风镜〗(名)[fēngjìng]
glasses worn as protection against sandstorm; sand-goggles

F

〖风浪〗(名)[fēnglàng]
①storm②crisis
〖风雷〗(名)[fēngléi]
wind and thunder
〖风力〗(名)[fēnglì]
wind force
〖风凉话〗(名)[fēngliánghuà]
irresponsible and carping comments
〖风流〗(形)[fēngliú]
①great and noble-hearted; distinguished and admirable ②loose; immoral
〖风马牛不相及〗
[fēngmǎniú bùxiāngjí]
have nothing in common with; totally unconnected; two different unrelated things
〖风貌〗(名)[fēngmào]
style and feature
〖风靡一时〗[fēngmǐyīshí]
be popular for a time
〖风平浪静〗[fēngpínglàngjìng]
the storm abates and the waves calm down-all is calm
〖风起云涌〗[fēngqǐyúnyǒng]
be raging; surge forward; spread like a storm
〖风气〗(名)[fēngqì]〔种 zhǒng〕
common practice
〖风趣〗(名、形)[fēngqù]
humorous; charming personality
〖风尚〗(名)[fēngshàng]
fashion of the times
〖风声鹤唳〗[fēngshēnghèlì]
be scared by the sigh of the wind and the cry of the cranes; (fig.) be scared
〖风霜〗(名)[fēngshuāng]
wind and frost; climatic hardships
〖风俗〗(名)[fēngsú]〔种 zhǒng〕
habits and customs; social customs
〖风调雨顺〗[fēngtiáoyǔshùn]
everything goes smoothly; favourable weather or condition
〖风头〗(名)[fēngtou]
limelight
〖风土人情〗[fēngtǔrénqíng]
local manners and practices
〖风味〗(名)[fēngwèi]
flavour
〖风险〗(名)[fēngxiǎn]〔场 chǎng〕
risk
〖风向〗(名)[fēngxiàng]
direction of wind
〖风言风语〗[fēngyánfēngyǔ]
gossip; an unfounded rumour
〖风雨〗(名)[fēngyǔ]〔场 chǎng〕
wind and rain; storm and stress
〖风雨飘摇〗[fēngyǔpiāoyáo]
unstable
〖风雨同舟〗[fēngyǔtóngzhōu]
in the same boat; stand together through storm and stress
〖风雨无阻〗[fēngyǔwúzǔ]
rain or shine (e.g. it will be done come rain or shine)
〖风云〗(名)[fēngyún]
winds and clouds; storm
〖风灾〗(名)[fēngzāi]〔场 chǎng〕
disaster of storm
〖风筝〗(名)[fēngzheng]〔只 zhī〕
kite

封(动、量)[fēng]
① seal; close up ② appoint ③ a measure word (e.g. for a letter)
〖封闭〗(动)[fēngbì]
seal up; close up; close down
〖封存〗(动)[fēngcún]
seal up for storage or safe-keeping
〖封底〗(名)[fēngdǐ]
back cover (of book)
〖封官许愿〗
[fēngguānxǔyuàn]
hand out official posts and make promises; offer high posts and other favours; promise official promotions
〖封建〗(形、名)[fēngjiàn]
feudal; feudalistic; feudalism
〖封建社会〗[fēngjiàn shèhuì]
feudal society
〖封建制度〗[fēngjiàn zhìdù]
feudal system
〖封建主义〗(名)[fēngjiàn zhǔyì]
feudalism
〖封面〗(名)[fēngmiàn]
cover
〖封山育林〗[fēngshān yùlín]
enclose the hill for natural afforestation
〖封锁〗(动)[fēngsuǒ]
block; seal off; blockade
〖封锁线〗(名)[fēngsuǒxiàn]
blocked line
〖封条〗(名)[fēngtiáo]
piece of paper stuck on door, etc. as seal

疯(形)[fēng]
insane; mad
〖疯疯癫癫〗(形)
[fēngfēngdiāndiān]
crazy; hysterical; frantic
〖疯狂〗(形)[fēngkuáng]
crazy; wild; frantic
〖疯子〗(名)[fēngzi]
madman

烽[fēng]
〖烽火〗(名)[fēnghuǒ]
war; flames of war
〖烽火连天〗[fēnghuǒliántiān]
the flames of war spread their conflagration far and wide

锋[fēng]
〖锋利〗(形)[fēnglì]
sharp
〖锋芒〗(名)[fēngmáng]
① the fine edge of spear or lance ② a biting or critical remark (fig.); spearhead
〖锋芒毕露〗[fēngmángbìlù]
self-asserted and prone to exhibit one's knowledge, etc.
〖锋芒所向〗
[fēngmángsuǒxiàng]
direct the spearhead against; focus the attack on

蜂(名)[fēng]
bees
〖蜂蜜〗(名)[fēngmì]
honey

〖蜂拥〗(动)[fēngyōng]
crowd on; flock; swarm

féng

逢(动)[féng]
meet; chance upon; come across

缝(动)[féng]
sew
另见 fèng
〖缝补〗(动)[féngbǔ]
mend; patch
〖缝纫〗(动)[féngrèn]
dressmaking
〖缝纫机〗(名)[féngrènjī]〔架 jià〕
sewing machine

F

fěng

讽[fěng]
〖讽刺〗(动)[fěngcì]
satirize

fèng

凤(名)[fèng]
phoenix
〖凤凰〗(名)[fènghuáng]
phoenix

奉(动)[fèng]
① have the honour to present (sth.) ② receive; follow (orders)
〖奉承〗(动)[fèngcheng]
flatter; sing one's praises; fawn on
〖奉告〗(动)[fènggào]
have the honour to inform
〖奉公守法〗[fènggōngshǒufǎ]
law-abiding
〖奉命〗[fèng mìng]
follow orders or instructions; under orders
〖奉陪〗(动)[fèngpéi]
keep (sb.) company; be together with
〖奉劝〗(动)[fèngquàn]
give a piece of advice; remonstrate
〖奉若神明〗[fèngruòshénmíng]
revere as sacred
〖奉送〗(动)[fèngsòng]
have the honour to present (sth.)
〖奉行〗(动)[fèngxíng]
carry out (order)

缝(名)[fèng]
crack; slit; seam
另见 féng
〖缝儿〗(名)[fèngr]〔条 tiáo〕
seam; open seam
〖缝隙〗(名)[fèngxì]
open seam; slit; slot

fó

佛(名)[fó]
Buddha
〖佛教〗(名)[Fójiào]
the Buddhist religion; Buddhism

fǒu

否(动、副)[fǒu]

decide in the negative; vote against; no; not; ...or not

〖否定〗(动)[fǒudìng]
decide in the negative; negate

〖否决〗(动)[fǒujué]
vote against

〖否决权〗(名)[fǒujuéquán]
veto

〖否认〗(动)[fǒurèn]
deny

〖否则〗(连)[fǒuzé]
or else; otherwise

fū

夫(名)[fū]
①husband ②man

〖夫妇〗(名)[fūfù]
man and wife; husband and wife

〖夫妻〗(名)[fūqī]
husband and wife

〖夫妻老婆店〗[fūqīlǎopodiàn]
mom-and-pop store; ma and pa store

〖夫人〗(名)[fūren]
①wife ②madam

肤[fū]

〖肤浅〗(形)[fūqiǎn]
skin-deep; superficial

〖肤色〗(名)[fūsè]
①complexion ②colour (e.g. people of all colours)

敷[fū]

〖敷衍〗(动)[fūyǎn]
be halfhearted about; perform one's duty perfunctorily or adopt an insincere attitude towards others

fú

伏(动)[fú]
①bend down; prostrate ②lie in concealment ③submit; cause to submit ④fall (e.g. rise and fall)

〖伏击〗(动)[fújī]
ambush

〖伏特〗(量)[fútè]
volt

〖伏天〗(名)[fútiān]
the hottest days of the year—first, second and third ten days after summer solstice, considered the hottest season

扶(动)[fú]
hold up; support

〖扶持〗(动)[fúchí]
support; help

〖扶老携幼〗[fúlǎoxiéyòu]
help the aged and the young

〖扶贫脱贫〗[fúpíntuōpín]
aid poverty-stricken regions to shake off poverty

〖扶手〗(名)[fúshǒu]
railing; hand-rail; armrest; banisters

〖扶植〗(动)[fúzhí]
nurse and strengthen; foster; back

〖扶助〗(动)[fúzhù]
foster; help; aid; assist

拂[fú]
〖拂晓〗(名)[fúxiǎo]
dawn

服(动)[fú]
① serve ② take; swallow (medicine) ③ convince
〖服从〗(动)[fúcóng]
obey; subordinate
〖服服帖帖〗(形)[fúfútiētiē]
obedient; resignedly
〖服气〗(动)[fúqì]
be convinced; accept inwardly
〖服务〗(动)[fúwù]
serve; render service
〖服务行业〗[fúwù hángyè]
service trades
〖服务员〗(名)[fúwùyuán]
service personnel; attendant
〖服务站〗(名)[fúwùzhàn]
service station; service centre
〖服役〗[fú yì]
service; do military service
〖服装〗(名)[fúzhuāng]
clothes; dress
〖服罪〗[fúzuì]
confess oneself to be guilty

俘(动)[fú]
capture
〖俘获〗(动)[fúhuò]
capture (booty)
〖俘虏〗(动、名)[fúlǔ]
capture; prisoner of war

浮(动)[fú]
① float; drift; appear on surface ② exceed; surpass; go beyond
〖浮雕〗(名)[fúdiāo]
bas-relief
〖浮动〗(动)[fúdòng]
① float ② be restless; unstable
〖浮动汇率〗[fúdònghuìlǜ]
floating exchange rate
〖浮光掠影〗[fúguānglüèyǐng]
reflected light and brushing shadow; (fig.) a dim impression which vanishes easily
〖浮华〗(形)[fúhuá]
extravagant; showy
〖浮夸〗(动)[fúkuā]
boast; exaggerate
〖浮力〗(名)[fúlì]
buoyancy
〖浮浅〗(形)[fúqiǎn]
shallow; superficial
〖浮现〗(动)[fúxiàn]
appear (of memory, image)
〖浮云〗(名)[fúyún]
passing clouds; symbol of insubstantiality
〖浮躁〗(形)[fúzào]
impetuous; restless
〖浮肿〗(动)[fúzhǒng]
swell

符(动)[fú]
conform; agree; coincide
〖符号〗(名)[fúhào]
marks; signs
〖符合〗(动)[fúhé]

be in keeping with; conform; tally with

幅(量)[fú]
a measure word (for painting, map)
〖幅度〗(名)[fúdù]
extent
〖幅员〗(名)[fúyuán]
size of territory

辐[fú]
〖辐射〗(动)[fúshè]
radiate

福(名)[fú]
happiness; good luck; prosperity
〖福利〗(名)[fúlì]
welfare; well-being

fǔ

抚[fǔ]
〖抚摩〗(动)[fǔmó]
stroke; fondle
〖抚恤〗(动)[fǔxù]
compensate; commiserate and help
〖抚养〗(动)[fǔyǎng]
bring up; be under (sb.'s) care
〖抚育〗(动)[fǔyù]
bring up;

斧(名)[fǔ]
axe
〖斧子〗(名)[fǔzi]〔把 bǎ〕
axe

俯(动)[fǔ]
bend
〖俯冲〗(动)[fǔchōng]
bend and dash ahead; dive (e.g. diving attack)
〖俯拾即是〗[fǔshíjíshì]
easily obtainable; available everywhere
〖俯首帖耳〗[fǔshǒutiē'ěr]
submissive; servile

釜[fǔ]
〖釜底抽薪〗[fǔdǐchōuxīn]
take away the firewood from under a cauldron to prevent the water from boiling; take drastic measures to deal with a situation (prevent disaster); a fundamental solution

辅[fǔ]
〖辅导〗(动)[fǔdǎo]
coach; guide
〖辅导员〗(名)[fǔdǎoyuán]
tutor; coach; instructor
〖辅音〗(名)[fǔyīn]
consonant
〖辅助〗(动)[fǔzhù]
assist; supplement

腐[fǔ]
〖腐败〗(形)[fǔbài]
corrupt; rotten
〖腐化〗(动)[fǔhuà]
corrupt; degenerate

F

〖腐烂〗(动)[fǔlàn]
vitiate; decay; rot
〖腐蚀〗(动)[fǔshí]
corrupt; be corroded; slowly worn out
〖腐朽〗(形)[fǔxiǔ]
decadent; rotten to the core

fù

讣[fù]
〖讣电〗(名)[fùdiàn]
obituary notice by telegram
〖讣告〗(名)[fùgào]
obituary notice

F

父(名)[fù]
father
〖父母〗(名)[fùmǔ]
father and mother; parents
〖父女〗(名)[fùnǚ]
father and daughter
〖父亲〗(名)[fùqīn]
father
〖父子〗(名)[fùzǐ]
father and son

付(动)[fù]
①give; hand over ②pay
〖付出〗(动)[fùchū]
pay out
〖付印〗(动)[fùyìn]
send to press
〖付诸东流〗[fùzhūdōngliú]
bury in oblivion; cast to the winds
〖付诸实施〗[fùzhūshíshī]
be carried out; put into execution

负(动、形)[fù]
① carry; shoulder ② owe ③ defeat ④ minus; negative
〖负担〗(动、名)[fùdān]
bear (burden); assume; undertake; shoulder burden; load; encumbrances
〖负电〗(名)[fùdiàn]
negative electricity
〖负号〗(名)[fùhào]
the minus sign
〖负荷〗(名)[fùhè]
load; capacity
〖负伤〗[fù shāng]
wounded; injured
〖负数〗(名)[fùshù]
(algebra) negative quantity; negative number
〖负隅顽抗〗[fùyúwánkàng]
resist desperately; make a last ditch fight
〖负约〗[fù yuē]
break one's promise; fail in treaty or obligation
〖负责〗(动、形)[fùzé]
responsible; be responsible
〖负债〗[fù zhài]
owe debts

妇(名)[fù]
woman
〖妇产科〗(名)[fùchǎnkē]
maternity department
〖妇女〗(名)[fùnǚ]
woman
〖妇女节〗(名)[Fùnǚjié]

Women's Day

附(动)[fù]
adhere to; attach to
〖附带〗(动)[fùdài]
① be supplementary; be appended to ② (do sth.) in passing
〖附和〗(动)[fùhè]
follow; echo; parrot; go along with
〖附加〗(动)[fùjiā]
add; supplement; attach; additional; supplementary
〖附件〗(名)[fùjiàn]
annex; appendix; enclosure
〖附近〗(名)[fùjìn]
neighbourhood; nearby
〖附录〗(名)[fùlù]
appendix
〖附设〗(动)[fùshè]
be attached or affiliated to
〖附属〗(动)[fùshǔ]
depend on; attach to; subordinate
〖附庸〗(名)[fùyōng]
rump; appendage; subservient towards

赴(动)[fù]
attend; go to
〖赴汤蹈火〗[fùtāngdǎohuǒ]
jump into hot water or walk through fire; (fig.) undaunted by danger; go through thick and thin

复(动)[fù]
① restore; return to sth. ② reply ③ multi-; poly-
〖复辟〗(动)[fùbì]
stage a come-back; restoration; resurgence
〖复查〗(动)[fùchá]
recheck
〖复仇〗[fù chóu]
revenge
〖复发〗(动)[fùfā]
recur; (old disease) comes back again
〖复古〗[fù gǔ]
restoration of ancient ways; back to the ancients
〖复合句〗(名)[fùhéjù]
complex sentence
〖复合元音〗[fùhé yuányīn]
compound vowel
〖复活〗(动)[fùhuó]
revive
〖复刊〗[fù kān]
re-issue (periodical)
〖复述〗(动)[fùshù]
retell
〖复数〗(名)[fùshù]
plural number
〖复习〗(动)[fùxí]
review
〖复写〗(动)[fùxiě]
duplicate; make copies
〖复兴〗(动)[fùxīng]
restore; revive
〖复印〗(动)[fùyìn]
Xerox; duplicate; photocopy
〖复印机〗(名)[fùyìnjī]
Xerox; duplicator; photocopier
〖复员〗(动)[fùyuán]

demobilize

〖复原〗(动)[fùyuán]
restore to health; restore

〖复杂〗(形)[fùzá]
complicated; complex

〖复杂化〗(动)[fùzáhuà]
complicate

〖复制〗(动)[fùzhì]
reproduce; duplicate

副(形、量)[fù]
① subsidiary; incidental; accessory ② vice-; deputy- ③ a measure word, set, pair (e.g. for spectacles; playing cards, gloves, etc.)

〖副本〗(名)[fùběn]
duplicate; copy; transcript

〖副产品〗(名)[fùchǎnpǐn]
by-products; subsidiary products

〖副词〗(名)[fùcí]
adverb

〖副刊〗(名)[fùkān]
supplement

〖副食〗(名)[fùshí]
foodstuff such as meat, fish, vegetable, etc.

〖副业〗(名)[fùyè]
side-line occupation

〖副作用〗(名)[fùzuòyòng]
deleterious effect; side-effect

赋(名)[fù]
①tax ②verse

〖赋税〗(名)[fùshuì]
tax; levy

〖赋予〗(动)[fùyǔ]
give; endow; entrust

富(形)[fù]
wealthy; rich; abundant

〖富丽〗(形)[fùlì]
grand; magnificent

〖富农〗(名)[fùnóng]
rich peasant (the term 富农 ref-ers to original class status, not present economic position)

〖富强〗(形)[fùqiáng]
prosperous and strong

〖富饶〗(形)[fùráo]
rich; bountiful

〖富庶〗(形)[fùshù]
rich and abundant

〖富有〗(形、动)[fùyǒu]
wealthy; be wealthy

〖富于〗(动)[fùyú]
be full of

〖富裕〗(形)[fùyù]
wealthy; well-to-do

〖富裕中农〗[fùyù zhōngnóng]
well-to-do middle peasants (the term 富裕中农 refers to original class status, not present economic position)

〖富余〗(形、动)[fùyu]
having enough to spare; have more to spare

〖富足〗(形)[fùzú]
rich; well-off

腹(名)[fù]

abdomen

〖腹背受敌〗[fùbèishòudí]

be attacked front and rear

覆 [fù]

〖覆盖〗(动)[fùgài]

cover

〖覆灭〗(动)[fùmiè]

collapse completely; downfall

〖覆没〗(动)[fùmò]

① (of ship) capsize ② annihilate

F

G

gā

旮[gā]

〖旮旯儿〗(名)[gālár]
an out of the way corner; a secluded spot

gāi

该(助动、动、代)[gāi]
① should; ought to ② owe (sb. sth.) ③ that (person, organisation, etc.)

gǎi

改(动)[gǎi]
① change ② correct ③ repent; amend

〖改编〗(动)[gǎibiān]
① (of lit. works) adapt; revise and rewrite ② regroup; reorganize (troops)

〖改变〗(动、名)[gǎibiàn]
change; alter

〖改朝换代〗[gǎicháohuàndài]
change of dynasty

〖改革〗(动、名)[gǎigé]
reform; change; innovation

〖改观〗(动)[gǎiguān]
present a new look; be quite different from

〖改过〗(动)[gǎiguò]
repent; reform

〖改过自新〗[gǎiguòzìxīn]
correct one's errors and make a fresh start; amend one's ways; turn over a new leaf

〖改行〗[gǎi háng]
change to new occupation

〖改换〗(动)[gǎihuàn]
change; transform; turn over

〖改悔〗(动)[gǎihuǐ]
repent; amend

〖改进〗(动、名)[gǎijìn]
improve; improvement

〖改良〗(动、名)[gǎiliáng]
reform; make only superficial changes; improve; reform; improvement

〖改良主义〗(名)[gǎiliángzhǔyì]
reformism
〖改期〗[gǎi qī]
change the date; change the scheduled time
〖改善〗(动、名)[gǎishàn]
improve; better (the state of affairs); improvement
〖改天换地〗[gǎitiānhuàndì]
transform heaven and earth; remake nature
〖改头换面〗[gǎitóuhuànmiàn]
change the outside only; make only superficial changes; disguise; camourflage
〖改弦更张〗[gǎixiángēngzhāng]
make a fresh start; change course
〖改邪归正〗[gǎixiéguīzhèng]
give up evil ways and return to the right; mend one's ways
〖改造〗(动)[gǎizào]
transform; remould
〖改正〗(动)[gǎizhèng]
correct
〖改锥〗(名)[gǎizhuī]〔把 bǎ〕
screw-driver
〖改组〗(动)[gǎizǔ]
reorganize; reshuffle

gài

盖(动、名)[gài]
①cover②build③cover; lid
〖盖棺论定〗[gàiguānlùndìng]
(lit.) when his coffin is covered all discussion about him can be settled; (fig.) only when a person is dead can he be finally judged and assessed
〖盖子〗(名)[gàizi]
cover of a container; lid

概[gài]
〖概况〗(名)[gàikuàng]
general conditions; basic facts
〖概括〗(动)[gàikuò]
generalize; summarize
〖概略〗(名、形)[gàilüè]
brief outline
〖概论〗(名)[gàilùn]
summary; outline
〖概念〗(名)[gàiniàn]
concept; notion; idea
〖概念化〗(动)[gàiniànhuà]
in abstract terms
〖概述〗(动)[gàishù]
deal with... in general outline
〖概数〗(名)[gàishù]
approximate number
〖概要〗(名)[gàiyào]
summary; outline

gān

干(形)[gān]
dried; dry
另见 gàn
〖干巴巴〗(形)[gānbābā]
dry; dull; insipid
〖干杯〗[gān bēi]
drink a toast
〖干瘪〗(形)[gānbiě]
colourless; dry and cracked; wizened

〖干脆〗(形)［gāncuì］
clearcut; straightforward; frank
〖干旱〗(形)［gānhàn］
dry spells; drought
〖干涸〗(动)［gānhé］
dried up
〖干净〗(形)［gānjìng］
①clean ②all finished
〖干枯〗(形)［gānkū］
withered
〖干粮〗(名)［gānliáng］
readymade food for journey
〖干扰〗(动、名)［gānrǎo］
interfere with; jam (broadcasts); interference
〖干涉〗(动)［gānshè］
interfere
〖干预〗(动)［gānyù］
intervene; meddle in
〖干燥〗(形)［gānzào］
dry

甘［gān］

〖甘拜下风〗［gānbàixiàfēng］
willingly acknowledge defeat
〖甘居中游〗［gānjūzhōngyóu］
rest content with remaining mid-stream without making further advance
〖甘苦〗(名)［gānkǔ］
weal and woe; joy and sorrow
〖甘心〗(动)［gānxīn］
be reconciled to; resign oneself to
〖甘心情愿〗［gānxīnqíngyuàn］
willingly and gladly
〖甘休〗(动)［gānxiū］
willing to let it go; take it lying down
〖甘愿〗(助动)［gānyuàn］
willing to
〖甘蔗〗(名)［gānzhe］
sugarcane

杆(名)［gān］

pole
另见 gǎn
〖杆子〗(名)［gānzi］〔根 gēn〕
pole

肝(名)［gān］

liver
〖肝胆相照，荣辱与共〗
［gāndǎnxiāngzhào，róngrǔyǔgòng］
treat each other with all sincerity and share weal and woe
〖肝火〗(名)［gānhuǒ］
irritability; irritation; fretfulness; peevishness
〖肝炎〗(名)［gānyán］
hepatitis
〖肝脏〗(名)［gānzàng］
the liver

尴［gān］

〖尴尬〗(形)［gāngà］
awkward; embarrasing

gǎn

杆(名、量)［gǎn］

① stick ② a measure word (usually for things with a barrel or stick)

另见 gān

赶(动) [gǎn]
①drive (a cart) ②hurry on or up
〖赶超〗(动) [gǎnchāo]
catch up with and surpass
〖赶车〗[gǎn chē]
drive a cart
〖赶集〗[gǎn jí]
go to the village fair
〖赶紧〗(副) [gǎnjǐn]
hurriedly
〖赶快〗(副) [gǎnkuài]
in a hurry; hurriedly; hurry up
〖赶路〗[gǎn lù]
hurry on one's way
〖赶忙〗(副) [gǎnmáng]
haste; hurriedly
〖赶任务〗[gǎn rènwù]
get one's work done hurriedly; hurry one's work
〖赶时髦〗[gǎn shímáo]
follow the fashions

敢(助动) [gǎn]
dare
〖敢于〗(动) [gǎnyú]
dare to
〖敢字当头〗[gǎnzìdāngtóu]
put daring above all else

感[gǎn]
〖感触〗(名) [gǎnchù]
stirring of emotion; deep feeling; move
〖感到〗(动) [gǎndào]
feel; realize
〖感动〗(动) [gǎndòng]
move; touch
〖感恩戴德〗[gǎn'ēndàidé]
be grateful for
〖感官〗(名) [gǎnguān]
organs of sense
〖感光〗[gǎn guāng]
affected by light; photo-sensitive
〖感化〗(动) [gǎnhuà]
convert (a person)
〖感激〗(动) [gǎnjī]
be grateful; be obliged; gratitude
〖感激涕零〗[gǎnjītìlíng]
so grateful as to shed tears
〖感觉〗(动、名) [gǎnjué]
sense; perceive; feel; sense of perception; sensation
〖感慨〗(名) [gǎnkǎi]
deeply touched
〖感冒〗(动、名) [gǎnmào]
catch cold; influenza
〖感情〗(名) [gǎnqíng]
feelings; emotion; sentiment
〖感情用事〗[gǎnqíngyòngshì]
give way to one's feelings; abandon oneself to emotion
〖感染〗(动) [gǎnrǎn]
①be infected by ②influence or be influenced by
〖感人〗(形) [gǎnrén]
moving; touching
〖感受〗(名、动) [gǎnshòu]
impression; be affected by; be impressed with
〖感叹词〗(名) [gǎntàncí]

G

interjection
〖感叹号〗(名)[gǎntànhào]
exclamation mark
〖感叹句〗(名)[gǎntànjù]
exclamatory sentence
〖感想〗(名)[gǎnxiǎng]
impression; feeling
〖感谢〗(动)[gǎnxiè]
thank; be grateful; be obliged
〖感性〗(名)[gǎnxìng]
the perceptual
〖感应〗(动)[gǎnyìng]
① (electr.) induct; induction ② be moved to response through the feelings and affections
〖感召〗(动)[gǎnzhào]
inspire; rally (sb.) to a worthy cause

G

gàn

干(动、名)[gàn]
① do; work; make ② trunk; stem
另见 gān
〖干部〗(名)[gànbù]
cadre
〖干活〗[gàn huó]
work; labour
〖干将〗(名)[gànjiàng]
a capable or daring man
〖干劲〗(名)[gànjìn]
vigour; energy; drive
〖干练〗(形)[gànliàn]
experienced in managing affairs
〖干事〗(名)[gànshi]
staff member; executive
〖干线〗(名)[gànxiàn]
trunk line; main line

gāng

刚(形、副)[gāng]
① hard; unyielding ② just; only just; barely
〖刚愎自用〗[gāngbìzìyòng]
obstinate and self-opinionated; set in one's ways
〖刚才〗(名)[gāngcái]
just; just now; a very short time ago
〖刚刚〗(副)[gānggāng]
just; as soon as; just now; a short while ago; no sooner
〖刚劲〗(形)[gāngjìng]
rigid; straight and powerful
〖刚强〗(形)[gāngqiáng]
firm and uncompromising
〖刚毅〗(形)[gāngyì]
resolute and firm; fortitude
〖刚直〗(形)[gāngzhí]
upright; upright and tenacious

肛[gāng]
〖肛门〗(名)[gāngmén]
anus

纲(名)[gāng]
① the main rope of a net ② key link
〖纲举目张〗[gāngjǔmùzhāng]
Once the key link is grasped, everything falls into place.
〖纲领〗(名)[gānglǐng]
programme
〖纲目〗(名)[gāngmù]

①outline; programme ②outline and details
〖纲要〗(名)[gāngyào]
programme; summary; outline

钢(名)[gāng]
steel
〖钢板〗(名)[gāngbǎn]〔块 kuài〕
①steel plate; steel sheet ②a stencil plate; steel engraving
〖钢笔〗(名)[gāngbǐ]〔枝 zhī〕
pen; fountain pen
〖钢材〗(名)[gāngcái]
rolled steel
〖钢锭〗(名)[gāngdìng]
steel ingot
〖钢管〗(名)[gāngguǎn]〔根 gēn〕
steel tube
〖钢筋〗(名)[gāngjīn]
steel bar
〖钢盔〗(名)[gāngkuī]〔顶 dǐng〕
steel helmet
〖钢钎〗(名)[gāngqiān]
jack hammer; drill
〖钢琴〗(名)[gāngqín]〔架 jià〕
piano
〖钢水〗(名)[gāngshuǐ]
molten steel
〖钢丝〗(名)[gāngsī]
steel wire
〖钢铁〗(名)[gāngtiě]
iron and steel

缸(名)[gāng]
crock; jar

gǎng

岗(名)[gǎng]
①mound ②sentry; a guard post
〖岗楼〗(名)[gǎnglóu]
watch tower
〖岗哨〗(名)[gǎngshào]
sentry; sentinel
〖岗位〗(名)[gǎngwèi]
post (e.g. stick to one's post)
〖岗位责任制〗[gǎngwèizérènzhì]
system of job (post) responsibility; system of specific individual responsibility for each part of a task

港(名)[gǎng]
port
〖港口〗(名)[gǎngkǒu]
port; harbour
〖港湾〗(名)[gǎngwān]
bay

gàng

杠(名)[gàng]
bar
〖杠杆〗(名)[gànggǎn]
lever
〖杠子〗(名)[gàngzi]〔根 gēn〕
bar; cudgel; a stout pole for two persons to carry things

gāo

高(形)[gāo]
high; tall (person)
〖高昂〗(形)[gāo'áng]
① (of voice, spirits) high ② expensive; dear
〖高傲〗(形)[gāo'ào]
arrogant; haughty; proud

〖高不可攀〗[gāobùkěpān]
too high to climb; sth.difficult to attain
〖高产〗(形)[gāochǎn]
high-yield
〖高产作物〗[gāochǎn zuòwù]
high-yield crops
〖高超〗(形)[gāochāo]
superb; exquisite
〖高潮〗(名)[gāocháo]
high tide; upsurge; climax
〖高大〗(形)[gāodà]
lofty; high and noble; tall
〖高等〗(形)[gāoděng]
high; advanced; high degree
〖高低〗(名)[gāodī]
height; pitch; a state of being superior or inferior
〖高低杠〗(名)[gāodīgàng]
uneven bars; asymmetrical bars
〖高地〗(名)[gāodì]
height; hill
〖高调〗(名)[gāodiào]
highpitch; bombastic words
〖高度〗(名、副)[gāodù]
height; a high degree; highly
〖高分子〗(名)[gāofēnzǐ]
high polymer
〖高峰〗(名)[gāofēng]
climax; peak
〖高高在上〗[gāogāozàishàng]
hold oneself aloof; sit up on high
〖高歌猛进〗[gāogēměngjìn]
march foward in triumph
〖高官厚禄〗[gāoguānhòulù]
high position and handsome salary
〖高贵〗(形)[gāoguì]
noble; elated
〖高呼〗(动)[gāohū]
shout
〖高级〗(形)[gāojí]
high-grade (steel); high-quality; senior; high-ranking; superb; high stage
〖高级社〗(名)[gāojíshè]
advanced agricultural producers' cooperative
〖高价〗(名)[gāojià]
high price
〖高架公路〗[gāojià gōnglù]
flyover; overpass
〖高架桥〗[gāojiàqiáo]
viaduct
〖高架铁路〗[gāojià tiělù]
overhead railway; elevated railroad
〖高见〗(名)[gāojiàn]
wise ideas
〖高精尖〗(形、名)[gāo jīng jiān]
high-grade, precision and advanced
〖高空作业〗[gāokōng zuòyè]
working in high altitude
〖高利贷〗(名)[gāolìdài]
usury
〖高利盘剥〗[gāolì pánbō]
exploit at high interest
〖高粱〗(名)[gāoliáng]
kaoliang; sorghum
〖高龄〗(名)[gāolíng]
advanced age
〖高炉〗(名)[gāolú]
blast furnace
〖高明〗(形)[gāomíng]

wise; brilliant; bright
〖高尚〗(形) [gāoshàng]
respectable; noble-minded
〖高烧〗(名) [gāoshāo]
high fever
〖高射炮〗(名) [gāoshèpào]
〔门 mén〕
anti-aircraft gun
〖高深〗(形) [gāoshēn]
profound; advanced
〖高耸〗(动) [gāosǒng]
lofty; high; towering
〖高速〗(形) [gāosù]
high speed; speedy
〖高速公路〗[gāosù gōnglù]
expressway; express highway
〖高谈阔论〗[gāotánkuòlùn]
harangue; loud and bombastic talk
〖高温〗(名) [gāowēn]
high temperature
〖高屋建瓴〗[gāowūjiànlíng]
press on irresistibly from a commanding height
〖高薪阶层〗[gāoxīn jiēcéng]
high-salaried stratum
〖高兴〗(形) [gāoxìng]
glad; pleased; happy; elated
〖高血压〗(名) [gāoxuèyā]
hypertension
〖高压〗(名) [gāoyā]
high pressure; high-handedly
〖高压线〗(名) [gāoyāxiàn]
high tension line
〖高原〗(名) [gāoyuán]
plateau
〖高瞻远瞩〗[gāozhānyuǎnzhǔ]
look far ahead and aim high; take a broad and long view; far-sighted
〖高涨〗(动) [gāozhǎng]
surge forward; run high
〖高枕无忧〗[gāozhěnwúyōu]
retire or rest without worries; (fig.) relax one's vigilance
〖高中〗(名) [gāozhōng]
senior middle school; high school

膏 (名) [gāo]
fat; grease; ointment; plaster
〖膏药〗(名) [gāoyao]〔帖 tiě〕
plaster (medicine)

gǎo

搞 (动) [gǎo]
do; make; get
〖搞鬼〗[gǎo guǐ]
play tricks

镐 (名) [gǎo]〔把 bǎ〕
pick

稿 (名) [gǎo]
manuscripts for publication
〖稿件〗(名) [gǎojiàn]
manuscripts for publication
〖稿纸〗(名) [gǎozhǐ]〔张 zhāng〕
manuscript paper
〖稿子〗(名) [gǎozi]〔篇 piān〕
manuscripts for publication

gào

告 (动) [gào]
① tell; inform ② announce ③

ask for; seek ④ sue; indict
〖告别〗(动) [gàobié]
take leave; bid farewell; say goodbye
〖告辞〗(动) [gàocí]
take leave; say goodbye
〖告急〗(动) [gàojí]
make an emergency request for help
〖告捷〗(动) [gàojié]
announce a victory; win a victory
〖告诫〗(动) [gàojiè]
warn; enjoin; counsel
〖告密〗[gào mì]
give secret information against sb.
〖告示〗(名)[gàoshi]〔张 zhāng〕
notice; notification
〖告诉〗(动) [gàosu]
tell; inform; make known
〖告终〗(动) [gàozhōng]
conclude; end up
〖告状〗[gào zhuàng]
① sue; indict ② bring a suit against; go to law; file a suit; bring an action against ③ lodge complaints; complain of one's grievances

gē

戈 (名) [gē]
spear; lance
〖戈壁〗(名) [gēbì]
the Gobi Desert

疙 [gē]
〖疙瘩〗(名) [gēda]〔个 gè〕
① pimple; knot ② knotty problem

哥 (名) [gē]
elder brother
〖哥哥〗(名) [gēge]
elder brother

胳 [gē]
〖胳膊〗(名) [gēbo]〔只 zhī〕
arm

搁 (动) [gē]
① place; lay; keep; preserve ② postpone; shelve; put aside
〖搁浅〗[gē qiǎn]
① run aground; run ashore ② be stranded
〖搁置〗(动) [gēzhì]
shelve; put off

割 (动) [gē]
cut; sever
〖割爱〗(动) [gē'ài]
give away or part with what one loves
〖割断〗(动) [gēduàn]
cut apart; chop up; lop off
〖割据〗(动) [gējù]
set up a separationist rule; set up a separate regime by force of arms
〖割裂〗(动) [gēliè]
carve up; sever; separate
〖割让〗(动) [gēràng]
cede (a territory)

鸽(名)[gē]
dove
〖鸽子〗(名)[gēzi]〔只 zhī〕
dove

歌(名)[gē]〔个 gè、支 zhī〕
song
〖歌唱〗(动)[gēchàng]
sing
〖歌词〗(名)[gēcí]〔首 shǒu〕
words of a song
〖歌功颂德〗[gēgōngsòngdé]
flattery and exaggerated praise; praise and eulogy
〖歌剧〗(名)[gējù]
opera
〖歌谱〗(名)[gēpǔ]
music of a song
〖歌曲〗(名)[gēqǔ]〔支 zhī〕
song
〖歌声〗(名)[gēshēng]
singing (e.g. a singing voice)
〖歌手〗(名)[gēshǒu]
singer
〖歌颂〗(动)[gēsòng]
eulogize; sing in praise of; extol
〖歌舞〗(名)[gēwǔ]
song and dance
〖歌谣〗(名)[gēyáo]〔首 shǒu〕
ballads (songs)
〖歌咏〗(名)[gēyǒng]
singing

gé

革(名、动)[gé]
①leather ②dismiss; transform
〖革除〗(动)[géchú]
excommunicate; get rid of; dismiss
〖革命〗(动、名)[gémìng]
make revolution; revolution
〖革命化〗(动)[gémìnghuà]
revolutionize
〖革命家〗(名)[gémìngjiā]
a revolutionary
〖革命浪漫主义〗
[gémìng làngmànzhǔyì]
revolutionary romanticism
〖革命乐观主义〗
[gémìng lèguān zhǔyì]
revolutionary optimism
〖革命派〗(名)[gémìngpài]
revolutionary group; revolutionaries
〖革命人道主义〗
[gémìng réndào zhǔyì]
revolutionary humanism
〖革命圣地〗[gémìng shèngdì]
sacred place of revolution
〖革命现实主义〗
[gémìng xiàn shí zhǔ yì]
revolutionary realism
〖革命性〗(名)[gémìngxìng]
revolutionary quality; revolutionary spirit
〖革命烈士〗(名)[gémìng liè shì]
revolutionary martyr
〖革命英雄主义〗
[gémìng yīng xióngzhǔyì]
revolutionary heroism
〖革命者〗(名)[gémìngzhě]
a revolutionary
〖革新〗(动、名)[géxīn]

renovate; transform; reform; innovation
〖革职〗[gé zhí]
dismiss; remove; discharge

阁(名)[gé]
① a chamber; a storied building ② the cabinet
〖阁楼〗(名)[gélóu]
garret
〖阁下〗(名)[géxià]
(Your, His) Excellency

格(名)[gé]
① square ② (gram.) case ③ form; pattern
〖格格不入〗[gégébùrù]
misfits; like square pegs in round holes; alien to
〖格局〗(名)[géjú]
style; manner; arrangement
〖格律〗(名)[gélǜ]
set rules
〖格式〗(名)[géshì]
form; pattern
〖格外〗(副)[géwài]
extraordinary; all the more
〖格言〗(名)[géyán]
maxim; proverb; saying

隔(动)[gé]
separate; partition; cut off
〖隔壁〗(名)[gébì]
next door
〖隔断〗(动)[géduàn]
cut off; separate
〖隔阂〗(名)[géhé]
estrangement; alienation; lack of understanding
〖隔绝〗(动)[géjué]
isolate; seal off; prevent... from
〖隔离〗(动)[gélí]
isolate
〖隔膜〗(名)[gémó]
① estrangement; uncongenial; lack of understanding ② diaphragm; septum

gè

个(量)[gè]
a measure word
〖个别〗(形)[gèbié]
(separate) individual; isolated; a few
〖个人〗(名)[gèrén]
individual; personal
〖个人英雄主义〗
[gèrén yīngxióng zhǔyì]
individual heroism
〖个人主义〗(名)[gèrénzhǔyì]
individualism
〖个体〗(名)[gètǐ]
individuality; individual
〖个体户〗(名)[gètǐhù]
individual entrepreneur; self-employed individual or household
〖个体经济〗[gètǐ jīngjì]
individual economy
〖个体劳动者〗[gètǐláodòng zhě]
individual labourer
〖个性〗(名)[gèxìng]
individuality; individual ch-

aracter; individual initiative

〖个子〗(名) [gèzi]
size (a person's stature)

各(代、副) [gè]
① each; every ② separately; respectively

〖各奔前程〗 [gèbènqiánchéng]
each goes his own way; each pursues his onward journey

〖各别〗(形) [gèbié]
different; separate; peculiar

〖各持己见〗 [gèchíjǐjiàn]
each persisting in his own opinion

〖各得其所〗 [gèdéqísuǒ]
each gets his due; each takes its proper place; each plays his proper role; some provision should be made for everyone

〖各个〗 [gè gè]
① each; every ② one by one

〖各个击破〗 [gègèjīpò]
crush one by one

〖各尽所能,按劳分配〗 [gèjìn suǒnéng, ànláofēnpèi]
from each according to his ability, to each according to his work

〖各尽所能,按需分配〗 [gèjìn suǒnéng, ànxūfēnpèi]
from each according to his ability, to each according to his needs

〖各就各位〗 [gèjiùgèwèi]
each to his own position

〖各式各样〗 [gèshìgèyàng]
all kinds of; various; various shades of; invarious ways

〖各抒己见〗 [gèshūjǐjiàn]
each expressing his own views

〖各行其是〗 [gèxíngqíshì]
act as one pleases; each goes his own ways

〖各有千秋〗 [gèyǒuqiānqiū]
each has its merits

〖各种〗 [gèzhǒng]
all sorts of; all varieties of; various

〖各自〗(代) [gèzì]
by oneself

〖各自为政〗 [gèzìwéizhèng]
each goes his own way; lack of coordination

gěi

给(动、介、助) [gěi]
give; offer, extend; for; to; by; with
另见 jǐ

〖给以〗(动) [gěiyǐ]
① give; offer ② deal with

〖给…以…〗 [gěi…yǐ…]
give...with...; deal...with...

gēn

根(名、量) [gēn]
① root ② a measure word, piece, stick, etc.

〖根本〗(名、形) [gēnběn]
① foundation ② root; basic; fundamental; radical; totally; entirely

〖根除〗(动)[gēnchú]
uproot; exterminate; eradicate
〖根底〗(名)[gēndǐ]
① basis; foundation ② the ins and outs
〖根基〗(名)[gēnjī]
foundation; basis
〖根据〗(动、名)[gēnjù]
base on; in accordance with; in the light of; basis; ground; reason
〖根据地〗(名)[gēnjùdì]
base area; base
〖根绝〗(动)[gēnjué]
exterminate; wipe out; eliminate
〖根深蒂固〗[gēnshēndìgù]
deeply rooted; deeply ingrained
〖根源〗(名)[gēnyuán]
source; origin; root
〖根治〗(动)[gēnzhì]
permanent control; fundamental solution

跟(动、介、连)[gēn]
① follow; acompany; catch up with ② to; from; with; and
〖跟前〗(名)[gēnqián]
in front of; nearby
〖跟随〗(动)[gēnsuí]
follow
〖跟头〗(名)[gēntou]
a fall; somersault
〖跟着〗(动、副)[gēnzhe]
follow; in the wake of; immediately; right away
〖跟踪〗(动)[gēnzōng]
tail after; follow in the track of; shadow (sb.)

gēng

更[gēng]
另见 gèng
〖更动〗(动)[gēngdòng]
modify; change
〖更改〗(动)[gēnggǎi]
alter; change
〖更换〗(动)[gēnghuàn]
replace; change
〖更替〗(动)[gēngtì]
substitute
〖更新〗(动)[gēngxīn]
renew
〖更衣室〗(名)[gēngyīshì]
dressing room
〖更正〗(动)[gēngzhèng]
make corrections; amend

耕(动)[gēng]
plough; cultivate
〖耕畜〗(名)[gēngchù]
draught animals
〖耕地〗(名)[gēngdì]
farmland; cultivated fields
〖耕具〗(名)[gēngjù]
farming tools
〖耕种〗(动)[gēngzhòng]
plough and sow; work on the farm

gěng

耿[gěng]
〖耿耿于怀〗[gěnggěngyúhuái]
sick at heart; stick in one's throat

〖耿直〗(形) [gěngzhí]
fair and just; upright

哽 [gěng]
〖哽咽〗(动) [gěngyè]
sob

梗 (名) [gěng]
the stem of a plant
〖梗概〗(名) [gěnggài]
outline
〖梗塞〗(动) [gěngsè]
obstruct
〖梗阻〗(动) [gěngzǔ]
impede; hinder; obstruct

gèng

更 (副) [gèng]
still; furthermore
另见 gēng
〖更加〗(副) [gèngjiā]
to a higher degree; still further; even more
〖更上一层楼〗
[gèngshàngyī cénglóu]
(lit.) go up a storey still higher; (fig.) strive for further improvement

gōng

工 (名) [gōng]
① industry; work ② man-days
〖工本〗(名) [gōngběn]
cost of production
〖工厂〗(名) [gōngchǎng]
factory; plant; mill; works
〖工潮〗(名) [gōngcháo]
worker strike
〖工程〗(名) [gōngchéng]
〔项 xiàng〕
construction work; project; job of work
〖工程兵〗(名) [gōngchéng bīng]
engineer corps
〖工程师〗(名) [gōngchéngshī]
engineer
〖工地〗(名) [gōngdì]
work site; construction site
〖工段〗(名) [gōngduàn]
working section
〖工分〗(名) [gōngfēn]
workpoint
〖工夫〗(名) [gōngfu]
① labour; effort; time ② ability; skill
〖工会〗(名) [gōnghuì]
trade union
〖工具〗(名) [gōngjù]
tool; instrument; means
〖工具书〗(名) [gōngjùshū]
〔本 běn〕
reference books (dictionary, etc.)
〖工龄〗(名) [gōnglíng]
working years; length of service
〖工农差别〗 [gōngnóng chābié]
difference between workers and peasants
〖工农联盟〗 [gōngnóngliánméng]
worker-peasant alliance; the alliance of workers and peasants
〖工人〗(名) [gōngrén]

G

worker
〖工人阶级〗(名)[gōngrénjiējí]
working class
〖工人运动〗[gōngrényùndòng]
labour movement; the workers' movement
〖工伤〗(名)[gōngshāng]
be injured while performing duty
〖工时〗(名)[gōngshí]
work hours
〖工事〗(名)[gōngshì]
defence works; entrenchment
〖工效〗(名)[gōngxiào]
working efficiency
〖工效挂钩〗[gōngxiàoguàgōu]
practice of linking pay to performance
〖工薪阶层〗[gōngxīnjiēcéng]
residents living off their salaries; salaried man
〖工序〗(名)[gōngxù]
working process
〖工业〗(名)[gōngyè]
industry
〖工业化〗(动)[gōngyèhuà]
industrialize; industrialization
〖工艺〗(名)[gōngyì]
technology; craftsmanship
〖工艺美术〗[gōngyì měishù]
industrial arts; arts and crafts
〖工艺品〗(名)[gōngyìpǐn]
product of craftsmanship
〖工贼〗(名)[gōngzéi]
scab; strike breaker; blackleg
〖工整〗(形)[gōngzhěng]
neat and orderly
〖工种〗(名)[gōngzhǒng]
kind of work; branch of work
〖工资〗(名)[gōngzī]
wage; salary
〖工作〗(动、名)[gōngzuò]
work; job
〖工作服〗(名)[gōngzuòfú]〔件 jiàn〕
overalls
〖工作面〗(名)[gōngzuòmiàn]
working faces
〖工作母机〗[gōngzuò mǔjī]
machine-tool
〖工作日〗(名)[gōngzuòrì]
working day

弓(名)[gōng]
bow
〖弓箭〗(名)[gōngjiàn]
bow and arrow

公(名)[gōng]
public
〖公安〗(名)[gōng'ān]
public security
〖公安部队〗[gōng'ān bùduì]
public security forces
〖公报〗(名)[gōngbào]
communiqué; bulletin
〖公倍数〗(名)[gōngbèishù]
common multiple
〖公布〗(动)[gōngbù]
issue; publish; announce
〖公尺〗(量)[gōngchǐ]
metre
〖公道〗(形)[gōngdào]

fair; just
〖公敌〗(名)[gōngdí]
enemy of the people; common enemy
〖公费〗(名)[gōngfèi]
free service (e.g. free medical treatment)
〖公费医疗〗[gōngfèi yīliáo]
free medical treatment
〖公分〗(量)[gōngfēn]
centimetre
〖公愤〗(名)[gōngfèn]
public indignation
〖公告〗(名)[gōnggào]
public announcement; bulletin; notice; communiqué
〖公公〗(名)[gōnggong]
father-in-law (husband's father)
〖公共〗(形)[gōnggòng]
public
〖公共汽车〗[gōnggòng qìchē]〔辆 liàng〕
bus
〖公关〗(名)[gōngguān]
public relation
〖公海〗(名)[gōnghǎi]
high seas
〖公函〗(名)[gōnghán]
official document
〖公积金〗(名)[gōngjījīn]
common reserve fund
〖公祭〗(动)[gōngjì]
public sacrifices; worship
〖公斤〗(量)[gōngjīn]
kilogram
〖公开〗(动、形)[gōngkāi]
open to the public; publicly
〖公款〗(名)[gōngkuǎn]
public funds
〖公里〗(量)[gōnglǐ]
kilometre
〖公理〗(名)[gōnglǐ]
①justice ②axioms
〖公历〗(名)[gōnglì]
the internationally current calender; Gregorian calendar
〖公粮〗(名)[gōngliáng]
public grain; agricultural tax
〖公路〗(名)[gōnglù]〔条 tiáo〕
highway
〖公论〗(名)[gōnglùn]
public opinion
〖公民〗(名)[gōngmín]
citizen
〖公民权〗(名)[gōngmínquán]
civic rights; rights of citizenship
〖公墓〗(名)[gōngmù]
public cemetery
〖公平〗(形)[gōngpíng]
just; fair
〖公仆〗(名)[gōngpú]
public servant
〖公顷〗(量)[gōngqǐng]
hectare
〖公然〗(副)[gōngrán]
openly; brazenly; undisguised
〖公认〗(动)[gōngrèn]
universally acknowledge or recognize
〖公审〗(动)[gōngshěn]
public trial
〖公使〗(名)[gōngshǐ]
minister (diplomatic representative accredited by one state

to another)

〚公式〛(名)[gōngshì]
formula

〚公事〛(名)[gōngshì]
public affairs; official business

〚公事公办〛[gōngshìgōngbàn]
do official business according to official principles; not to let personal consideration interfere with one's execution of public duty

〚公式化〛(动)[gōngshìhuà]
formularize; formulate; formularization

〚公司〛(名)[gōngsī]
company

〚公私合营〛[gōngsī héyíng]
jointly run by the state and private owner; joint state-private owned enterprises

〚公文〛(名)[gōngwén]
official document

〚公物〛(名)[gōngwù]
public property; public asset

〚公务员〛(名)[gōngwùyuán]
public servant

〚公演〛(动)[gōngyǎn]
perform in public

〚公益金〛(名)[gōngyìjīn]
public welfare fund

〚公用〛[gōng yòng]
for public use; for common use; communal

〚公有〛[gōng yǒu]
publicly owned

〚公有制〛(名)[gōngyǒuzhì]
public ownership

〚公寓〛(名)[gōngyù]
apartment house

〚公元〛(名)[gōngyuán]
A.D.

〚公园〛(名)[gōngyuán]
park

〚公约〛(名)[gōngyuē]
pact; convention; pledge

〚公约数〛(名)[gōngyuēshù]
common factor

〚公允〛(形)[gōngyǔn]
fair and just

〚公债〛(名)[gōngzhài]
government bonds

〚公正〛(形)[gōngzhèng]
just; impartial

〚公证〛(名)[gōngzhèng]
notarization

〚公证处〛(名)[gōngzhèngchù]
notary office

〚公众〛(名)[gōngzhòng]
the public

〚公转〛(动)[gōngzhuàn]
revolve (e.g. round the sun)

功(名)[gōng]
① meritorious deeds; merit ② virtue; effect

〚功绩〛(名)[gōngjī]
merits; feat; achievement

〚功课〛(名)[gōngkè]
lessons

〚功劳〛(名)[gōngláo]
meritorious deeds; achievement; credit; service

〚功利主义〛(名)[gōnglìzhǔyì]
utilitarianism

〚功能〛(名)[gōngnéng]

function
〖功勋〗(名)[gōngxūn]
meritorious deeds (done for the nation)
〖功用〗(名)[gōngyòng]
function; use

攻(动)[gōng]
attack
〖攻打〗(动)[gōngdǎ]
attack (a place held by the enemy)
〖攻读〗(动)[gōngdú]
study hard; take great pains in study
〖攻击〗(动)[gōngjī]
attack
〖攻坚战〗(名)[gōngjiānzhàn]
battle of storming heavily fortified points
〖攻克〗(动)[gōngkè]
attack and capture; capture
〖攻其不备〗[gōngqíbùbèi]
attack where ... is not prepared
〖攻势〗(名)[gōngshì]
offensive
〖攻无不克〗[gōngwúbùkè]
all conquering attack
〖攻心〗[gōng xīn]
① conquer the mind; work on a person's soft spot to bring him to terms ② cause a shock; produce loss of conciousness

供(动)[gōng]
supply; provide; enshrine
另见 gòng
〖供不应求〗[gōngbùyìngqiú]
supply falls short of demand
〖供给〗(动)[gōngjǐ]
supply; provide; furnish
〖供求〗[gōngqiú]
supply and demand
〖供销〗[gōng xiāo]
supply and marketing
〖供销合作社〗
[gōngxiāohézuòshè]
supply and marketing co-operative
〖供需见面,双向选择〗
[gōngxūjiànmiàn, shuāngxiàngxuǎnzé]
graduates and companies meeting face to face and choosing as both see fit — a system applied in work assignment of graduates
〖供养〗(动)[gōngyǎng]
provide for the needs of one's parents or elders
〖供应〗(动)[gōngyìng]
supply; provide

宫(名)[gōng]
palace
〖宫灯〗(名)[gōngdēng]
palace lantern (a decorative ceiling lamp)
〖宫殿〗(名)[gōngdiàn]〔座 zuò〕
palace
〖宫廷〗(名)[gōngtíng]
royal court
〖宫廷政变〗

[gōngtíng zhèngbiàn]
palace coup

恭 [gōng]
〖恭敬〗(形) [gōngjìng]
respectful
〖恭惟〗(动) [gōngwei]
flatter

gǒng

巩 [gǒng]
〖巩固〗(形、动) [gǒnggù]
firm; solid; stable; consolidated; consolidate; strengthen

拱 (名) [gǒng]
an arch
〖拱桥〗(名)[gǒngqiáo]〔座 zuò〕
arched bridge

gòng

共 (形、动) [gòng]
① common; mutual ② total
〖共产党〗(名)[gòngchǎndǎng]
communist party
〖共产党员〗(名)
[gòngchǎndǎngyuán]
member of the communist party
〖共产国际〗[Gòngchǎn Guójì]
Comintern; Communist International
〖共产主义〗(名)[gòngchǎnzhǔyì]
communism
〖共和国〗(名) [gònghéguó]
republic
〖共鸣〗(名) [gòngmíng]
① acoustic resonance; resonance ② sympathy; echo
〖共事〗(动) [gòngshì]
work together
〖共同〗(形) [gòngtóng]
common; joint
〖共同市场〗[gòngtóngshìchǎng]
Common Market
〖共性〗(名) [gòngxìng]
common characteristics; general character

贡 [gòng]
〖贡献〗(动、名) [gòngxiàn]
contribute; render service; contribution

供 (动) [gòng]
confess
另见 gōng
〖供词〗(名) [gòngcí]
confession
〖供认〗(动) [gòngrèn]
confess

gōu

勾 (动) [gōu]
① expunge ② arouse ③ sketch
另见 gòu
〖勾搭〗(动) [gōuda]
ally oneself with; collude with
〖勾画〗(动) [gōuhuà]
roughly sketch out
〖勾结〗(动) [gōujié]
collude with; collaborate with; work hand in glove; conspire with
〖勾销〗(动) [gōuxiāo]

cancel; blot out; expunge; wipe out
〖勾心斗角〗[gōuxīndòujiǎo]
scheme against each other
〖勾引〗(动)[gōuyǐn]
induce; entice; seduce; lure

沟(名)[gōu]〔条 tiáo〕
ditch; gully
〖沟壑〗(名)[gōuhè]
gully; valley
〖沟渠〗(名)[gōuqú]
ditch; irrigation channel
〖沟通〗(动)[gōutōng]
connect; communicate

钩(名、动)[gōu]
hook
〖钩子〗(名)[gōuzi]
hook

篝[gōu]
〖篝火〗(名)[gōuhuǒ]
campfire

gǒu

苟[gǒu]
〖苟安〗(动)[gǒu'ān]
seek momentary ease
〖苟且〗(形)[gǒuqiě]
careless; muddling along
〖苟且偷安〗[gǒuqiětōu'ān]
seek ease and comfort at the expense of principle
〖苟延残喘〗[gǒuyáncánchuǎn]
eke out a meagre existence; try to prolong one's exhausted panting

狗(名)[gǒu]〔只 zhī〕
dog
〖狗急跳墙〗[gǒujítiàoqiáng]
a cornered dog will leap over a wall in desperation; be driven to extremities
〖狗腿子〗(名)[gǒutuǐzi]
lackey; henchman
〖狗血喷头〗[gǒuxuèpēntóu]
curse someone very thoroughly; pour out a torrent of abuse
〖狗仗人势〗[gǒuzhàngrénshì]
(term of abuse) the dog takes advantage of its master's power; play the bully with the backing of a powerful person

gòu

勾[gòu]
另见 gōu
〖勾当〗(名)[gòudàng]
fraudulent deal

构[gòu]
〖构成〗(动)[gòuchéng]
consist of; constitute; form; formulate
〖构词法〗(名)[gòucífǎ]
word formation; morphology
〖构件〗(名)[gòujiàn]
assembly piece
〖构思〗(动)[gòusī]
meditate; compose one's thoughts
〖构图〗[gòu tú]

compose
〖构造〗(名、动)[gòuzào]
structure; construction; construct; make up of

购(动)[gòu]
buy
〖购买〗(动)[gòumǎi]
buy; purchase
〖购买力〗(名)[gòumǎilì]
purchasing power
〖购置〗(动)[gòuzhì]
buy (big and durable items)

够(动、形)[gòu]
① reach ② enough; sufficient
〖够本〗[gòu běn]
enough to repay the cost price
〖够受的〗[gòu shòu de]
enough to bear

媾[gòu]
〖媾和〗(动)[gòuhé]
negotiate for peace

gū

估(动)[gū]
estimate
〖估计〗(动、名)[gūjì]
estimate; calculate; size up; appraise
〖估价〗[gū jià]
evaluate; appraise
〖估量〗(动)[gūliáng]
estimate; take it into account; appraise

沽[gū]
〖沽名钓誉〗[gūmíngdiàoyù]
buy reputation and fish for praise; fish for fame and reputation

姑(名)[gū]
aunt (father's sisters)
〖姑父〗(名)[gūfu]
uncle (husband of father's sister)
〖姑姑〗(名)[gūgu]
aunt (father's sisters)
〖姑娘〗(名)[gūniang]
girl
〖姑且〗(副)[gūqiě]
temporarily; for the time being; provisionally
〖姑息〗(动)[gūxī]
tolerate; indulge; appease
〖姑息养奸〗[gūxīyǎngjiān]
indulge the evil-doers; purposely tolerate bad things

孤(形)[gū]
lonely
〖孤傲〗(形)[gū'ào]
aloof and arrogant
〖孤单〗(形)[gūdān]
lonely
〖孤独〗(形)[gūdú]
solitary; lonely
〖孤儿〗(名)[gū'ér]
orphan
〖孤芳自赏〗[gūfāngzìshǎng]
narcissistic
〖孤家寡人〗[gūjiāguǎrén]

a man isolated from the masses; totally isolated; isolationist
〖孤军〗(名)[gūjūn]
an army being isolated and cut off from help
〖孤苦伶仃〗[gūkǔlíngdīng]
lonely and miserable
〖孤立〗(动、形)[gūlì]
isolate; isolated
〖孤立无援〗[gūlìwúyuán]
isolated and helpless; isolated and abandoned
〖孤零零〗(形)[gūlínglíng]
alone; helpless
〖孤陋寡闻〗[gūlòuguǎwén]
solitary and inexperienced; ill-informed
〖孤僻〗(形)[gūpì]
eccentric; peculiar
〖孤掌难鸣〗[gūzhǎngnánmíng]
(lit.) one cannot clap with one hand; (fig.) one who stands alone has no power
〖孤注一掷〗[gūzhùyīzhì]
risk all on a single throw; make a last desperate effort

辜[gū]
〖辜负〗(动)[gūfù]
fail to live up to; disappoint the hopes of

gǔ

古(形)[gǔ]
ancient
〖古代〗(名)[gǔdài]
ancient times
〖古典〗(名)[gǔdiǎn]
classical; classic
〖古典文学〗[gǔdiǎn wénxué]
classical literature
〖古董〗(名)[gǔdǒng]
antiques; curios
〖古怪〗(形)[gǔguài]
strange; peculiar
〖古迹〗(名)[gǔjī]
historical sites; places of historical interests; historic monuments
〖古籍〗(名)[gǔjí]
ancient books
〖古今中外〗[gǔjīnzhōngwài]
in ancient or in modern times, in China or elsewhere; for all times and for all countries
〖古老〗(形)[gǔlǎo]
old; ancient
〖古人〗(名)[gǔrén]
the ancients
〖古诗〗(名)[gǔshī]〔首 shǒu〕
ancient poem
〖古往今来〗[gǔwǎngjīnlái]
from ancient to modern times
〖古为今用〗[gǔwéijīnyòng]
make the past serve the present
〖古文〗(名)[gǔwén]
the classical style of writing
〖古物〗(名)[gǔwù]
historical relics; antiques

谷(名)[gǔ]
①valley ②grain

G

〖谷物〗(名)[gǔwù]
cereals
〖谷子〗(名)[gǔzi]〔粒 lì〕
millet

股(名、量)[gǔ]
① thigh ② share ③ a measure word, strand (for hair, rope), whiff (of fresh air), group (for persons, bandits, etc.), current (e.g. a counter or adverse current)
〖股本〗(名)[gǔběn]
capital stock; share capital; equity capital
〖股东〗(名)[gǔdōng]
shareholder; stockholder
〖股份〗(名)[gǔfèn]
shareholding
〖股份制〗(名)[gǔfènzhì]
shareholding enterprise system
〖股价〗(名)[gǔjià]
share prices; stock prices
〖股金〗(名)[gǔjīn]
money paid for shares in a partnership or cooperative
〖股民〗(名)[gǔmín]
investor
〖股票〗(名)[gǔpiào]〔张 zhāng〕
shares; stocks
〖股票交易所〗(名)[gǔpiàojiāoyìsuǒ]
stock exchange
〖股权〗(名)[gǔquán]
stock right; shareholder's right
〖股市〗(名)[gǔshì]
stock market
〖股息〗(名)[gǔxī]
dividend

骨(名)[gǔ]
bone
〖骨干〗(名)[gǔgàn]
mainstay; hard core; backbone
〖骨骼〗(名)[gǔgé]
skeleton
〖骨灰〗(名)[gǔhuī]
ashes
〖骨科〗(名)[gǔkē]
orthopedics
〖骨膜〗(名)[gǔmó]
periosteum
〖骨气〗(名)[gǔqì]
moral integrity; loftiness
〖骨肉〗(名)[gǔròu]
blood relationship
〖骨瘦如柴〗[gǔshòurúchái]
emaciated like a stick; lean as a lath; thin as a rake
〖骨髓〗(名)[gǔsuǐ]
marrow
〖骨头〗(名)[gǔtou]
bone
〖骨折〗(名、动)[gǔzhé]
fracture of bones; break (one's) bones
〖骨子里〗(名)[gǔzilǐ]
in one's heart; by nature

蛊[gǔ]
〖蛊惑人心〗[gǔhuòrénxīn]
confuse and poison people's minds; resort to demagogy

鼓(名、动)[gǔ]
①drum②rouse; pout; inflate
〖鼓吹〗(动)[gǔchuī]
(derog.)advocate; advertise; play up; agitate
〖鼓动〗(动)[gǔdòng]
agitate; instigate; urge
〖鼓风机〗(名)[gǔfēngjī]
blower; blowing machine
〖鼓励〗(动)[gǔlì]
encourage; inspire
〖鼓舞〗(动、名)[gǔwǔ]
inspire; encourage; stimulate
〖鼓掌〗[gǔ zhǎng]
applaud
〖鼓足干劲〗[gǔzúgànjìn]
go all out; exert the utmost effort

gù

固[gù]
〖固步自封〗[gùbùzìfēng]
stand still and cease to make progress
〖固定〗(动、形)[gùdìng]
fix; fixed; static; stable
〖固然〗(副)[gùrán]
it's true that...; although; though; of course
〖固体〗(名)[gùtǐ]
solid
〖固有〗(动)[gùyǒu]
inherent
〖固执〗(动、形)[gùzhí]
stubborn; obstinate
〖固执己见〗[gùzhíjǐjiàn]
stick stubbornly to one's own opinion

故(名、形、连)[gù]
①cause; reason②old; past③therefore; intentionally
〖故步自封〗[gùbùzìfēng]
ultra-conservative and self-satisfied; stand still and cease to make progress
〖故都〗(名)[gùdū]
ancient capital
〖故宫〗(名)[gùgōng]
former imperial palace
〖故伎重演〗[gùjìchóngyǎn]
repetition of the old dodge; up to one's old tricks
〖故居〗(名)[gùjū]
former residence
〖故弄玄虚〗[gùnòngxuánxū]
use intrigues and tricks
〖故事〗(名)[gùshi]〔个 gè〕
story; tale
〖故事片〗(名)[gùshipiàn]〔部 bù〕
feature film
〖故乡〗(名)[gùxiāng]
hometown; native place; birthplace
〖故意〗(形)[gùyì]
intentional; purposely; deliberately
〖故障〗(名)[gùzhàng]
out of order

顾(动)[gù]
①care for②look about
〖顾此失彼〗[gùcǐshībǐ]

G

take care of one matter while forgetting the other; unable to attend to everything at once
〖顾忌〗(动)[gùjì]
be misgiven; misgivings
〖顾客〗(名)[gùkè]
customer; client; shopper
〖顾虑〗(动、名)[gùlǜ]
worry; apprehensions; misgivings
〖顾名思义〗[gùmíngsīyì]
from the name you know what it implies
〖顾全大局〗[gùquándàjú]
take the interests of the whole into account; consideration for the general interests
〖顾问〗(名)[gùwèn]
adviser

G

雇(动)[gù]
hire
〖雇工〗(名)[gùgōng]
hired labour
〖雇农〗(名)[gùnóng]
hired farm labourers
〖雇佣〗(动)[gùyōng]
hire
〖雇佣劳动〗[gùyōng láodòng]
hiring of labour
〖雇员〗(名)[gùyuán]
employee
〖雇主〗(名)[gùzhǔ]
employer

guā

瓜(名)[guā]
melon
〖瓜分〗(动)[guāfēn]
carve up; partition
〖瓜葛〗(名)[guāgé]
interrelations
〖瓜熟蒂落〗[guāshúdìluò]
a melon falls when it is ripe
〖瓜子儿〗(名)[guāzǐr]
melon seeds

刮(动)[guā]
① scrape ② blow
〖刮风〗[guā fēng]
(of wind) blow
〖刮脸〗[guā liǎn]
shave
〖刮脸刀〗(名)[guāliǎndāo]
razor

呱(象声)[guā]
onomatopoeia, quack; croak
〖呱呱〗(象声)[guāguā]
onomatopoeia, quack; croak

guǎ

寡(形)[guǎ]
few
〖寡妇〗(名)[guǎfu]
widow
〖寡头〗(名)[guǎtóu]
oligarch; magnate; boss

guà

挂(动)[guà]
① hang up; suspend; put up ② be caught (by a hook, nail, etc.) ③

put on record; register
〖挂彩〗[guà cǎi]
wounded (in battle)
〖挂钩〗[guà gōu]
link up; establish contact
〖挂号〗[guà hào]
register
〖挂号信〗(名)[guàhàoxìn]
registered letter
〖挂念〗(动)[guàniàn]
worry over (sb.); long for
〖挂帅〗[guà shuài]
put...in command; take command
〖挂图〗(名)[guàtú]〔幅 fú〕
wall chart
〖挂羊头卖狗肉〗[guàyángtóumàigǒuròu]
hang out a sheep's head when what one is selling is dog's meat; selling dog's meat under the label of a sheep's head
〖挂一漏万〗[guàyīlòuwàn]
record one item while leaving out ten thousand; incomplete and full of ommissions

guāi

乖(形)[guāi]
① (of a child) obedient ② quick-witted

guǎi

拐(动)[guǎi]
① turn ② lame
〖拐棍〗(名)[guǎigùn]〔根 gēn〕
walking stick
〖拐弯〗[guǎi wān]
making turns
〖拐弯抹角〗[guǎiwānmòjiǎo]
speak or write in a roundabout way; beat about the bush

guài

怪(形、动)[guài]
① strange; abnormal ② blame; rebuke
〖怪不得〗[guài bu de]
① not to be blamed ② no wonder
〖怪话〗(名)[guàihuà]
unprincipled complaints and remarks
〖怪模怪样〗[guàimúguàiyàng]
peculiar; queer; odd; strange
〖怪僻〗(形)[guàipì]
(of persons) eccentric; odd; queer
〖怪物〗(名)[guàiwu]
monster

guān

关(动、名)[guān]
① close; shut ② concern; relate to; have reference to ③ pass; passage ④ crucial moment; turning point
〖关闭〗(动)[guānbì]
close down; shut
〖关怀〗(动)[guānhuái]
be concerned about; solicitude; be in the thoughts of
〖关键〗(名)[guānjiàn]
pivot; key; crux; linchpin
〖关节〗(名)[guānjié]

①joint links ②articulation
〖关节炎〗(名)[guānjiéyán]
arthritis
〖关联〗(动、名)[guānlián]
be related or interconnected; connections (of problems, etc.)
〖关门主义〗(名)[guānménzhǔyì]
closed-doorism; closed-door sectarianism
〖关切〗(动)[guānqiè]
deeply concerned about
〖关税〗(名)[guānshuì]
customs duties; tariffs
〖关头〗(名)[guāntóu]
critical point; juncture
〖关系〗(名、动)[guānxì]
relation; relationship; be related to; concern
〖关心〗(动)[guānxīn]
show concern for; be concerned about
〖关押〗(动)[guānyā]
put into prison; take into custody
〖关于〗(介)[guānyú]
about; concerning; regarding; on
〖关照〗(动)[guānzhào]
①take care of; take sth. into account ②inform
〖关注〗(动)[guānzhù]
pay close attention to; be intensely concerned about

观[guān]

〖观测〗(动)[guāncè]
observe and survey; prognosticate through careful observation
〖观察〗(动)[guānchá]
observe; view; examine
〖观察员〗(名)[guāncháyuán]
observer
〖观潮派〗(名)[guāncháopài]
one who takes a wait-and-see attitude
〖观点〗(名)[guāndiǎn]
point of view; approach
〖观感〗(名)[guāngǎn]
impression; view
〖观光〗(动)[guānguāng]
make a sight-seeing trip
〖观看〗(动)[guānkàn]
watch; inspect
〖观礼〗(动)[guānlǐ]
review (a parade)
〖观礼台〗(名)[guānlǐtái]
rostrum; reviewing stand
〖观摩〗(动)[guānmó]
see the good in and learn from each other
〖观念〗(名)[guānniàn]
idea; notion; concept
〖观赏〗(动)[guānshǎng]
watch and enjoy
〖观望〗(动)[guānwàng]
①take a wait-and-see attitude ②look (around)
〖观众〗(名)[guānzhòng]
audience

官(名)[guān]

official; officer
〖官方〗(名)[guānfāng]

official

〖官架子〗(名) [guānjiàzi]
superior airs assumed by officials

〖官吏〗(名) [guānlì]
government official in old society

〖官僚〗(名) [guānliáo]
bureaucrat

〖官僚主义〗(名)[guānliáozhǔyì]
bureaucracy

〖官僚资本〗[guānliáo zīběn]
bureaucrat-capital

〖官僚资本主义〗
[guānliáo zī běnzhǔyì]
bureaucratic capitalism

〖官僚资产阶级〗
[guānliáo zīchǎnjiējí]
bureaucrat-capitalist class

〖官气〗(名) [guānqì]
official airs

〖官腔〗(名) [guānqiāng]
official jargon

〖官司〗(名) [guānsi]
law suits; case

〖官样文章〗
[guānyàngwénzhāng]
red tape; useless official formalities; official paper

〖官员〗(名) [guānyuán]
government official;official

冠 [guān]

另见 guàn

〖冠冕堂皇〗
[guānmiǎntánghuáng]
(derog.)ostentations; dignified in form but insincere in substance

鳏 [guān]

〖鳏寡孤独〗[guānguǎgūdú]
widower, widow, orphan and elderly and childless people (disabled and supportless)

guǎn

管 (动、介) [guǎn]

① be in charge of; take care of; govern;manage;control ② guarantee ③ a preposition similar to the preposition "把", but used exclusively in the pattern "管…叫…"

〖管保〗(动) [guǎnbǎo]
guarantee

〖管道〗(名) [guǎndào]
piping

〖管教〗(动) [guǎnjiào]
teach; instruct; educate

〖管理〗(动) [guǎnlǐ]
manage; administrate

〖管事〗(形) [guǎnshì]
efficient; effective; useful

〖管辖〗(动) [guǎnxiá]
subject to the jurisdiction of; exercise control over; be under the rule of

〖管弦乐〗(名) [guǎnxiányuè]
orchestral music

〖管用〗(形) [guǎnyòng]
effective

〖管制〗(动) [guǎnzhì]
control; put under surveillance

〖管子〗(名)[guǎnzi]
pipe; tube

guàn

贯[guàn]
〖贯彻〗(动)[guànchè]
carry through; implement
〖贯彻始终〗[guànchèshǐ zhōng]
carry on to the end; thorough implementation
〖贯穿〗(动)[guànchuān]
run through (all processes); continue through; be shot through and through with
〖贯通〗(动)[guàntōng]
① have a thorough understanding; cover ②interconnect; be connected
〖贯注〗(动)[guànzhù]
concentrate; be imbued with; be absorbed in

冠[guàn]
另见 guān
〖冠军〗(名)[guànjūn]
champion (in games and sports)

惯(形、动)[guàn]
habitual;usual;customary ①be accustomed to; be prone to; be used to ②spoil; over-indulgent
〖惯匪〗(名)[guànfěi]
bandits with long records; inveterate bandits
〖惯技〗(名)[guànjì]
customary tactic
〖惯例〗(名)[guànlì]
customary practice; convention
〖惯性〗(名)[guànxìng]
inertia
〖惯于〗(动)[guànyú]
be used to

盥[guàn]
〖盥洗〗(动)[guànxǐ]
wash hands and face
〖盥洗室〗(名)[guànxǐshì]
toilet; wash-room; lavatory

灌(动)[guàn]
fill; pour in; irrigate
〖灌溉〗(动)[guàngài]
irrigate
〖灌木〗(名)[guànmù]
shrubs; bush
〖灌输〗(动)[guànshū]
① (of water) pour or pump into ②imbue; instil into
〖灌注〗(动)[guànzhù]
pour into; fill

罐(名)[guàn]
jug; jar; pot
〖罐头〗(名)[guàntou]
canned food
〖罐子〗(名)[guànzi]〔个 gè〕
pot; jar

guāng

光(名、动、副)[guāng]
①light ②bare; naked ③only; merely; solely; alone

〖光彩〗(名、形) [guāngcǎi]
brilliance; splendour; glory; honour; bright; brilliant
〖光彩夺目〗[guāngcǎiduómù]
brightness dazzles the eyes
〖光辐射〗(名) [guāngfúshè]
light radiation
〖光合作用〗[guānghézuòyòng]
activism
〖光滑〗(形) [guānghuá]
smooth; sleek
〖光辉〗(名、形) [guānghuī]
glory; splendour; radiance; splendid; glorious
〖光景〗(名) [guāngjǐng]
① landscape; view; scene ② circumstances; situation; condition
〖光临〗(动) [guānglín]
come; arrive (polite form)
〖光溜溜〗(形) [guāngliūliū]
smooth; slippery; naked
〖光芒〗(名) [guāngmáng]
brilliance
〖光明〗(形) [guāngmíng]
bright; brilliant
〖光明磊落〗[guāngmínglěiluò]
frank and forthright
〖光明正大〗[guāngmíngzhèngdà]
be open and above board; frank and upright; just and honourable
〖光年〗(量) [guāngnián]
light year
〖光谱〗(名) [guāngpǔ]
spectrum
〖光荣〗(名、形) [guāngróng]
glory; honour; glorious
〖光速〗(名) [guāngsù]
speed of light
〖光天化日〗[guāngtiānhuàrì]
broad daylight
〖光秃秃〗(形) [guāngtūtū]
barren; bald; bare
〖光线〗(名) [guāngxiàn]
ray of light
〖光学〗(名) [guāngxué]
optics
〖光焰〗(名) [guāngyàn]
brilliance
〖光阴〗(名) [guāngyīn]
time
〖光源〗(名) [guāngyuán]
light source
〖光泽〗(名) [guāngzé]
lustre

guǎng

广(形) [guǎng]
broad; extensive
〖广播〗(动) [guǎngbō]
broadcast
〖广播电台〗[guǎngbō diàntái]
broadcasting station
〖广播剧〗[guǎngbō jù]
broadcast play
〖广播体操〗[guǎngbō tǐcāo]
gymnastics done to music (through radio)
〖广博〗(形) [guǎng bó]
wide range of (knowledge); extensive (reading, experience); erudite
〖广场〗(名) [guǎngchǎng]

square
〖广大〗(形) [guǎngdà]
broad; wide; large
〖广度〗(名) [guǎngdù]
breadth
〖广泛〗(形) [guǎngfàn]
extensive; widespread
〖广告〗(名) [guǎnggào]
advertisement
〖广开言路〗[guǎngkāiyánlù]
encourage the free airing of views
〖广阔〗(形) [guǎngkuò]
broad; wide
〖广阔天地〗[guǎngkuò tiāndì]
wide prospect; vast areas
〖广义〗(名) [guǎngyì]
broad sense

G

guàng

逛(动) [guàng]
stroll; visit (a park)

guī

归(动) [guī]
①return ②belong to; be due to
〖归队〗[guī duì]
①rejoin one's unit ②return to one's original occupation
〖归根结底〗[guīgēnjiédǐ]
in the final analysis
〖归功〗(动) [guīgōng]
give the credit to...; attribute...to
〖归还〗(动) [guīhuán]
return (what is borrowed)
〖归结〗(动) [guījié]
①reduce... (to a question of); come to a conclusion ② in the end; in the final analysis
〖归咎〗(动) [guījiù]
lay the blame on; blame; attribute
〖归纳〗(动) [guīnà]
infer by induction
〖归宿〗(名) [guīsù]
the end results of
〖归心似箭〗[guīxīnsìjiàn]
a mind bent on returning is like an arrow; anxious to return home as soon as possible
〖归于〗(动) [guīyú]
①result in ②ascribe to; be due to
〖归罪〗(动) [guīzuì]
lay the blame on; shift the responsibility on to (others)

龟(名) [guī] [只 zhī]
tortoise
〖龟甲〗(名) [guījiǎ]
shell of the tortoise
〖龟缩〗(动) [guīsuō]
hide like the tortoise withdrawing its head into its shell

规[guī]
〖规程〗(名) [guīchéng]
rules and regulations
〖规定〗(动、名) [guīdìng]
formulate; define rules; regulations
〖规范〗(名、形) [guīfàn]
model; standard; standardized

〖规格〗(名) [guīgé]
specifications
〖规划〗(动、名) [guīhuà]
work out a plan; project; programme
〖规矩〗(形、名) [guīju]
well-behaved; rules
〖规律〗(名) [guīlǜ]
law
〖规律性〗(名) [guīlǜxìng]
systematic; in accordance with the law of development; law
〖规模〗(名) [guīmó]
scale
〖规劝〗(动) [guīquàn]
admonish; persuade; offer advice to
〖规则〗(名) [guīzé]
rules and regulations
〖规章〗(名) [guīzhāng]
rules; regulations

闺 [guī]
〖闺女〗(名) [guīnü]
①girl ②daughter

瑰 [guī]
〖瑰丽〗(形) [guīlì]
very beautiful; elegant

guǐ

轨 (名) [guǐ]
①rail; track; road; path ②order; method; way; rules
〖轨道〗(名) [guǐdào]
①track; rails ②order; way; method; rules ③orbit

诡 [guǐ]
〖诡辩〗(动) [guǐbiàn]
sophisticate; resort to sophistry
〖诡计〗(名) [guǐjì]
trick; scheme
〖诡计多端〗[guǐjìduōduān]
full of schemes and tricks; wily
〖诡秘〗(形) [guǐmì]
secret
〖诡诈〗(形) [guǐzhà]
crafty

鬼 (名) [guǐ]
①ghost; devil; spirit; apparition ②trick
〖鬼把戏〗[guǐ bǎxì]
malicious intrigue
〖鬼鬼祟祟〗(形) [guǐguǐsuìsuì]
stealthily
〖鬼话〗(名) [guǐhuà]
utter nonsense; deception
〖鬼迷心窍〗[guǐmíxīnqiào]
possessed by ghosts
〖鬼蜮〗(名) [guǐyù]
demon
〖鬼子〗(名) [guǐzi]
devil

guì

柜 (名) [guì]
cupboard; wardrobe
〖柜台〗(名) [guìtái]
counter
〖柜子〗(名) [guìzi]〔个 gè〕
cupboard; wardrobe

刽[guì]
〖刽子手〗(名)[guìzishǒu]
executioner; killer; hang-man; butcher

贵(形)[guì]
① expensive; dear ② honourable ③ precious
〖贵宾〗(名)[guìbīn]
honoured guest
〖贵客〗(名)[guìkè]
honoured guest
〖贵姓〗[guì xìng]
May I know your name?
〖贵重〗(形)[guìzhòng]
valuable; precious
〖贵族〗(名)[guìzú]
aristocrat; noble

G

桂[guì]
〖桂花〗(名)[guìhuā]
sweet-scented osmanthus

跪(动)[guì]
sweet-scented osmanthus

gǔn

滚(动)[gǔn]
① roll; tumble ② get out
〖滚动〗(动)[gǔndòng]
roll; tumble
〖滚瓜烂熟〗[gǔnguālànshú]
(of reading or recitation) very fluent and well versed
〖滚滚〗(形)[gǔngǔn]
rushing; torrential
〖滚热〗(形)[gǔnrè]
boiling hot
〖滚珠〗(名)[gǔnzhū]
ball (for ball bearing)
〖滚珠轴承〗[gǔnzhūzhóuchéng]
ball bearing

gùn

棍(名)[gùn]
stick; cudgel
〖棍子〗(名)[gùnzi]〔根 gēn〕
stick; club; baton

guō

锅(名)[guō]〔口 kǒu〕
cooking-pot
〖锅炉〗(名)[guōlú]
boiler

guó

国(名)[guó]
country; nation; state
〖国宾〗(名)[guóbīn]
state guest
〖国策〗(名)[guócè]
state policy
〖国产〗[guó chǎn]
home-made
〖国都〗(名)[guódū]
the capital of a country
〖国度〗(名)[guódù]
country; nation
〖国法〗(名)[guófǎ]
national laws; the law of the land
〖国防〗(名)[guófáng]
national defense

〖国歌〗(名)[guógē]
national anthem
〖国画〗(名)[guóhuà]〔幅 fú〕
traditional Chinese painting
〖国徽〗(名)[guóhuī]
national emblem
〖国籍〗(名)[guójí]
nationality
〖国计民生〗[guójìmínshēng]
the national economy and the people's livelihood
〖国际〗(名)[guójì]
international
〖国际法〗(名)[guójìfǎ]
international law
〖国际歌〗(名)[Guójìgē]
the Internationale
〖国际惯例〗[guójìguànlì]
international practice
〖国际音标〗[guójì yīnbiāo]
the International Phonetic Alphabet (I.P.A.)
〖国际主义〗(名)[guójìzhǔyì]
internationalism
〖国家〗(名)[guójiā]
country; state; nation
〖国家机器〗[guójiā jīqì]
state apparatus
〖国家资本主义〗[guójiāzībĕnzhǔyì]
state-capitalism
〖国界〗(名)[guójiè]
national boundaries
〖国境〗(名)[guójìng]
territorial limits; border
〖国库〗(名)[guókù]
national treasury
〖国库券〗(名)[guókùquàn]
treasury bill (T.B.)
〖国民〗(名)[guómín]
people of a country; nation
〖国民党〗(名)[guómíndǎng]
the Kuomintang
〖国民经济〗[guómín jīngjì]
national economy
〖国民收入〗[guómín shōurù]
national income
〖国内〗(名)[guónèi]
inside the country; domestic; internal; home (e.g. home affairs); civil
〖国旗〗(名)[guóqí]〔面 miàn〕
national flag
〖国庆节〗(名)[guóqìngjié]
national day
〖国事〗(名)[guóshì]
state affairs
〖国书〗(名)[guóshū]
letter of credence
〖国体〗(名)[guótǐ]
form of state; the state system
〖国土〗(名)[guótǔ]
national territory
〖国外〗(名)[guówài]
abroad
〖国务院〗(名)[guówùyuàn]
the state council
〖国宴〗(名)[guóyàn]
state banquet
〖国营〗[guó yíng]
state-owned; government operated
〖国营经济〗[guóyíng jīngjì]
state-owned economy; state en-

terprise
〖国有〗[guó yǒu]
state-owned; nationalized
〖国有化〗(动)[guóyǒuhuà]
nationalize; nationalization

guǒ

果(名)[guǒ]
fruit; result; outcome
〖果断〗(形)[guǒduàn]
resolute
〖果脯〗(名)[guǒfǔ]
dried fruits processed with sugar
〖果敢〗(形)[guǒgǎn]
resolute and daring
〖果酱〗(名)[guǒjiàng]
jam
〖果然〗(副)[guǒrán]
as expected; sure enough
〖果实〗(名)[guǒshí]
① fruit ② gain; fruit
〖果树〗(名)[guǒshù]〔棵 kē〕
fruit trees
〖果园〗(名)[guǒyuán]
orchard
〖果真〗(副)[guǒzhēn]
true to promise; as expected; really

guò

过(动、名、尾)[guò]
① pass over or through; pass by ② surpass ③ error; fault ④ a suffix used to express a completed action or past experience
〖过不去〗[guò bu qù]
① cannot pass through ② be hard on (sb.) ③ feel sorry for...
〖过场〗(名)[guòchǎng]
① interlude ② mere formality
〖过程〗(名)[guòchéng]
process; course
〖过错〗(名)[guòcuò]
error; fault
〖过道〗(名)[guòdào]
corridor
〖过得去〗[guò de qù]
can pass through; passable
〖过度〗(形)[guòdù]
excessive; over-
〖过渡〗(动)[guòdù]
pass over; transition
〖过渡时期〗[guòdù shíqī]
transition period
〖过分〗(形)[guòfèn]
excessive
〖过关〗[guò guān]
① go through a mountain pass ② pass the test of
〖过河拆桥〗[guòhéchāiqiáo]
(lit.) remove the plank after crossing the bridge; (fig.) devoid of all gratitude; ingratitude
〖过活〗(动)[guòhuó]
make a living
〖过火〗(形)[guòhuǒ]
excessive; carry things too far; overdo; overstep the limits
〖过激〗(形)[guòjī]
excessively; ultra-
〖过来〗[guò lái]

come over
〖过虑〗(动) [guòlǜ]
be overanxious; worry too much; worry needlessly
〖过滤〗(动) [guòlǜ]
filter
〖过敏〗(形、动) [guòmǐn]
allergic; over-sensitive; allergy
〖过目〗 [guò mù]
go over; look over; read over; glance over
〖过年〗 [guò nián]
① celebrate New Year's Day ② after New Year's Day
〖过期〗 [guò qī]
overdue; out of date
〖过去〗(名) [guòqù]
the past; previous
〖过去〗 [guò qù]
cross over; go over; pass through
〖过日子〗 [guò rìzi]
make a living
〖过剩〗(动) [guòshèng]
surplus
〖过失〗(名) [guòshī]
error
〖过时〗 [guò shí]
out-of-date; obsolete; outmoded
〖过问〗(动) [guòwèn]
intervene; take action on; take an interest in
〖过细〗(形) [guòxì]
careful
〖过意不去〗 [guòyì bù qù]
feel uneasy; Sorry!
〖过硬〗 [guò yìng]
become truly proficient in; pass the test
〖过于〗(副) [guòyú]
too much; over-; excessively

hā

哈(动、象声、叹)[hā]
① exhale ② onomatopoeia,ha ha! (sound of laughter) ③ interjection used to express satisfaction
〖哈哈大笑〗[hāhā dàxiào]
hearty laughter
〖哈欠〗(名)[hāqian]
yawn

hāi

咳(叹)[hāi]
interjection expressing sorrow, surprise, etc.
另见 ké

hái

还(副)[hái]
still; still more; yet
另见 huán
〖还是〗(副)[háishì]
①still ②or ③it's better...

孩[hái]
〖孩子〗(名)[háizi]
child

hǎi

海(名)[hǎi]
sea
〖海岸〗(名)[hǎi'àn]
coast; shore
〖海岸线〗(名)[hǎi'ànxiàn]
coastline
〖海拔〗(名)[hǎibá]
above sea-level
〖海报〗(名)[hǎibào]
poster
〖海滨〗(名)[hǎibīn]
seashore
〖海潮〗(名)[hǎicháo]
the tides
〖海带〗(名)[hǎidài]
kelp (an edible seaweed)
〖海盗〗(名)[hǎidào]
pirate
〖海底〗(名)[hǎidǐ]

bottom of the sea
〖海底捞月〗[hǎidǐlāoyuè]
(lit.) dredge for the moon in the sea; (fig.) useless effort; a fruitless attempt
〖海防〗(名) [hǎifáng]
coastal defense
〖海港〗(名) [hǎigǎng]
harbour; seaport
〖海关〗(名) [hǎiguān]
customs house
〖海军〗(名) [hǎijūn]
navy
〖海枯石烂〗[hǎikūshílàn]
(lit.) (until) the seas run dry and the rocks decay; (fig.) an oath of unchanging fidelity
〖海阔天空〗[hǎikuòtiānkōng]
(lit.) the sea is wide and the sky is boundless; (fig.) (talk) at random and without direction
〖海绵〗(名) [hǎimián]
sponge
〖海面〗(名) [hǎimiàn]
the surface of the sea
〖海鸥〗(名) [hǎi'ōu]〔只 zhī〕
sea gull
〖海参〗(名) [hǎishēn]
sea cucumber; sea slug
〖海市蜃楼〗[hǎishìshènlóu]
mirage
〖海滩〗(名) [hǎitān]
beach
〖海外〗(名) [hǎiwài]
overseas; abroad
〖海湾〗(名) [hǎiwān]
gulf; bay
〖海味〗(名) [hǎiwèi]
sea food
〖海峡〗(名) [hǎixiá]
straits
〖海啸〗(名) [hǎixiào]
tidal wave
〖海燕〗(名) [hǎiyàn]〔只 zhī〕
petrel
〖海洋〗(名) [hǎiyáng]
ocean
〖海洋权〗(名) [hǎiyángquán]
maritime right
〖海洋性气候〗
[hǎiyángxìng qìhòu]
oceanic climate; marine climate
〖海域〗(名) [hǎiyù]
marine area
〖海员〗(名) [hǎiyuán]
seaman
〖海运〗(名) [hǎiyùn]
sea transportation

hài

骇 [hài]
〖骇人听闻〗[hàiréntīngwén]
(of news, incident, etc.) shocking; terrifying

害 (动、名) [hài]
injure; make sb. suffer; damage; harm
〖害虫〗(名) [hàichóng]
pest
〖害处〗(名) [hàichu]
harm
〖害怕〗(动) [hàipà]
fear; be afraid of

〖害人虫〗(名)[hàirénchóng]
pest; vermin
〖害羞〗(形)[hàixiū]
shy; bashful

hān

酣(形)[hān]
rapturous
〖酣睡〗(动)[hānshuì]
sleep soundly
〖酣战〗(动、名)[hānzhàn]
rage a fierce battle; a desperate battle

憨[hān]
〖憨厚〗(形)[hānhòu]
simple and honest

hán

含(动)[hán]
contain; be filled with; imply
〖含糊〗(形)[hánhu]
obscure; vague; equivocal; ambiguous
〖含混〗(形)[hánhùn]
ambiguous; equivocal
〖含沙射影〗[hánshāshèyǐng]
insinuate; insinuation
〖含蓄〗(形)[hánxù]
restrained but suggestive in speech or writing
〖含义〗(名)[hányì]
content; significance; implication

函(名)[hán]
letter
〖函授〗(名)[hánshòu]
correspondence course; lessons by correspondence
〖函数〗(名)[hánshù]
(math.) function

涵[hán]
〖涵洞〗(名)[hándòng]
tunnel
〖涵养〗(名)[hányǎng]
the virtue of patience

寒(形)[hán]
cold
〖寒潮〗(名)[háncháo]
cold wave
〖寒带〗(名)[hándài]
(geog.) the frigid zones
〖寒假〗(名)[hánjià]
winter vacation
〖寒冷〗(形)[hánlěng]
bitterly cold
〖寒流〗(名)[hánliú]
cold wave
〖寒酸〗(形)[hánsuān]
shabby
〖寒心〗(形)[hánxīn]
dampened; dismayed; disappointed
〖寒暄〗(动)[hánxuān]
make small talk; commonplaces of conversation about the weather, etc.
〖寒战〗(名)[hánzhàn]
shiver; quiver; trembling

H

hǎn

罕 [hǎn]
〖罕见〗(形) [hǎnjiàn]
rare; unusual; uncommon

喊 (动) [hǎn]
shout; yell
〖喊话〗[hǎnhuà]
shouting; talk through loudspeaker
〖喊叫〗(动) [hǎnjiào]
shout; yell; howl

hàn

汉 [hàn]
〖汉奸〗(名) [hànjiān]
Chinese traitor
〖汉语〗(名) [Hànyǔ]
Chinese language
〖汉语拼音方案〗
[Hànyǔpīnyīn fāng'àn]
scheme for the Chinese Phonetic Alphabet
〖汉字〗(名) [Hànzì]
Chinese character

汗 (名) [hàn]〔滴 dī〕
sweat; perspiration
〖汗流浃背〗[hànliújiābèi]
soaked through with sweat
〖汗马功劳〗[hànmǎgōngláo]
achievements in war; exploits; laboriously achieved merit
〖汗衫〗(名)[hànshān]〔件 jiàn〕
shirt
〖汗水〗(名) [hànshuǐ]
sweat; perspiration

旱 (形、动) [hàn]
dry
〖旱涝保收〗[hànlàobǎoshōu]
sure to get high yields irrespective of drought or waterlogging
〖旱灾〗(名) [hànzāi]
drought

捍 [hàn]
〖捍卫〗(动) [hànwèi]
defend; safeguard

悍 [hàn]
〖悍然〗(副) [hànrán]
brazenly; flagrantly

焊 (动) [hàn]
weld
〖焊接〗(动) [hànjiē]
connect by welding

háng

行 (名、量) [háng]
① line; row ② a branch of trade ③ a measure word (for row, column, line)
另见 xíng
〖行家〗(名) [hángjia]
expert; a person who is skilled in certain line
〖行列〗(名) [hángliè]
ranks; column
〖行情〗(名) [hángqíng]

market prices
〖行业〗(名) [hángyè]
a branch of trade; occupation

航 [háng]
〖航标〗(名) [hángbiāo]
buoy
〖航程〗(名) [hángchéng]
flying or sailing range
〖航道〗(名) [hángdào]
channel; waterway
〖航海〗(名) [hánghǎi]
navigation
〖航空〗(名) [hángkōng]
aviation
〖航空母舰〗[hángkōngmǔjiàn]
aircraft carrier
〖航线〗(名) [hángxiàn]
air or navigation line
〖航向〗(名) [hángxiàng]
the direction in which...is heading
〖航行〗(动) [hángxíng]
sail; navigate
〖航运〗(名) [hángyùn]
sea or river transportation

hāo

薅 (动) [hāo]
weed; pull out weeds (usu. with hand)

háo

号 (动) [háo]
howl; wail
另见 hào
〖号啕大哭〗[háotáodàkū]
wail loudly; cry loudly; utter a loud cry

毫 [háo]
〖毫不〗(副) [háobù]
not the least bit; without the slightest
〖毫毛〗(名) [háomáo] [根 gēn]
hair
〖毫升〗(量) [háoshēng]
millilitre
〖毫无〗[háowú]
by no means; devoid of; without the least; not in the least; not the slightest

豪 [háo]
〖豪放〗(形) [háofàng]
gallant-minded
〖豪华〗(形) [háohuá]
luxurious; sumptuous
〖豪杰〗(名) [háojié]
warrior; hero
〖豪迈〗(形) [háomài]
gallant; magnificent; militant
〖豪情〗(名) [háoqíng]
lofty sentiments
〖豪情壮志〗[háoqíngzhuàngzhì]
lofty spirit and soaring determination
〖豪绅〗(名) [háoshēn]
evil gentry
〖豪爽〗(形) [háoshuǎng]
generous and broadminded
〖豪言壮语〗[háoyánzhuàngyǔ]
militant and lofty words
〖豪壮〗(形) [háozhuàng]

heroic; daring; bold

壕(名)[háo]
trench
〖壕沟〗(名)[háogōu][条 tiáo]
ditch; trench

hǎo

好(形、副)[hǎo]
① good; well ② easy ③ how; very ④ so as to be able to; so that (one) could
另见 hào
〖好比〗(动)[hǎobǐ]
be like; as; just like
〖好吃〗(形)[hǎochī]
good to eat; delicious; tasty
〖好处〗(名)[hǎochu]
benefit; goodness; use
〖好歹〗(名、副)[hǎodǎi]
① danger (usually referring to some contingency) ② in any case; any way; anyhow; come what may
〖好感〗(名)[hǎogǎn]
good impression
〖好汉〗(名)[hǎohàn]
wise man; worthy man; hero
〖好好儿〗(副)[hǎohǎor]
① good; normal ② industriously; properly; thoroughly
〖好久〗(名)[hǎojiǔ]
long time
〖好看〗(形)[hǎokàn]
goodlooking
〖好人好事〗[hǎorénhǎoshì]
good personalities and good deeds
〖好容易〗(副)[hǎoróngyì]
with much difficulty
〖好手〗(名)[hǎoshǒu]
a very capable person; past master
〖好似〗(动)[hǎosì]
look like; seem
〖好听〗(形)[hǎotīng]
pleasant to the ear; fine sounding
〖好玩儿〗(形)[hǎowánr]
interesting; playful
〖好闻〗(形)[hǎowén]
good to smell
〖好像〗(动)[hǎoxiàng]
(look) as if; look like
〖好笑〗(形)[hǎoxiào]
funny
〖好些〗(形)[hǎoxiē]
a good many
〖好心〗(名)[hǎoxīn]
goodwilled; kind-hearted; well-intentioned
〖好样的〗(名)[hǎoyàngde]
a fine person; a worthy man; a good sort
〖好意〗(名)[hǎoyì]
goodwill; well-intentioned
〖好在〗(连)[hǎozài]
luckily; fortunately
〖好转〗(动)[hǎozhuǎn]
turn for the better

hào

号(名)[hào]
① sign; mark ② number ③ bugle

④date
另见 háo
〖号称〗(动)[hàochēng]
①designate ②is said to be; be reputedly for
〖号角〗(名)[hàojiǎo]
clarion call; a bugle horn
〖号令〗(名)[hàolìng]
order; command
〖号码〗(名)[hàomǎ]
number
〖号召〗(动、名)[hàozhào]
call upon; call

好(动)[hào]
be fond of; like
另见 hǎo
〖好高骛远〗[hàogāowùyuǎn]
crave something high and out of reach
〖好客〗(形)[hàokè]
hospitable
〖好奇〗(形)[hàoqí]
curious
〖好强〗(形)[hàoqiáng]
not willing to lag behind
〖好胜〗(形)[hàoshèng]
love of preeminence
〖好恶〗(名)[hàowù]
love-hate
〖好逸恶劳〗[hàoyìwùláo]
love ease, dislike work
〖好战〗(形)[hàozhàn]
war-like

耗(动)[hào]
waste
〖耗费〗(动、名)[hàofèi]
consume; consumption

浩[hào]
〖浩大〗(形)[hàodà]
great (e.g. expense); gigantic; powerful
〖浩荡〗(形)[hàodàng]
grand; mighty
〖浩瀚〗(形)[hàohàn]
expansive; limitless

hē

呵(动、叹)[hē]
①exhale ②an interjection expressing surprise
〖呵斥〗(动)[hēchì]
reprimand

喝(动)[hē]
drink
另见 hè

hé

禾[hé]
〖禾苗〗(名)[hémiáo]
grain seedling; rice-shoots

合(动)[hé]
①close; shut ②combine; join; meet ③coincide; conform; be in keeping with; correspond
〖合并〗(动)[hébìng]
merge; amalgamate
〖合不来〗[hébulái]
not be in harmony with; hard to

H

get alongtogether
〖合唱〗(动、名)[héchàng]
chorus
〖合成〗(动)[héchéng]
synthesize; compose
〖合成词〗(名)[héchéngcí]
compound word
〖合成纤维〗[héchéng xiānwéi]
synthetic fibre
〖合成橡胶〗[héchéng xiàngjiāo]
synthetic rubber
〖合得来〗[hédelái]
be in harmony with; be on good terms
〖合订本〗(名)[hédìngběn]
one-volume edition; bound volume
〖合法〗(形)[héfǎ]
legal; legitimate; lawful
〖合法化〗(动)[héfǎhuà]
legalize
〖合格〗(形)[hégé]
qualified; up to the standard
〖合股〗[hégǔ]
joint-stock; share
〖合伙〗[héhuǒ]
seek partnership with; collude with
〖合金〗(名)[héjīn]
alloy
〖合金钢〗(名)[héjīngāng]
alloy steel
〖合理〗(形)[hélǐ]
reasonable; rational
〖合理化〗(动)[hélǐhuà]
rationalize
〖合流〗(动)[héliú]
join forces with; cast one's lot with; collaborate with
〖合龙〗(动)[hélóng]
link up; meet
〖合情合理〗[héqínghélǐ]
reasonable and just
〖合适〗(形)[héshì]
suitable; fit
〖合算〗(形)[hésuàn]
reasonable in price; worth
〖合同〗(名)[hétong]
contract
〖合营〗(动)[héyíng]
jointly owned (enterprises)
〖合影〗[hé yǐng]
taking a group photo
〖合影〗(名)[héyǐng]
group photo
〖合奏〗(动、名)[hézòu]
play a chorus; chorus
〖合作〗(动)[hézuò]
co-operate; collaborate
〖合作化〗(动)[hézuòhuà]
collectivization (agriculture)
〖合作社〗(名)[hézuòshè]
co-operatives
〖合作医疗〗[hézuòyīliáo]
co-operative medical service

何[hé]

〖何必〗(副)[hébì]
why on earth; why should
〖何尝〗(副)[hécháng]
it's not that...but
〖何等〗(副)[héděng]
①how (=very) ②what kind of
〖何妨〗(副)[héfáng]

why not
〖何苦〗(副) [hékǔ]
① for what earthly reason ② totally unnecessary
〖何况〗(连) [hékuàng]
besides; furthermore
〖何其毒也〗[héqídúyě]
how vicious it is
〖何其相似乃尔〗
[héqíxiāngsìnǎi'ěr]
what a striking likeness
〖何去何从〗[héqùhécóng]
(decide) on what path to follow; which to reject and which to accept; where to go
〖何如〗[hérú]
how about
〖何谓〗[héwèi]
what is meant by
〖何以〗[héyǐ]
why
〖何在〗[hézài]
where is...

和(名、形、连、介) [hé]
① peace; amity; amiable; harmonious ② and; to; with
另见 huó huò
〖和蔼〗(形) [hé'ǎi]
peaceable; amiable; kindly
〖和风细雨〗[héfēngxìyǔ]
(lit.) gentle breeze and mild rain; (fig.) not be rough
〖和好〗(动) [héhǎo]
become reconciled with (sb.); iron out a dispute
〖和缓〗(形) [héhuǎn]
conciliatry; moderate; mild
〖和解〗(动) [héjiě]
reconcile; settlement by meditation
〖和睦〗(形) [hémù]
friendly; harmonious
〖和平〗(名) [hépíng]
peace
〖和平共处〗[hépínggòngchǔ]
peaceful coexistence
〖和平共处五项原则〗
[hépínggòngchǔwǔxiàngyuánzé]
Five Principles of Peaceful Coexistence: mutual respect for territorial integrity and sovereignty, mutual non-aggression, non-interference in each other's internal affairs, equality and mutual benefit and peaceful coexistence
〖和平演变〗[hépíngyǎnbiàn]
peaceful evolution
〖和气〗(形) [héqì]
friendly; placid
〖和谈〗(名) [hétán]
peace negotiations
〖和谐〗(形) [héxié]
harmonious
〖和颜悦色〗[héyányuèsè]
amiable manner; benign countenance
〖和约〗(名) [héyuē]
peace treaty

河(名) [hé] 〔条 tiáo〕
river
〖河床〗(名) [héchuáng]

river bed
〖河堤〗(名)[hédī]
river embankment; dyke
〖河流〗(名)[héliú]
rivers
〖河山〗(名)[héshān]
rivers and mountains (territory of a country)
〖河水〗(名)[héshuǐ]
river waters

荷[hé]
〖荷花〗(名)[héhuā]〔朵 duǒ〕
lotus flower

核(名)[hé]
nucleus; kern
〖核保护伞〗[hébǎohùsǎn]
nuclear protective umbrella
〖核弹头〗[hédàntóu]
nuclear warhead
〖核定〗(动)[hédìng]
grant after due consideration
〖核对〗(动)[héduì]
verify; check
〖核讹诈〗[héézhà]
nuclear blackmail
〖核垄断〗[hélǒngduàn]
nuclear monopoly
〖核实〗(动)[héshí]
verify; check up
〖核算〗(动)[hésuàn]
estimate; calculate; (economic) accounting
〖核桃〗(名)[hétao]
walnut
〖核武器〗[héwǔqì]
nuclear weapons
〖核心〗(名)[héxīn]
nucleus; hard core
〖核装置〗[hézhuāngzhì]
nuclear device
〖核子〗(名)[hézǐ]
nucleus

盒(名、量)[hé]
① box ② a measure word (e.g. a box of...)
〖盒子〗(名)[hézi]
box

hè

贺(动)[hè]
greet
〖贺词〗(名)[hècí]
speech of greeting
〖贺电〗(名)[hèdiàn]
message of greeting
〖贺年〗[hè nián]
New Year greetings
〖贺喜〗[hèxǐ]
congratulate on happy occasion
〖贺信〗(名)[hèxìn]〔封 fēng〕
letter of greeting

喝(动)[hè]
shout
另见 hē
〖喝彩〗[hècǎi]
applaud

赫[hè]
〖赫赫有名〗[hèhèyǒumíng]
have a great reputation

褐(形)[hè]
brown
〖褐色〗(名)[hèsè]
brown colour

hēi

黑(形)[hēi]
①black; dark ②sinister
〖黑暗〗(形)[hēi'àn]
dark
〖黑白片〗(名)[hēibáipiàn]
black and white film
〖黑板〗(名)[hēibǎn]〔块 kuài〕
blackboard
〖黑板报〗(名)[hēibǎnbào]
blackboard newspaper
〖黑洞洞〗(形)[hēidōngdōng]
very dark; pitch-dark
〖黑话〗(名)[hēihuà]
gangsters' slang; double-talk; malicious words
〖黑货〗(名)[hēihuò]
contraband goods; sinister stuff
〖黑名单〗(名)[hēimíngdān]
black list
〖黑色〗(名)[hēisè]
black colour
〖黑市交易〗[hēishìjiāoyì]
off-the-books deal; trading illegally on the black market
〖黑体字〗(名)[hēitǐzì]
bold-face type
〖黑夜〗(名)[hēiyè]
night
〖黑油油〗(形)[hēiyōuyōu]
intense dark; black

嘿(叹)[hēi]
an interjection used: ① to arouse attention ② to express content, satisfaction ③ to express surprise

hén

痕[hén]
〖痕迹〗(名)[hénjī]
mark; trace; stamp; vestige; track

hěn

狠(形)[hěn]
① relentless; cruel ② firm; resolute (e.g. firmly grasp)
〖狠毒〗(形)[hěndú]
malicious
〖狠心〗(形)[hěnxīn]
cruel; ruthless

很(副)[hěn]
very; quite

hèn

恨(动)[hèn]
hate; be exasperated
〖恨不得〗(副)[hènbude]
very anxious to; vexed at not being able to; wish only one could
〖恨铁不成钢〗
[hèntiěbùchéng gāng]
(lit.) wish iron could turn into steel at once; (fig.) be strict to someone in the hope that

he could be better or change for the better immediately

hēng

哼(动、叹)[hēng]
① hum ② an interjection expressing dissatisfaction or distrust

héng

恒[héng]
〖恒心〗(名)[héngxīn]
persistence; constancy
〖恒星〗(名)[héngxīng]〔颗 kē〕
fixed star

横(形、动、名)[héng]
horizontal; crosswise; span; cross; trans-; across
另见 hèng
〖横冲直撞〗
[héngchōngzhí zhuàng]
reckless action; colliding with (vehicles, etc.) in every direction
〖横渡〗(动)[héngdù]
cross; ferry or sail across; traverse
〖横幅〗(名)[héngfú]
streamer
〖横贯〗(动)[héngguàn]
go through from (east to west)
〖横扫〗(动)[héngsǎo]
sweep away or across
〖横竖〗(副)[héngshù]
any way; by all means
〖横行霸道〗[héngxíngbàdào]
ride roughshod over; play the bully
〖横征暴敛〗[héngzhēngbàoliǎn]
exorbitant taxes and levies; ruthless taxation

衡[héng]
〖衡量〗(动)[héngliáng]
measure; estimate; judge

hèng

横(形)[hèng]
unreasonable; savage
另见 héng
〖横暴〗(形)[hèngbào]
brutal; tyrannical; high-handed
〖横财〗(名)[hèngcái]
ill-gotten gains; underhand gains

hōng

轰(动、象声)[hōng]
① drive out ② bomb; bombard ③ onomatopoeia, bang, crash (sound of explosion, thunder, etc.)
〖轰动〗(动)[hōngdòng]
stir; create a sensation; be astir
〖轰轰烈烈〗(形)
[hōnghōng lièliè]
stormy and heroic; stirring and seething
〖轰击〗(动)[hōngjī]
bombard
〖轰隆〗(象声)[hōnglōng]
onomatopoeia, bang, crash, ro-

ar (sound of thunder, explosion, etc.)
〖轰鸣〗(动)[hōngmíng]
roar (of guns, etc.)
〖轰炸〗(动)[hōngzhà]
bomb
〖轰炸机〗(名)[hōngzhàjī]〔架 jià〕
bomber

哄[hōng]
另见 hǒng
〖哄动〗(动)[hōngdòng]
cause a sensation; stir; bestir
〖哄抬〗(动)[hōngtái]
force up (prices)
〖哄堂大笑〗[hōngtáng dàxiào]
the people of the whole house burst out into laughter; fit of laughter

烘(动)[hōng]
dry at a fire
〖烘托〗(动)[hōngtuō]
① set off in contrast ② paint around an outline to make the object prominent

hóng

红(形)[hóng]
① red ② (fig.) revolutionary
〖红包〗(名)[hóngbāo]
red packet (covert payment or bribery)
〖红宝石〗(名)[hóngbǎoshí]
ruby
〖红茶〗(名)[hóngchá]
black tea
〖红灯〗(名)[hóngdēng]〔盏 zhǎn〕
red lantern; red light in traffic lights
〖红光满面〗[hóngguāngmǎnmiàn]
beaming with health; glowing with health
〖红军〗(名)[Hóngjūn]
the Red Army
〖红领巾〗(名)[hónglǐngjīn]
① red scarf worn by Young Pioneers ② the Young Pioneers
〖红旗〗(名)[hóngqí]〔面 miàn〕
red flag; red banner
〖红润〗(形)[hóngrùn]
rosy (e.g. cheeks)
〖红色〗(名)[hóngsè]
red colour
〖红糖〗(名)[hóngtáng]
brown sugar
〖红彤彤〗(形)[hóngtōngtōng]
bright red
〖红外线〗(名)[hóngwàixiàn]
infrared rays
〖红十字会〗(名)[hóngshízìhuì]
the Red Cross
〖红星〗(名)[hóngxīng]〔颗 kē〕
red star
〖红血球〗(名)[hóngxuèqiú]
red corpuscle; erythrocytes
〖红药水〗(名)[hóngyàoshuǐ]
mercurochrome
〖红缨枪〗(名)[hóngyīngqiāng]〔枝 zhī〕red-tasselled spear

宏[hóng]
〖宏大〗(形)[hóngdà]

great; grand
〖宏观〗(形、名)[hóngguān]
macro; macroscopic
〖宏观调控〗[hóngguāntiáokòng]
macro-control
〖宏图〗(名)[hóngtú]
far-reaching plans; grandiose plans
〖宏伟〗(形)[hóngwěi]
magnificent; grand (prospects)

虹(名)[hóng]
rainbow

洪[hóng]
〖洪亮〗(形)[hóngliàng]
(of voice) loud and clear
〖洪流〗(名)[hóngliú]
powerful current; tide
〖洪炉〗(名)[hónglú]
crucible
〖洪水〗(名)[hóngshuǐ]
flood; inundation

鸿[hóng]
〖鸿沟〗(名)[hónggōu]〔道 dào〕
gap; chasm
〖鸿毛〗(名)[hóngmáo]
swan's-down; feather

hǒng

哄(动)[hǒng]
coax; lull
另见 hōng
〖哄骗〗(动)[hǒngpiàn]
cheat by fine words

hóu

喉(名)[hóu]
throat
〖喉咙〗(名)[hóulóng]
throat
〖喉舌〗(名)[hóushé]
mouthpiece; spokesmen

猴(名)[hóu]
monkey
〖猴子〗(名)[hóuzi]〔只 zhī〕
monkey

hǒu

吼(动)[hǒu]
roar; bellow
〖吼叫〗(动)[hǒujiào]
roar

hòu

后(名)[hòu]
back; behind; rear
〖后备〗(名)[hòubèi]
reserves
〖后备军〗(名)[hòubèijūn]
reserve force
〖后边〗(名)[hòubian]
rear; back
〖后代〗(名)[hòudài]
succeeding generations; descendants
〖后盾〗(名)[hòudùn]
backing; support
〖后发制人〗[hòufāzhìrén]
gain mastery by striking only after the enemy has struck

〖后方〗(名)[hòufāng]
rear (area)
〖后顾之忧〗[hòugùzhīyōu]
fear of attack from behind
〖后果〗(名)[hòuguǒ]
consequence
〖后患〗(名)[hòuhuàn]
disastrous consequences; aftermaths
〖后悔〗(形、动)[hòuhuǐ]
repent; regret; remorseful
〖后悔莫及〗[hòuhuǐmòjí]
too late to regret it
〖后记〗(名)[hòujì]
postscript (of a book or article)
〖后继有人〗[hòujìyǒurén]
have qualified successors
〖后进〗(形)[hòujìn]
lag behind
〖后来〗(名)[hòulái]
afterwards; later on
〖后来居上〗[hòuláijūshàng]
late-comers become the first; the new comers have overtaken the old hands
〖后浪推前浪〗
[hòulàngtuīqiánlàng]
each wave pushing at the one ahead
〖后路〗(名)[hòulù]〔条 tiáo〕
① back route ② way of escape; room for retreat
〖后面〗(名)[hòumiàn]
① back ② later ③ behind
〖后年〗(名)[hòunián]
the year after next
〖后起之秀〗[hòuqǐzhīxiù]
the outstanding up-and-coming people
〖后勤〗(名)[hòuqín]
logistics service; rear-service
〖后人〗(名)[hòurén]
successors
〖后台〗(名)[hòutái]
① backstage ② behind-the-scenes boss; supporter
〖后天〗(名)[hòutiān]
① the day after tomorrow ② a posterior
〖后头〗(名)[hòutou]
behind; back
〖后退〗(动)[hòutuì]
retreat; evacuate
〖后遗症〗(名)[hòuyízhèng]
after-effect
〖后裔〗(名)[hòuyì]
descendants; posterity
〖后者〗(名)[hòuzhě]
the latter

厚(形)[hòu]
thick
〖厚此薄彼〗[hòucǐbóbǐ]
discriminate against some and favour others
〖厚道〗(形)[hòudao]
decent; sincere and considerate
〖厚度〗(名)[hòudù]
thickness
〖厚古薄今〗[hòugǔbójīn]
stress the past more than the present
〖厚今薄古〗[hòujīnbógǔ]

stress the present more than the past
〖厚实〗(形)[hòushi]
①thick and solid ②rich; well-off
〖厚颜无耻〗[hòuyánwúchǐ]
have the cheek to...; have no sense of shame

侯(动)[hòu]
wait
〖候补〗(动)[hòubǔ]
alternate
〖候车室〗(名)[hòuchēshì]
waiting-room (of railway station, etc.)
〖候选人〗(名)[hòuxuǎnrén]
candidate

hū

呼(动、象声)[hū]
①call; cry out; shout ②exhale ③onomatopoeia, whistle; hiss (for sound of wind, flame, etc.)
〖呼喊〗(动)[hūhǎn]
cry; call; shout
〖呼号〗(动)[hūháo]
wail
〖呼唤〗(动)[hūhuàn]
call to
〖呼喇喇〗(象声)[hūlālā]
onomatopoeia (sound of fluttering of flags, sound of flapping, etc.)
〖呼声〗(名)[hūshēng]
voice; outcry
〖呼吸〗(动)[hūxī]
respirate; breathe
〖呼啸〗(动)[hūxiào]
scream
〖呼应〗(动)[hūyìng]
respond to; echo
〖呼吁〗(动)[hūyù]
appeal; call for

忽[hū]
〖忽而〗(副)[hū'ér]
now...now...; suddenly
〖忽略〗(动)[hūlüè]
neglect; ignore
〖忽然〗(副)[hūrán]
suddenly; abruptly; unexpectedly
〖忽视〗(动)[hūshì]
overlook; neglect; ignore

hú

囫[hú]
〖囫囵吞枣〗[húlúntūnzǎo]
(lit.) swallow up a date in one gulp; (fig.) gulp down without thought

狐(名)[hú]
fox
〖狐假虎威〗[hújiǎhǔwēi]
the fox borrows the tiger's terror; (fig.) assume someone else's authority to browbeat others
〖狐狸〗(名)[húli]〔只 zhī〕
fox
〖狐群狗党〗[húqúngǒudǎng]
a gang of scoundrels

〖狐疑〗(动、名)[húyí]
suspicion; distrust

弧(名)[hú]
arc
〖弧度〗(名)[húdù]
radian
〖弧光〗(名)[húguāng]
(electr.) arc
〖弧形〗(名)[húxíng]
bowshape; arc-shape

胡(副)[hú]
nonsensical
〖胡椒粉〗(名)[hújiāofěn]
powdered pepper
〖胡萝卜〗(名)[húluóbo]
carrot
〖胡闹〗(动)[húnào]
keep up one's wrong doing; indulge in an unreasonable altercation; behave recklessly
〖胡琴〗(名)[húqín]〔把 bǎ〕
Chinese violin with two strings
〖胡说〗(动)[húshuō]
talk nonsense
〖胡说八道〗[húshuōbādào]
talk nonsense or rubbish
〖胡同〗(名)[hútòng]〔条 tiáo〕
lane
〖胡言乱语〗[húyánluànyǔ]
talk nonsense
〖胡子〗(名)[húzi]
beard; moustache
〖胡作非为〗[húzuòfēiwéi]
run amuck; criminal actions

壶(名、量)[hú]〔把 bǎ〕
kettle; pot

湖(名)[hú]
lake
〖湖泊〗(名)[húpō]
lakes in general

蝴[hú]
〖蝴蝶〗(名)[húdié]〔只 zhī〕
butterfly

糊(动)[hú]
① be burnt; be singed ② paste
〖糊口〗(动)[húkǒu]
make a living
〖糊里糊涂〗[húlihútú]
muddy (ideas); with minds in a haze
〖糊涂〗(形)[hútu]
muddle headed

hǔ

虎(名)[hǔ]〔只 zhī〕
tiger
〖虎口〗(名)[hǔkǒu]
① (lit.) tiger's mouth; (fig.) a dangerous place ② area between thumb and index finger
〖虎视眈眈〗[hǔshìdāndān]
glare at fiercely (with covetous desire)
〖虎头蛇尾〗[hǔtóushéwěi]
begin with tigerish energy but peter out towards the end; a brave beginning but a weak end-

ing

〖虎穴〗(名)[hǔxué]
tiger's den—a very dangerous place

hù

互[hù]

〖互不侵犯条约〗[hùbùqīnfàntiáoyuē]
treaty of mutual non-aggression

〖互惠〗[hùhuì]
reciprocal

〖互利〗[hùlì]
mutual benefit

〖互通有无〗[hùtōngyǒuwú]
mutual help to make up what the other lacks; help supply each other's wants

〖互相〗(副)[hùxiāng]
mutually; each other

〖互助〗(动)[hùzhù]
aid mutually

〖互助组〗(名)[hùzhùzǔ]
mutual-aid team

户(量)[hù]
a measure word, household

〖户口〗(名)[hùkǒu]
① household ② registered residence

〖户口簿〗(名)[hùkǒubù]
permanent residence booklet

〖户头〗(名)[hùtóu]
(bank) account

护(动)[hù]
protect

〖护理〗(动)[hùlǐ]
nurse; look after

〖护士〗(名)[hùshi]
nurse

〖护送〗(动)[hùsòng]
escort

〖护照〗(名)[hùzhào]
passport

怙[hù]

〖怙恶不悛〗[hù'èbùquān]
persist in evil and not repent; sticking to one's arbitrary habits; remain impenitent and keep to one's wrong doing

huā

花(动、名)[huā][朵 duǒ]
① spend; use ② (of eye-sight) become dim, blurred or dizzy ③ colourful; variegated; coloured ④ flower

〖花白〗(形)[huābái]
(of hair, beard, etc,) greyish

〖花瓣〗(名)[huābàn]
flower petals

〖花边〗(名)[huābiān]
lace

〖花布〗(名)[huābù]
printed calico

〖花茶〗(名)[huāchá]
perfumed tea

〖花朵〗(名)[huāduǒ]
blossom; a cluster of flowers

〖花费〗(动)[huāfèi]
spend; use up

H

〖花岗岩〗(名)[huāgāngyán]
granite
〖花花绿绿〗(形)[huāhuālùlù]
multi-coloured; colourful
〖花花世界〗[huāhuāshìjiè]
a world of self-indulgent luxury
〖花镜〗(名)[huājìng]〔副 fù〕
presbyopic eyeglasses; spectacles for people with long sight
〖花卷儿〗(名)[huājuǎnr]
steamed roll (made of wheat flour)
〖花篮〗(名)[huālán]〔只 zhī〕
flower baskets; baskets of flowers
〖花炮〗(名)[huāpào]
fireworks; fire cracker
〖花盆儿〗(名)[huāpénr]〔个 gè〕
flower pot
〖花瓶〗(名)[huāpíng]〔个 gè〕
flower vase
〖花圈〗(名)[huāquān]
wreath
〖花色品种〗[huāsèpǐnzhǒng]
colours and patterns; varieties
〖花生〗(名)[huāshēng]
peanut
〖花生米〗(名)[huāshēngmǐ]
〔粒 lì〕shelled peanut
〖花束〗(名)[huāshù]
bouquet
〖花言巧语〗[huāyánqiǎoyǔ]
honeyed or deceiving words
〖花样〗(名)[huāyàng]
①pattern; design; style; variations ②tricks
〖花园〗(名)[huāyuán]
garden
〖花招〗(名)[huāzhāo]
trick

哗(象声)[huā]
onomatopoeia, (tinkle, rattle sound of flowing water or chains, etc.)
另见 huá
〖哗哗〗(象声)[huāhuā]
onomatopoeia (the sound of flowing water; splish-splash)

huá

划(动)[huá]
①paddle ②scratch; cut
另见 huà
〖划船〗[huáchuán]
paddle a boat; row
〖划算〗[huásuàn]
be to one's profit; be worthwhile doing sth.; pay

华[huá]
〖华表〗(名)[huábiǎo]
decorative pillar
〖华而不实〗[huá'érbùshí]
flashy without substance
〖华丽〗(形)[huálì]
gorgeous
〖华侨〗(名)[huáqiáo]
overseas Chinese

哗[huá]

H

另见 huā
〖哗然〗(形)[huárán]
clamorous
〖哗众取宠〗[huázhòngqǔchǒng]
impress people by claptrap; curry favour by claptrap

滑(形、动)[huá]
slippery; slip
〖滑冰〗[huábīng]
skate
〖滑稽〗(形)[huájī]
ridiculous; ludicrous
〖滑轮〗(名)[huálún]
pulley
〖滑坡〗[huápō]
① landslide; landslip ② declining; downhill; slump
〖滑梯〗(名)[huátī]
slide for children to play on
〖滑头〗(形)[huátóu]
cunning
〖滑翔〗(动)[huáxiáng]
glid; and wheel round
〖滑翔机〗(名)[huáxiángjī]
glider; gliding plane
〖滑雪〗[huáxuě]
ski

huà

化(动、尾)[huà]
change; convert; transform; (suffix) -ize; -ization
〖化肥〗(名)[huàféi]
fertilizer
〖化公为私〗[huàgōngwéisī]
appropriate public property
〖化合〗(动)[huàhé]
combine in chemical process; chemical combination
〖化合反应〗[huàhéfǎnyìng]
reaction of combination
〖化合物〗(名)[huàhéwù]
(chem.) compound
〖化身〗(名)[huàshēn]
reincarnation; personification
〖化石〗(名)[huàshí]
fossil
〖化险为夷〗[huàxiǎnwéiyí]
come out safely from danger
〖化学〗(名)[huàxué]
chemistry
〖化学变化〗[huàxuébiànhuà]
chemical change
〖化学反应〗[huàxuéfǎnyìng]
chemical reaction
〖化学方程式〗[huàxuéfāngchéngshì]
chemical equation
〖化学工业〗[huàxuégōngyè]
chemical industry
〖化学武器〗[huàxuéwǔqì]
weapon of chemical warfare
〖化学纤维〗[huàxuéxiānwéi]
chemical fibre; synthetic fibre
〖化学元素〗[huàxuéyuánsù]
chemical element
〖化验〗(动)[huàyàn]
chemical examination
〖化整为零〗[huàzhěng wéilíng]
break up the whole into parts
〖化装〗(动)[huàzhuāng]
dress in disguise; make-up

划(动)[huà]
draw; classify
另见 huá
〖划分〗(动)[huàfēn]
divide; set apart
〖划清〗(动)[huàqīng]
draw a clear line between
〖划时代〗[huàshídài]
epoch-making

画(动、名)[huà]
〔张 zhāng、幅 fú〕
①draw; paint; drawings; paintings ②strokes of a character
〖画报〗(名)[huàbào]〔本 běn〕
pictorial
〖画饼充饥〗[huàbǐngchōngjī]
draw a cake to satisfy one's hunger
〖画家〗(名)[huàjiā]
painter
〖画刊〗(名)[huàkān]
pictorial magazine
〖画廊〗(名)[huàláng]
gallery
〖画龙点睛〗[huàlóngdiǎnjīng]
(lit.) put in the eyeballs in painting a dragon; (fig.) a critical touch
〖画面〗(名)[huàmiàn]
① the general appearance of a work of art in respect of light, colour and composition ② picture (of film)
〖画皮〗(名)[huàpí]
mask; disguise
〖画片〗(名)[huàpiàn]〔张 zhāng〕
small reprints of paintings
〖画蛇添足〗[huàshétiānzú]
(lit.) paint a snake with feet added to it; (fig.) ruin the effect by adding what is superfluous
〖画像〗(名)[huàxiàng]
〔张 zhāng〕portrait
〖画展〗(名)[huàzhǎn]
art exhibition

话(名)[huà]〔句 jù〕
speech; talk; words
〖话别〗(动)[huàbié]
say goodbye; make one's farewells
〖话柄〗(名)[huàbǐng]
target or material for gossip
〖话剧〗(名)[huàjù]
play; modern drama
〖话题〗(名)[huàtí]
topic (for discussion or conversation)

huái

怀(名、动)[huái]
①bosom ②cherish; harbour
〖怀抱〗(名、动)[huáibào]
embrace; (be in) the arms of...
〖怀表〗(名)[huáibiǎo]
pocket watch
〖怀恨〗(动)[huáihèn]
have resentment in one's heart; nurse hatred against
〖怀念〗(动)[huáiniàn]
cherish the memory of

〖怀疑〗(动、名)[huáiyí]
suspect; suspicion
〖怀孕〗[huáiyùn]
pregnancy
〖怀着〗(动)[huáizhe]
cherish; harbour; be filled with

槐(名)[huái]
locust; acacia
〖槐树〗(名)[huáishù][棵 kē]
locust; acacia

huài

坏(形)[huài]
bad
〖坏处〗(名)[huàichu]
harm; adverse effect
〖坏蛋〗(名)[huàidàn]
"bad egg"; a villain; a rascal; scoundrel
〖坏分子〗(名)[huàifènzǐ]
bad element
〖坏人〗(名)[huàirén]
bad man; bad element

huān

欢[huān]
〖欢畅〗(形)[huānchàng]
happy; cheerful
〖欢呼〗(动)[huānhū]
cheer; acclaim; applaud; hail
〖欢聚一堂〗[huānjùyītáng]
a happy gathering; get together joyously
〖欢乐〗(形)[huānlè]
happy; delighted; elated
〖欢声雷动〗[huānshēngléidòng]
thunderous cheers
〖欢送〗(动)[huānsòng]
see off; send off
〖欢腾〗(动)[huānténg]
be overjoyed; rejoice; be elated
〖欢天喜地〗[huāntiānxǐdì]
extremely delighted; filled with joy
〖欢喜〗(形)[huānxǐ]
① happy ② like; be fond of
〖欢笑〗(动)[huānxiào]
laugh heartily
〖欢心〗(名)[huānxīn]
love; appreciation; (win one's) favour
〖欢欣鼓舞〗[huānxīnggǔwǔ]
be elated and inspired
〖欢迎〗(动)[huānyíng]
welcome; greet

huán

还(动)[huán]
return
另见 hái
〖还击〗(动)[huánjī]
fight back; counter-attack; deal counter blows
〖还礼〗[huánlǐ]
① return the salute; return courtesy
〖还手〗[huánshǒu]
fight or hit back; give returning blows
〖还原〗[huányuán]
reduce; restore; return to ori-

H

ginal shape or position

环(名)[huán]
①ring②the key to
〖环保〗(名)[huánbǎo]
environmental protection
〖环抱〗(动)[huánbào]
encircle; surround
〖环顾〗(动)[huángù]
look round
〖环节〗(名)[huánjié]
link
〖环境〗(名)[huánjìng]
conditions; environment; circumstances
〖环球〗(名)[huánqiú]
around the world; the whole world
〖环绕〗(动)[huánrào]
go round; centre on
〖环视〗(动)[huánshì]
look round
〖环行〗(动)[huánxíng]
go round a certain place

huǎn

缓(动、形)[huǎn]
be slow; postpone; slow
〖缓兵之计〗[huǎnbīngzhījì]
measures to stave off an attack; stalling tactics
〖缓冲〗(动)[huǎnchōng]
buffer; lessen
〖缓和〗(动、形)[huǎnhé]
allay; moderate; mitigate; detente; relax
〖缓慢〗(形)[huǎnmàn]
very slow
〖缓期〗[huǎnqī]
postpone

huàn

幻[huàn]
〖幻灯〗(名)[huàndēng]
lantern slides
〖幻觉〗(名)[huànjué]
hallucination
〖幻灭〗(动)[huànmiè]
disillusion; shatter
〖幻想〗(动、名)[huànxiǎng]
illusion

换(动)[huàn]
change; exchange
〖换班〗[huànbān]
relieve guard; change shifts
〖换工〗[huàngōng]
exchange of labour
〖换算〗(动)[huànsuàn]
convert
〖换汤不换药〗
[huàntāngbù huànyào]
old wine in new bottles
〖换文〗[huànwén]
exchange notes
〖换文〗(名)[huànwén]
exchanged notes

唤(动)[huàn]
call
〖唤起〗(动)[huànqǐ]
arouse; call
〖唤醒〗(动)[huànxǐng]
awaken

涣[huàn]
〖涣散〗(形、动)[huànsàn]
dissipate; sap; dissipated; demobilized

患(动)[huàn]
suffer (from illness); be distressed in mind
〖患病〗[huànbìng]
be afflicted with a disease; fall ill; suffer from illness
〖患得患失〗[huàndéhuànshī]
worry about personal gain and loss
〖患难〗(名)[huànnàn]
adversity; hardship
〖患难与共〗[huànnànyǔgòng]
stick together through thick and thin; share weal and woe
〖患者〗(名)[huànzhě]
patient

焕[huàn]
〖焕发〗(形、动)[huànfā]
sparkling; sparkle; brim over with
〖焕然一新〗[huànrányīxīn]
spick and span; take on an altogether new aspect

豢[huàn]
〖豢养〗(动)[huànyǎng]
nurture; groom; foster

huāng

荒(形)[huāng]
① fantastic; absurd ② famine (year)
〖荒诞〗(形)[huāngdàn]
fantastic; ludicrous
〖荒诞无稽〗[huāngdànwújī]
absurdity
〖荒地〗(名)[huāngdì]
wasteland
〖荒废〗(动)[huāngfèi]
① fall into disuse; lay waste ② neglect and become unproficient
〖荒凉〗(形)[huāngliáng]
desolate
〖荒谬〗(形)[huāngmiù]
absurd; ridiculous
〖荒谬绝伦〗[huāngmiùjuélún]
absurd in the highest degrees; nothing could be more ridiculous; sheer nonsense
〖荒年〗(名)[huāngnián]
crop failures; famine years
〖荒山〗(名)[huāngshān]
barren hills
〖荒疏〗(形)[huāngshū]
uncultivated (land); neglect and become unproficient; (get) out of practice
〖荒唐〗(形)[huāngtáng]
absurd; mythical
〖荒芜〗(形)[huāngwú]
(of land) overgrown with underbrush from lack of management
〖荒野〗(名)[huāngyě]
wilderness
〖荒淫无耻〗[huāngyínwúchǐ]
given to debauchery; dissipation

慌(形) [huāng]
flurried; nervous
〖慌乱〗(形) [huāngluàn]
be alarmed and bewildered
〖慌忙〗(形) [huāngmáng]
flustered; hurried
〖慌张〗(形) [huāngzhāng]
helter-skelter; nervous

huáng

皇 [huáng]
〖皇帝〗(名) [huángdì]
emperor

黄(形) [huáng]
yellow
〖黄豆〗(名) [huángdòu] 〔粒 lì〕
soybean
〖黄瓜〗(名) [huángguā]
cucumber
〖黄昏〗(名) [huánghūn]
dusk
〖黄金〗(名) [huángjīn]
gold
〖黄金时代〗[huángjīn shídài]
golden age
〖黄色〗(名、形) [huángsè]
① yellow colour; yellow ② decadent; obscene
〖黄土〗(名) [huángtǔ]
loess
〖黄油〗(名) [huángyóu]
① butter ② lubricating oil

惶 [huáng]
〖惶惶〗(形) [huánghuáng]
alarmed; nervous
〖惶惶不可终日〗
[huánghuáng bùkězhōngrì]
be kept in a state of constant nervousness; be on tenterhooks all the time
〖惶惑〗(形) [huánghuò]
perplexed and alarmed
〖惶恐〗(形) [huángkǒng]
fear; alarmed

蝗 [huáng]
〖蝗虫〗(名) [huángchóng]
locust (insect)

磺 [huáng]
〖磺胺〗(名) [huáng'ān]
sulphanilamide

huǎng

恍 [huǎng]
〖恍惚〗(形) [huǎnghū]
illusory
〖恍然大悟〗[huǎngrándàwù]
suddenly realize

谎(名) [huǎng]
lie; falsehood
〖谎话〗(名) [huǎnghuà]
lie
〖谎言〗(名) [huǎngyán]
lie

幌 [huǎng]
〖幌子〗(名) [huǎngzi]
① signboard ② under the guise

H

of; pretext; smokescreen

huàng

晃 (动) [huàng]
sway
〖晃荡〗(动) [huàngdang]
sway
〖晃动〗(动) [huàngdòng]
shake
〖晃悠〗(形、动) [huàngyou]
swinging; swing

huī

灰 (名、形) [huī]
①ash ②grey
〖灰暗〗(形) [huī'àn]
obscure; dim; dismal
〖灰白〗(形) [huībái]
grey and white; greyish
〖灰尘〗(名) [huīchén]
dust
〖灰烬〗(名) [huījìn]
ashes
〖灰溜溜〗(形) [huīliūliū]
dispirited
〖灰色〗(名) [huīsè]
grey coloured
〖灰心〗(形) [huīxīn]
disheartened; dispirited
〖灰心丧气〗[huīxīnsàngqì]
downhearted; downcast

诙 [huī]
〖诙谐〗(形) [huīxié]
humorous

挥 (动) [huī]
wave
〖挥动〗(动) [huīdòng]
wave
〖挥发〗(动) [huīfā]
evaporate
〖挥霍〗(动) [huīhuò]
spend extravagantly; spend freely
〖挥金如土〗[huījīnrútǔ]
spend money like dirt
〖挥手〗[huīshǒu]
wave one's arm
〖挥舞〗(动) [huīwǔ]
wave; brandish

恢 [huī]
〖恢复〗(动) [huīfù]
restore; regain; recover; rehabilitate; resume

辉 [huī]
〖辉煌〗(形) [huīhuáng]
glorious; splendid; brilliant
〖辉映〗(动) [huīyìng]
reflect; illuminate; shine

徽 [huī]
〖徽章〗(名) [huīzhāng] [枚 méi]
badge

huí

回 (动、量) [huí]
①return; come back ②a measure word (a chapter in story, number of times, e.g. once, twice, etc.)

H

〖回拜〗(动)[huíbài]
pay a return visit
〖回避〗(动)[huíbì]
evade; avoid confrontation with; bypass
〖回潮〗(动、名)[huícháo]
reverse; stage a come-back; backwash; reflux; a come-back
〖回答〗(动、名)[huídá]
answer; reply
〖回电〗(名)[huídiàn]
reply by telegram
〖回访〗(动)[huífǎng]
return a visit
〖回复〗(动)[huífù]
① reply ② restore
〖回顾〗(动)[huígù]
look back
〖回归线〗(名)[huíguīxiàn]
[条 tiáo] tropic
〖回合〗(名)[huíhé]
rounds (e.g. boxing)
〖回击〗(动)[huíjī]
counterattack; fight back
〖回家〗[huíjiā]
go home
〖回敬〗(动)[huíjìng]
reciprocate; offer sth. in return
〖回绝〗(动)[huíjué]
turn down; reject
〖回来〗[huílái]
come back
〖回民〗(名)[Huímín]
Hui (national minority of China)
〖回去〗[huí qù]
go back
〖回升〗(动)[huíshēng]
rise up again
〖回声〗(名)[huíshēng]
echo
〖回收〗(动)[huíshōu]
redeem (productive use of cast-off things)
〖回头〗(副)[huítóu]
in a moment; later on
〖回味〗(动)[huíwèi]
① after taste ② realize through recollection
〖回响〗(动)[huíxiǎng]
echo
〖回想〗(动)[huíxiǎng]
recall
〖回心转意〗[huíxīnzhuǎnyì]
repent; change one's mind
〖回信〗(名)[huíxìn]
reply by letter
〖回旋〗(动)[huíxuán]
① gyrate; go round and round ② (room for) manoeuvre
〖回忆〗(动)[huíyì]
recollect
〖回忆录〗(名)[huíyìlù]
memoirs
〖回音〗(名)[huíyīn]
① letter of reply ② echo

huǐ

悔[huǐ]
〖悔改〗(动)[huǐgǎi]
mend one's ways
〖悔过〗(动)[huǐguò]
repent
〖悔过自新〗[huǐguòzìxīn]

repent and start anew
〖悔恨〗(动) [huǐhèn]
lament over
〖悔悟〗(动) [huǐwù]
awake to one's errors
〖悔之不及〗[huǐzhībùjí]
too late to repent

毁(动) [huǐ]
destroy; damage
〖毁坏〗(动) [huǐhuài]
damage; destroy
〖毁灭〗(动) [huǐmiè]
wipe out; exterminate

huì

汇(动) [huì]
① flow into; gather together ② transmit; remit (money)
〖汇报〗(动、名) [huìbào]
report; give an account of a report
〖汇编〗(名、动) [huìbiān]
assemble; collect and edit
〖汇兑〗(动) [huìduì]
remit (money)
〖汇费〗(名) [huìfèi]
remittance fee
〖汇合〗(动) [huìhé]
merge with; flow together; confluence
〖汇集〗(动) [huìjí]
pool; concourse (of rivers, people, etc.); come together
〖汇款〗[huìkuǎn]
remit money
〖汇款〗(名) [huìkuǎn]
remittance
〖汇率〗(名) [huìlǜ]
rate of exchange
〖汇总〗(动) [huìzǒng]
gather together

讳 [huì]
〖讳疾忌医〗[huìjíjìyī]
conceal a malady for fear of taking medicine; conceal one's illness and be reluctant to be cured; (fig.) conceal one's shortcomings and be reluctant to overcome them
〖讳莫如深〗[huìmòrúshēn]
carefully conceal or avoid mentioning

会(名、动、助动) [huì]
① meeting ② association; society ③ have the ability to; good at; know; understand ④ can; will (do, speak, sing, etc.)
另见 kuài
〖会餐〗(动) [huìcān]
dine together
〖会场〗(名) [huìchǎng]
place of meeting
〖会费〗(名) [huìfèi]
membership dues (of a union, association, etc.)
〖会合〗(动) [huìhé]
meet; join
〖会话〗(动、名) [huìhuà]
converse; dialogue; conversation
〖会集〗(动) [huìjí]

H

assemble
〖会见〗(动) [huìjiàn]
meet with
〖会客〗[huì kè]
see visitors
〖会客室〗(名) [huìkèshì]
reception room
〖会面〗[huìmiàn]
meet each other
〖会师〗(动) [huìshī]
join forces
〖会谈〗(动) [huìtán]
confer with; hold talks; negotiate
〖会同〗(动) [huìtóng]
join; be together with
〖会晤〗(动) [huìwù]
meet
〖会演〗(动) [huìyǎn]
hold a festival (of stage shows)
〖会议〗(名) [huìyì]
meeting; conference
〖会意〗(动) [huìyì]
silently appreciate
〖会员〗(名) [huìyuán]
member of an association, union, etc.; membership
〖会战〗(动、名) [huìzhàn]
engage in a decisive battle; general engagement
〖会诊〗(动) [huìzhěn]
(med.) have consultation

诲 [huì]
〖诲人不倦〗[huìrénbùjuàn]
never tired of teaching others; teach with tireless zeal

绘 (动) [huì]
draw; paint
〖绘画〗(名) [huìhuà]
drawing; painting
〖绘声绘色〗[huìshēnghuìsè]
vividly portrayed or depicted
〖绘图〗[huìtú]
draw a design
〖绘制〗(动) [huìzhì]
draw

贿 [huì]
〖贿赂〗(动、名) [huìlù]
bribe

烩 (动) [huì]
braise (cooking)

彗 [huì]
〖彗星〗(名) [huìxīng] [颗 kē]
comet

晦 [huì]
〖晦涩〗(形) [huìsè]
obscure in meaning

hūn

昏 (动) [hūn]
faint
〖昏暗〗(形) [hūn'àn]
dark; dim
〖昏沉〗(形) [hūnchén]
①dismal; dim ②muddled
〖昏花〗(形) [hūnhuā]

H

dim-sighted
〖昏迷〗(动) [hūnmí]
faint
〖昏天黑地〗[hūntiānhēidì]
in total darkness
〖昏庸〗(形) [hūnyōng]
stupid; idiotic

荤 (形) [hūn]
meat dishes
〖荤菜〗(名) [hūncài]
meat dishes

婚 (名) [hūn]
marriage
〖婚姻〗(名) [hūnyīn]
marriage
〖婚姻法〗(名) [hūnyīnfǎ]
marriage law

hún

浑 (形) [hún]
turbid; confused
〖浑厚〗(形) [húnhòu] honest
〖浑身〗(名) [húnshēn]
whole body

馄 [hún]
〖馄饨〗(名) [húntún]
stuffed dumplings

魂 (名) [hún]
soul
〖魂不附体〗[húnbùfùtǐ]
be scared out of one's wits

hùn

混 (动) [hùn]
muddle along; infiltrate; confuse
〖混纺〗(名) [hùnfǎng]
mixed fabric
〖混合〗(动) [hùnhé]
mix
〖混乱〗(形) [hùnluàn]
chaotic; disorderly
〖混凝土〗(名) [hùnníngtǔ]
cement
〖混水摸鱼〗[hùnshuǐmōyú]
fish in troubled waters
〖混同〗(动) [hùntóng]
confuse...with
〖混为一谈〗[hùnwéiyītán]
① equate...with... ② mix the two together
〖混淆〗(动) [hùnxiáo]
confuse; mix up
〖混淆黑白〗[hùnxiáohēibái]
juggle black and white; turn things upside down
〖混淆是非〗[hùnxiáoshìfēi]
confuse right and wrong
〖混淆视听〗[hùnxiáoshìtīng]
confuse the public
〖混杂〗(动) [hùnzá]
mix
〖混战〗(动) [hùnzhàn]
fight tangled warfare
〖混浊〗(形) [hùnzhuó]
muddy

huō

豁 (动) [huō]

①do sth. at all costs; stop at no sacrifices; ②crack
另见 huò
〖豁出去〗[huōchuqu]
stop at no sacrifices
〖豁口〗(名)[huōkǒu]
a crack; an opening (in a wall, city wall, etc.)

huó

和(动)[huó]
mix
另见 hé huò

活(动、形、名)[huó]
①live; alive; living ②work
〖活动〗(动、名)[huódòng]
①act ②activity; action
〖活动家〗(名)[huódòngjiā]
protagonist; man of action
〖活该〗(动)[huógāi]
it serves you right!
〖活力〗(名)[huólì]
vitality
〖活灵活现〗[huólínghuóxiàn]
vividly portray; tone it up with colour and life
〖活路〗(名)[huólù]〔条 tiáo〕
way out
〖活命〗(名)[huómìng]
survival
〖活泼〗(形)[huópo]
lively; vigorous
〖活塞〗(名)[huósāi]
piston
〖活生生〗(形)[huóshēngshēng]
vivid; lively
〖活像〗(动)[huóxiàng]
remarkably like; just like
〖活页〗(名)[huóyè]
loose-leaf
〖活跃〗(动、形)[huóyuè]
be active; spring into life; active; lively; animated
〖活字印刷〗[huózìyìnshuā]
movable-type printing; block-printing

huǒ

火(名、动)[huǒ]
①fire ②fall into a rage; become enraged; get angry
〖火把〗(名)[huǒbǎ]
torch
〖火柴〗(名)[huǒchái]〔盒 hé〕
match
〖火车〗(名)[huǒchē]〔列 liè〕
train
〖火车头〗(名)[huǒchētóu]
locomotive
〖火海〗(名)[huǒhǎi]
a sea of flames
〖火海刀山〗[huǒhǎidāoshān]
a sea of flames and a mountain of swords
〖火候〗(名)[huǒhou]
①strength of a fire (for cooking, etc.) ②critical moment
〖火花〗(名)[huǒhuā]
sparks
〖火化〗(动)[huǒhuà]
cremate
〖火箭〗(名)[huǒjiàn]
rocket

〖火警〗(名)[huǒjǐng]
an outbreak of fire; fire alarm
〖火炬〗(名)[huǒjù]
torch
〖火坑〗(名)[huǒkēng]
fiery pit; (fig.) extremely miserable situation
〖火辣辣〗(形)[huǒlālā]
fiery
〖火力〗(名)[huǒlì]
fire-power
〖火力点〗(名)[huǒlìdiǎn]
firing point
〖火力发电〗[huǒlì fā diàn]
thermo-electricity generation
〖火炉〗(名)[huǒlú]
stove; furnace
〖火苗〗(名)[huǒmiáo]
flame
〖火气〗(名)[huǒqì]
anger; bad temper
〖火热〗(形)[huǒrè]
fieryhot
〖火山〗(名)[huǒshān]
volcano
〖火上浇油〗[huǒshàngjiāoyóu]
pour oil on the flames
〖火烧眉毛〗[huǒshāoméimáo]
the fire is singeing the eyebrows; (fig.) extremely urgent
〖火烧〗(名)[huǒshao]
pancake
〖火石〗(名)[huǒshí]
flint
〖火速〗(副)[huǒsù]
at express speed
〖火腿〗(名)[huǒtuǐ]
ham
〖火线〗(名)[huǒxiàn]
front; fighting line
〖火星〗(名)[huǒxīng]〔颗 kē〕
① sparks ② the planet Mars
〖火焰〗(名)[huǒyàn]
flame
〖火药〗(名)[huǒyào]
gun-powder
〖火灾〗(名)[huǒzāi]
conflagration; fire-disaster
〖火葬〗(动)[huǒzàng]
cremate
〖火中取栗〗[huǒzhōngqǔlì]
pull chestnuts out of the fire
〖火种〗(名)[huǒzhǒng]
tinder

伙(名、量)[huǒ]
group; band
〖伙伴〗(名)[huǒbàn]
companion; partner
〖伙房〗(名)[huǒfáng]
kitchen
〖伙计〗(名)[huǒji]
(archaic) shop assistant
〖伙食〗(名)[huǒshí]
food (in a unit or institute)
〖伙同〗(动)[huǒtóng]
collude with; gang up with

huò

或(连、副)[huò]
or
〖或许〗(副)[huòxǔ]
perhaps
〖或者〗(连、副)[huòzhě]
or

H

和(动)[huò]
mix (earth into mud)
另见 hé huó
〖和稀泥〗[huòxīní]
(lit.) mix mud; (fig.) blur the line between right and wrong

货(名)[huò]
goods
〖货币〗(名)[huòbì]
currency
〖货币交换〗[huòbìjiāohuàn]
the exchange of currency
〖货舱〗(名)[huòcāng]
stowage; the hold (of a ship)
〖货车〗(名)[huòchē]
freight car
〖货架子〗(名)[huòjiàzi]
shelf; fixtures for goods
〖货色〗(名)[huòsè]
①goods (as referring to the variety or quality) ②rubbish (of person, things or ideas); stuff
〖货物〗(名)[huòwù]
goods
〖货源〗(名)[huòyuán]
commodity supply
〖货运〗(名)[huòyùn]
freight transport
〖货真价实〗[huòzhēnjiàshí]
① genuine goods at a fair price; ② out and out

获(动)[huò]
gain; obtain
〖获得〗(动)[huòdé]
get; attain
〖获胜〗[huòshèng]
win (victory)
〖获悉〗(动)[huòxī]
learn (news, etc.)

祸(名)[huò]
misfortune
〖祸根〗(名)[huògēn]
source of trouble; root of evil
〖祸国殃民〗[huòguóyāngmín]
wreck the country and ruin the people
〖祸害〗(名、动)[huòhài]
evil; bane; bring disaster to
〖祸首〗(名)[huòshǒu]
arch-criminal; principal criminal

霍[huò]
〖霍然〗(副)[huòrán]
suddenly

豁[huò]
另见 huō
〖豁达〗(形)[huòdá]
broadminded
〖豁亮〗(形)[huòliàng]
spacious and bright
〖豁免〗(动)[huòmiǎn]
exempt
〖豁免权〗(名)[huòmiǎnquán]
right of immunity
〖豁然〗(副)[huòrán]
broadened and brightened
〖豁然开朗〗[huòránkāilǎng]
suddenly broadened and brightened

jī

几[jī]

另见jǐ

〖几乎〗(副)[jīhū]
almost; nearly

讥[jī]

〖讥讽〗(动)[jīfěng]
satirize

〖讥笑〗(动)[jīxiào]
ridicule; jeer; make fun of; laugh at

击(动)[jī]

hit; knock; render a blow

〖击败〗(动)[jībài]
defeat

〖击毙〗(动)[jībì]
kill (in fighting)

〖击毁〗(动)[jīhuǐ]
destroy

〖击剑〗(名)[jījiàn]
sword fighting; fencing

〖击溃〗(动)[jīkuì]
defeat utterly; crush; put to rout; smash

〖击落〗(动)[jīluò]
shoot down

〖击破〗(动)[jīpò]
rout; crush; frustrate

〖击伤〗(动)[jīshāng]
wound; injure

〖击退〗(动)[jītuì]
repulse; drive back; rebuff

〖击一猛掌〗[jīyīměngzhǎng]
give a shove

饥(形)[jī]

hungry

〖饥饿〗(形)[jī'è]
hungry

〖饥寒〗(名)[jīhán]
hunger and cold

〖饥寒交迫〗[jīhánjiāopò]
(live in) hunger and cold

〖饥荒〗(名)[jīhuāng]
famine

机[jī]

〖机场〗(名)[jīchǎng]
airport
〖机车〗(名)[jīchē]
locomotive
〖机床〗(名)[jīchuáng]〔台 tái〕
machine tools
〖机动〗(形)[jīdòng]
mobile; flexible; manoeuvre
〖机耕〗[jīgēng]
mechanized ploughing
〖机构〗(名)[jīgòu]
①organization; set-up ②institution
〖机关〗(名)[jīguān]
organization; offices; institute
〖机关枪〗(名)[jīguānqiāng]
〔挺 tǐng〕machine gun
〖机会〗(名)[jīhuì]
opportunity; chance
〖机会主义〗(名)[jīhuìzhǔyì]
opportunism
〖机井〗(名)[jījǐng]〔眼 yǎn〕
electric pump well
〖机警〗(形)[jījǐng]
alert; watchful
〖机灵〗(形)[jīling]
quick-witted; clever
〖机密〗(形、名)[jīmì]
secret; confidential
〖机敏〗(形)[jīmǐn]
witty; dexterous; alert
〖机能〗(名)[jīnéng]
function
〖机器〗(名)[jīqì]〔台 tái、架 jià〕
machine
〖机械〗(名、形)[jīxiè]
machinery; machines; mechanical
〖机械化〗(动)[jīxièhuà]
(mechanization)mechanize
〖机械唯物主义〗
[jīxièwéiwù zhǔyì]
mechanical materialism
〖机械运动〗[jīxièyùndòng]
mechanical motion
〖机要〗(形)[jīyào]
confidential
〖机油〗(名)[jīyóu]
lubricant
〖机遇〗(名)[jīyù]
favourable circumstances; opportunity
〖机制〗(名)[jīzhì]
mechanism
〖机智〗(形)[jīzhì]
quick-witted

肌[jī]

〖肌肉〗(名)[jīròu]
muscle

鸡(名)[jī]〔只 zhī〕

fowls; hen or cock
〖鸡蛋〗(名)[jīdàn]〔个 gè〕
hen's egg
〖鸡毛蒜皮〗[jīmáosuànpí]
trifles; trivialities

奇[jī]

另见 qí
〖奇数〗(名)[jīshù]
odd number

J

迹[jī]
〖迹象〗(名)[jīxiàng]
trace; hint

积(动、名)[jī]
①accumulate ② (math.)product of multiplication; accumulation
〖积肥〗[jīféi]
stock up manure; collect fertilizer; manure accumulation
〖积极〗(形)[jījí]
active; positive
〖积极分子〗[jījífènzǐ]
activist
〖积极性〗(名)[jījíxìng]
initiative; enthusiasm
〖积聚〗(动)[jījù]
aggregate; accumulate
〖积累〗(动)[jīlěi]
accumulate; cumulate
〖积少成多〗[jīshǎochéngduō]
economy in trifles ensures abundance; from small increments comes abundance
〖积蓄〗(动、名)[jīxù]
save; accumulate; savings
〖积压〗(动)[jīyā]
overstock
〖积攒〗(动)[jīzǎn]
save; hoard; stock up

基[jī]
〖基本〗(形)[jīběn]
basic; fundamental; essential
〖基本词汇〗[jīběn cíhuì]
basic vocabulary
〖基本功〗(名)[jīběngōng]
basic training; essential skill
〖基本建设〗[jīběn jiànshè]
capital construction
〖基本粒子〗[jīběn lìzǐ]
fundamental particle
〖基本路线〗[jīběn lùxiàn]
basic line
〖基本矛盾〗[jīběn máodùn]
basic contradiction; fundamental contradiction
〖基本上〗(副)[jīběnshang]
basically; fundamentally
〖基层〗(名)[jīcéng]
basic level or unit; grassroots
〖基础〗(名)[jīchǔ]
base; foundation
〖基地〗(名)[jīdì]
base; the base area
〖基点〗(名)[jīdiǎn]
vital point; starting point; base
〖基调〗(名)[jīdiào]
keynote
〖基督教〗(名)[jīdūjiào]
Christianity
〖基金〗(名)[jījīn]
fund

畸[jī]
〖畸形〗(名)[jīxíng]
deformity

激(动)[jī]
stir; arouse
〖激昂〗(形)[jī'áng]

fervent and excited; emotionally wrought up
〖激荡〗(动)[jīdàng]
stir; rouse
〖激动〗(形、动)[jīdòng]
excited; stir; exciting; agitate
〖激发〗(动)[jīfā]
arouse
〖激愤〗(形)[jīfèn]
irritated
〖激光〗(名)[jīguāng]
laser
〖激光唱机〗(名)[jīguāngchàngjī]
CD player; laser record player
〖激光唱片〗(名)[jīguāngchàng piàn]
CD (compact disc); laser record; laser disc
〖激化〗(动)[jīhuà]
intensify; deepen
〖激进〗(形)[jījìn]
radical; drastic
〖激励〗(动)[jīlì]
inspire; encourage
〖激烈〗(形)[jīliè]
violent; drastic; intense
〖激流〗(名)[jīliú]
torrent
〖激怒〗(动)[jīnù]
annoy; irritate; enrage
〖激情〗(名)[jīqíng]
strong emotions
〖激素〗(名)[jīsù]
hormone
〖激增〗(动)[jīzēng]
increase greatly
〖激战〗(名、动)[jīzhàn]
fierce battle; wage an intensive struggle

jí

及(动、连)[jí]
①reach ②and; as well as
〖及格〗[jígé]
pass (an examination); up to the standard
〖及时〗(形)[jíshí]
in or on time
〖及早〗(副)[jízǎo]
as early as possible

吉[jí]
〖吉普车〗(名)[jípǔchē]〔辆 liàng〕
jeep
〖吉祥〗(名、形)[jíxiáng]
luck; auspicious; propitious
〖吉祥物〗(名)[jíxiángwù]
mascot

岌[jí]
〖岌岌可危〗[jíjíkěwēi]
in imminent danger

级(量)[jí]
a measure word, rank; grade; step; rung
〖级别〗(名)[jíbié]
rank; grade; class
〖级数〗(名)[jíshù]
series (e.g. arithmetical series)

极(名、副)[jí]

J

extreme; utmost; extremely
〖极点〗(名)[jídiǎn]
farthest point
〖极度〗(形)[jídù]
extreme; intemperate
〖极端〗(名、形)[jíduān]
extreme; radical; out-and-out
〖极力〗(副)[jílì]
spare no effort; do the utmost
〖极其〗(副)[jíqí]
very; highly
〖极为〗(副)[jíwéi]
extremely
〖极限〗(名)[jíxiàn] limit

即(动)[jí]

be; approach; that is
〖即便〗(连)[jíbiàn]
even if
〖即或〗(连)[jíhuò]
even though
〖即将〗(副)[jíjiāng]
soon; in no time; nearly
〖即刻〗(副)[jíkè]
at once; immediately
〖即日〗(名)[jírì]
① the very day ② in the next few days
〖即使〗(连)[jíshǐ]
even if
〖即席〗[jíxí]
on-the-spot

急(形)[jí]

①urgent; swift; hurriedly ② impatient; impetuous
〖急促〗(形)[jícù]
①short and quick (e.g. breaths) ②short (time)
〖急电〗(名)[jídiàn]
an urgent telegram
〖急风暴雨〗[jífēngbàoyǔ]
violent storm
〖急救〗(动)[jíjiù]
give first aid treatment
〖急剧〗(形)[jíjù]
abrupt; drastic
〖急流〗(名)[jíliú]
rushing currents
〖急忙〗(形)[jímáng]
in a great hurry; hurriedly
〖急迫〗(形)[jípò]
hasty; urgent
〖急起直追〗[jíqǐzhízhuī]
make haste and catch up with
〖急切〗(形)[jíqiè]
pressing; instant
〖急速〗(副)[jísù]
speedy; at great speed
〖急先锋〗(名)[jíxiānfēng]
champion of; be in the van; shock force
〖急性〗(名)[jíxìng]
acute
〖急性病〗(名)[jíxìngbìng]
① acute disease ② impetuosity; impatience
〖急需〗(动)[jíxū]
be badly in need of
〖急于〗(动)[jíyú]
eager (to do sth.)
〖急躁〗(形)[jízào]
impetuous
〖急诊〗(名)[jízhěn]
(med.) emergency case

〖急中生智〗[jízhōngshēngzhì]
have quick wits in emergency
〖急转直下〗[jízhuǎnzhíxià]
go into a precipitous decline

疾[jí]
〖疾病〗(名)[jíbìng]
sickness; illness
〖疾驰〗(动)[jíchí]
gallop away at full speed
〖疾风劲草〗[jífēngjìngcǎo]
the strong wind reveals the strength of the grass; (fig.) only those who are firm and resolute can withstand severe trials
〖疾苦〗(名)[jíkǔ]
misery; suffering; difficulty

棘[jí]
〖棘手〗(形)[jíshǒu]
difficult; thorny knotty

集(动)[jí]
assemble; gather together
〖集合〗(动)[jíhé]
assemble; muster; rally
〖集会〗[jíhuì]
hold a meeting; assembly; mass rally
〖集结〗(动)[jíjié]
concentrate; mass
〖集聚〗(动)[jíjù]
assemble in one place
〖集权〗[jíquán]
centralize; centralization of state power
〖集市〗(名)[jíshì]
(country) market
〖集思广益〗[jísīguǎngyì]
good at gathering all useful opinions; have a ready ear to the opinion (of the masses); collect opinions from the masses and benefit thereby
〖集体〗(名)[jítǐ]
collective
〖集体化〗(动)[jítǐhuà]
collectivization
〖集体经济〗[jítǐjīngjì]
collective economy
〖集体所有制〗[jítǐsuǒyǒuzhì]
collective ownership
〖集体舞〗(名)[jítǐwǔ]
group dance
〖集体主义〗(名)[jítǐzhǔyì]
collectivism
〖集团〗(名)[jítuán]
group; clique; bloc
〖集训〗(动)[jíxùn]
bring people together for training
〖集邮〗[jíyóu]
collect postage stamps; stamp collecting; philately
〖集约〗(形)[jíyuē]
intensive
〖集约经营〗[jíyuējīngyíng]
intensive management
〖集镇〗(名)[jízhèn]
town
〖集中〗(动、形)[jízhōng]
concentrate; centralized
〖集中营〗(名)[jízhōngyíng]
concentration camp
〖集装箱〗(名)[jízhuāngxiāng]

container
〖集子〗(名)[jízi]
a collection of writings

籍[jí]
〖籍贯〗(名)[jíguàn]
native place

jǐ

几(数)[jǐ]
several; how many
另见 jī
〖几何〗(名)[jǐhé]
①geometry ②how many? how much?
〖几何级数〗[jǐhéjíshù]
geometric progression

挤(动、形)[jǐ]
squeeze; extract; crowded

给[jǐ]
另见 gěi
〖给养〗(名)[jǐyǎng]
provisions; subsistence; supplies
〖给予〗(动)[jǐyǔ]
present; supply; offer; give; render

脊(名)[jǐ]
spine; ridge
〖脊背〗(名)[jǐbèi]
back
〖脊椎动物〗[jǐzhuīdòngwù]
the vertebrates
〖脊椎骨〗(名)[jǐzhuīgǔ]
the vertebrae; the back bone

jì

计(名、动)[jì]
①calculate; reckon; count ②stratagem; plan
〖计策〗(名)[jìcè]
device; stratagem; policy
〖计划〗(名、动)[jìhuà]
plan; devise
〖计划经济〗[jìhuàjīngjì]
planned economy
〖计划生育〗[jìhuàshēngyù]
family planning
〖计划性〗(名)[jìhuàxìng]
planning
〖计较〗(动)[jìjiào]
①dispute; find fault with ②be concerned for (e.g. personal gain); bother about
〖计量〗(动)[jìliàng]
measure; estimate
〖计谋〗(名)[jìmóu]
scheme; plot; stratagem
〖计算〗(动)[jìsuàn]
calculate; reckon
〖计算尺〗(名)[jìsuànchǐ]
slide rule
〖计算机〗(名)[jìsuànjī]〔台 tái〕
computer
〖计算器〗(名)[jìsuànqì]〔台 tái〕
calculator

记(动)[jì]
①memorize; keep in mind ②record; note; write down
〖记得〗(动)[jìde]

remember
〖记分〗[jì fēn]
keep the score
〖记工〗[jìgōng]
recording work-points
〖记功〗[jìgōng]
give credit for meritorious work
〖记过〗[jìguò]
give a demerit
〖记号〗(名)[jìhao]
sign; mark
〖记录〗(动、名)[jìlù]
① take notes; record ② minutes (of meeting) ③ record (sports)
〖记录片〗(名)[jìlùpiàn]〔部 bù〕
documentary film
〖记取〗(动)[jìqǔ]
remember (advice); bear in mind; learn (e.g. a lesson)
〖记性〗(名)[jìxing]
memory
〖记叙〗(动)[jìxù]
narrate
〖记忆〗(动、名)[jìyì]
memorize; remember; memory
〖记忆力〗(名)[jìyìlì]
memory power
〖记忆犹新〗[jìyìyóuxīn]
fresh in mind; the memory is still fresh
〖记载〗(动)[jìzǎi]
put down in writing; record
〖记者〗(名)[jìzhě]
newspaper reporter; journalist; correspondent
〖记住〗(动)[jìzhù]
bear in mind; remember

伎[jì]
〖伎俩〗(名)[jìliǎng]
ruse; trick; subterfuge

纪[jì]
〖纪律〗(名)[jìlǜ]
discipline
〖纪律性〗(名)[jìlǜxìng]
sense of discipline
〖纪念〗(动、名)[jìniàn]
commemorate; souvenir; commemoration
〖纪念碑〗(名)[jìniànbēi]
monument; cenotaph
〖纪念册〗(名)[jìniàncè]〔本 běn〕
souvenir album
〖纪念品〗(名)[jìniànpǐn]
souvenir
〖纪念日〗(名)[jìniànrì]
anniversaries of important events; anniversary
〖纪念章〗(名)[jìniànzhāng]〔枚 méi〕
memorial badge
〖纪要〗(名)[jìyào]
summary; minutes (of meeting)
〖纪元〗(名)[jìyuán]
the beginning of a reign or an era; epoch

技[jì]
〖技能〗(名)[jìnéng]
ability; skill
〖技巧〗(名)[jìqiǎo]
skill
〖技术〗(名)[jìshù]
technique

〖技术革新〗[jìshùgéxīn]
technical innovation
〖技术员〗(名)[jìshùyuán]
technical personnel; technician
〖技艺〗(名)[jìyì]
feat; skill; stunt

忌(动)[jì]

① envy ② fear; be afraid of ③ avoid; abstain (from wine, smoking, etc.)
〖忌妒〗(动)[jìdu]
be jealous of; envy
〖忌讳〗(动)[jìhuì]
taboo

季(名)[jì]

season
〖季度〗(名)[jìdù]
quarter of a year
〖季节〗(名)[jìjié]
season

既(连)[jì]

since; as well as...
〖既得利益〗[jìdélìyì]
benefit already acquired; the rights already secured
〖既定〗[jìdìng]
given; already committed; already decided
〖既然〗(连)[jìrán]
since
〖既往不咎〗[jìwǎngbùjiù]
let bygones be bygones; be let off for one's past misdeeds
〖既…也…〗[jì…yě…]
both...and...
〖既…又…〗[jì…yòu…]
...also...

觊[jì]

〖觊觎〗(动)[jìyú]
covet; desire eagerly (sth. that one should not obtain)

继[jì]

〖继承〗(动)[jìchéng]
fall heir to; inherit; carry forward (the revolutionary tradition); take over
〖继承权〗(名)[jìchéngquán]
right of inheritance
〖继而〗(副)[jì'ér]
after this
〖继父〗(名)[jìfù]
step-father
〖继母〗(名)[jìmǔ]
step-mother
〖继任〗(动)[jìrèn]
succeed (sb.) in office
〖继往开来〗[jìwǎngkāilái]
carry forward the undertakings of the predecessor and open up a new road for future
〖继续〗(动)[jìxù]
continue

寄(动)[jì]

① send by post ② entrust to; place hopes on
〖寄存〗(动)[jìcún]
hand over for safekeeping

〖寄居〗(动)[jìjū]
put up at another person's house
〖寄生〗(动)[jìshēng]
on or within another organism; (of persons) depend on another for a living; be parasitical
〖寄生虫〗(名)[jìshēngchóng]
parasites
〖寄宿〗(动)[jìsù]
have lodgings
〖寄托〗(动)[jìtuō]
entrust to the care of; pin one's hopes on
〖寄予〗(动)[jìyǔ]
place (hope or confidence) in

寂[jì]
〖寂静〗(形)[jìjìng]
silent; quiet
〖寂寞〗(形)[jìmò]
lonely

jiā

J

加(动)[jiā]
add; increase; plus
〖加班〗[jiābān]
work overtime; work extra hours
〖加倍〗[jiābèi]
① double (an amount) ② redouble (efforts)
〖加法〗(名)[jiāfǎ]
(math.) addition
〖加工〗(动)[jiāgōng]
process into a finished product
〖加紧〗(动)[jiājǐn]
accelerate; intensify; step up
〖加剧〗(动)[jiājù]
intensify; heighten
〖加快〗(动)[jiākuài]
speed up
〖加强〗(动)[jiāqiáng]
strengthen; consolidate
〖加热〗[jiārè]
heat up
〖加入〗(动)[jiārù]
join; enter
〖加深〗(动)[jiāshēn]
deepen; intensify
〖加数〗(名)[jiāshù]
(math.) a number to be added to another; addend
〖加速〗(动)[jiāsù]
speed up
〖加速度〗(名)[jiāsùdù]
acceleration; rate of acceleration
〖加速运动〗[jiāsùyùndòng]
accelerated motion
〖加以〗(动、连)[jiāyǐ]
① give...to; render; deal ② besides; in addition to
〖加油〗[jiāyóu]
① pep up; cheer (game player) ② refuel
〖加重〗(动)[jiāzhòng]
increase (in weight, degree, etc.)

夹(动)[jiā]
① clip; take with tweezers ② mix with; insert between; contain
另见 jiá
〖夹边〗(名)[jiābiān]

(geom.) included side
〖夹道欢迎〗[jiādàohuānyíng]
welcoming crowds lining the streets; a grand roadside welcome
〖夹攻〗(动)[jiāgōng]
make a pincer movement against (the enemy); pincer attacks; pincers around (e.g. the enemy)
〖夹角〗(名)[jiājiǎo]
(geom.) included angle
〖夹生饭〗(名)[jiāshēngfàn]
half-cooked rice
〖夹杂〗(动)[jiāzá]
mix up; blend
〖夹子〗(名)[jiāzi]
clips; tongs; pincers; pliers

佳[jiā]
〖佳话〗(名)[jiāhuà]
matters of great interest; charming stories
〖佳节〗(名)[jiājié]
a happy occasion; a joyful festival
〖佳音〗(名)[jiāyīn]
good news

枷[jiā]
〖枷锁〗(名)[jiāsuǒ]
fetters; shackles

家(名、尾)[jiā]
① family; househlod ② home; house; residence ③ a suffix (for such words as writer, artist, etc.)
〖家常〗(名)[jiācháng]
① domestic affairs; home affairs ② commonplace
〖家常便饭〗[jiāchángbiànfàn]
① ordinary meal ② daily lot
〖家畜〗(名)[jiāchù]
domestic animals
〖家当〗(名)[jiādàng]
family property; family possession
〖家伙〗(名)[jiāhuo]
① tool or weapon ② what a fellow! ③ scoundrel
〖家家〗[jiājiā]
every family
〖家家户户〗[jiājiāhùhù]
each and every family
〖家具〗(名)[jiājù]
furniture
〖家眷〗(名)[jiājuàn]
family (wife and children)
〖家破人亡〗[jiāpòrénwáng]
with the family broken up and decimated
〖家禽〗(名)[jiāqín]
fowl
〖家史〗(名)[jiāshǐ]
history of a family
〖家属〗(名)[jiāshǔ]
one's dependents; families
〖家庭〗(名)[jiātíng]
family; home
〖家务〗(名)[jiāwù]
family affairs; home affairs
〖家乡〗(名)[jiāxiāng]
native place
〖家信〗(名)[jiāxìn]〔封 fēng〕
letters from home
〖家喻户晓〗[jiāyùhùxiǎo]

known to every family
〖家园〗(名)[jiāyuán]
native place; home
〖家长〗(名)[jiāzhǎng]
parents of a child; head of a family
〖家族〗(名)[jiāzú]
clan

嘉[jiā]
〖嘉奖〗(动)[jiājiǎng]
praise; reward

jiá

夹(形)[jiá]
lined (e.g. jacket)
另见 jiā

jiǎ

甲(名)[jiǎ]
① first class ② the first of the ten stems; number one ③ a natural or artificial shell
〖甲板〗(名)[jiǎbǎn]
the deck of a ship
〖甲骨文〗(名)[jiǎgǔwén]
inscriptions on oracle bones
〖甲克〗(名)[jiǎkè]
jacket
〖甲状腺〗(名)[jiǎzhuàngxiàn]
(physiol.) the thyroid gland

钾(名)[jiǎ]
(chem.) potassium
〖钾肥〗(名)[jiǎféi]
potassium fertilizer

假(形)[jiǎ]
false; spurious; pseudo; sham
另见 jià
〖假充〗(动)[jiǎchōng]
pass oneself off as; pose as
〖假定〗(动、名)[jiǎdìng]
assume; suppose; presume
〖假公济私〗[jiǎgōngjìsī]
promote one's private interests under the guise of serving the public
〖假借〗(动)[jiǎjiè]
using various guises; (do sth.) in the name of
〖假冒伪劣〗[jiǎmàowěiliè]
counterfeit and shoddy (products)
〖假面具〗(名)[jiǎmiànjù]
① mask ② hypocrisy
〖假如〗(连)[jiǎrú]
supposing that; if
〖假若〗(连)[jiǎruò]
supposing that; if
〖假设〗(名、动)[jiǎshè]
assume; suppose; presume
〖假使〗(连)[jiǎshǐ]
if; in case
〖假想〗(名、动)[jiǎxiǎng]
fancy; hypothesis
〖假象〗(名)[jiǎxiàng]
feint; false appearance; false impression
〖假惺惺〗(形)[jiǎxīngxīng]
hypocritical
〖假造〗(动)[jiǎzào]
counterfeit; fake
〖假装〗(动)[jiǎzhuāng]

feint; disguise; pretend; sham

jià

价(名)[jià]
price
〖价格〗(名)[jiàgé]
price
〖价值〗(名)[jiàzhí]
value
〖价值规律〗[jiàzhíguīlǜ]
law of value

驾(动)[jià]
drive; sail (a ship); fly (an airplane)
〖驾驶〗(动)[jiàshǐ]
drive; pilot
〖驾驶员〗(名)[jiàshǐyuán]
driver; pilot
〖驾驭〗(动)[jiàyù]
keep hold of the reins; dominate

架(动、量)[jià]
① lay on a frame; put up; prop up ② a measure word (for machine, T.V. set, aeroplane, etc.)
〖架空〗(动)[jiàkōng]
① built or supported on stilts; aerial ② become nominal; render (sb.) powerless
〖架设〗(动)[jiàshè]
put up; erect
〖架式〗(名)[jiàshi]
posture; pose
〖架子〗(名)[jiàzi]
① a supporting framework; mantle ② arrogance; haughtiness; airs

假(名)[jià]
leave; holiday
另见 jiǎ
〖假期〗(名)[jiàqī]
holidays; vacation
〖假日〗(名)[jiàrì]
holiday
〖假条〗(名)[jiàtiáo]
leave certificate (e.g. sick leave certificate)

嫁(动)[jià]
① (of a girl) marry ② transfer; shift
〖嫁祸于人〗[jiàhuòyúrén]
put blame on others; transfer the evil to another
〖嫁接〗(动)[jiàjiē]
graft

jiān

尖(名、形)[jiān]
a sharp point; sharp; pointed
〖尖兵〗(名)[jiānbīng]
vanguard; trail-blazer
〖尖刀〗(名)[jiāndāo]〔把 bǎ〕
dagger; sharp knife
〖尖端〗(名、形)[jiānduān]
the highest point; the pinnacle; the most advanced
〖尖端放电〗[jiānduānfàngdiàn]
point discharge
〖尖刻〗(形)[jiānkè]
(of words, speech) sharp; acr-

J

imonious
〖尖锐〗(形)[jiānruì]
sharp; pointed; acute

奸(形)[jiān]
treacherous; wicked; sinister
〖奸商〗(名)[jiānshāng]
profiteer; unscrupulous merchant
〖奸细〗(名)[jiānxi]
a spy; secret agent
〖奸险〗(形)[jiānxiǎn]
crafty and dangerous
〖奸诈〗(形)[jiānzhà]
crafty

歼(动)[jiān]
wipe out; annihilate; exterminate;
〖歼击机〗(名)[jiānjījī]〔架 jià〕
fighter (aeroplane)
〖歼灭〗(动)[jiānmiè]
annihilate; destroy
〖歼灭战〗(名)[jiānmièzhàn]
battle of annihilation

J

坚[jiān]
〖坚壁清野〗[jiānbìqīngyě]
strengthen one's defence works and clear the fields
〖坚持〗(动)[jiānchí]
persist in; adhere to; hold fast to; insist on; uphold
〖坚持不懈〗[jiānchíbùxiè]
persistent; perseveringly; unremittingly; firm adherence
〖坚定〗(形、动)[jiāndìng]
steady; firm; resolute; determined; affirm
〖坚定不移〗[jiāndìngbùyí]
firm and resolute; unswerving; persistently
〖坚固〗(形)[jiāngù]
solid; firm; hard
〖坚决〗(形)[jiānjué]
determined; resolute
〖坚苦卓绝〗[jiānkǔzhuōjué]
overcome great difficulties with surpassing bravery; most arduous (struggle)
〖坚强〗(形)[jiānqiáng]
staunch; firm; resolute
〖坚忍不拔〗[jiānrěnbùbá]
firm and indomitable; stubbornly and unyieldingly
〖坚如磐石〗[jiānrúpánshí]
firm as rock; rock-firm; monolithic
〖坚实〗(形)[jiānshí]
solid; strong
〖坚守〗(动)[jiānshǒu]
guard securely; hold fast (position)
〖坚信〗(动)[jiānxìn]
firmly believe
〖坚毅〗(形)[jiānyì]
resolute; with firm determination
〖坚硬〗(形)[jiānyìng]
hard; strong and tough
〖坚贞〗(形)[jiānzhēn]
faithful and firm
〖坚贞不屈〗[jiānzhēnbùqū]
stand firm and unyielding

间(量)[jiān]
a measure word (for room)
另见 jiàn

肩(名)[jiān]
shoulder
〖肩膀〗(名)[jiānbǎng]
shoulder
〖肩负〗(动)[jiānfù]
carry (a burden); shoulder; assume (responsibility for)

艰[jiān]
〖艰巨〗(形)[jiānjù]
extremely difficult; very tough; heavy
〖艰苦〗(形)[jiānkǔ]
hard and arduous; hard and bitter
〖艰难〗(形)[jiānnán]
difficult; hardship
〖艰难险阻〗[jiānnánxiǎnzǔ]
difficulties and dangers
〖艰深〗(形)[jiānshēn]
difficult to understand
〖艰险〗(形)[jiānxiǎn]
difficult and dangerous; perilous
〖艰辛〗(形)[jiānxīn]
arduous

监[jiān]
〖监察〗(动)[jiānchá]
supervise; control
〖监督〗(动)[jiāndū]
supervise
〖监护〗(动)[jiānhù]
serve as a guardian for
〖监视〗(动)[jiānshì]
keep a close watch over; keep an eye on
〖监视器〗(名)[jiānshìqì]
monitor
〖监狱〗(名)[jiānyù]
jail; prison

兼(动)[jiān]
combine; concurrently
〖兼备〗(动)[jiānbèi]
be qualified for both or more
〖兼并〗(动)[jiānbìng]
annex (territory, etc.)
〖兼顾〗(动)[jiāngù]
give consideration to both; give attention to both...and ...
〖兼课〗[jiānkè]
doing teaching work besides one's own work
〖兼任〗(动)[jiānrèn]
hold concurrent post; concurrently
〖兼收并蓄〗[jiānshōubìngxù]
swallow anything and everything uncritically
〖兼听则明,偏信则暗〗
[jiāntīngzémíng,piānxìnzé'àn]
listen to both sides and you will be enlightened,heed only one side and you will be benighted
〖兼语句〗(名)[jiānyǔjù]
pivotal sentence; telescopic sentence

〖兼职〗[jiānzhí]
(hold) concurrent jobs

缄 [jiān]

〖缄默〗(动)[jiānmò]
keep silent and say nothing

煎 (动)[jiān]

fry (e.g. fish)
〖煎熬〗(动)[jiān'áo]
① fry in oil or boil in water ② (fig.) endure long hardships and sufferings

jiǎn

拣 (动)[jiǎn]

① choose; select ② pick up

茧 (名)[jiǎn]

the cocoon of the silk worm

俭 [jiǎn]

〖俭朴〗(形)[jiǎnpǔ]
frugal and simple (e.g. living a simple life)
〖俭省〗(形)[jiǎnshěng]
frugal; economical

捡 (动)[jiǎn]

pick up

检 (动)[jiǎn]

check; examine
〖检查〗(动、名)[jiǎnchá]
check; inspect; check up
〖检察官〗(名)[jiǎncháguān]
public procurator
〖检察院〗(名)[jiǎncháyuàn]
procuratorate
〖检点〗(动)[jiǎndiǎn]
keep watch over one's words or deeds
〖检举〗(动)[jiǎnjǔ]
expose (illegal acts, misconduct, etc.)
〖检讨〗(动、名)[jiǎntǎo]
examine one's own mistakes; self-criticism
〖检修〗(动)[jiǎnxiū]
overhaul
〖检验〗(动)[jiǎnyàn]
examine; inspect; test
〖检疫〗(动)[jiǎnyì]
quarantine
〖检阅〗(动)[jiǎnyuè]
review (troops, parade, etc.)
〖检字法〗(名)[jiǎnzìfǎ]
the rule for finding a character in a dictionary

减 (动)[jiǎn]

take away; deduct; reduce
〖减产〗[jiǎnchǎn]
decrease in output; drop in cropyields
〖减低〗(动)[jiǎndī]
reduce
〖减法〗(名)[jiǎnfǎ]
subtraction
〖减免〗(动)[jiǎnmiǎn]
free from; exempt
〖减轻〗(动)[jiǎnqīng]
extenuate; mitigate; lighten;

J

reduce
〖减弱〗(动)[jiǎnruò]
become weaker; wane
〖减色〗[jiǎnsè]
lose colour by fading; detract from; deteriorate; become less attractive
〖减少〗(动)[jiǎnshǎo]
reduce; take away from a quantity; lessen
〖减数〗(名)[jiǎnshù]
(math.) subtrahend
〖减缩〗(动)[jiǎnsuō]
reduce; decrease; retrench
〖减退〗(动)[jiǎntuì]
diminish; reduce; drop (in temperature)
〖减租减息〗[jiǎnzūjiǎnxī]
reduction of rent and interest

剪(动)[jiǎn]
cut with scissors
〖剪裁〗(动)[jiǎncái]
cut cloth to make dress or suit; cutting
〖剪彩〗[jiǎncǎi]
the ceremony of cutting the ribbon (to open...)
〖剪刀〗(名)[jiǎndāo]〔把 bǎ〕
scissors
〖剪辑〗(名、动)[jiǎnjí]
editing (film)
〖剪贴〗(名、动)[jiǎntiē]
① paper cutting ② cut out and paste
〖剪纸〗(名)[jiǎnzhǐ]
scissorcut; paper-cut
〖剪子〗(名)[jiǎnzi]〔把 bǎ〕
scissors

简(形)[jiǎn]
simple; brief
〖简报〗(名)[jiǎnbào]
bulletin
〖简便〗(形)[jiǎnbiàn]
simple and convenient
〖简称〗(动、名)[jiǎnchēng]
abbreviated term
〖简单〗(形)[jiǎndān]
simple; sketchy
〖简单化〗(动)[jiǎndānhuà]
over-simplify
〖简单句〗(名)[jiǎndānjù]
simple sentence
〖简短〗(形)[jiǎnduǎn]
short and brief
〖简化〗(动)[jiǎnhuà]
simplify
〖简化汉字〗[jiǎnhuà Hànzì]
simplified Chinese characters
〖简洁〗(形)[jiǎnjié]
terse and concise
〖简历〗(名)[jiǎnlì]
resume; profile; vitae
〖简练〗(形)[jiǎnliàn]
succinct; terse; concise
〖简陋〗(形)[jiǎnlòu]
rough (e.g. accomodation); simple
〖简略〗(形)[jiǎnlüè]
simple; brief; terse
〖简明〗(形)[jiǎnmíng]
concise; simple and clear
〖简明扼要〗[jiǎnmíng'èyào]

brief and concise
〖简明新闻〗[jiǎnmíngxīnwén]
news in brief
〖简谱〗(名)[jiǎnpǔ]
Chinese solfa musical notation
〖简体字〗(名)[jiǎntǐzì]
simplified characters
〖简写〗(名)[jiǎnxiě]
abbreviated characters; simplified writing
〖简讯〗(名)[jiǎnxùn]
brief news
〖简要〗(形)[jiǎnyào]
concise; brief and to the point
〖简易〗(形)[jiǎnyì]
simple and easy; elementary
〖简直〗(副)[jiǎnzhí]
absolutely; virtually; nothing less than

碱(名)[jiǎn]
alkaline
〖碱性〗(名)[jiǎnxìng]
alkaline

J

jiàn

见(动)[jiàn]
see
〖见报〗[jiànbào]
appeared in newspaper; issued in newspaper
〖见缝插针〗[jiànfèngchāzhēn]
seize every opportunity to do (sth.)
〖见怪〗(动)[jiànguài]
blame
〖见机行事〗[jiànjīxíngshì]
take cue and act accordingly; act according to circumstances
〖见解〗(名)[jiànjiě]
understanding; opinion
〖见面〗[jiànmiàn]
come face to face; meet
〖见识〗(名、动)[jiànshi]
① insight; general knowledge
② gain more experience
〖见闻〗(名)[jiànwén]
what one sees and hears; general knowledge; experience
〖见习〗(动)[jiànxí]
learn through practice
〖见效〗(动)[jiànxiào]
obtain results; effective; fruitful
〖见异思迁〗[jiànyìsīqiān]
wish to change one's mind the moment one sees something different
〖见证〗(名)[jiànzhèng]
evidence; proof

件(量)[jiàn]
a measure word, piece; article; item

间(动)[jiàn]
separate; divide
另见 jiān
〖间谍〗(名)[jiàndié]
spy; espionage
〖间断〗(动)[jiànduàn]
interrupt; breach; intermission; inconsecutive
〖间隔〗(动、名)[jiàngé]

①divide②interval;space; gap
〖间或〗(副)[jiànhuò]
sometimes
〖间接〗(形)[jiànjiē]
indirect
〖间苗〗[jiànmiáo]
thin out young plants
〖间隙〗(名)[jiànxì]
①cleft; gap②interval; break
〖间歇〗(名)[jiànxiē]
intermittence;pause
〖间作〗(动)[jiànzuò]
intercropping; inter-plant

饯 [jiàn]
〖饯别〗(动)[jiànbié]
give a farewell party
〖饯行〗(动)[jiànxíng]
give a farewell dinner

建 (动)[jiàn]
build; construct; establish
〖建都〗[jiàndū]
found a capital
〖建国〗[jiànguó]
create a new nation; reconstruct the nation
〖建交〗[jiànjiāo]
establish diplomatic relations with
〖建军〗[jiànjūn]
the founding of an army; build an army
〖建立〗(动)[jiànlì]
establish; set up; build
〖建设〗(动、名)[jiànshè]
build; construction
〖建设性〗(名)[jiànshèxìng]
constructive; positive
〖建树〗(动)[jiànshù]
set up; contribute
〖建议〗(名、动)[jiànyì]
suggestion; proposal; propose
〖建制〗(名)[jiànzhì]
general term for organization and administrative system
〖建筑〗(名、动)[jiànzhù]
construction; building; build; construct
〖建筑物〗(名)[jiànzhùwù]
building; edifice; structure

贱 (形)[jiàn]
cheap; mean

剑 (名)[jiàn]〔把 bǎ〕
sword
〖剑拔弩张〗[jiànbánǔzhāng]
sabre-rattling; ready for a show-down

健 [jiàn]
〖健步〗[jiànbù]
walk with firm strides; vigorous steps
〖健康〗(形、名)[jiànkāng]
healthy; health
〖健美〗(形、名)[jiànměi]
bodybuilding
〖健美操〗(名)[jiànměicāo]
bodybuilding exercises; aerobics
〖健全〗(形、动)[jiànquán]
① sound and hale ② perfect;

put...on a sound footing
〖健身房〗(名)[jiànshēnfáng]
gym; gymnasium
〖健谈〗(形)[jiàntán]
talkative; loquacious
〖健忘〗(形)[jiànwàng]
forgetful; oblivious
〖健在〗(动)[jiànzài]
still alive and in good health (refering to elderly people); still going strong
〖健壮〗(形)[jiànzhuàng]
vigorous and healthy; hale and hearty

舰(名)[jiàn]〔艘 sōu〕
naval vessels
〖舰队〗(名)[jiànduì]
fleet
〖舰艇〗(名)[jiàntǐng]〔艘 sōu〕
naval vessels

渐(副)[jiàn]
gradually; step by step; little by little
〖渐变〗(动)[jiànbiàn]
gradually change
〖渐渐〗(副)[jiànjiàn]
gradually
〖渐进〗(动)[jiànjìn]
make gradual improvement; advance step by step

践[jiàn]
〖践踏〗(动)[jiàntà]
trample underfoot

鉴[jiàn]
〖鉴别〗(动)[jiànbié]
distinguish
〖鉴定〗(动、名)[jiàndìng]
① evaluate; evaluation; appraisal ② differentiate; discern; judge
〖鉴戒〗(名)[jiànjiè]
take warning from an occurrence
〖鉴赏〗(动)[jiànshǎng]
discern and appreciate; connoisseur
〖鉴于〗(动)[jiànyú]
in consideration of; in view of

箭(名)[jiàn]〔枝 zhī〕
arrow
〖箭步〗(名)[jiànbù]
quick strides
〖箭在弦上〗[jiànzàixiánshàng]
(lit.) the arrow is already on the string; (fig.) it must happen; a point of no return

jiāng

江(名)[jiāng]〔条 tiáo〕
large river
〖江河日下〗[jiānghérìxià]
fast deteriorating; going from bad to worse
〖江湖〗(名)[jiānghú]
far and near; everywhere; from place to place (archaic)
〖江米〗(名)[jiāngmǐ]
glutinous rice
〖江南〗(名)[jiāngnán]
regions south of the Yangtze

River
〖江山〗(名)[jiāngshān]
national territory

将(介、副)[jiāng]
① by; with ② just; about to ③ have (sth.) done
另见 jiàng
〖将功赎罪〗[jiānggōngshúzuì]
make amends for one's crimes by good deeds
〖将计就计〗[jiāngjìjiùjì]
turn a person's trick against him
〖将近〗(动)[jiāngjìn]
near; be on the verge; impending
〖将就〗(动)[jiāngjiu]
have to make do with
〖将军〗(名)[jiāngjūn]
(mil.) general
〖将来〗(名)[jiānglái]
in the future; in time to come
〖将信将疑〗[jiāngxìnjiāngyí]
half believing, half doubting; half-believe
〖将要〗(副)[jiāngyào]
will; be going to

姜(名)[jiāng]〔块 kuài〕
ginger

僵(形)[jiāng]
stiff; still; rigid
〖僵持〗(动)[jiāngchí]
arrive at a deadlock; be stalled
〖僵化〗(动)[jiānghuà]
petrify; rigidity; inflexible
〖僵局〗(名)[jiāngjú]
deadlock; impasse
〖僵尸〗(名)[jiāngshī]
corpse
〖僵死〗(动)[jiāngsǐ]
harden or stiffen; petrify
〖僵硬〗(形)[jiāngyìng]
numb and rigid; inflexible

疆[jiāng]
〖疆界〗(名)[jiāngjiè]〔条 tiáo〕
boundaries; border
〖疆土〗(名)[jiāngtǔ]
territory of a country
〖疆域〗(名)[jiāngyù]
national territory

jiǎng

讲(动)[jiǎng]
speak; talk
〖讲稿〗(名)[jiǎnggǎo]〔篇 piān〕
a written speech
〖讲话〗[jiǎnghuà]
talk; give a speech
〖讲话〗(名)[jiǎnghuà]
talk; speech
〖讲解〗(动)[jiǎngjiě]
explain
〖讲究〗(动、形)[jiǎngjiu]
① carefully (make efforts to) study and perfect ② be particular about...; pay attention to
〖讲课〗[jiǎngkè]
give lectures; give lessons
〖讲理〗[jiǎnglǐ]
be reasonable
〖讲排场〗[jiǎngpáichǎng]

love ostentation; showy
〖讲求〗(动)[jiǎngqiú]
study carefully; devote particular care to; choose carefully
〖讲授〗(动)[jiǎngshòu]
teach; lecture
〖讲述〗(动)[jiǎngshù]
describe; recount; relate
〖讲台〗(名)[jiǎngtái]
lecture platform
〖讲坛〗(名)[jiǎngtán]
rostrum; podium; dais
〖讲学〗[jiǎngxué]
lecture
〖讲演〗(动、名)[jiǎngyǎn]
give a lecture; a lecture
〖讲义〗(名)[jiǎngyì]
lecture notes; teaching material
〖讲座〗(名)[jiǎngzuò]
lecture

奖(名、动)[jiǎng]
prize; reward; praise
〖奖惩〗(名)[jiǎngchéng]
reward and punishment
〖奖金〗(名)[jiǎngjīn]
bonuses
〖奖励〗(动、名)[jiǎnglì]
commend; reward; award; commendation
〖奖品〗(名)[jiǎngpǐn]
award; prize
〖奖学金〗(名)[jiǎngxuéjīn]
scholarship; exhibition
〖奖章〗(名)[jiǎngzhāng]〔枚 méi〕
medal
〖奖状〗(名)[jiǎngzhuàng]
〔张 zhāng〕citation

桨(名)[jiǎng]
an oar; a paddle

jiàng

降(动)[jiàng]
fall; drop; descend
另见 xiáng
〖降半旗〗[jiàngbànqí]
flag flown at half-mast
〖降低〗(动)[jiàngdī]
reduce; lower; debase
〖降级〗[jiàngjí]
reduce in rank; demote
〖降价〗[jiàngjià]
cut price; reduce price
〖降临〗(动)[jiànglín]
condescend
〖降落〗(动)[jiàngluò]
alight; land (of airplanes); descend
〖降落伞〗(名)[jiàngluòsǎn]
parachute
〖降生〗(动)[jiàngshēng]
be born
〖降温〗[jiàngwēn]
drop in temperature; cool down

将(名)[jiàng]
commander
另见 jiāng
〖将领〗(名)[jiànglǐng]
generals
〖将士〗(名)[jiàngshì]
commanders and fighters

浆[jiàng]
〖浆糊〗(名)[jiànghu]〔瓶 píng〕
paste

酱(名)[jiàng]
sauce
〖酱油〗(名)[jiàngyóu]
soy sauce

jiāo

交(动)[jiāo]
① hand in; turn over ② make friends with
〖交班〗[jiāobān]
pass work on to the next shift
〖交叉〗(动)[jiāochā]
intersect; intercross; cross
〖交差〗[jiāochāi]
report on what one has done in line of duty
〖交错〗(动)[jiāocuò]
overlap; interlace
〖交代〗(动)[jiāodài]
① hand over ② explain; give an account of...
〖交底〗[jiāodǐ]
confide a secret to (sb.); confide to (sb.) what one has in mind
〖交锋〗[jiāofēng]
cross swords with; engage each other (in a battle or ball game)
〖交付〗(动)[jiāofù]
turn over; hand over; deliver
〖交工〗[jiāogōng]
finish the construction
〖交换〗(动)[jiāohuàn]
exchange
〖交际〗(名、动)[jiāojì]
social intercourse
〖交加〗(动)[jiāojiā]
take place all at once
〖交接〗(动)[jiāojiē]
① contact ② handover and take over
〖交界〗(动)[jiāojiè]
boundary; border; frontier
〖交卷〗[jiāojuàn]
① hand in examination paper ② fulfil; accomplish; finish (e.g. work)
〖交流〗(动)[jiāoliú]
exchange (e.g. cultural exchange)
〖交流电〗(名)[jiāoliúdiàn]
(electr.) alternating current
〖交纳〗(动)[jiāonà]
pay (e.g. tax)
〖交情〗(名)[jiāoqing]
friendship; mutual affection
〖交涉〗(动)[jiāoshè]
negotiate; discuss terms; deal with
〖交谈〗(动)[jiāotán]
talk with
〖交替〗(动)[jiāotì]
① come one after another ② alternate; by turns
〖交通〗(名)[jiāotōng]
communication; traffic
〖交头接耳〗[jiāotóujiē'ěr]
whisper into each other's ears
〖交往〗(动)[jiāowǎng]
associate with; have dealings with

〖交响乐〗(名)[jiāoxiǎngyuè]
symphony
〖交心〗[jiāoxīn]
heart-to-heart talk; confide what one has in mind
〖交易〗(名)[jiāoyì]
transaction;business deal; trade
〖交游〗(动)[jiāoyóu]
make friends
〖交织〗(动)[jiāozhī]
interlace; overlap

郊[jiāo]

〖郊区〗(名)[jiāoqū]
suburban areas
〖郊外〗(名)[jiāowài]
outskirts; suburbs
〖郊游〗(动)[jiāoyóu]
outing; excursion

浇(动)[jiāo]

sprinkle with water; water
〖浇灌〗(动)[jiāoguàn]
irrigate; water

J

骄[jiāo]

〖骄傲〗(形)[jiāoào]
arrogant; proud; conceited
〖骄横〗(形)[jiāohèng]
insufferably arrogant; extremely overbearing
〖骄气〗(名、形)[jiāoqì]
arrogant; proud; unbearably conceited
〖骄阳〗(名)[jiāoyáng]
scorching sun
〖骄纵〗(动)[jiāozòng]
arrogant and wild;proud and ungovernable

娇(形)[jiāo]

① squeamish; pernickety ② beautiful
〖娇嫩〗(形)[jiāonen]
young and delicate; frail; delicate
〖娇气〗(名、形)[jiāoqì]
finicky airs; squeamish; pernickety
〖娇生惯养〗
[jiāoshēngguàn yǎng]
brought up in easy circumstances by doting parents; spoilt

胶(名)[jiāo]

glue
〖胶布〗(名)[jiāobù]
adhesive plaster
〖胶合〗(动)[jiāohé]
cement (sth.); glue (sth.)
〖胶卷〗(名)[jiāojuǎn]〔卷 juǎn〕
film (undeveloped)
〖胶水〗(名)[jiāoshuǐ]〔瓶 píng〕
liquid glue
〖胶鞋〗(名)[jiāoxié]〔双 shuāng〕
rainshoes; rubber boots; plimsoll

教(动)[jiāo]

teach
另见 jiào
〖教书〗[jiāo shū]
teach

〖教书育人〗[jiāoshūyùrén]
impart knowledge to students while giving them political and ideological education; impart knowledge and educate people
〖教学〗[jiāo xué]
teaching

焦(形)[jiāo]
①scorched ②anxious
〖焦点〗(名)[jiāodiǎn]
focal point; focus; heart of the matter
〖焦黄〗(形)[jiāohuáng]
dry and yellowish
〖焦急〗(形)[jiāojí]
very anxious and restless; worried
〖焦虑〗(形)[jiāolǜ]
very worried; extremely anxious
〖焦炭〗(名)[jiāotàn]
coke
〖焦头烂额〗[jiāotóulàn'é]
(lit.) smash heads and scorch brows; (fig.) land in a hot spot
〖焦土〗(名)[jiāotǔ]
scorched earth
〖焦躁〗(形)[jiāozào]
anxious and fretful

jiáo

嚼(动)[jiáo]
chew; masticate

jiǎo

角(名)[jiǎo]
①horn ②corner ③angle
另见 jué
〖角度〗(名)[jiǎodù]
(geom.) angular magnitude; the size of angle
〖角落〗(名)[jiǎoluò]
corner

侥[jiǎo]
〖侥幸〗(形)[jiǎoxìng]
through good luck; by a narrow margin

狡[jiǎo]
〖狡辩〗(动)[jiǎobiàn]
quibble about; use specious arguments to defend oneself; resort to sophistry
〖狡猾〗(形)[jiǎohuá]
slippery; sly; cunning
〖狡诈〗(形)[jiǎozhà]
deceitful; cunning

饺[jiǎo]
〖饺子〗(名)[jiǎozi]
ravioli; (meat) dumplings

绞(动)[jiǎo]
wring; twist
〖绞尽脑汁〗[jiǎojìnnǎozhī]
rack one's brains
〖绞索〗(名)[jiǎosuǒ]〔条 tiáo〕
noose
〖绞痛〗(形)[jiǎotòng]
extremely painful

矫[jiǎo]

〖矫健〗(形)[jiǎojiàn]
robust; vigorous
〖矫捷〗(形)[jiǎojié]
agile; nimble
〖矫揉造作〗[jiǎoróuzàozuò]
artificial; unnatural; made-up
〖矫枉过正〗[jiǎowǎngguòzhèng]
(lit.)straighten the crooked beyond the straight; (fig)exceed the proper limits in righting a wrong; go beyond the proper limits in righting a wrong
〖矫正〗(动)[jiǎozhèng]
make corrections; improve; set right

皎 [jiǎo]
〖皎洁〗(形)[jiǎojié]
clean; unsullied

脚 (名)[jiǎo]〔只 zhī〕
① the foot ② the leg or base on which a thing stands or rests
〖脚本〗(名)[jiǎoběn]
script; scenario
〖脚步〗(名)[jiǎobù]
footstep
〖脚跟〗(名)[jiǎogēn]
the heel
〖脚镣〗(名)[jiǎoliào]
shackles; ankle chains
〖脚踏两只船〗
[jiǎotàliǎngzhī chuán]
straddle two boats; riding two horses at same time;keeping irons in the fire
〖脚踏实地〗[jiǎotàshídì]
do solid work; down-to-earth
〖脚印〗(名)[jiǎoyìn]
footprints
〖脚指头〗(名)[jiǎozhítou]
toe
〖脚注〗(名)[jiǎozhù]
footnote

搅 (动)[jiǎo]
stir; mix
〖搅拌〗(动)[jiǎobàn]
mix; stir
〖搅动〗(动)[jiǎodòng]
stir
〖搅乱〗(动)[jiǎoluàn]
confuse; befuddle; throw into disorder
〖搅扰〗(动)[jiǎorǎo]
disturb; upset; harrass; stir up

剿 (动)[jiǎo]
annihilate; wipe out (the enemy); suppress

缴 (动)[jiǎo]
① pay (tax);hand over ② capture
〖缴获〗(动、名)[jiǎohuò]
capture; seize
〖缴纳〗(动)[jiǎonà]
pay(tax,duties,fees,dues,etc.)
〖缴械〗[jiǎoxiè]
disarm; lay down one's arms

jiào

叫 (动、介)[jiào]

call; ask; send for; order; summon
〖叫喊〗(动)[jiàohǎn]
cry; shout; call out; yell
〖叫唤〗(动)[jiàohuan]
call out; yell; utter shrill cry
〖叫苦连天〗[jiàokǔliántiān]
constantly complain; ventilate one's endless grievances; keep on pouring out one's hard lot
〖叫门〗[jiàomén]
call at the door; knock at the door
〖叫嚷〗(动)[jiàorǎng]
bluster; clamour; raise a hue and cry; yell
〖叫嚣〗(动)[jiàoxiāo]
clamour; make a din; declare blatantly
〖叫做〗(动)[jiàozuò]
term; name; call; brand as; be known as

觉(名)[jiào]
sleep
另见 jué

校(动)[jiào]
①correct; proofread ②contest; compare
另见 xiào
〖校对〗(动)[jiàoduì]
proofread

轿(名)[jiào]
sedan-chair
〖轿车〗(名)[jiàochē]〔辆 liàng〕
car; saloon (car)

较(介、副)[jiào]
compare; comparatively; in comparison with
〖较量〗(动)[jiàoliàng]
match; compare (e.g. strength, skill); contest

教(名)[jiào]
①education; teaching ②religion
另见 jiāo
〖教案〗(名)[jiào'àn]
a teaching plan
〖教材〗(名)[jiàocái]
teaching material (textbook, etc.); text
〖教程〗(名)[jiàochéng]
curriculum; course
〖教导〗(动、名)[jiàodǎo]
teach; instruct; teaching; instruction
〖教导员〗(名)[jiàodǎoyuán]
(mil.) political director
〖教改〗(名)[jiàogǎi]
educational reform
〖教工〗(名)[jiàogōng]
teaching and administrative staff (of a school)
〖教具〗(名)[jiàojù]
teaching aids
〖教科书〗(名)[jiàokēshū]
[本 běn] textbook
〖教练〗(名、动)[jiàoliàn]
coach; teach; instruct

〖教师〗(名)[jiàoshī]
teacher
〖教室〗(名)[jiàoshì]
classroom
〖教士〗(名)[jiàoshì]
priest; clergyman
〖教授〗(名、动)[jiàoshòu]
①professor ②teach; instruct; coach; lecture
〖教唆〗(动)[jiàosuō]
incite; instigate; abet
〖教唆犯〗(名)[jiàosuōfàn]
abettor; instigator
〖教堂〗(名)[jiàotáng]
church; cathedral
〖教条〗(名)[jiàotiáo]
dogmas
〖教条主义〗(名)[jiàotiáo zhǔyì]
dogmatism
〖教徒〗(名)[jiàotú]
follower of religion; believer
〖教学〗(名)[jiàoxué]
teaching
〖教学法〗(名)[jiàoxuéfǎ]
teaching methodology; pedagogy
〖教学相长〗[jiàoxuéxiāngzhǎng]
both teachers and students make progress by learning from each other
〖教训〗(动、名)[jiàoxun]
①teach; educate ②(learn) a lesson; teach (sb.) a lesson; reproach; rebuke
〖教研室〗(名)[jiàoyánshì]
teaching and research section
〖教研组〗(名)[jiàoyánzǔ]
teaching and research group
〖教养〗(动、名)[jiàoyǎng]
bring up; upbringing
〖教益〗(名)[jiàoyì]
beneficial advice
〖教育〗(动、名)[jiàoyù]
education; educate
〖教员〗(名)[jiàoyuán]
teacher

jiē

阶[jiē]

〖阶层〗(名)[jiēcéng]
social strata
〖阶地〗(地)[jiēdì]
terrace
〖阶段〗(名)[jiēduàn]
period; stage; phase
〖阶级〗(名)[jiējí]
class
〖阶级斗争〗[jiējídòuzhēng]
class struggle
〖阶级性〗(名)[jiējíxìng]
class nature; class character
〖阶梯〗(名)[jiētī]
steps; ladder
〖阶梯教室〗[jiētī jiàoshì]
lecture theatre
〖阶下囚〗(名)[jiēxiàqiú]
prisoner; captive

结(动)[jiē]

bear (fruit)
另见 jié
〖结实〗(形)[jiēshi]
strong; stout; robust; sturdy

接(动)[jiē]

connect; touch with

J

〖接班〗[jiēbān]
take over (e.g. shift)
〖接班人〗(名)[jiēbānrén]
successor
〖接触〗(动)[jiēchù]
contact; get in touch with
〖接待〗(动)[jiēdài]
receive; accommodate; reception
〖接待室〗(名)[jiēdàishì]
reception room
〖接到〗(动)[jiēdào]
receive
〖接二连三〗[jiē'èrliánsān]
one after the other; repeatedly
〖接管〗(动)[jiēguǎn]
take over
〖接轨〗[jiēguǐ]
bring into line with (e.g. international norms, practices, etc.)
〖接济〗(动)[jiējì]
support; help; supply
〖接见〗(动)[jiējiàn]
receive sb.
〖接交〗(动)[jiējiāo]
hand over (e.g. work)
〖接近〗(动)[jiējìn]
come close to; approach; draw near
〖接力〗(名)[jiēlì]
relay (e.g. relay race)
〖接连〗(副)[jiēlián]
one after another; consecutively; in succession; repeatedly
〖接纳〗(动)[jiēnà]
accept; take up; admit
〖接洽〗(动)[jiēqià]
contact (someone) to discuss sth.; deal with
〖接壤〗(动)[jiērǎng]
border on; be neighbor
〖接生〗(动)[jiēshēng]
assist with childbirth; act as midwife
〖接收〗(动)[jiēshōu]
take over; accept
〖接受〗(动)[jiēshòu]
accept; succumb
〖接替〗(动)[jiētì]
take someone's place; replace sb.
〖接头〗[jiētóu]
get into contact with (sb.)
〖接吻〗[jiēwěn]
kiss
〖接应〗(动)[jiēyìng]
①act in coordination ②supply
〖接着〗(动、连)[jiēzhe]
①take; accept (with one's hand) ②next; after that; following

揭(动)[jiē]
uncover; lay bare; expose
〖揭穿〗(动)[jiēchuān]
expose; uncover; disclose
〖揭发〗(动)[jiēfā]
bring to light; expose; lay bare
〖揭盖子〗[jiēgàizi]
take the lid off; bring...into the open
〖揭竿而起〗[jiēgān'érqǐ]
rise in rebellion
〖揭开〗(动)[jiēkāi]

uncover; reveal
〖揭露〗(动)[jiēlù]
expose; unmask
〖揭幕〗[jiēmù]
raise the curtain; inaugurate
〖揭破〗(动)[jiēpò]
unmask; disclose
〖揭示〗(动)[jiēshì]
① set forth; announce; enunciate ② make intelligible
〖揭晓〗(动)[jiēxiǎo]
announce the results

街(名)[jiē]〔条 tiáo〕
street
〖街道〗(名)[jiēdào]〔条 tiáo〕
① street ② residential district; neighborhood
〖街坊〗(名)[jiēfang]
neighbourhood
〖街谈巷议〗[jiētánxiàngyì]
casual conversation; street gossip
〖街头巷尾〗[jiētóuxiàngwěi]
all over the city; in all parts of the city

J

jié

节(名、量)[jié]
① section ② festival ③ joint ④ a measure word, part, period, paragraph, section, etc.
〖节俭〗(形)[jiéjiǎn]
economical; frugal
〖节录〗(动)[jiélù]
excerpt
〖节目〗(名)[jiémù]〔个 gè〕
programme; item
〖节气〗(名)[jiéqi]
the 24 periods of 15 days each which make a year; solar terms
〖节日〗(名)[jiérì]
festival
〖节省〗(动)[jiéshěng]
save; use something sparingly
〖节外生枝〗[jiéwàishēngzhī]
canse complications; raise side issues
〖节衣缩食〗[jiéyīsuōshí]
live frugally; sparing food and clothing
〖节余〗(名、动)[jiéyú]
remainder; left-overs
〖节育〗[jiéyù]
birth control
〖节约〗(动)[jiéyuē]
practise economy; economize
〖节制〗(动)[jiézhì]
limit; regulate; control; restrict
〖节奏〗(名)[jiézòu]
rhythm

劫(动)[jié]
① rob; plunder ② threaten
〖劫持〗(动)[jiéchí]
hold under duress
〖劫掠〗(动)[jiélüè]
plunder; rob

杰[jié]
〖杰出〗(形)[jiéchū]
excellent; outstanding; distinguished

〖杰作〗(名)[jiézuò]
masterpiece

洁[jié]
〖洁白〗(形)[jiébái]
pure white; clean
〖洁净〗(形)[jiéjìng]
clean; pure

结(动、名)[jié]
connect; knot; joint; tie
另见 jiē
〖结冰〗[jiébīng]
freeze
〖结成〗(动)[jiéchéng]
unite; form; enter into
〖结构〗(名)[jiégòu]
construction; structure
〖结果〗(名、副)[jiéguǒ]
result; consequence; bear fruit; as a result
〖结合〗(动)[jiéhé]
combine; integrate with; in coordination with
〖结核〗(名)[jiéhé]
tuberculosis; T.B.
〖结婚〗[jiéhūn]
marry; get married
〖结交〗(动)[jiéjiāo]
associate with; make acquaintance with
〖结晶〗(名、动)[jiéjīng]
crystallization; crystallize
〖结局〗(名)[jiéjú]
end; result; outcome
〖结论〗(名)[jiélùn]
conclusion
〖结盟〗[jiéméng]
ally with
〖结社〗[jiéshè]
form a society or association
〖结识〗(动)[jiéshí]
become acquainted with
〖结束〗(动)[jiéshù]
finish; terminate; end up
〖结算〗(动)[jiésuàn]
balance account
〖结尾〗(名)[jiéwěi]
end; finals
〖结业〗[jié yè]
finish school
〖结余〗(名)[jiéyú]
surplus; excess
〖结扎〗(动)[jiézā]
stitch; tie up (med.)
〖结账〗[jiézhàng]
pay bills;clearing (of account);settle balance;settle one's accounts

捷(形)[jié]
① fast; speedy ② win victory
〖捷报〗(名)[jiébào]
news of victory
〖捷径〗(名)[jiéjìng]
shortest path; shortcut
〖捷足先登〗[jiézúxiāndēng]
the fastest reaches the goal first

截(动、量)[jié]
①cut up (piece) ②intercept ③ a measure word, portion, part, etc.

〖截断〗(动)[jiéduàn]
cut into pieces; cut off; block
〖截击〗(动)[jiéjī]]
block and attack; intercept
〖截面〗(名)[jiémiàn]
cross-section
〖截然〗(副)[jiérán]
obviously; abruptly; entirely
〖截肢〗[jiézhī]
amputate
〖截止〗(动)[jiézhǐ]
stop
〖截至〗(动)[jiézhì]
up to (a certain time)

竭(动)[jié]
① deplete; exhaust ② exert
〖竭力〗(副)[jiélì]
do one's utmost; do one's best

jiě

姐(名)[jiě]
elder sister
〖姐夫〗(名)[jiěfu]
brother-in-law (husband of one's elder sister)
〖姐姐〗(名)[jiějie]
elder sister
〖姐妹〗(名)[jiěmèi]
sisters

解(动、名)[jiě]
① understand; comprehend; explain ② untie ③ get rid of; relieve of
〖解饱〗[jiěbǎo]
allay hunger
〖解除〗(动)[jiěchú]
relieve of; get rid of; remove
〖解答〗(动)[jiědá]
answer
〖解冻〗[jiědòng]
defreeze; (of ice) thaw
〖解饿〗[jiě è]
free (sb.) from hunger
〖解乏〗[jiěfá]
alleviate tiredness
〖解放〗(动、名)[jiěfàng]
liberate; emancipate; emancipation; liberation
〖解放军〗(名)[jiěfàngjūn]
liberation army
〖解放区〗(名)[jiěfàngqū]
liberated area
〖解放思想〗[jiěfàngsīxiǎng]
emancipate one's mind; emancipate ideologically
〖解放战争〗[jiěfàngzhànzhēng]
liberation war
〖解雇〗(动)[jiěgù]
dismiss; sack; fire
〖解救〗(动)[jiějiù]
give relief to; save
〖解决〗(动)[jiějué]
settle; solve
〖解渴〗[jiěkě]
slake thirst; quench
〖解闷〗[jiěmèn]
kill time; find distraction
〖解剖〗(动)[jiěpōu]
dissect; analyse
〖解散〗(动)[jiěsàn]
dismiss; scatter; break up; disperse; dissolve

〖解释〗(动、名)[jiěshì]
explain; expound; explanation
〖解说〗(动)[jiěshuō]
explain
〖解体〗(动)[jiětǐ]
disintegrate; fall into pieces
〖解脱〗(动)[jiětuō]
free from; extricate...from
〖解围〗[jiěwéi]
① raise siege ② save...from embarrassment
〖解析几何〗[jiěxījǐhé]
analytical geometry

jiè

介[jiè]
〖介词〗(名)[jiècí]
preposition
〖介入〗(动)[jièrù]
take sides in; intervene; involve
〖介绍〗(动)[jièshào]
introduce; recommend
〖介意〗(动)[jièyì]
care; mind (e.g. do you mind?)

戒(动)[jiè]
guard against; keep a watchful eye on...
〖戒备〗(动)[jièbèi]
watchfulness; guard against; be on the alert against
〖戒骄戒躁〗[jièjiāojièzào]
be on guard against conceit and impetuosity; guard against pride and haste
〖戒心〗(名)[jièxīn]
be on guard against
〖戒严〗(动)[jièyán]
proclaim martial law; curfew; place guards around
〖戒指〗(名)[jièzhi]
(finger) ring

届(量)[jiè]
a measure word, session, term, etc.
〖届时〗(副)[jièshí]
when the time comes

界(名)[jiè]
limit; boundary; terminus
〖界限〗(名)[jièxiàn]
① limit; confine ② demarcation line
〖界线〗(名)[jièxiàn]
① boundary line ② demarcation line

借(动)[jiè]
borrow; lend
〖借贷〗(动)[jièdài]
borrow money
〖借刀杀人〗[jièdāoshārén]
use A's knife to kill B; use other people to cause harm to sb.
〖借故〗[jiègù]
take...as a pretext
〖借光〗[jièguāng]
ask a favour
〖借鉴〗(动、名)[jièjiàn]
draw from certain experience; use as an example;
〖借口〗(动、名)[jièkǒu]

on the pretext of...; excuse
〖借款〗[jiè kuǎn]
borrow money
〖借款〗(名)[jièkuǎn]
loan
〖借题发挥〗[jiètífāhuī]
play on the theme of; seize on a theme as a false pretex to express one's own view
〖借条〗(名)[jiètiáo]〔张 zhāng〕
promissory note—I.O.U.
〖借以〗(动)[jièyǐ]
by means of; so as to; for the purpose of
〖借助〗(动)[jièzhù]
presume on; ask assistance for; by the help of...

jīn

斤(量)[jīn]
jin; Chinese measure of weight; 1 jin=1/2Kg.
〖斤斤计较〗[jīnjīnjìjiào]
think about narrow personal gains and losses; minute squaring of accounts; square accounts in every detail

今(名)[jīn]
the present time; today
〖今后〗(名)[jīnhòu]
from now on; future
〖今年〗(名)[jīnnián]
this year
〖今天〗(名)[jīntiān]
today
〖今昔〗(名)[jīnxī]
present and past
〖今朝〗(名)[jīnzhāo]
today; in the present time

金(名)[jīn]
gold
〖金笔〗(名)[jīnbǐ]〔枝 zhī〕
fountain pen (with a gold nip)
〖金碧辉煌〗[jīnbìhuīhuáng]
magnificent; splendid
〖金刚石〗(名)[jīngāngshí]
diamond
〖金黄〗(形)[jīnhuáng]
golden yellow
〖金科玉律〗[jīnkēyùlǜ]
infallible law; golden rule
〖金钱〗(名)[jīnqián]
money
〖金融〗(名)[jīnróng]
finance
〖金色〗(名)[jīnsè]
golden colour
〖金属〗(名)[jīnshǔ]
metal
〖金文〗(名)[jīnwén]
inscription on ancient bronze vessels
〖金星〗(名)[jīnxīng]
(planet) Venus
〖金鱼〗(名)[jīnyú]〔条 tiáo〕
goldfish
〖金字塔〗(名)[jīnzìtǎ]
pyramid

津[jīn]
〖津津有味〗[jīnjīnyǒuwèi]

do something with zest or relish; with enormous gusto
〖津贴〗(名、动)[jīntiē]
allowance; subsidy; subsidize

矜[jīn]
〖矜持〗(形)[jīnchí]
behave awkwardly; in an unnatural way

筋(名)[jīn]
sinew
〖筋斗〗(名)[jīndǒu]
somer sault
〖筋骨〗(名)[jīngǔ]
muscle and bone; person's physique (bones and sinews)

禁(动)[jīn]
be able to withstand or endure
另见 jìn
〖禁不起〗[jīnbuqǐ]
cannot withstand
〖禁不住〗[jīn bu zhù]
① can not withstand ② be unable to help (doing sth.)
〖禁得起〗[jīndeqǐ]
be able to withstand or endure
〖禁得住〗[jīndezhù]
be able to withstand or endure
〖禁受〗(动)[jīnshòu]
suffer; undergo; go through

襟(名)[jīn]
the lapel of a coat
〖襟怀坦白〗[jīnhuáitǎnbái]
largeness of mind

jǐn

仅(副)[jǐn]
only; merely
〖仅仅〗(副)[jǐnjǐn]
only; alone

尽(动)[jǐn]
be limited to
另见 jìn
〖尽管〗(副、连)[jǐnguǎn]
in spite; despite; even though; nonetheless; nevertheless; for all that
〖尽快〗(副)[jǐnkuài]
as soon as possible
〖尽量〗(副)[jǐnliàng]
the best of one's ability; as full as possible; spare no effort
〖尽先〗(副)[jǐnxiān]
give priority to

紧(形、动)[jǐn]
tighten; tight
〖紧凑〗(形)[jǐncòu]
concise and to the point; tightly packed or arranged
〖紧急〗(形)[jǐnjí]
urgent; critical (moment); emergent
〖紧密〗(形)[jǐnmì]
close
〖紧迫〗(形)[jǐnpò]
pressing; urgent
〖紧俏〗(形)[jǐnqiào]

well sold and in short supply; hard-to-get (commodity)
〖紧缩〗(动)[jǐnsuō]
cut down
〖紧要〗(形)[jǐnyào]
important; essential; critical
〖紧张〗(形)[jǐnzhāng]
critical; tense; intense

锦(名)[jǐn]
tapestry; embroidered work
〖锦标〗(名)[jǐnbiāo]
championship; a trophy
〖锦标赛〗(名)[jǐnbiāosài]
championships
〖锦旗〗(名)[jǐnqí]〔面 miàn〕
embroidered flag
〖锦上添花〗[jǐnshàngtiānhuā]
more flowers on the brocade; gild refined gold; embellish what is already beautiful
〖锦绣〗(名)[jǐnxiù]
rich brocade
〖锦绣山河〗[jǐnxiùshānhé]
beautiful land

谨[jǐn]
〖谨慎〗(形)[jǐnshèn]
careful; cautious
〖谨小慎微〗[jǐnxiǎoshènwēi]
cautious and meticulous; timorous and meticulous; over-cautious

jìn

尽(动)[jìn]
① exert; put forth ② use up completely
另见 jǐn
〖尽力〗[jìnlì]
to the best of one'sability; exert
〖尽情〗(副)[jìnqíng]
elatedly
〖尽人皆知〗[jìnrénjiēzhī]
it is widely known; known to all
〖尽善尽美〗[jìnshànjìnměi]
the best there is; it's perfection itself; try one's best (to do sth.) to perfection
〖尽心〗[jìnxīn]
with all one's heart
〖尽兴〗(动)[jìnxìng]
to one's heart's content
〖尽职〗[jìnzhí]
faithfully carry out one's duties

进(动)[jìn]
① go ahead; move forward; advance ② enter; come in; make way into
〖进步〗(形、动)[jìnbù]
progressive; make progress; progress
〖进程〗(名)[jìnchéng]
developments; progress; course
〖进度〗(名)[jìndù]
progress
〖进而〗(连)[jìn'ér]
furthermore
〖进犯〗(动)[jìnfàn]
invade; intrude
〖进攻〗(动)[jìngōng]

J

attack; assault
〖进化〗(动)[jìnhuà]
evolve; evolution
〖进化论〗(名)[jìnhuàlùn]
theory of evolution; evolutionism
〖进军〗(动)[jìnjūn]
march on; advance; push on (to an area)
〖进口〗(动)[jìnkǒu]
import; trade in
〖进口货〗(名)[jìnkǒuhuò]
imported goods
〖进来〗[jìnlái]
come in; enter
〖进取〗(动)[jìnqǔ]
endeavour to make improvement; make much more progress
〖进去〗[jìnqù]
go in; enter
〖进入〗(动)[jìnrù]
make way into; enter
〖进退两难〗[jìntuìliǎngnán]
in a dilemma; be between two fires
〖进退维谷〗[jìntuìwéigǔ]
find oneself in a dilemma
〖进行〗(动)[jìnxíng]
proceed with; go ahead; carry on
〖进行曲〗(名)[jìnxíngqǔ]
march (music)
〖进修〗(动)[jìnxiū]
pursue further studies
〖进一步〗[jìnyībù]
go a step further
〖进展〗(动)[jìnzhǎn]
advance; improve; progress; make headway; develop
〖进驻〗(动)[jìnzhù]
garrison; get into position

近(形)[jìn]

①near; nearby ②recent; current
〖近代〗(名)[jìndài]
modern (times, etc.)
〖近郊〗(名)[jìnjiāo]
suburbs; outskirts
〖近况〗(名)[jìnkuàng]
the current situation
〖近来〗(名)[jìnlái]
recently; not long ago; of late
〖近日〗(名)[jìnrì]
recent days; recently
〖近视〗(名、形)[jìnshì]
shortsighted
〖近水楼台〗[jìnshuǐlóutái]
(lit.) waterfront towers get the moonlight first; (fig.) a person in a favourable position wins favour first
〖近似〗(动)[jìnsì]
look like; be similar
〖近似值〗(名)[jìnsìzhí]
approximate value

劲(名)[jìn]

strength; effort
另见 jìng
〖劲头〗(名)[jìntóu]
①strength ②zeal; enthusiasm

浸(动)[jìn]

immerse; soak
〖浸透〗(动)[jìntòu]

saturated through and through with
〖浸种〗[jìn zhǒng]
soak seeds

禁(动)[jìn]
①prohibit; forbid ②take into custody; lock up
另见 jīn
〖禁闭〗(名)[jìnbì]
imprison; detain; lock up
〖禁锢〗(动)[jìngù]
jail; lock up; put under custody
〖禁忌〗(动)[jìnjì]
taboo
〖禁绝〗(动)[jìnjué]
absolutely prohibit
〖禁令〗(名)[jìnlìng]
legal restriction; forbidden; prohibition law
〖禁区〗(名)[jìnqū]
out of bounds area; forbidden area; off limits
〖禁运〗(动)[jìnyùn]
embargo
〖禁止〗(动)[jìnzhǐ]
forbid; prohibit; ban

jīng

茎(名)[jīng]
stem; stalk of a plant

京(名)[jīng]
①capital (of a country); metropolis ②Peking
〖京剧〗(名)[jīngjù]
Peking opera

经(名、动)[jīng]
① classics ② longitude ③ manage; handle ④ go or pass through
〖经不起〗[jīngbuqǐ]
cannot withstand (sth.)
〖经常〗(形)[jīngcháng]
often; consistent; usual
〖经得起〗[jīngdeqǐ]
can stand (sth.)
〖经典〗(名)[jīngdiǎn]
classics; classical
〖经度〗(名)[jīngdù]
longitude
〖经费〗(名)[jīngfèi][笔 bǐ]
expenditure; expenses; fund
〖经风雨,见世面〗
[jīngfēngyǔ, jiànshìmiàn]
face the world and brave the storm
〖经管〗(动)[jīngguǎn]
manage; be in charge of
〖经过〗(动、名)[jīngguò]
pass through; process
〖经纪人〗(名)[jīngjìrén]
broker; middleman; agent
〖经济〗(名、形)[jīngjì]
economy; economic; economical
〖经济过热〗[jīngjìguòrè]
overheated economic development
〖经济基础〗[jīngjìjīchǔ]
economic base; economic foundation
〖经济实体〗[jīngjìshítǐ]
economic entity
〖经济特区〗[jīngjìtèqū]
special economic zone

〖经济危机〗[jīngjìwēijī]
economic crisis
〖经济作物〗[jīngjìzuòwù]
industrial crops
〖经久不息〗[jīngjiǔbùxī]
prolonged (applause, ovation, etc.)
〖经理〗(名)[jīnglǐ]
manager
〖经历〗(动、名)[jīnglì]
experience; undergo; go through; career
〖经商〗[jīngshāng]
be in the business; engage in business; go into business
〖经手〗[jīngshǒu]
responsible for; pass through one's hands
〖经受〗(动)[jīngshòu]
undergo; suffer; go through
〖经销〗(动)[jīngxiāo]
sell on commission; deal in; distribute
〖经心〗(形)[jīngxīn]
carefully
〖经验〗(名)[jīngyàn]
experience
〖经验主义〗(名)[jīngyànzhǔyì]
empiricism
〖经营〗(动)[jīngyíng]
manage; run

荆[jīng]
〖荆棘〗(名)[jīngjí]
brambles

惊(动)[jīng]
frighten; startle
〖惊动〗(动)[jīngdòng]
trouble; disturb; startle; shock
〖惊弓之鸟〗[jīnggōngzhīniǎo]
birds startled by the mere twang of a bowstring; nervously alert
〖惊慌〗(形)[jīnghuāng]
alarmed; startled
〖惊慌失措〗[jīnghuāngshīcuò]
state of panic; panic and confusion
〖惊恐〗(形)[jīngkǒng]
scared; frightened
〖惊恐万状〗[jīngkǒngwànzhuàng]
panic-stricken
〖惊奇〗(形)[jīngqí]
surprised; astonished
〖惊人〗(形)[jīngrén]
astonishing; surprising
〖惊叹〗(动)[jīngtàn]
exclaim in surprise
〖惊叹号〗(名)[jīngtànhào]
exclamation mark
〖惊涛骇浪〗[jīngtāohàilàng]
tempestuous storm; fierce and frightening storm
〖惊天动地〗[jīngtiāndòngdì]
earth-shaking
〖惊喜〗(形)[jīngxǐ]
pleasantly surprised
〖惊险〗(形)[jīngxiǎn]
thrilling
〖惊心动魄〗[jīngxīndòngpò]
soul-stirring; breath-taking
〖惊醒〗(动)[jīngxǐng]
wake up; be wakened in fright
〖惊讶〗(形)[jīngyà]

surprised; alarmed
〖惊异〗(形)[jīngyì]
astonished

旌[jīng]
〖旌旗〗(名)[jīngqí]
banners or flags

晶[jīng]
〖晶体〗(名)[jīngtǐ]
crystal
〖晶体管〗(名)[jīngtǐguǎn]
transistor
〖晶莹〗(形)[jīngyíng]
radiant crystalline

兢[jīng]
〖兢兢业业〗[jīngjīngyèyè]
do things in a careful and thoroughgoing manner

精(形)[jīng]
fine;essential; exquisite; excellent; refined
〖精兵简政〗[jīngbīngjiǎnzhèng]
better troops and simpler administration; fewer and better troops and simpler administration
〖精彩〗(形)[jīngcǎi]
excellent (e.g.show); brilliant
〖精打细算〗[jīngdǎxìsuàn]
very careful in reckoning; accurate in calculation; with great care in reckoning
〖精雕细刻〗[jīngdiāoxìkè]
give something careful revision; meticulous work; elaborate
〖精读〗(动)[jīngdú]
intensive study or reading
〖精干〗(形)[jīnggàn]
ingenious and capable; efficient;
〖精耕细作〗[jīnggēngxìzuò]
intensive cultivation; intensive and meticulous farming
〖精悍〗(形)[jīnghàn]
capable; sharp
〖精华〗(名)[jīnghuá]
fine essence; quintessence (of classical philosophy);the cream (of the nation)
〖精简〗(动)[jīngjiǎn]
cut down (the number of the personnel); simplify
〖精简机构〗[jīngjiǎnjīgòu]
simplify the administrative structure
〖精力〗(名)[jīnglì]
energy; physical and mental vitality
〖精练〗(形)[jīngliàn]
well trained; refined
〖精良〗(形)[jīngliáng]
at the highest grade or the best quality
〖精美〗(形)[jīngměi]
elegant and refined; of the finest quality; exquisite
〖精密〗(形)[jīngmì]
exact; precise; comprehensive
〖精密度〗(名)[jīngmìdù]
precision
〖精明〗(形)[jīngmíng]

smart; bright; brilliant
〖精明强干〗[jīngmíngqiánggàn]
ingenious and capable
〖精疲力竭〗[jīngpílìjié]
completely exhausted; tired out
〖精辟〗(形)[jīngpì]
incisive; profound
〖精巧〗(形)[jīngqiǎo]
skilful; delicate
〖精确〗(形)[jīngquè]
accurate; precise
〖精锐〗(形)[jīngruì]
crack (troops, etc.)
〖精神〗(名、形)[jīngshen]
spirit; spiritual; vigorous
〖精神病〗(名)[jīngshénbìng]
mental disease
〖精神贵族〗[jīngshénguìzú]
intellectual aristocrat
〖精神焕发〗[jīngshénhuànfā]
in high spirits; vigorous; brimming with energy
〖精神面貌〗[jīngshénmiànmào]
mental outlook
〖精神食粮〗[jīngshénshíliáng]
nourishment for mind; intellectual food
〖精神文明〗[jīngshénwénmíng]
spiritual civilization; cultural and ideological progress
〖精髓〗(名)[jīngsuǐ]
quintessence
〖精通〗(动)[jīngtōng]
proficient in; be versed in; master
〖精细〗(形)[jīngxì]
fine; delicate
〖精心〗(形)[jīngxīn]
carefully; meticulous
〖精益求精〗[jīngyìqiújīng]
perfect one's skill constantly; be constantly perfecting one's skill
〖精湛〗(形)[jīngzhàn]
① exquisite; skilful ② deep; profound
〖精致〗(形)[jīngzhì]
of fine workmanship
〖精装〗(名)[jīngzhuāng]
deluxe or high quality edition; hard-cover books

鲸(名)[jīng]
whale
〖鲸吞〗(动)[jīngtūn]
annex; swallow up; devour
〖鲸鱼〗(名)[jīngyú]
whale

jǐng

井(名)[jǐng]〔眼 yǎn、口 kǒu〕
well
〖井井有条〗[jǐngjǐngyǒutiáo]
arranged in good order
〖井然〗(形)[jǐngrán]
well arranged; in good order; tidy
〖井田制〗(名)[jǐngtiánzhì]
the nine-square system of dividing the land

颈[jǐng]
〖颈项〗(名)[jǐngxiàng]
neck

景(名)[jǐng]
scenery; scene; sight
〖景况〗(名)[jǐngkuàng]
state of affairs; condition
〖景气〗(形)[jǐngqì]
economic prosperity; boom
〖景色〗(名)[jǐngsè]
landscape; scenery
〖景泰蓝〗(名)[jǐngtàilán]
cloisonne
〖景物〗(名)[jǐngwù]
the beautiful scene before one's eyes; lovely prospects
〖景象〗(名)[jǐngxiàng]
prospects
〖景仰〗(动)[jǐngyǎng]
admire; respect
〖景致〗(名)[jǐngzhì]
especially beautiful scenery or scene

警(名)[jǐng]
police
〖警报〗(名)[jǐngbào]
combat alert; alarm
〖警察〗(名)[jǐngchá]
police; policeman
〖警告〗(动、名)[jǐnggào]
①warn; warning ②put on guard ③caution (punishment)
〖警戒〗(动)[jǐngjiè]
①be vigilant; guard against ②warn; counsel
〖警句〗(名)[jǐngjù]
a brilliant sentence; epigram
〖警觉〗(名)[jǐngjué]
alert
〖警惕〗(动、名)[jǐngtì]
maintain vigilance; be on the look out; vigilance
〖警卫〗(动、名)[jǐngwèi]
post sentries (around...); guards; troops on duty
〖警钟〗(名)[jǐngzhōng]
①an alarm bell ②warning

jìng

劲[jìng]
另见 jìn
〖劲敌〗(名)[jìngdí]
redoutable enemy
〖劲旅〗(名)[jìnglǚ]
crack troops
〖劲松〗(名)[jìngsōng]
a sturdy pine

净(形)[jìng]
clean; pure
〖净化〗(动)[jìnghuà]
purify
〖净重〗(名)[jìngzhòng]
net weight

径[jìng]
〖径直〗(副)[jìngzhí]
directly; straightforward
〖径自〗(副)[jìngzì]
direct personal action (e.g. without permission).

痉[jìng]
〖痉挛〗(动)[jìngluán]
convulsions; convulsive cont-

ractions

竞[jìng]

〖竞赛〗(动)[jìngsài]
compete; contest; competition
〖竞选〗(动)[jìngxuǎn]
campaign; run for (e.g. office)
〖竞争〗(动)[jìngzhēng]
compete;contend; struggle for; competition
〖竞争力〗(名、形)[jìngzhēnglì]
competitive

竟(副)[jìng]

①ultimately; finally ②whole; from begining to end
〖竟然〗(副)[jìngrán]
even; go to the length of; go so far as to

敬(动)[jìng]

① respect; hold in veneration ② offer sth. respectfully;present with respect
〖敬爱〗(动)[jìng'ài]
love and respect; esteem
〖敬而远之〗[jìng'éryuǎnzhī]
stay at a respectful distance from; keep someone at a respectable distance
〖敬礼〗[jìnglǐ]
salute
〖敬佩〗(动)[jìngpèi]
admire and respect; esteem
〖敬献〗(动)[jìngxiàn]
present; offer with respect
〖敬仰〗(动)[jìngyǎng]
have the highest admiration for
〖敬意〗(名)[jìngyì]
salute; regards; esteem; respects; tribute
〖敬祝〗(动)[jìngzhù]
offer respectful wishes (to sb.)

静(形)[jìng]

silent; quiet
〖静电〗(名)[jìngdiàn]
electrostatic
〖静电感应〗[jìngdiàngǎnyìng]
electrostatic induction
〖静脉〗(名)[jìngmài]
veins
〖静悄悄〗(形)[jìngqiāoqiāo]
quietly; silently
〖静止〗(动)[jìngzhǐ]
static; stationary; motionless

境(名)[jìng]

①boundary; border ②locality; area ③situation; condition
〖境地〗(名)[jìngdì]
(living or working) conditions; situation
〖境界〗(名)[jìngjiè]
①boundaries; border ②condition; extent; state (of mind)
〖境况〗(名)[jìngkuàng]
situation; condition
〖境内〗(名)[jìngnèi]
within the territory or area
〖境遇〗(名)[jìngyù]
circumstance; situation

镜(名)[jìng]
a mirror
〖镜头〗(名)[jìngtóu]
① a camera lens ② shots (motion picture)
〖镜子〗(名)[jìngzi]〔面 miàn〕
a mirror; spectacles; glasses

jiǒng

迥[jiǒng]
〖迥然〗(副)[jiǒngrán]
utterly; entirely

炯[jiǒng]
〖炯炯〗(形)[jiǒngjiǒng]
shining brightly; sparkling

窘(形)[jiǒng]
① poor ② embarrassed; awkward
〖窘迫〗(形)[jiǒngpò]
① find it difficult to make ends meet ② be in a difficult or embarrassing position

J

jiū

纠(动)[jiū]
correct (a mistake)
〖纠察〗(名)[jiūchá]
pickets
〖纠缠〗(动)[jiūchán]
entangle; pester
〖纠纷〗(名)[jiūfēn]
quarrel; dispute; conflict
〖纠葛〗(名)[jiūgé]
entanglement; dispute; complication
〖纠集〗(动)[jiūjí]
(derog.) gather; pull together; muster
〖纠正〗(动)[jiūzhèng]
correct (a mistake); amend; rectify

究[jiū]
〖究竟〗(名、副)[jiūjìng]
① the whys and wherefores; the reasons for sth. ② after all; anyway; whatever

揪(动)[jiū]
hold fast; clutch; grasp

jiǔ

九(数)[jiǔ]
① nine ② many; plenty
〖九牛二虎之力〗
[jiǔniú'èrhǔzhīlì]
(lit.) the strength of two tigers and nine oxen; (fig.) great strength
〖九牛一毛〗[jiǔniúyīmáo]
a drop in the ocean
〖九死一生〗[jiǔsǐyīshēng]
(lit.) nine chances to die and one chance to live; (fig.) a narrow escape (of one's life); a close shave
〖九霄云外〗[jiǔxiāoyúnwài]
the farthest limits of the sky; (fling to) the four winds
〖九一八事变〗[JiǔYībāShìbiàn]
the Incident of September 18, 1931—On September 18, 1931, the

Japanese "Kwantung Army" in northeastern China seized Shenyang. Under Chiang Kaishek's order of "absolute non-resistance", the Chinese troops at Shenyang and elsewhere in the Northeast (the Northeastern Army) withdrew to the south of Shanhaikuan, and consequently the Japanese forces rapidly occupied the provinces of Liaoning, Kirin and Heilungkiang. This act of Japanese aggression has become known as the "September 18th Incident".
〖九月〗(名)[jiǔyuè]
September

久(形)[jiǔ]
for a long time
〖久经〗(动)[jiǔjīng]
have gone through... a long time; long standing
〖久远〗(形)[jiǔyuǎn]
long ago or distant future

酒(名)[jiǔ]
alcoholic beverages or drinks
〖酒杯〗(名)[jiǔbēi][个 gè]
wine cup or glass
〖酒会〗(名)[jiǔhuì]
cocktail party
〖酒精〗(名)[jiǔjīng]
alcohol; spirits
〖酒席〗(名)[jiǔxí]
a formal banquet

jiù

旧(形)[jiù]
old; former; past
〖旧居〗(名)[jiùjū]
the former dwelling place; former residence
〖旧历〗(名)[jiùlì]
lunar calendar

救(动)[jiù]
① save (a person from danger, etc.) ② help; assist
〖救国〗[jiùguó]
rescue the country; save the nation; national salvation
〖救护〗(动)[jiùhù]
give first aid to; come to the rescue of
〖救荒〗[jiùhuāng]
provide disaster relief
〖救火〗[jiùhuǒ]
put out fire
〖救济〗(动)[jiùjì]
give relief to; provide relief for
〖救命〗[jiùmìng]
save a person's life; life-saving
〖救世主〗(名)[jiùshìzhǔ]
the Saviour
〖救死扶伤〗[jiùsǐfúshāng]
heal the wounded, rescue the dying
〖救亡〗(动)[jiùwáng]
save the nation from subjugation; national salvation
〖救星〗(名)[jiùxīng]

liberator; saviour
〖救灾〗[jiùzāi]
give relief aid; disaster relief

就(动、副、连)[jiù]
① assume; take up; start doing (sth.) ② expression of finality; that is; must; will ③ then; soon
〖就地〗(副)[jiùdì]
on the spot; locally
〖就地取材〗[jiùdìqǔcái]
obtain raw materials locally; use local materials
〖就近〗(副)[jiùjìn]
at close quarters; nearby
〖就事论事〗[jiùshìlùnshì]
take the matter on its merits; be pragmatic
〖就是〗(连)[jiùshì]
① even if ② simply; just
〖就是说〗[jiùshìshuō]
that is to say...
〖就算〗(连)[jiùsuàn]
granted that; even if
〖就绪〗(动)[jiùxù]
be in good order; be completed
〖就业〗[jiùyè]
take up employment; begin a job
〖就义〗(动)[jiùyì]
lay down one's life for a just cause; die a martyr
〖就职〗[jiùzhí]
take up post; assume duty

舅(名)[jiù]
maternal uncle
〖舅舅〗(名)[jiùjiu]
maternal uncle
〖舅母〗(名)[jiùmu]
aunt (wife of mother's brother)

jū

拘(动)[jū]
arrest; seize
〖拘谨〗(形)[jūjǐn]
cautious; over-reserved
〖拘留〗(动)[jūliú]
detain; hold in custody
〖拘泥〗(形)[jūnì]
formal; stiff
〖拘束〗(形)[jūshù]
restrained; inhibited; awkward; not at ease

居(动)[jū]
live; reside; dwell
〖居高临下〗[jūgāolínxià]
commanding height
〖居功〗[jūgōng]
claim credit (for oneself)
〖居留〗(动)[jūliú]
reside; stay
〖居民〗(名)[jūmín]
resident; inhabitant
〖居然〗(副)[jūrán]
even; have the audacity to; go so far as
〖居心〗[jūxīn]
intend (to do sth.); bent on
〖居心叵测〗[jūxīnpǒcè]
with ulterior motives; harbour evil intent towards

〖居住〗(动)[jūzhù]
live; reside; inhabit

鞠[jū]

〖鞠躬〗[jūgōng]
bow (in respect)
〖鞠躬尽瘁,死而后已〗
[jūgōngjìncuì, sǐ'érhòuyǐ]
bending one's backs to the task until one's dying day; give one's all (to the service of the people)

jú

局(名、量)[jú]

① bureau; department ② a measure word (for chess game, table-tennis, etc.)
〖局部〗(名)[júbù]
partial; in part; local
〖局促〗(形)[júcù]
① narrow and small ② brief; short (of time) ③ stand on ceremony
〖局面〗(名)[júmiàn]
condition; situation
〖局势〗(名)[júshì]
situation; state of affairs
〖局限〗(动)[júxiàn]
be limited to; limitation;
〖局限性〗(名)[júxiànxìng]
limitations; being narrow

菊(名)[jú]

chrysanthemum
〖菊花〗(名)[júhuā][朵 duǒ]
chrysanthemum blossom

橘(名)[jú]

orange
〖橘子〗(名)[júzi]
orange (fruit)

jǔ

咀[jǔ]

〖咀嚼〗(动)[jǔjué]
chew; munch

沮[jǔ]

〖沮丧〗(形)[jǔsàng]
dispirited; depressed; dejected

矩[jǔ]

〖矩形〗(名)[jǔxíng]
rectangle

举(动)[jǔ]

hold up; raise
〖举办〗(动)[jǔbàn]
① sponsor ② hold; conduct; open
〖举报〗(动)[jǔbào]
report an offence to the authorities; turn sb. in
〖举动〗(名)[jǔdòng]
behaviour; conduct
〖举国〗(名)[jǔguó]
the whole country
〖举例〗[jǔlì]
give examples; cite an instance; for example
〖举目〗[jǔmù]
look up
〖举棋不定〗[jǔqíbùdìng]

(lit.)hesitate in making a move at chess; (fig.) indecisive; hesitating; wavering
〖举世〗(名)[jǔshì]
the whole world; all the world
〖举世闻名〗[jǔshìwénmíng]
be known to all the world; world renowned; world famous
〖举行〗(动)[jǔxíng]
take place; hold; stage
〖举一反三〗[jǔyīfǎnsān]
derive or infer other things from one fact; make inferences by analogy
〖举止〗(名)[jǔzhǐ]
behaviour; manner
〖举重〗(名)[jǔzhòng]
weight-lifting
〖举足轻重〗[jǔzúqīngzhòng]
be in an important position; play a pivotal role; carry a big weight in

jù

巨(形)[jù]
great; huge; giant (size)
〖巨大〗(形)[jùdà]
huge; immense
〖巨额〗(名)[jù'é]
a huge sum of (money)
〖巨幅〗(名)[jùfú]
huge (portrait)
〖巨型〗(名)[jùxíng]
large (model); giant; mammoth

句(名、量)[jù]
① sentence ② a measure word, sentence
〖句号〗(名)[jùhào]
a full stop
〖句型〗(名)[jùxíng]
sentence pattern
〖句子〗(名)[jùzi]
sentence

拒(动)[jù]
resist; reject
〖拒绝〗(动)[jùjué]
reject; refuse; turn down

具[jù]
〖具备〗(动)[jùbèi]
measure up to; possess
〖具体〗(形)[jùtǐ]
concrete; specific; actual
〖具体化〗(动)[jùtǐhuà]
embody; be specific
〖具有〗(动)[jùyǒu]
be provided with; possess

俱(副)[jù]
all
〖俱乐部〗(名)[jùlèbù]
club

剧(名)[jù]
drama
〖剧本〗(名)[jùběn]
a play; script
〖剧场〗(名)[jùchǎng]
theatre
〖剧烈〗(形)[jùliè]
violent; acute; drastic

〖剧情〗(名)[jùqíng]
dramatic plot
〖剧团〗(名)[jùtuán]
theatrical troupe; ensemble
〖剧院〗(名)[jùyuàn]
theatre
〖剧种〗(名)[jùzhǒng]
types of opera

据(动)[jù]
occupy; take possession of
〖据点〗(名)[jùdiǎn]
strong-hold; fortified points; foothold
〖据说〗[jùshuō]
allegedly; be said to; it is said that
〖据为己有〗[jùwéijǐyǒu]
take forceful possession of; have all to oneself; make something one's own

惧[jù]
〖惧怕〗(动)[jùpà]
fear; frighten
〖惧色〗(名)[jùsè]
appearance of being scared

距(介)[jù]
in between; remote from
〖距离〗(名、介)[jùlí]
① space; distance between two points ② discrepancy

飓[jù]
〖飓风〗(名)[jùfēng]
hurricane; typhoon

锯(名、动)[jù]〔把 bǎ〕
saw
〖锯齿〗(名)[jùchǐ]
the teeth of a saw

聚(动)[jù]
gather together; assemble; herd...together
〖聚会〗(动)[jùhuì]
gather together; meet
〖聚集〗(动)[jùjí]
gather together; assemble
〖聚精会神〗[jùjīnghuìshén]
concentrate one's attention
〖聚居〗(动)[jùjū]
live closely together; live in a compact community

juān

捐(动、名)[juān]
① contribute ② tax; duty
〖捐款〗(名)[juānkuǎn]
contribute money
〖捐躯〗(动)[juānqū]
lay down one's life for a just cause
〖捐税〗(名)[juānshuì]
taxes
〖捐献〗(动)[juānxiàn]
contribute
〖捐赠〗(动)[juānzèng]
donation; contribute; offer

juǎn

卷(动、量)[juǎn]
① roll up ② a measure word, roll

另见 juàn
〖卷入〗(动)[juǎnrù]
be drawn into; be involved in
〖卷舌元音〗[juǎnshéyuányīn]
retroflex vowels
〖卷土重来〗[juǎntǔchónglái]
stage a comeback
〖卷扬机〗(名)[juǎnyángjī]
hoisting machine; a hoist

juàn

卷(名、量)[juàn]
① examination paper ② a measure word, volume
另见 juǎn
〖卷子〗(名)[juànzi]
examination paper

绢(名)[juàn]
plain silk

圈(名)[juàn]
a pen (for cattle, sheep, etc.)
另见 quān

J

眷[juàn]
〖眷属〗(名)[juànshǔ]
family (wife and children, etc.)

juē

撅(动)[juē]
① stick up (in the air) ② break off (a branch)

jué

决(动、副)[jué]
①decide ②breach; crack ③certainly; absolutely (usu. negative)
〖决不〗[juébù]
certainly not; in no way; by no means; never
〖决策〗(动、名)[juécè]
①decide on (a plan, etc.); decision ②policy-making
〖决定〗(动、名)[juédìng]
decide; determine; decision
〖决定性〗(名)[juédìngxìng]
decisive; crucial
〖决断〗(动)[juéduàn]
make a firm decision
〖决口〗[juékǒu]
breach; crack; gap
〖决裂〗(动)[juéliè]
break with; rupture
〖决然〗(副)[juérán]
decidedly; resolutely; firmly
〖决赛〗(动、名)[juésài]
(sports) finals
〖决胜〗(动)[juéshèng]
strive to win the decisive battle; make a final bid for victory
〖决算〗(动、名)[juésuàn]
final accounts; financial statement; balance account
〖决心〗(名)[juéxīn]
determination; resolve; make up one's mind
〖决心书〗(名)[juéxīnshū]
letter expressing one's determination; written pledge
〖决议〗(名)[juéyì]

resolution; decision; resolve
〖决战〗(动、名)[juézhàn]
fight a decisive battle; decisive battle; pitched battle

诀[jué]
〖诀窍〗(名)[juéqiào]
secret to success; key to success

抉[jué]
〖抉择〗(动)[juézé]
choose; select; make a choice from alternatives

角(名)[jué]
① actor ② role (in drama or cinema)
另见 jiǎo
〖角色〗(名)[juésè]
role (in drama or cinema)
〖角逐〗(动)[juézhú]
tussle; contend for; compete with...for mastery; rivalry

觉(动)[jué]
feel; be aware
另见 jiào
〖觉察〗(动)[juéchá]
sense; discern; discover
〖觉得〗(动)[juéde]
feel
〖觉悟〗(动、名)[juéwù]
be aware; realise; consciousness
〖觉醒〗(动)[juéxǐng]
consciousness; awareness; awakening

绝(动、副)[jué]
① end; break off ② run out of; exhaust ③ very; definitely; absolutely
〖绝对〗(形)[juéduì]
absolute; pure; sheer
〖绝对化〗(动)[juéduìhuà]
absolutely; render absolute
〖绝对真理〗[juéduì zhēnlǐ]
absolute truth
〖绝对值〗(名)[juéduìzhí]
absolute magnitude
〖绝迹〗[juéjī]
completely disappear
〖绝技〗(名)[juéjì]
a superb skill
〖绝交〗[juéjiāo]
break off relations with; sever relations with
〖绝境〗(名)[juéjìng]
in hopeless straits; doom; impasse
〖绝句〗(名)[juéjù]
four-lined verse with five or seven characters to each line
〖绝路〗[juélù]
heading for doom; taking the road to ruin
〖绝路〗(名)[juélù]
doom; dead end; catastrophe
〖绝密〗(形)[juémì]
top secret; strictly confidential
〖绝妙〗(形)[juémiào]
marvellous; excellent; wonder-

ful
〖绝食〗[juéshí]
hunger strike
〖绝望〗[juéwàng]
have no hope for; despair; lose all hope for
〖绝无仅有〗[juéwújǐnyǒu]
extremely rare; exceptional; unusual
〖绝育〗[juéyù]
sterilization; be sterilized
〖绝缘〗(动)[juéyuán]
insulate; insulation; isolate
〖绝缘体〗(名)[juéyuántǐ]
an insulator; insulating material
〖绝种〗[juézhǒng]
become extinct

倔[jué]
〖倔强〗(形)[juéjiàng]
obstinate; stubborn; resolute

掘(动)[jué]
dig; excavate
〖掘进〗(动)[juéjìn]
tunnel
〖掘墓人〗(名)[juémùrén]
grave-digger
〖掘土机〗(名)[juétǔjī]
bulldozer

崛[jué]
〖崛起〗(动)[juéqǐ]
tower upwards

攫[jué]
〖攫取〗(动)[juéqǔ]
seize; grab

jūn

军(名)[jūn]
①military; army ②corps
〖军备〗(名)[jūnbèi]
armaments
〖军队〗(名)[jūnduì]
(mil.)troops; army; forces
〖军阀〗(名)[jūnfá]
warlord
〖军费〗(名)[jūnfèi]
military expenses
〖军官〗(名)[jūnguān]
officer
〖军国主义〗(名)[jūnguózhǔyì]
militarism
〖军火〗(名)[jūnhuǒ]
munitions
〖军火商〗(名)[jūnhuǒshāng]
munition makers and dealers
〖军纪〗(名)[jūnjì]
military discipline
〖军舰〗(名)[jūnjiàn]〔艘 sōu〕
warship
〖军民〗[jūnmín]
army and people; soldiers and civilians
〖军旗〗(名)[jūnqí]〔面 miàn〕
army flag
〖军区〗(名)[jūnqū]
military area
〖军人〗(名)[jūnrén]
military man; serviceman; military personnel
〖军事〗(名)[jūnshì]

J

military affairs
〖军事家〗(名)[jūnshìjiā]
military strategist
〖军事基地〗[jūnshìjīdì]
military bases
〖军属〗(名)[jūnshǔ]
army-man's family
〖军衔〗(名)[jūnxián]
military rank
〖军心〗(名)[jūnxīn]
hearts of the troops; the morale of the army
〖军训〗(名)[jūnxùn]
military training
〖军用〗[jūnyòng]
for use by the military
〖军乐〗(名)[jūnyuè]
military band (music)
〖军长〗(名)[jūnzhǎng]
corps commander
〖军种〗(名)[jūnzhǒng]
armed services
〖军转民〗[jūnzhuǎnmín]
transfer from military production to civil production
〖军装〗(名)[jūnzhuāng]〔套 tào〕
military uniform

均(形)[jūn]
equal; even; balanced
〖均等〗(动)[jūnděng]
on an equal footing
〖均衡〗(动)[jūnhéng]
balance
〖均势〗(名)[jūnshì]
balance of power; relative equilibrium of forces
〖均匀〗(形)[jūnyún]
even; uniform

君(代、名)[jūn]
①you (archaic) ②king; emperor

jùn

俊(形)[jùn]
talented; smart; bright; good-looking

郡(名)[jùn]
an administrative district
〖郡县制〗(名)[jùnxiànzhì]
prefectural system (archaic)

峻[jùn]
〖峻岭〗(名)[jùnlǐng]
steep mountain
〖峻峭〗(形)[jùnqiào]
(of mountain, cliff) precipitous

骏[jùn]
〖骏马〗(名)[jùnmǎ]〔匹 pǐ〕
a fine horse

竣(动)[jùn]
finish; complete; end
〖竣工〗[jùngōng]
finish construction

J

kā

咖[kā]
〖咖啡〗(名)[kāfēi]
coffee

kǎ

卡(动)[kǎ]
be choked; be stuck
〖卡车〗(名)[kǎchē]〔辆 liàng〕
truck; lorry
〖卡尺〗(名)[kǎchǐ]
caliper
〖卡片〗(名)[kǎpiàn]
〔张 zhāng〕
card

咔[kǎ]
〖咔叽〗(名)[kǎjī]
(cloth) khaki

kāi

开(动)[kāi]
open; start
〖开办〗(动)[kāibàn]
set up;start; establish; open up
〖开采〗(动)[kāicǎi]
mine; extract; exploit
〖开场〗[kāi chǎng]
opening of a show
〖开场白〗(名)[kāichǎngbái]
opening speech or remarks
〖开车〗[kāi chē]
drive a vehicle
〖开诚布公〗[kāichéngbùgōng]
frank and straightforward
〖开除〗(动)[kāichú]
discharge;expel;dismiss;sack
〖开创〗(动)[kāichuàng]
found;start;establish;usher in
〖开刀〗[kāi dāo]
(surgical) operation; operate
〖开导〗(动)[kāidǎo]
enlighten;explain and
convince
〖开动〗(动)[kāidòng]
start; operate; set into motion;

supply the motivating power
〖开端〗(名)[kāiduān] the beginning; the inauguration (of affairs, relations, etc.)
〖开发〗(动)[kāifā]
open up; exploit; tap
〖开发区〗(名)[kāifāqū]
development zone (area)
〖开饭〗[kāi fàn]
have meal served
〖开方〗[kāi fāng]
(math.) work out a square or cube
〖开放〗(动)[kāifàng]
①blossom ②(of park, exhibition, etc.) be open
〖开放政策〗[kāifàng zhèngcè]
open policy; policy of opening to the outside world
〖开赴〗(动)[kāifù]
set out for; be on the way to; move to
〖开工〗[kāigōng]
go into operation
〖开关〗(名)[kāiguān]
electric switch; mechanical control button
〖开国〗[kāiguó]
the founding of a new state power
〖开航〗(动)[kāiháng]
① open up a sea route or airline ② set sail; cast off (ship)
〖开花〗[kāi huā]
①blossom ②crack; pop (e.g. popcorn)
〖开荒〗[kāi huāng]
reclaim land; open up waste land
〖开会〗[kāi huì]
hold a meeting; attend a meeting
〖开火〗[kāi huǒ]
open fire
〖开垦〗(动)[kāikěn]
reclaim land; bring wasteland under cultivation
〖开矿〗[kāi kuàng]
open mines
〖开阔〗(形、动)[kāikuò]
wide; broad
〖开朗〗(形)[kāilǎng]
open-minded
〖开路〗[kāi lù]
open a new road; lead the way; pave the way
〖开门〗[kāi mén]
open door
〖开门见山〗[kāiménjiànshān]
(lit.) the door opens on a view of mountains; (fig.) put it bluntly; no beating about the bush; come straight to the point
〖开明〗(形)[kāimíng]
enlightened
〖开幕〗[kāi mù]
inaugurate; opening (ceremony)
〖开炮〗[kāi pào]
open fire with guns; shelling; gunfire
〖开辟〗(动)[kāipì]
open up; usher in; create; break new ground; pave (the way); blaze the trail
〖开窍〗[kāi qiào]
come to understand; be enlightened
〖开山〗[kāi shān]
quarry stones; build roads by

blasting mountains
〖开设〗(动)[kāishè]
establish; found; start (shop, hospital)
〖开始〗(动)[kāishǐ]
begin; start; begin with
〖开水〗(名)[kāishuǐ]
boiled water
〖开通〗(形)[kāitong]
enlightened
〖开头〗[kāi tóu]
beginning; start; at the outset of
〖开脱〗(动)[kāituō]
extricate (oneself) from...; absolve (sb. of his responsibility)
〖开拓〗(动)[kāituò]
carve out; open up (e.g. large tracts of farmland)
〖开外〗(名)[kāiwài]
beyond; over (more than a certain number, usually refering to a person's age)
〖开玩笑〗[kāi wánxiào]
make a joke
〖开销〗(动、名)[kāixiāo]
①pay out ②expenses
〖开小差〗[kāi xiǎochāi]
①desert (post) ②absent-minded
〖开心〗(形)[kāixīn]
happy; joyous; pleasant
〖开学〗[kāi xué]
opening of a school term
〖开演〗(动)[kāiyǎn]
(of plays, cinemas) start
〖开夜车〗[kāiyèchē]
work late into the night
〖开源节流〗[kāiyuánjiéliú]
open up the source and reglate the flow; develop rsources and be economical
〖开凿〗(动)[kāizáo]
dig; cut (a canal, etc.); tunnel
〖开展〗(动)[kāizhǎn]
carry out; develop; launch; promote
〖开张〗[kāi zhāng]
(of shops) open for business; make a start
〖开支〗(动、名)[kāizhī]
spend; cost; expenditure; expenses

kǎi

凯 [kǎi]
〖凯歌〗(名)[kǎigē]
paean of victory; song of victory
〖凯旋〗(动)[kǎixuán]
return in triumph

楷 [kǎi]
〖楷书〗(名)[kǎishū]
pattern of characters written in formal style

kān

刊 (名)[kān]
journal; publications
〖刊登〗(动)[kāndēng]
publish (news, story)
〖刊物〗(名)[kānwù]
journal; periodical; publications

〖刊印〗(动)[kānyìn]
print
〖刊载〗(动)[kānzǎi]
publish; print

看(动)[kān]
① look after ② watch
另见 kàn
〖看管〗(动)[kānguǎn]
①take care of; look after ②put in prison
〖看守〗(动)[kānshǒu]
guard; watch; keep a look out

勘[kān]
〖勘测〗(动)[kāncè]
survey
〖勘察〗(动)[kānchá]
prospect
〖勘探〗(动)[kāntàn]
prospect; survey; examine on the spot; investigate
〖勘误〗[kānwù]
corrigendum; correct printing errors

kǎn

坎(名)[kǎn]
〖坎坷〗(形)[kǎnkě]
upsand downs (usu. fig.)

砍(动)[kǎn]
hew; chop; hack

kàn

看(动)[kàn]
① look; watch ② see (friend, doctor, film, etc.) ③ read
另见 kān
〖看病〗[kànbìng]
① receive or examine a patient ② consult a doctor
〖看不起〗[kànbuqǐ]
look down upon; despise; belittle
〖看穿〗(动)[kànchuān]
see through; be disillusioned
〖看待〗(动)[kàndài]
view; as sess; look at; treat
〖看得起〗[kàndeqǐ]
look up to; attach great importance to...; hold in high esteem
〖看法〗(名)[kànfǎ]
view; opinion; the way one looks at sth.; approach
〖看风使舵〗[kànfēngshǐduò]
trim the sails to the wind
〖看见〗(动)[kànjiàn]
(actually) see; can see
〖看来〗(连)[kànlái]
appear; take on the appearence of; seem; look like
〖看破〗(动)[kànpò]
see through (trick, falseness)
〖看齐〗(动)[kànqí]
① keep a breast of; keep pace with ②follow the example
〖看望〗(动)[kànwàng]
visit
〖看中〗(动)[kànzhòng]
pickout; select; take a liking to
〖看重〗(动)[kànzhòng]

think highly of; value (of person)

kāng

康[kāng]
〖康庄大道〗[kāngzhuāngdàdào]
broadpath; broad road

慷[kāng]
〖慷慨〗(形)[kāngkǎi]
generous
〖慷慨激昂〗[kāngkǎijī'áng]
in lofty and energetic spirit; out of the fullness of one's heart

糠(名)[kāng]
husk; chaff

káng

扛(动)[káng]
carry; shoulder; undertake
〖扛活〗[káng huó]
(one who) worked as a farmhand for a landlord or rich peasant in the old societykàng

K

kàng

抗(动)[kàng]
resist; oppose; struggle against
〖抗暴〗[kàng bào]
the struggle against tyranny
〖抗旱〗[kàng hàn]
fight against drought
〖抗击〗(动)[kàngjī]
resist
〖抗拒〗(动)[kàngjù]
resist; oppose; frustrate
〖抗美援朝〗
[kàngMěiyuánCháo]
Resist U.S. Aggression and Aid Korea
〖抗日根据地〗
[KàngRìGēnjùdì]
the anti-Japanese-base areas; the base areas in the War of Resistance against Japanese Aggression
〖抗日救亡运动〗
[Kàng Rì Jiù wáng Yùndòng]
the Movement for Resisting Japanese Aggression and Saving the Nation
〖抗日军政大学〗
[Kàng Rì Jūn zhèng Dàxué]
the Chinese People's Anti-Japanese Military and Political College
〖抗日战争〗
[Kàng Rì Zhàn zhēng]
the War of Resistance against Japanese Aggression
〖抗生素〗(名)[kàngshēngsù]
anti-biotics
〖抗议〗(动)[kàngyì]
protest; protest against
〖抗战〗(动)[kàngzhàn]
the War of Resistance against Japanese Aggression (1937—1945)

炕(名)[kàng]

heated brick bed (in North China)

kǎo

考(动)[kǎo]
test; examine; investigate
〖考查〗(动)[kǎochá]
investigate; study (facts, conditions); subject (sb.) to a good test; examine; judge; test fully...
〖考察〗(动)[kǎochá]
investigate; study
〖考古〗(名)[kǎogǔ]
archaeology
〖考核〗(动)[kǎohé]
checkup
〖考究〗(动、形)[kǎojiu]
① closely examine; thoroughly study ② be particular about; pay attention to
〖考虑〗(动)[kǎolǜ]
consider; think over; ponder over
〖考勤〗(动)[kǎoqín]
(of work, study) check attendance
〖考试〗(动、名)[kǎoshì]
sit for an examination; examination; test
〖考验〗(动、名)[kǎoyàn]
test; ordeal
〖考证〗(动)[kǎozhèng]
research; study of data

拷[kǎo]
〖拷贝〗(名)[kǎobèi]
copy or print (of film)
〖拷打〗(动)[kǎodǎ]
subject to a beating; torture; beat up
〖拷机〗(名)[kǎojī]
pager; beeper

烤(动)[kǎo]
roast
〖烤面包〗(名)[kǎomiànbāo]
toast
〖烤鸭〗(名)[kǎoyā]
roast duck

kào

靠(动)[kào]
rely on; depend; lean on
〖靠岸〗[kào àn]
along the shore
〖靠边〗[kào biān]
on the side
〖靠不住〗[kào bu zhù]
undependable; unreliable
〖靠得住〗[kào de zhù]
reliable; dependable; trustworthy
〖靠近〗(动)[kàojìn]
be near by; be close to; come over to (the people)
〖靠拢〗(动)[kàolǒng]
be drawn to; come close to
〖靠山〗(名)[kàoshān]
patron; standby; supporter; protector; mainstays

kē

苛(形)[kē]

harsh
〖苛刻〗(形)[kēkè]
stern; harsh
〖苛求〗(动)[kēqiú]
ask too much; be too exacting

科(名)[kē]
class; branch of study; section
〖科技〗(名)[kējì]
science and technology
〖科教片〗(名)[kējiàopiàn]
scientific and educational film
〖科目〗(名)[kēmù]
branch of study; subject
〖科学〗(名、形)[kēxué]
science; scientific
〖科学家〗(名)[kēxuéjiā]
scientist
〖科学试验〗[kēxué shìyàn]
scientific experiment
〖科学性〗(名)[kēxuéxìng]
scientific spirit
〖科学院〗(名)[kēxuéyuàn]
Academy of Sciences
〖科学种田〗
[kēxué zhòng tián]
plant in a scientific way
〖科研〗(名)[kēyán]
scientific research

棵(量)[kē]
a measure word (for tree, etc.)

颗(量)[kē]
a measure word, grain (e.g. one grain of)
〖颗粒〗(名)[kēlì]
a round piece; grains (of sand, etc.)

瞌[kē]
〖瞌睡〗(名)[kēshuì]
nap; doze

kē

壳(名)[ké]
shell (e.g. seashell)

咳(动)[ké]
cough
另见 hāi
〖咳嗽〗(动)[késou]
cough

kě

可(助动、副)[kě]
①may; can ②very; really; so
〖可爱〗(形)[kě'ài]
lovable; lovely; charming
〖可悲〗(形)[kěbēi]
deplorable; pitiable
〖可不是〗[kěbushì]
that's right; that's it
〖可乘之机〗[kěchéngzhījī]
(give sb.) an opening to exploit; avail oneself of the opportunity to...
〖可耻〗(形)[kěchǐ]
ignominious; shameful; despicable
〖可歌可泣〗[kěgēkěqì]
heroic and moving; laudable

K

〖可观〗(形)[kěguān]
appreciable; considerable
〖可贵〗(形)[kěguì]
valuable; worth; precious; fine
〖可恨〗(形)[kěhèn]
hateful
〖可见〗(连)[kějiàn]
it is obvious that; it can be seen that; it is apparent that
〖可靠〗(形)[kěkào]
reliable; trustworthy; dependable
〖可可〗(名)[kěkě]
cocoa
〖可控硅〗(名)[kěkòngguī]
controlable silicon
〖可口〗(形)[kěkǒu]
tasty; delicious
〖可怜〗(形、动)[kělián]
pitiable; pitiful; pity
〖可能〗(形、名、助动)[kěnéng]
possible; possibility; maybe
〖可能性〗(名)[kěnéngxìng]
possibility; potentiality
〖可怕〗(形)[kěpà]
horrible; terrible
〖可巧〗(副)[kěqiǎo]
happen to; as it happens
〖可取〗(形)[kěqǔ]
worth having; useful
〖可是〗(连)[kěshì]
but
〖可塑性〗(名)[kěsùxìng]
plasticity
〖可望而不可即〗
[kěwàng'ér bùkějí]
be beyond reach; within sight but beyond reach
〖可恶〗(形)[kěwù]
hateful; wicked; disgusting
〖可惜〗(形)[kěxī]
unfortunately; pitiful
〖可笑〗(形)[kěxiào]
ridiculous; absurd
〖可心〗(形)[kěxīn]
nice; pleasing; just as one would like; admirable
〖可行〗(形)[kěxíng]
feasible; workable
〖可行性〗(名)[kěxíngxìng]
feasibility
〖可疑〗(形)[kěyí]
suspicious; questionable; dubious
〖可以〗(助动、形)[kěyǐ]
①may; can ②will do; good enough; passable

渴 (形)[kě]
thirsty; eager
〖渴望〗(动)[kěwàng]
yearn; eagerly hope for; long for; thirst for

kè

克 (动、量)[kè]
①surmount; overcome ②cotrol; restrain ③ a measure word, gram
〖克敌制胜〗[kèdízhìshèng]
defeat the enemy and win victory
〖克分子〗(名)[kèfēnzǐ]
grammolecule; mole

〖克服〗(动)[kèfú]
surmount; overcome
〖克己奉公〗[kèjǐfènggōng]
wholehearted devotion to public duty
〖克制〗(动)[kèzhì]
restrain; restrict; control (oneself)

刻(动、量)[kè]
① carve ② a measure word, a quarter (of an hour)
〖刻板〗(形)[kèbǎn]
mechanical; inflexible; dogmatic
〖刻薄〗(形)[kèbó]
acrimonious; acrid; harsh
〖刻不容缓〗[kèbùrónghuǎn]
very urgent; pressing
〖刻骨仇恨〗[kègǔ chóuhèn]
bitter hatred; nourish or harbour a deep hatred for
〖刻画〗(动)[kèhuà]
portray; depict
〖刻苦〗(形)[kèkǔ]
painstaking; industrious

客(名)[kè]
guest; visitor
〖客车〗(名)[kèchē]〔列 liè〕
passenger train
〖客观〗(名、形)[kèguān]
objectivity; objective
〖客观唯心主义〗
[kèguān wéixīnzhǔyì]
objective idealism
〖客观主义〗(名)[kèguānzhǔyì]
jectivism
〖客轮〗(名)[kèlún]〔艘 sōu〕
passenger boat
〖客气〗(形)[kèqi]
polite; civil
〖客人〗(名)[kèrén]
guest; visitor
〖客厅〗(名)[kètīng]
sitting-room; drawing-room

课(名、量)[kè]
① lesson; classwork ② a measure word (e.g. lesson)
〖课本〗(名)[kèběn]
text book
〖课程〗(名)[kèchéng]
curriculum; course
〖课堂〗(名)[kètáng]
classroom
〖课题〗(名)[kètí]
main topic; subject
〖课外〗(名)[kèwài]
extracurricular
〖课文〗(名)[kèwén]〔篇 piān〕
lessons in a textbook

kěn

肯(助动)[kěn]
be willing (to)
〖肯定〗(动、形)[kěndìng]
① affirm; approve; assert ② affirmative; positive; determined
〖肯干〗(形)[kěngàn]
hard-working; industrious

垦(动)[kěn]

reclaim (land)
〖垦荒〗[kěn huāng]
reclaim waste-land

恳[kěn]
〖恳切〗(形)[kěnqiè]
sincere
〖恳求〗(动)[kěnqiú]
implore; entreat

啃(动)[kěn]
bite; chew

kēng

坑(名)[kēng]
a pit; a sunken hole in ground
〖坑道〗(名)[kēngdào]
tunnel
〖坑害〗(动)[kēnghài]
make false accusation; frame up

吭(动)[kēng]
sing or shout
〖吭气〗[kēngqì]
talk
〖吭声〗[kēngshēng]
utter a sound

铿[kēng]
〖铿锵〗(形)[kēngqiāng]
jangling

kōng

空(形、名、副)[kōng]
①empty; blank ②the open air; sky ③fruitlessly; in vain
另见 kòng
〖空洞〗(形)[kōngdòng]
devoid of content
〖空洞无物〗[kōngdòngwúwù]
void of content (of speech, writing, etc.)
〖空话〗(名)[kōnghuà]
empty or meaningless talk
〖空间〗(名)[kōngjiān]
space
〖空军〗(名)[kōngjūn]
air force
〖空口无凭〗[kōngkǒuwúpíng]
oral expressions cannot be taken as proof; a verbal statement is no evidence; oral evidence is no proof
〖空旷〗(形)[kōngkuàng]
open; wide; spacious
〖空气〗(名)[kōngqì]
①air ②atmosphere
〖空前〗(形)[kōngqián]
never before; unprecedented
〖空前绝后〗[kōngqiánjuéhòu]
without parallel in history; without either precedent or sequel
〖空前未有〗[kōngqiánwèiyǒu]
it has never been known bfore; without precedent
〖空谈〗(动、名)[kōngtán]
①prattle about; talk aimlessly; gossip ②prating; idle talk; empty talk
〖空调〗(名)[kōngtiáo]
airconditioning
〖空调机〗(名)[kōngtiáojī]

K

airconditioner
〖空头〗(形)[kōngtóu]
phoney (writer, etc.)
〖空头支票〗[kōngtóu zhīpiào]
① dishonoured cheque ② empty promise; lip service
〖空投〗(动)[kōngtóu]
airdrop
〖空袭〗(动)[kōngxí]
airraid
〖空想〗(动、名)[kōngxiǎng]
be under illusion; illusion; fantasy
〖空心〗[kōng xīn]
hollow; tubular
〖空虚〗(形)[kōngxū]
vacant; empty; void of content
〖空中〗(名)[kōngzhōng]
in the air
〖空中楼阁〗[kōngzhōnglóugé]
castle in the air; ivory towers

kǒng

孔 (名、量)[kǒng]
① opening; hole ② a measure word (for well, etc.)
〖孔雀〗(名)[kǒngquè]〔只 zhī〕
peacock

恐 [kǒng]
〖恐怖〗(形)[kǒngbù]
horrible; terrible
〖恐吓〗(动)[kǒnghè]
terrify; frighten; intimidate
〖恐慌〗(形)[kǒnghuāng]
panicky; panic stricken
〖恐惧〗(动)[kǒngjù]
frighten; fear; dread
〖恐怕〗(副)[kǒngpà]
perhaps; (I am) afraid...

kòng

空 (动、名)[kòng]
① empty; leave sth. empty ② leisure
另见 kōng
〖空白〗(名)[kòngbái]
blank
〖空白点〗(名)[kòngbáidiǎn]
blankness
〖空额〗(名)[kòng'é]
vacancy
〖空隙〗(名)[kòngxì]
an empty space; gap; loophole
〖空闲〗(名、动)[kòngxián]
free time; leisure; not busy
〖空余〗(名)[kòngyú]
leisure; unoccupied
〖空子〗(名)[kòngzi]
① an unoccupied place; an opening ② chance; opportunity; loophole

控 [kòng]
〖控告〗(动)[kònggào]
bring a complaint before the court against; level a charge against (sb.); charge sb. with
〖控诉〗(动)[kòngsù]
accuse; bring an accusation against
〖控制〗(动)[kòngzhì]
control; dominate; contain
〖控制论〗(名)[kòngzhìlùn]

cybernetics

kōu

抠(动)[kōu]
scrape (a hole)

kǒu

口(名、量)[kǒu]
① mouth; hole ② outlet; pass ③ a measure word (for person, pig, well, etc.)
〖口才〗(名)[kǒucái]
eloquence; the ability to talk
〖口吃〗(形)[kǒuchī]
stutter
〖口齿〗(名)[kǒuchǐ]
the ability to talk
〖口袋〗(名)[kǒudài]
① a bag ② coat pocket
〖口供〗(名)[kǒugòng]
confession; testimony; deposition
〖口号〗(名)[kǒuhào]
slogan; catchword
〖口技〗(名)[kǒujì]
an entertainment by vocat imitation
〖口径〗(名)[kǒujìng]
calibre; gauge; aperture
〖口诀〗(名)[kǒujué]
rhyme for a formula; mnemonic
〖口角〗(名)[kǒujué]
quarrel
〖口口声声〗
[kǒukǒushēngshēng]
glibly (profess, say, anounce); keep on proclaiming; say sth. repeatedly
〖口粮〗(名)[kǒuliáng]
rations; provisions; food grain
〖口令〗(名)[kǒulìng]
password; word of command
〖口蜜腹剑〗[kǒumìfùjiàn]
(lit.) honey in mouth and dagger in heart; honey on one's lips and murder in one's heart; (fig.) a mouth that praises and a hand that kills
〖口气〗(名)[kǒuqì]
tone (e.g. speak in high tone); a manner of speaking
〖口腔〗(名)[kǒuqiāng]
oral cavity
〖口若悬河〗[kǒuruòxuánhé]
glibly; loquacious; nimble of speech
〖口哨儿〗(名)[kǒushàor]
whistle; whistling
〖口实〗(名)[kǒushí]
basis or material (for gossip)
〖口试〗(名、动)[kǒushì]
oral examination; have an oral test
〖口是心非〗[kǒushìxīnfēi]
say yes and mean no; say one thing and mean another
〖口头〗(名)[kǒutóu]
verbal; oral
〖口头禅〗(名)[kǒutóuchán]
pet phrase
〖口味〗(名)[kǒuwèi]
taste; flavour
〖口吻〗(名)[kǒuwěn]
tone of speech
〖口信〗(名)[kǒuxìn]

oral message
〖口形〗(名)[kǒuxíng]
mouth position
〖口译〗(名、动)[kǒuyì]
interpretation; interpret
〖口音〗(名)[kǒuyīn]
accent
〖口语〗(名)[kǒuyǔ]
spoken language
〖口罩〗(名)[kǒuzhào]
mouthmask
〖口子〗(名)[kǒuzi]
an opening (wound); a crack

kòu

扣 (动)[kòu]
① fasten; button up ② deduct ③ detain
〖扣除〗(动)[kòuchú]
deduct; take off
〖扣留〗(动)[kòuliú]
detain
〖扣帽子〗[kòu màozi]
tag (sb.) with a label; be branden as
〖扣押〗(动)[kòuyā]
detain (person)
〖扣子〗(名)[kòuzi]〔个 gè〕
① a knot ② a button

kū

枯 (形)[kū]
dried; withered; dried up
〖枯槁〗(形)[kūgǎo]
dried and withered
〖枯黄〗(形)[kūhuáng]
withered; wilted
〖枯竭〗(动)[kūjié]
dry up (spring of water, of thought, etc.); exhaust
〖枯萎〗(动)[kūwěi]
dry up; wither
〖枯燥〗(形)[kūzào]
dry and dull; uninteresting

哭 (动)[kū]
weep; cry
〖哭哭啼啼〗(形)[kūkūtítí]
wail and whine; keep on weeping
〖哭泣〗(动)[kūqì]
weep; sob

窟 [kū]
〖窟窿〗(名)[kūlong]
a hole (in wall, etc.)

骷 [kū]
〖骷髅〗(名)[kūlóu]
skeleton

kǔ

苦 (形、名、副)[kǔ]
painful; bitter; sufferings; painstakingly
〖苦处〗(名)[kǔchu]
suffering; plight; distress
〖苦功〗(名)[kǔgōng]
painstaking effort
〖苦口婆心〗[kǔkǒupóxīn]
advice in earnest words and with good intention
〖苦闷〗(形)[kǔmèn]
gloomy

〖苦难〗(名)[kǔnàn]
hardships; calamity; sufferings
〖苦恼〗(形)[kǔnǎo]
worried; vexed; anxious; distressed
〖苦水〗(名)[kǔshuǐ]
① bitter water ② untold sufferings
〖苦头〗(名)[kǔtóu]
bitterness; sufferings
〖苦心〗(名)[kǔxīn]
taking great pains (in doing sth.); painstaking
〖苦心孤诣〗[kǔxīngūyì]
take great pains (in doing sth.)
〖苦战〗(动)[kǔzhàn]
engage in hard battle
〖苦衷〗(名)[kǔzhōng]
difficulty; embarrassment

kù

库(名)[kù]
treasury; depot; warehouse
〖库存〗(名、动)[kùcún]
stocks; stores; store up
〖库房〗(名)[kùfáng]
storehouse

裤(名)[kù]
trousers
〖裤衩〗(名)[kùchǎ]〔条 tiáo〕
underpants
〖裤腿〗(名)[kùtuǐ]
trouserlegs
〖裤子〗(名)[kùzi]〔条 tiáo〕
trousers

酷[kù]
〖酷爱〗(动)[kù'ài]
have an ardent love for
〖酷热〗(形)[kùrè]
exceedingly hot
〖酷暑〗(名)[kùshǔ]
torrid summer heat
〖酷刑〗(名)[kùxíng]
torture; severe punishment

kuā

夸(动)[kuā]
① brag; boast ② praise
〖夸大〗(动)[kuādà]
exaggerate; over-emphasize
〖夸奖〗(动)[kuājiǎng]
praise
〖夸口〗[kuā kǒu]
boast; brag
〖夸夸其谈〗[kuākuāqítán]
indulge in verbiage; big words; rant
〖夸耀〗(动)[kuāyào]
show off; brag about
〖夸张〗(动)[kuāzhāng]
brag; exaggerate; boast

kuǎ

垮(动)[kuǎ]
break down; collapse
〖垮台〗[kuǎ tái]
break down; fall down

kuà

挎(动)[kuà]
hang; sling; dangle

〖挎包〗(名)[kuàbāo]
haversack; knapsack

跨 (动)[kuà]
stride; cross
〖跨度〗(名)[kuàdù]
span; stretch; flypast
〖跨国公司〗[kuàguó gōngsī]
transnational corporation
〖跨越〗(动)[kuàyuè]
pass; cross

kuài

会 [kuài]
另见 huì
〖会计〗(名)[kuàijì]
accountant
〖会计师事务所〗
[kuàijìshīshìwùsuǒ]
CPA firm; accounting firm
〖会计电算化〗
[kuàijìdiànsuànhuà]
electronic data processing accounting

块 (名、量)[kuài]
①a piece of; ②a measure word, piece, lump (e.g. a cake of soap)

K

快 (形)[kuài]
quick; fast
〖快板儿〗(名)[kuàibǎnr]
clappertalk; clapper verses
〖快报〗(名)[kuàibào]
quick news bulletin; newsflash
〖快餐〗(名)[kuàicān]
fast food; quick meal
〖快餐店〗(名)[kuàicāndiàn]
snack bar; fast food outlet
〖快车〗(名)[kuàichē]
express train
〖快感〗(名)[kuàigǎn]
a feeling of joy or satisfaction
〖快活〗(形)[kuàihuo]
joyful; happy
〖快乐〗(形)[kuàilè]
happy
〖快马加鞭〗[kuàimǎjiābiān]
at high speed; with the greatest urgency
〖快慢〗(名)[kuàimàn]
rate of speed
〖快速〗(形)[kuàisù]
fast; highspeed
〖快食面〗(名)[kuàishímiàn]
instant noodles
〖快慰〗(形)[kuàiwèi]
elated

脍 [kuài]
〖脍炙人口〗[kuàizhìrénkǒu]
on everybody's lips; popular

筷 (名)[kuài]
chopsticks
〖筷子〗(名)[kuàizi]
〔双 shuāng〕chopsticks

kuān

宽 (形)[kuān]
①wide; broad② lenient; tolerant

〖宽敞〗(形)[kuānchang]
spacious
〖宽绰〗(形)[kuānchuo]
①spacious ②welloff
〖宽打窄用〗[kuāndǎzhǎiyòng]
budget liberally and spend sparingly
〖宽大〗(形、动)[kuāndà]
generous; be lenient
〖宽度〗(名)[kuāndù]
width
〖宽广〗(形)[kuānguǎng]
wide; spacious
〖宽宏大量〗
[kuānhóngdàliàng]
broadminded and generous
〖宽厚〗(形)[kuānhòu]
generous; kind
〖宽阔〗(形)[kuānkuò]
broad
〖宽容〗(动)[kuānróng]
tolerate; be lenient to
〖宽恕〗(动)[kuānshù]
forgive; tolerate
〖宽慰〗(形)[kuānwèi]
comforting
〖宽银幕电影〗
[kuānyínmùdiànyǐng]
wide screen film; cinemascope
〖宽裕〗(形)[kuānyù]
rich; welloff
〖宽窄〗(名)[kuānzhǎi]
width

kuǎn

款(名)[kuǎn]〔笔 bǐ〕
money
〖款待〗(动)[kuǎndài]
entertain
〖款项〗(名)[kuǎnxiàng]
money
〖款子〗(名)[kuǎnzi]
money; (a good) sum

kuāng

筐(名)[kuāng]
basket
〖筐子〗(名)[kuāngzi]〔个 gè〕
basket

kuáng

狂(形)[kuáng]
mad; insane; crazy
〖狂吠〗(动)[kuángfèi]
bark
〖狂风〗(名)[kuángfēng]
gale
〖狂欢〗(动)[kuánghuān]
hold carnival; have a lively celebration
〖狂澜〗(名)[kuánglán]
roaring waves
〖狂热〗(形)[kuángrè]
frantic; feverish; frenzied
〖狂人〗(名)[kuángrén]
madman; maniac
〖狂妄〗(形)[kuángwàng]
arrogant; preposterous
〖狂妄自大〗[kuángwàngzìdà]
be arrogant and conceited
〖狂言〗(名)[kuángyán]
crazy remarks

kuàng

旷(动、形)[kuàng]
①desert; skip ②spacious; wide; open
〖旷工〗[kuàng gōng]
skip work
〖旷课〗[kuàng kè]
skip school
〖旷日持久〗[kuàngrìchíjiǔ]
a long drawnout; drag on
〖旷野〗(名)[kuàngyě]
wilderness

况[kuàng]
〖况且〗(连)[kuàngqiě]
furthermore; moreover

矿(名)[kuàng]
mine
〖矿藏〗(名)[kuàngcáng]
deposit; mineral reserves; mine
〖矿产〗(名)[kuàngchǎn]
mineral products; mine
〖矿工〗(名)[kuànggōng]
miner
〖矿井〗(名)[kuàngjǐng]
mine pit
〖矿山〗(名)[kuàngshān]
mining area; mining
〖矿石〗(名)[kuàngshí]
ore
〖矿物〗(名)[kuàngwù]
mineral

框(名)[kuàng]
frame
〖框框〗(名)[kuàngkuang]
① frame ② conventions
〖框子〗(名)[kuàngzi]
jamb; frame

kuī

亏(动、介)[kuī]
① lose ② thanks to; owing to
〖亏本〗(动)[kuīběn]
lose money in business; lose one's capital; unprofitable
〖亏得〗(介)[kuīde]
it is fortunate that...
〖亏损〗(动、名)[kuīsǔn]
lose money; loss; deficit; lossmaking

岿[kuī]
〖岿然〗(副)[kuīrán]
immutable

窥[kuī]
〖窥测〗(动)[kuīcè]
conjecture; spy out
〖窥伺〗(动)[kuīsì]
spy into; peep
〖窥探〗(动)[kuītàn]
spy over

kuí

葵[kuí]
〖葵花〗(名)[kuíhuā]〔朵 duǒ〕
sunflower

魁[kuí]
〖魁伟〗(形)[kuíwěi]

well built; stately
〖魁梧〗(形)[kuíwú]
well built (of a person)

kuǐ

傀[kuǐ]
〖傀儡〗(名)[kuǐlěi]
puppet

kuì

溃[kuì]
〖溃败〗(动)[kuìbài]
defeat
〖溃烂〗(动)[kuìlàn]
fester; ulcerate
〖溃散〗(动)[kuìsàn]
disperse; fall apart
〖溃疡〗(名)[kuìyáng]
ulcer

愧[kuì]
〖愧色〗(名)[kuìsè]
shame

kūn

昆[kūn]
〖昆虫〗(名)[kūnchóng]
insect

kǔn

捆(动、量)[kǔn]
①tie up; bind up ②a measure word (firewood, books, etc.)

kùn

困(形)[kùn]
①weary; tired ②hard pressed; difficult
〖困惑〗(形)[kùnhuò]
perplexed; bewildered; puzzled
〖困境〗(名)[kùnjìng]
dilemma; difficult position
〖困倦〗(形)[kùnjuàn]
tired
〖困苦〗(形)[kùnkǔ]
distressed; in poverty and distress
〖困难〗(形、名)[kùnnan]
difficult; hard pressed; hardship; difficulty
〖困守〗(动)[kùnshǒu]
be hemmed in
〖困兽犹斗〗[kùnshòuyóudòu]
even a trapped beast struggleskuò

kuò

扩(动)[kuò]
expand
〖扩充〗(动)[kuòchōng]
expand; extend; enlarge
〖扩大〗(动)[kuòdà]
enlarge; increase
〖扩建〗(动)[kuòjiàn]
enlarge; expand
〖扩军〗[kuò jūn]
arms expansion
〖扩军备战〗[kuò jūn bèi zhàn]
arms expansion and war preparations
〖扩散〗(动)[kuòsàn]
spread; proliferate (nuclear weapons)

K

〖扩音机〗(名)[kuòyīnjī]
microphone
〖扩音器〗(名)[kuòyīnqì]
amplifier; loudspeaker
〖扩展〗(动)[kuòzhǎn]
expand; dilate
〖扩张〗(动)[kuòzhāng]
expand; extend
〖扩张主义〗(名)[kuòzhāngzhǔyì]
expansionism

括(动)[kuò]

include; consist
〖括号〗(名)[kuòhào]
brackets
〖括弧〗(名)[kuòhú]
parenthesis

阔(形)[kuò]

broad; wide
〖阔别〗(动)[kuòbié]
be parted for a long time
〖阔步〗[kuòbù]
stride; take long steps
〖阔绰〗(形)[kuòchuò]
luxurious
〖阔气〗(形)[kuòqi]
luxurious; extravagant

K

lā

拉(动)[lā]
pull; drag; tug; haul
〖拉丁美洲〗(名)[Lādīngměizhōu]
Latin America
〖拉丁字母〗[Lādīngzìmǔ]
Latin alphabet; Roman alphabet
〖拉肚子〗[lādùzi]
have loose bowels; suffer from diarrhoea
〖拉拉扯扯〗[lālāchěchě]
(lit.)tug; (fig.)exchange flattery and favours
〖拉力〗(名)[lālì]
tensile force; pull; drawing force
〖拉练〗(动)[lāliàn]
route march (e.g. military training)
〖拉链儿〗(名)[lāliànr]
zipper; zip fastener
〖拉拢〗(动)[lālǒng]
draw...in; pull (sb.) over to (one's side); be roped in (by...); inveigle (sb. into doing sth.)
〖拉杂〗(形)[lāzá]
disconnected; rambling; ill organized

垃[lā]
〖垃圾〗(名)[lājī]
garbage; rubbish; refuse

lǎ

喇[lǎ]
〖喇叭〗(名)[lǎba]
trumpet; horn; (coll.) loud speaker

là

落(动)[là]
① leave out; be missing ② leave behind ③ fall; drop; lag (behind)
另见 luò

腊 [là]
〖腊月〗(名)[làyuè]
the 12th lunar month

蜡 (名)[là]
①wax ②candle
〖蜡版〗(名)[làbǎn]
mimeograph stencil; (cut) a stencil
〖蜡笔〗(名)[làbǐ] 〔枝 zhī〕
crayon
〖蜡黄〗(形)[làhuáng]
waxen; wax yellow; sallow
〖蜡纸〗(名)[làzhǐ] 〔张 zhāng〕
①wax paper ②mimeograph stencil
〖蜡烛〗(名)[làzhú] 〔枝 zhī〕
candle

辣 (形)[là]
① peppery; hot ② (of smell or taste) burn; bite; pungent
〖辣椒〗(名)[làjiāo]
hot pepper
〖辣手〗(形)[làshǒu]
hard nut (to crack)

la

啦(助)[la]
a modal particle

L

lái

来 (动、助)[lái]
① come; arrive; be here ② about; around (e.g. about fifty metres away)
〖来宾〗(名)[láibīn]
visitor; guest
〖来不及〗[láibují]
too late; there isn't enough time (to do sth.)
〖来得及〗[lái de jí]
have time; there is still enough time (to do...)
〖来函〗(名)[láihán]
letter that has arrived; letter received by...
〖来回〗(名、副)[láihuí]
① go to (a place) and come back; make a round trip ② to and fro; back and forth
〖来历〗(名)[láilì]
antecedents; background; origin
〖来临〗(动)[láilín]
approach; come; arrive
〖来龙去脉〗[láilóngqùmài]
origin and course of development; from beginning to end; whole process
〖来年〗(名)[láinián]
next year; the coming year
〖来日方长〗[láirìfāngcháng]
the day is yet to come for ...; there's ample time ahead; there will be time for that
〖来头〗(名)[láitou]
① (of person) background; backing; connections ② source
〖来往〗(动、名)[láiwǎng]
① come and go ② intercourse; dealings; transaction
〖来信〗(名)[láixìn]
incoming letter

〖来由〗(名)[láiyóu]
cause; reason
〖来源〗(名)[láiyuán]
cause; reason; source
〖来自〗(动)[láizì]
come from

lài

赖(动、形)[lài]
① depend; rely ② hold on (to a place); hang on (in a place) ③ deny (one's error, etc.); go back on one's words ④ shift the blame on (to) some one else ⑤ poor; nogood (e.g. crops)
〖赖以〗(动)[làiyǐ]
rely; depend

lán

拦(动)[lán]
block; bar; hold back
〖拦洪坝〗(名)[lánhóngbà]
flood-control dam; dam
〖拦截〗(动)[lánjié]
intercept
〖拦路〗[lánlù]
block the way
〖拦路虎〗(名)[lánlùhǔ]
obstacle; stumbling block
〖拦阻〗(动)[lánzǔ]
block; obstruct; hinder; hold back; intercept

栏(名)[lán]
railing
〖栏杆〗(名)[lángān]
railing; balustrade; banisters

阑[lán]
〖阑尾炎〗(名)[lánwěiyán]
appendicitis

蓝(形)[lán]
blue
〖蓝色〗(名)[lánsè]
blue
〖蓝图〗(名)[lántú]
blueprint

谰[lán]
〖谰言〗(名)[lányán]
slander; calumny

褴[lán]
〖褴褛〗(形)[lánlǚ]
shabby; ragged

篮(名、量)[lán]
① basket ② a measure word, basketful
〖篮球〗(名)[lánqiú]〔个 gè〕
basketball
〖篮子〗(名)[lánzi]〔个 gè〕
basket

lǎn

懒(形)[lǎn]
① lazy; indolent; slothful ② sluggish; languid
〖懒得〗(助动)[lǎnde]
reluctant to; not in a mood to; do not feel like
〖懒惰〗(形)[lǎnduò]
lazy

〖懒汉〗(名)[lǎnhàn]
lazybones; idler
〖懒散〗(形)[lǎnsǎn]
slothful; sluggish; negligent
〖懒洋洋〗(形)[lǎnyāngyāng]
listless; languid

làn

烂(动、形)[làn]
①go bad; rot; rotten ②wear out (clothes) ③overcooked or thoroughly cooked
〖烂漫〗(形)[lànmàn]
bright coloured; brilliant
〖烂熟〗(形)[lànshú]
① (of food) thoroughly cooked; (of fruit) thoroughly ripe ② learn...thoroughly
〖烂摊子〗(名)[làntānzi]
shambles; mess; situation which is difficult to rectify

滥[làn]
〖滥用〗(动)[lànyòng]
abuse; use indiscriminately; misuse
〖滥竽充数〗[lànyúchōngshù]
hold a position without qualification; merely make up the number

láng

狼(名)[láng]〔只 zhī〕
wolf
〖狼狈〗(形)[lángbèi]
awkward;embarrassing; in a dilemma
〖狼狈为奸〗[lángbèiwéijiān]
collude in evil doing; work hand in glove with; as partners in crime
〖狼藉〗(形)[lángjí]
messy chaotic; in utter disorder
〖狼吞虎咽〗[lángtūnhǔyàn]
gobble up; wolf (down); devour
〖狼心狗肺〗[lángxīngǒufèi]
① ungrateful ② wolf-hearted; brutal and cold blooded
〖狼子野心〗[lángzǐyěxīn]
wolish ambition; aggressive designs

榔[láng]
〖榔头〗(名)[lángtou]〔把 bǎ〕
hammer

lǎng

朗[lǎng]
〖朗读〗(动)[lǎngdú]
read aloud
〖朗诵〗(动)[lǎngsòng]
recite; read with expression

làng

浪(名)[làng]
wave
〖浪潮〗(名)[làngcháo]
tide; wave
〖浪费〗(动)[làngfèi]
waste; be extravagant; squander
〖浪花〗(名)[lànghuā]
spray; spindrift

〖浪漫主义〗(名)
[làngmàn zhǔyì]
romanticism
〖浪头〗(名)[làngtou]
①wave ②fashion; currents

lāo

捞(动)[lāo]
①dredge up; drag for; scoop up (from water) ②gain; get; acquire
〖捞稻草〗[lāo dàocǎo]
try in vain to extricate oneself from dangers of difficulties
〖捞取〗(动)[lāoqǔ]
reap; gain
〖捞一把〗[lāo yī bǎ]
rake in some profit

láo

劳[láo]
〖劳动〗(动)[láodòng]
work; labour; physical labour; manual labour
〖劳动改造〗[láodòng gǎizào]
reform (of criminals) through labour
〖劳动教养〗
[láodòng jiàoyǎng]
labour education and rehabilitation; rehabilitation through labour
〖劳动节〗(名)[Láodòngjié]
May Day
〖劳动竞赛〗[láodòng jìngsài]
labour emulation; emulation drive
〖劳动力〗(名)[láodònglì]
① labour power; labour force; labour ② capacity for work
〖劳动模范〗[láodòngmófàn]
model worker
〖劳动日〗(名)[láodòngrì]
workday
〖劳动者〗(名)[láodòngzhě]
worker; labourer
〖劳工〗(名)[láogōng]
labourer (a term used in old society)
〖劳驾〗[láo jià]
① excuse me ② would you mind...?; can you do me a favour?
〖劳苦〗(形)[láokǔ]
toilsome
〖劳累〗(形)[láolèi]
tired; exhausted; fatigue
〖劳力〗(名)[láolì]
① labour; manpower ② capacity for work
〖劳碌〗(形)[láolù]
burdensome; toilsome
〖劳民伤财〗[láomínshāngcái]
waste manpower and material resources; waste energy and money
〖劳神〗[láo shén]
①take the trouble to ② overtax or exert (oneself)
〖劳务输出〗[láowùshūchū]
export of labour service
〖劳役〗(名)[láoyì]
forced labour; penal servitude
〖劳逸结合〗[láoyìjiéhé]
alternate work with rest and recreation

L

〖劳资关系〗[láozīguānxì]
relations between labour and capital

牢(名、形)[láo]
①prison ②firm; secure
〖牢不可破〗[láobùkěpò]
indestructible; unbreakable
〖牢房〗(名)[láofáng]
prison
〖牢记〗(动)[láojì]
keep firmly in mind; keep (sth.) always at heart
〖牢固〗(形)[láogù]
firm; secure
〖牢靠〗(形)[láokào]
firm; solid
〖牢骚〗(名)[láosāo]
discontent; complaint; grievances

唠[láo]
〖唠叨〗(动、形)[láodao]
nag; keep repeating the same thing; nagging

lǎo

老(形、副、头)[lǎo]
①old; aged ②outdated ③always ④prefix
〖老百姓〗(名)[lǎobǎixìng]
ordinary civilian; common people
〖老板〗(名)[lǎobǎn]
shop keeper; boss
〖老伴儿〗(名)[lǎobànr]
husband or wife (of an old couple)
〖老本〗(名)[lǎoběn]
capital (first investment)
〖老大难〗(名)[lǎodànán]
big, difficult and longstanding problem; a hard nut to crack
〖老大娘〗(名)[lǎodàniáng]
a respectful form of address for an old woman
〖老大爷〗(名)[lǎodàyé]
a respectful form of address for an old man
〖老当益壮〗
[lǎodāngyìzhuàng]
more vigorous with age; the older, the more energetic
〖老调〗(名)[lǎodiào]
worn-out theme; the same old story; old tune
〖老虎〗(名)[lǎohǔ][只 zhī]
tiger
〖老化〗(动)[lǎohuà]
worn out
〖老家〗(名)[lǎojiā]
old home; native place
〖老奸巨猾〗[lǎojiānjùhuá]
an old hand at trickery and deception; "sly old fox"
〖老茧〗(名)[lǎojiǎn]
callous
〖老练〗(形)[lǎoliàn]
experienced; seasoned
〖老龄化〗(动、名)[lǎolínghuà]
aging of the population
〖老马识途〗[lǎomǎshítú]
(lit.) an old horse knows the way; (of experienced people) know the ropes

〖老年〗(名)[lǎonián]
old age
〖老农〗(名)[lǎonóng]
old peasant; veteran peasant
〖老婆〗(名)[lǎopo]
(coll.) wife
〖老气横秋〗[lǎoqìhéngqiū]
lacking in youthful vigour
〖老前辈〗(名)[lǎoqiánbèi]
senior; elder; predecessor
〖老人〗(名)[lǎorén]
①old people; the aged ②elderly parents; grandparents
〖老人家〗(名)[lǎorenjia]
a term of respect for an old man or woman
〖老弱残兵〗[lǎoruòcánbīng]
those (soldiers) who are old, weak, ill or disabled
〖老少〗(名)[lǎoshào]
the old and the young
〖老生常谈〗
[lǎoshēngchángtán]
platitudes; cliches
〖老师〗(名)[lǎoshī]
teacher
〖老实〗(形)[lǎoshi]
honest; well behaved
〖老手〗(名)[lǎoshǒu]
a person with rich experience; an old hand; old timer
〖老鼠〗(名)[lǎoshǔ]〔只 zhī〕
mouse; rat
〖老鼠过街,人人喊打〗
[lǎoshǔguòjiē, rénrénhǎndǎ]
like rats running across the street with everyone shouting "kill them!"
〖老太太〗(名)[lǎotàitai]
a term of respect for an old woman
〖老头儿〗(名)[lǎotóur]
an old man; old chap
〖老乡〗(名)[lǎoxiāng]
fellow villager; townsman
〖老小〗(名)[lǎoxiǎo]
grown ups and children (in a family)
〖老羞成怒〗[lǎoxiūchéngnù]
enraged at having been disgraced
〖老爷〗(名)[lǎoye]
maternal grandfather
〖老一套〗[lǎoyītào]
old ways; old practice; the same old story; trite
〖老一辈〗[lǎoyībèi]
older generation
〖老鹰〗(名)[lǎoyīng]
black-eared kite; hawk; eagle
〖老子〗(名)[lǎozi]
① (coll.) father ② regard oneself as the number one auhority

lào

涝(形、动)[lào]
waterlogging

烙(动)[lào]
① brand (with hot iron) ② iron (clothes, etc.) ③ bake
〖烙饼〗(名)[làobǐng]
〔张 zhāng〕pancake
〖烙铁〗(名)[làotie]
① iron (for ironing clothes,

L

etc.) ②welding iron
〖烙印〗(名)[làoyìn]
brand

lè

乐(动)[lè]
①be happy or glad ②laugh; joy
另见 yuè
〖乐观〗(形)[lèguān]
optimistic; hopeful
〖乐观主义〗(名)[lèguānzhǔyì]
optimism
〖乐趣〗(名)[lèqù]
delight; pleasure; joy
〖乐意〗(助动)[lèyì]
be willing to; ready to...; want
〖乐于〗(动)[lèyú]
be glad or happy to
〖乐园〗(名)[lèyuán]
paradise; land of promise

勒[lè]
另见 lēi
〖勒令〗(动)[lèlìng]
order sb. to do one's bidding
〖勒索〗(动)[lèsuǒ]
extort (money, food, etc.)

le

了(助、尾)[le]
① particle, expression of completion or change of an acion
② suffix, expression of completion of an action
另见 liǎo liào

lēi

勒(动)[lēi] ① strap (sth. tight); strangle ②rein in
另见 lè

léi

雷(名)[léi]
①thunder ②(mil.) mine
〖雷达〗(名)[léidá]
radar
〖雷厉风行〗[léilìfēngxíng]
(lit.) be enforced with the power of a thunder bolt and the speed of lightning; (fig.) vigorously and speedily
〖雷鸣〗[léi míng]
① thunder clap ② a loud sound like thunder clapping
〖雷霆万钧〗[léitíngwànjūn]
as powerful as a thunder bolt
〖雷同〗(形)[léitóng]
indentical (copy or echo what others have said)
〖雷雨〗(名)[léiyǔ]
thunder storm

lěi

垒(动)[lěi]
build by piling up (as bricks)
〖垒球〗(名)[lěiqiú] 〔个 gè〕
baseball

累[lěi]
另见 lèi
〖累积〗(动)[lěijī]
accumulate
〖累进〗(动)[lěijìn]

progress; build up gradually
〖累累〗(形)[lěilěi]
①cluster; heap ②innumerble

磊[lěi]
〖磊落〗(形)[lěiluò]
open and above-board

lèi

泪(名)[lèi]
tears; tear drops
〖泪痕〗(名)[lèihén]
tear stains
〖泪花〗(名)[lèihuā]
tears in one's eyes
〖泪水〗(名)[lèishuǐ]
tear

类(名、量)[lèi]
kind; class; category; like
〖类别〗(名)[lèibié]
classification; category
〖类似〗(形)[lèisì]
similar; resembling
〖类推〗(动)[lèituī]
resson by analogy; analogize
〖类型〗(名)[lèixíng]
type; class

累 (动)[lèi]
①tired; fatigued; weary ②overwork; exhaust
另见lěi

léng

棱(名)[léng]
edge; angular; corner
〖棱角〗(名)[léngjiǎo]
①sharp ②edge; corner
〖棱镜〗(名)[léngjìng]
prism

lěng

冷(形)[lěng]
cold; cool
〖冷冰冰〗(形)[lěngbīngbīng]
cold as ice
〖冷不防〗(副)[lěngbufáng]
unawares; off guard
〖冷藏〗(动)[lěngcáng]
keep in cold storage; refrigerate
〖冷场〗[lěng chǎng]
an embarrassing pause; awkward silence (at a meeting, etc.)
〖冷嘲热讽〗[lěngcháorèfěng]
burning satire and freezing irony
〖冷淡〗(形)[lěngdàn]
indifferent; cold; indifferent attitude; be cold shouldered
〖冷冻〗(动)[lěngdòng]
freeze
〖冷汗〗(名)[lěnghàn]
cold sweat
〖冷箭〗(名)[lěngjiàn]
(lit.) arrow shot from a hiding place; (fig.) a stab in the back
〖冷静〗(形)[lěngjìng]
calm; sober
〖冷酷〗(形)[lěngkù]
grim; unfeeling; hardhearted
〖冷落〗(形)[lěngluò]
①cold shouldered; slighted ②

desolate

〖冷门〗(名)[lěngmén]

① an unexpected winner; dark horse ② a profession, trade or branch of learning that receives little attention or interest, or is not in great demand

〖冷气〗(名)[lěngqì]

cold air; air conditioning

〖冷清〗(形)[lěngqing]

quiet and dreary; desolate; quiet and isolated

〖冷却〗(动)[lěngquè]

cool down; cooling (system)

〖冷食〗(名)[lěngshí]

cold drinks and snacks

〖冷水〗(名)[lěngshuǐ]

cold water; unboiled water

〖冷飕飕〗(形)[lěngsōusōu]

chilling; chilly; piercing (wind); biting cold

〖冷笑〗(动)[lěngxiào]

sneer; laugh scornfully

〖冷眼〗(名)[lěngyǎn]

① cool and objective ② cold and indifferent

〖冷眼旁观〗[lěngyǎnpángguān]

look on coldly; look on as a bystander; take a detached point of view

L

〖冷饮〗(名)[lěngyǐn]

cold drinks

〖冷遇〗(名)[lěngyù]

cold shoulder; cold reception

〖冷战〗(名)[lěngzhàn]

the cold war

lèng

愣(形、动)[lèng]

① become dazed; become stupefied ② rash; reckless; foolhardy

〖愣头愣脑〗[lèngtóulèngnǎo]

foolhardy

lí

厘(量)[lí]

a measure word ① one thousandth of a Chinese foot or chi (尺) ② one thousandth of a Chinese ounce or liang (两) ③ one hundredth of a mou (亩) ④ one thousandth of a yuan (元)

〖厘米〗(量)[límǐ]

centimetre

离(动、介)[lí]

① leave; be away from ② from; away; off

〖离别〗(动)[líbié]

part; leave

〖离婚〗[lí hūn]

get a divorce

〖离间〗(动)[líjiàn]

sow discord; drive a wedge between; set one person against the other; sow dissension

〖离开〗(动)[líkāi]

① leave; depart ② deviate from

〖离奇〗(形)[líqí]

fantastic; odd; strange; extraordinary

〖离散〗(动)[lísàn]

disperse; be separated from one another; be scattered about
〖离乡背井〗[líxiāngbèijǐng]
leave one's native place; be away from home
〖离心离德〗[líxīnlídé]
dissension and discord; disunity
〖离心力〗(名)[líxīnlì]
centrifugal force
〖离职〗[lí zhí]
leave one's post
〖离子〗(名)[lízǐ]
ion

梨(名)[lí]〔个 gè〕
pear

犁(名、动)[lí]
plough

黎[lí]
〖黎明〗(名)[límíng]
dawn; daybreak

篱[lí]
〖篱笆〗(名)[líba]
fence; hedge

lǐ

礼(名)[lǐ]
①ceremony ②gifts
〖礼服〗(名)[lǐfú]〔套 tào〕
ceremonial dress; formal attire
〖礼花〗(名)[lǐhuā]
firework display at celebrations
〖礼节〗(名)[lǐjié]
formality; courtesy; etiquette; protocol
〖礼貌〗(名)[lǐmào]
politeness; manners; courtesy
〖礼炮〗(名)[lǐpào]
gun salute; salvo
〖礼品〗(名)[lǐpǐn]
presents; gifts
〖礼品券〗(名)[lǐpǐnquàn]
gift coupon; gift certificate
〖礼让〗(动)[lǐràng]
give precedence to sb. out of courtesy or thoughtfulness
〖礼尚往来〗[lǐshàngwǎnglái]
courtesy demands reciprocity
〖礼堂〗(名)[lǐtáng]
auditorium; assembly hall; hall
〖礼物〗(名)[lǐwù]
presents; gifts
〖礼仪〗(名)[lǐyí]
etiquette; deportment; rite
〖礼仪小姐〗[lǐyíxiǎojiě]
Miss Deportment
〖礼遇〗(名)[lǐyù]
polite reception; treat with courtesy

里(名、量)[lǐ]
①lining ②inside ③inner ④a measure word, li (a Chinese measure—500 metres)
〖里边〗(名)[lǐbian]
inside; in; within
〖里程〗(名)[lǐchéng]

mileage
〖里程碑〗(名)[lǐchéngbēi]
milestone
〖里面〗(名)[lǐmiàn]
interior; inside
〖里通外国〗[lǐtōngwàiguó]
have illicit or treacherous relations with a foreign country
〖里头〗(名)[lǐtou]
inside; interior
〖里应外合〗[lǐyìngwàihé]
coordinated attack from within and without
〖里子〗(名)[lǐzi]
lining

理(名、动)[lǐ]
①reason; logic; truth ②put in order; tidy ③acknowledge; pay attention to
〖理财〗[lǐcái]
manage money matters; manage financial affairs
〖理财之道〗[lǐcáizhīdào]
way of managing financial affairs
〖理睬〗(动)[lǐcǎi]
take notice of; heed
〖理发〗[lǐ fà]
haircut; have a hair cut
〖理发馆〗(名)[lǐfàguǎn]
barber shop; the barber's; the hairdresser's
〖理发员〗(名)[lǐfàyuán]
barber; hairdresser
〖理工科大学〗[lǐgōngkēdàxué]
college (university) of science and engineering
〖理会〗(动)[lǐhuì]
① comprehend; understand ② take notice of
〖理解〗(动)[lǐjiě]
understand; apprehend; comprehend; grasp
〖理科〗(名)[lǐkē]
science; science department
〖理亏〗(形)[lǐkuī]
unjustifiable; in the wrong
〖理论〗(名)[lǐlùn]
theory; thesis
〖理屈词穷〗[lǐqūcíqióng]
unable to advance any more arguments to defend oneself; find oneself devoid of all argument
〖理事〗(名)[lǐshì]
member of a council; director
〖理事会〗(名)[lǐshìhuì]
council; board of directors
〖理顺〗(动)[lǐshùn]
rationalize; straighten out
〖理所当然〗[lǐsuǒdāngrán]
only right and natural; a matter of course; it stands to reason
〖理想〗(名、形)[lǐxiǎng]
ideal; aspiration
〖理性〗(名)[lǐxìng]
rational; reason
〖理由〗(名)[lǐyóu]
reason; ground; argument
〖理直气壮〗[lǐzhíqìzhuàng]
with right on one's side; bold and selfconfident
〖理智〗(名)[lǐzhì]

intellect; reason

lì

力(名)[lì]
power; strength; force
〖力不从心〗[lìbùcóngxīn]
strength not equal to one's will; ability falls behind one's wishes
〖力量〗(名)[lìliàng]
①physical strength ②power; strength; force
〖力气〗(名)[lìqì]
strength; effort
〖力求〗(动)[lìqiú]
do one's best to; strive to; make every effort to
〖力图〗(动)[lìtú]
try hard to; strive to
〖力学〗(名)[lìxué]
mechanics
〖力争〗(动)[lìzhēng]
strive for; endeavour; struggle hard
〖力争上游〗[lìzhēngshàngyóu]
aim high

历[lì]
〖历程〗(名)[lìchéng]
course; progress
〖历次〗(名)[lìcì]
various (occasions, events, etc.)
〖历代〗(名)[lìdài]
successive dynasties; past dynasties
〖历法〗(名)[lìfǎ]
calendar
〖历届〗(名)[lìjiè]
all previous (sessions, etc.); record
〖历来〗(名)[lìlái]
always; all along; all through the ages; for ages
〖历年〗(名)[lìnián]
over the years; in past years
〖历史〗(名)[lìshǐ]
history; historical
〖历史剧〗(名)[lìshǐjù]
historical drama
〖历史唯物主义〗
[lìshǐ wéiwù zhǔyì]
historical materialism
〖历史唯心主义〗
[lìshǐ wéixīn zhǔyì]
historical idealism

厉[lì]
〖厉害〗(形)[lìhai]
fierce; terrible; formidable; serious
〖厉行〗(动)[lìxíng]
strictly carry out; practise

立(动)[lì]
①stand ②erect; set up ③exist; subsist
〖立场〗(名)[lìchǎng]
(class) stand; position; standpoint
〖立党为公〗[lìdǎngwèigōng]
build a party for the interests of the vast majority
〖立法〗[lì fǎ]

L

legislation; legislative
〖立方〗(名)[lìfāng]
cube
〖立方米〗(量)[lìfāngmǐ]
cubic metre
〖立功〗[lì gōng]
perform deeds of merit; render meritorious service
〖立功赎罪〗[lìgōngshúzuì]
perform meritorious service to atone for one's crimes; make amends for their crimes by good deeds
〖立即〗(副)[lìjí]
at once; immediately; promptly
〖立刻〗(副)[lìkè]
immediately; at once; instantly
〖立体〗(名)[lìtǐ]
solid; three dimensional
〖立体电影〗[lìtǐdiànyǐng]
stereoscopic film
〖立体几何〗[lìtǐ jǐhé]
solid geometry
〖立体声〗(名)[lìtǐshēng]
stereophony; stereo
〖立志〗[lì zhì]
be determined;aim at (doing sth.); aim to (do sth.)
〖立锥之地〗[lìzhuīzhīdì]
(lit.)a place just big enough to stick an awl; (fig.)an extremely small place
〖立足〗(动)[lìzú]
gain a foothold; be on a... footing; base oneself on
〖立足点〗(名)[lìzúdiǎn]
foothold; footing; stand

利(名)[lì]
profit; interest
〖利弊〗(名)[lìbì]
advantages and disadvantages
〖利害〗(名)[lìhài]
gains and losses; interest
〖利害〗(形)[lìhai]
fierce; powerful; terrible; formidable
〖利令智昏〗[lìlìngzhìhūn]
selfinterest blinds the eyes; greed blinds or tends to make one do foolish things
〖利率〗(名)[lìlǜ]
rate of interest
〖利落〗(形)[lìluo]
brisk; agile; nimble
〖利润〗(名)[lìrùn]
profit
〖利税〗(名)[lìshuì]
profit and tax
〖利索〗(形)[lìsuo]
brisk; agile; nimble; deft; dexterious
〖利息〗(名)[lìxī]
interest
〖利益〗(名)[lìyì]
interest; benefit; gain; profit
〖利用〗(动)[lìyòng]
use; make use of; utilize; take advantage of; exploit
〖利诱〗(动)[lìyòu]
lure by promise of gain
〖利欲熏心〗[lìyùxūnxīn]
blinded by cupidity; obsessed with the desire for gain; overcome by covetousness

沥[lì]
〖沥青〗(名)[lìqīng]
pitch; asphalt; bitumen

例(名)[lì] example; instance
〖例会〗(名)[lìhuì]
regular meeting
〖例假〗(名)[lìjià]
①official holidays; legal holidays ②menstrual period
〖例句〗(名)[lìjù]
sentence as an example; model sentence
〖例如〗(动)[lìrú]
for instance; such as; for example; e.g.
〖例题〗(名)[lìtí]
illustrative sentence; example
〖例外〗(名、动)[lìwài]
exception; make an exception of
〖例行〗(形)[lìxíng]
routine; regular
〖例行公事〗[lìxínggōngshì]
routine business; mere formality
〖例证〗(名)[lìzhèng]
proof; evidence; example; case in point; demonstration
〖例子〗(名)[lìzi][个 gè]
example; instance

隶[lì]
〖隶书〗(名)[lìshū]
clerical script; official script in ancient China (one of the four main styles of Chinese calligraphy)
〖隶属〗(动)[lìshǔ]
under the command of; subordinate to

荔[lì]
〖荔枝〗(名)[lìzhī]
lichee (fruit)

栗[lì]
〖栗子〗(名)[lìzi]
chestnut

粒(量)[lì]
a measure word, grain, dosage, etc.
〖粒子〗(名)[lìzǐ]
particle

痢[lì]
〖痢疾〗(名)[lìji]
dysentery

li

哩(助)[li]
a modal particle

liǎ

俩(数量)[liǎ]
two; both

lián

连(动、名)[lián]
① link; join; connect ② (mil.) company

〖连词〗(名)[liáncí]
(gram.) conjunction
〖连带〗(动)[liándài]
connect; in relation with
〖连队〗(名)[liánduì]
(mil.) company
〖连动句〗(名)[liándòngjù]
verbal construction in series
〖连贯〗(动)[liánguàn]
① link up; piece together; hang together ② coherent; consistent (of writing)
〖连环〗[lián huán]
chain of rings
〖连环画〗(名)[liánhuánhuà]
series of pictures telling a story; picture story book
〖连接〗(动)[liánjiē]
join; link
〖连累〗(动)[liánlěi]
implicate; involve; get (sb.) into trouble
〖连忙〗(副)[liánmáng]
hastily; promptly; at once
〖连绵〗(动)[liánmián]
continue uninterruptedly; go on and on; in succession
〖连年〗(名)[liánnián]
successive years; consecutive years; for years running; year after year
〖连篇累牍〗[liánpiānlěidú]
pages and pages; volumes; at great length; keep on repeating
〖连日〗(名)[liánrì]
for days on end; day after day
〖连锁反应〗[liánsuǒ fǎnyìng]
chain reaction
〖连锁商店〗
[liánsuǒ shāngdiàn]
chain store
〖连同〗(连)[liántóng]
together with; along with
〖连写〗(动)[liánxiě]
joining of syllables in writing
〖连续〗(动)[liánxù]
consecutive; successive; continuous
〖连夜〗(名)[liányè]
before the night was out; that very night
〖连载〗(动)[liánzǎi]
publish in instalments; serialize
〖连长〗(名)[liánzhǎng]
company commander
〖连着〗(动)[liánzhe]
① continue ② connect; link

怜[lián]
〖怜悯〗(动)[liánmǐn]
take pity on; have compassion for
〖怜惜〗(动)[liánxī]
take pity on; have pity for

帘[lián]
〖帘子〗(名)[liánzi]
hanging screen; screen; curtain

联(动)[lián]
unite; join; ally oneself with
〖联邦〗(名)[liánbāng]
federation; union

〖联播〗(动)[liánbō]
radio hookup; broadcast over national radio network
〖联产承包〗
[liánchǎnchéngbāo]
contract system that links remuneration with output
〖联合〗(动)[liánhé]
unite; ally; join with
〖联合公报〗
[liánhé gōngbào]
joint communique
〖联合国〗(名)[Liánhéguó]
the United Nations
〖联合声明〗[liánhé shēngmíng]
joint statement
〖联合收割机〗[liánhé shōugējī]
combine harvester
〖联欢〗(动)[liánhuān]
have get together; have a gathering
〖联结〗(动)[liánjié]
join; link; connect
〖联络〗(动)[liánluò]
establish contact; liaison
〖联盟〗(名)[liánméng]
alliance; coalition; league
〖联名〗[lián míng]
jointly signed
〖联席会议〗[liánxí huìyì]
joint conference; joint council; joint meeting
〖联系〗(动、名)[liánxì]
contact; get in touch with; connect; (have) ties (with)
〖联想〗(动、名)[liánxiǎng]
associate (sth.) with; an association of ideas
〖联运〗(动)[liányùn]
through transport; through traffic; through (e.g. bus, train, etc.)

廉(形)[lián]
① honest ② cheap
〖廉价〗(名)[liánjià]
cheap; low-priced; inexpensive
〖廉洁〗(形)[liánjié]
honest, not corrupt; morally clean
〖廉洁奉公〗[liánjiéfènggōng]
be honest in performing official duties; perform one's official duties honestly
〖廉政〗[liánzhèng]
clean and honest government

镰(名)[lián]
sickle
〖镰刀〗(名)[liándāo]〔把 bǎ〕
sickle

liǎn

脸(名)[liǎn]
face; countenance
〖脸盆〗(名)[liǎnpén]〔个 gè〕
washbasin
〖脸皮〗(名)[liǎnpí]
face-saving; personal consideration
〖脸色〗(名)[liǎnsè]
① complexion ② expression; look

L

liàn

练(动)[liàn]
train; practise; drill
〖练兵〗[liàn bīng]
train troops; training
〖练习〗(动、名)[liànxí]
①practise ②exercise
〖练习本〗(名)[liànxíběn]
〔本 běn〕exercise book

炼(动)[liàn]
smelt; refine; temper
〖炼钢〗[liàn gāng]
steel-making; steel-smelting
〖炼焦〗[liàn jiāo]
coking
〖炼铁〗[liàn tiě]
iron smelting; iron-making
〖炼油〗[liàn yóu]
oil refining; refining of petroleum

恋[liàn]
〖恋爱〗(动、名)[liàn'ài]
love; be in love
〖恋恋不舍〗[liànliànbùshě]
reluctant to part

链(名)[liàn]
chain
〖链子〗(名)[liànzi]〔条 tiáo〕
chain; (of bicycle) roller chain

liáng

良(形)[liáng]
①good; able; good quality ②kind
〖良好〗(形)[liánghǎo]
good; fine
〖良田〗(名)[liángtián]
fertile farmland
〖良心〗(名)[liángxīn]
conscience
〖良种〗(名)[liángzhǒng]
picked seed; high quality seed; fine strain; fine breed

凉(形)[liáng]
cool; cold
〖凉快〗(形)[liángkuai]
nice and cool; delightfully cool
〖凉爽〗(形)[liángshuǎng]
nice and cool; pleasantly cool
〖凉水〗(名)[liángshuǐ]
cold water
〖凉鞋〗(名)[liángxié]
〔双 shuāng〕
sandals

梁(名)[liáng]
beam

量(动)[liáng]
measure
另见 liàng
〖量具〗(名)[liángjù]
measuring tools

粮(名)[liáng]
grain; provisions; food

〖粮仓〗(名)[liángcāng]
granary; barn
〖粮草〗(名)[liángcǎo]
food and fodder; army provisions; rations and forage
〖粮店〗(名)[liángdiàn]
grain shop; provisions store
〖粮食〗(名)[liángshi]〔粒 lì〕
grain; cereals; staple food
〖粮食作物〗[liángshi zuòwù]
cereal crops; grain crops

liǎng

两(数、量)[liǎng]
① two; both ② a few; some ③ one tenth of a jin(so grams)
〖两败俱伤〗[liǎngbàijùshāng]
neither side wins; both sides suffer
〖两重性〗(名)[liǎngchóngxìng]
duality; dual character; dual nature
〖两次运球〗[liǎngcì yùnqiú]
double dribble
〖两点论〗(名)[liǎngdiǎnlùn]
theory of one divided up into two
〖两极分化〗[liǎngjí fēnhuà]
polarization
〖两脚规〗(名)[liǎngjiǎoguī]
① compasses ②dividers
〖两面派〗(名)[liǎngmiànpài]
double dealer; double faced
〖两面三刀〗[liǎngmiànsāndāo]
double dealing
〖两栖动物〗[liǎngqī dòngwù]
amphibian
〖两讫〗[liǎngqì]
the goods are delivered and the bill is cleared
〖两全其美〗[liǎngquánqíměi]
to the satisfaction of both parties; satisfying both demands
〖两手〗(名)[liǎngshǒu]
① two hands ② dual tactics
〖两条腿走路〗
[liǎng tiáo tuǐ zǒu lù]
walk on two legs (e.g. the policy of walking on two legs)
〖两袖清风〗[liǎngxiùqīngfēng]
(of an official) havec lean hands; remain uncorrupted
〖两翼〗(名)[liǎngyì]
both wings; both flanks

liàng

亮(形)[liàng]
bright; luminous
〖亮光〗(名)[liàngguāng]
light
〖亮晶晶〗(形)[liàngjīngjīng]
sparkling; twinkling; glistening
〖亮堂〗(形)[liàngtang]
① bright; light ② clear; enlightened
〖亮相〗[liàngxiàng]
① strike a pose on the stage ② state one's views; declare one's position ③ (of a new product) appear on the market

谅[liàng]

〖谅解〗(动)[liàngjiě]
be tolerant and understanding

辆(量)[liàng]
a measure word (for automobiles, etc.)

量(名、动)[liàng]
①capacity ②quantity; amount; volume; output ③esimate; weigh
另见 liáng
〖量变〗(名)[liàngbiàn]
quantitative change
〖量词〗(名)[liàngcí]
a measure word; unit word; classifier
〖量力〗[liàng lì]
according to one's ability and strength
〖量体裁衣〗[liàngtǐcáiyī]
cut the garment according to the figure; fit the dress to the figure

liāo

撩(动)[liāo]
raise; lift up

liáo

辽[liáo]
〖辽阔〗(形)[liáokuò]
vast expanses; very extensive; boundless
〖辽远〗(形)[liáoyuǎn]
far away; remote

疗[liáo]
〖疗效〗(名)[liáoxiào]
healing effect
〖疗养〗(动)[liáoyǎng]
recuperate; convalesce
〖疗养院〗(名)[liáoyǎngyuàn]
sanatorium

聊(动)[liáo]
chat; free talk
〖聊天〗[liáo tiān]
chat; have a free and easy talk

寥[liáo]
〖寥廓〗(形)[liáokuò]
broad and farreaching; immensity
〖寥寥无几〗[liáoliáowújǐ]
very few; scanty

嘹[liáo]
〖嘹亮〗(形)[liáoliàng]
(person's voice) clear; resonant; reverberant

缭[liáo]
〖缭乱〗(形)[liáoluàn]
confused; confounded
〖缭绕〗(动)[liáorǎo]
①encircle ②linger in the air

燎(动)[liáo]
blaze up; set fire to
〖燎原〗[liáo yuán]
start a prairie fire; prairie on fire

liǎo

了(动)[liǎo]
①end up ②understand; know
另见 le liào
〖了不得〗[liǎobude]
something serious; grave
〖了不起〗[liǎobuqǐ]
swell with pride; far from common
〖了解〗(动)[liǎojiě]
understand; know; grasp
〖了如指掌〗[liǎorúzhǐzhǎng]
know it like the palm of one's own hand
〖了事〗[liǎo shì]
make an end of; end up (e.g. end up in nothing definite)

潦[liǎo]
〖潦草〗(形)[liǎocǎo]
rough; careless

liào

了[liào]
另见 le liǎo
〖了望〗(动)[liàowàng]
observe

料(动、名)[liào]
①predict; guess ②material
〖料理〗(动)[liàolǐ]
look after; arrange; set in order
〖料想〗(动)[liàoxiǎng]
imagine;conceive;figure (sth.) to (oneself)

镣(名)[liào]
shackles
〖镣铐〗(名)[liàokào]
shackles

liè

列(动、量)[liè]
①line up; enumerate ②a measure word (train)
〖列车〗(名)[lièchē]
a train
〖列队〗[liè duì]
line up
〖列举〗(动)[lièjǔ]
list; enumerate; bring up one by one
〖列宁主义〗(名)[Lièníngzhǔyì]
Leninism
〖列强〗(名)[lièqiáng]
the big powers (formerly referred to the imperialist powers)
〖列席〗(动)[lièxí]
be observer at conference

劣(形)[liè]
bad; inferior
〖劣等〗(形)[lièděng]
inferiority
〖劣根性〗(名)[liègēnxìng]
bad characteristics
〖劣势〗(名)[lièshì]
inferiority
〖劣质〗(名、形)[lièzhì]
inferior quality;low grade; shoddy

烈(形)[liè]

fierce; furious; raging
〖烈火〗(名)[lièhuǒ]
raging flames
〖烈日〗(名)[lièrì]
scorching sun
〖烈士〗(名)[lièshì]
martyr;those who died for the revolution
〖烈属〗(名)[lièshǔ]
family members of those who died for the revolution; family of a martyr
〖烈性〗(名)[lièxìng]
① violent temper ② strong (wine)

猎[liè]
〖猎狗〗(名)[liègǒu]〔只 zhī〕
hunting dog
〖猎奇〗(动)[lièqí]
(usually derog.)hunt for novelty
〖猎枪〗(名)[lièqiāng]〔枝 zhī〕
hunting gun
〖猎取〗(动)[lièqǔ]
① gained by hunting ② seize
〖猎人〗(名)[lièrén]
hunter
〖猎手〗(名)[lièshǒu]
hunter (usually referring to a skilled hunter)

L

裂(动)[liè]
split; break
〖裂缝〗(名)[lièfèng]
a crack; an opening
〖裂痕〗(名)[lièhén]
split; crack
〖裂口〗(名)[lièkǒu]
an opening made by force (e.g. gash, crack)
〖裂纹〗(名)[lièwén]
small surface cracks

lín

邻[lín]
〖邻邦〗(名)[línbāng]
neighbouring country
〖邻国〗(名)[línguó]
neighbouring country
〖邻近〗(名、动)[línjìn]
close to; near or nearby
〖邻居〗(名)[línjū]
neighbour

林(名)[lín]
forest; wood
〖林立〗(动)[línlì]
(fig.) standing like a forest; a forest of...
〖林业〗(名)[línyè]
forestry
〖林阴道〗(名)[línyīndào]
〔条 tiáo〕a shady wooded road

临(动)[lín]
befall; come about
〖临别〗(动)[línbié]
at parting; when leaving
〖临床〗[línchuáng]
clinical treatment
〖临近〗(动)[línjìn]
approach; close by
〖临渴掘井〗[línkějuéjǐng]
(lit.) begin to sink well when

feeling thirsty; (fig.) do a thing at the last minute
〖临时〗(形)[línshí]
provisional; temporary
〖临时代办〗[línshí dàibàn]
charge d'affaires ad interim
〖临时工〗(名)[línshígōng]
casual labourer; emporary worker; transient worker
〖临危不惧〗[línwēibùjù]
be undaunted in the face of perils
〖临阵磨枪〗[línzhènmóqiāng]
(lit.) start sharpening one's spear just before going into battle; (fig.) do things at the last minute

淋(动)[lín]
take a shower; be caught (in the rain)
〖淋巴〗(名)[línbā]
lymph
〖淋漓〗(形)[línlí]
① vivid and moving ② roundly
〖淋漓尽致〗[línlíjìnzhì]
(fig.) very incisive; deep and vivid
〖淋浴〗(名)[línyù]
shower bath

琳[lín]
〖琳琅满目〗[línlángmǎnmù]
dazzling; glittering; glistening

磷(名)[lín]
phosphorus
〖磷肥〗(名)[línféi]
phosphorus; phosphate fertilizer

lǐn

凛[lǐn]
〖凛冽〗(形)[lǐnliè]
biting cold; freezing cold
〖凛凛〗(形)[lǐnlǐn]
①stern and severe ②biting cold
〖凛然〗(形)[lǐnrán]
aweinspiring

lìn

吝[lìn]
〖吝啬〗(形)[lìnsè]
miserly; stingy
〖吝惜〗(动)[lìnxī]
stint; save or spare (effort, etc)

líng

伶[líng]
〖伶俐〗(形)[línglì]
clear headed; intelligent; perspicacious

灵(形)[líng]
① intelligent; clever ② efficacious
〖灵便〗(形)[língbiàn]
light and convenient; handy
〖灵感〗(名)[línggǎn]
inspiration

〖灵魂〗(名)[línghún]
soul
〖灵活〗(形)[línghuó]
flexible; agile
〖灵活性〗(名)[línghuóxìng]
flexibility
〖灵机一动〗[língjīyīdòng]
a bright idea occurs; hit upon a good idea
〖灵柩〗(名)[língjiù]
hearse
〖灵敏〗(形)[língmǐn]
intelligent; quick-witted; smart
〖灵巧〗(形)[língqiǎo]
clever dexterous
〖灵通〗(形)[língtōng]
well informed
〖灵验〗(形)[língyàn]
efficacious; effective

玲[líng]
〖玲珑〗(形)[línglóng]
cleverly carved; intricate (carving)

铃(名)[líng]
bell

凌[líng]
〖凌晨〗(名)[língchén]
early dawn; daybreak
〖凌驾〗(动)[língjià]
domineer; override; lord it over
〖凌空〗(动)[língkōng]
soar; fly high
〖凌厉〗(形)[línglì]
quick and forceful
〖凌乱〗(形)[língluàn]
in great disorder; in a mess
〖凌辱〗(动)[língrǔ]
humiliate
〖凌云〗(动)[língyún]
fly in the sky

陵[líng]
〖陵墓〗(名)[língmù]
mausoleum; tomb
〖陵园〗(名)[língyuán]
cemetery

菱(名)[líng]
water chestnut
〖菱形〗(名)[língxíng]
rhombus

零(数、形)[líng]
① fractional (number) ② zero
〖零花〗(名、动)[línghuā]
pocket money; make small purchases
〖零活儿〗(名)[línghuór]
odd jobs
〖零件〗(名)[língjiàn]
spare parts
〖零乱〗(形)[língluàn]
disordered; messy
〖零七八碎〗[língqībāsuì]
small separate pieces; odd pieces; odds and ends
〖零钱〗(名)[língqián]
small change
〖零敲碎打〗[língqiāosuìdǎ]
piecemeal approach

L

〖零散〗(形)[língsǎn]
incomplete in a set
〖零食〗(名)[língshí]
titbits (eating between meals)
〖零售〗(动)[língshòu]
retail
〖零碎〗(形)[língsuì]
remnants; odd pieces; left over; fragmentary
〖零星〗(形)[língxīng]
sporadic; in pieces; in fragments; odds and ends
〖零用〗(名、动)[língyòng]
be used for small purchases; a little pocket money

lǐng

领(动、名)[lǐng]
① lead ② collar
〖领带〗(名)[lǐngdài]〔条 tiáo〕
necktie; tie
〖领导〗(动、名)[lǐngdǎo]
lead; leader; leadership
〖领导班子〗[lǐngdǎo bānzi]
a leading group
〖领导权〗(名)[lǐngdǎoquán]
leadership
〖领海〗(名)[lǐnghǎi]
territorial inland sea; territorial waters
〖领航〗(动)[lǐngháng]
pilot or guide; give direction or navigation
〖领会〗(动)[lǐnghuì]
grasp; understand; comprehend
〖领教〗(动)[lǐngjiào]
① have had enough experience of...; have the pleasure of seeing... ② seek for advice
〖领空〗(名)[lǐngkōng]
air space; territorial inland air
〖领取〗(动)[lǐngqǔ]
receive what is due
〖领事〗(名)[lǐngshì]
consul
〖领事馆〗(名)[lǐngshìguǎn]
consulate
〖领头〗[lǐng tóu]
take the lead
〖领土〗(名)[lǐngtǔ]
territory
〖领悟〗(动)[lǐngwù]
comprehend; realise
〖领先〗(动)[lǐngxiān]
take the lead; be in the lead
〖领袖〗(名)[lǐngxiù]
leader
〖领域〗(名)[lǐngyù]
national territory; sphere
〖领章〗(名)[lǐngzhāng]
insignia; collar tablet
〖领子〗(名)[lǐngzi]
collar

lìng

另(形、副)[lìng]
another; other
〖另起炉灶〗[lìngqǐlúzào]
make a fresh start
〖另外〗(形、副)[lìngwài]
① separate; separately ② apart from; besides; other
〖另眼看待〗[lìngyǎnkàndài]

L

①see... in a new light ②regard (sb.) favourably

令(动、名)[lìng]
order or instruct; orders; instruction; law
〖令人发指〗[lìngrénfàzhǐ]
make one's hair stand on end with anger
〖令人作呕〗[lìngrénzuò'ǒu]
nauseate; make one sick

liū

溜(动)[liū]
slink off; slip away; slope off; sneak away
〖溜冰〗(名、动)[liū bīng]
ice skating
〖溜达〗(动)[liūda]
stroll; go for a walk

liú

浏[liú]
〖浏览〗(动)[liúlǎn]
go over; browse; glance over

留(动)[liú]
stay; remain
〖留级〗(名、动)[liú jí]
fail in same grade at school
〖留恋〗(动)[liúliàn]
reluctant to part with; long for; hanker after
〖留念〗(动)[liúniàn]
give something on parting as a souvenir
〖留情〗[liú qíng]
show consideration; mercy
〖留神〗[liú shén]
be on the lookout; alert; be wary; vigilant
〖留声机〗(名)[liúshēngjī]
gramophone
〖留守〗(动)[liúshǒu]
person assigned to stay behind to perform rear service
〖留心〗[liú xīn]
be careful; pay attention
〖留学〗(动)[liúxué]
study abroad; be abroad for further study
〖留学生〗(名)[liúxuéshēng]
students studying abroad
〖留言〗(名)[liú yán]
leave word; leave a message with
〖留意〗[liú yì]
take precaution; be careful; keep in mind
〖留有余地〗[liúyǒuyúdì]
leave room for; make allowance for

流(动)[liú]
flow
〖流弊〗(名)[liúbì]
malpractice
〖流产〗[liú chǎn]
miscarriage; abortion; abortive
〖流畅〗(形)[liúchàng]
fluent
〖流传〗(动)[liúchuán]
spread; get about; be in circu-

L

lation; hand down
〖流窜〗(动)[liúcuàn]
run amuck
〖流弹〗(名)[liúdàn]
stray bullet
〖流动〗(动)[liúdòng]
float; fluid; mobile; circulate
〖流毒〗(动、名)[liúdú]
poison; evil effect
〖流感〗(名)[liúgǎn]
influenza
〖流寇〗(名)[liúkòu]
roving rebels
〖流寇主义〗(名)[liúkòuzhǔyì]
roving rebel ideology
〖流浪〗(动)[liúlàng]
wander about; rove
〖流离〗(动)[liúlí]
live the life of a refugee
〖流离失所〗[liúlíshīsuǒ]
become destitute and homeless
〖流利〗(形)[liúlì]
fluent; glib; smooth
〖流露〗(动)[liúlù]
show unintentionally
〖流落〗(动)[liúluò]
become destitute and drift ab-out
〖流氓〗(名)[liúmáng]
riffraff; gangster
〖流派〗(名)[liúpài]
schools; branch; sect
〖流失〗(动)[liúshī]
shift
〖流水〗(名)[liúshuǐ]
flowing water
〖流水不腐,户枢不蠹〗[liúshuǐ bùfǔ, hùshūbùdù]
running water does not go stale and door hinges do not become worm-eaten; running water is never stale and a door hinge is never worm-eaten
〖流水线〗(名)[liúshuǐxiàn]
assembly line
〖流水账〗(名)[liúshuǐzhàng]
daytoday account
〖流水作业〗[liúshuǐ zuòyè]
streamlined method of work
〖流速〗(名)[liúsù]
volume of flow
〖流通〗(动)[liútōng]
circulate
〖流亡〗(动)[liúwáng]
exile; live in exile abroad; fl-ee
〖流线型〗(名)[liúxiànxíng]
streamline
〖流星〗(名)[liúxīng]〔颗 kē〕
meteor
〖流行〗(动、形)[liúxíng]
be prevalent to; popular; cur-rent
〖流血〗[liú xuè]
bloodshed
〖流言蜚语〗[liúyánfēiyǔ]
rumours and gossip
〖流域〗(名)[liúyù]
river valley or reaches

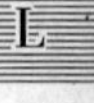

硫(名)[liú]
sulphur
〖硫磺〗(名)[liúhuáng]
sulphur

〖硫酸〗(名)[liúsuān]
sulphate

瘤 (名)[liú]
tumour
〖瘤子〗(名)[liúzi]〔个 gè〕
tumour

liǔ

柳 (名)[liǔ]
willow
〖柳树〗(名)[liǔshù]〔棵 kē〕
willow tree

liù

六 (数)[liù]
six
〖六书〗(名)[liùshū]
the six principles of formation of Chinese script
〖六一国际儿童节〗
[Liù Yī GuójìÉrtóngjié]
"June 1st" the International Children's Day
〖六月〗(名)[liùyuè]
June

lóng

龙 (名)[lóng]
dragon
〖龙飞凤舞〗[lóngfēifèngwǔ]
(of calligraphy) quick and forceful
〖龙井茶〗(名)[lóngjǐngchá]
Longjing tea
〖龙腾虎跃〗[lóngténghǔyuè]
dragon leaps and tiger bounds
〖龙头〗(名)[lóngtóu]
① dragon head; bellwether ② water tap

聋 (动、形)[lóng]
deafen; deaf
〖聋哑〗(形)[lóngyǎ]
deaf and dumb
〖聋子〗(名)[lóngzi]
a deaf person

隆 [lóng]
〖隆冬〗(名)[lóngdōng]
deep winter
〖隆隆〗(象声)[lónglóng]
onomatopoeia, booming; rumbling
〖隆重〗(形)[lóngzhòng]
solemn; grand (e.g. reception); ceremonious

lǒng

垄 (名、量)[lǒng]
① a rise in land ② a measure word, a mound
〖垄断〗(动)[lǒngduàn]
monopolize
〖垄断资本〗[lǒngduàn zīběn]
monopoly capital
〖垄断资产阶级〗
[lǒngduàn zī chǎnjiējí]
monopoly bourgeoisie

笼 [lǒng]
〖笼络〗(动)[lǒngluò]

L

win control over; halter
〖笼统〗(形)[lǒngtǒng]
in general terms; indiscriminately
〖笼罩〗(动)[lǒngzhào]
hover over; be enveloped by

lóu

喽[lóu]
〖喽罗〗(名)[lóuluó]
paltry followers; stooges; hangerson; pawns

楼(名)[lóu]〔座 zuò〕
storied building; tower
〖楼房〗(名)[lóufáng]
building
〖楼面〗(名)[lónmiàn]
floor
〖楼梯〗(名)[lóutī]
staircase

lǒu

搂(动)[lǒu]
embrace; hug

篓(名)[lǒu]
basket
〖篓子〗(名)[lǒuzi]〔个 gè〕
basket

lòu

陋[lòu]
〖陋习〗(名)[lòuxí]
vulgar habits

漏(动)[lòu]
leak out; disclose
〖漏洞〗(名)[lòudòng]
flaw
〖漏洞百出〗[lòudòngbǎichū]
full of loopholes
〖漏斗〗(名)[lòudǒu]
a funnel for liquids
〖漏网〗[lòu wǎng]
escape from the net; escape undetected

露(动)[lòu]
expose
另见 lù
〖露马脚〗[lòu mǎjiǎo]
① (usu. derog.) reveal cloven hoof ② let the cat out of the bag
〖露头〗[lòu tóu]
emerge; appear

lú

芦[lú]
〖芦苇〗(名)[lúwěi]
reed

炉(名、量)[lú]
① stove; furnace ② a measure word
〖炉火纯青〗[lúhuǒchúnqīng]
absolute purity; complete mastery
〖炉灶〗(名)[lúzào]
kitchen range; oven
〖炉子〗(名)[lúzi]〔个 gè〕

L

stove

lǔ

卤(名)[lǔ]
rock salt; natural salt on land

掳[lǔ]
〖掳掠〗(动)[lǔlüè]
carry away by force (of person or things); loot

鲁[lǔ]
〖鲁莽〗(形)[lǔmǎng]
reckless; rough and rash; hot-headed

lù

陆(名)[lù]
land
〖陆地〗(名)[lùdì]
land
〖陆军〗(名)[lùjūn]
army; the land force
〖陆路〗(名)[lùlù]
road; by land
〖陆续〗(副)[lùxù]
in sucession; continually; one after the other

录(动)[lù]
record (a speech)
〖录取〗(动)[lùqǔ]
select persons qualified for sth; admit (e.g. student to college)
〖录像〗[lùxiàng]
video recording
〖录像带〗(名)[lùxiàngdài]
video tape; video cassette
〖录像机〗(名)[lùxiàngjī]
video recorder; video cassette recorder
〖录音〗[lù yīn]
make recording
〖录音带〗(名)[lùyīndài]
tape; magnetic tape
〖录音机〗(名)[lùyīnjī]
recorder (e.g. tape recorder)

鹿(名)[lù]〔只 zhī〕
deer
〖鹿茸〗(名)[lùróng]
cartilaginous part of root of antler

路(名)[lù]〔条 tiáo〕
road
〖路程〗(名)[lùchéng]
journey; road
〖路费〗(名)[lùfèi]
travel expenses
〖路过〗(动)[lùguò]
pass by
〖路口〗(名)[lùkǒu]
the junction of streets and roads
〖路上〗(名)[lùshang]
on the way
〖路途〗(名)[lùtú]
① road; way ② distance of the journey
〖路线〗(名)[lùxiàn]
line

〖路牌〗(名)[lùpái]
street nameplate
〖路遥知马力〗[lùyáozhīmǎlì]
the strength of a horse is tested by the distance travelled; a long journey tests a horse's strength
〖路子〗(名)[lùzi]
way; method

露(名、动)[lù]
①dew ②expose; lay bare
另见 lòu
〖露骨〗(形)[lùgǔ]
become quite open; bareface; undisguisedly; bluntly
〖露水〗(名)[lùshui]
dew
〖露宿〗(动)[lùsù]
pass the night in the open
〖露天〗(形)[lùtiān]
open air
〖露营〗(动)[lùyíng]
camp in the open

lǘ

驴(名)[lǘ]〔头 tóu〕
donkey

lǚ

捋(动)[lǚ]
stroke (e.g. one's own beard)
另见 luō

旅(名)[lǚ]
brigade
〖旅程〗(名)[lǚchéng]
journey
〖旅费〗(名)[lǚfèi]
travelling expenses
〖旅馆〗(名)[lǚguǎn]
hotel
〖旅居〗(动)[lǚjū]
stay abroad
〖旅客〗(名)[lǚkè]
traveller
〖旅社〗(名)[lǚshè]
hotel
〖旅途〗(名)[lǚtú]
during travel
〖旅行〗(动)[lǚxíng]
travel; journey; take a trip; make a tour
〖旅行袋〗(名)[lǚxíngdài]〔个 gè〕
travelling bag
〖旅行社〗(名)[lǚxíngshè]
travel service
〖旅游〗(名)[lǚyóu]
tourism
〖旅长〗(名)[lǚzhǎng]
brigadier

屡(副)[lǚ]
often; repeatedly
〖屡次〗(副)[lǚcì]
repeatedly; time and again; one after another
〖屡次三番〗[lǚcìsānfān]
time and again; again and again; with iteration
〖屡见不鲜〗[lǚjiànbùxiān]
it is not strange when one has often seen it; it is often seen
〖屡教不改〗[lǚjiàobùgǎi]

refuse to correct one's errors after repeated education; refuse to mend one's way despite repeated education

履[lǚ]
〖履历〗(名)[lǚlì]
record of experiences; career
〖履行〗(动)[lǚxíng]
carry out; perform (e.g. duty); put into effect

lǜ

律[lǜ]
〖律师〗(名)[lǜshī]
lawyer
〖律师事务所〗[lǜshīshìwùsuǒ]
law office; lawyer's firm
〖律诗〗(名)[lǜshī]〔首 shǒu〕
a poem of eight lines either five or seven characters each with a strict tonal pattern

绿(形)[lǜ]
green
〖绿茶〗(名)[lǜchá]
green tea
〖绿灯〗(名)[lǜdēng]
green light (e.g. traffic)
〖绿豆〗(名)[lǜdòu]
green peas
〖绿化〗(动)[lǜhuà]
clothe with greenery; make green; afforestation
〖绿色〗(名)[lǜsè]
green colour
〖绿色食品〗[lǜsèshípǐn]
green food stuffs
〖绿油油〗(形)[lǜyōuyōu]
dark green
〖绿洲〗(名)[lǜzhōu]
oasis

luán

孪[luán]
〖孪生〗(形)[luánshēng]
twin

luǎn

卵(名)[luǎn]
egg
〖卵黄〗(名)[luǎnhuáng]
yolk
〖卵石〗(名)[luǎnshí]
cobble; pebble
〖卵翼〗(动)[luǎnyì]
(derog.) brood; be shielded by

luàn

乱(形)[luàn]
disorder
〖乱窜〗(动)[luàncuàn]
run amuck
〖乱哄哄〗(形)[luànhōnghōng]
noisy; boisterous; tumultuous
〖乱七八糟〗[luànqībāzāo]
at sixes and sevens; topsy-turvy
〖乱子〗(名)[luànzi]
disturbances; trouble

lüè

掠(动)[lüè]

①plunder ②flash; streak; dash; flit

〖掠夺〗(动)[lüèduó]
plunder; rob; pillage

略(形、副)[lüè]
briefly; slightly

〖略微〗(副)[lüèwēi]
just a little; slightly

lūn

抡(动)[lūn]
swing

lún

伦[lún]

〖伦理〗(名)[lúnlǐ]
ethics

沦[lún]

〖沦亡〗(动)[lúnwáng]
(of a country) perish

〖沦陷〗(动)[lúnxiàn]
be occupied (territory); be fallen (into the enemy's hand)

轮(名、动、量)[lún]
①wheel ②take turns ③a measure word, shift, round, etc.

〖轮班〗[lún bān]
shift; rotation; in turn

〖轮船〗(名)[lúnchuán]
〔艘 sōu〕ship; steamer; steamship

〖轮渡〗(名)[lúndù]
ferry

〖轮换〗(动)[lúnhuàn]
go by turns

〖轮廓〗(名)[lúnkuò]
outline; clearly defined; contour; frame; rough sketch

〖轮流〗(动)[lúnliú]
in turn; take turns; by turns

〖轮休〗(动)[lúnxiū]
have holiday by turns

〖轮训〗(动)[lúnxùn]
receive training in rotation

〖轮子〗(名)[lúnzi]〔个 gè〕
wheel

〖轮作〗(动)[lúnzuò]
crop rotation

lùn

论(动)[lùn]
①discuss ②regard...as ③deal with

〖论处〗(动)[lùnchǔ]
decide; judge

〖论点〗(名)[lùndiǎn]
proposition; thesis; argument

〖论调〗(名)[lùndiào]
argument; view; tone

〖论断〗(名)[lùnduàn]
thesis; proposition; conclusion

〖论据〗(名)[lùnjù]
basis of argument

〖论述〗(动)[lùnshù]
deal with; elaborate; speak or write in detail; expound

〖论说〗(动)[lùnshuō]
talk about

〖论坛〗(名)[lùntán]

comment; review; forum
〖论文〗(名)[lùnwén]〔篇 piān〕
essay; thesis; treatise
〖论战〗(名、动)[lùnzhàn]
controversy; polemics; debate
〖论争〗(名、动)[lùnzhēng]
controvert; debate
〖论证〗(动)[lùnzhèng]
expound and prove
〖论著〗(名)[lùnzhù]
published works
〖论资排辈〗[lùnzīpáibèi]
give top priority to seniority

luō

啰[luō]
〖啰嗦〗(形、动)[luōsuō]
talkative; verbose; prolix

捋(动)[luō]
rub one's hand along or over sth.
另见 lǚ

luó

罗(名)[luó]
a net; gauze
〖罗列〗(动)[luóliè]
list (phenomenon, etc.)
〖罗盘〗(名)[luópán]
compass
〖罗网〗(名)[luówǎng]
a net; snare; trammels

萝[luó]
〖萝卜〗(名)[luóbo]
turnip

逻[luó]
〖逻辑〗(名)[luójí]
logic

锣(名)[luó]
gong
〖锣鼓〗(名)[luógǔ]
drum and gong
〖锣鼓喧天〗[luógǔxuāntiān]
sound of gongs and drums during celebration

骡(名)[luó]
mule
〖骡子〗(名)[luózi]〔头 tóu〕
mule

螺[luó]
〖螺母〗(名)[luómǔ]
nut
〖螺丝钉〗(名)[luósīdīng]
screw
〖螺旋〗(名)[luóxuán]
spiral

luò

骆[luò]
〖骆驼〗(名)[luòtuo]〔峰 fēng〕
camel

络[luò]
〖络绎不绝〗[luòyìbùjué]
keep coming or going; uninterruptedly

落(动)[luò]

①fall;drop down ②be placed on
另见 là

〖落成〗(动)[luòchéng]
complete; finish (e.g. construction)

〖落后〗(形、动)[luòhòu]
fall behind; backward; lag behind

〖落户〗[luò hù]
settle down

〖落花流水〗[luòhuāliúshuǐ]
(smash) into pieces

〖落脚〗[luò jiǎo]
stop for a rest

〖落井下石〗[luòjǐngxiàshí]
drop stones on (sb.) who has fallen into a well

〖落空〗[luò kōng]
nothing comes of it;come to naught; come to nothing

〖落款〗(名)[luòkuǎn]
put one's signature to...

〖落落大方〗[luòluòdàfāng]
very poised and unstrained

〖落实〗(动)[luòshí]
take concrete measures to ensure the implementation of; carry out

〖落水狗〗(名)[luòshuǐgǒu]
the dog in the water

〖落体运动〗[luòtǐ yùndòng]
falling action

〖落网〗[luò wǎng]
(of criminal) be arrested

〖落伍〗[luò wǔ]
(fall) behind the ranks;lag behind

〖落选〗[luòxuǎn]
fail to be elected

L

mā

妈(名)[mā]
mother
〖妈妈〗(名)[māma]
mama

抹(动)[mā]
wipe clean
另见 mǒ mò
〖抹布〗(名)[mābù]
rag

má

麻(名、形)[má]
① hemp; flax of various kinds ② numb
〖麻痹〗(形)[mábì]
① be numbed ② lack of vigilance
〖麻痹大意〗[mábìdàyì]
be caught off guard; lack of vigilance
〖麻布〗(名)[mábù]
linen
〖麻袋〗(名)[mádài]
hempen sack; gunny sack
〖麻烦〗(形、动)[máfan]
① troublesome; annoying ② trouble; bother (e.g. may I trouble you...)
〖麻利〗(形)[máli]
quick-witted; snappy
〖麻木〗(形)[mámù]
numbed
〖麻木不仁〗[mámùbùrén]
be numbed; apathetic
〖麻雀〗(名)[máquè]〔只 zhī〕
sparrow0
〖麻绳〗(名)[máshéng]〔条 tiáo〕
hempen cord
〖麻疹〗(名)[mázhěn]
measles
〖麻醉〗(动)[mázuì]
anaesthetize
〖麻醉剂〗(名)[mázuìjì]
drug; anaesthetic

mǎ

马(名)[mǎ]〔匹 pǐ〕
horse
〖马鞍〗(名)[mǎ'ān]
saddle
〖马车〗(名)[mǎchē]〔辆 liàng〕
horse carriage
〖马达〗(名)[mǎdá]
motor
〖马到成功〗[mǎdàochénggōng]
accomplish immediately; immediate success
〖马灯〗(名)[mǎdēng]〔盏 zhǎn〕
storm lantern
〖马后炮〗(名)[mǎhòupào]
belated effort
〖马虎〗(形)[mǎhu]
perfunctory; careless; sloppy
〖马克思主义〗(名)
[Mǎkèsī zhǔyì]
Marxism
〖马拉松〗(名)[mǎlāsōng]
marathon race
〖马力〗(量)[mǎlì]
horsepower
〖马路〗(名)[mǎlù]〔条 tiáo〕
avenue; road; street
〖马前卒〗(名)[mǎqiánzú]
pawn; foot soldier
〖马上〗(副)[mǎshàng]
instantly; at once
〖马桶〗(名)[mǎtǒng]
night stool
〖马戏〗(名)[mǎxì]
circus

玛[mǎ]
〖玛瑙〗(名)[mǎnǎo]
agate

码(动、量)[mǎ]
①pile up ②a measure word, yard
〖码头〗(名)[mǎtou]
dock; wharf

蚂[mǎ]
〖蚂蜂〗(名)[mǎfēng]〔只 zhī〕
hornet
〖蚂蚁〗(名)[mǎyǐ]〔只 zhī〕
ant
〖蚂蚁啃骨头〗[mǎyǐkěngútou]
ants gnawing at a bone (e.g. making huge machine with small machine-tools)

mà

骂(动)[mà] scold; curse

ma

吗(助)[ma]
modal particle, indeterminate questioning tone

嘛(助)[ma]
modal particle

mái

埋(动)[mái]
bury
另见 mán
〖埋藏〗(动)[máicáng]
bury; hide away
〖埋伏〗(动、名)[máifú]

M

ambush; lie in wait for
〚埋没〛(动)[máimò]
fail to bring out; stifle
〚埋头〛[máitóu]
bury (oneself) in; immers (oneself) in
〚埋头苦干〛[máitóukǔgàn]
hard-working; industrious
〚埋葬〛(动)[máizàng]
bury; burial

mǎi

买(动)[mǎi]
buy; purchase
〚买办〛(名)[mǎibàn]
comprador
〚买办资产阶级〛
[mǎibàn zī chǎnjiējí]
comprador bourgeoisie
〚买方市场〛[mǎifāngshìchǎng]
buyer's market
〚买卖〛(名)[mǎimai]
trade; deal

mài

迈(动)[mài]
stride
〚迈步〛[màibù]
stride forward
〚迈进〛(动)[màijìn]
move forward with big strides

麦(名)[mài]
wheat
〚麦浪〛(名)[màilàng]
waves in wheat field caused by breeze
〚麦苗〛(名)[màimiáo]
wheat seedling
〚麦收〛(名)[màishōu]
wheat harvest
〚麦芽糖〛(名)[màiyátáng]
malt dust
〚麦种〛(名)[màizhǒng]
wheat seeds
〚麦子〛(名)[màizi]〔粒 lì〕
wheat

卖(动)[mài]
sell
〚卖方市场〛[màifāngshìchǎng]
seller's market
〚卖国〛[màiguó]
betray one's country; selling out the country
〚卖国贼〛(名)[màiguózéi]
traitor
〚卖国主义〛(名)[màiguózhǔyì]
national betrayal
〚卖劲〛[màijìn]
do one's utmost; make great effort
〚卖力〛[màilì]
make great efforts; work hard
〚卖命〛[mài mìng]
① sweat one's guts out; sweat blood ② throw away one's life
〚卖弄〛(动)[màinong]
show off
〚卖身契〛(名)[màishēnqì]
indenture by which one sells oneself or family
〚卖身投靠〛[màishēn tóukào]
sell oneself for personal gains

脉(名)[mài]
pulse
〖脉搏〗(名)[màibó]
pulse beat
〖脉络〗(名)[màiluò]
① general term for vein and artery ② line of thoughts

mán

埋[mán]
另见 mái
〖埋怨〗(动)[mányuàn]
grumble; complain; blame

蛮[mán]
〖蛮不讲理〗[mánbùjiǎnglǐ]
refuse to listen to reason; arrogant and unreasonable
〖蛮干〗(动)[mángàn]
act rashly
〖蛮横〗(形)[mánhèng]
arrogant and unreasonable; arbitrary; overbearing

馒[mán]
〖馒头〗(名)[mántou]〔个 gè〕
steamed bread

瞒(动)[mán]
hoodwink
〖瞒上欺下〗[mánshàngqīxià]
hoodwink those above bully those below
〖瞒天过海〗[mántiānguòhǎi]
cross the sea under camouflage; (fig.)try to get away with it under false pretences

mǎn

满(形、动)[mǎn]
① full ② fill up
〖满不在乎〗[mǎnbùzàihu]
take it for nothing; not care a fig
〖满城风雨〗[mǎnchéngfēngyǔ]
like a storm over the whole city; (news) spread all over
〖满怀〗(动)[mǎnhuái]
be filled with (confidence, etc.)
〖满面春风〗[mǎnmiànchūnfēng]
face beaming with smiles; face radiates happiness
〖满腔〗(名)[mǎnqiāng]
full of (e.g. enthusiasm); be filled with
〖满堂红〗[mǎntánghóng]
all-round accomplishment; triumph on all fronts
〖满意〗(动、形)[mǎnyì]
satisfy; satisfaction; be content with
〖满员〗[mǎn yuán]
capacity filled; keep at full strength
〖满载〗(动)[mǎnzài]
fully loaded
〖满载而归〗[mǎnzài'érguī]
come home fully loaded with...
〖满足〗(动)[mǎnzú]
satisfy; content
〖满座〗[mǎn zuò]
capacity audiences; whole aud-

ience; full house

màn

谩[màn]
〖谩骂〗(动)[mànmà]
abuse vilify; rail at; swear at; calumnies

蔓[màn]
〖蔓延〗(动)[mànyán]
spread

漫(动)[màn]
flood; spread over
〖漫不经心〗[mànbùjīngxīn]
inattentive; careless
〖漫步〗(动)[mànbù]
stroll
〖漫长〗(形)[màncháng]
long; lengthy; endless
〖漫画〗(名)[mànhuà]
cartoon
〖漫山遍野〗[mànshānbiànyě]
all over themountains and wilderness; over hill and dale
〖漫谈〗(动)[màntán]
have a casual conversation
〖漫天〗(形)[màntiān]
the whole sky

慢(形)[màn]
slow
〖慢车〗(名)[mànchē]
slow train; stopping train
〖慢慢腾腾〗(形)
[mànmantēngtēng]
very slow
〖慢条斯理〗[màntiáosīlǐ]
very slowly and unperturbed
〖慢性〗(名)[mànxìng]
chronic
〖慢性病〗(名)[mànxìngbìng]
① chronic disease ② disease of dilatoriness

máng

忙(形)[máng]
busy
〖忙碌〗(形)[mánglù]
busy
〖忙乱〗(形)[mángluàn]
pressing and disorderly

盲[máng]
〖盲肠炎〗(名)[mángchángyán]
appendicitis
〖盲从〗(动)[mángcóng]
follow blindly
〖盲动〗(动)[mángdòng]
act blindly
〖盲动主义〗(名)
[mángdòngzhǔyì]
putschism
〖盲流〗(名)[mángliú]
blind inflow (influx) into the city; blind migrants
〖盲目〗(形)[mángmù]
① blind ② without clear understanding
〖盲目性〗(名)[mángmùxìng]
blindly and uncritically; blindness
〖盲人〗(名)[mángrén]

blind person
〖盲文〗(名)[mángwén]
symbols for the blind; braille

茫[máng]
〖茫茫〗(形)[mángmáng]
far and wide; large and boundless
〖茫然〗(形)[mángrán]
not knowing what to do; completely at sea
〖茫无头绪〗[mángwútóuxù]
confused and without a clue

mǎng

莽[mǎng]
〖莽撞〗(形)[mǎngzhuàng]
reckless; headstrong

蟒(名)[mǎng]〔条 tiáo〕
boa; constrictor; python

māo

猫(名)[māo]〔只 zhī〕
cat
〖猫论〗(名)[māolùn]
theory that it doesn't matter if it's a white cat or a black one so long as it can catch mice
〖猫头鹰〗(名)[māotóuyīng]
〔只 zhī〕owl

máo

毛(名、量)[máo]
① hair; fur ② a measure word, money unit, (e.g. 1mao=10 cents)
〖毛笔〗(名)[máobǐ]〔枝 zhī〕
writing brush
〖毛病〗(名)[máobìng]
weakness; trouble; malady
〖毛玻璃〗(名)[máobōlí]
frosted glass
〖毛糙〗(形)[máocao]
coarse
〖毛骨悚然〗[máogǔsǒngrán]
make one's hair stand on end; horror stricken
〖毛巾〗(名)[máojīn]〔条 tiáo〕
towel
〖毛孔〗(名)[máokǒng]
pore
〖毛利〗(名)[máolì]
gross profit
〖毛料〗(名)[máoliào]
woolen fabric
〖毛毛雨〗(名)[máomaoyǔ]
fine rain
〖毛茸茸〗(形)[máorōngrōng]
soft like fur
〖毛手毛脚〗[máoshǒumáojiǎo]
flurried in movement; rough handed
〖毛遂自荐〗[Máosuìzìjiàn]
(fig.) self recommendation; recommend oneself (e.g. for a post)
〖毛细管〗(名)[máoxìguǎn]
capillary
〖毛线〗(名)[máoxiàn]
woolen yarn; knitting wool
〖毛衣〗(名)[máoyī]〔件 jiàn〕
woolen jacket; woolen sweater

M

〖毛泽东思想〗(名)[Máozé dōngsīxiǎng]
Mao Tsetung Thought
〖毛织品〗(名)[máozhīpǐn]
woolen fabrics

矛(名)[máo]
spear
〖矛盾〗(名、形)[máodùn]
contradiction; conflict; contradictory
〖矛头〗(名)[máotóu]
spear head

茅[máo]
〖茅塞顿开〗[máosèdùnkāi]
become enlightened all of a sudden; at once become enlightened
〖茅台酒〗(名)[máotáijiǔ]〔瓶 píng〕
Maotai (a famous wine)
〖茅屋〗(名)[máowū]〔间 jiān〕
thatched house; cottage

锚(名)[máo]
anchor

蟊[máo]
〖蟊贼〗(名)[máozéi]
pernicious enemies of the people

mǎo

铆(动)[mǎo]
rivet
〖铆钉〗(名)[mǎodīng]
rivet

mào

茂(形)[mào]
luxuriant
〖茂密〗(形)[màomì]
thick; heavy (growth of trees)
〖茂盛〗(形)[màoshèng]
luxuriant; plentiful (foliage, etc.); thriving

冒(动)[mào]
① (smoke) send up; burst ② brave; risk ③ assume false identity; act under false pretences
〖冒充〗(动)[màochōng]
pretend to be; pass oneself off as
〖冒犯〗(动)[màofàn]
violate openly; insult; give offence
〖冒号〗(名)[màohào]
colon
〖冒火〗[màohuǒ]
be enraged; flare up; angry
〖冒尖〗(动)[màojiān]
stand out; be conspicuous
〖冒尖户〗(名)[màojiānhù]
conspicuous person or household with a high income through honest labour
〖冒进〗(动)[màojìn]
adventurous advance; advance adventurously or regardlessly
〖冒昧〗(形)[màomèi]
take the liberty of; presumptu-

ous

〖冒名〗[mào míng]
act under false name

〖冒牌〗[mào pái]
forge a trademark (of goods)

〖冒失〗(形)[màoshi]
rash; thoughtless

〖冒天下之大不韪〗
[màotiānxiàzhīdàbùwěi]
defy the universal will of the people; risk universal condemnation

〖冒险〗[mào xiǎn]
run the risk; lay oneself open to danger

〖冒险主义〗(名)[màoxiǎnzhǔyì]
adventurism

贸[mào]

〖贸然〗(副)[màorán]
heedlessly; recklessly; without hesitation

〖贸易〗(名)[màoyì]
trade

帽(名)[mào]
cap; hat

〖帽徽〗(名)[màohuī]
emblem on a cap

〖帽檐〗(名)[màoyán]
hat brim

〖帽子〗(名)[màozi]〔顶 dǐng〕
cap

貌(名)[mào]
appearance

〖貌合神离〗[màohéshénlí]
one in appearance but each going his own way

〖貌似〗(动)[màosì]
appear to be; seem

méi

没(动、副)[méi]
have not; no
另见 mò

〖没关系〗[méi guānxi]
① do not matter ② have nothing to do with

〖没精打采〗[méijīngdǎcǎi]
in low spirits

〖没趣〗(形)[méiqù]
awkward; embarrasing

〖没什么〗[méi shénme]
nothing serious; never mind; that's all right

〖没说的〗[méi shuōde]
① no argument about it ② nothing to say against

〖没有〗(动、副)[méiyǒu]
devoid of; without; have not

玫[méi]

〖玫瑰〗(名)[méigui]
rose

枚(量)[méi]
a measure word, a countable piece (for coin, badge, etc.)

眉(名)[méi]
eyebrow

〖眉飞色舞〗[méifēisèwǔ]
jubilantly; gloatingly; exultantly
〖眉开眼笑〗[méikāiyǎnxiào]
face melt in smiles; all smiles; beam with satisfaction
〖眉毛〗(名)[méimao]
eyebrow
〖眉目〗(名)[méimù]
① looks ② clue; arrangcment
〖眉头〗(名)[méitóu]
brows

梅(名)[méi]
plum
〖梅花〗(名)[méihuā][朵 duǒ]
plum flower

媒[méi]
〖媒介〗(名)[méijiè]
transmitter (of disease, new ideas); intermidiate

煤(名)[méi]
coal
〖煤矿〗(名)[méikuàng]
coal mine
〖煤气〗(名)[méiqì]
coal gas
〖煤气灶〗(名)[méiqìzào]
gas range; gas cooker
〖煤炭〗(名)[méitàn]
coal
〖煤油〗(名)[méiyóu]
kerosene

霉(名)[méi]
mildew; mold
〖霉菌〗(名)[méijūn]
mold; mould
〖霉烂〗(动)[méilàn]
become mildewed; deteriorate; decay

měi

每(代、副)[měi]
every; each; per
〖每到〗[měi dào]
every time; whenever
〖每逢〗[měi féng]
every (certain day); when
〖每况愈下〗[měikuàngyùxià]
from bad to worse; deteriorate
〖每每〗(副)[měiměi]
often; all the time
〖每日每时〗[měi rì měi shí]
daily and hourly

美(形)[měi]
beautiful; pretty
〖美不胜收〗[měibùshèngshōu]
too beautiful to be absorbed all at once
〖美德〗(名)[měidé]
fine personality
〖美感〗(名)[měigǎn]
sense of beauty
〖美观〗(形)[měiguān]
nice looking; external beauty
〖美好〗(形)[měihǎo]
good and desirable; fine; wonderful
〖美化〗(动)[měihuà]
prettify; embellish

〖美丽〗(形)[měilì]
beautiful
〖美满〗(形)[měimǎn]
happy
〖美妙〗(形)[měimiào]
wonderful; bright; excellent
〖美容〗(名)[měiróng]
cosmetology; art of facial make-up
〖美容院〗(名)[měiróngyuàn]
beauty parlour; beauty shop
〖美术〗(名)[měishù]
fine arts
〖美术字〗(名)[měishùzì]
words written in an artistic way
〖美味〗(名)[měiwèi]
delicious or tasty food
〖美学〗(名)[měixué]
esthetics
〖美中不足〗[měizhōngbùzú]
some blemishes in an apparently perfect thing; with some slight imperfection

mèi

妹(名)[mèi]
younger sister
〖妹夫〗(名)[mèifu]
brother-in-law (husband of younger sister)
〖妹妹〗(名)[mèimei]
younger sister

媚(动)[mèi]
flatter; fawn
〖媚外〗[mèiwài]
fawn on foreigners

魅[mèi]
〖魅力〗(名)[mèilì]
attraction; draw

mēn

闷(形、动)[mēn]
①stuffy; suffocative
另见 mèn
〖闷热〗(形)[mēnrè]
hot and stuffy
〖闷头儿〗[mēn tóur]
silent and absorbed (in work)

mén

门(名、量)[mén]〔扇 shàn〕
① door; gate ② a measure word (e.g. branch of study)
〖门户〗(名)[ménhù]
①door ②doorway
〖门槛〗(名)[ménkǎn]
threshold
〖门口〗(名)[ménkǒu]
doorway; threshold; doorstep
〖门帘〗(名)[ménlián]
door-screen
〖门路〗(名)[ménlu]
ways of doing things; tricks of trade
〖门面〗(名)[ménmiàn]
shop front
〖门牌〗(名)[ménpái]
house number
〖门市部〗(名)[ménshìbù]

sales department; retail department

〖门庭若市〗[méntíngruòshì]
(lit.) the courtyard is as crowded as a market-place; (fig.) as busy as a market-place

〖门徒〗(名)[méntú]
disciple; follower

〖门外汉〗(名)[ménwàihàn]
layman; greenhorn

〖门诊〗(名)[ménzhěn]
outpatient department

扪(动)[mén]
feel; lay hand on

〖扪心自问〗[ménxīnzìwèn]
examine one's own conscience and ask oneself; self-examination

mèn

闷(形)[mèn]
①depressed ②airtight
另见 mēn

〖闷闷不乐〗[mènmènbùlè]
depressive; unhappy

〖闷气〗(名)[mènqì]
depression; melancholy; low spirits

焖(动)[mèn]
simmer over slow fire (a method of cooking)

men

们(尾)[men]
plural particle (for people, not things)

mēng

蒙(动)[mēng]
①guess ②cheat; deceive
另见 méng

〖蒙蒙亮〗(形)[mēngmēngliàng]
at dawn

〖蒙骗〗(动)[mēngpiàn]
deceive

méng

萌[méng]

〖萌芽〗(动)[méngyá]
①budding sprout ②rudiment

蒙(动)[méng]
①cover ②receive; suffer from ③ignorant
另见 mēng

〖蒙蔽〗(动)[méngbì]
hoodwink; fuddle; mislead

〖蒙混〗(动)[ménghùn]
slip by

〖蒙胧〗(形)[ménglóng]
drowsy

〖蒙昧〗(形)[méngmèi]
ignorant

〖蒙蒙〗(形)[méngméng]
drizzly

〖蒙受〗(动)[méngshòu]
be favoured; suffer (e.g. humiliation, losses)

盟(名)[méng]
alliance

〖盟国〗(名)[méngguó]
allies
〖盟约〗(名)[méngyuē]
treaty of alliance

朦[méng]
〖朦胧〗(形)[ménglóng]
misty; hazy; dim (e.g. moonlight)

měng

猛(形)[měng]
① valiant; fierce ② sudden
〖猛烈〗(形)[měngliè]
fierce; furious; violent
〖猛然〗(副)[měngrán]
suddenly
〖猛兽〗(名)[měngshòu]
beasts of prey
〖猛醒〗(动)[měngxǐng]
realize suddenly

锰(名)[měng]
manganese
〖锰钢〗(名)[měnggāng]
manganese steel

mèng

梦(名)[mèng]
dream
〖梦话〗(名)[mènghuà]
① talking in a dream ② nonsense; raving
〖梦见〗(动)[mèngjiàn]
dream
〖梦境〗(名)[mèngjìng]
dream world
〖梦寐以求〗[mèngmèiyǐqiú]
(lit.) try to get even in one's dream; (fig.) hanker after
〖梦乡〗(名)[mèngxiāng]
dreamland
〖梦想〗(动、名)[mèngxiǎng]
daydream; hope in vain; illusion
〖梦呓〗(名)[mèngyì]
① talking in dream ② arrant nonsense

mī

眯(动)[mī]
(eyes) close into a narrow slit; squint

mí

弥[mí]
〖弥补〗(动)[míbǔ]
① make up (e.g. deficiency); make amends (e.g. for past mistakes) ② fill (e.g. cracks)
〖弥漫〗(动)[mímàn]
widespread
〖弥天大谎〗[mítiāndàhuǎng]
blatant lie; gross lie; gross untruth

迷(动)[mí]
① lose way ② mislead
〖迷航〗[mí háng]
lose way in the sea
〖迷糊〗(形)[míhu]
unclear; muddle
〖迷惑〗(动)[míhuò]

puzzle; delude; befuddle
〖迷恋〗(动)[míliàn]
be enamoured with; indulge in; be intoxicated with
〖迷路〗[mí lù]
① have lost one's way ② (fig.) lose one's bearings
〖迷茫〗(形)[mímáng]
extensive and indistinct
〖迷梦〗(名)[míméng]
fond dreams
〖迷失〗(动)[míshī]
lose one's bearings
〖迷途〗(名)[mítú]
wrong path
〖迷雾〗(名)[míwù]
heavy mist
〖迷信〗(动、名)[míxìn]
place blind faith in; worship; superstition

谜(名)[mí]
① riddle ② puzzle; conundrum; mystery
〖谜语〗(名)[míyǔ]〔个 gè〕
puzzle; riddle

糜[mí]
〖糜烂〗(形)[mílàn]
rotten; decadent

mǐ

米(名、量)[mǐ]〔粒 lì〕
① rice ② a measure word, metre
〖米饭〗(名)[mǐfàn]
rice
〖米黄〗(形)[mǐhuáng]
dull yellow
〖米粒〗(名)[mǐlì]
rice grain
〖米色〗(名)[mǐsè]
buff (colour)
〖米汤〗(名)[mǐtāng]
rice soup

靡[mǐ]
〖靡靡之音〗[mǐmǐzhīyīn]
demoralizing music; decadent music

mì

泌[mì]
〖泌尿科〗(名)[mìniàokē]
department of urinary diseases

秘[mì]
〖秘诀〗(名)[mìjué]
key to success
〖秘密〗(形、名)[mìmì]
secret; confidential
〖秘书〗(名)[mìshū]
secretary

密(形)[mì]
dense; thick
〖密度〗(名)[mìdù]
① concentration ② density
〖密封〗(动)[mìfēng]
airtight; sealing off
〖密集〗(形)[mìjí]
be highly concentrated; closely concentre; bring together thick and fast

〖密件〗(名)[mìjiàn]
secret document
〖密码〗(名)[mìmǎ]
secret code
〖密密层层〗(形)[mìmicéngcéng]
layer upon layer
〖密密麻麻〗(形)[mìmimámá]
very dense
〖密谋〗(动)[mìmóu]
conspire
〖密切〗(形)[mìqiè]
close (relationship, etc.)
〖密实〗(形)[mìshi]
close and solid
〖密植〗(动)[mìzhí]
close planting

幂 (名)[mì]
(math.) power

蜜 (名)[mì]
honey
〖蜜蜂〗(名)[mìfēng]〔只 zhī〕
honey bee
〖蜜饯〗(名)[mìjiàn]
sugarpreserved fruit

mián

绵 [mián]
〖绵绸〗(名)[miánchóu]
cotton pongee
〖绵亘〗(动)[miángèn]
extend
〖绵绵〗(形)[miánmián]
continuous; uninterrupted
〖绵软〗(形)[miánruǎn]
soft and tensile
〖绵延〗(动)[miányán]
extend; continue
〖绵羊〗(名)[miányáng]〔只 zhī〕
sheep

棉 (名)[mián]
cotton
〖棉袄〗(名)[mián'ǎo]〔件 jiàn〕
cotton-padded jacket
〖棉被〗(名)[miánbèi]〔床 chuáng〕
cotton-padded quilt
〖棉布〗(名)[miánbù]
cotton cloth
〖棉纺〗(名)[miánfǎng]
cotton textile
〖棉花〗(名)[miánhua]
cotton
〖棉裤〗(名)[miánkù]〔条 tiáo〕
cotton-padded trousers
〖棉毛裤〗(名)[miánmáokù]〔条 tiáo〕
long cotton underpants
〖棉毛衫〗(名)[miánmáoshān]〔件 jiàn〕
long cotton sleeved vest
〖棉纱〗(名)[miánshā]
cotton yarn
〖棉线〗(名)[miánxiàn]
cotton thread
〖棉衣〗(名)[miányī]〔件 jiàn〕
cotton-padded coat; cotton padded clothes
〖棉织品〗(名)[miánzhīpǐn]
cotton fabrics

miǎn

免 (动)[miǎn]

①be free from; be relieved from (work) ② excuse;save (embarrassment)

〖免不得〗[miǎn bu de]
cannot help

〖免不了〗[miǎn bu liǎo]
unavoidable

〖免除〗(动)[miǎnchú]
dismiss; remove; avoid

〖免得〗(连)[miǎnde]
so as to avoid; lest; in case

〖免费〗[miǎn fèi]
free of charge

〖免检〗[miǎnjiǎn]
be exempt from inspection

〖免税商店〗[miǎnshuìshāngdiàn]
duty free shop

〖免疫力〗(名)[miǎnyìlì]
immunity from disease

勉 [miǎn]

〖勉励〗(动)[miǎnlì]
inspire; encourage

〖勉强〗(形、动)[miǎnqiǎng]
reluctant; do sth. unwillingly; compel; force

〖勉为其难〗[miǎnwéiqínán]
manage to do what is beyond one's power

缅 [miǎn]

〖缅怀〗(动)[miǎnhuái]
recall

腼 [miǎn]

〖腼腆〗(形)[miǎntiǎn]
embarrassed; blushing; shy

miàn

面 (名、量)[miàn]

① face surface ② flour ③ noodles ④ a measure word (for flat things, mirror, flag, etc.)

〖面包〗(名)[miànbāo]
bread

〖面红耳赤〗[miànhóng'ěrchì]
blush to the roots; crimson with shame or anger

〖面积〗(名)[miànjī]
area

〖面孔〗(名)[miànkǒng]
a person's face

〖面临〗(动)[miànlín]
encounter; be confronted with

〖面貌〗(名)[miànmào]
face; looks; appearance

〖面面俱到〗[miànmiànjùdào]
in every way; every detail thought of

〖面面相觑〗[miànmiànxiāngqù]
look at each other in astonishment

〖面目〗(名)[miànmù]
countenance; looks

〖面目全非〗[miànmùquánfēi]
beyond recognition

〖面目一新〗[miànmùyīxīn]
assume a completly new appearance; the new atmosphere that prevails...

〖面前〗(名)[miànqián]
front; in the face of

〖面色〗(名)[miànsè]
complexion

〖面生〗(形)[miànshēng]

unfamiliar
〖面试〗(名)[miànshì]
interview; audition
〖面熟〗(形)[miànshú]
familiar
〖面条〗(名)[miàntiáo]
noodles
〖面子〗(名)[miànzi]
① surface ② face-saving; for prestige reasons

miáo

苗(名)[miáo]〔棵 kē〕
sprout; seedling
〖苗圃〗(名)[miáopǔ]
seedling nursery
〖苗条〗(形)[miáotiao]
slender
〖苗头〗(名)[miáotou]
sign; indication

描(动)[miáo]
portray; describe; sketch
〖描画〗(动)[miáohuà]
portray
〖描绘〗(动)[miáohuì]
depict by words or painting
〖描摹〗(动)[miáomó]
trace (painting or design)
〖描写〗(动)[miáoxiě]
describe; portray; depict

瞄(动)[miáo]
aim
〖瞄准〗(动)[miáozhǔn]
take aim; direct

miǎo

秒(名)[miǎo]
(of time) second; (of degree) second
〖秒针〗(名)[miǎozhēn]
second hand (of clock or watch)

渺[miǎo]
〖渺茫〗(形)[miǎománg]
① dim and remote; hazy; indistinct ② uncertain
〖渺小〗(形)[miǎoxiǎo]
tiny; negligible; paltry

藐[miǎo]
〖藐视〗(动)[miǎoshì]
despise; look down upon

miào

妙(形)[miào]
wonderful; remarkable

庙(名)[miào]〔座 zuò〕
temple

miè

灭(动)[miè]
① annihilate; wipe out ② extinguish; put out
〖灭顶之灾〗[mièdǐngzhīzāi]
be drowned; in danger of being swamped
〖灭火机〗(名)[mièhuǒjī]
fire extinguisher
〖灭迹〗[miè jī]
obliterate traces

〖灭绝〗(动)[mièjué]
destroy completely;annihilate
〖灭口〗[miè kǒu]
silence a witness (e.g. of a crime)
〖灭亡〗(动)[mièwáng]
penish; doom

蔑[miè]
〖蔑视〗(动)[mièshì]
show contempt; despise; ignore

mín

民(名)[mín]
people
〖民办〗[mín bàn]
run by the local people; community-run
〖民兵〗(名)[mínbīng]
people's militia
〖民愤〗(名)[mínfèn]
indignation among the people; wrath of the masses
〖民歌〗(名)[míngē]〔首 shǒu〕
folk song
〖民工〗(名)[míngōng]
civilian workers (builders); peasant workers (builders)
〖民间〗(名)[mínjiān]
① folk (e.g. story, song, dance) ② among the people
〖民间团体〗[mínjiān tuántǐ]
non-governmental organization
〖民间文学〗[mínjiān wénxué]
folk literature
〖民间艺术〗[mínjiān yìshù]
folk arts
〖民警〗(名)[mínjǐng]
people's policeman
〖民事〗(名、形)[mínshì]
civil; relating to civil law
〖民心〗(名)[mínxīn]
popular support; popular sentiments
〖民谣〗(名)[mínyáo]〔首 shǒu〕
ballad
〖民意〗(名)[mínyì]
popular opinion; will of the people
〖民意测验〗[mínyìcèyàn]
poll; public opinion poll
〖民用〗[mín yòng]
civilian; civil
〖民乐〗(名)[mínyuè]
folk music
〖民众〗(名)[mínzhòng]
masses
〖民主〗(名、形)[mínzhǔ]
democracy; democratic
〖民主党派〗[mínzhǔ dǎngpài]
democratic parties
〖民主改革〗[mínzhǔ gǎigé]
democratic reforms
〖民主集中制〗
[mínzhǔjízhōngzhì]
democratic centralism
〖民族〗(名)[mínzú]
nationality; national
〖民族革命〗[mínzúgémìng]
national revolution
〖民族解放运动〗
[mínzú jiěfàng yùndòng]
national liberation movement
〖民族统一战线〗
[mínzú tǒngyī zhànxiàn]

the national united front
〖民族形式〗[mínzú xíngshì]
national form
〖民族英雄〗[mínzú yīngxióng]
national heroes
〖民族主义〗(名)[mínzúzhǔyì]
nationalism
〖民族资产阶级〗
[mínzú zīchǎn jiējí]
national bourgeoisie
〖民族自决〗[mínzú zìjué]
national self-determination
〖民族自治〗[mínzú zìzhì]
national autonomy

mǐn

敏[mǐn]
〖敏感〗(形)[mǐngǎn]
sensitive; keen feeling
〖敏捷〗(形)[mǐnjié]
quick response to; agile
〖敏锐〗(形)[mǐnruì]
sharp; keen; penetrating

míng

名(名、量)[míng]
① name② in the name of③ fame; reputation ④ a measure word (for person)
〖名不副实〗[míngbùfùshí]
more in name than in reality; unworthy of the name
〖名不虚传〗[míngbùxūchuán]
have a well-deserved reputation
〖名册〗(名)[míngcè]
personnel roster; record of names
〖名产〗(名)[míngchǎn]
famous product
〖名称〗(名)[míngchēng]
name by which person or thing is called; term
〖名词〗(名)[míngcí]
①word; term②noun
〖名次〗(名)[míngcì]
order of selection
〖名存实亡〗[míngcúnshíwáng]
non-existent except in name; exist in name only
〖名单〗(名)[míngdān]〔张 zhāng〕
name list
〖名额〗(名)[míng'é]
the given number (of persons)
〖名副其实〗[míngfùqíshí]
worthy of the name; in reality as well as in name
〖名利〗(名)[mínglì]
(personal) fame and gain
〖名列前茅〗[mínglièqiánmáo]
come out in front
〖名目〗(名)[míngmù]
name; title; label
〖名牌〗(名)[míngpái]
famous brand
〖名片〗(名)[míngpiàn]
visiting card; calling card
〖名气〗(名)[míngqì]
reputation; fame
〖名人〗(名)[míngrén]
famous persons
〖名声〗(名)[míngshēng]
fame; renown
〖名胜〗(名)[míngshèng]
places of historic interest

〖名堂〗(名)[míngtang]
①variety②fruitful result
〖名望〗(名)[míngwàng]
reputation
〖名言〗(名)[míngyán]
epigram; famous saying; proverb
〖名义〗(名)[míngyì]
①in the name of; in the capacity of ②in name
〖名誉〗(名)[míngyù]
①reputation②honorary
〖名著〗(名)[míngzhù]
famous works
〖名字〗(名)[míngzi]
persons' names

明(形)[míng]
open; clear; bright; clear-sighted
〖明白〗(形、动)[míngbai]
①apparent②clear;understand
〖明摆着〗[míng bǎizhe]
plain and clear; evident
〖明辨是非〗[míngbiànshìfēi]
distinguish right from wrong
〖明察秋毫〗[míngcháqiūháo]
detect the minutest detail in everything
〖明澈〗(形)[míngchè]
crystal clear
〖明灯〗(名)[míngdēng]
beacon
〖明晃晃〗(形)[mínghuānghuāng]
clear; glaring
〖明火执仗〗[mínghuǒzhízhàng]
open robbery; conduct activities openly (evil doings)
〖明快〗(形)[míngkuài]
perspicacious; perspicuous
〖明朗〗(形)[mínglǎng]
bright; forthright
〖明亮〗(形)[míngliàng]
①shining②discerning
〖明了〗(动、形)[míngliǎo]
understand; clear-cut
〖明媚〗(形)[míngmèi]
bright and beautiful
〖明明〗(副)[míngmíng]
clearly
〖明目张胆〗[míngmùzhāngdǎn]
in a bare-faced way; brazenly; openly
〖明年〗(名)[míngnián]
next year
〖明枪暗箭〗[míngqiāng'ànjiàn]
attack by overt and covert means
〖明确〗(形、动)[míngquè]
explicit; definite; clear; understand clearly
〖明日〗(名)[míngrì]
tomorrow
〖明天〗(名)[míngtiān]
tomorrow
〖明晰〗(形)[míngxī]
perspicuous; clear-cut
〖明显〗(形)[míngxiǎn]
obvious; evident
〖明信片〗(名)[míngxìnpiàn]
〔张 zhāng〕postcard
〖明哲保身〗[míngzhébǎoshēn]
be worldly wise and play safe
〖明知故犯〗[míngzhīgùfàn]

commit mistakes deliberately
〖明智〗(形)[míngzhì]
wise; sagacious

鸣(动)[míng]
① make sound ② voice;air (e.g. opinion)
〖鸣锣开道〗[míngluókāidào]
(lit.) sound the gongs to clear the way for; (fig.) pave the way for

冥[míng]
〖冥思苦想〗[míngsīkǔxiǎng]
cudgel one's brains
〖冥想〗(动)[míngxiǎng]
contemplate

铭[míng]
〖铭记〗(动)[míngjì]
remember; bear in mind
〖铭刻〗(动)[míngkè]
engrave

瞑[míng]
〖瞑目〗(动)[míngmù]
close the eyes (death)

mìng

命(动、名)[mìng]
① give order ② life
〖命根子〗(名)[mìnggēnzi]
lifeline; one's very life
〖命令〗(名、动)[mìnglìng]
order; command
〖命脉〗(名)[mìngmài]
lifeblood
〖命名〗[mìng míng]
assign name
〖命题〗[mìng tí]
thesis
〖命运〗(名)[mìngyùn]
destiny; fate
〖命中〗(动)[mìngzhòng]
hit the aim

miù

谬[miù]
〖谬论〗(名)[miùlùn]
fallacy
〖谬误〗(名)[miùwù]
falsehood

mō

摸(动)[mō]
feel with the hand
〖摸底〗[mō dǐ]
feel out; try to find out the truth
〖摸索〗(动)[mōsuǒ]
grope for; in quest of (truth)

mó

模[mó]
另见 mú
〖模范〗(名)[mófàn]
model (e.g. workers); example
〖模仿〗(动)[mófǎng]
imitate; copy
〖模糊〗(形)[móhu]
obscure; vague; blurred
〖模棱两可〗[móléngliǎngkě]
in an equivocal way; cut both

ways; shift and hedge; ambiguous (attitude)
〖模拟〗(动)[mónǐ]
imitate; simulate; mock
〖模式〗(名)[móshì]
pattern; type, model
〖模特儿〗(名)[mótèr]
model
〖模型〗(名)[móxíng]
model; pattern

摩[mó]
〖摩擦〗(动)[mócā]
① rub together ② conflict; friction
〖摩擦力〗(名)[mócālì]
friction
〖摩拳擦掌〗[móquáncāzhǎng]
roll up one's sleeves for battle; clench fists in preparation for fight or hard work
〖摩托车〗(名)[mótuōchē]
〔辆 liàng〕motorcycle

磨(动)[mó]
① rub ② polish
另见 mò
〖磨蹭〗(形、动)[móceng]
① the rubbing of one thing against another ② idle at work; slack ③ pester (e.g. pester sb. for sth.)
〖磨床〗(名)[móchuáng]
grinder
〖磨练〗(动)[móliàn]
steel; temper
〖磨灭〗(动)[mómiè]
dull; blunt
〖磨损〗(动)[mósǔn]
breakdown due to friction

蘑[mó]
〖蘑菇〗(名)[mógu]
mushroom

魔(名)[mó]
devil
〖魔鬼〗(名)[móguǐ]
monster; devil
〖魔力〗(名)[mólì]
magic hold; spell-binding power
〖魔术〗(名)[móshù]
juggling
〖魔爪〗(名)[mózhǎo]
claws; evil talons

mǒ

抹(动)[mǒ]
① wipe; blot out ② rub...on; apply...to
另见 mā mò
〖抹杀〗(动)[mǒshā]
ignore; negate; deny; write off

mò

末(名)[mò]
① end; final; the last ② dust; powder
〖末了〗(名)[mòliǎo]
at the end
〖末路〗(名)[mòlù]
doom; the end

〖末日〗(名)[mòrì]
the end; doom
〖末梢〗(名)[mòshāo]
the end of...
〖末尾〗(名)[mòwěi]
end of (e.g. event, thing); tail end of
〖末叶〗(名)[mòyè]
last part of century or dynasty

没(动)[mò]
cover; submerge
另见 méi
〖没落〗(动)[mòluò]
decline
〖没收〗(动)[mòshōu]
confiscate

抹(动)[mò]
①daub; plaster
②skirt; bypass
另见 mā mǒ

沫(名)[mò]
bubbles

茉[mò]
〖茉莉〗(名)[mòlì]
jasmine

陌[mò]
〖陌生〗(形)[mòshēng]
strange

莫(副)[mò]
not
〖莫不〗(副)[mòbù]
might it not be ...; perhaps; probably
〖莫大〗(形)[mòdà]
most important
〖莫非〗(副)[mòfēi]
unless; could it be...?
〖莫名其妙〗[mòmíngqímiào]
difficult to guess what it is all about; inexplicable
〖莫如〗(连)[mòrú]
it would be better
〖莫若〗(连)[mòruò]
nothing better than
〖莫须有〗[mòxūyǒu]
fabulous; spurious; concocted
〖莫衷一是〗[mòzhōngyīshì]
difficult to tell what is right

磨(名、动)[mò]
①mill② friction; grind
另见 mó
〖磨房〗(名)[mòfáng]
mill house
〖磨盘〗(名)[mòpán]
mill stone

漠[mò]
〖漠不关心〗[mòbùguānxīn]
indifferent
〖漠漠〗(形)[mòmò]
①nonchalant ②silent
〖漠然〗(形)[mòrán]
apathetic; indifferent
〖漠视〗(动)[mòshì]
look down upon; ignore; regard as unimportant

墨(名)[mò]
ink; stationery
〖墨盒〗(名)[mòhé]〔个 gè〕
ink box
〖墨迹未干〗[mòjìwèigān]
scarcely has the ink dried; the ink has hardly dried
〖墨镜〗(名)[mòjìng]〔副 fù〕
sun glasses
〖墨绿〗(形)[mòlǜ]
dark green
〖墨守成规〗[mòshǒuchéngguī]
stick to the established practice; follow stereotyped routine
〖墨水〗(名)[mòshuǐ]〔瓶 píng〕
fluid ink
〖墨汁〗(名)[mòzhī]
prepared liquid ink

默[mò]
〖默哀〗(动)[mò'āi]
silence (mourning)
〖默不作声〗[mòbùzuòshēng]
silent
〖默默无闻〗[mòmòwúwén]
not known to public
〖默契〗(形、名)[mòqì]
tacit understanding
〖默然〗(形)[mòrán]
speechless
〖默认〗(动)[mòrèn]
recognize tacitly
〖默写〗(动)[mòxiě]
dictate
〖默许〗(动)[mòxǔ]
approve tacitly

móu

牟[móu]
〖牟利〗[móu lì]
make profits
〖牟取〗(动)[móuqǔ]
try to get (e.g. profits)

谋(动)[móu]
plan; plot
〖谋害〗(动)[móuhài]
plan to harm
〖谋划〗(动)[móuhuà]
plan and contrive
〖谋求〗(动)[móuqiú]
plan to achieve
〖谋杀〗(动)[móushā]
try to kill; attempt murder
〖谋生〗(动)[móushēng]
make a living

mǒu

某(代)[mǒu]
a certain (e.g. person or place)

mú

模(名)[mú]
model
另见 mó
〖模具〗(名)[mújù]
pattern; model
〖模样〗(名)[múyàng]
shape; looks
〖模子〗(名)[múzi]
mould

mǔ

母(名)[mǔ]
①mother ②female of species
〖母亲〗(名)[mǔqīn]
mother
〖母校〗(名)[mǔxiào]
Alma Mater
〖母音〗(名)[mǔyīn]
vowel

牡[mǔ]
〖牡丹〗(名)[mǔdān]
peony

亩(量)[mǔ]
a measure word mou
〖亩产〗(名)[mǔchǎn]
per mou yield

mù

木(名、形)[mù]
①timber; wood ②insensitive
〖木板〗(名)[mùbǎn]〔块 kuài〕
wooden board
〖木材〗(名)[mùcái]
timber
〖木筏〗(名)[mùfá]
wooden raft
〖木工〗(名)[mùgōng]
carpenter
〖木刻〗(名)[mùkè]
wood carving
〖木料〗(名)[mùliào]
timber
〖木偶〗(名)[mù'ǒu]
wooden figure; puppet
〖木偶戏〗(名)[mù'ǒuxì]
puppet show
〖木排〗(名)[mùpái]
raft
〖木器〗(名)[mùqì]
wooden furniture
〖木然〗(形)[mùrán]
benumbed
〖木炭〗(名)[mùtàn]
charcoal
〖木头〗(名)[mùtou]〔块 kuài〕
wood; wood block
〖木星〗(名)[mùxīng]〔颗 kē〕
planet Jupiter
〖木已成舟〗[mùyǐchéngzhōu]
what's done is done

目(名)[mù]
①eye ②catalogue
〖目标〗(名)[mùbiāo]
aim; goal; target; object
〖目不转睛〗[mùbùzhuǎnjīng]
stare continuously
〖目瞪口呆〗[mùdèngkǒudāi]
stunned; dumbfounded
〖目的〗(名)[mùdì]
aim; objective; goal
〖目睹〗(动)[mùdǔ]
witness
〖目光〗(名)[mùguāng]
sight; vision
〖目击〗(动)[mùjī]
witness
〖目空一切〗[mùkōngyīqiè]
look down upon all
〖目录〗(名)[mùlù]
contents (of book); catalogue

〖目前〗(名)[mùqián]
the present
〖目中无人〗[mùzhōngwúrén]
look down on everyone

沐[mù]
〖沐浴〗(动)[mùyù]
bathe; be bathed in

牧(动)[mù]
tend (sheep, cow, etc.)
〖牧草〗(名)[mùcǎo]
plant grown as food for cattle; fodder grass
〖牧场〗(名)[mùchǎng]
livestock farm; pasture land
〖牧歌〗(名)[mùgē]〔首 shǒu〕
pastoral song
〖牧民〗(名)[mùmín]
herdsman
〖牧童〗(名)[mùtóng]
cowherd; shepherd
〖牧畜〗(名)[mùxù]
livestock; cattle breeding
〖牧业〗(名)[mùyè]
animal husbundary; livestock
〖牧主〗(名)[mùzhǔ]
herdowner

募(动)[mù]
enlist (e.g. soldiers)
〖募捐〗(动)[mùjuān]
raise funds

墓(名)[mù]
grave; tomb

幕(名、量)[mù]
① curtain ② a measure word, scene, act, etc.
〖幕后〗(名)[mùhòu]
behind-the-scenes; back stage

睦[mù]
〖睦邻〗[mù lín]
good neighbour

暮[mù]
〖暮年〗(名)[mùnián]
declining years
〖暮气〗(名)[mùqì]
spirit of decline
〖暮色〗(名)[mùsè]
view of sunset

ná

拿(动、介)[ná]
①carry; take; take hold of ② seize; capture ③make use of; by means of
〖拿…来说〗[ná…láishuō]
take...for example
〖拿手〗(形)[náshǒu]
be good at
〖拿手好戏〗[náshǒuhǎoxì]
one's forte; one's specialty; one's favourite game
〖拿主意〗[ná zhǔyi]
make up one's mind

nǎ

哪(代)[nǎ]
which...?
另见 na
〖哪个〗(代)[nǎge]
which one?
〖哪里〗(代)[nǎli]
①where? ②wherever
〖哪怕〗(连)[nǎpà]
even if; even though
〖哪儿〗(代)[nǎr]
where?
〖哪些〗(代)[nǎxiē]
which?
〖哪样〗(代)[nǎyàng]
what kind?

nà

那(代、连)[nà]
that; which
〖那个〗(代)[nàge]
that one
〖那里〗(代)[nàli]
over there
〖那么〗(代、连)[nàme]
such
〖那么点儿〗[nàmediǎnr]
so little; so few
〖那么些〗[nàmexiē]
so much; so many
〖那么着〗[nàmezhe]
like that; in that way

N

〖那儿〗(代) [nàr]
there
〖那些〗(代) [nàxiē]
those
〖那样〗(代) [nàyàng]
so; in such a manner

呐 [nà]
〖呐喊〗(动) [nàhǎn]
utter loud shout in support; acclaim

纳 (动) [nà]
accept; take in
〖纳闷儿〗[nàmènr]
be baffled; be in doubt and confused
〖纳入〗(动) [nàrù]
bring within; fit into; be placed in
〖纳税〗[nà shuì]
pay a tax
〖纳新〗[nà xīn]
take in the fresh; admit new members (e.g. into the Party)

na

哪 (助) [na]
a modal particle
另见 nǎ

nǎi

乃 [nǎi]
〖乃至〗(连) [nǎizhì]
even

奶 (名) [nǎi]
① milk ② a woman's breasts ③ suckle; breast feed
〖奶粉〗(名) [nǎifěn]
milk powder
〖奶奶〗(名) [nǎinai]
① grandmother ② respectful term of address used by young people to a woman of about their grandmothers' age
〖奶油〗(名) [nǎiyóu]
cream

nài

耐 (动) [nài]
be resistant to; endure; last
〖耐烦〗(形) [nàifán]
patient
〖耐火材料〗[nàihuǒcáiliào]
heat-resistant material; refractory material
〖耐久〗(形) [nàijiǔ]
durable; capable of standing wear and tear
〖耐劳〗[nài láo]
can endure hardship; good stamina
〖耐心〗(形) [nàixīn]
patient; forbearing; tolerant
〖耐性〗(名) [nàixìng]
patience
〖耐用〗(形) [nàiyòng]
durable; capable of standing wear and tear

nán

男 (名) [nán]
men

〖男男女女〗[nánnánnǚnǚ]
crowds of men and women
〖男女〗(名) [nánnǚ]
men and women
〖男女平等〗[nánnǚpíngděng]
sex equality; equality of men and women
〖男人〗(名) [nánrén]
① adult (male) ② (coll.) husband
〖男声〗(名) [nánshēng]
male voice
〖男性〗(名) [nánxìng]
masculine sex; male

南 (名) [nán]
south
〖南边〗(名) [nánbian]
the south
〖南昌起义〗[NánchāngQǐyì]
the Nanchang Uprising (1927)
〖南方〗(名) [nánfāng]
the southern part
〖南瓜〗(名) [nánguā] [个 gè]
pumpkin
〖南极〗(名) [nánjí]
South Pole
〖南极洲〗(名) [Nánjízhōu]
Antarctic
〖南美洲〗(名) [Nánměizhōu]
South America
〖南腔北调〗[nánqiāngběidiào]
talk with a strong local accent
〖南辕北辙〗[nányuánběizhé]
(lit.) go south by driving the chariot north; (fig.) diametrically opposite; heading in the wrong direction
〖南征北战〗[nánzhēngběizhàn]
fight north and south (all over the country)

难 (形) [nán]
difficult; hard
另见 nàn
〖难产〗(动) [nánchǎn]
① (of child-birth) difficult labour ② difficult to get results
〖难处〗(名) [nánchu]
① difficulties ② hard to get along with
〖难道〗(副) [nándào]
is it possible...? could it possibly be...? does it mean ...?
〖难得〗(形) [nándé]
hard to get (e.g. sth. precious); rare; scarce
〖难度〗(名) [nándù]
extent of difficulty; difficulty
〖难怪〗(动、连) [nánguài]
① not to blame ② small wonder that; that's why; little wonder that
〖难关〗(名) [nánguān]
difficult position; impasse; predicament; barrier
〖难过〗(动、形) [nánguò]
① feel miserable or dejected; feel sorry; be filled with pain ② hard up; uncomfortable; difficult to make ends meet
〖难堪〗(形) [nánkān]
① embarrassing ② unbearable;

hard to endure
〖难看〗(形)[nánkàn]
①ugly; not good to look at; not a nice sight ②disgraceful
〖难免〗(形)[nánmiǎn]
cannot help; unavoidable
〖难能可贵〗[nánnéngkěguì]
it is praiseworthy for one who has achieved sth. difficult
〖难受〗(形)[nánshòu]
unbearable; distressed
〖难说〗(动、形)[nánshuō]
①hard to say ②not sure; not certain
〖难题〗(名)[nántí]
knotty problem; baffling problem; a hard nut to crack
〖难听〗(形)[nántīng]
unpleasant to hear
〖难为〗(动)[nánwei]
①make it difficult for; embarrass ②express sympathy to sb. for...
〖难为情〗(形)[nánwéiqíng]
shy; ashamed; embarrassing
〖难闻〗(形)[nánwén]
ill-smelling; stinking
〖难以置信〗[nányǐzhìxìn]
unbelievable; hard to believe; incredible

nàn

难(名)[nàn]
disaster; calamity
另见 nán
〖难民〗(名)[nànmín]
refugee
〖难兄难弟〗[nànxiōngnàndì]
①fellow sufferers; brothers in suffering ②one as bad as the other; tweedledum and tweedledee

náng

囊(名)[náng]
bag; case; sack; purse
〖囊括〗(动)[nángkuò]
muster; embrace everything; all embracing
〖囊肿〗(名)[nángzhǒng]
a benign tumour

náo

挠(动)[náo]
①disturb; interrupt; interfere ②scratch ③bend

nǎo

恼(动)[nǎo]
①be annoyed ②be angry
〖恼恨〗(动)[nǎohèn]
be irritated and filled with hatred
〖恼火〗(动)[nǎohuǒ]
be enraged; lose patience; be annoyed
〖恼怒〗(动)[nǎonù]
be irritated and angry
〖恼人〗(形)[nǎorén]
irritating
〖恼羞成怒〗[nǎoxiūchéngnù]
so ashamed that one is incited to anger; fly into a rage with shame

脑(名)[nǎo]
the brain
〖脑袋〗(名)[nǎodai]
the head
〖脑海〗(名)[nǎohǎi]
the brain; the mind
〖脑筋〗(名)[nǎojīn]
brains; mental ability
〖脑力劳动〗[nǎolì láodòng]
mental labour; brain work
〖脑膜〗(名)[nǎomó]
the three membranes that envelop the brain and the spinal cord
〖脑膜炎〗(名)[nǎomóyán]
meningitis
〖脑体倒挂〗[nǎotǐdàoguà]
income of the manual labourers being higher than that of mental workers; reversal of the relation between mental workers and physical labourers
〖脑炎〗(名)[nǎoyán]
encephalitis
〖脑溢血〗(名)[nǎoyìxuè]
cerebral apoplexy; cerebral haemorrhage
〖脑子〗(名)[nǎozi]
① the brain ② mental power

nào

闹(动)[nào]
① create disturbance; kick up a fuss; raise an uproar ② suffer from; troubled by ③ carry out; cause...to happen
〖闹别扭〗[nào bièniu]
be at odds
〖闹病〗[nào bìng]
be ill
〖闹肚子〗[nào dùzi]
suffer from diarrhoea
〖闹革命〗[nào gémìng]
make revolution
〖闹哄哄〗(形)[nàohōnghōng]
noisy; boisterous
〖闹脾气〗[nào píqi]
show ill temper; lose temper
〖闹情绪〗[nào qíngxù]
ill-tempered
〖闹市〗(名)[nàoshì]
downtown area; busy streets
〖闹事〗[nào shì]
cause trouble; create disturbances
〖闹腾〗(动)[nàoteng]
① create trouble; create disturbances ② kick up a fuss
〖闹意见〗[nào yìjiàn]
quarrel dispute
〖闹着玩儿〗[nàozhewánr]
do sth. for the fun of it
〖闹钟〗(名)[nàozhōng]
alarm clock

ne

呢(助)[ne]
modal particle
另见 ní

nèi

内(名)[nèi]
inner part; inside
〖内部〗(名)[nèibù]

N

internal parts; within; inner
〖内海〗(名)[nèihǎi]
inland sea
〖内涵〗(名)[nèihán]
intension; connotation
〖内行〗(形、名)[nèiháng]
one who knows how; in one's element; one who knows the ropes
〖内河〗(名)[nèihé]
inland waterway; inland river
〖内讧〗(名)[nèihòng]
internal dissension; internal conflicts; internal troubles
〖内奸〗(名)[nèijiān]
hidden traitor
〖内角〗(名)[nèijiǎo]
an interior angle
〖内疚〗(形)[nèijiù]
prickings of conscience; self-reproach
〖内科〗(名)[nèikē]
medical department
〖内联外引〗[nèiliánwàiyǐn]
introduce investment from abroad and establish lateral ties at home
〖内幕〗(名)[nèimù]
inside story
〖内切〗(动)[nèiqiē]
be tangent internally
〖内勤〗(名)[nèiqín]
office personnel (e.g. mil.)
〖内情〗(名)[nèiqíng]
inside information (of story); affairs not known to the outside world
〖内燃机〗(名)[nèiránjī]
diesel engine
〖内燃机车〗[nèirán jīchē]
diesel locomotive
〖内容〗(名)[nèiróng]
content (of a book, etc.); substance
〖内外交困〗[nèiwàijiāokùn]
beset with difficulties both at home and abroad
〖内线〗(名)[nèixiàn]
① interiorlines ② extension line (e.g.telephone)
〖内项〗(名)[nèixiàng]
inner term
〖内销〗(动)[nèixiāo]
sell in the home market (of homemade goods)
〖内心〗(名)[nèixīn]
inner being; in one's heart of hearts
〖内衣〗(名)[nèiyī]〔件 jiàn〕
underwear
〖内因〗(名)[nèiyīn]
internal cause
〖内应〗(名)[nèiyìng]
uprising from inside; support from inside
〖内在〗(形)[nèizài]
inside; internal; inner
〖内脏〗(名)[nèizàng]
internal organs of the body
〖内债〗(名)[nèizhài]〔笔 bǐ〕
goverment bonds
〖内战〗(名)[nèizhàn]
civil war
〖内政〗(名)[nèizhèng]
internal affairs

nèn

嫩(形)[nèn]
tender; soft
〖嫩黄〗(形)[nènhuáng]
light yellow
〖嫩绿〗(形)[nènlǜ]
light green

néng

能(助动)[néng]
can; be able to
〖能动〗(形)[néngdòng]
conscious activity; active
〖能干〗(形)[nénggàn]
able; capable
〖能够〗(助动)[nénggòu]
can; be able to
〖能官能民〗[néngguānnéngmín]
can be either an official or common people
〖能力〗(名)[nénglì]
ability; capability
〖能量〗(名)[néngliàng]
capacity; energy (e. g. atomic energy)
〖能耐〗(名)[néngnai]
capability; ableness
〖能上能下〗[néngshàngnéngxià]
able to work both at the top and down below; (of cadres) who can work at both higher or lower levels
〖能手〗(名)[néngshǒu]
expert; a good hand at...
〖能文能武〗[néngwénnéngwǔ]
skilled both in literary talents and military arts; able to do both mental and manual labour
〖能源〗(名)[néngyuán]
energy sources

ní

尼[ní]
〖尼龙〗(名)[nílóng]
nylon

呢(名)[ní]
a kind of woolen fabric
另见 ne
〖呢绒〗(名)[níróng]
woolen textiles
〖呢子〗(名)[nízi]
a kind of woolen fabric

泥(名)[ní]
mud
〖泥巴〗(名)[níbā]
mud; muck; mire
〖泥浆〗(名)[níjiāng]
mud
〖泥坑〗(名)[níkēng]
quagmire; swamp
〖泥塑〗(名)[nísù]
clay figure modelling
〖泥潭〗(名)[nítán]
swamp; quagmire
〖泥土〗(名)[nítǔ]
mud and soil

霓[ní]
〖霓虹灯〗(名)[níhóngdēng]
neon light

nǐ

拟(动)[nǐ]

draft; fix
〖拟订〗(动)[nǐdìng]
draw up; work out; map out

你(代)[nǐ]
you
〖你们〗(代)[nǐmen]
you (pl.)
〖你死我活〗[nǐsǐwǒhuó]
life-and-death (e.g. struggle)

nì

逆(动)[nì]
go against; be contrary to; adverse
〖逆差〗(名)[nìchā]
deficit; unfavorable balance; adverse balance
〖逆耳〗(形)[nì'ěr]
unpleasant to hear
〖逆风〗[nì fēng]
contrary wind; adverse wind
〖逆流〗(名)[nìliú]
adverse current; counter-current
〖逆时针方向〗
[nìshízhēnfāngxiàng]
anti-clockwise
〖逆水行舟〗[nìshuǐxíngzhōu]
sail against the current; sail in the head tide

匿(动)[nì]
hide; conceal
〖匿名〗[nìmíng]
anonymous

腻(形)[nì]
tired of; sick of
〖腻烦〗(形)[nìfan]
boring; annoying; tiresome

溺[nì]
〖溺爱〗(动)[nì'ài]
spoil (e.g. child)

niān

拈(动)[niān]
take; pick up (with two or three fingers)
〖拈轻怕重〗[niānqīngpàzhòng]
prefer the light and shirk the heavy

nián

年(名)[nián]
①year ②person's age
〖年成〗(名)[niáncheng]
the result of a year's harvest
〖年初〗(名)[niánchū]
the beginning of a year
〖年代〗(名)[niándài]
years
〖年底〗(名)[niándǐ]
the end of a year
〖年度〗(名)[niándù]
annual; yearly
〖年份〗(名)[niánfèn]
①a particular year ②age; vintage
〖年糕〗(名)[niángāo]〔块 kuài〕
New Year cake made of glutinous rice flour
〖年画〗(名)[niánhuà]〔张 zhāng〕

new year pictures; new year paintings

〖年级〗(名)[niánjí]
grade or class in a school

〖年纪〗(名)[niánjì]
person's age

〖年景〗(名)[niánjǐng]
harvest condition

〖年龄〗(名)[niánlíng]
age (e.g. person, plant)

〖年迈〗(形)[niánmài] advanced in age; old-aged

〖年轻〗(形)[niánqīng]
young

〖年头〗(名)[niántóu]
① condition of the times ② the result of the harvest

〖年限〗(名)[niánxiàn]
a fixed number of years

〖年夜饭〗(名)[niányèfàn]
family reunion meal on the eve of the lunar New Year

〖年月〗(名)[niányuè]
condition of the times; years

〖年终〗(名)[niánzhōng]
the end of a year

粘(形)[nián]
glutinous; gluey; sticky
另见 zhān

〖粘土〗(名)[niántǔ]
clay

niǎn

捻(动)[niǎn]
twist something with fingers

撵(动)[niǎn]
① drive away ② pursue

碾(动)[niǎn]
grind crush; pound; polish or husk

〖碾子〗(名)[niǎnzi]
a mill for husking grain or rice

niàn

念(动)[niàn]
① long; yearn ② read; study

〖念叨〗(动)[niàndao]
harp on sth; grumble

〖念念不忘〗[niànniànbùwàng]
bear in mind constantly; cling to

〖念书〗[niàn shū]
study or read; study in school; receive an education

〖念头〗(名)[niàntou]
idea; thought; notion

niáng

娘(名)[niáng]
mother

〖娘家〗(名)[niángjia]
a married woman's maiden home

〖娘子军〗(名)[niángzǐjūn]
women's detachment

niàng

酿(动)[niàng]
cause something to mature gradually

〖酿酒〗[niàng jiǔ]
distil wine

N

〖酿造〗(动)[niàngzào]
make by fermentation

niǎo

鸟(名)[niǎo]〔只 zhī〕
birds
〖鸟瞰〗(动、名)[niǎokàn]
look down from above; bird's-eye-view
〖鸟枪〗(名)[niǎoqiāng]〔枝 zhī〕
gun used for killing birds; air-rifle; shot-gun

袅[niǎo]
〖袅袅〗(形)[niǎoniǎo]
curling upward; delicate and graceful

niào

尿(名、动)[niào]
urine; pass water
〖尿素〗(名)[niàosù]
urinate; urea

niē

捏(动)[niē]
pinch; knead with the fingers
〖捏一把汗〗[niē yì bǎ hàn]
be seized with fear or deep concern
〖捏造〗(动)[niēzào]
fabricate; trump up; make up; concoct

nín

您(代)[nín]
(polite form of address) you (second person singular)

níng

宁[níng]
另见 nìng
〖宁静〗(形)[níngjìng]
tranquil

拧(动)[níng]
①wring ②pinch
另见 nǐng

狞[níng]
〖狞笑〗(动)[níngxiào]
smile hideously and hypocritically

柠[níng]
〖柠檬〗(名)[níngméng]
lemon

凝(动)[níng]
① congeal; freeze; solidify ② fix (e.g. attention)
〖凝成〗(动)[níngchéng]
solidify
〖凝固〗(动)[nínggù]
solidify; coagulate
〖凝固点〗(名)[nínggùdiǎn]
freezing point; solidification point
〖凝结〗(动)[níngjié]
① condense ② stalemate; cement
〖凝聚〗(动)[níngjù]
coagulate; solidity; cohesion
〖凝聚力〗(名)[níngjùlì]

rallying force; cohesive force
〖凝神〗(形)[níngshén]
fully concentrating
〖凝视〗(动)[níngshì]
stare at; look intently
〖凝思〗(动)[níngsī]
meditate; be buried in thought
〖凝滞〗(动)[níngzhì]
slow-moving;not flowing freely; blocked up

nǐng

拧(动)[nǐng]
wrench; twist; pull violently
另见 níng

nìng

宁[nìng]
另见 níng
〖宁可〗(连)[nìngkě]
would rather; have rather; prefer... to...
〖宁缺毋滥〗[nìngquēwùlàn]
would rather leave the post vacant than have it filled by anybody unqualified for it; would rather go without than make do with anything not up to the mark
〖宁死不屈〗[nìngsǐbùqū]
rather die than submit or surrender
〖宁愿〗(连)[nìngyuàn]
would rather; prefer

niú

牛(名)[niú]〔头 tóu〕
cattle
〖牛痘〗(名)[niúdòu]
vaccine; vaccination
〖牛犊〗(名)[niúdú]
a calf
〖牛劲〗(名)[niújìn]
① as strong as an ox ② the temperament of an ox-stubborness
〖牛奶〗(名)[niúnǎi]
cow's milk
〖牛皮〗(名)[niúpí]
ox hide; leather
〖牛脾气〗(名)[niúpíqi]
the temperament of an ox-stubborness
〖牛肉〗(名)[niúròu]
beef
〖牛市〗(名)[niúshì]
bull market (referring to the rise of prices at the stock market)

niǔ

扭(动)[niǔ]
twist; wrench; turn round
〖扭亏为盈〗[niǔkuīwéiyíng]
turn loss into gain; go from loss-incurring to profit-making
〖扭捏〗(形)[niǔnie]
bashful
〖扭转〗(动)[niǔzhuǎn]
reverse;turn back (e.g.the tide);divert;head...away from...

忸[niǔ]
〖忸怩〗(形)[niǔní]
bashful

N

纽[niǔ]
〖纽带〗(名)[niǔdài]
ties (e.g.ties of friendship)
〖纽扣〗(名)[niǔkòu]〔个 gè〕
button

niù

拗(动、形)[niù]
cause to change; stubborn
另见 ào
〖拗不过〗[niù bu guò]
cannot persuade one to give up (e.g. his stubborness)

nóng

农(名)[nóng]
farming
〖农产品〗(名)[nóngchǎnpǐn]
farm products
〖农场〗(名)[nóngchǎng]
farm
〖农村〗(名)[nóngcūn]
countryside; rural district
〖农会〗(名)[nónghuì]
peasants' association
〖农活〗(名)[nónghuó]
farm work
〖农具〗(名)[nóngjù]
farm implements
〖农林牧副渔全面发展〗[nóng línmùfùyúquánmiànfāzhǎn]
over-all development of farming, forestry, animal husbandry, side occupations and fishery
〖农忙〗[nóng máng]
busy farming season
〖农民〗(名)[nóngmín]
peasants
〖农民起义〗[nóngmín qǐyì]
peasant uprising
〖农民战争〗[nóngmínzhànzhēng]
peasant warfare
〖农奴〗(名)[nóngnú]
serfs
〖农奴主〗(名)[nóngnúzhǔ]
serf owner
〖农田〗(名)[nóngtián]
farm land
〖农田基本建设〗[nóngtián jīběn jiànshè]
capital construction on the farms
〖农田水利〗[nóngtián shuǐlì]
water conservancy
〖农闲〗[nóng xián]
slack farming season
〖农谚〗(名)[nóngyàn]
proverbs relating to farming
〖农药〗(名)[nóngyào]
insecticide
〖农业〗(名)[nóngyè]
agriculture; farming
〖农事〗(名)[nóngshì]
farm work; farming
〖农时〗(名)[nóngshí]
farming season
〖农渠〗(名)[nóngqú]
field ditch
〖农业技术〗[nóngyè jìshù]
agricultural technology; agrotechnique
〖农艺师〗(名)[nóngyìshī]

agronomist

〖农业合作化〗[nóngyèhézuòhuà]

movement for agricultural co-operation

〖农转非〗[nóngzhuǎnfēi]

change from having rural residence registration to city or town residence registration

〖农作物〗(名)[nóngzuòwù]

the agricultural produce (crop, plant, fruit, etc.)

浓(形)[nóng]

thick; heavy; dense

〖浓度〗(名)[nóngdù]

density of concentration

〖浓厚〗(形)[nónghòu]

① thick and heavy ② deep (e.g. emotion)

〖浓眉〗(名)[nóngméi]

thick eyebrows

〖浓密〗(形)[nóngmì]

dense

〖浓缩〗(动)[nóngsuō]

condense

〖浓郁〗(形)[nóngyù]

rich and fragrant

〖浓重〗(形)[nóngzhòng]

thick and heavy

脓(名)[nóng]

pus

〖脓肿〗(名)[nóngzhǒng]

abscess

nòng

弄(动)[nòng]

① play with ② make; do ③ obtain; acquire; secure

〖弄假成真〗[nòngjiǎchéngzhēn]

pretence has become reality; say in fun what is fulfilled in earnest

〖弄巧成拙〗[nòngqiǎochéngzhuō]

try to be clever but turn out the contrary; cunning outwits itself

〖弄虚作假〗[nòngxūzuòjiǎ]

resort to deception

nú

奴[nú]

〖奴才〗(名)[núcai]

vassal; stooge; flunkey

〖奴化〗(动)[núhuà]

enslave

〖奴隶〗(名)[núlì]

slave

〖奴隶社会〗[núlì shèhuì]

slave society

〖奴隶主〗(名)[núlìzhǔ]

slave-owner

〖奴隶主义〗(名)[núlìzhǔyì]

slavishness; servility

〖奴仆〗(名)[núpú]

servant

〖奴颜婢膝〗[núyánbìxī]

bend one's knees before...; servility; subservience

〖奴颜媚骨〗[núyánmèigǔ]

servile; flattery; sycophancy

〖奴役〗(动)[núyì]

enslave; bondage

N

nǔ

努[nǔ]

〖努力〗(动、形)[nǔlì]
exert; strive; endeavour; make great effort; energetic

nù

怒[nù]

〖怒不可遏〗[nùbùkě'è]
anger knows no bounds

〖怒潮〗(名)[nùcháo]
angry waves; raging tide

〖怒冲冲〗(形)[nùchōngchōng]
in a great rage

〖怒发冲冠〗[nùfàchōngguān]
he was so angry that his hair stood on end

〖怒吼〗(动)[nùhǒu]
roar aloud; howl; bellow

〖怒火〗(名)[nùhuǒ]
anger; rage; fury

〖怒目而视〗[nùmù'érshì]
glare; angry look; stare at with angry eyes

〖怒气〗(名)[nùqì]
anger; fury; wrath

〖怒视〗(动)[nùshì]
look at with angry eyes

〖怒涛〗(名)[nùtāo]
angry waves

nǚ

女(名)[nǚ]
female

〖女儿〗(名)[nǚ'ér]
daughter; girl

〖女工〗(名)[nǚgōng]
women workers

〖女强人〗(名)[nǚqiángrén]
woman of exceptional talent and ability

〖女人〗(名)[nǚrén]
woman

〖女声〗(名)[nǚshēng]
woman's (solo); women's (chorus)

〖女士〗(名)[nǚshì]
lady; miss

〖女性〗(名)[nǚxìng]
the female

〖女婿〗(名)[nǚxu]
son-in-law

〖女子〗(名)[nǚzǐ]
a girl or woman

nuǎn

暖(形)[nuǎn]
warm

〖暖烘烘〗(形)[nuǎnhōnghōng]
comfortably warm

〖暖壶〗(名)[nuǎnhú]〔个 gè〕
thermos bottle

〖暖和〗(形)[nuǎnhuo]
warm

〖暖流〗(名)[nuǎnliú]
warm current

〖暖瓶〗(名)[nuǎnpíng]〔个 gè〕
thermos bottle

〖暖气〗(名)[nuǎnqì]
① warmth; heat ② central heating

nüè

疟[nüè]

〖疟疾〗(名)[nüèji]
malaria

虐[nüè]
〖虐待〗(动)[nüèdài]
ill-treat; maltreatment

nuó

挪(动)[nuó]
move; remove
〖挪动〗(动)[nuódòng]
move; remove
〖挪用〗(动)[nuóyòng]
embezzle

nuò

诺[nuò]
〖诺言〗(名)[nuòyán]
promise

懦[nuò]
〖懦夫〗(名)[nuòfū]
coward
〖懦弱〗(形)[nuòruò]
weak (e.g. in character)

糯[nuò]
〖糯米〗(名)[nuòmǐ]
glutinous rice

O

ò

哦(叹)[ò]
(*int.*), Oh!

ōu

欧[ōu]
〖欧姆〗(量)[ōumǔ]
a measure word, ohm
〖欧洲〗(名)[ōuzhōu]
Europe

殴[ōu]
〖殴打〗(动)[ōudǎ]
① beat up ② fight with fists

ǒu

呕[ǒu]
〖呕吐〗(动)[ǒutù]
vomit
〖呕心沥血〗[ǒuxīnlìxuè]
make painstaking efforts

偶[ǒu]
〖偶尔〗(副)[ǒu'ěr]
occasionally; not habitually
〖偶然〗(形)[ǒurán]
occasional; casual; accidental
〖偶然性〗(名)[ǒuránxìng]
by chance or coincidence
〖偶数〗(名)[ǒushù]
even number
〖偶像〗(名)[ǒuxiàng]
an idol (superstitious image)

藕(名)[ǒu]
lotus roots
〖藕断丝连〗[ǒuduànsīlián]
(lit.) a section of arrowroot is separated, but the clinging fibre remains; (fig.) relations not entirely severed
〖藕粉〗(名)[ǒufěn]
arrowroot powder

P

pā

趴(动)[pā]
lie on one's face; crouch down

pá

扒(动)[pá]
① scratch ② rake (together); harrow (up)
另见 bā
〖扒手〗(名)[páshǒu]
pickpocket

爬(动)[pá]
crawl; climb
〖爬虫〗(名)[páchóng]
reptiles
〖爬格子〗[págézi]
take up writing as a career
〖爬行动物〗[páxíng dòngwù]
reptiles
〖爬行主义〗(名)[páxíngzhǔyì]
the doctrine of trailing behind at a snail's pace

耙(名)[pá]〔把 bǎ〕
a rake; a harrow

pà

怕(动、副)[pà]
fear; be frightened; fear of; afraid of
〖怕人〗(形)[pàrén]
① shy ② terrifying
〖怕羞〗[pà xiū]
bashful; shy

pāi

拍(动、名)[pāi]
① beat; clap; tap lightly ② take (a photo) ③ send (a telegram) ④ (of music) a beat
〖拍板〗(动)[pāibǎn]
have the final say; have the last word
〖拍卖〗(动)[pāimài]
auction off sth.; sell sth. by an auction

〖拍摄〗(动)[pāishè]
take photo; photograph
〖拍手〗[pāi shǒu]
clap hands
〖拍手称快〗
[pāishǒuchēngkuài]
clap hands to express one's satisfaction; gleefully hail
〖拍照〗(动)[pāizhào]
have photograph taken
〖拍子〗(名)[pāizi]〔个 gè、副 fù〕
① bat or racquet ② baton (music) ③ (fly) swatter

pái

排(动、名、量)[pái]
① drain (off, away) ② row ③ (mil.) platoon ④ a measure word (a volley of shots, row of house, etc.)
〖排版〗[pái bǎn]
compose type
〖排比〗(名)[páibǐ]
the toric (parallel construction or form)
〖排场〗(名)[páichǎng]
display of splendour; impressive sights (e.g. gatherings)
〖排斥〗(动)[páichì]
shut out; exclude; eject; discriminate against
〖排除〗(动)[páichú]
① exclude; dispel ② overcome; surmount
〖排队〗[pái duì]
① line up; queue up ② classify; list
〖排骨〗(名)[páigǔ]
pork ribs
〖排灌〗(动)[páiguàn]
drain and irrigate
〖排挤〗(动)[páijǐ]
squeeze out; edge out; exclude; push out
〖排涝〗[pái lào]
drain waterlogged farmland
〖排练〗(动)[páiliàn]
rehearse
〖排列〗(动)[páiliè]
arrange in order; rank; place
〖排球〗(名)[páiqiú]〔个 gè〕
① volley-ball (game) ② volley-ball
〖排山倒海〗[páishāndǎohǎi]
(lit.) topple mountains and drain seas; (fig.) sweeping world with the momentum of an avalanche; mighty; tremendous; irresistible
〖排外〗[pái wài]
① anti-foreign ② sectarian-tendencies in external relations leading to exclusiveness towards people out side the group or clique
〖排泄〗(动)[páixiè]
excrete; let off
〖排演〗(动)[páiyǎn]
rehearse
〖排印〗(动)[páiyìn]
set up and print from type
〖排长〗(名)[páizhǎng]
platoon leader
〖排字〗[pái zì]
set up type

徘[pái]
〖徘徊〗(动)[páihuái]
①hover; linger ②hesitate

牌(名)[pái]
①tablet; signboard ②playing cards
〖牌价〗(名)[páijià]
fixed price; market quotation; market price
〖牌照〗(名)[páizhào]
license
〖牌子〗(名)[páizi]
brand; label; trademark

pài

派(动、名、量)[pài]
①dispatch; send (e.g. someone on mission) ②school of thought; groups of beliefs ③a measure word (for faction, school, etc.)
〖派别〗(名)[pàibié]
(of thought or beliefs) categories; schools; clique; faction
〖派出所〗(名)[pàichūsuǒ]
local police station
〖派遣〗(动)[pàiqiǎn]
send someone on mission; dispatch
〖派生〗(动)[pàishēng]
derive from; derivative
〖派系〗(名)[pàixì]
clique; faction

pān

攀(动)[pān]
climb
〖攀比〗(动)[pānbǐ]
compete with others to see who is superior; keep up with the Joneses
〖攀登〗(动)[pāndēng]
climb up; scale
〖攀折〗(动)[pānzhé]
break (branches)

pán

盘(名、动、量)[pán]
①a tray; dish; plate ②investigate ③ circle around; twist about ④ a measure word, plate (e.g. a plate of...)
〖盘剥〗(动)[pánbō]
exploit; usurious
〖盘查〗(动)[pánchá]
examine thoroughly; interrogate
〖盘点〗(动)[pándiǎn]
make an inventory; take stock
〖盘根错节〗[pángēncuòjié]
(lit.) (of trees) with twisting roots and intercrossing branches; (fig.) (of conditions) complex and difficult; entangled
〖盘货〗[pán huò]
take stock; stock-taking
〖盘踞〗(动)[pánjù]
occupy; entrench
〖盘算〗(动)[pánsuàn]
calculate; premeditate
〖盘问〗(动)[pánwèn]
interrogate; question
〖盘旋〗(动)[pánxuán]

①circle around ②linger; tarry
〖盘子〗(名)[pánzi]〔个 gè〕
plate; saucer

磐 [pán]
〖磐石〗(名)[pánshí]
monolith; rock

P

pàn

判 (动)[pàn]
①judge; make a decision ② evaluate; appraise ③ differentiate; distinguish
〖判断〗(动、名)[pànduàn]
judge; determine; assertain; judgement
〖判决〗(动)[pànjué]
bring in a verdict; judgement; verdict
〖判刑〗[pàn xíng]
pass sentence; sentence (person)

盼 (动)[pàn]
hope; long for; look forward to
〖盼头〗(名)[pàntou]
hope; prospect
〖盼望〗(动)[pànwàng]
hope; yearn for; long for

叛 (动)[pàn]
betray
〖叛变〗(动)[pànbiàn]
betray; turn traitor
〖叛国〗[pàn guó]
turn traitor to one's country
〖叛乱〗(动)[pànluàn]
revolt; rebel; mutiny
〖叛卖〗(动)[pànmài]
commit acts of treachery; betray
〖叛逆〗(名)[pànnì]
treason; betrayal; rebel
〖叛徒〗(名)[pàntú]
traitor; renegade

畔 (名)[pàn]
boundary; side (e. g. roadside); bank (of lake or river)

pāng

滂 [pāng]
〖滂沱〗(形)[pāngtuó]
torrential; pouring

páng

彷 [páng]
〖彷徨〗(动)[pánghuáng]
hesitate; uncertain

庞 [páng]
〖庞大〗(形)[pángdà]
colossal; huge; massive
〖庞然大物〗[pángrándàwù]
① colossus, formidable giant ② huge monster
〖庞杂〗(形)[pángzá]
disorderly and motley

旁 (名)[páng]
side
〖旁边〗(名)[pángbiān]
nearby position; right by

〖旁观〗(动)[pángguān]
observe from the sidelines; look on with folded arms
〖旁观者清〗[pángguānzhěqīng]
the on looker is always clear-minded; an onlooker sees clearly; an onlooker sees most
〖旁门〗(名)[pángmén]
sidegate
〖旁敲侧击〗[pángqiāocèjī]
beat about the bush; attack by innuendo
〖旁人〗(代)[pángrén]
others
〖旁若无人〗[pángruòwúrén]
(lit.)as if no one was nearby; (fig.) ①expressions of pride, haughtiness; overweening ② behave in a natural way
〖旁听〗(动)[pángtīng]
①attend (a lecture) in the capacity of an associate student ②be present (at a conference) as an observer
〖旁听生〗(名)[pángtīngshēng]
auditor
〖旁证〗(名)[pángzhèng]
circumstantial evidence; side witness

膀[páng]
〖膀胱〗(名)[pángguāng]
bladder

磅[páng]
另见 bàng
〖磅礴〗(形)[pángbó]
overwhelming; grand; majestic

螃[páng]
〖螃蟹〗(名)[pángxiè]〔只 zhī〕
crab

pàng

胖(形)[pàng]
fat; plump
〖胖乎乎〗(形)[pànghūhū]
plump
〖胖子〗(名)[pàngzi]
fatty; a fat person

pāo

抛(动)[pāo]
throw; cast; fling
〖抛锚〗[pāo máo]
cast anchor; (of cars) get stuck midway
〖抛弃〗(动)[pāoqì]
throw away; abandon; discard; get rid of
〖抛售〗(动)[pāoshòu]
undersell; dump; sell at low prices
〖抛物线〗(名)[pāowùxiàn]
parabola
〖抛砖引玉〗[pāozhuānyǐnyù]
cast away a brick and attract a jadestone; throw a sprat to catch a whale

páo

刨(动)[páo]
dig
另见 bào

P

P

咆[páo]
〖咆哮〗(动)[páoxiào]
rage and roar (e. g. like a lion)

炮[páo]
另见 pào
〖炮制〗(动)[páozhì]
dish up; cook up

pǎo

跑(动)[pǎo]
run
〖跑步〗[pǎo bù]
run; jogging
〖跑道〗(名)[pǎodào]〔条 tiáo〕
①athletic track ②runway
〖跑龙套〗[pǎo lóngtào]
utility man; general handiman
〖跑腿儿〗[pǎo tuǐr]
footman; messenger; run an errand

pào

泡(名、动)[pào]
① blister ② bulb ③ bubble ④ soak; steep
〖泡沫〗(名)[pàomò]
foam; froth
〖泡沫塑料〗[pàomò sùliào]
foam plastics
〖泡影〗(名)[pàoyǐng]
①bubble ②an illusion

炮(名)[pào]
①firecrackers ②artillery
另见 páo
〖炮兵〗(名)[pàobīng]
an artilleryman; artillery
〖炮弹〗(名)[pàodàn]〔发 fā〕
shell
〖炮灰〗(名)[pàohuī]
cannon fodder
〖炮火〗(名)[pàohuǒ]
gunfire
〖炮楼〗(名)[pàolóu]〔座 zuò〕
gun turret
〖炮声〗(名)[pàoshēng]
the sound of artillery

pēi

胚[pēi]
〖胚胎〗(名)[pēitāi]
embryo

péi

陪(动)[péi]
accompany; keep company with
〖陪伴〗(动)[péibàn]
keep company with
〖陪衬〗(名、动)[péichèn]
contrast; serve as a contrast
〖陪同〗(动)[péitóng]
accompany; keep company with

培(动)[péi]
bring up; cultivate
〖培训〗(动)[péixùn]
train; cultivate
〖培养〗(动)[péiyǎng]
bring up; foster; cultivate
〖培育〗(动)[péiyù]
grow; breed; bring up
〖培植〗(动)[péizhí]

cultivate; foster

赔(动)[péi]
①compensate②suffer a loss
〖赔本〗[péi běn]
run at a loss
〖赔偿〗(动)[péicháng]
compensate; make compensation
〖赔款〗[péi kuǎn]
pay indemnity
〖赔款〗(名)[péikuǎn]
indemnities
〖赔礼〗[péi lǐ]
apologize
〖赔罪〗[péi zuì]
apologize; make an apology

pèi

佩[pèi]
〖佩带〗(动)[pèidài]
carry; wear
〖佩服〗(动)[pèifú]
admire; have a high opinion of (sb.)

配(动)[pèi]
①breed; artificial insemination②compose; blend; arrange; match③be worthy; deserve
〖配备〗(动)[pèibèi]
furnish with; equip
〖配搭〗(动)[pèidā]
①adjust; arrange②supplement; add to
〖配电〗[pèi diàn]
lay on electricity
〖配额〗(名)[pèi'é]
quota
〖配合〗(动)[pèihé]
coordinate; be in harmony with
〖配给〗(动)[pèijǐ]
ration out; put on rations
〖配件〗(名)[pèijiàn]
accessories; parts
〖配角儿〗(名)[pèijuér]
minor roles; supporting actors
〖配套〗[pèi tào]
serialize
〖配音〗[pèi yīn]
dubbing (e.g. motion picture)
〖配种〗[pèi zhǒng]
breeding

pēn

喷(动)[pēn]
spray; sprinkle; spit out
〖喷薄〗(形)[pēnbó]
gush forth
〖喷壶〗(名)[pēnhú]〔把 bǎ〕
sprinkler
〖喷漆〗[pēn qī]
spray-paint
〖喷气发动机〗[pēnqì fādòngjī]
jet engine
〖喷气式飞机〗[pēnqìshì fēijī]
〔架 jià〕jet-plane
〖喷泉〗(名)[pēnquán]
fountain
〖喷洒〗(动)[pēnsǎ]
spray; sprinkle
〖喷射〗(动)[pēnshè]
jet
〖喷嚏〗(名)[pēntì]
sneeze

P

〖喷雾器〗(名)[pēnwùqì]
sprayer

pén

盆(名)[pén]
basin
〖盆地〗(名)[péndì]
(geog.) basin

P

pēng

抨[pēng]
〖抨击〗(动)[pēngjī]
flay; attack vigorously; censure

烹(动)[pēng]
cook; cuisine
〖烹调〗(动)[pēngtiáo]
cooking; cuisine

澎[pēng]
〖澎湃〗(形)[pēngpài]
surging; rising (tide)

péng

朋[péng]
〖朋友〗(名)[péngyou]
friend

棚(名)[péng]
shed
〖棚子〗(名)[péngzi]
shed

蓬[péng]
〖蓬勃〗(形)[péngbó]
vigorous; surging; going full steam ahead
〖蓬松〗(形)[péngsōng]
fluffy

膨[péng]
〖膨胀〗(动)[péngzhàng]
inflate; swell; expand
〖膨胀系数〗[péngzhàng xìshù]
coefficient of expansion

pěng

捧(动、量)[pěng]
① hold up with both hands ② applaud in public ③ a measure word (for sth. which can be held in both hands, e.g. a handful of peanuts)
〖捧场〗[pěng chǎng]
lavish praise on; flatter; sing praise to
〖捧腹大笑〗[pěngfùdàxiào]
split one's sides with laughter

pèng

碰(动)[pèng]
① knock against; collide ② encounter; meet ③ have a try at it
〖碰杯〗[pèng bēi]
clink glasses with
〖碰壁〗[pèng bì]
run one's head against a stone wall; meet with a rebuff
〖碰钉子〗[pèng dīngzi]
receive serious rebuff; run into snags
〖碰见〗(动)[pèngjiàn]

run into; chance upon; meet
〖碰巧〗(副)[pèngqiǎo]
coincidentally
〖碰头〗[pèng tóu]
meet to (discuss sth.); put (our) heads together

pī

批(动、量)[pī]
①criticize; comment ②slap ③a measure word (batch, lot, group, etc.)
〖批驳〗(动)[pībó]
refute; rebut
〖批发〗(动)[pīfā]
wholesale
〖批改〗(动)[pīgǎi]
correct
〖批号〗(名)[pīhào]
lot number; batch number
〖批量〗[pīliàng]
batch, lot
〖批判〗(动、名)[pīpàn]
criticize; repudiate; criticism; repudiation
〖批评〗(动、名)[pīpíng]
criticize; criticism
〖批示〗(动、名)[pīshì]
write an official comment; official comments
〖批语〗(名)[pīyǔ]
comments
〖批阅〗(动)[pīyuè]
read or see official documents with remarks
〖批注〗(动、名)[pīzhù]
annotate with comments; annotation
〖批准〗(动)[pīzhǔn]
sanction; endorse; approve

披(动)[pī]
①wear ②split; crack
〖披荆斩棘〗[pījīngzhǎnjí]
open a way by breaking through bramble and thistle; clear away obstacles in one's way; blaze one's way through all the difficulties
〖披露〗(动)[pīlù]
①announce; publish ②disclose
〖披星戴月〗[pīxīngdàiyuè]
(of work or travel) get up by starlight, but not knock off (work) till the moon rises; start early in the morning and continue till late at night

砒[pī]
〖砒霜〗(名)[pīshuāng]
arsenic

劈(动)[pī]
① split; slice; chop into pieces ② scold to one's face ③ (blow) direct in the face
另见 pǐ
〖劈山造田〗[pī shān zào tián]
level mountains to make fields
〖劈头盖脸〗[pītóugàiliǎn]
① right in the face ② shower down

霹[pī]

〖霹雳〗(名)[pīlì]
descriptive of crashing thunder; lightning flash

pí

皮(名)[pí]
skin; hide; fur; leather
〖皮袄〗(名)[pí'ǎo]〔件 jiàn〕
leather jacket
〖皮包〗(名)[píbāo]〔个 gè〕
leather bag
〖皮包公司〗[píbāogōngsī]
paper company; dummy corporation
〖皮带〗(名)[pídài]〔条 tiáo〕
leather belt; leather girdle
〖皮肤〗(名)[pífū]
skin
〖皮革〗(名)[pígé]
hides; leather
〖皮货〗(名)[píhuò]
hide; fur goods
〖皮科〗(名)[píkē]
department of skin diseases
〖皮毛〗(名)[pímáo]
①hide; leather; fur ②superficiality
〖皮棉〗(名)[pímián]
ginned cotton
〖皮球〗(名)[píqiú]〔个 gè〕
(leather) ball
〖皮鞋〗(名)[píxié]〔双 shuāng〕
leather shoes
〖皮子〗(名)[pízi]
hide; leather; fur

毗[pí]
〖毗连〗(动)[pílián]
adjoin; be adjacent
〖毗邻〗(动)[pílín]
adjoin (of neighbours); neighbouring

疲[pí]
〖疲惫〗(形)[píbèi]
tired; weary
〖疲乏〗(形)[pífá]
exhausted; worn out
〖疲倦〗(形)[píjuàn]
weary; fatigued
〖疲劳〗(形)[píláo]
fatigued; tired; weary
〖疲软〗(形)[píruǎn]
weak; sluggish; bearish
〖疲塌〗(形)[píta]
inertia
〖疲于奔命〗[píyúbēnmìng]
be kept constantly on the run; be fully occupied

啤[pí]
〖啤酒〗(名)[píjiǔ]
〔杯 bēi、瓶 píng〕beer

琵[pí]
〖琵琶〗(名)[pípá]
pipa, Chinese lute

脾(名)[pí]
spleen
〖脾气〗(名)[píqi]
temperament; temper

pǐ

匹(量)[pǐ]

a measure word (bale of cloth, horse, etc.)
〖匹敌〗(动)[pǐdí]
match; equal in force

痞[pǐ]
〖痞子〗(名)[pǐzi]
riffraff

劈(动)[pǐ]
split
另见 pī
〖劈柴〗(名)[pǐchái]
splitting firewood

癖[pǐ]
〖癖好〗(名)[pǐhào]
take special liking to (sth.); special or favourite hobby

pì

屁(名)[pì]
wind (from bowels); fart
〖屁股〗(名)[pìgu]
the buttocks

辟(动)[pì]
① create; pave ② refute (e. g. rumour)
〖辟谣〗[pì yáo]
deny a rumour; refute slanders

媲[pì]
〖媲美〗(动)[pìměi]
be on a par with; compare favourably with

僻[pì]
〖僻静〗(形)[pìjìng]
quiet and out-of-the-way

譬[pì]
〖譬如〗(动)[pìrú]
take for example

P

piān

偏(形、副)[piān]
slanting; be inclined to; be partial to
〖偏爱〗(动)[piān'ài]
be partial to; favour
〖偏差〗(名)[piānchā]
deviation; errors
〖偏方〗(名)[piānfāng]
local folk prescription
〖偏废〗(动)[piānfèi]
over-emphasize one thing to the neglect of the other
〖偏激〗(形)[piānjī]
go to extremes
〖偏见〗(名)[piānjiàn]
prejudice; bias
〖偏旁〗(名)[piānpáng]
the right and left parts of a character
〖偏僻〗(形)[piānpì]
out-of-the-way
〖偏偏〗(副)[piānpiān]
① deliberately ② against expectation ③ by coincidence
〖偏袒〗(动)[piāntǎn]
take sides with; be partial to
〖偏听偏信〗[piāntīngpiānxìn]
be partial to; believe in one-

sided story

〖偏向〗(动、名)[piānxiàng]
deviation

〖偏心〗(形)[piānxīn]
lack of impartiality; be partial to

〖偏正结构〗[piān zhèng jiégòu]
(gram.) modified-modifier construction

〖偏重〗(动)[piānzhòng]
have a bias towards; be inclined to; tend to

篇(量)[piān]
a measure word (for an article, etc.)

〖篇幅〗(名)[piānfu]
the length of an article

〖篇目〗(名)[piānmù]
chapter heading

〖篇章〗(名)[piānzhāng]
literary piece; writing in general

翩[piān]

〖翩翩〗(形)[piānpiān]
gracefully moving; flying; dancing

pián

便[pián]
另见 biàn

〖便宜〗(形、动)[piányi]
① cheap (price) ② get away with

piàn

片(名、量)[piàn]
① slice ② a measure word (for tablet, stretch and used after "一" to describe scenery, atmosphere, sound, feeling, etc.)

〖片段〗(名)[piànduàn]
chapter; section; fragment; part (usually referring to writing, novel, drama, etc.)

〖片刻〗(名)[piànkè]
a short moment

〖片面〗(形)[piànmiàn]
one-sided; unilateral

〖片面性〗(名)[piànmiànxìng]
one-sidedness

骗(动)[piàn]
deceive; cheat

〖骗局〗(名)[piànjú]
fraud; swindling; double dealing; trickery

〖骗取〗(动)[piànqǔ]
gain something by cheating

〖骗子〗(名)[piànzi]
deceiver; swindler; juggler; charlatan

piāo

剽[piāo]

〖剽悍〗(形)[piāohàn]
brave and prompt in action

〖剽窃〗(动)[piāoqiè]
plagiarize

漂(动)[piāo]
drift
另见 piǎo piào

〖漂浮〗(动)[piāofú]

float about
〖漂流〗(动)[piāoliú]
drift about

飘(动)[piāo]
flow about; drift about; flatter; fly
〖飘泊〗(动)[piāobó]
drift aimlessly; have no fixed abode
〖飘荡〗(动)[piāodàng]
① drift about ② flutter
〖飘浮〗(动)[piāofú]
float about
〖飘渺〗(形)[piāomiǎo]
misty; unrealistic; obscure
〖飘飘然〗(形)[piāopiāorán]
be carried away with one's own importance
〖飘扬〗(动)[piāoyáng]
flutter; fly in the wind
〖飘摇〗(动)[piāoyáo]
drift about

piáo

瓢(名)[piáo]
dried gourd serving as dipper
〖瓢泼大雨〗[piáopō dàyǔ]
torrential rain; downpour

piǎo

漂(动)[piǎo]
bleach
另见 piāo piào
〖漂白〗(动)[piǎobái]
bleach

瞟(动)[piǎo]
wink at; cast a glance at

piào

票(名)[piào]〔张 zhāng〕
ticket
〖票贩子〗(名)[piàofànzi]
ticket scalper
〖票房价值〗[piàofángjiàzhí]
box-office value
〖票据〗(名)[piàojù]
note; bill

漂[piào]
另见 piāo piǎo
〖漂亮〗(形)[piàoliang]
① good-looking; beautiful ② brilliant; smart; bright
〖漂亮话〗(名)[piàolianghuà]
fine words; high-sounding words

piē

撇(动)[piē]
cast aside; leave behind
另见 piě
〖撇开〗(动)[piēkāi]
bypass; put aside

piě

撇(动、名)[piě]
① throw; hurl ② strokes (of a character)
另见 piē

pīn

拼(动)[pīn]

P

① assemble; put together ② do sth. desperately
〖拼凑〗(动)[pīncòu]
① scrape together ② patch up; piece together
〖拼命〗[pīn mìng]
risk one's life for; put up a desperate fight; do sth. desperately
〖拼盘儿〗(名)[pīnpánr]
cold hors d'oeuvre (usu. assorted cold meat)
〖拼死〗(副)[pīnsǐ]
desperately; frantically
〖拼写〗(动)[pīnxiě]
spell (a word)
〖拼音〗[pīn yīn]
phonetic transcriptions
〖拼音文字〗[pīnyīn wénzì]
a phonetic language
〖拼音字母〗[pīnyīn zìmǔ]
phonetic alphabet

pín

贫(形)[pín]
① poor ② lack; short of
〖贫病交迫〗[pínbìng jiāopò]
suffering from both poverty and sickness; sick as well as poor
〖贫齿动物〗[pínchǐ dòngwù]
edentate animal; edentate
〖贫乏〗(形)[pínfá]
needy; meagre; thin
〖贫雇农〗(名)[píngùnóng]
poor peasants and farm labourers
〖贫寒〗(形)[pínhán]
poor
〖贫化〗[pínhuà]
dilution
〖贫瘠〗(形)[pínjí]
poor; arid
〖贫苦〗(形)[pínkǔ]
poor; poverty
〖贫困〗(形)[pínkùn]
poor and hard up; impoverished
〖贫民〗(名)[pínmín]
poor people
〖贫民窟〗(名)[pínmínkū]
slums
〖贫农〗(名)[pínnóng]
poor peasants (the term poor peasants refers to original class status, not present economic position)
〖贫穷〗(形)[pínqióng]
poor; poverty; privation
〖贫血〗(名)[pínxuè]
anaemia
〖贫嘴〗[pínzuǐ]
garrulous, loquacious
〖贫嘴薄舌〗[pínzuǐ bóshé]
garrulous and sharp-tongued

频[pín]
〖频繁〗(形)[pínfán]
continuous; frequent
〖频率〗(名)[pínlǜ]
frequency

pǐn

品(名)[pǐn]
① goods; articles ② grade; class ③ variety; character (of person)

〖品德〗(名)[pǐndé]
quality (of person)
〖品格〗(名)[pǐngé]
character of person
〖品头论足〗[pǐntóulùnzú]
find faults with
〖品行〗(名)[pǐnxíng]
personal conduct
〖品质〗(名)[pǐnzhì]
quality; character
〖品种〗(名)[pǐnzhǒng]
range of variety

pìn

聘[pìn]
〖聘请〗(动)[pìnqǐng]
engage; employ; invite
〖聘任〗(动)[pìnrèn]
engage; appoint to a position
〖聘书〗(名)[pìnshū]
letter of appointment

pīng

乒[pīng]
〖乒乓〗(象声)[pīngpāng]
onomatopoeia (for sound of hail)
〖乒乓球〗(名)[pīngpāngqiú]
〔个 gè〕ping-pong ball

píng

平(形、动)[píng]
① flat ② common; ordinary ③ balanced; even ④ level (e. g. a piece of ground) ⑤ pacify; restore to normal
〖平安〗(形)[píng'ān]
peaceful; safe
〖平白无故〗[píngbáiwúgù]
without any reason
〖平常〗(名、形)[píngcháng]
ordinary; common; usual
〖平淡〗(形)[píngdàn]
uninteresting; dull
〖平等〗(形、名)[píngděng]
equal; equality
〖平等互利〗[píngděng hùlì]
reciprocity based on equality; equality and mutual benefit
〖平地〗(名)[píngdì]
flat ground; level ground
〖平定〗(动)[píngdìng]
put down; quell; suppress; pacify
〖平凡〗(形)[píngfán]
ordinary; undistinguished; common
〖平方〗(名)[píngfāng]
square
〖平方公里〗(量)[píngfānggōnglǐ]
square kilometre
〖平方米〗(量)[píngfāngmǐ]
square metre
〖平房〗(名)[píngfáng]〔间 jiān〕
one-storied house
〖平分〗(动)[píngfēn]
divide equally
〖平分秋色〗[píngfēnqiūsè]
divide equally between two
〖平衡〗(动、名)[pínghéng]
balance; equilibrium
〖平衡木〗(名)[pínghéngmù]
beam (gymnastics)
〖平滑〗(形)[pínghuá]

P

smooth
〖平静〗(形)[píngjìng]
quiet; tranquil
〖平均〗(动)[píngjūn]
equalize; average
〖平均主义〗(名)[píngjūnzhǔyì]
equalitarianism
〖平炉〗(名)[pínglú]
open hearth furnace
〖平面〗(名)[píngmiàn]
flat surface; plain
〖平面几何〗[píngmiàn jǐhé]
plane geometry
〖平铺直叙〗[píngpūzhíxù]
monotonous; uninteresting; flat; dull (of writing)
〖平起平坐〗[píngqǐpíngzuò]
on an equal footing
〖平日〗(名)[píngrì]
at ordinary times; normal days
〖平生〗(名)[píngshēng]
① life time ② has never before...; never have...
〖平时〗(名)[píngshí]
usually; in peace time; in normal times
〖平素〗(名)[píngsù]
in normal days
〖平坦〗(形)[píngtǎn]
plain and level (e.g. road)
〖平稳〗(形)[píngwěn]
steady; safe; even; smooth
〖平息〗(动)[píngxī]
put down; stamp out
〖平心静气〗[píngxīnjìngqì]
dispassionately; calmly
〖平信〗(名)[píngxìn]〔封 fēng〕
ordinary mail
〖平行〗(动)[píngxíng]
① parallel ② on an equal footing ③ of equal rank
〖平行四边形〗
[píngxíng sìbiānxíng]
parallelogram
〖平行线〗(名)[píngxíngxiàn]
〔条 tiáo〕parallel lines
〖平易近人〗[píngyìjìnrén]
amicable; well-disposed; easy to get along with
〖平原〗(名)[píngyuán]
plain
〖平整〗(形、动)[píngzhěng]
① neat ② level (e.g. a piece of ground)
〖平装〗(名)[píngzhuāng]
ordinary packing

评(动)[píng]
criticize; judge
〖评比〗(动)[píngbǐ]
compare; appraise
〖评定〗(动)[píngdìng]
judge; evaluate
〖评分〗[píngfēn]
give a mark; mark; grade
〖评估〗(动、名)[pínggū]
evaluate; estimate
〖评价〗(动、名)[píngjià]
evaluate; appraise; assess; evaluation; appraisal
〖评奖〗[píng jiǎng]
the granting of awards through discussion
〖评理〗[píng lǐ]
reason out sth.

〖评论〗(动、名)[pínglùn]
comment; commentary
〖评论员〗(名)[pínglùnyuán]
commentator
〖评判〗(动)[píngpàn]
pass judgement; decide
〖评审〗(动)[píngshěn]
examine and appraise (sb's work, scientific research, etc.)
〖评选〗(动)[píngxuǎn]
appraise and elect
〖评议〗(动)[píngyì]
appraise; discuss
〖评语〗(名)[píngyǔ]
comment
〖评注〗(动、名)[píngzhù]
edition with comments

苹[píng]
〖苹果〗(名)[píngguǒ]〔个 gè〕
apple

凭(动、连)[píng]
① base on; rely on; depend on; make use of ② no matter what; never mind; in spite of
〖凭借〗(动)[píngjiè]
rely on; resort to
〖凭据〗(名)[píngjù]
evidence; basis for belief
〖凭空〗(副)[píngkōng]
without ground or basis; groundlessly
〖凭信〗(动)[píngxìn]
trust (a person)
〖凭证〗(名)[píngzhèng]
evidence

屏[píng]
〖屏风〗(名)[píngfēng]
〔扇 shàn〕a screen
〖屏障〗(名)[píngzhàng]
① frontier defence; outpost ② mountain range

瓶(名)[píng]
① jar; bottle; vase; jug ② a measure word (a bottle of)
〖瓶颈〗(名)[píngjǐng]
bottle-neck
〖瓶子〗(名)[píngzi]〔个 gè〕
bottle

pō

坡(名)[pō]
slope

泼(动)[pō]
splash; pour out
〖泼辣〗(形)[pōlà]
① pungent ② clear-cut; have a lot of drive
〖泼冷水〗[pō lěngshuǐ]
pour cold water; discourage; dampen one's spirits

颇(副)[pō]
rather; fairly; somewhat; pretty; to a certain degree

pó

婆(名)[pó]
old woman
〖婆婆〗(名)[pópo]

husband's mother

pò

迫(动)[pò]
force; compel
〖迫不及待〗[pòbùjídài]
hurriedly; in haste; brook no delay
〖迫害〗(动)[pòhài]
persecute
〖迫近〗(动)[pòjìn]
close; near; get close to
〖迫切〗(形)[pòqiè]
urgent; imminent; pressing
〖迫使〗(动)[pòshǐ]
enforce; coerce; compel; oblige
〖迫在眉睫〗[pòzàiméijié]
imminent; approaching

破(动、形)[pò]
① break; damage ② spend ③ reveal; lay bare
〖破案〗[pò àn]
solve a case; bring a case to book
〖破产〗[pò chǎn]
bankruptcy; ruin; be wrecked
〖破除〗(动)[pòchú]
do away with; abolish
〖破釜沉舟〗[pòfǔchénzhōu]
burn one's boats; fight with one's back against the wall
〖破格〗[pò gé]
make an exception for
〖破坏〗(动)[pòhuài]
destroy; undermine; wreck; sabotage
〖破获〗(动)[pòhuò]
unearth; uncover
〖破旧立新〗[pòjiùlìxīn]
destroy the old and establish the new; eradicate the old and foster the new
〖破烂〗(形、名)[pòlàn]
torndown; ragged; tumble-down; rags; rubbish
〖破例〗[pò lì]
as an exception
〖破裂〗(动)[pòliè]
split; break
〖破落〗(动)[pòluò]
fall into decline
〖破灭〗(动)[pòmiè]
vanish
〖破碎〗(动)[pòsuì]
break into pieces
〖破天荒〗[pòtiānhuāng]
epoch-making; unprecedented; for the first time
〖破绽〗(名)[pòzhàn]
loopholes; weak point
〖破折号〗(名)[pòzhéhào]
dash ("—")

魄[pò]
〖魄力〗(名)[pòlì]
courage; vigour

pōu

剖(动)[pōu]
① cut open; dissect ② analyze
〖剖析〗(动)[pōuxī]
explain; dissect

pū

扑(动)[pū]

①pounce; jump on; rush toward ②touch lightly; tap
〖扑克牌〗(名)[pūkèpái]
playing cards
〖扑空〗[pū kōng]
miss a punch; fail to get what one wants
〖扑灭〗(动)[pūmiè]
stamp out; put down; extinguish
〖扑通〗(象声)[pūtōng]
onomatopoeia, plop (for sound of sth. dropping into water)

铺(动)[pū]
spread; pave
另见 pù
〖铺床〗[pū chuáng]
make the bed
〖铺盖〗(名)[pūgài]
bedding
〖铺设〗(动)[pūshè]
spread out
〖铺张〗(形)[pūzhāng]
extravagant

pú

仆(名)[pú]
servant
〖仆从〗(名)[púcóng]
servant; hangers-on

匍[pú]
〖匍匐〗(动)[púfú]
crawl; edge forward

葡[pú]
〖葡萄〗(名)[pútáo]
grapes
〖葡萄糖〗(名)[pútáotáng]
glucose

pǔ

朴[pǔ]
〖朴实〗(形)[pǔshí]
simple; direct; honest
〖朴素〗(形)[pǔsù]
simple; plain

普[pǔ]
〖普遍〗(形)[pǔbiàn]
universal
〖普遍性〗(名)[pǔbiànxìng]
universal nature; universality
〖普查〗(名)[pǔchá]
general survey
〖普及〗(动、形)[pǔjí]
①popularize; reach all ②widely diffused; universal
〖普通〗(形)[pǔtōng]
common; ordinary
〖普通话〗(名)[pǔtōnghuà]
common spoken language
〖普选〗(名、动)[pǔxuǎn]
general election
〖普照〗(动)[pǔzhào]
illuminate

谱(名、动)[pǔ]
musical notation
〖谱写〗(动)[pǔxiě]
write melody for

P

pù

铺(名)[pù]
①bed②shop
另见 pū
〖铺位〗(名)[pùwèi]
berth; stall

〖铺子〗(名)[pùzi]
shop

瀑[pù]
〖瀑布〗(名)[pùbù]
waterfall

qī

七(数)[qī]
seven
〖七零八落〗[qīlíngbāluò]
scattered here and there; in ruins; in confusion
〖七拼八凑〗[qīpīnbācòu]
improvise desperately; scrape together; a patchwork without order
〖七七事变〗[Qī Qī Shìbiàn]
the July 7th. Incident of 1937—it marks the beginning of the Chinese people's heroic War of Resistance against Japanese Aggression which lasted for eight years
〖七上八下〗[qīshàngbāxià]
in a mental flurry of indecision
〖七手八脚〗[qīshǒubājiǎo]
too many cooks spoil the broth
〖七一〗[Qī Yī]
"July 1"—the birthday of the Communist Party of China (1921)
〖七月〗(名)[qīyuè]
July

妻(名)[qī]
wife
〖妻离子散〗[qīlízǐsàn]
broken up family; break up family
〖妻子〗(名)[qīzi]
wife

栖[qī]
〖栖身〗(动)[qīshēn]
dwell; obtain shelter
〖栖息〗(动)[qīxī]
dwell; dwell for rest

凄[qī]
〖凄惨〗(形)[qīcǎn]
sad; hard up; miserable; op-

pressed

〖凄厉〗(形)[qīlì]
forlorn and bitter; biting; shrilling

〖凄凉〗(形)[qīliáng]
gloomy and forlorn; miserable

期(名、量)[qī]

①a period(e.g. time) ②a measure word(for periodical, training course)

〖期待〗(动)[qīdài]
① look forward to ② wait in hope

〖期货〗(名)[qīhuò]
futures

〖期间〗(名)[qījiān]
period; term; time

〖期刊〗(名)[qīkān]
a periodical

〖期票〗(名)[qīpiào]
promissory note; term bill

〖期求〗(动)[qīqiú]
crave for

〖期望〗(动)[qīwàng]
hope; expect; look forward to; count on

〖期限〗(名)[qīxiàn]
time limit

欺(动)[qī]

cheat; bully; humiliate; browbeat

〖欺负〗(动)[qīfu]
bully; browbeat

〖欺瞒〗(动)[qīmán]
cheat; deceive; hide from

〖欺骗〗(动)[qīpiàn]
deceive; swindle; hoodwink

〖欺人太甚〗[qīréntàishèn]
bully others too much

〖欺人之谈〗[qīrénzhītán]
deceitful talk; lie

〖欺软怕硬〗[qīruǎnpàyìng]
browbeat the weak and fear the strong; cringe before the strong and bully the weak

〖欺侮〗(动)[qīwǔ]
bully; humiliate

〖欺压〗(动)[qīyā]
bully and oppress; ride roughshod over sb./sth.

〖欺诈〗(动)[qīzhà]
cheat; deceive

漆(名、动)[qī]

paint; lacquer; varnish; coat with varnish

〖漆黑〗(形)[qīhēi]
pitch dark

〖漆黑一团〗[qīhēiyītuán]
be completely in the dark; be quite hopeless

〖漆器〗(名)[qīqì]
lacquerware

qí

齐(形)[qí]

①neat; tidy ②together; complete

〖齐备〗(动)[qíbèi]
all ready; all complete

〖齐全〗(形)[qíquán]
complete

〖齐心〗(形)[qíxīn]
be of one heart
〖齐心协力〗[qíxīnxiélì]
work as one man; be of one heart

其(代)[qí]
his; her; its; their; that
〖其次〗(名)[qícì]
① next in importance; secondary ② next
〖其间〗(名)[qíjiān]
between; during; within (a period of time)
〖其实〗(副)[qíshí]
in reality; as a matter of fact; actually; in truth
〖其他〗(代)[qítā]
others; the other
〖其余〗(代)[qíyú]
the remaining; the rest
〖其中〗(名)[qízhōng]
inside; among (a group); of which

奇(形)[qí]
strange; surprise
另见 jī
〖奇耻大辱〗[qíchǐdàrǔ]
crying shame and crowning humiliation
〖奇怪〗(形)[qíguài]
strange; odd; curious; astonishing; funny
〖奇观〗(名)[qíguān]
impressive sight; remarkable spectacle; picturesque
〖奇货可居〗[qíhuòkějū]
hoarding; a rare commodity worth hoarding to corner the market
〖奇迹〗(名)[qíjì]
miracle; wonderful achievement
〖奇妙〗(形)[qímiào]
wonderful; marvellous
〖奇谈〗(名)[qítán]
strange talk or theory
〖奇谈怪论〗[qítánguàilùn]
strange tale and absurd argument; fantastic stories and theories
〖奇特〗(形)[qítè]
striking; unusual
〖奇闻〗(名)[qíwén]
strange story
〖奇袭〗(动)[qíxí]
raid; surprise attack
〖奇形怪状〗
[qíxíngguàizhuàng]
strange sight; peculiar appearance
〖奇异〗(形)[qíyì]
strange; wonderful; remarkable
〖奇装异服〗[qízhuāngyìfú]
strange fashions; fancy clothes; peculiar dress

歧[qí]
〖歧路〗(名)[qílù]
a forked road; crossroads
〖歧视〗(动)[qíshì]
discriminate against; discrimination
〖歧途〗(名)[qítú]

wrong path
〖歧义〗(名)[qíyì]
ambiguous word or a word with two or more possible meanings

祈 [qí]
〖祈祷〗(名、动)[qídǎo]
a prayer; pray
〖祈求〗(动)[qíqiú]
entreat earnestly; earnestly hope for
〖祈使句〗(名)[qíshǐjù]
(gram.) imperative sentence

畦 (名、量)[qí]
① furrow ② a measure word (e.g. one furrow of vegetables)

崎 [qí]
〖崎岖〗(形)[qíqū]
uneven; rough; rugged (area)

骑 (动)[qí]
ride (especially on horseback, bicycle, etc.)
〖骑兵〗(名)[qíbīng]
cavalry
〖骑虎难下〗[qíhǔnánxià]
(lit.) he who rides a tiger finds it difficult to dismount; (fig.) a situation from which it is difficult to extricate oneself
〖骑墙〗[qí qiáng]
sit on the fence; taking no side

棋 (名)[qí]
a game of chess
〖棋逢对手〗[qíféngduìshǒu]
(lit.) equal match in a game of chess; one comes across one's equal in a game of chess; (fig.) equal match; one is just as strong or good as the other
〖棋盘〗(名)[qípán]
chess board
〖棋子〗(名)[qízǐ]〔个 gè〕
chess pieces; chessmen; draughtsmen

旗 (名)[qí]〔面 miàn〕
flag; banner
〖旗杆〗(名)[qígān]〔根 gēn〕
flagpole
〖旗鼓相当〗[qígǔxiāngdāng]
be equal to; be a match for; be well matched in strength
〖旗号〗(名)[qíhào]
(lit.) army standard or banner; (fig.) (under) the signboard or pretext of
〖旗开得胜〗[qíkāidéshèng]
win victory as soon as one's banner is displayed; triumphantly ... at one stroke
〖旗手〗(名)[qíshǒu]
standard bearer
〖旗帜〗(名)[qízhì]
① flag; banner ② good example; model
〖旗帜鲜明〗[qízhìxiānmíng]
unfurl a radiant banner; a clear-cut stand
〖旗子〗(名)[qízi]〔面 miàn〕

flag; banner

qǐ

乞 [qǐ]
〖乞丐〗(名)[qǐgài]
beggar
〖乞怜〗(动)[qǐlián]
piteously beg help
〖乞灵〗(动)[qǐlíng]
resort to; seek help from
〖乞求〗(动)[qǐqiú]
pass the hat round; go begging; fall on one's knees

岂(副)[qǐ]
an adverb expressing rhetorical question
〖岂不〗(副)[qǐbù]
wouldn't it ...; would it not ...
〖岂非〗(副)[qǐfēi]
wouldn't it be ...; would it not be ...
〖岂有此理〗[qǐyǒucǐlǐ]
how could such a thing be possible; fantastic; sheer nonsense
〖岂有他哉〗[qǐyǒutāzāi]
how can it be otherwise

企 [qǐ]
〖企求〗(动)[qǐqiú]
expect; seek; be after
〖企事业〗(名)[qǐshìyè]
enterprises and institutions
〖企图〗(动、名)[qǐtú]
attempt; try
〖企业〗(名)[qǐyè]
enterprise; undertaking
〖企业家〗(名)[qǐyèjiā]
entrepreneur; enterpriser
〖企业精神〗[qǐyèjīngshén]
entrepreneurship
〖企业文化〗[qǐyèwénhuà]
corporate culture

杞 [qǐ]
〖杞人忧天〗[qǐrényōutiān]
(lit.) the man of Chi worried in case the sky should fall; (fig.) unnecessary worry; neurotic worry

启 [qǐ]
〖启发〗(动、名)[qǐfā]
enlighten; inspire; arouse; enlightenment; inspiration
〖启发式〗(名)[qǐfāshì]
method of developing (e.g. students') initiative
〖启蒙〗(动)[qǐméng]
enlighten
〖启示〗(动、名)[qǐshì]
enlighten; enlightenment; teaching
〖启事〗(名)[qǐshì]
notice

起(动、量)[qǐ]
① stand up; get up; rise; cause to rise; start ② a measure word (batch, time, group, etc.)
〖起笔〗(名)[qǐbǐ]
the first stroke of a character
〖起步〗(动)[qǐbù]

be in the initial stage
〖起草〗(动)[qǐcǎo]
draft out; map out; sketch
〖起程〗(动)[qǐchéng]
start on journey
〖起初〗(名)[qǐchū]
at first; at the beginning
〖起床〗[qǐ chuáng]
get up from bed
〖起点〗(名)[qǐdiǎn]
starting point
〖起飞〗(动)[qǐfēi]
take off (e.g.aeroplane)
〖起伏〗[qǐ fú]
ups and downs
〖起航〗(动)[qǐháng]
weigh anchor; set sail (of ships)
〖起哄〗(动)[qǐhòng]
kick up a fuss
〖起家〗[qǐ jiā]
① begin an undertaking; build up a fortune ② start off
〖起劲〗(形)[qǐjìn]
enthusiastic; excited; in high spirits
〖起来〗[qǐ lái]
① stand up; get up ② arise; get on the move
〖起码〗(形)[qǐmǎ]
minimum; at least; rudimentary
〖起色〗(名)[qǐsè]
recuperate (e.g. from illness); improve (illness, work, etc.)
〖起身〗[qǐ shēn]
① start a journey ② get up in the morning
〖起诉〗(动)[qǐsù]
sue; prosecute
〖起诉书〗(名)[qǐsùshū]
indictment; bill of complaint
〖起头儿〗[qǐ tóur]
at first; beginning
〖起先〗(名)[qǐ xiān]
at first
〖起义〗(动、名)[qǐyì]
stage an uprising; uprising; insurrection
〖起因〗(名)[qǐyīn]
cause; as a result of
〖起源〗(名、动)[qǐyuán]
beginning; source; birth; originate in; arise from
〖起重机〗(名)[qǐzhòngjī]
crane (machine)
〖起…作用〗[qǐ…zuòyòng]
play a ... part in; serve as

qì

气(名、动)[qì]
① air; gas; breath ② get angry
〖气昂昂〗(形)[qì'áng'áng]
high morale; high spirits
〖气冲冲〗(形)[qìchōngchōng]
enraged; angry
〖气喘〗[qì chuǎn]
be short of breath; gasp; suffer from asthma
〖气氛〗(名)[qìfēn]
atmosphere; air
〖气愤〗(形)[qìfèn]
angry; indignant
〖气概〗(名)[qìgài]
spirit; heroic manner; heroic bearing; interpidity
〖气功〗(名)[qìgōng]

qigong; breathing exercise; qigong system of meditational exercise used to treat physical and spiritual harmony

〖气管〗(名)[qìguǎn]
windpipe; trachea

〖气管炎〗(名)[qìguǎnyán]
bronchitis

〖气候〗(名)[qìhòu]
climate; weather

〖气呼呼〗(形)[qìhūhū]
angrily; gasp out (e.g. in anger)

〖气急败坏〗[qìjíbàihuài]
breathless and excited; worked up

〖气节〗(名)[qìjié]
integrity; fine quality

〖气力〗(名)[qìlì]
physical strength; effort

〖气量〗(名)[qìliàng]
degree of broadmindedness or narrow-mindedness (of a person)

〖气流〗(名)[qìliú]
current of air

〖气馁〗(形)[qìněi]
down-hearted; lose heart; become dejected

〖气派〗(名)[qìpài]
airs; manner; style

〖气魄〗(名)[qìpò]
spirit; courage; oaring; boldness

〖气球〗(名)[qìqiú]〔个 gè〕
balloon

〖气色〗(名)[qìsè]
complexion

〖气势〗(名)[qìshì]
spiritedness; spirit

〖气势磅礴〗[qìshìpángbó]
majestic and momentous

〖气势汹汹〗[qìshìxiōngxiōng]
ferociously; overbearing attitude

〖气态〗(名)[qìtài]
gaseous

〖气体〗(名)[qìtǐ]
gaseous body; gas

〖气味〗(名)[qìwèi]
flavour; smell; taste (also fig.)

〖气味相投〗[qìwèixiāngtóu]
congenial to

〖气温〗(名)[qìwēn]
air temperature

〖气息〗(名)[qìxī]
①breath ②flavour; taste

〖气息奄奄〗[qìxīyǎnyǎn]
dying; gasping; fainting; at the end of one's resources

〖气象〗(名)[qìxiàng]
① climatic phenomena ② atmosphere; air; spirit

〖气象台〗(名)[qìxiàngtái]
meteorological observatory; weather station

〖气象万千〗[qìxiàngwànqiān]
magnificent and very varied sights

〖气象站〗(名)[qìxiàngzhàn]
weather station

〖气压〗(名)[qìyā]
air pressure

〖气焰〗(名)[qìyàn]
arrogance

〖气质〗(名)[qìzhì]
disposition; aptitude; deportment; character

〖气壮如牛〗[qìzhuàngrúniú]
strong as an ox
〖气壮山河〗[qìzhuàngshānhé]
sublime and heroic

迄 [qì]
〖迄今〗[qì jīn]
to this day

弃(动)[qì]
abandon; forsake
〖弃暗投明〗[qì'àntóumíng]
forsake the darkness and cross over to the light
〖弃权〗[qì quán]
abstention; abstain; waive

汽(名)[qì]
steam; vapour
〖汽车〗(名)[qìchē]〔辆 liàng〕
automobile
〖汽笛〗(名)[qìdí]
steam whistle
〖汽化〗(动)[qìhuà]
vaporize
〖汽水〗(名)[qìshuǐ]〔瓶 píng〕
aerated waters; mineral waters
〖汽油〗(名)[qìyóu]
gasoline; petrol

泣(动)[qì]
sob
〖泣不成声〗[qìbùchéngshēng]
weep bitterly

契(名)[qì]
contracts; agreements
〖契约〗(名)[qìyuē]〔张 zhāng〕
contracts; agreements; (title) deeds

器 [qì]
〖器材〗(名)[qìcái]
equipment; materials and equipment; appliances
〖器官〗(名)[qìguān]
physical organ
〖器具〗(名)[qìjù]
utensil; appliances; furniture; apparatus
〖器皿〗(名)[qìmǐn]
kitchenware; utensils; container
〖器械〗(名)[qìxiè]
① apparatus ② military weapons
〖器乐〗(名)[qìyuè]
instrumental music
〖器重〗(动)[qìzhòng]
regard highly

qiā

掐(动)[qiā]
① press hard (e.g. between finger and thumb) ② pinch; nip

qià

恰 [qià]
〖恰当〗(形)[qiàdàng]
fitting and proper; right in degree or extent
〖恰好〗(副)[qiàhǎo]

Q

exactly right
〖恰恰〗(副)[qiàqià]
just; exactly
〖恰巧〗(副)[qiàqiǎo]
by chance
〖恰如其分〗[qiàrúqífèn]
just right; well measured; to a proper extent; according to the specific conditions

洽 [qià]
〖洽商〗(动)[qiàshāng]
negotiate or discuss
〖洽谈〗(动)[qiàtán]
talk over; discuss

qiān

千(数)[qiān]
thousand
〖千百万〗(数)[qiānbǎiwàn]
millions
〖千变万化〗[qiānbiànwànhuà]
myriads of changes; kaleidoscopic change
〖千差万别〗[qiānchāwànbié]
different in a thousand and one ways
〖千疮百孔〗
[qiānchuāngbǎikǒng]
riddled with a thousand gaping wounds; heavily damaged; a hopeless mess
〖千锤百炼〗[qiānchuíbǎiliàn]
well experienced; has gone through fire and water; steeled and tempered
〖千方百计〗[qiānfāngbǎijì]
in a thousand and one ways; leave no stone unturned; do all in one's power
〖千军万马〗[qiānjūnwànmǎ]
a powerful army
〖千钧一发〗[qiānjūnyīfà]
(lit.) a thousand catties hang upon one hair; (fig.) extremely delicate and dangerous situation
〖千卡〗(量)[qiānkǎ]
kilocalorie
〖千克〗(量)[qiānkè]
kilogram
〖千里迢迢〗[qiānlǐtiáotiáo]
from afar
〖千难万险〗[qiānnánwànxiǎn]
untold hardships and risks
〖千篇一律〗[qiānpiānyīlǜ]
(of writing) repetitious; monotonous; all alike; stereotyped
〖千奇百怪〗[qiānqíbǎiguài]
exceedingly strange; very wonderful; all sorts of strange things
〖千秋万代〗[qiānqiūwàndài]
forever; through the ages
〖千丝万缕〗[qiānsīwànlǚ]
a thousand and one links or ties
〖千头万绪〗[qiāntóuwànxù]
a host of miscellaneous problems
〖千瓦〗(量)[qiānwǎ]
kilowatt (kw.)
〖千万〗(数、副)[qiānwàn]
① ten million ② be sure (e. g.

to bear it in mind)
〖千辛万苦〗[qiānxīnwànkǔ]
untold hardships; all kinds of hardships
〖千言万语〗[qiānyánwànyǔ]
a host of words
〖千载难逢〗[qiānzǎinánféng]
an opportunity of a thousand years; an extremely rare opportunity; once in a blue moon
〖千真万确〗[qiānzhēnwànquè]
absolutely true; one can swear it is true
〖千周〗(量)[qiānzhōu]
kilocycle

阡 [qiān]
〖阡陌〗(名)[qiānmò]
crisscross of paths separating farms

迁(动)[qiān]
① move to another place ② change into
〖迁就〗(动)[qiānjiù]
accomodate; give in to
〖迁居〗(动)[qiānjū]
move into another house
〖迁移〗(动)[qiānyí]
remove; migrate; shift

牵(动)[qiān]
① pull; drag ② involve; draw in
〖牵扯〗(动)[qiānchě]
drag into; involve
〖牵动〗(动)[qiāndòng]
involve; affect
〖牵挂〗(动)[qiānguà]
remember fondly; be concerned; worry over
〖牵累〗(动)[qiānlěi]
involve in
〖牵连〗(动)[qiānlián]
implicate; drag into trouble; have connections with
〖牵强〗(形)[qiānqiǎng]
farfetched
〖牵强附会〗[qiānqiǎngfùhuì]
stretch the sense
〖牵涉〗(动)[qiānshè]
involve; be linked up with
〖牵线搭桥〗[qiānxiàndāqiáo]
act as a go-between (an intermediate)
〖牵引〗(动)[qiānyǐn]
pull; draw; draft; haul
〖牵引力〗(名)[qiānyǐnlì]
traction; tractive power
〖牵制〗(动)[qiānzhì]
tie down; contain; hinder; pin down; restrain

铅(名)[qiān]
lead
〖铅版〗(名)[qiānbǎn]〔块 kuài〕
type plate
〖铅笔〗(名)[qiānbǐ]〔枝 zhī〕
pencil
〖铅球〗(名)[qiānqiú]〔个 gè〕
shot (for sport)
〖铅印〗(动)[qiānyìn]
print from lead type
〖铅字〗(名)[qiānzì]
lead type; printing type

谦[qiān]

〖谦让〗(动)[qiānràng]
be modest

〖谦虚〗(形)[qiānxū]
modest

〖谦逊〗(形)[qiānxùn]
modest; unobtrusive; unassuming

签(动)[qiān]
sign

〖签到〗[qiān dào]
sign in on arrival at meeting or office

〖签订〗(动)[qiāndìng]
sign; conclude (e. g. an agreement)

〖签发〗(动)[qiānfā]
authorize and despatch (documents, etc.)

〖签名〗[qiān míng]
sign one's name

〖签名〗(名)[qiānmíng]
signature

〖签署〗(动)[qiānshǔ]
sign; affix one's signature

〖签证〗(名)[qiānzhèng]
visa

〖签字〗[qiān zì]
sign (e. g. treaty); affix one's signature

〖签字〗(名)[qiānzì]
signature

qián

前(名)[qián]
①in front; forward ②former; previous; of earlier times

〖前辈〗(名)[qiánbèi]
older generations; predecessors

〖前边〗(名)[qiánbian]
in front of; lie ahead of

〖前车之鉴〗[qiánchēzhījiàn]
(lit.) the overturned cart in front serves as a warning to the carts behind; (fig.) it is well to profit by the folly of others; one should take warning from another's mistake

〖前程〗(名)[qiánchéng]
prospects; future career

〖前导〗(名)[qiándǎo]
pioneer; one who shows the way

〖前额〗(名)[qián'é]
the forehead

〖前方〗(名)[qiánfāng]
①the front (battle) ②the place ahead; right in front

〖前赴后继〗[qiánfùhòujì]
advance wave upon wave

〖前功尽弃〗[qiángōngjìnqì]
all previous work is wasted; all labour lost; waste all the previous efforts

〖前后〗(名)[qiánhòu]
① front and back ② round the time of ③ on all sides; in every direction

〖前进〗(动)[qiánjìn]
①advance; press ahead; go forward ②make progress

〖前景〗(名)[qiánjǐng]
①vista; landscape ②prospe-

ct; future
〖前列〗(名)[qiánliè]
foremost; forefront
〖前面〗(名)[qiánmiàn]
① ahead; in front of ② (what is mentioned) above; supra
〖前年〗(名)[qiánnián]
the year before last
〖前怕狼,后怕虎〗
[qiánpàláng, hòupàhǔ]
fear the wolf in front and the tiger behind; nervous and indecisive
〖前驱〗(名)[qiánqū]
forerunner; vanguard; precursor
〖前人〗(名)[qiánrén]
the people of the past; former people
〖前任〗(名)[qiánrèn]
predecessor; former (e. g. minister)
〖前哨〗(名)[qiánshào]
the foreward patrol; sentry; outpost; forward units
〖前身〗(名)[qiánshēn]
the precursor of an organization
〖前所未有〗[qiánsuǒwèiyǒu]
unprecedented; such as never previously existed
〖前提〗(名)[qiántí]
prerequisite; precondition; premise
〖前天〗(名)[qiántiān]
the day before yesterday
〖前头〗(名)[qiántou]
① in front; ahead ② before
〖前途〗(名)[qiántú]
prospect; future
〖前往〗(动)[qiánwǎng]
head toward; go to; proceed to
〖前卫〗(名)[qiánwèi]
① vanguard ② half back (football)
〖前无古人〗[qiánwúgǔrén]
unprecedented; unparalleled
〖前夕〗(名)[qiánxī]
① the night before last ② eve
〖前线〗(名)[qiánxiàn]
the battle front
〖前夜〗(名)[qiányè]
the night before last; eve
〖前者〗(名)[qiánzhě]
the former
〖前奏〗(名)[qiánzòu]
① prelude (music) ② prelude to an event

虔 [qián]
〖虔诚〗(形)[qiánchéng]
pious; devout

钱 (名)[qián]
money; a measure word (for Chinese herbal medicine)
〖钱包〗(名)[qiánbāo]〔个 gè〕
purse; wallet
〖钱币〗(名)[qiánbì]
coin
〖钱财〗(名)[qiáncái]
wealth; money

钳 (名)[qián]
pincers; pliers

〖钳工〗(名)[qiángōng]
fitter
〖钳制〗(动)[qiánzhì]
pin down
〖钳子〗(名)[qiánzi]〔把 bǎ〕
pincers; pliers

掮 [qián]
〖掮客〗(名)[qiánkè]
broker

乾 [qián]
〖乾坤〗(名)[qiánkūn]
the universe

潜(动)[qián]
hide; go under
〖潜藏〗(动)[qiáncáng]
hide
〖潜伏〗(动)[qiánfú]
lie low; live in hiding; fallow
〖潜力〗(名)[qiánlì]
potentiality; latent capacity
〖潜入〗(动)[qiánrù]
sneak in; enter secretly
〖潜水〗[qián shuǐ]
swim underwater; dive
〖潜水艇〗(名)[qiánshuǐtǐng]
submarine
〖潜逃〗(动)[qiántáo]
abscond
〖潜移默化〗[qiányímòhuà]
a silent transforming influence; be unconsciously influenced
〖潜泳〗(名)[qiányǒng]
swim underwater
〖潜在〗(动)[qiánzài]
latent; lurking; potential

黔 [qián]
〖黔驴技穷〗[qiánlǘjìqióng]
at one's wits end; at the end of one's tether

qiǎn

浅(形)[qiǎn]
shallow; superficial; not deep or profound
〖浅薄〗(形)[qiǎnbó]
superficial; shallow
〖浅近〗(形)[qiǎnjìn]
plain, simple
〖浅陋〗(形)[qiǎnlòu]
meagre; shallow
〖浅显〗(形)[qiǎnxiǎn]
plain; easy to understand
〖浅易〗(形)[qiǎnyì]
simple and easy

遣 [qiǎn]
〖遣返〗(动)[qiǎnfǎn]
repatriate
〖遣散〗(动)[qiǎnsàn]
disband
〖遣送〗(动)[qiǎnsòng]
send (sb.) away; repatriate

谴 [qiǎn]
〖谴责〗(动)[qiǎnzé]
denounce; condemn

qiàn

欠(动)[qiàn]

①owe(debt, gratitude, etc.)
②short of; lacking in
〖欠缺〗(动)[qiànquē]
be deficient in; be short of
〖欠条〗(名)[qiàntiáo]
IOU; a bill signed in acknowledgement of debt
〖欠债〗(名)[qiànzhài]
debt due; outstanding accounts

Q

歉[qiàn]
〖歉收〗(动)[qiànshōu]
have poor harvest; have bad crops
〖歉意〗(名)[qiànyì]
ill at ease; sorry

qiāng

枪(名)[qiāng]〔枝 zhī〕
gun; rifle; pistol
〖枪毙〗(动)[qiāngbì]
execute by shooting
〖枪杆〗(名)[qiānggǎn]
gun
〖枪林弹雨〗[qiānglíndànyǔ]
amidst gunfire; heavy fire(war)
〖枪杀〗(动)[qiāngshā]
kill by shooting
〖枪支〗(名)[qiāngzhī]
guns

腔(名)[qiāng]
①mouth cavity ②(speech)accent
〖腔调〗(名)[qiāngdiào]
① tone of speech ② melody or tune

qiáng

强(形)[qiáng]
①strong; powerful ②good
另见 qiǎng
〖强暴〗(形、名)[qiángbào]
violent; brutal; tyranny
〖强大〗(形)[qiángdà]
powerful; mighty
〖强盗〗(名)[qiángdào]
robber; bandit
〖强调〗(动)[qiángdiào]
lay great stress on; emphasize
〖强度〗(名)[qiángdù]
intensity; strength
〖强国〗(名)[qiángguó]
a powerful nation; great powers
〖强化〗(动)[qiánghuà]
strengthen
〖强加〗(动)[qiángjiā]
force on; impose upon
〖强加于人〗[qiángjiāyúrén]
impose one's views upon others; foist one's views on others
〖强奸〗(动)[qiángjiān]
rape
〖强健〗(形)[qiángjiàn]
physically strong
〖强烈〗(形)[qiángliè]
① sharp; strong; intensive ② violent; ardent
〖强权〗(名)[qiángquán]
power
〖强盛〗(形)[qiángshèng]
prosperous; strong
〖强行〗(副)[qiángxíng]
by force
〖强硬〗(形)[qiángyìng]

unyielding; strong
〖强占〗(动)[qiángzhàn]
occupy by force
〖强制〗(动)[qiángzhì]
compel; force
〖强壮〗(形)[qiángzhuàng]
strong; powerful; sturdy; well-built

墙(名)[qiáng]〔堵 dǔ〕
wall
〖墙报〗(名)[qiángbào]〔期 qī〕
wall newspaper
〖墙壁〗(名)[qiángbì]
wall
〖墙角〗(名)[qiángjiǎo]
corner of wall
〖墙脚〗(名)[qiángjiǎo]
① foot of wall ② foundation; cornerstone

qiǎng

抢(动)[qiǎng]
① rob; loot; take by force ② vie with each other to be the first ③ make a rush for
〖抢渡〗(动)[qiǎngdù]
rush across (e.g. a river)
〖抢夺〗(动)[qiǎngduó]
loot; grab; plunder; seize
〖抢劫〗(动)[qiǎngjié]
loot; rob; plunder
〖抢救〗(动)[qiǎngjiù]
rush to rescue; rush to save; give first aid treatment
〖抢收〗(动)[qiǎngshōu]
rush harvest
〖抢先〗[qiǎng xiān]
compete to be the first
〖抢险〗[qiǎng xiǎn]
rush to deal with an emergency
〖抢修〗(动)[qiǎngxiū]
rush to repair
〖抢种〗(动)[qiǎngzhòng]
plant in a rush

强[qiǎng]
另见 qiáng
〖强辩〗(动)[qiǎngbiàn]
resort to sophistry in self-justification
〖强词夺理〗[qiǎngcíduólǐ]
quibble; use lame arguments and perverted logic
〖强迫〗(动)[qiǎngpò]
compel; force
〖强求〗(动)[qiǎngqiú]
insist on (e. g. having sth. done); by means of compulsion
〖强人所难〗[qiǎngrénsuǒnán]
make sb.do what is beyond his power or against his will

qiāo

悄[qiāo]
〖悄悄〗(副)[qiāoqiāo]
silently; stealthily

锹(名)[qiāo]〔把 bǎ〕
a shovel

敲(动)[qiāo]
knock

Q

〖敲打〗(动)[qiāodǎ]
beat; strike
〖敲骨吸髓〗[qiāogǔxīsuǐ]
suck the lifeblood
〖敲门砖〗(名)[qiāoménzhuān]
(lit.)brick for knocking at gate; (fig.)ways and means to seek favour
〖敲诈〗(动)[qiāozhà]
blackmail; extort
〖敲诈勒索〗[qiāozhàlèsuǒ]
blackmail and impose exactions on

qiáo

乔[qiáo]
〖乔装打扮〗[qiáozhuāngdǎbàn]
disguise oneself

侨[qiáo]
〖侨胞〗(名)[qiáobāo]
fellow countrymen who live abroad
〖侨汇〗(名)[qiáohuì]
remittances from fellow countrymen abroad
〖侨居〗(动)[qiáojū]
live abroad
〖侨民〗(名)[qiáomín]
those living abroad and retaining their own nationality; foreign residents

桥(名)[qiáo]〔座 zuò〕
bridge
〖桥洞〗(名)[qiáodòng]
archway in a bridge
〖桥墩〗(名)[qiáodūn]
abutment; foundation piers
〖桥梁〗(名)[qiáoliáng]
〔座 zuò〕bridge; girders of a bridge
〖桥头堡〗(名)[qiáotóubǎo]
① bridgehead ② a salient point in battle line

憔[qiáo]
〖憔悴〗(形)[qiáocuì]
weary looking; worn-out

瞧(动)[qiáo]
see; look
〖瞧不起〗[qiáo bu qǐ]
have no regard for; look down upon
〖瞧得起〗[qiáo de qǐ]
have high regard for (person); hold sb. in esteem
〖瞧见〗(动)[qiáojiàn]
see

qiǎo

巧(形)[qiǎo]
① intelligent; clever ② skilful; dexterous ③ be a coincidence
〖巧夺天工〗[qiǎoduótiāngōng]
art beats nature
〖巧合〗(动)[qiǎohé]
by chance; by coincidence
〖巧克力〗(名)[qiǎokèlì]
chocolate
〖巧立名目〗[qiǎolìmíngmù]
concoct various pretexts; in-

vent all sorts of names
〖巧妙〗(形)[qiǎomiào]
clever; wonderful; ingenious
〖巧取豪夺〗[qiǎoqǔháoduó]
obtain by force or deception; rob by force or by trick

qiào

俏(形)[qiào]
handsome; beautiful
〖俏皮〗(形)[qiàopi]
① cheeky; humorous; witty
② beautiful; nice looking
〖俏皮话〗(名)[qiàopihuà]
witty; sarcastic remarks

峭 [qiào]
〖峭壁〗(名)[qiàobì]
cliff; precipice

窍 [qiào]
〖窍门〗(名)[qiàomén]
secret of success; skilful method

翘(动)[qiào]
lift up; turn up; curl up
〖翘尾巴〗[qiào wěiba]
be cocky; wag one's tail in the air

qiē

切(动)[qiē]
cut
另见 qiè
〖切除〗(动)[qiēchú]
cut off; sever
〖切磋〗(动)[qiēcuō]
study and learn by mutual discussion
〖切磋琢磨〗[qiēcuōzhuómó]
weigh and consider; study carefully and learn by mutual discussion
〖切断〗(动)[qiēduàn]
cut off; disconnect; sever
〖切削〗(动)[qiēxiāo]
cut

qié

茄 [qié]
〖茄子〗(名)[qiézi]〔个 gè〕
eggplant; aubergine

qiě

且(副、连)[qiě]
for the present; for a while; as well as

qiè

切(动、副)[qiè]
① fit; correspond to ② make sure; by all means
另见 qiē
〖切齿〗(形)[qièchǐ]
grind one's teeth in hatred or anger
〖切肤之痛〗[qièfūzhītòng]
sorrow like cutting one's flesh; sorrow hits home
〖切合实际〗[qièhé shíjì]
correspond to; suit the actual

condition of

〖切记〗(动)[qièjì]
be sure to remember; always remember

〖切身〗(形)[qièshēn]
personal; intimate; firsthand; vital (e.g. interest)

〖切实〗(形)[qièshí]
practical; correspond to; solid

〖切中要害〗[qièzhòngyàohài]
hit the nail on the head

Q

怯(形)[qiè]
timid; coward; nervous

〖怯懦〗(形)[qiènuò]
timid; timorous

〖怯弱〗(形)[qièruò]
timid

窃(动)[qiè]
steal

〖窃据〗(动)[qièjù]
entrench; seize

〖窃取〗(动)[qièqǔ]
steal; usurp

〖窃听器〗(名)[qiètīngqì]
tapping device; bugging device

惬[qiè]

〖惬意〗(形)[qièyì]
pleasing; satisfying

qīn

钦[qīn]

〖钦差大臣〗[qīnchāidàchén]
an imperial envoy

〖钦佩〗(动)[qīnpèi]
admire; respect; esteem; think highly of

侵[qīn]

〖侵犯〗(动)[qīnfàn]
encroach upon; intrude; violate

〖侵害〗(动)[qīnhài]
violate; infringe upon

〖侵略〗(动)[qīnlüè]
invade; aggression

〖侵略战争〗[qīnlüèzhànzhēng]
war of aggression

〖侵略者〗(名)[qīnlüèzhě]
aggressors; invaders

〖侵权〗[qīnquán]
tort; infringement

〖侵入〗(动)[qīnrù]
invade; intrude

〖侵蚀〗(动)[qīnshí]
corrupt; corrode; make inroads on

〖侵袭〗(动)[qīnxí]
encroach upon; make a sneaking attack on

〖侵占〗(动)[qīnzhàn]
① seize; occupy by force ② invade and occupy

亲(形、动)[qīn]
① closely related ② kiss ③ intimate ④ personal
另见 qìng

〖亲爱〗(形)[qīn'ài]
dear; beloved

〖亲笔〗(名、副)[qīnbǐ]
written by one's own hand; in one's own handwriting
〖亲近〗(形)[qīnjìn]
intimate; close
〖亲口〗(副)[qīnkǒu]
(told) by person himself; told personally
〖亲密〗(形)[qīnmì]
very intimate; close
〖亲戚〗(名)[qīnqi]
relative; kinsmen
〖亲切〗(形)[qīnqiè]
warm; cordial; sincere; heartily
〖亲热〗(形)[qīnrè]
warm and affectionate; devoted
〖亲人〗(名)[qīnrén]
relative; kinsfolk
〖亲身〗(副)[qīnshēn]
personal; in person
〖亲生〗(形)[qīnshēng]
parents or children of one's own
〖亲手〗(副)[qīnshǒu]
with one's own hand
〖亲属〗(名)[qīnshǔ]
relatives
〖亲眼〗(副)[qīnyǎn]
with one's own eyes
〖亲友〗(名)[qīnyǒu]
friends and relatives
〖亲者痛,仇者快〗
[qīnzhětòng, chóuzhěkuài]
sadden those near and dear to us and gladden the enemy
〖亲自〗(副)[qīnzì]
personally; in person

qín

琴(名)[qín]
a general term for stringed instruments (including piano)

勤(形)[qín]
① diligent; industrious; hard-working ② often
〖勤奋〗(形)[qínfèn]
hardworking; diligent
〖勤工俭学〗[qíngōngjiǎnxué]
part-time work and part-time study
〖勤俭〗(形)[qínjiǎn]
industrious and frugal; industrious and economical
〖勤俭建国〗[qínjiǎn jiànguó]
build the country through hard work and thrift; build the country with industry and frugality
〖勤俭节约〗[qínjiǎn jiéyuē]
be industrious and practise economy
〖勤谨〗(形)[qínjin]
dutiful and industrious
〖勤恳〗(形)[qínkěn]
diligent and consciencious
〖勤快〗(形)[qínkuai]
diligent; hard-working
〖勤劳〗(形)[qínláo]
hard-working; industrious
〖勤勉〗(形)[qínmiǎn]
earnest and diligent
〖勤务员〗(名)[qínwùyuán]
orderlies; service personnel
〖勤学苦练〗[qínxuékǔliàn]
study and practise hard

qīng

青(形)[qīng]
blue; green; black; dark(depending on what it modifies)
〖青菜〗(名)[qīngcài]
green vegetable; greens
〖青出于蓝而胜于蓝〗[qīngchūyúlán'érshèngyúlán]
(lit.)blue is extracted from the indigo plant but is bluer than it;(fig.)the pupil learns from and outdoes his teacher
〖青春〗(名)[qīngchūn]
youth
〖青红皂白〗[qīnghóngzàobái]
(make no)distinction between black and white or right and wrong
〖青黄不接〗[qīnghuángbùjiē]
between seasons when the crops is still in the blade and the old stock is consumed; a temporary shortage
〖青年〗(名)[qīngnián]
youth
〖青纱帐〗(名)[qīngshāzhàng]
the "green curtain" of tall crops(e.g. sorghum fields)
〖青蛙〗(名)[qīngwā]〔只 zhī〕
frog

轻(形、动)[qīng]
①light ②slight; belittle
〖轻便〗(形)[qīngbiàn]
easy and convenient; light; handy
〖轻敌〗[qīng dí]
underestimate the enemy; belittle the enemy
〖轻而易举〗[qīng'éryìjǔ]
easy to undertake; easily
〖轻浮〗(形)[qīngfú]
frivolous; light (e.g. conduct); flighty
〖轻工业〗(名)[qīnggōngyè]
light industry
〖轻举妄动〗[qīngjǔwàngdòng]
act rashly; take reckless actions
〖轻快〗(形)[qīngkuài]
①light-hearted ②light-footed
〖轻描淡写〗[qīngmiáodànxiě]
touch lightly on; mild comments
〖轻蔑〗(形)[qīngmiè]
despising; contemptuous
〖轻飘飘〗(形)[qīngpiāopiāo]
light as a feather
〖轻巧〗(形)[qīngqiǎo]
①agile; nimble; delicate ②handy; portable
〖轻声〗(名)[qīngshēng]
neutral tone
〖轻视〗(动)[qīngshì]
look down upon; make light of; slight
〖轻率〗(形)[qīngshuài]
rash; hasty
〖轻松〗(形)[qīngsōng]
relaxed; easy mind; light(work)
〖轻微〗(形)[qīngwēi]
slight; light
〖轻信〗(动)[qīngxìn]
give credence to; believe easily; take for granted

〖轻易〗(形)[qīngyì]
①simple and easy ②casual(e.g. attitude)
〖轻重〗(名)[qīngzhòng]
①weight ②relative importance ③proper limit
〖轻重缓急〗[qīngzhònghuǎnjí]
in order of importance and urgency; order of priority
〖轻装〗(名)[qīngzhuāng]
light packs; lightly equipped (with essentials)

氢(名)[qīng]
hydrogen
〖氢弹〗(名)[qīngdàn]〔枚 méi〕
hydrogen bomb

倾(动)[qīng]
① incline ② collapse ③ exhaust
〖倾家荡产〗[qīngjiādàngchǎn]
lose one's entire fortune; reduce to poverty and ruin
〖倾盆大雨〗[qīngpén dàyǔ]
pouring rain; torrential downpour
〖倾诉〗(动)[qīngsù]
get sth. off one's chest; make a clean breast of
〖倾听〗(动)[qīngtīng]
hear out; listen attentively
〖倾向〗(动、名)[qīngxiàng]
be inclined to; tend to; tendency; proneness
〖倾向性〗(名)[qīngxiàngxìng]
tendency
〖倾销〗(动)[qīngxiāo]
dump(e.g. goods)
〖倾斜〗(形)[qīngxié]
inclined
〖倾泻〗(动)[qīngxiè]
flow out; flood
〖倾轧〗(动)[qīngyà]
have internal dissension; infighting
〖倾注〗(动)[qīngzhù]
① pour down ② concentrate ... on ...

清(形、动)[qīng]
①pure; clean ②clear; clear up; check up
〖清白〗(形)[qīngbái]
pure; unsullied
〖清查〗(动)[qīngchá]
comb out; detect; investigate; inquire into; examine
〖清澈〗(形)[qīngchè]
clear; lucid
〖清晨〗(名)[qīngchén]
the early hours; dawn
〖清除〗(动)[qīngchú]
clear out; weed out
〖清楚〗(形)[qīngchu]
clear; lucid
〖清脆〗(形)[qīngcuì]
clear
〖清单〗(名)[qīngdān]
detailed list or account
〖清淡〗(形)[qīngdàn]
① quiet and simple ② mild (flavour); weak ③slack(e.g. season)

〖清点〗(动)[qīngdiǎn]
take an inventory; make a list; check up
〖清高〗(形)[qīnggāo]
self-contained; pure and lofty
〖清规戒律〗[qīngguījièlǜ]
taboos and commandments; outmoded rules; regulations and conventions
〖清洁〗(形)[qīngjié]
clean
〖清净〗(形)[qīngjìng]
quiet and peaceful
〖清静〗(形)[qīngjìng]
quiet; tranquil
〖清理〗(动)[qīnglǐ]
① check up ② clean up; put in order ③ sort out
〖清凉〗(形)[qīngliáng]
fresh and cool
〖清爽〗(形)[qīngshuǎng]
① cool and refreshing ② feeling good and fit
〖清水衙门〗[qīngshuǐyámen]
work unit which has no outside income; one who is above bribery
〖清算〗(动)[qīngsuàn]
settle accounts; clear off account; rid; liquidate
〖清谈〗(名)[qīngtán]
empty talk; impractical discussion
〖清晰〗(形)[qīngxī]
clear and precise
〖清洗〗(动)[qīngxǐ]
purge; eliminate; comb out
〖清闲〗(形)[qīngxián]
be at leisure
〖清香〗(形)[qīngxiāng]
freshly fragrant
〖清新〗(形)[qīngxīn]
delightfully fresh
〖清醒〗(形、动)[qīngxǐng]
sober; sane; clear headed; return to one's senses; get sober
〖清秀〗(形)[qīngxiù]
delicate
〖清一色〗[qīngyīsè]
all of one suit; all of the same colour; a homogeneous body
〖清音〗(名)[qīngyīn]
voiceless consonants
〖清早〗(名)[qīngzǎo]
early morning

蜻 [qīng]

〖蜻蜓〗(名)[qīngtíng]〔只 zhī〕
dragonfly
〖蜻蜓点水〗[qīngtíngdiǎnshuǐ]
touch superficially; skim over one's work

qíng

情(名)[qíng]

① feelings ② condition
〖情报〗(名)[qíngbào]
information; intelligence
〖情不自禁〗[qíngbùzìjìn]
be tempted to; cannot help; overcome by one's feelings
〖情调〗(名)[qíngdiào]
sentimental appeal; sentimental tone or mood

〖情感〗(名)[qínggǎn]
emotion; feelings; sensibilities
〖情节〗(名)[qíngjié]
① plot or details (of a story, etc.) ② details of a case
〖情景〗(名)[qíngjǐng]
general aspect
〖情况〗(名)[qíngkuàng]
circumstances; conditions; state of affairs; situation
〖情理〗(名)[qínglǐ]
reasonableness; reason
〖情面〗(名)[qíngmiàn]
face saving; sensibility; personal consideration
〖情投意合〗[qíngtóuyìhé]
agree in opinion; suit each other perfectly; mutual affection and agreement
〖情形〗(名)[qíngxing]
general condition; situation
〖情绪〗(名)[qíngxù]
sentiment; disposition; spirit; morale (e. g. of troops)
〖情谊〗(名)[qíngyì]
friendship
〖情意〗(名)[qíngyì]
cordiality; love and affection
〖情由〗(名)[qíngyóu]
the details and cause of a matter
〖情愿〗(助动)[qíngyuàn]
be willing to; wish to; would rather

晴(形)[qíng]
clear (e. g. sky); fair; fine (weather)
〖晴空万里〗[qíngkōngwànlǐ]
clear open sky
〖晴朗〗(形)[qínglǎng]
bright and clear (weathear)
〖晴纶〗(名)[qínglún]
orlon
〖晴天霹雳〗[qíngtiānpīlì]
a bolt from the blue
〖晴雨表〗(名)[qíngyǔbiǎo]
barometer

qǐng

顷(量)[qǐng]
a measure word for land
〖顷刻〗(名)[qǐngkè]
in a short instant

请(动)[qǐng]
① request; ask for ② invite
〖请便〗[qǐng biàn]
do as you please
〖请假〗[qǐng jià]
ask for leave
〖请教〗(动)[qǐngjiào]
ask for advice; learn from
〖请客〗[qǐng kè]
invite someone (to dinner, etc.)
〖请求〗(动、名)[qǐngqiú]
beg; request; ask for; begging
〖请示〗(动)[qǐngshì]
ask for instructions; ask instructions from
〖请帖〗(名)[qǐngtiě]
invitation card
〖请问〗(动)[qǐngwèn]

may I ask...
〖请愿〗[qǐng yuàn]
petition
〖请坐〗[qǐng zuò]
sit down please

qìng

庆(动)[qìng]
celebrate; congratulate
〖庆典〗(名)[qìngdiǎn]
celebration
〖庆贺〗(动)[qìnghè]
congratulate; celebrate
〖庆幸〗(动)[qìngxìng]
rejoice (e. g. over a narrow escape)
〖庆祝〗(动)[qìngzhù]
celebrate; congratulate

亲 [qìng]
另见 qīn
〖亲家〗(名)[qìngjia]
relatives by marriage; families related by marriage

罄 [qìng]
〖罄竹难书〗[qìngzhúnánshū]
(lit.) (usu. crime) too numerous to inscribe on all bamboo strips; (fig.) too numerous to be listed in one book

qióng

穷(形)[qióng]
① poor; impoverished ② exhausted; hard pressed; pushed to limit
〖穷光蛋〗[qióngguāngdàn]
pauper; poor wretch
〖穷兵黩武〗[qióngbīngdúwǔ]
wage sanguinary wars; militaristic and aggressive (e. g. policy)
〖穷尽〗(形)[qióngjìn]
exhaustion (of resources)
〖穷苦〗(形)[qióngkǔ]
poverty stricken
〖穷困〗(形)[qióngkùn]
poor; impoverished
〖穷奢极欲〗[qióngshējíyù]
have every luxury; live off the fat of the land
〖穷途末路〗[qióngtúmòlù]
at one's last gasp; at the end of one's tether; driven into an impasse
〖穷乡僻壤〗[qióngxiāngpìrǎng]
the remote hinterland; the remotest corners of the countryside
〖穷凶极恶〗[qióngxiōngjí'è]
in a vicious and unrestrained way; ferocious; fiendish; wickedness and evil carried to the utmost degree
〖穷则思变〗[qióngzésībiàn]
poverty gives rise to the desire for change

qiū

丘(名)[qiū]
a mound; hillock
〖丘陵〗(名)[qiūlíng]

an earthen mound; hill

秋(名)[qiū]
autumn; the fall
〖秋风扫落叶〗
[qiūfēngsǎoluòyè]
(lit.)the autumn wind sweeping the dead leaves; (fig.)irresistible force
〖秋耕〗(名)[qiūgēng]
plough in autumn
〖秋毫无犯〗[qiūháowúfàn]
do not cause the slightest damage(e.g. to the people); forbid the slightest violation of (e.g. the people's interest)
〖秋后蚂蚱〗[qiūhòumàzha]
(lit.)locust in late autumn; (fig.)the days are numbered
〖秋季〗(名)[qiūjì]
autumn
〖秋千〗(名)[qiūqiān]
a swing
〖秋收〗(名)[qiūshōu]
harvest in autumn; autumn harvest
〖秋收起义〗[Qiūshōu Qǐyì]
Autumn Harvest Uprising This famous Uprising under the leadership of Comrade Mao Tsetung was launched in September 1927 by the people's armed forces of Hsiushui, Pinghsiang, Pingkiang and Liuyang Counties on the HunanKiangsi border, who formed the 1st Division of the First Workers' and Peasants' Revolutionary Army. Comrade Mao Tsetung led this force to the Chingkang Mountains where a revolutionary base was established.
〖秋天〗(名)[qiūtiān]
autumn
〖秋种〗(名)[qiūzhòng]
autumn sowing

qiú

囚[qiú]
〖囚犯〗(名)[qiúfàn]
prisoner
〖囚禁〗(动)[qiújìn]
imprison; put in prison

求(动)[qiú]
beg; request; try to obtain; require
〖求得〗(动)[qiúdé]
obtain
〖求和〗[qiú hé]
① sue for peace ② try to have the game ended in a draw
〖求救〗(动)[qiújiù]
cry for help; seek help
〖求情〗[qiú qíng]
ask a favour; appeal to another's mercy; plead with
〖求全〗(动)[qiúquán]
(usually derog.)ask for perfection
〖求同存异〗[qiútóngcúnyì]
seek common ground while reserving differences
〖求学〗(动)[qiúxué]

go to school or college for further studies
〖求援〗(动)[qiúyuán]
ask for help
〖求证〗(动)[qiúzhèng]
prove that...
〖求之不得〗[qiúzhībùdé]
just what one wished for; exceedingly welcome

泅(动)[qiú]
swim
〖泅水〗[qiú shuǐ]
swim

酋[qiú]
〖酋长〗(名)[qiúzhǎng]
tribal chieftain; chieftain

球(名)[qiú]〔个 gè〕
a ball; a ball game; a sphere
〖球场〗(名)[qiúchǎng]
playground for any kind of ball games
〖球迷〗(名)[qiúmí]
a ball game fan
〖球面〗(名)[qiúmiàn]
(math.) surface of sphere; spherical surface
〖球拍〗(名)[qiúpāi]
a racket; a bat
〖球赛〗(名)[qiúsài]
a ball match
〖球体〗(名)[qiútǐ]
spheroid
〖球鞋〗(名)[qiúxié]〔双 shuāng〕
shoes for games

qū

区(名)[qū]
region; area; district
〖区别〗(动、名)[qūbié]
distinguish between; draw a distinction between; difference
〖区分〗(动)[qūfēn]
differentiate between
〖区划〗(名)[qūhuà]
seperate into classes or categories; the division of regions
〖区委〗(名)[qūwěi]
district party committee
〖区域〗(名)[qūyù]
area; region

曲[qū]
另见qǔ
〖曲解〗(动)[qūjiě]
distort; twist; misinterpret; misrepresent
〖曲线〗(名)[qūxiàn]
curve
〖曲线运动〗[qūxiànyùndòng]
zigzag course; curvilinear motion
〖曲折〗(形)[qūzhé]
circuitous; intricate; ups and downs
〖曲直〗(名)[qūzhí]
right and wrong

驱[qū]
〖驱除〗(动)[qūchú]
drive away; exterminate; expel
〖驱使〗(动)[qūshǐ]
① dictate; order about ② imp-

el; drive
〖驱逐〗(动)[qūzhú]
expel; oust
〖驱逐出境〗[qūzhú chūjìng]
deportation; expel (sb.) from a country
〖驱逐舰〗(名)qūzhújiàn]
〔艘 sōu〕a destroyer

屈(动)[qū]
① bent ② bow down; submit ③ be in the wrong
〖屈服〗(动)[qūfú]
submit; give way; bow to; yield to
〖屈辱〗(名)[qūrǔ]
humiliation; disgrace
〖屈膝〗(动)[qūxī]
knuckle down; succumb; give in
〖屈指可数〗[qūzhǐkěshǔ]
not many; only a few to count

躯[qū]
〖躯干〗(名)[qūgàn]
the trunk (physical)
〖躯体〗(名)[qūtǐ]
the human body

趋[qū]
〖趋势〗(名)[qūshì]
trend; tendency
〖趋向〗(名、动)[qūxiàng]
directional trend; tendency; head toward; tend to

qú

渠(名)[qú]〔条 tiáo〕
drain; canal
〖渠道〗(名)[qúdào]〔条 tiáo〕
channel; irrigationcanal; drain

qǔ

曲(名)[qǔ]
song; drama; opera
另见 qū
〖曲调〗(名)[qǔdiào]
melody of song; tune
〖曲高和寡〗[qǔgāohèguǎ]
songs of a highbrow type will find very few people to join in the chorus
〖曲艺〗(名)[qǔyì]
ballad singing and story telling
〖曲子〗(名)[qǔzi]〔支 zhī〕
tune; melody

取(动)[qǔ]
① take; get; obtain; aim for ② select for
〖取材〗(动)[qǔcái]
acquire material (for writing)
〖取长补短〗[qǔchángbǔduǎn]
overcome one's weaknesses by learning from each other's strong points
〖取代〗(动)[qǔdài]
replace; step into the shoes of; take over
〖取道〗(动)[qǔdào]
by way of
〖取得〗(动)[qǔdé]
obtain; get
〖取缔〗(动)[qǔdì]

ban; outlaw; prohibit; forbid; suppress
〖取而代之〗[qǔ'érdàizhī]
replace; take someone's place; take over
〖取经〗[qǔ jīng]
seek for experience
〖取决〗(动)[qǔjué]
depend on; be decided by; hinge on
〖取暖〗(动)[qǔnuǎn]
warm(oneself) up
〖取其精华,去其糟粕〗
[qǔqíjīng huá, qùqízāopò]
select the refined and discard the crude
〖取巧〗(动)[qǔqiǎo]
manipulate; take advantage of the situation; skilful management
〖取舍〗(动)[qǔshě]
(decide what to) assimilate and (what to) discard
〖取胜〗(动)[qǔshèng]
win victory
〖取消〗(动)[qǔxiāo]
cancel; negate; liquidate; abolish; do away with; repeal
〖取笑〗(动)[qǔxiào]
make fun of
〖取之不尽,用之不竭〗
[qǔzhī bùjìn, yòngzhībùjié]
inexhaustible(sources)

娶(动)[qǔ]
marry(a wife)

qù

去(动)[qù]
①go to; leave for ②be done for; lost; gone ③get rid of; discard
〖去粗取精〗[qùcūqǔjīng]
discard the dross and select the essential
〖去掉〗(动)[qùdiào]
do away with; get rid of; abandon
〖去路〗(名)[qùlù]
exit; the way to advance
〖去年〗(名)[qùnián]
last year
〖去声〗(名)[qùshēng]
the fourth tone
〖去世〗(动)[qùshì]
pass away; die
〖去伪存真〗[qùwěicúnzhēn]
eliminate the false and retain the true
〖去向〗(名)[qùxiàng]
heading for

趣[qù]
〖趣味〗(名)[qùwèi]
interest

quān

圈(名、动)[quān]
① a circle; ring ② encircle; fence in; draw a circle over
另见 juàn
〖圈套〗(名)[quāntào]
a trap

〖圈子〗(名)[quānzi]
circle

quán

权(名)[quán]
power; (law) right; influence
〖权衡〗(动)[quánhéng]
judge and weigh (importance); weigh and consider
〖权力〗(名)[quánlì]
power and authority; power
〖权利〗(名)[quánlì]
right; privilege
〖权势〗(名)[quánshì]
power and influence
〖权术〗(名)[quánshù]
intrigue; plot; means
〖权威〗(名)[quánwēi]
authority
〖权限〗(名)[quánxiàn]
limits of authority; within the power or right of
〖权宜之计〗[quányízhījì]
temporary expedient; stopgap measure; makeshift
〖权益〗(名)[quányì]
legal rights; inviolable rights

全(形、副)[quán]
① whole ② complete; perfectly; completely; all
〖全部〗(名)[quánbù]
the whole; all; the complete
〖全程〗(名)[quánchéng]
the entire journey; the whole journey
〖全都〗(副)[quándōu]
all; completely
〖全方位〗(形)[quánfāngwèi]
all directional; comprehensive
〖全副〗(形)[quánfù]
full (e.g. fully equipped); whole set of
〖全国〗(形)[quánguó]
national; across the nation; whole country
〖全国一盘棋〗[quánguóyīpánqí]
co-ordinate all the activities of the nation as in a chess game; all-round considerations and arrangements for the nation as a whole
〖全会〗(名)[quánhuì]
plenary session; plenum
〖全集〗(名)[quánjí]
the complete works (of an author)
〖全局〗(名)[quánjú]
whole situation; the situation as a whole
〖全力〗(名)[quánlì]
with whole strength; do everything in one's power; all-out
〖全力以赴〗[quánlìyǐfù]
go all out; make every effort to; do one's utmost
〖全貌〗(名)[quánmào]
the entire outlook
〖全面〗(形)[quánmiàn]
overall; allround; all-out
〖全民〗(名)[quánmín]
whole people; entire people
〖全民所有制〗
[quánmínsuǒyǒuzhì]

ownership by the whole people
〖全能〗(名)[quánnéng]
allround; almighty
〖全盘〗(名)[quánpán]
overall; whole; entire; comprehensive
〖全球〗(名)[quánqiú]
the whole world; the entire globe
〖全权〗(名)[quánquán]
full powers; plenipotentiary
〖全权代表〗[quánquándàibiǎo]
plenipotentiary
〖全神贯注〗
[quánshénguànzhù]
be absorbed in; be utterly concentrated on
〖全体〗(名)[quántǐ]
all; entire; whole
〖全心全意〗[quánxīnquányì]
heart and soul; whole-heartedly

泉(名)[quán]
spring
〖泉水〗(名)[quánshuǐ]
spring; spring water
〖泉眼〗(名)[quányǎn]
point in ground from which spring water issues
〖泉源〗(名)[quányuán]
springs; sources

拳(名)[quán]
fist
〖拳击〗(名)[quánjī]
punch with fist; box
〖拳头〗(名)[quántóu]〔个 gè〕
fist; blow by fist
〖拳头产品〗[quántóuchǎnpǐn]
highly competitive product

痊 [quán]
〖痊愈〗(动)[quányù]
fully recover from illness

quǎn

犬(名)[quǎn]
dog
〖犬牙交错〗[quǎnyájiāocuò]
jigsaw pattern

quàn

劝(动)[quàn]
persuade
〖劝导〗(动)[quàndǎo]
exhort; induce; persuade
〖劝告〗(动、名)[quàngào]
advise; persuade; remonstrate; advice; admonition
〖劝解〗(动)[quànjiě]
remonstrate; persuade
〖劝说〗(动)[quànshuō]
persuade
〖劝阻〗(动)[quànzǔ]
dissuade from; discourage from

券(名)[quàn]〔张 zhāng〕
certificate; ticket; coupon

quē

缺(动)[quē]
①need ②be short of; lack
〖缺点〗(名)[quēdiǎn]

shortcoming; weak point; defect
〖缺额〗(名)[quē'é]
a vacancy; deficiency
〖缺乏〗(动)[quēfá]
lack of
〖缺口〗(名)[quēkǒu]
breach; gap
〖缺门〗(名)[quēmén]
gap
〖缺欠〗(名、动)[quēqiàn]
defect; deficiency; imperfection; drawback
〖缺勤〗(动)[quēqín]
be absent from work
〖缺少〗(动)[quēshǎo]
be lack of
〖缺席〗(动)[quēxí]
be absent from (meeting, etc.)
〖缺陷〗(名)[quēxiàn]
defect; shortcoming; imperfection; drawback

qué

瘸(动、形)[qué]
lame
〖瘸子〗(名)[quézi]
a cripple

què

却(副)[què]
yet; but

确[què]
〖确保〗(动)[quèbǎo]
make sure; secure; guarantee
〖确定〗(动)[quèdìng]
affirm; fix; set
〖确立〗(动)[quèlì]
establish; build up
〖确切〗(形)[quèqiè]
①precise and definite ②solid
〖确认〗(动)[quèrèn]
affirm
〖确实〗(形)[quèshí]
exact; true; certain; solid
〖确信〗(动)[quèxìn]
be sure; be confident
〖确凿〗(形)[quèzáo]
established; sound; ironclad (e.g. fact)

qún

裙(名)[qún]
skirt
〖裙带关系〗[qúndài guānxì]
nepotism
〖裙子〗(名)[qúnzi]〔条 tiáo〕
skirt

群(名、量)[qún]
①crowd; group ②a measure word (for person, animal, etc.)
〖群策群力〗[qúncèqúnlì]
collective wisdom and efforts
〖群岛〗(名)[qúndǎo]
archipelago
〖群氓〗(名)[qúnméng]
mob
〖群魔乱舞〗[qúnmóluànwǔ]
evil spirits of all kinds dance in a riotous revelry
〖群起而攻之〗
[qúnqǐ'érgōngzhī]

rally together to attack
〖群言堂〗(名)[qúnyántáng]
rule by the voice of many
〖群众〗(名)[qúnzhòng]
masses
〖群众关系〗[qúnzhòngguānxì]
relationship with the masses
〖群众观点〗
[qúnzhòngguāndiǎn]
mass viewpoint q
〖群众路线〗[qúnzhòng lùxiàn]
mass line
〖群众性〗(名)[qúnzhòngxìng]
mass character
〖群众运动〗
[qúnzhòng yùndòng]
mass movement
〖群众组织〗[qúnzhòng zǔzhī]
mass organization

rán

然[rán]

〖然而〗(连)[rán'ér]
but; yet; however; nevertheless

〖然后〗(副)[ránhòu]
then; afterwards

燃[rán]

〖燃料〗(名)[ránliào]
fuel

〖燃眉之急〗[ránméizhījí]
(lit.) as urgent as eyebrows on fire; (fig.) very urgent; emergency

〖燃烧〗(动)[ránshāo]
burn; set on fire

rǎn

染(动)[rǎn]
① dye ② contract; get infected with; catch (e.g. illness)

〖染料〗(名)[rǎnliào]
dye; dyestuff

〖染色〗[rǎnsè]
dye

〖染指〗(动)[rǎnzhǐ]
have a hand in; meddle in (for gain); poke one's nose in; come in for a share

rāng

嚷[rāng]
另见 rǎng

〖嚷嚷〗(动)[rāngrang]
make a row; bawl; make much noise

ráng

瓤(名)[ráng]
the juicy part of watery fruits (e.g. melon, orange, etc.)

rǎng

嚷(动)[rǎng]
shout; yell; clamo
另见 rāng

ràng

让(动、介)[ràng]
① concede; make way for; offer hospitality ② cede; transfer ③ let; permit; allow
〖让步〗[ràngbù]
make concession; compromise
〖让利〗[rànglì]
cut profits(to promote sales)
〖让路〗[rànglù]
make way(for sb.)
〖让座〗[ràng zuò]
give up one's seat(to sb.)

ráo

饶(动)[ráo]
forgive; pardon
〖饶恕〗(动)[ráoshù]
forgive; pardon; excuse

rǎo

扰[rǎo]
〖扰乱〗(动)[rǎoluàn]
cause havoc with; mess up; perturb; disturb

rào

绕(动)[rào]
entwine; intertwine; revolve; steer clear of
〖绕圈子〗[ràoquānzi]
take a roundabout (way); beat about the bush
〖绕远儿〗[ràoyuǎnr]
take a round about way

rě

惹(动)[rě]
nettle; annoy; irritate
〖惹不起〗[rě buqǐ]
dare not provoke
〖惹得起〗[rě deqǐ]
dare nettle
〖惹祸〗[rěhuò]
court trouble(disasters)
〖惹事〗[rě shì]
create trouble
〖惹是生非〗[rěshìshēngfēi]
provoke mischief

rè

热(形、动)[rè]
① hot ② heat(sth.) ③ show warmth of feeling
〖热爱〗(动)[rè'ài]
love ardently; love heartily
〖热潮〗(名)[rècháo]
upsurge
〖热忱〗(名)[rèchén]
enthusiasm; zeal
〖热带〗(名)[rèdài]
the torrid zone; the tropics
〖热点〗(名)[rèdiǎn]
hot spot; hot point; explosive issue
〖热电厂〗(名)[rèdiànchǎng]
thermo-electric plant
〖热核反应〗[rèhéfǎnyìng]
thermonuclear reaction
〖热烘烘〗(形)[rèhōnghōng]
① stirring; (fig.) nice and warm ② affectionate

〖热火〗(形)[rèhuo]
deeply attached to; seething
〖热火朝天〗[rèhuǒcháotiān]
burning with ardour; stirring and seething with activity
〖热泪盈眶〗[rèlèiyíngkuàng]
one's eyes brim over with warm, excited tears; warm tears well up in one's eyes
〖热量〗(名)[rèliàng]
heat capacity; warmth
〖热烈〗(形)[rèliè]
warm; enthusiastic; heartily; fervent; ardent
〖热门〗(形)[rèmén]
popular; in great demand
〖热闹〗(形、名)[rènao]
① (where it is) abustle and astir; noisy; boisterous; bustling ② lively; jolly; animated; exciting ③ a noisy and amusing show
〖热能〗(名)[rènéng]
thermal energy
〖热切〗(形)[rèqiè]
warm and cordial; ardent; earnest
〖热情〗(名、形)[rèqíng]
warmth; fervent spirit; devotion; enthusiastic
〖热水〗(名)[rèshuǐ]
hot water
〖热水袋〗(名)[rèshuǐdài]
[个 gè] hot water bottle
〖热水瓶〗(名)[rèshuǐpíng]
[个 gè] thermos flask
〖热望〗(动)[rèwàng]
hope fervently; long for earnestly
〖热线〗(名)[rèxiàn]
hot line
〖热心〗(名)[rèxīn]
enthusiasm; earnestness; ardour; zeal
〖热心肠〗(名)[rèxīncháng]
warm-hearted
〖热血〗(名)[rèxuè]
hot blood
〖热源〗(名)[rèyuán]
heat source
〖热中〗(动)[rèzhōng]
hanker for; bent on; intent on

rén

人(名)[rén]
person; human beings; people
〖人才〗(名)[réncái]
men of talent; men of ability
〖人称〗(名)[rénchēng]
(gram.) (the first, second or third) person
〖人称代词〗[rénchēngdàicí]
personal pronoun
〖人次〗(量)[réncì]
men-times
〖人定胜天〗[réndìngshèngtiān]
it is man's will, not heaven, that decides
〖人浮于事〗[rénfúyúshì]
superfluous staff; overstaffed
〖人格〗(名)[réngé]
personality; character
〖人格化〗(动)[réngéhuà]
personify
〖人工〗(名)[réngōng]

① done by man; artificial ② a calculating unit of the amount of work done (e.g. man hours)
〖人工降雨〗[réngōngjiàngyǔ]
artificial rain fall
〖人家〗(名)[rénjiā]
household
〖人家〗(代)[rénjia]
a pronoun which can replace first or third person
〖人间〗(名)[rénjiān]
the world of men
〖人口〗(名)[rénkǒu]
population
〖人类〗(名)[rénlèi]
mankind
〖人力〗(名)[rénlì]
manpower; manual labour
〖人们〗(名)[rénmen]
a general term for a great number of people (e.g. they)
〖人民〗(名)[rénmín]
people
〖人民币〗(名)[rénmínbì]
Renminbi (currency of the People's Republic of China)
〖人民代表大会〗
[rénmín dài biǎo dàhuì]
the people's congress
〖人命〗(名)[rénmìng]
human life
〖人民民主专政〗
[rénmínmínzhǔzhuānzhèng]
people's democratic dictatorship
〖人民内部矛盾〗
[rénmínnèibùmáodùn]
contradictions among the people
〖人民战争〗[rénmínzhànzhēng]
people's war
〖人情〗(名)[rénqíng]
① human relationship ② a favour ③ reason ④ gift; present
〖人人〗[rénrén]
everybody
〖人山人海〗[rénshānrénhǎi]
huge crowds
〖人身〗(名)[rénshēn]
the human body; person
〖人参〗(名)[rénshēn]
ginseng
〖人生〗(名)[rénshēng]
the life of man
〖人生观〗(名)[rénshēngguān]
one's outlook on life; philosophy of life
〖人士〗(名)[rénshì]
personages; public figures
〖人事〗(名)[rénshì]
personnel affairs
〖人所共知〗[rénsuǒgòngzhī]
it is common knowledge that ...; it is widely known
〖人为〗[rénwéi]
artificial; man-made
〖人物〗(名)[rénwù]
① personage; a notable figure ② characters (in a play, novel, etc.)
〖人心〗(名)[rénxīn]
the feelings of the people
〖人心所向〗[rénxīnsuǒxiàng]
the feelings of the people are for ...
〖人心向背〗[rénxīnxiàngbèi]

R

the people are for or against ...
〖人行道〗(名)[rénxíngdào]
〔条 tiáo〕pavement; sidewalk
〖人性〗(名)[rénxìng]
humanity; human nature
〖人选〗(名)[rénxuǎn]
candidate
〖人烟〗(名)[rényān]
household
〖人影儿〗(名)[rényǐngr]
① the shadow of man ② living soul
〖人员〗(名)[rényuán]
personnel
〖人云亦云〗[rényúnyìyún]
repeat word for word what others say; parrot others
〖人造地球卫星〗[rénzàodìqiúwèixīng]〔颗 kē〕
man-made earth satellite
〖人造胰岛素〗[rénzàoyídǎosù]
artificial insulin
〖人证〗(名)[rénzhèng]
testimony given by a witness
〖人种〗(名)[rénzhǒng]
the human species; a person's race

仁(形、名)[rén]
① benevolent; benevolence ② the core, kernel or pip (of fruits, nuts, etc.)
〖仁慈〗(形)[réncí]
benevolent; merciful
〖仁政〗(名)[rénzhèng]
the policy of benevolence
〖仁至义尽〗[rénzhìyìjìn]
exercise great restraint and exert one's utmost effort; magnanimous

rěn

忍(动)[rěn]
endure; suffer; tolerate
〖忍不住〗[rěnbuzhù]
unbearable; unable to restrain (oneself); pass the limits of endurance
〖忍得住〗[rěndezhù]
endurable; put up with; bearable
〖忍耐〗(动)[rěnnài]
be tolerant of; endure; put up with
〖忍气吞声〗[rěnqìtūnshēng]
swallow insults in meek submission
〖忍受〗(动)[rěnshòu]
suffer; endure; undergo; bear
〖忍无可忍〗[rěnwúkěrěn]
be driven past the limits of forbearance; come to the end of one's patience
〖忍心〗[rěnxīn]
pitiless; hard-hearted

rèn

刃(名)[rèn]
the cutting edge of a knife or sword
〖刃具〗(名)[rènjù]
cutter

认(动)[rèn]
①recognize; understand; realise ② take (sb.) for ...; adopt ③admit (e.g. defeat)
〖认得〗(动)[rènde]
know (e.g. sb.); recognize
〖认定〗(动)[rèndìng]
affirm; identify ... with ...
〖认可〗(动)[rènkě]
approve; give legal force to
〖认领〗(动)[rènlǐng]
claim (sth.) one has lost and is found by others
〖认生〗(形)[rènshēng]
(of a child) feeling shy (before a stranger)
〖认识〗(动、名)[rènshi]
understand; comprehend; be familiar with; be aware of; cognition; knowledge
〖认识论〗(名)[rènshilùn]
theory of knowledge
〖认输〗[rènshū]
admit defeat
〖认为〗(动)[rènwéi]
take for; regard as
〖认贼作父〗[rènzéizuòfù]
take foes for parents; take enemies for benefactors
〖认账〗[rènzhàng]
confess what one has done or said
〖认真〗(形)[rènzhēn]
earnest; serious (e.g. attitude)
〖认罪〗[rènzuì]
acknowledge one's guilt; plead guilty

任(动、名、介)[rèn]
①appoint; assign ②responsibility; duty ③let
〖任何〗(代)[rènhé]
any; whatever
〖任劳任怨〗[rènláorènyuàn]
work hard without complaint
〖任免〗(动)[rènmiǎn]
appoint and dismiss
〖任命〗(动)[rènmìng]
appoint; nominate
〖任凭〗(动、连)[rènpíng]
let (sb.) take his course; no matter what; despite
〖任期〗(名)[rènqī]
term of service
〖任人摆布〗[rènrénbǎibù]
be at the mercy of; under someone's thumb
〖任人唯亲〗[rènrénwéiqīn]
appoint people by favouritism
〖任人唯贤〗[rènrénwéixián]
appoint people on their merits
〖任务〗(名)[rènwù]
an assigned task; duties
〖任性〗(形)[rènxìng]
capricious; unrestrained; intractable
〖任意〗(副)[rènyì]
just as one wishes; wilfully; arbitrarilly; at will
〖任用〗(动)[rènyòng]
appoint; assign
〖任职〗[rènzhí]
take office

〖任重道远〗[rènzhòngdàoyuǎn]
shoulder a heavy responsibility and embark on a long journey

韧(形)[rèn]
pliable; flexible
〖韧性〗(名)[rènxìng]
① tenacity ② flexibility

妊[rèn]
〖妊娠〗(动)[rènshēn]
be pregnant

rēng

扔(动)[rēng]
throw; cast; hurl
〖扔掉〗(动)[rēngdiào]
throw away; cast aside; discard

réng

仍(副)[réng]
still; yet
〖仍旧〗(副)[réngjiù]
yet; still; as before
〖仍然〗(副)[réngrán]
as usual; as before

rì

日(名)[rì]
① the sun ② date; day
〖日报〗(名)[rìbào]
a daily newspaper
〖日薄西山〗[rìbóxīshān]
(lit.) sinking fast just like the sun setting behind the western hills; (fig.) in one's latter days
〖日常〗(形)[rìcháng]
day-to-day; usual; daily; everyday
〖日程〗(名)[rìchéng]
a daily schedule; agenda for the day
〖日光〗(名)[rìguāng]
sunshine; sunlight; rays of the sun
〖日光灯〗(名)[rìguāngdēng]
fluorescent light; daylight lamp
〖日光浴〗(名)[rìguāngyù]
sun bath
〖日积月累〗[rìjīyuèlěi]
by gradual accumulation; day's and month's multiplying
〖日记〗(名)[rìjì][篇 piān]
diary
〖日见〗(副)[rìjiàn]
shows or reveals day after day
〖日历〗(名)[rìlì]
a calendar
〖日暮途穷〗[rìmùtúqióng]
in one's decline; on one's last legs; head for doom
〖日期〗(名)[rìqī]
a date
〖日食〗(名)[rìshí]
eclipse of the sun; solar eclipse
〖日新月异〗[rìxīnyuèyì]
constant changes; change rapidly; bring about new changes day after day
〖日夜〗(名)[rìyè]
day and night

〖日以继夜〗[rìyǐjìyè]
night and day
〖日益〗(副)[rìyì]
more and more; with each passing day; day by day
〖日用品〗(名)[rìyòngpǐn]
daily necessities; articles of daily use
〖日子〗(名)[rìzi]
① day; date; a particular day ② time ③ life; living condition

róng

荣(形)[róng]
① prosperous; thriving ② honourable
〖荣幸〗(形)[róngxìng]
honoured; honourable
〖荣誉〗(名)[róngyù]
honour; an honourable reputation
〖荣誉军人〗[róngyùjūnrén]
disabled soldiers

绒(名)[róng]
cotton; silk or woolen goods
〖绒裤〗(名)[róngkù]〔条 tiáo〕
felted under trousers
〖绒衣〗(名)[róngyī]〔件 jiàn〕
felted undershirt

容(动)[róng]
①tolerate; allow; permit ②contain; hold
〖容光焕发〗[róngguānghuànfā]
glowing with health and in high spirits
〖容积〗(名)[róngjī]
volume as measured in cubic units
〖容量〗(名)[róngliàng]
capacity
〖容貌〗(名)[róngmào]
(a person's) facial appearance and expression
〖容纳〗(动)[róngnà]
contain; hold (e.g. many people)
〖容器〗(名)[róngqì]
container
〖容忍〗(动)[róngrěn]
tolerate; endure; stand
〖容许〗(动)[róngxǔ]
permit; allow
〖容易〗(形)[róngyì]
easy; be liable to; likely

溶(动)[róng]
dissolve in water
〖溶化〗(动)[rónghuà]
melt; thaw; dissolve
〖溶剂〗(名)[róngjì]
solvent
〖溶解〗(动)[róngjiě]
dissolve; thaw; melt; disintegrate
〖溶液〗(名)[róngyè]
fluid

熔(动)[róng]
smelt; fuse
〖熔点〗(名)[róngdiǎn]
the smelting point
〖熔化〗(动)[rónghuà]

smelt; fuse
〖熔炉〗(名)[rónglú]〔个 gè〕
crucible

融[róng]
〖融合〗(动)[rónghé]
amalgamate; blend; merge together; melt together
〖融化〗(动)[rónghuà]
melt; thaw
〖融会贯通〗[rónghuìguàntōng]
full comprehension; thorough understanding
〖融解〗(动)[róngjiě]
melt; fuse; fiquefy; dissolve
〖融洽〗(形)[róngqià]
harmonious
〖融资〗[róngzī]
finance; financing

rǒng

冗[rǒng]
〖冗长〗(形)[rǒngcháng]
lengthy; tediously long; cumbersome (e.g. writings; speeches)

róu

柔(形)[róu]
weak; flexible; pliant; soft; mild
〖柔和〗(形)[róuhé]
soft; mild; gentle
〖柔软〗(形)[róuruǎn]
soft; flexible; easily bent

揉(动)[róu]
rub

蹂[róu]
trample; tread on
〖蹂躏〗(动)[róulìn]
trample upon; ravage; crush under one's feet

ròu

肉(名)[ròu]
①meat; flesh ②the edible part of certain fruits
〖肉搏〗(动)[ròubó]
hand-to-hand combat; close quarter fighting
〖肉麻〗(形)[ròumá]
disgusting; nauseating; sickening
〖肉松〗(名)[ròusōng]
dried fluffy meat

rú

如(动)[rú]
①be like; similar to ②compare favourably; be as good as
〖如常〗[rúcháng]
commonplace; ordinary; as usual
〖如出一辙〗[rúchūyīzhé]
one and the same; identical; originate from the same source
〖如此〗(代)[rúcǐ]
such; like this
〖如此而已〗[rúcǐ'éryǐ]
that is what it all adds up to; that is all there is to it
〖如法炮制〗[rúfǎpáozhì]

follow suit; be modelled on
〖如故〗[rúgù]
① as usual; as before ② be like old friends
〖如果〗(连)[rúguǒ]
if; supposing that
〖如何〗(代)[rúhé]
how? what?
〖如虎添翼〗[rúhǔtiānyì]
just like adding wings to a tiger
〖如火如荼〗[rúhuǒrútú]
flaring like a fire set to dry tinder; momentous; imposing; grand; roaring
〖如获至宝〗[rúhuòzhìbǎo]
as if one has gained treasured possessions
〖如饥似渴〗[rújīsìkě]
seek eagerly; thirst for (e.g. revolutionary theory)
〖如今〗(名)[rújīn]
nowadays; these days
〖如期〗[rúqī]
in time; as scheduled
〖如丧考妣〗[rúsàngkǎobǐ]
as bereaved as at the loss of one's parents
〖如上〗[rúshàng]
as above
〖如实〗[rúshí]
accurately; truthfully
〖如释重负〗[rúshìzhòngfù]
just like a big load has been taken off one's mind
〖如同〗(动)[rútóng]
similar to; like
〖如下〗[rúxià]
as follows
〖如意〗(形)[rúyì]
as one wishes; as one likes it; according to one's wishes
〖如鱼得水〗[rúyúdéshuǐ]
(lit.) like fish in water; (fig.) one's desire is gratified
〖如愿以偿〗[rúyuànyǐcháng]
obtain what is desired; achieve what one wishes

儒(名)[rú]
Confucianism; Confucianist
〖儒艮〗[rúgèn]
dugong
〖儒家〗(名)[Rújiā]
Confucianists; Confucian school
〖儒生〗(名)[rúshēng]
Confucian scholars

蠕[rú]
〖蠕动〗(动)[rúdòng]
wriggling

rǔ

乳(名)[rǔ]
① the breasts ② milk
〖乳房〗(名)[rǔfáng]
the breasts
〖乳牛〗(名)[rǔniú]
[头 tóu] a milk cow
〖乳汁〗(名)[rǔzhī]
milk
〖乳制品〗(名)[rǔzhìpǐn]
dairy products

辱[rǔ]
〖辱骂〗(动)[rǔmà]
vilify; abuse; revile

rù

入(动)[rù]
enter; go into; come in or into
〖入不敷出〗[rùbùfūchū]
the income falls short of the expenditure
〖入超〗(动)[rùchāo]
adverse trade balance; trade deficit; import excess
〖入境〗[rùjìng]
enter country; entry (e.g. visa)
〖入口〗(名)[rùkǒu]
entrance
〖入门〗[rù mén]
(learn) the ABC of ...; ushered into a subject; cross the threshold
〖入迷〗[rùmí]
become fascinated; be obsessed by
〖入侵〗(动)[rùqīn]
invade
〖入神〗[rùshén]
be deeply absorbed in
〖入手〗(动)[rùshǒu]
begin; start; get under way; take ... as the point of departure
〖入睡〗(动)[rùshuì]
fall asleep
〖入伍〗[rùwǔ]
enlist; enroll; join the army
〖入席〗[rùxí]
take one's seat
〖入学〗[rùxué]
(for school) enrol; enrolment

褥(名)[rù]
a mattress
〖褥子〗(名)[rùzi]〔条 tiáo〕
a mattress

ruǎn

软(形)[ruǎn]
soft
〖软化〗(动)[ruǎnhuà]
soften up; attenuate
〖软和〗(形)[ruǎnhuo]
comfortable; cosy; soft and tender
〖软件〗(名)[ruǎnjiàn]
software
〖软绵绵〗(形)[ruǎnmiánmián]
velvety; feathery
〖软弱〗(形)[ruǎnruò]
weak; feeble
〖软弱性〗(名)[ruǎnruòxìng]
weakness; flabbiness
〖软席〗(名)[ruǎnxí]
soft (cushioned) seats
〖软饮料〗(名)[ruǎnyǐnliào]
soft drinks
〖软硬兼施〗[ruǎnyìngjiānshī]
couple persuasion with force; combine harsh and mild moasures
〖软着陆〗[ruǎnzhuólù]
soft landing

ruì

锐[ruì]

R

〖锐角〗(名)[ruìjiǎo]
an acute angle
〖锐利〗(形)[ruìlì]
keen; sharp; pointed
〖锐气〗(名)[ruìqì]
(man with) brains and drive; elan

瑞 [ruì]
〖瑞雪〗(名)[ruìxuě]
timely snow

rùn

闰 [rùn]
〖闰年〗(名)[rùnnián]
leap year; a year with an intercalary month
〖闰月〗(名)[rùnyuè]
the intercalary month in a lunar leap year

润 (形)[rùn]
soft to the touch; moist; moisten
〖润滑〗(形)[rùnhuá]
lubricating
〖润滑油〗(名)[rùnhuáyóu]
lubricating grease; lubricating oil
〖润色〗(动)[rùnsè]
larded with; give the final polish to

ruò

若 (连)[ruò]
①if; in case; and... ②as if
〖若非〗(连)[ruòfēi]
had it not been
〖若干〗(数)[ruògān]
① how much? how many? ② a certain number or amount
〖若即若离〗[ruòjíruòlí]
seemingly attached (e.g. to each other)
〖若是〗(连)[ruòshì]
if; supposing
〖若无其事〗[ruòwúqíshì]
as if nothing had happened

弱 (形)[ruò]
weak; feeble
〖弱点〗(名)[ruòdiǎn]
weakness; weak points
〖弱国〗(名)[ruòguó]
weak countries
〖弱肉强食〗[ruòròuqiángshí]
the weak will stand an easy prey to the strong; jungle law
〖弱小〗(形)[ruòxiǎo]
small and weak
〖弱者〗(名)[ruòzhě]
the weak

sā

撒(动)[sā]
let go; cast (e.g. a net)
另见 sǎ

〖撒谎〗[sāhuǎng]
tell a lie; make up a story

〖撒娇〗[sājiāo]
behave in a spoiled manner; act in a pettishly charming manner

〖撒手〗[sāshǒu]
① let go the hand; relinquish one's hold on ② wash one's hands off the matter; give it up; refuse to take any further interest in

sǎ

洒(动)[sǎ]
① splash; sprinkle; spill ② scatter; litter

撒(动)[sǎ]
① cast; spread ② scatter; spill
另见 sā

sà

飒[sà]

〖飒飒〗(象声)[sàsà]
onomatopoeia, sound of whistling wind or rustling leaves

〖飒爽〗(形)[sàshuǎng]
bright and brave

sāi

腮(名)[sāi]
the jaws

塞(动、名)[sāi]
① stuff; cram; pack ② stop up; block up; close up
另见 sè

〖塞子〗(名)[sāizi]〔个 gè〕
stopper; cork

sài

赛(动)[sài]

contest; compete
〖赛跑〗[sàipǎo]
race
〖赛球〗[sàiqiú]
play a ball game match

sān

三(数)[sān]
three
〖三八国际劳动妇女节〗
[SānBāGuójìLáodòngFùnǚjié]
The March Eighth International Working Women's Day
〖三八红旗手〗
[SānBāHóngqíshǒu]
"March 8th" red banner winner (pace-setter) — female model worker or woman who has made great achievement in her work
〖三包〗(名)[sānbāo]
three guarantees— repair, exchange or return of a product
〖三部曲〗[sānbùqǔ]
trilogy
〖三叉戟〗(名)[sānchājǐ]
trident
〖三叉神经〗(名)
[sānchāshénjīng]
trigeminal nerve
〖三岔路口〗[sānchālùkǒu]
a fork in the road; a junction of three roads
〖三长两短〗
[sānchángliǎngduǎn]
unexpected misfortune; sth. unfortunate, esp. death
〖三重〗[sānchóng]
triple, threefold
〖三重唱〗(名)[sānchóngchàng]
(vocal) trio
〖三重奏〗(名)[sānchóngzòu]
(instrumental) trio
〖三度空间〗[sāndùkōngjiān]
three-dimensional space
〖三大纪律,八项注意〗
[sāndàjìlǜ, bāxiàngzhùyì]
the Three Main Rules of Discipline and the Eight Points for Attention—The Three Main Rules of Discipline are as follows: ①Obey orders in all your actions. ② Don't take a single needle or piece of thread from the masses. ③ Turn in everything captured. The Eight Points for Attention are as follows: ① Speak politely, ② Pay fairly for what you buy. ③ Return everything you borrow. ④ Pay for anything you damage. ⑤ Don't hit or swear at people. ⑥ Don't damage crops. ⑦ Don't take liberties with women. ⑧ Don't ill-treat captives.
〖三番五次〗[sānfānwǔcì]
time and again; many a time; repeatedly
〖三伏〗(名)[sānfú]
three periods of ten days each after luner solstice — hottest days
〖三废〗(名)[sānfèi]
the three wastes—factory fumes, polluted run-off water, and residue wastes

〖三个臭皮匠,合成一个诸葛亮〗[sāngechòupíjiàng héchéngyīge zhūgěliàng]
three cobblers with their wits combined equal ZhugeLiang the master mind—the wisdom of the masses exceeds that of the wisest individual
〖三角〗(名)[sānjiǎo]
triangle; trigonometry
〖三角函数〗[sānjiǎohánshù]
trigonometric function
〖三角架〗(名)[sānjiǎojià]
tripod
〖三角形〗(名)[sānjiǎoxíng]
triangle
〖三角洲〗(名)[sānjiǎozhōu]
delta
〖三九〗(名)[sānjiǔ]
the third nine days after winter solstice—coldest days
〖三句话不离本行〗[sānjùhuàbùlíběnháng]
talk shop wherever one goes; can hardly open one's mouth without talking shop
〖三军〗(名)[sānjūn]
three armed services-the army, navy and air force
〖三来一补〗[sānláiyībǔ]
three processing industries and one compensation-processing raw materials on the client's demand, assembling parts for the client, processing according to the client's samples, and doing compensation trade with foreign clients
〖三令五申〗[sānlìngwǔshēn]
have repeately is sued orders; repeated orders and instructions
〖三轮车〗(名)[sānlúnchē]
〔辆 liàng〕①pedicab ②three-wheeled cart
〖三秋〗(名)[sānqiū]
general term for Autumn harvesting, sowing and ploughing
〖三三两两〗
[sānsānliǎngliǎng]
in twos and threes
〖三天打鱼,两天晒网〗
[sāntiāndǎyú,liǎngtiānshài wǎng]
spend three days fishing and two days drying nets; by fits and starts
〖三色堇〗[sānsèjǐn]
pansy
〖三通〗[sāntōng]
exchanges of mails, trade, air and shipping services
〖三无人员〗[sānwúrényuán]
transients without proper work, lawful identification or permanent address
〖三峡工程〗[sānxiágōngchéng]
Three Gorges Project
〖三夏〗(名)[sānxià]
general term for summer harvesting, sowing and ploughing
〖三心二意〗[sānxīn'èryì]
undecided; hesitant; manyminded
〖三言两语〗[sānyánliǎngyǔ] a few words spoken

S

〖三月〗(名)[sānyuè]
March
〖三资企业〗[sānzīqǐyè]
enterprises in three forms of ventures—Sino-foreign joint ventures, co-operative businesses, and exclusively foreign-funded enterprises
〖三自一包〗[sānzìyībāo]
plots of land for private use, free markets, and enterprises with sole responsibility for their own profits and losses; program of fixing output quotas on a household basis

sǎn

伞(名)[sǎn]〔把 bǎ〕
umbrella
〖伞兵〗(名)[sǎnbīng]
paratrooper; parachuter

散(动、形)[sǎn]
disband; scattered; loose
另见 sàn
〖散光〗(名)[sǎnguāng]
astigmatic; astigmatism
〖散漫〗(形)[sǎnmàn]
① undisciplined ② unorganized; scattered
〖散文〗(名)[sǎnwén]〔篇 piān〕
prose; essay; sketch
〖散装〗[sǎnzhuāng]
loose packed; load in bulk

sàn

散(动)[sàn]
① break up; disperse ② spread; scatter
另见 sǎn
〖散布〗(动)[sànbù]
scatter; spread; disseminate; diffuse
〖散步〗[sànbù]
take a stroll; take a walk
〖散场〗[sànchǎng]
the show ends and the audience files out
〖散发〗(动)[sànfā]
① distribute; parcel out ② give off; spread
〖散会〗[sànhuì]
the meeting is closed; the meeting breaks up
〖散失〗(动)[sànshī]
get lost; vanish
〖散心〗[sànxīn]
ease up; lighten; amuse (e.g. oneself); be carefree

sāng

丧(名)[sāng]
funeral
另见 sàng
〖丧事〗(名)[sāngshì]
things to do with a funeral
〖丧钟〗(名)[sāngzhōng]
(death) knell

桑(名)[sāng]
mulberry
〖桑树〗(名)[sāngshù]〔棵 kē〕
mulberry

sǎng

嗓 [sǎng]
〖嗓门〗(名)[sǎngmén]
voice pitch
〖嗓子〗(名)[sǎngzi]
throat

sàng

丧 (动)[sàng]
lose
另见 sāng
〖丧家之犬〗[sàngjiāzhīquǎn]
stray dogs; homeless dogs
〖丧命〗[sàngmìng]
lose life
〖丧气〗(形)[sàngqì]
downcast; dispirited; disheart ened
〖丧权辱国〗[sàngquánrǔguó]
humiliate the nation and forfeit its sovereignty; national betrayal; forfeit sovereignty and bring humiliation to the country
〖丧失〗(动)[sàngshī]
lose; forfeit
〖丧心病狂〗
[sàngxīnbìngkuáng]
become frenzied; become perverse

sāo

骚 [sāo]
〖骚动〗(动)[sāodòng]
disturb; harass; ferment; riots
〖骚乱〗(动、名)[sāoluàn]
disturb; make trouble; disturbance; riot; chaos
〖骚扰〗(动)[sāorǎo]
cause trouble; disturb

臊 (形)[sāo]
rank-smelling; the smell of foxes

sǎo

扫 (动)[sǎo]
① sweep ② erase; eliminate; sweep out
另见 sào
〖扫除〗(动)[sǎochú]
sweep away; clear away; erase; eliminate
〖扫荡〗(动)[sǎodàng]
mop up; destroy; wipe out
〖扫地〗[sǎodì]
sweep the floor
〖扫雷〗[sǎoléi]
mine clearance; sweep mines
〖扫盲〗[sǎománg]
eliminate (wipe out) illiteracy
〖扫描〗(动)[sǎomiáo]
scan; scanning
〖扫墓〗[sǎomù]
visit grave
〖扫射〗(动)[sǎoshè]
strafe
〖扫尾〗[sǎowěi]
finish; the end of
〖扫兴〗(形)[sǎoxìng]
disappointed; disappointing

S

嫂(名)[sǎo]
wife of one's elder brother
〖嫂子〗(名)[sǎozi]
wife of one's elder brother

sào

扫[sào]
另见 sǎo
〖扫帚〗(名)[sàozhou]〔把 bǎ〕
broom

sè

色(名)[sè]
① colour ② complexion ③ quality
〖色彩〗(名)[sècǎi]
① shade of colour ② spectrum; colouration tendency
〖色厉内荏〗[sèlìnèirěn]
tough-looking out side but really timid within; strong looking outside but brittle within; fierce of visage but faint of heart
〖色盲〗(名)[sèmáng]
colour blindness
〖色情〗(名)[sèqíng]
salacity; carnal desire; lust
〖色泽〗(名)[sèzé]
lustre

涩(形)[sè]
(astringent in taste) not smooth; rough-going

塞[sè]
另见 sāi
〖塞擦音〗(名)[sècāyīn]
affricatives
〖塞音〗(名)[sèyīn]
plosives

sēn

森[sēn]
〖森林〗(名)[sēnlín]
forest
〖森严〗(形)[sēnyán]
severe

sēng

僧[sēng]
〖僧侣〗(名)[sēnglǚ]
monks; priests

shā

杀(动)[shā]
① kill; slaughter ② fight (e.g. one's way out) ③ weaken
〖杀风景〗[shāfēngjǐng]
spoil the landscape; (fig.) dampen one's enthusiasm
〖杀害〗(动)[shāhài]
kill; slaughter; murder
〖杀鸡取卵〗[shājīqǔluǎn]
(lit.) kill the hen to get all its eggs; (fig.) be after only immediate interests
〖杀菌〗[shājūn]
disinfect
〖杀戮〗(动)[shālù]
slaughter
〖杀气腾腾〗[shāqìténgténg]

S

make a bellicose remark
〖杀人不见血〗[shārénbùjiànxiě]
destroy a person by smooth strategy; obtain an objective by underhand means
〖杀人不眨眼〗
[shārénbùzhǎyǎn]
murder ... in cold blood; kill or slaughter (people) without blinking
〖杀伤〗(动)[shāshāng]
inflict casualties
〖杀一儆百〗[shāyījǐngbǎi]
execute one man to warn a hundred; (fig.) punish one as an example to others

沙(名)[shā]
sand
〖沙发〗(名)[shāfā]
sofa
〖沙龙〗(名)[shālóng]
salon
〖沙漠〗(名)[shāmò]
desert
〖沙滩〗(名)[shātān]
sandbank; sandy stretch
〖沙土〗(名)[shātǔ]
sandy soil
〖沙文主义〗(名)[shāwénzhǔyì]
chauvinism
〖沙眼〗(名)[shāyǎn]
trachoma
〖沙子〗(名)[shāzi]
sand

纱(名)[shā]
yarn; gauze
〖纱布〗(名)[shābù]
gauze
〖纱窗〗(名)[shāchuāng]
screen window
〖纱锭〗(名)[shādìng]
(cotton) spindles

刹(动)[shā]
halt; check
另见 chà
〖刹车〗[shāchē]
apply brakes; brake

砂(名)[shā]
sand
〖砂轮〗(名)[shālún]
emery wheel
〖砂糖〗(名)[shātáng]
granulated sugar

煞(动)[shā]
① be brought to an end ② tie
另见 shà
〖煞尾〗[shāwěi]
end up sth.; put sth. to an end

鲨[shā]
〖鲨鱼〗(名)[shāyú][条 tiáo]
shark

shá

啥(代)[shá]
what

shǎ

傻(形)[shǎ]

S

foolish; silly; foolhardy
〖傻瓜〗(名)[shǎguā]
fool; blockhead
〖傻瓜相机〗[shǎguāxiàngjī]
idiot camera; automatic miniature camera; foolproof camera
〖傻子〗(名)[shǎzi]
fool; idiot

shà

煞[shà]
另见 shā
〖煞白〗(形)[shàbái]
deadly pale
〖煞费苦心〗[shàfèikǔxīn]
cudgel or rack one's brains; painstakingly
〖煞有介事〗[shàyǒujièshì]
pull a sanctimonious face; pretend to be serious

霎[shà]
〖霎时间〗(名)[shàshíjiān]
a short moment

shāi

筛(动)[shāi]
sift
〖筛选〗(动)[shāixuǎn]
screen out; make selection
〖筛子〗(名)[shāizi]〔个 gè〕
sieve

shài

晒(动)[shài] sun; dry

shān

山(名)[shān]〔座 zuò〕
①mountain ②hill
〖山坳〗(名)[shān'ào]
level ground in the moutains or hills
〖山地〗(名)[shāndì]
mountainous area; mountainous regions
〖山峰〗(名)[shānfēng]〔座 zuò〕
mountaintop; peak
〖山冈〗(名)[shāngāng]
hill
〖山歌〗(名)[shāngē]〔支 zhī〕
folk song
〖山沟〗(名)[shāngōu]
valley
〖山谷〗(名)[shāngǔ]
valley
〖山河〗(名)[shānhé]
①mountain and river; general topography ②country; territory
〖山洪〗(名)[shānhóng]
mountain torrents
〖山货〗(名)[shānhuò]
sundries; rustic articles of wood and bamboo ...
〖山脚〗(名)[shānjiǎo]
the foot of a mountain
〖山岭〗(名)[shānlǐng]
mountain range
〖山麓〗(名)[shānlù]
the foot of a mountain
〖山峦〗(名)[shānluán]
mountain range
〖山脉〗(名)[shānmài]

mountain range
〖山明水秀〗[shānmíngshuǐxiù]
beautiful mountains and rivers
〖山南海北〗[shānnánhǎiběi]
the four corners of the land
〖山坡〗(名)[shānpō]
mountain or hill slope
〖山穷水尽〗[shānqióngshuǐjìn]
at the end of one's rope; come to an end
〖山区〗(名)[shānqū]
mountainous area
〖山水〗(名)[shānshuǐ]
landscape
〖山头〗(名)[shāntóu]
hill top; up in the hills
〖山崖〗(名)[shānyá]
cliff
〖山腰〗(名)[shānyāo]
halfway up a mountain or a hill
〖山雨欲来风满楼〗
[shānyǔyùláifēngmǎnlóu]
the turbulent wind precedes the mountain storm; the gale is raging and the storm is about to burst
〖山珍海味〗[shānzhēnhǎiwèi]
delicacies from mountains and seas

删(动)[shān]

delete; cut out; write off; strike out
〖删除〗(动)[shānchú]
delete; cut out
〖删繁就简〗[shānfánjiùjiǎn]
simplifying complicated material
〖删改〗(动)[shāngǎi]
① delete ② change; revise
〖删节〗(动)[shānjié]
abridge; chop out
〖删节号〗(名)[shānjiéhào]
abridgement mark

珊[shān]

〖珊瑚〗(名)[shānhú]
coral

舢[shān]

〖舢板〗(名)[shānbǎn]〔只 zhī〕
sampan (small boat)

扇(动)[shān]

fan
另见 shàn
〖扇动〗(动)[shāndòng]
instigate; engage in agitation; incite
〖扇风点火〗[shānfēngdiǎnhuǒ]
fan up the fire; stir up; make trouble

shǎn

闪(名、动)[shǎn]

① dodge; duck; start aside ② sparkle; glitter ③ flash; flicker
〖闪电〗(名)[shǎndiàn]
lightening
〖闪光〗(名)[shǎnguāng]
light flash; sparkle
〖闪烁〗(动)[shǎnshuò]
flicker; twinkle

〖闪耀〗(动)[shǎnyào]
flash; sparkle

shàn

苫(动)[shàn]
cover

扇(量)[shàn]
a measure word (for door or window)
另见 shān
〖扇子〗(名)[shànzi]〔把 bǎ〕
fan

善(形)[shàn]
① kind; good and honest ② be good at; skilled in; know how (e.g. to make good use) ③ be liable to; be apt to
〖善后〗(名)[shànhòu]
redress; rehabilitate; make good what comes after
〖善良〗(形)[shànliáng]
kind; good and honest
〖善心〗(名)[shànxīn]
kindhearted; good intentions
〖善意〗(名)[shànyì]
well intentioned; goodwill; sincere
〖善于〗(动)[shànyú]
be good at; be adept at; know how to

擅[shàn]
〖擅长〗(动)[shàncháng]
be good at; be expert at
〖擅自〗(副)[shànzì]
arbitrarily; take the liberty; take it upon oneself to

膳[shàn]
〖膳费〗(名)[shànfèi]
boarding fees
〖膳食〗(名)[shànshí]
meals

赡[shàn]
〖赡养〗(动)[shànyǎng]
support financially (e.g. parents); provide (sb.) with daily necessities

shāng

伤(动、名)[shāng]
① wound; injure; ② hurt; harm
〖伤风〗(动、名)[shāngfēng]
catch cold
〖伤害〗(动)[shānghài]
do harm to; hurt; impair
〖伤痕〗(名)[shānghén]
scar
〖伤口〗(名)[shāngkǒu]
wound
〖伤脑筋〗[shāngnǎojīn]
cause sb. enough headaches; take great deal of thinking
〖伤势〗(名)[shāngshì]
condition of injury or wound
〖伤亡〗(动、名)[shāngwáng]
wounded and killed; casualty
〖伤心〗[shāng xīn]
sad; grievous; heart-broken
〖伤员〗(名)[shāngyuán]
wounded soldier; the wounded

商(名)[shāng]
commerce; trade
〖商标〗(名)[shāngbiāo]
trade mark
〖商场〗(名)[shāngchǎng]
bazaar; market
〖商店〗(名)[shāngdiàn]
shop; stores
〖商定〗(动)[shāngdìng]
make decision through discussion or consultation
〖商贩〗(名)[shāngfàn]
pedlar
〖商行〗(名)[shāngháng]
trading company; commercial firm
〖商号〗(名)[shānghào]
business firm; business establishment
〖商量〗(动)[shāngliáng]
discuss; talk (things) over ...; put (our) heads together
〖商品〗(名)[shāngpǐn]
commercial product; commodity
〖商品房〗[shāngpǐnfáng]
housing for sale
〖商品经济〗[shāngpǐnjīngjì]
commodity economy
〖商品粮〗[shāngpǐnliáng]
commodity grain
〖商品制度〗[shāngpǐnzhìdù]
commodity system
〖商洽〗(动)[shāngqià]
discuss together; talk over; confer
〖商情〗(名)[shāngqíng]
market conditions; business information
〖商榷〗(动)[shāngquè]
counsel; consult; confer with
〖商人〗(名)[shāngrén]
merchant; tradesman; businessman
〖商谈〗(动)[shāngtán]
discuss; talk over
〖商讨〗(动)[shāngtǎo]
discuss; counsel; negotiate
〖商务〗(名)[shāngwù]
commercial affairs
〖商业〗(名)[shāngyè]
commerce
〖商业街〗[shāngyèjiē]
shopping street
〖商业区〗[shāngyèqū]
business quarter
〖商议〗(动)[shāngyì]
consult each other; discuss
〖商酌〗(动)[shāngzhuó]
discuss

墒(名)[shāng]
moisture in the top soil
〖墒情〗(名)[shāngqíng]
moisture holding capacity in the top soil

shǎng

赏(动)[shǎng]
award; reward; bestow
〖赏赐〗(动)[shǎngcì]
give; bestow; vouchsafe
〖赏罚分明〗[shǎngfáfēnmíng]
never hesitate to award or punish (sb.) when he deserves
〖赏识〗(动)[shǎngshí]

treasure or praise; appreciate

晌(名)[shǎng]

a period in a day

〖晌午〗(名)[shǎngwu]

noon

shàng

上(名、动)[shàng]

①top ②go up; mount ③go to

〖上班〗[shàngbān]

go to work; go on duty

〖上边〗(名)[shàngbian]

above; over; upper

〖上策〗(名)[shàngcè]

wise policy; best policy; good way

S

〖上层〗(名)[shàngcéng]

upper strata

〖上层建筑〗[shàngcéngjiànzhù]

super structure

〖上窜下跳〗[shàngcuànxiàtiào]

run clandestine errands up and down the line

〖上当〗[shàngdàng]

be taken in; be fooled; be duped

〖上等〗(形)[shàngděng]

superior grade; first class

〖上帝〗(名)[shàngdì]

god

〖上吊〗[shàngdiào]

hang oneself

〖上冻〗[shàngdòng]

freeze; get frozen

〖上火〗[shànghuǒ]

get angry; get inflamed

〖上级〗(名)[shàngjí]

(bodies or people) in higher positions of responsibility; higher authorities; next higher level

〖上缴〗(动)[shàngjiǎo]

turn in sth. (e.g. profits) to a higher level

〖上进〗(名)[shàngjìn]

progress

〖上课〗[shàngkè]

have class; attend class

〖上空〗(名)[shàngkōng]

airspace; high up in the air

〖上来〗[shànglái]

come up

〖上梁不正下梁歪〗[shàngliángbùzhèng xiàliángwāi]

(lit.) if the upper beam is not straight, the lower one will go aslant; (fig.) when those above behave unworthily, those below will do the same

〖上马〗[shàngmǎ]

(lit.) mount the horse; (fig.) make a start on (a project, etc.); set something (usu. the construction of a project) going

〖上门服务〗[shàngménfúwù]

make house calls; come to the customer's house to render service

〖上面〗(名)[shàngmian]

above; top

〖上去〗[shàng qù]

go up

〖上任〗[shàngrèn]

take up an official post; assume office

〖上身〗(名)[shàngshēn]
upper part of body
〖上升〗(动)[shàngshēng]
go up; rise; grow
〖上声〗(名)[shàngshēng] 又读[shǎngshēng]
the third tone
〖上市〗[shàngshì]
be in season; be in (usu. vegetables, fruits, etc.); on the market
〖上述〗[shàngshù]
what is mentioned above; as said or narrated above
〖上税〗[shàngshuì]
pay tax
〖上诉〗(动)[shàngsù]
appeal to a higher court
〖上台〗[shàngtái]
① go on the stage ② come into power; take office
〖上头〗(名)[shàngtou]
① leading body at a higher level ② at the top of ...
〖上文〗(名)[shàngwén]
the preceding context
〖上午〗(名)[shàngwǔ]
before noon
〖上下〗(名)[shàngxià]
① about (usu. after a number) ② good and bad ③ high and low
〖上行下效〗[shàngxíngxiàxiào]
those in subordinate positions will follow the example set by their superiors
〖上旬〗(名)[shàngxún]
the first ten days of the month; the early part of the month
〖上演〗(动)[shàngyǎn]
give a public performance; on show
〖上衣〗(名)[shàngyī]〔件 jiàn〕
jacket; coat
〖上瘾〗[shàngyǐn]
be addicted (to sth.); get into the habit (of doing sth.); habit forming
〖上映〗[shàngyìng]
show (a film); screen; be on; run
〖上游〗(名)[shàngyóu]
① upper stream; upper reaches (of a river); the upper river valley ② (fig.) aiming high
〖上装〗[shàngzhuāng]
① make up (for a theatrical performance) ② upper outer garment; jacket
〖上座〗(名)[shàngzuò]
seat of honour

尚(副)[shàng]
still; yet
〖尚且〗(连)[shàngqiě]
① more over ② still less ③ let alone; to say nothing of; not to speak of; not to mention
〖尚未〗(副)[shàngwèi]
not yet; cannot yet

shāo

捎(动)[shāo]
carry; bring along
〖捎带〗(动)[shāodài]

S

bring; carry along

烧(动)[shāo]
①burn②cook(rice,etc.); boil (water, etc.)③have a fever
〖烧杯〗(名)[shāobēi]〔个 gè〕
beaker
〖烧火〗[shāohuǒ]
fire(e.g. a furnace); look after the fire
〖烧酒〗(名)[shāojiǔ]
strong liquor

稍(副)[shāo]
slightly; rather; just a little
〖稍微〗(副)[shāowēi]
just a little; rather; slightly

S

shāo

勺(名)[sháo]
spoon; dipper; ladle
〖勺子〗(名)[sháozi]〔把 bǎ〕
spoon; dipper; ladle

芍[sháo]
〖芍药〗(名)[sháoyao]
a peony like flower

韶[sháo]
〖韶光〗(名)[sháoguāng]
① beautiful springtime ② glorious youth

shǎo

少(形、动)[shǎo]
① few; little; seldom ② lose; short of
另见 shào
〖少不了〗[shǎobuliǎo]
necessary; essential; cannot do without
〖少而精〗[shǎoérjīng]
fewer but better; less but better; condensed and concentrated(e.g. teaching content)
〖少见多怪〗[shǎojiànduōguài]
less seen, more strange; one who has seen very little finds everything strange
〖少数〗(名)[shǎoshù]
minority; a small number
〖少数民族〗[shǎoshùmínzú]
minority nationalities; national minorities
〖少许〗(形)[shǎoxǔ]
little; few

shào

少[shào]
另见 shǎo
〖少年〗(名)[shàonián]
teenager; youngster; juvenile
〖少年犯〗(名)[shàoniánfàn]
juvenile delinquent
〖少年宫〗(名)[shàoniángōng]
palace of young pioneers; children's palace
〖少年先锋队〗
[shàoniánxiānfēngduì]
the Young Pioneers
〖少女〗(名)[shàonǚ]
young girl

哨(名)[shào]
① sentinel; sentry ② whistle
〖哨兵〗(名)[shàobīng]
sentinel; sentry
〖哨所〗(名)[shàosuǒ]
outposts; post; sentry-box
〖哨子〗(名)[shàozi]
whistle

shē

奢 [shē]
〖奢侈〗(形)[shēchǐ]
luxurious; extravagant
〖奢侈品〗(名)[shēchǐpǐn]
luxury goods; luxuries
〖奢华〗(形)[shēhuá]
luxurious; pompous
〖奢望〗(名)[shēwàng]
wild hope; extravagant wish; expecting too much

赊(动)[shē]
sell on credit; give credit
〖赊购〗(动)[shēgòu]
buy on credit

shé

舌(名)[shé]
tongue
〖舌根音〗(名)[shégēnyīn]
velar
〖舌尖音〗(名)[shéjiānyīn]
blade-alveolar
〖舌面音〗(名)[shémiànyīn]
palatal consonant
〖舌头〗(名)[shétou]
tongue

折(动)[shé]
① break off (e.g.the branch broke off) ② lose (e.g. profit and loss)
另见 zhē zhé

蛇(名)[shé][条 tiáo]
snake

shě

舍(动)[shě]
give up; part with; abandon
〖舍本逐末〗[shěběnzhúmò]
grasp the shadow instead of the essence; penny wise, pound foolish
〖舍不得〗[shěbude]
loath to give up; grudge; stingy; reluctant to part with
〖舍得〗(动)[shěde]
be willing to give up; generous
〖舍己为公〗[shějǐwèigōng]
sacrifice oneself for the interests of the people
〖舍己为人〗[shějǐwèirén]
sacrifice oneself for others
〖舍近求远〗[shějìnqiúyuǎn]
give up what is within reach and seek after sth. unreachable; unpracticable
〖舍死忘生〗[shěsǐwàngshēng]
lay down one's life for ...

shè

设(动)[shè]
① set up; build up ② try to;

manage ③ suppose; assume
〖设备〗(名)[shèbèi]
equipment; facilities; apparatus
〖设法〗[shèfǎ]
use proper means; take steps; endeavour; try to
〖设防〗[shèfáng]
set up patrol or defense
〖设计〗(动、名)[shèjì]
design; draw up a plan; project
〖设立〗(动)[shèlì]
establish; set up; form; found
〖设身处地〗[shèshēnchǔdì]
place oneself in others' position
〖设施〗(名)[shèshī]
installation (e.g. supply installation); (fortified) position
〖设想〗(动、名)[shèxiǎng]
① assume; envisage; imagination ② be considerate of
〖设置〗(动)[shèzhì]
arrange; place (e.g. obstacles)

社(名)[shè]
commune
〖社会〗(名)[shèhuì]
society
〖社会存在〗[shèhuìcúnzài]
social existance; social being
〖社会地位〗[shèhuìdìwèi]
social status
〖社会分工〗[shèhuìfēngōng]
social division of labour
〖社会公德〗[shèhuìgōngdé]
social moral
〖社会工作〗[shèhuìgōngzuò]
social work; public activities
〖社会关系〗[shèhuìguānxì]
① social connections ② personal social relations (including relatives and friends)
〖社会活动〗[shèhuìhuódòng]
social activities
〖社会科学〗[shèhuìkēxué]
social sciences
〖社会青年〗[shèhuìqīngnián]
unemployed, out-of-school youth
〖社会意识〗[shèhuìyìshí]
social consciousness
〖社会主义〗(名)[shèhuìzhǔyì]
socialism
〖社会主义初级阶段〗
[shèhuìzhǔyìchūjíjiēduàn]
the primary stage of socialism
〖社会主义革命〗
[shèhuìzhǔyìgémìng]
socialist revolution
〖社会主义建设〗
[shèhuìzhǔyìjiànshè]
socialist construction
〖社稷〗[shèjì]
the god of the land and the god of grain—the state; the country
〖社交〗(名)[shèjiāo]
social intercourse
〖社论〗(名)[shèlùn]〔篇 piān〕
editorial
〖社团〗(名)[shètuán]
mass organizations; body of persons; corporation

射(动)[shè]
①shoot ②radiate(e.g. rays); cast(e.g. light) ③inject
〖射击〗(动)[shèjī]
shoot
〖射箭〗[shèjiàn]
shoot with an arrow; shooting an arrow
〖射流〗(名)[shèliú]
efflux; jet
〖射线〗(名)[shèxiàn]
ray

涉[shè]
〖涉及〗(动)[shèjí]
involve; be concerned with; touch upon
〖涉猎〗(动)[shèliè]
read widely but in a cursory way
〖涉外〗[shèwài]
concerning foreign affairs or foreign nationals
〖涉外婚姻〗[shèwàihūnyīn]
marriage of a Chinese to a foreigner or vice versa

赦(动)[shè]
pardon
〖赦免〗(动)[shèmiǎn]
(law) pardon

摄(动)[shè]
①absorb ②photograph
〖摄取〗(动)[shèqǔ]
absorb
〖摄氏温度计〗[shèshìwēndùjì]
Celsius thermometer
〖摄像〗[shèxiàng]
videotape
〖摄像机〗(名)[shèxiàngjī]
video camera; pickup camera
〖摄影〗[shèyǐng]
photograph
〖摄影机〗(名)[shèyǐngjī]
camera; cinecamera
〖摄制〗(动)[shèzhì]
shoot(e.g. film)

慑[shè]
〖慑于〗(动)[shèyú]
fear

shēn

申[shēn]
〖申办〗(动)[shēnbàn]
apply for permission to do sth.; apply to host sth.
〖申报〗(动)[shēnbào]
declare sth. to the customs or to the income tax office
〖申报单〗(名)[shēnbàodān]
declaration form
〖申辩〗(动)[shēnbiàn]
defend oneself; plead or rebut in defence
〖申斥〗(动)[shēnchì]
rebuke; reproach; scold
〖申明〗(动)[shēnmíng]
try to clear the matter up; avow; make a statement
〖申请〗(动)[shēnqǐng]
apply for; request
〖申请书〗(名)[shēnqǐngshū]
a letter of application

〖申述〗(动)[shēnshù]
explain ; state one's position; assure

伸(动)[shēn]
stretch; reach out
〖伸懒腰〗[shēnlǎnyāo]
stretch oneself; give a stretch
〖伸手〗[shēnshǒu]
(lit.)stretch out one's arm; (fig.)self-seeking
〖伸缩〗(动)[shēnsuō]
flexible
〖伸缩性〗(名)[shēnsuōxìng]
flexibility
〖伸展〗(动)[shēnzhǎn]
expand ; extend
〖伸张〗(动)[shēnzhāng]
expand

身(名)[shēn]
body
〖身败名裂〗[shēnbàimíngliè]
lose all standing and reputation; bring ruin and shame upon
〖身边〗(名)[shēnbiān]
(have sb.or sth.)by; (have sth.) in hand
〖身材〗(名)[shēncái]
stature ; figure; form; posture
〖身长〗(名)[shēncháng]
a person's height
〖身份〗(名)[shēnfen]
(person's) social status
〖身份证〗(名)[shēnfenzhèng]
ID card; identity card; identification card
〖身价〗(名)[shēnjià]
(person's) social status
〖身经百战〗[shēnjīngbǎizhàn]
veteran fighters who have experienced many battles; go through many battles; battle tested
〖身量〗(名)[shēnliang]
height
〖身临其境〗[shēnlínqíjìng]
be present on the spot
〖身躯〗(名)[shēnqū]
body ; build (e.g. a man of strong build); figure
〖身上〗(名)[shēnshang]
(he) has ... with (him); bodily
〖身世〗(名)[shēnshì]
life; condition or situation of living
〖身体〗(名)[shēntǐ]
body
〖身体力行〗[shēntǐlìxíng]
set an example by personally taking part; put into practice and work really hard
〖身心〗(名)[shēnxīn]
heart and soul
〖身子〗(名)[shēnzi]
① body ② pregnancy

呻[shēn]
〖呻吟〗(动)[shēnyín]
groan

绅[shēn]
〖绅士〗(名)[shēnshì]
gentry

S

深(形)[shēn]
deep; profound
〖深奥〗(形)[shēn'ào]
profound; deep
〖深长〗(形)[shēncháng]
profound and far-reaching; penetrating
〖深沉〗(形)[shēnchén]
profound; deep
〖深仇大恨〗[shēnchóudàhèn]
with immense hatred; bitter and deep-seated hatred
〖深度〗(名)[shēndù]
depth
〖深更半夜〗[shēngēngbànyè]
in the dead hour of the night; late at night
〖深耕〗(动)[shēngēng]
deep ploughing
〖深耕细作〗[shēngēngxìzuò]
deep ploughing and careful cultivation
〖深厚〗(形)[shēnhòu]
profound; deep (e.g. friendship)
〖深化〗(动)[shēnhuà]
deepen
〖深究〗(动)[shēnjiū]
go deeply into the matter
〖深刻〗(形)[shēnkè]
profound; penetrating; incisive; deep-going
〖深谋远虑〗[shēnmóuyuǎnlǜ]
far sightedeness; great forethought; foresight
〖深浅〗(名)[shēnqiǎn]
depth
〖深切〗(形)[shēnqiè]
profound; earnest; sincere
〖深情〗(名)[shēnqíng]
deep-rooted friendship; deep feeling; profound feeling
〖深情厚谊〗[shēnqínghòuyì]
profound sentiments of friendship; deep-rooted friendship
〖深入〗(动、形)[shēnrù]
go deep among; go deep into; deepen; deep-going; in a thorough going way
〖深入浅出〗[shēnrùqiǎnchū]
(of an article or a speech) complicated content but plain in words; treat difficult matters in a simple and explicit way
〖深入人心〗[shēnrùrénxīn]
strike deep roots in the hearts of the people
〖深山〗(名)[shēnshān]
deep in the mountain
〖深思〗(动)[shēnsī]
think deeply; ponder over
〖深思熟虑〗[shēnsīshúlǜ]
deep consideration; ponder deeply; weigh and consider
〖深邃〗[shēnsuì]
①deep ②profound; abstruse; recondite
〖深意〗[shēnyì]
profound meaning
〖深恶痛绝〗[shēnwùtòngjué]
hate deeply; implacable hatred; cherish a bitter hatred for
〖深信〗(动)[shēnxìn]
firmly believe; be deeply convinced

S

〖深夜〗(名)[shēnyè]
late in the night; in the dead of night
〖深渊〗(名)[shēnyuān]
abyss
〖深远〗(形)[shēnyuǎn]
far-reaching; profound
〖深造〗(动)[shēnzào]
take a more advanced course of study or training
〖深重〗(形)[shēnzhòng]
heavy; grave; severe

shén

什 [shén]
〖什么〗(代)[shénme]
what
〖什么的〗(代)[shénmede]
such as; and soon

神 (名)[shén]
god
〖神采〗(名)[shéncǎi]
glamour; spirit (in appearance)
〖神采奕奕〗[shéncǎiyìyì]
beaming and buoyant in spirits; in high spirits
〖神出鬼没〗[shénchūguǐmò]
my steriously appear and disappear; act swiftly and wittily
〖神乎其神〗[shénhūqíshén]
make ... as sth. miraculous; miraculous
〖神话〗(名)[shénhuà]
fairy tale; myths; fable
〖神经〗(名)[shénjīng]
nerves
〖神经病〗(名)[shénjīngbìng]
① neurosis ② mental disorder
〖神经过敏〗[shénjīngguòmǐn]
① neuroticism ② neurotic; oversensitive
〖神经科〗(名)[shénjīngkē]
department of neurology
〖神经衰弱〗[shénjīngshuāiruò]
nervous debility; neurasthenia
〖神秘〗(形)[shénmì]
mystical; mysterious
〖神奇〗(形)[shénqí]
magical; mysterious
〖神气〗(形、名)[shénqì]
① facial expression ② vigorous; in high spirit ③ over-weening; pride; arrogance
〖神情〗(名)[shénqíng]
look; expression; appearance
〖神色〗(名)[shénsè]
look; countenance
〖神圣〗(形)[shénshèng]
sacred
〖神速〗(形)[shénsù]
amazingly fast; with lightning speed
〖神态〗(名)[shéntài]
look; expression
〖神通〗(名)[shéntōng]
magical power; infinitely powerful
〖神往〗(动)[shénwǎng]
be carried away by ...
〖神志〗(名)[shénzhì]
state of mind
〖神州〗(名)[shénzhōu]

referring to China

shěn

审(动)[shěn]
①review; examine; check over ②place on trial; handle a case
〖审查〗(动)[shěnchá]
review; examine; investigate; inspect; check over
〖审定〗(动)[shěndìng]
check and decide
〖审核〗(动)[shěnhé]
examine and pass on
〖审计〗(动)[shěnjì]
audit
〖审美〗[shěnměi]
aesthetic
〖审判〗(动)[shěnpàn]
place on trial; judge
〖审批〗(动)[shěnpī]
examine and endorse; check and approve
〖审问〗(动)[shěnwèn]
cross examine; interrogate
〖审讯〗(动)[shěnxùn]
cross examine; interrogate

婶(名)[shěn]
wife of one's father's younger brother
〖婶母〗(名)[shěnmǔ]
wife of one's father's younger brother

shèn

肾(名)[shèn]
the kidney
〖肾炎〗(名)[shènyán]
nephritis

甚(副)[shèn]
very; very much; extremely
〖甚而〗(连)[shèn'ér]
even; go so far as to; go to the length of
〖甚或〗(连)[shènhuò]
even; go so far as to
〖甚嚣尘上〗
[shènxiāochénshàng]
make a lot of noise; the dust and din of ... fill the air; a great clamour has arisen; widespread clamours
〖甚至〗(连)[shènzhì]
go so far as to; even

渗(动)[shèn]
seep through
〖渗入〗(动)[shènrù]
infiltrate; penetrate
〖渗透〗(动)[shèntòu]
①infiltrate; permeate ②percolate; osmose

慎[shèn]
〖慎重〗(形)[shènzhòng]
careful; cautious; prudent

shēng

升(动、量)[shēng]
①go up; rise ②be promoted; upgrade ③a measure word, litre
〖升华〗(动)[shēnghuá]
sublimate

S

〖升级〗[shēngjí]
be promoted to higher post; upgrade; move sb. (e.g. students) up to higher grades
〖升学〗[shēngxué]
go for further study
〖升值〗[shēngzhí]
revaluation

生(动、形)[shēng]
① be born ② grow; produce; bring forth ③ exist; live ④ raw ⑤ unfamiliar
〖生搬硬套〗[shēngbānyìngtào]
apply mechanically; mechanical application
〖生病〗[shēngbìng]
fall ill; get ill; be taken ill
〖生产〗(动、名)[shēngchǎn]
①produce; manufacture; make; yield production ②give birth to
〖生辰〗[shēngchén]
birthday
〖生成物〗[shēngchéngwù]
product; resultant
〖生根〗[shēnggēn]
take root; strike root
〖生计〗[shēngjì]
means of livelihood; livelihood
〖生产方式〗
[shēngchǎnfāngshì]
mode of production
〖生产关系〗[shēngchǎn guānxì]
the relations of production
〖生产过剩〗
[shēngchǎnguòshèng]
overproduction
〖生产力〗(名)[shēngchǎnlì]
productive forces
〖生产率〗(名)[shēngchǎnlǜ]
①productivity ②production efficacy
〖生产资料〗[shēngchǎnzīliào]
means of production
〖生词〗(名)[shēngcí]
new words
〖生存〗(动)[shēngcún]
exist; survive; live; existence
〖生动〗(形)[shēngdòng]
vivid; lively
〖生活〗(动、名)[shēnghuó]
① live ②everyday matters; livelihood; life; living ③living conditions; well-being
〖生活资料〗[shēnghuózīliào]
means of livelihood
〖生火〗[shēng huǒ]
make a fire; light a fire
〖生理〗(名)[shēnglǐ]
physiology
〖生力军〗(名)[shēnglìjūn]
fresh reinforcement; new and positive force
〖生龙活虎〗[shēnglónghuóhǔ]
extremely forceful and lively; full of vigour
〖生命〗(名)[shēngmìng]
life
〖生命力〗(名)[shēngmìnglì]
vitality; life-force
〖生命线〗(名)[shēngmìngxiàn]
life-line; lifeblood
〖生怕〗(动)[shēngpà]

fear; be afraid; lest
〖生僻〗(形)[shēngpì]
(of words, etc.) rarely used
〖生平〗(名)[shēngpíng]
all one's life; lifetime
〖生气〗[shēngqì]
get angry; anger
〖生气〗(名)[shēngqì]
vigorous spirit; life
〖生气勃勃〗[shēngqìbóbó]
vigorous; dynamic; full of vigour and vitality
〖生前〗(名)[shēngqián]
while person was living
〖生人〗(名)[shēngrén]
stranger
〖生日〗(名)[shēngri]
birthday
〖生手〗(名)[shēngshǒu]
an inexperienced hand; a new hand
〖生疏〗(形)[shēngshū]
unfamiliar; unacquainted; hardly know...; getting rusty
〖生死存亡〗[shēngsǐcúnwáng]
a matter of life and death
〖生死与共〗[shēngsǐyǔgòng]
share life and death; through thick and thin
〖生态〗(名)[shēngtài]
ecology; modes of life and relation to their environment
〖生态平衡〗
[shēngtàipínghéng]
ecological balance (equilibrium)
〖生态系统〗[shēngtàixìtǒng]
ecosystem
〖生铁〗(名)[shēngtiě]
pig iron; cast iron
〖生吞活剥〗[shēngtūnhuóbō]
(lit.) swallow raw and whole; (fig.) mechanically learn (sth.) or take (other's experience)
〖生物〗(名)[shēngwù]
living creatures or plants; biology
〖生效〗[shēngxiào]
come into force; become effective
〖生锈〗[shēngxiù]
rust; rusty
〖生意〗(名)[shēngyi]
trade; do business
〖生硬〗(形)[shēngyìng]
rigid; stiff; arbitrary; inflexible
〖生育〗(动)[shēngyù]
give birth to and raise (children)
〖生长〗(动)[shēngzhǎng]
grow; grow up
〖生殖〗(动)[shēngzhí]
generate; reproduce
〖生字〗(名)[shēngzì]〔个gè〕
new word; unlearned character

声(名)[shēng]
voice; noise; sound
〖声波〗(名)[shēngbō]
sound waves
〖声称〗(动)[shēngchēng]
(usu. derog.) claim; allege
〖声带〗(名)[shēngdài]
① vocal chord ② sound track
〖声调〗(名)[shēngdiào]

tone
〖声东击西〗[shēngdōngjīxī]
making a feint to the east but attack in the west
〖声泪俱下〗[shēnglèijùxià]
pour oneself out in tears
〖声名狼藉〗[shēngmínglángjí]
discredited; unsavoury; notorious; a bad reputation
〖声明〗(动、名)[shēngmíng]
declare; make a statement; pronouncement
〖声母〗(名)[shēngmǔ]
the initial of a syllable
〖声色〗(名)[shēngsè]
voice and countenance (of person)
〖声势〗(名)[shēngshì]
threatening force; prestige and influence; spirited atmosphere
〖声势浩大〗[shēngshìhàodà]
a large threatening force
〖声嘶力竭〗[shēngsīlìjié]
shout oneself hoarse
〖声速〗(名)[shēngsù]
the speed of sound
〖声讨〗(动)[shēngtǎo]
denounce
〖声望〗(名)[shēngwàng]
prestige; popularity; reputation
〖声响〗(名)[shēngxiǎng]
sound; noise
〖声学〗(名)[shēngxué]
acoustics
〖声音〗(名)[shēngyīn]
voice; noise; sound
〖声誉〗(名)[shēngyù]
prestige; reputation
〖声援〗(动)[shēngyuán]
declare in support of; declare to be on the side of
〖声源〗(名)[shēngyuán]
source of sound
〖声乐〗(名)[shēngyuè]
vocal music
〖声张〗(动)[shēngzhāng]
make known

牲[shēng]
〖牲畜〗(名)[shēngchù]
domestic animals; livestock
〖牲口〗(名)[shēngkou]
cattle; livestock

笙(名)[shēng]
a gourd-shaped hand musical instrument with a row of reed pipes

shéng

绳(名)[shéng]〔条 tiáo〕
a rope
〖绳索〗(名)[shéngsuǒ]
a rope
〖绳子〗(名)[shéngzi]〔条 tiáo〕
rope; cord; string

shěng

省(名、动)[shěng]
① province ② economise; be thrifty
〖省得〗(连)[shěngde]

save the trouble of ...; so that one won't ...
〖省份〗(名)[shěngfèn]
province
〖省会〗(名)[shěnghuì]
provincial capital
〖省力〗[shěnglì]
save energy
〖省略〗(动)[shěnglüè]
omit; leave out
〖省事〗[shěngshì]
convenient; save trouble
〖省委〗(名)[shěngwěi]
the provincial party committee
〖省心〗[shěngxīn]
save a lot of bother

shèng

圣[shèng]
〖圣诞节〗(名)[Shèngdànjié]
Christmas
〖圣地〗(名)[shèngdì]
sacred place

胜(动)[shèng]
①victorious; win; triumph over
〖胜利〗(动、名)[shènglì]
win; victory; triumph
〖胜任〗(动)[shèngrèn]
competent; be well qualified to do sth.

盛(形)[shèng]
①prosperous; grand ②profound; kind ③popular
另见 chéng
〖盛产〗(动)[shèngchǎn]
abound in; be rich in
〖盛大〗(形)[shèngdà]
grand; gala
〖盛典〗(名)[shèngdiǎn]
grand ceremony
〖盛会〗(名)[shènghuì]
grand occasion; impressive gathering; distinguished gathering
〖盛开〗(动)[shèngkāi]
be in full bloom
〖盛况〗(名)[shèngkuàng]
prosperity; grandeur
〖盛名〗(名)[shèngmíng]
renown; well-known
〖盛气凌人〗[shèngqìlíngrén]
arrogant; overbearing; domineering
〖盛情〗(名)[shèngqíng]
courtesy; hospitality; kindness
〖盛夏〗(名)[shèngxià]
midsummer
〖盛行〗(动)[shèngxíng]
become popular; prevail; become current; be in vogue
〖盛装〗(名)[shèngzhuāng]
festival clothes

剩(动)[shèng]
leave as remainder; ... left over by ...; remain
〖剩余〗(动、名)[shèngyú]
remain; left over; surplus; remains; remainder
〖剩余价值〗[shèngyú jiàzhí]
surplus value

shī

尸(名)[shī]
corpse
〖尸骸〗(名)[shīhái]
corpse
〖尸体〗(名)[shītǐ]〔具 jù〕
corpse; dead body

失(动)[shī]
① lose ② fail ③ break(e.g. promise); neglect(e.g. duty)
〖失败〗(动、名)[shībài]
defeat; fail; fall through; failure
〖失策〗[shīcè]
make a wrong decision; miscalculation
〖失常〗(形)[shīcháng]
abnormal
〖失传〗(动)[shīchuán]
be lost through the generations
〖失当〗(形)[shīdàng]
inappropriate; improper
〖失道寡助〗[shīdàoguǎzhù]
an unjust cause finds meagre support
〖失地〗(名)[shīdì]
lost territory
〖失掉〗(动)[shīdiào]
lose; outlive; miss; be deprived of
〖失魂落魄〗[shīhúnluòpò]
be scared out of one's wits
〖失火〗[shīhuǒ]
catch fire
〖失礼〗[shīlǐ]
have no manners; unmannered
〖失利〗[shīlì]
suffer setback; lose ground
〖失灵〗[shīlíng]
fail to work effectively; be out of gear; ineffective
〖失密〗[shīmì]
let out a secret
〖失眠〗[shīmián]
lose sleep; insomnia
〖失明〗[shīmíng]
lose one's sight; become blind
〖失去〗(动)[shīqù]
lose; miss
〖失散〗(动)[shīsàn]
be scattered; break up; disperse
〖失事〗[shīshì]
accident; mishap
〖失手〗[shīshǒu]
a slip of the hand
〖失守〗(动)[shīshǒu]
fall to the enemy; ... has fallen
〖失算〗(动)[shīsuàn]
miscalculate; make a mistaken move or decision
〖失调〗(动)[shītiáo]
① out of balance; be out of proportion ② ailment
〖失望〗[shīwàng]
① be disappointed ② give up all hope; hopelessness
〖失物〗(名)[shīwù]
lost property
〖失误〗(动)[shīwù]
make a mistake; miss
〖失陷〗(动)[shīxiàn]
be occupied by the enemy; fall

into enemy hands
〖失效〗[shīxiào]
become invalid; lose efficiency; cease to be in force; become null and void
〖失信〗[shīxìn]
break promise; breach of promise
〖失学〗[shīxué]
unable to continue one's studies
〖失言〗[shīyán]
make a slip of the tongue
〖失业〗[shīyè]
lose one's job; unemployment; out of work
〖失职〗[shīzhí]
neglect of duty
〖失主〗(名)[shīzhǔ]
owner of lost property
〖失踪〗[shīzōng]
disappear; lose traces of; missing; vanish
〖失足〗[shīzú]
take a false step; go astray; be misguided

师(名)[shī]
①teacher; master ②(mil.) division
〖师出无名〗[shīchūwúmíng]
there is no excuse for the campaign; carry out a campaign without any justifiable reason
〖师范〗(名)[shīfàn]
teacher's school or college
〖师傅〗(名)[shīfu]
master (e.g. master-worker)
〖师长〗(名)[shīzhǎng]
①divisional commander ②teachers (respectful term for teacher)
〖师资〗(名)[shīzī]
teaching staff

诗(名)[shī]〔首 shǒu〕
poetry; poem; verse
〖诗歌〗(名)[shīgē]〔首 shǒu〕
poem
〖诗篇〗(名)[shīpiān]
poem
〖诗人〗(名)[shīrén]
poet
〖诗意〗(名)[shīyì]
poetic sentiment

施(动)[shī]
①apply ②bestow
〖施肥〗[shīféi]
apply fertilizer or manure
〖施工〗[shīgōng]
construction; work (e.g. schedule); building (e.g. section)
〖施加〗(动)[shījiā]
bring or exert (e.g. pressure); exercise ... over
〖施行〗(动)[shīxíng]
enforce; carry out; apply
〖施展〗(动)[shīzhǎn]
display; give full play to; use

狮(名)[shī]
lion
〖狮子〗(名)[shīzi]〔头 tóu〕
lion

湿(形)[shī]
wet; moist
〖湿度〗(名)[shīdù]
degree of humidity
〖湿淋淋〗(形)[shīlīnlīn]
dripping wet
〖湿润〗(形)[shīrùn]
humid; moist
〖湿疹〗(名)[shīzhěn]
a kind of skin disease with boils

嘘(叹)[shī]
an interjection, whistling sound

shí

十(数)[shí]
ten
〖十恶不赦〗[shí'èbùshè]
unpardonable crimes; guilty beyond forgiveness
〖十二月〗(名)[shí'èryuè]
December
〖十冬腊月〗[shídōnglàyuè]
the winter months
〖十分〗(副)[shífēn]
very; extremely; fully; completely; perfectly
〖十拿九稳〗[shínájiǔwěn]
be quite certain of
〖十全十美〗[shíquánshíměi]
flawless and perfect; perfect
〖十万〗(数)[shíwàn]
a hundred thousand
〖十万火急〗[shíwànhuǒjí]
extremely urgent
〖十一国庆节〗
[ShíYīGuóqìngjié]
October 1—National Day of the People's Republic of China
〖十一月〗(名)[shíyīyuè]
November
〖十月〗(名)[shíyuè]
October
〖十月革命〗[ShíyuèGémìng]
the October Revolution
〖十字路口〗[shízìlùkǒu]
cross roads
〖十足〗(形)[shízú]
hundred percent; sheer; to the hilt; outright

石(名)[shí]
stone; rock
另见 dàn
〖石沉大海〗[shíchéndàhǎi]
like a stone sunk into the sea; produce no reaction
〖石雕〗(名)[shídiāo]
stone carvings
〖石膏〗(名)[shígāo]
gypsum
〖石膏像〗(名)[shígāoxiàng]
gypsum statue
〖石灰〗(名)[shíhuī]
lime; quicklime
〖石灰石〗(名)[shíhuīshí]
lime stone
〖石匠〗(名)[shíjiàng]
stone mason
〖石窟〗(名)[shíkū]
stone cave
〖石蜡〗(名)[shílà]
paraffin

〖石棉〗(名)[shímián]
asbestos
〖石蕊〗(名)[shíruǐ]
litmus
〖石头〗(名)[shítou]〔块 kuài〕
stone; rock
〖石油〗(名)[shíyóu]
petroleum

时(名)[shí]
①time; period; stage; age ②season ③chance; occasion
〖时常〗(副)[shícháng]
often; frequently; now and then; from time to time
〖时代〗(名)[shídài]
epoch; era; age; period
〖时而〗(副)[shí'ér]
sometimes; now ... now
〖时分〗(名)[shífèn]
time (early, late)
〖时光〗(名)[shíguāng]
time
〖时候〗(名)[shíhou]
①time; when ②duration
〖时机〗(名)[shíjī]
circumstances; occasion; juncture
〖时间〗(名)[shíjiān]
time; duration
〖时间表〗(名)[shíjiānbiǎo]
timetable; schedule
〖时间词〗(名)[shíjiāncí]
word denoting time
〖时间性〗(名)[shíjiānxìng]
limited to a period only; period of time suitable for a certain event
〖时节〗(名)[shíjié]
①season ②at a moment when; at a time when
〖时局〗(名)[shíjú]
current situation; present (political) situation
〖时刻〗(名)[shíkè]
①time; hour ②all the time; always
〖时令〗(名)[shílìng]
seasonal regulation; seasonal changes
〖时髦〗(形)[shímáo]
fashionable; vogue
〖时期〗(名)[shíqī]
period; stage
〖时起时伏〗[shíqǐshífú]
vary in intensity from time to time; now rise and now fall
〖时时〗(副)[shíshí]
every now and then; often
〖时事〗(名)[shíshì]
current affairs
〖时事述评〗[shíshìshùpíng]
comment on current affairs
〖时兴〗(形、动)[shíxīng]
fashionable; come into fashion
〖时宜〗(名)[shíyí]
appropriate to the occasion; at an appropriate time
〖时针〗(名)[shízhēn]
clock-hand; hour-hand
〖时装〗(名)[shízhuāng]
current fashion in dress

识(动)[shí]
recognize; know; understand
〖识别〗(动)[shíbié]

distinguish; judge; tell ... from ...

〖识破〗(动)[shípò]

see through; recognize; be brought to light; uncover

〖识字〗[shízì]

can read; learn to read

实(形)[shí]

①true; honest ②concrete; solid

〖实词〗(名)[shící]

notional word

〖实话〗(名)[shíhuà]

(tell) the truth

〖实惠〗(形、名)[shíhuì]

①practical ②substantial benefit

〖实际〗(名、形)[shíjì]

reality; realistic; real; true; actual; practical; practicable

〖实践〗(动)[shíjiàn]

put in practice; practise; carry into effect

〖实践性〗(名)[shíjiànxìng]

practice; practicality

〖实况〗(名)[shíkuàng]

actualities; occurence on the spot; reality

〖实况电视转播〗[shíkuàngdiànshìzhuǎnbō]

live televised

〖实力〗(名)[shílì]

real strength; actual strength of forces

〖实权〗(名)[shíquán]

real power; actual power

〖实施〗(动)[shíshī]

carry out; put into effect; implement; apply

〖实事求是〗[shíshìqiúshì]

seek truth from facts; in a practical way

〖实数〗(名)[shíshù]

real number

〖实体〗(名)[shítǐ]

entity

〖实物〗(名)[shíwù]

real objects; ... in kind

〖实习〗(动)[shíxí]

practise what one has learned; take practical course

〖实现〗(动)[shíxiàn]

realize ; come true; bring into being

〖实效〗(名)[shíxiào]

real results; efficacy

〖实行〗(动)[shíxíng]

carry out; do actually; practise; execute; enforce

〖实验〗(动、名)[shíyàn]

test; experiment

〖实验室〗(名)[shíyànshì]

laboratory

〖实业家〗(名)[shíyèjiā]

industrialist

〖实用〗(形)[shíyòng]

practical; applicable

〖实用主义〗(名)[shíyòngzhǔyì]

pragmatism

〖实在〗(形)[shízài]

real; actual; true

〖实质〗(名)[shízhì]

nature; substance; essence

拾(动、数)[shí]

①pick up ②tidy up ③ten
〖拾掇〗(动)[shíduo]
①tidy up ②repair
〖拾取〗(动)[shíqǔ]
pick up

食(名)[shí]
eat; edible (e.g. oils)
〖食道〗(名)[shídào]
oesophagus
〖食粮〗(名)[shíliáng]
food; foodstuff; grain
〖食品〗(名)[shípǐn]
edible things in general; foodstuffs
〖食谱〗(名)[shípǔ]
menu; recipe
〖食堂〗(名)[shítáng]
dining room
〖食物〗(名)[shíwù]
food; foodstuffs
〖食物中毒〗[shíwùzhòngdú]
food poisoning
〖食言〗[shíyán]
go back on one's word; break one's promise
〖食用〗(动)[shíyòng]
edible (e.g. edible oil)
〖食油〗(名)[shíyóu]
edible oil
〖食欲〗(名)[shíyù]
appetite
〖食指〗(名)[shízhǐ]
forefinger

shǐ

史(名)[shǐ]
history
〖史册〗(名)[shǐcè]
history books; historical works
〖史料〗(名)[shǐliào]
historical data
〖史诗〗(名)[shǐshī]
historical epic
〖史实〗(名)[shǐshí]
historical facts
〖史无前例〗[shǐwúqiánlì]
without parallel in history; unprecedented
〖史学〗(名)[shǐxué]
historical studies; historical science; science of history

矢[shǐ]
〖矢口否认〗[shǐkǒufǒurèn]
flatly deny

使(动、介)[shǐ]
make; let
〖使不得〗[shǐbude]
①cannot be used ②will not do
〖使得〗(动)[shǐde]
①can be used ②will do ③effect; make
〖使馆〗(名)[shǐguǎn]
embassy
〖使节〗(名)[shǐjié]
envoy
〖使劲〗[shǐjìn]
put out strength; make effort; exert
〖使命〗(名)[shǐmìng]
mission

〖使团〗(名)[shǐtuán]
diplomatic corps
〖使用〗(动)[shǐyòng]
use; apply; employ; exercise
〖使用价值〗[shǐyòng jiàzhí]
use value
〖使用寿命〗[shǐyòngshòumìng]
service life
〖使者〗(名)[shǐzhě]
emissary; messenger; envoy

始(动)[shǐ]
begin; start
〖始末〗(名)[shǐmò]
from beginning to end
〖始终〗(名、副)[shǐzhōng]
from beginning to end; always
〖始终不渝〗[shǐzhōngbùyú]
unswervingly; consistantly

屎(名)[shǐ]
excrements; dung

shì

士[shì]
〖士兵〗(名)[shìbīng]
soldier
〖士气〗(名)[shìqì]
morale; fighting spirit

氏[shì]
〖氏族〗(名)[shìzú]
clan(e.g. clan society)

示[shì]
〖示范〗(动、名)[shìfàn]
demonstrate; set example; show; model; example
〖示弱〗(动)[shìruò]
show one's weakness
〖示威〗(动)[shìwēi]
demonstrate
〖示意〗(动)[shìyì]
give sign; hint
〖示意图〗(名)[shìyìtú]
sketch scheme; schematic drawing
〖示众〗(动)[shìzhòng]
expose to all; proclaim to all

世(名)[shì]
① life-time ② generations ③ the world
〖世代〗(名)[shìdài]
generations
〖世故〗(名、形)[shìgù]
the ways of the world; worldly-wise; sophisticated
〖世纪〗(名)[shìjì]
century
〖世界〗(名)[shìjiè]
world; earth; global
〖世界观〗(名)[shìjièguān]
world outlook
〖世界屋脊〗[shìjièwūjǐ]
the roof of the world
〖世界语〗(名)[Shìjièyǔ]
Esperanto
〖世面〗(名)[shìmiàn]
world affairs; the world (e.g. see much of the world)
〖世上无难事,只怕有心人〗
[shìshàngwúnánshì,

zhǐpàyǒuxīnrén]
nothing is difficult in the world for anyone who sets his mind on it
〖世上无难事,只要肯登攀〗
[shì shàngwúnánshì, zhǐyàokěndēngpān]
nothing is hard in this world if you dare to scale the heights
〖世世代代〗[shìshìdàidài]
generation after generation; age after age
〖世袭〗(动)[shìxí]
inherit; hereditary

市 (名)[shì]
①market; trade ②city
〖市场〗(名)[shìchǎng]
market
〖市场经济〗[shìchǎngjīngjì]
market economy
〖市郊〗(名)[shìjiāo]
suburb
〖市侩〗(名)[shìkuài]
gigman; philistine
〖市民〗(名)[shìmín]
townspeople; ordinary residents
〖市区〗(名)[shìqū]
urban area
〖市容〗(名)[shìróng]
appearance of the city
〖市委〗(名)[shìwěi]
municipal party committee
〖市镇〗(名)[shìzhèn]
town; small town
〖市政〗(名)[shìzhèng]
municipal administration

式 (名)[shì]
form; type
〖式样〗(名)[shìyàng]
type; style; pattern
〖式子〗(名)[shìzi]
form; formula; expression

似 [shì]
另见 sì
〖…似的〗(助)[…shìde]
like; as

势 [shì]
〖势必〗(副)[shìbì]
bound to; certainly; inevitably
〖势不两立〗[shìbùliǎnglì]
irreconcilable; mutually exclusive; implacable hostility
〖势均力敌〗[shìjūnlìdí]
balance of forces; all square; be in equilibrium
〖势力〗(名)[shìlì]
force; power; influence
〖势力范围〗[shìlìfànwéi]
spheres of influence
〖势能〗(名)[shìnéng]
potential energy
〖势如破竹〗[shìrúpòzhú]
(overp ower the enemy) like splitting bamboo; irresistible; be ever victorious
〖势头〗(名)[shìtóu]
impetus; momentum

事(名)[shì]
affair; matter; thing; business
〖事半功倍〗[shìbàngōngbèi]
get double results with half the effort
〖事倍功半〗[shìbèigōngbàn]
get half the results with double the effort
〖事变〗(名)[shìbiàn]
event; incident
〖事端〗(名)[shìduān]
event
〖事故〗(名)[shìgù]
accident; trouble
〖事过境迁〗[shìguòjìngqiān]
when the event is over the circumstances are different
〖事后〗(名)[shìhòu]
after the event; afterwards
〖事迹〗(名)[shìjì]
record of events; deed
〖事件〗(名)[shìjiàn]
event; occurrence; incident; happening
〖事例〗(名)[shìlì]
case; example
〖事前〗(名)[shìqián]
prior to the event; in advance; beforehand
〖事情〗(名)[shìqing]〔件 jiàn〕
affair; event; thing; matter
〖事实〗(名)[shìshí]
fact
〖事态〗(名)[shìtài]
situation
〖事务〗(名)[shìwù]
business; things; affair
〖事务主义〗(名)[shìwùzhǔyì]
routinism
〖事先〗(名)[shìxiān]
prior; before the event; in advance
〖事项〗(名)[shìxiàng]
item of business
〖事业〗(名)[shìyè]
cause; undertaking
〖事业单位〗[shìyèdānwèi]
nonprofit institution
〖事业心〗[shìyèxīn]
dedication; devotion to one's work
〖事宜〗(名)[shìyí]
subject dealt with; affair
〖事由〗(名)[shìyóu]
reason; cause
〖事与愿违〗[shìyǔyuànwéi]
events don't turn out the way one wishes
〖事在人为〗[shìzàirénwéi]
man is the determining factor in doing things

试(动)[shì]
① try; experiment ② test
〖试点〗(名)[shìdiǎn]
experiments made at selected point
〖试管〗(名)[shìguǎn]
test tube
〖试剂〗(名)[shìjì]
reagent
〖试金石〗(名)[shìjīnshí]
touch stone
〖试探〗(动)[shìtàn]

S

feel out; sound out
〖试图〗(动)[shìtú]
try; attempt
〖试问〗(动)[shìwèn]
may I ask ...?
〖试行〗(动)[shìxíng]
try; test
〖试验〗(动、名)[shìyàn]
experiment; test
〖试验田〗(名)[shìyàntián]
[块 kuài] experimental farm plot
〖试用〗(动)[shìyòng]
① try out; test ② on probation
〖试纸〗(名)[shìzhǐ]
litmus paper
〖试制〗(动)[shìzhì]
trial produce; trial manufacture

视[shì]
〖视察〗(动)[shìchá]
inspect
〖视而不见〗[shì'érbùjiàn]
look at but not see; turn a blind eye to; shut one's eyes to
〖视觉〗(名)[shìjué]
vision
〖视力〗(名)[shìlì]
power of vision
〖视死如归〗[shìsǐrúguī]
defy death; look death calmly in the face
〖视线〗(名)[shìxiàn]
line of vision
〖视野〗(名)[shìyě]
visual field

拭[shì]
〖拭目以待〗[shìmùyǐdài]
watchful; wait and see

柿[shì]
〖柿子〗(名)[shìzi][个 gè]
persimmon

是(动)[shì]
correct; right
〖…是的〗(助)[…shìde]
like; as
〖是非〗(名)[shìfēi]
rights and wrongs
〖是否〗[shìfǒu]
is it true or isn't it? whether ... or ...

适[shì]
〖适当〗(形)[shìdàng]
proper; suitable; fit
〖适得其反〗[shìdéqífǎn]
on the contrary; be just the reverse; exactly the opposite
〖适度〗(形)[shìdù]
appropriate; proper
〖适合〗(动)[shìhé]
suit; fit in with; accommodate to; conform with
〖适可而止〗[shìkě'érzhǐ]
stop where it reaches the limit; not to overdo; be satisfied with what is proper
〖适口〗(形)[shìkǒu]
pleasing to the taste; tasty
〖适量〗(形)[shìliàng]
an appropriate amount

〖适龄〗(名)[shìlíng]
come of age (e.g. school age child)
〖适时〗(形)[shìshí]
opportune; timely; well-timed; in good time
〖适宜〗(形)[shìyí]
proper; appropriate
〖适应〗(动)[shìyìng]
adapt to; adjust to; meet with; suit the needs of
〖适用〗(形)[shìyòng]
applicable; suitable for
〖适中〗(形)[shìzhōng]
not extreme; moderate

室(名)[shì]
room

逝[shì]
〖逝世〗(动)[shìshì]
pass away; die

释(动)[shì]
① explain ② dispel ③ release
〖释放〗(动)[shìfàng]
set free; release
〖释义〗[shì yì]
explanation of the meaning

嗜[shì]
〖嗜好〗(名)[shìhào]
special love of certain things; hobby; partiality; weakness for; be addicted

誓[shì]
〖誓词〗(名)[shìcí]
pledge
〖誓师〗(动)[shìshī]
pledge (e.g. a pledge meeting); oath (e.g. oath-taking rally)
〖誓死〗(副)[shìsǐ]
defy death (to do sth.); vow to
〖誓言〗(名)[shìyán]
oath; vow

shōu

收(动)[shōu]
① collect ② take back; recover ③ receive; obtain ④ finish
〖收报机〗(名)[shōubàojī]
receiver
〖收兵〗[shōu bīng]
withdraw troops
〖收藏〗(动)[shōucáng]
collect and keep
〖收成〗(名)[shōucheng]
harvest; yield
〖收发〗[shōufā]
receive and dispatch
〖收复〗(动)[shōufù]
recover; recapture
〖收割〗(动)[shōugē]
harvest; reap
〖收工〗[shōugōng]
finish work
〖收购〗(动)[shōugòu]
buy up; purchase in large quantities
〖收归国有〗[shōuguīguóyǒu]
nationalize
〖收回〗(动)[shōuhuí]
① take back; recover ② revoke;

annul
〖收获〗(动、名)[shōuhuò]
①harvest; yield; crop ②results
〖收集〗(动)[shoují]
collect; gather
〖收据〗(名)[shōujù]
receipt
〖收敛〗(动)[shōuliǎn]
put restraint on; lessen
〖收留〗(动)[shōuliú]
take in; accept sb. and provide with support
〖收拢〗(动)[shōulǒng]
close in
〖收罗〗(动)[shōuluó]
collect; gather
〖收买〗(动)[shōumǎi]
buy off; buy over
〖收容〗(动)[shōuróng]
accept; admit
〖收入〗(动、名)[shōurù]
①take (sth.) in ②income
〖收拾〗(动)[shōushi]
①clear up; tidy up ②repair
〖收缩〗(动)[shōusuō]
①shrink; contract ②shorten; reduce
〖收条〗(名)[shōutiáo]
〔张 zhāng〕receipt
〖收听〗(动)[shōutīng]
listen into
〖收尾〗[shōuwěi]
ending of affair
〖收效〗[shōuxiào]
have result; bear fruit; produce effect
〖收益〗(名)[shōuyì]
benefit; gains; profits
〖收音机〗(名)[shōuyīnjī]
〔架 jià〕radio
〖收支〗(名)[shōuzhī]
revenue and expenditure; income and expenses

shǒu

手(名)[shǒu]
hand
〖手背〗(名)[shǒubèi]
back of the hand
〖手笔〗(名)[shǒubǐ]
personal handwriting
〖手臂〗(名)[shǒubì]
arm
〖手表〗(名)[shǒubiǎo]
〔块 kuài〕wrist-watch
〖手册〗(名)[shǒucè]〔本 běn〕
handbook
〖手电筒〗(名)[shǒudiàntǒng]
flashlight
〖手段〗(名)[shǒuduàn]
①means; measure ②tricks; manoeuvres
〖手法〗(名)[shǒufǎ]
①skill; method ②tricks; manoeuvres
〖手风琴〗(名)[shǒufēngqín]
accordion
〖手稿〗(名)[shǒugǎo]
manuscript
〖手工〗(名)[shǒugōng]
handmade; make sth. by hand
〖手工业〗(名)[shǒugōngyè]
handicraft
〖手工艺〗(名)[shǒugōngyì]

handicraft; craftsmanship
〖手迹〗(名)[shǒujì]
original handscript; handwriting
〖手脚〗(名)[shǒujiǎo]
move; motion
〖手巾〗(名)[shǒujīn]〔条 tiáo〕
towel
〖手绢儿〗(名)[shǒujuànr]
〔块 kuài〕handkerchief
〖手铐〗(名)[shǒukào]
handcuffs
〖手榴弹〗(名)[shǒuliúdàn]
〔颗 kē〕handgrenade
〖手忙脚乱〗
[shǒumángjiǎoluàn]
in a great bustle; thrown into confusion
〖手枪〗(名)[shǒuqiāng]
〔枝 zhī〕pistol
〖手巧〗[shǒuqiǎo]
skilful; nimble; light-handed
〖手软〗[shǒuruǎn]
tender hearted
〖手势〗(名)[shǒushì]
hand gesture
〖手术〗(名)[shǒushù]
(med.) operation
〖手套〗(名)[shǒutào]〔副 fù〕
gloves
〖手提包〗(名)[shǒutíbāo]
〔个 gè〕handbag
〖手头〗(名)[shǒutóu]
① on hand ② financial condition
〖手腕〗(名)[shǒuwàn]
trick; manoeuvres; stratagem
〖手无寸铁〗[shǒuwúcùntiě]
unarmed; barehanded
〖手舞足蹈〗[shǒuwǔzúdǎo]
dance with joy
〖手心〗(名)[shǒuxīn]
centre of palm; palm
〖手续〗(名)[shǒuxù]
procedure; formalities
〖手艺〗(名)[shǒuyì]
manual skill; handicraft skill
〖手印〗(名)[shǒuyìn]
fingerprint
〖手札〗(名)[shǒuzhá]
letter written with one's own hand
〖手掌〗(名)[shǒuzhǎng]
palm of hand
〖手杖〗(名)[shǒuzhàng]
walking stick
〖手纸〗(名)[shǒuzhǐ]
toilet paper
〖手指〗(名)[shǒuzhǐ]
finger
〖手足〗(名)[shǒuzú]
(lit.) hand and feet; (fig.) brothers
〖手足无措〗[shǒuzúwúcuò]
at a loss what to do; panic-stricken

守(动)[shǒu]
① guard; defend ② look after ③ observe
〖守敌〗(名)[shǒudí]
enemy troops who are on the defensive; defence troops of the enemy
〖守法〗[shǒufǎ]
abide by the law; law-abiding

S

〖守候〗(动)[shǒuhòu]
①wait; look for ②look after; take care of
〖守护〗(动)[shǒuhù]
guard; protect
〖守旧〗(形)[shǒujiù]
conservative
〖守口如瓶〗[shǒukǒurúpíng]
tight-lipped; keep a secret
〖守势〗(名)[shǒushì]
on the defensive; defensive op-eration
〖守卫〗(动)[shǒuwèi]
guard; defend
〖守则〗(名)[shǒuzé]
rules; regulations
〖守株待兔〗[shǒuzhūdàitù]
(lit.)stand by a tree stump waiting for a hare to dash it-self against it; (fig.)wait for gains without pains

首(名、量)[shǒu]
①head ②leader; chief ③a mea-sure word(for poem, song, etc.)
〖首创〗(动)[shǒuchuàng]
initiate; begin; start
〖首创精神〗
[shǒuchuàngjīngshén]
initiative
〖首当其冲〗
[shǒudāngqíchōng]
the first to be affected; bear the brunt of
〖首都〗(名)[shǒudū]
capital
〖首恶〗(名)[shǒu'è]
chief criminal; ringleader
〖首府〗(名)[shǒufǔ]
capital of an autonomous reg-ion
〖首届〗[shǒujiè]
first batch; first meeting
〖首领〗(名)[shǒulǐng]
chieftain; heads
〖首脑〗(名)[shǒunǎo]
heads; leading figures; chief personalities
〖首屈一指〗[shǒuqūyīzhǐ]
top the world (in a certain re-spect); the first
〖首饰〗(名)[shǒushi]
ornaments(e.g. ring)
〖首尾〗(名)[shǒuwěi]
beginning and end
〖首位〗(名)[shǒuwèi]
first place; precedence over
〖首席〗(名)[shǒuxí]
first place; seat of honour
〖首先〗(名、副)[shǒuxiān]
first of all; in the first place; above all; primarily
〖首相〗(名)[shǒuxiàng]
prime minister
〖首要〗(形)[shǒuyào]
foremost; primary; cardinal
〖首长〗(名)[shǒuzhǎng]
leading cadres of higher ranks

shòu

寿(名)[shòu]
age of person; longevity
〖寿辰〗(名)[shòuchén]
(respectful term for) birthday

〖寿命〗(名)[shòumìng]
age of a person

受(动)[shòu]
receive; suffer
〖受潮〗[shòucháo]
damp affected
〖受宠若惊〗
[shòuchǒngruòjīng]
receive favour with unexpected excitement; feel over-whelmingly flattered
〖受害〗[shòuhài]
suffer injury; come to harm; suffer damage; be hurt
〖受害者〗(名)[shòuhàizhě]
victim; sufferer
〖受贿〗[shòuhuì]
accept bribe
〖受惊〗[shòujīng]
frightened
〖受苦〗[shòukǔ]
suffer bitterness; go through hardships
〖受累〗[shòulèi]
① suffer from tiredness ② be involved in (e.g. trouble)
〖受凉〗[shòuliáng]
catch cold
〖受命〗(动)[shòumìng]
be charged with; be ordered to; under orders
〖受难〗[shòunàn]
suffer hardships or disasters
〖受骗〗[shòupiàn]
be deceived
〖受气〗[shòuqì]
submit to the bullying of
〖受权〗(动)[shòuquán]
accept authority; be authorized by
〖受伤〗[shòushāng]
be hurt; be injured; be wounded
〖受益〗[shòuyì]
profit from; benefit by
〖受援国〗(名)[shòuyuánguó]
recipient country
〖受罪〗[shòuzuì]
suffer (e.g. torture, trouble)

授(动)[shòu]
① award; entrust; vest ② teach
〖授奖〗[shòujiǎng]
award prize
〖授命〗(动)[shòumìng]
charge sb. with a duty; order sb. to do sth.
〖授权〗(动)[shòuquán]
authorize
〖授意〗(动)[shòuyì]
hint; prompt
〖授予〗(动)[shòuyǔ]
award; invest

售(动)[shòu]
sell
〖售货员〗(名)[shòuhuòyuán]
salesman; shop assistant
〖售票员〗(名)[shòupiàoyuán]
ticket seller; conductor (e.g. bus)

兽[shòu]
〖兽行〗(名)[shòuxíng]
brutality

〖兽性〗(名)[shòuxìng]
bestial nature
〖兽医〗(名)[shòuyī]
veterinary

瘦(形)[shòu]
thin
〖瘦弱〗(形)[shòuruò]
thin and weak
〖瘦小〗(形)[shòuxiǎo]
thin and small

shū

书(名)[shū]〔本 běn〕
①book ②letter ③documents
〖书包〗(名)[shūbāo]〔个 gè〕
schoolboy's satchel
〖书报〗(名)[shūbào]
books and newspapers
〖书本〗(名)[shūběn]
book
〖书呆子〗(名)[shūdāizi]
bookworm
〖书店〗(名)[shūdiàn]
bookshop
〖书法〗(名)[shūfǎ]
handwriting; calligraphy
〖书籍〗(名)[shūjí]
books; works
〖书记〗(名)[shūjì]
secretary
〖书架〗(名)[shūjià]〔个 gè〕
book-shelf
〖书刊〗(名)[shūkān]
books and magazines
〖书库〗(名)[shūkù]
room for storing books
〖书面〗(名)[shūmiàn]
written form
〖书面语〗(名)[shūmiànyǔ]
written language
〖书名号〗(名)[shūmínghào]
editorial marks for books or articles—"《》"or"〈〉"
〖书目〗(名)[shūmù]
catalogue of books
〖书评〗(名)[shūpíng]
commentary of a book; book review
〖书签〗(名)[shūqiān]
bookmark
〖书生气〗(名)[shūshēngqì]
academic; bookishness
〖书写〗(动)[shūxiě]
write
〖书信〗(名)[shūxìn]
letter
〖书桌〗(名)[shūzhuō]
〔张 zhāng〕desk

抒(动)[shū]
express
〖抒发〗(动)[shūfā]
express; pour out (e. g. feelings)
〖抒情〗[shūqíng]
express feelings
〖抒情诗〗(名)[shūqíngshī]
〔首 shǒu〕lyric poetry

枢[shū]
〖枢纽〗(名)[shūniǔ]
pivot; axis; key position

S

叔(名)[shū]
uncle
〖叔叔〗(名)[shūshu]
uncle (father's younger brother); uncle(a child's form of address for any person about his father's age)

殊[shū]
〖殊不知〗[shūbùzhī]
the fact is that ...
〖殊死〗(形)[shūsǐ]
desperate (e.g. fight, struggle)
〖殊途同归〗[shūtútóngguī]
different roads lead to the same goal

S

梳(动)[shū]
comb
〖梳子〗(名)[shūzi]〔把 bǎ〕
comb

舒(动)[shū]
open up; stretch out
〖舒畅〗(形)[shūchàng]
comfortable; ease of mind
〖舒服〗(形)[shūfu]
comfortable; nice; refreshing
〖舒适〗(形)[shūshì]
comfortable; ease
〖舒坦〗(形)[shūtan]
at ease; comfortable
〖舒心〗(形)[shūxīn]
feel happy
〖舒展〗(动、形)[shūzhǎn]
①stretch ②comfortable

疏[shū]
〖疏忽〗(形、动)[shūhu]
negligent; relax vigilance against; overlook
〖疏散〗(动)[shūsàn]
disperse; spread out
〖疏通〗(动)[shūtōng]
dredge
〖疏远〗(形、动)[shūyuǎn]
estranged; (keep) at arm's length; alienate

输(动)[shū]
①transmit; transfer; transport ②lose
〖输出〗(动)[shūchū]
export
〖输入〗(动)[shūrù]
import
〖输送〗(动)[shūsòng]
transport; send; deliver
〖输血〗[shūxuè]
blood transfusion
〖输油管〗(名)[shūyóuguǎn]〔条 tiáo〕 oil transmission tube; oil pipe-line

蔬[shū]
〖蔬菜〗(名)[shūcài]
vegetable

shú

赎(动)[shú]
ransom; redeem; atone
〖赎买政策〗[shúmǎizhèngcè]
policy of redemption; buyout policy

〖赎罪〗[shúzuì]
atone for one's crimes

熟(形)[shú]
① ripe; mature ② familiar ③ skilled; experienced
〖熟练〗(形)[shúliàn]
skilled; experienced
〖熟路〗(名)[shúlù]
familiar route
〖熟能生巧〗[shúnéngshēngqiǎo]
practice makes perfect
〖熟人〗(名)[shúrén]
old acquaintance
〖熟识〗(动)[shúshi]
be familiar with; acquaint oneself with
〖熟视无睹〗[shúshìwúdǔ]
turn a blind eye to; take no notice of; ignore
〖熟铁〗(名)[shútiě]
wrought iron
〖熟悉〗(动)[shúxī]
know well; familiarize with
〖熟习〗(动)[shúxí]
know well; be skilful at
〖熟语〗(名)[shúyǔ]
idiom
〖熟字〗(名)[shúzì]
familiar word

shǔ

暑(名)[shǔ]
hot; hot weather; summer heat
〖暑假〗(名)[shǔjià]
summer vacation
〖暑天〗(名)[shǔtiān]
the hot summer; the dog-days

属(动)[shǔ]
belong to; come within (the category of)
〖属地〗(名)[shǔdì]
annexed territory; colony
〖属实〗[shǔshí]
turn out true; be verified
〖属性〗(名)[shǔxìng]
nature; attribute
〖属于〗(动)[shǔyú]
belong to; pertain to; be part of

署(动)[shǔ]
sign; affix one's signature
〖署名〗[shǔmíng]
signature; sign one's name

鼠(名)[shǔ][只 zhī]
rat; mouse
〖鼠目寸光〗[shǔmùcùnguāng]
short-sightedness; see only what is under one's nose

数(动)[shǔ]
count
另见 shù
〖数不着〗[shǔbuzháo]
not qualified; not important enough
〖数得着〗[shǔdezháo]
good quality; outstanding
〖数九〗[shǔjiǔ]
start counting every ninth day from winter solstice until 9×9=

81 days when winter is over
〖数一数二〗[shǔyīshǔ'èr]
count at the top; among the best; outstanding

曙[shǔ]
〖曙光〗(名)[shǔguāng]
the first light of day; dawn

shù

术[shù]
〖术语〗(名)[shùyǔ]
jargon; technical term; terminology

束(动、量)[shù]
①tie; tie up ②a measure word (bale, bunch, etc.)
〖束缚〗(动)[shùfù]
constraint; rigid control; bind; fetter
〖束手待毙〗[shùshǒudàibì]
wait for death with tied hands; resign oneself to extinction
〖束手无策〗[shùshǒuwúcè]
can do nothing to help; be at a loss what to do
〖束之高阁〗[shùzhīgāogé]
shelve a matter; brush (sth.) aside

述(动)[shù]
narrate; relate
〖述评〗(名)[shùpíng]
narrate; comment
〖述说〗(动)[shùshuō]
tell; give an account of
〖述语〗(名)[shùyǔ]
predicate
〖述职〗[shùzhí]
(of an ambassador) report work

树(名、动)[shù]〔棵 kē〕
① tree ② plant; cultivate ③ set up
〖树碑立传〗[shùbēilìzhuàn]
glorify sb. by singing the praises of his life (nowadays usu. derog.)
〖树丛〗(名)[shùcóng]
grove; thicket
〖树倒猢狲散〗[shùdǎohúsūnsàn]
monkeys scatter when the tree falls; rats leave a sinking ship
〖树敌〗[shùdí]
incur enmity
〖树干〗(名)[shùgàn]
tree trunk
〖树立〗(动)[shùlì]
set up; establish; build
〖树林〗(名)[shùlín]
woods
〖树苗〗(名)[shùmiáo]〔棵 kē〕
saplings
〖树木〗(名)[shùmù]
trees in general
〖树梢〗(名)[shùshāo]
tree top
〖树阴〗(名)[shùyīn]
shade of a tree
〖树枝〗(名)[shùzhī]
tree branches

竖(形、动、名)[shù]

①vertical; longitudinal ②stand up; set upright ③vertical stroke
〖竖立〗(动)[shùlì]
stand up; set upright; hold aloft

数(名)[shù] number
另见 shǔ
〖数词〗(名)[shùcí]
numeral
〖数额〗(名)[shù'é]
number; quota
〖数据〗(名)[shùjù]
data; datum
〖数据库〗(名)[shùjùkù]
data base; data bank
〖数量〗(名)[shùliàng]
quantity
〖数目〗(名)[shùmù]
number
〖数学〗(名)[shùxué]
mathematics
〖数值〗(名)[shùzhí]
number; numerical value
〖数字〗(名)[shùzì]
①numeral ②figure ③quota
〖数字计算机〗[shùzìjìsuànjī]
digital computer

漱(动)[shù]
wash; clean; rinse out
〖漱口〗[shùkǒu]
rinse out (one's mouth)

shuā

刷(动、象声)[shuā]
①brush clean; scrub ②onomatopoeia (sound of heavy rain, etc.)
〖刷洗〗(动)[shuāxǐ]
clean; wash out
〖刷新〗(动)[shuāxīn]
renovate; set (e.g. new record)
〖刷子〗(名)[shuāzi]〔把 bǎ〕
brush

shuǎ

耍(动)[shuǎ]
play; juggle
〖耍花招〗[shuǎhuāzhāo]
play tricks; resort to stratagems; manoeuvre
〖耍赖〗(动)[shuǎlài]
be deliberately dishonest
〖耍弄〗(动)[shuǎnòng]
①make a fool of ②play
〖耍手腕〗[shuǎshǒuwàn]
play a trick; manoeuvre; juggle with

shuāi

衰(形)[shuāi]
decline; weakening
〖衰败〗(动)[shuāibài]
decline; be on the wane
〖衰老〗(形)[shuāilǎo]
grow old; go out
〖衰落〗(动)[shuāiluò]
decline; be on the wane
〖衰弱〗(形)[shuāiruò]
old and weak; weak
〖衰退〗(动)[shuāituì]
decline; depress

〖衰亡〗(动)[shuāiwáng]
wither away; die out

摔(动)[shuāi]
① fall ② throw or dash down
〖摔打〗(动)[shuāidǎ]
give hard knocks; treat roughly
〖摔交〗[shuāijiāo]
wrestle; wrestling

shuǎi

甩(动)[shuǎi]
fling; cast away; crack (whip)

shuài

率(动)[shuài]
lead (e.g. an army)
〖率领〗(动)[shuàilǐng]
lead (e.g. an army)

shuān

闩(动、名)[shuān]
door bolt

拴(动)[shuān]
tie; fasten

shuàn

涮(动)[shuàn]
wash; rinse

shuāng

双(形、量)[shuāng]
① double; both; a pair of ② a measure word, pair (for hands, socks, shoes, etc.)
〖双边〗(名)[shuāngbiān]
bilateral
〖双重〗(名)[shuāngchóng]
double; two fold
〖双唇音〗(名)[shuāngchúnyīn]
labial
〖双方〗(名)[shuāngfāng]
two sides; mutual; both sides
〖双杠〗(名)[shuānggàng]
horizontal bars
〖双关〗(动)[shuāngguān]
a word or phrase with double meanings
〖双管齐下〗[shuāngguǎnqíxià]
do two things at the same time; a pincer drive with ...
〖双轨〗(名)[shuāngguǐ]
double track
〖双数〗(名)[shuāngshù]
even number
〖双向〗(名)[shuāngxiàng]
two-way; bi-directional
〖双向选择〗
[shuāngxiàngxuǎnzé]
two-way selection; mutual choice-referring to employer and employee choosing each other in the job interview

霜(名)[shuāng]
frost
〖霜冻〗(名)[shuāngdòng]
frost; frostbite

shuǎng

爽(形)[shuǎng]

refreshing

〖爽快〗(形)[shuǎngkuai]

① cool and refreshing; comfortable; cheerful; invigorating ② candid; outspoken; straightforward

〖爽朗〗(形)[shuǎnglǎng]

① crisp and dry (e.g. air) ② cheerful; invigorating

shuí

谁(代)[shuí]

who; whom

shuǐ

水(名)[shuǐ]

water

〖水坝〗(名)[shuǐbà]

dam

〖水泵〗(名)[shuǐbèng]〔台 tái〕

water pump

〖水彩〗(名)[shuǐcǎi]

water colour

〖水产〗(名)[shuǐchǎn]

marine products; aquatic products

〖水产业〗(名)[shuǐchǎnyè]

marine production; aquatic production

〖水车〗(名)[shuǐchē]

paddle irrigation wheel; water wheel

〖水到渠成〗[shuǐdàoqúchéng]

(lit.) canal is formed when water comes; (fig.) sth. achieved when conditions are ripe

〖水稻〗(名)[shuǐdào]

rice

〖水滴石穿〗[shuǐdīshíchuān]

(lit.) constant dripping wears through the stone; (fig.) a small repeated action can have a big result

〖水电站〗(名)[shuǐdiànzhàn]

〔座zuò〕hydraulic electric station; water power station; hydropower station

〖水分〗(名)[shuǐfèn]

moisture; humidity

〖水管子〗(名)[shuǐguǎnzi]

water tube

〖水果〗(名)[shuǐguǒ]

fruit

〖水壶〗(名)[shuǐhú]〔把 bǎ〕

kettle

〖水库〗(名)[shuǐkù]

reservoir

〖水力〗(名)[shuǐlì]

water power

〖水力发电〗[shuǐlìfādiàn]

hydroelectric power

〖水利〗(名)[shuǐlì]

water conservancy; irrigation

〖水利工程〗[shuǐlìgōngchéng]

water conservancy project

〖水利化〗(动)[shuǐlìhuà]

build water conser vancy works on an extensive scale; bring all farmland under irrigation

〖水龙头〗(名)[shuǐlóngtóu]

water tap

〖水落石出〗[shuǐluòshíchū]

(lit.) the rock emerges as the water sinks; (fig.) the truth will prevail in the end; everything is thrashed out

〖水泥〗(名)[shuǐní]

cement

〖水平〗(名)[shuǐpíng]

① level ② standard; level

〖水平面〗(名)[shuǐpíngmiàn]

horizontal plane; sea level

〖水平线〗(名)[shuǐpíngxiàn]

horizon; water level; horizontal line

〖水渠〗(名)[shuǐqú]〔条 tiáo〕

canal; irrigation ditch

〖水乳交融〗[shuǐrǔjiāoróng]

mix well like milk and water; get along well with each other

〖水深火热〗[shuǐshēnhuǒrè]

(lit.) in deep water or hot fire; (fig.) keep in suffering; an abyss of suffering

〖水手〗(名)[shuǐshǒu]

sailor; seaman

〖水塔〗(名)[shuǐtǎ]〔座 zuò〕

water tower

〖水田〗(名)[shuǐtián]

irrigated land; irrigated fields

〖水土〗(名)[shuǐtǔ]

① water and soil ② climate (e.g. climate does not agree with person)

〖水土保持〗[shuǐtǔ bǎochí]

water and soil conservancy; conservation of water and soil

〖水土流失〗[shuǐtǔliúshī]

soil erosion; water losses and soil erosion

〖水位〗(名)[shuǐwèi]

water level

〖水文〗(名)[shuǐwén]

hydrology

〖水泄不通〗[shuǐxièbùtōng]

watertight; be besieged so closely that not a drop of water could have trickled through; (road) so jammed as to be impassible

〖水星〗(名)[shuǐxīng]

(planet) Mercury

〖水银〗(名)[shuǐyín]

mercury

〖水域〗(名)[shuǐyù]

body of water

〖水源〗(名)[shuǐyuán]

the source of water

〖水灾〗(名)[shuǐzāi]

flood

〖水闸〗(名)[shuǐzhá]

floodgate; waterlock

〖水涨船高〗[shuǐzhǎngchuángāo]

when the river rises the boat floats high

〖水蒸气〗(名)[shuǐzhēngqì]

steam; vapour

〖水中捞月〗[shuǐzhōnglāoyuè]

(lit.) catch the moon in the water; (fig.) fish in the air; a fruitless attempt; in vain

shuì

税 (名)[shuì]

taxes; duty

〖税收〗(名)[shuìshōu]

revenue from tax; taxation

睡(动)[shuì]
sleep
〖睡觉〗[shuìjiào]
go to sleep; go to bed
〖睡眠〗(名)[shuìmián]
sleep
〖睡衣〗(名)[shuìyī]〔件 jiàn〕
pyjamas

shùn

顺(形、动)[shùn]
① smooth; convenient ② obedient; submit to
〖顺便〗(副)[shùnbiàn]
at convenience; without extra effort; by the way; offhand
〖顺从〗(动)[shùncóng]
obey; submit
〖顺当〗(形)[shùndang]
smooth; unhindered; plain sailing
〖顺耳〗(形)[shùn'ěr]
pleasing to the ear
〖顺风〗[shùnfēng]
with the wind; leeward
〖顺口〗(形)[shùnkǒu]
① (of speech) fluent ② without hesitation; casual ③ agreeable to taste
〖顺口溜〗(名)[shùnkǒuliū]
improvised verse; doggerel
〖顺利〗(形)[shùnlì]
without a hitch; smooth; unhindered; plain sailing
〖顺流而下〗[shùnliú'érxià]
go downstream; go with the current
〖顺路〗(形)[shùnlù]
① (doing sth.) on the way or lying on one's route
〖顺手〗(形)[shùnshǒu]
① without extra trouble; without hindrance ② be at home in sth. ③ within easy reach
〖顺手牵羊〗
[shùnshǒuqiānyáng]
(lit.) lead away the sheep in passing; (fig.) picking up others' things in passing; spirit sth. away
〖顺水〗[shùnshuǐ]
with the current
〖顺水推舟〗[shùnshuǐtuīzhōu]
swim with the current; do sth. with the prevailing climate or tendency
〖顺心〗(形)[shùnxīn]
in agreement with what one wants
〖顺序〗(名)[shùnxù]
in proper order or sequence
〖顺延〗(动)[shùnyán]
postpone
〖顺眼〗(形)[shùnyǎn]
pleasing to the eye

瞬 [shùn]
〖瞬息〗(名)[shùnxī]
in the twinkling of an eye
〖瞬息万变〗[shùnxīwànbiàn]
full of changes in the twinkling of an eye; great changes have taken place in a twinkle

shuō

说(动)[shuō]

S

① say; remark ② explain; elucidate ③ criticise
〖说不定〗[shuōbudìng]
perhaps; it is hard to say
〖说不过去〗[shuōbuguòqù]
unreasonable
〖说不上〗[shuōbushàng]
① unqualified to be mentioned as such ② hard to say
〖说穿〗(动)[shuōchuān]
expose (e.g. a secret)
〖说法〗(名)[shuōfa]
way of saying
〖说服〗(动)[shuōfú]
persuade; convince ... by reasoning; bring round
〖说话〗[shuōhuà]
talk; speak
〖说谎〗[shuōhuǎng]
tell a lie
〖说教〗(动)[shuōjiào]
preach; preaching
〖说理〗[shuōlǐ]
talk reason; reasoning
〖说明〗(动、名)[shuōmíng]
explain; define; exposition
〖说明书〗(名)[shuōmíngshū]
[张 zhāng] ① synopsis ② instructions
〖说情〗[shuōqíng]
put in a good word (e.g. for sb.)
〖说说笑笑〗[shuōshuōxiàoxiào]
just have a pleasant talk together
〖说闲话〗[shuōxiánhuà]
gossip
〖说一不二〗[shuōyībù'èr]
mean what one says; have the final say

shuò

硕 [shuò]
〖硕果〗(名)[shuòguǒ]
(lit.) fruits; (fig.) great achievements

sī

司 (名)[sī]
department in a ministry
〖司法〗(名)[sīfǎ]
the judiciary; judicial
〖司机〗(名)[sījī]
driver
〖司空见惯〗[sīkōngjiànguàn]
it is quite common for; a matter of repeated occurrence
〖司令〗(名)[sīlìng]
commander
〖司令部〗(名)[sīlìngbù]
headquarters
〖司令员〗(名)[sīlìngyuán]
commanding officer
〖司仪〗(名)[sīyí]
master of ceremony

丝 (名)[sī]
silk
〖丝绸〗(名)[sīchóu]
silks
〖丝绸之路〗[sīchóuzhīlù]
the Silk Road
〖丝毫〗(副)[sīháo]
the slightest; in the least; at all
〖丝绵〗(名)[sīmián]

silk floss; silk-wadding
〖丝织品〗(名)[sīzhīpǐn]
silks; silk fabrics

私(名)[sī]
selfish; private
〖私愤〗(名)[sīfèn]
personal grudge; personal spite
〖私货〗(名)[sīhuò]
contraband; contraband goods
〖私利〗(名)[sīlì]
selfish interests; personal gains
〖私人〗(名)[sīrén]
private; (in) private capacity
〖私生活〗[sīshēnghuó]
private life
〖私下〗(副)[sīxià]
privately; in private
〖私心〗(名)[sīxīn]
self-seeking; selfish ideas; selfish motive
〖私营〗[sīyíng]
privately owned
〖私营经济〗[sīyíngjīngjì]
private sector of the economy
〖私有〗[sīyǒu]
private ownership
〖私有制〗(名)[sīyǒuzhì]
system of private ownership; private ownership
〖私自〗(副)[sīzì]
privately; without permission; secretly

思(动)[sī]
①think; ponder ②remember fondly; miss
〖思潮〗(名)[sīcháo]
trend of thought; ideological trend
〖思考〗(动)[sīkǎo]
think carefully; meditate; ruminate
〖思量〗(动)[sīliang]
weigh and consider; reckon
〖思路〗(名)[sīlù]
thread of thought
〖思念〗(动)[sīniàn]
remember fondly; feel the absence of
〖思索〗(动)[sīsuǒ]
ponder; think
〖思维〗(名)[sīwéi]
thought; mind
〖思想〗(名)[sīxiǎng]
thought; thinking; ideas; ideologically
〖思想斗争〗[sīxiǎng dòuzhēng]
ideological struggle; struggle in mind
〖思想家〗(名)[sīxiǎngjiā]
thinker
〖思想评论〗[sīxiǎngpínglùn]
ideological review
〖思想性〗(名)[sīxiǎngxìng]
ideological level; ideological content
〖思绪〗(名)[sīxù]
①train of thought ②mood

斯[sī]
〖斯文〗(形)[sīwen]
elegant; refined (e.g. manners)

厮[sī]
〖厮杀〗(动)[sīshā]
fight

撕(动)[sī]
tear
〖撕毁〗(动)[sīhuǐ]
tear to pieces; tear up

嘶[sī]
〖嘶哑〗(形)[sīyǎ]
hoarse

sǐ

死(动、形)[sǐ]
die; dead; death
〖死板〗(形)[sǐbǎn]
rigid; stiff; inflexible
〖死不改悔〗[sǐbùgǎihuǐ]
not to repent even onto death; flatly refuse to correct one's errors; stubbornly refuse to mend one's ways
〖死不瞑目〗[sǐbùmíngmù]
cannot die in peace; die with injustice unredressed or with one's wishes not fulfilled
〖死党〗(名)[sǐdǎng]
sworn follower
〖死得其所〗[sǐdéqísuǒ]
die a worthy death
〖死敌〗(名)[sǐdí]
sworn enemies; deadly enemy
〖死对头〗[sǐduìtou]
deadly enemy; irreconcilable opponents; determined antagonist
〖死胡同〗[sǐhútòng]
blind alley; impasse
〖死灰复燃〗[sǐhuīfùrán]
like dying embers that flare up
〖死活〗(名、副)[sǐhuó]
① (disregard) of the fate of ② utterly
〖死记硬背〗[sǐjì yìngbèi]
memorize mechanically
〖死角〗(名)[sǐjiǎo]
dead angle
〖死里逃生〗[sǐlǐtáoshēng]
narrow escape; escape death by a hair's breadth
〖死路〗(名)[sǐlù]
blind alley; impasse; road to destruction
〖死难〗(动)[sǐnàn]
die tragic death; die in action for a cause
〖死气沉沉〗[sǐqìchénchén]
lifeless; spiritless; dull; dreary
〖死去活来〗[sǐqùhuólái]
half dead; struck down with grief
〖死尸〗(名)[sǐshī]〔具 jù〕
corpse; dead body
〖死守〗(动)[sǐshǒu]
hold on to the last; defend at all cost
〖死亡〗(动)[sǐwáng]
die; breathe one's last; meet one's doom; death
〖死心〗[sǐxīn]
give up hope; be reconciled to
〖死心塌地〗[sǐxīntādì]
be dead set on; out-and-out

S

〖死心眼儿〗[sǐxīnyǎnr]
one-track-minded; pig-headed
〖死刑〗(名)[sǐxíng]
death penalty; capital punishment; death sentence
〖死有余辜〗[sǐyǒuyúgū]
crime deserves more than death
〖死罪〗(名)[sǐzuì]
death penalty

sì

四(数)[sì]
four
〖四边形〗(名)[sìbiānxíng]
quadrangle; quadrilateral
〖四方〗(名、形)[sìfāng]
①square ②all corners; everywhere
〖四分五裂〗[sìfēnwǔliè]
torn a part by disunity; badly split
〖四化〗(名)[sìhuà]
four modernizations (of industry, agriculture, national defence, and science and technology)
〖四季〗(名)[sìjì]
the four seasons
〖四郊〗[sìjiāo]
suburbs; out skirts
〖四面〗(名)[sìmiàn]
four sides; all round
〖四面八方〗[sìmiànbāfāng]
far and near; in all directions; everywhere; thick and fas t
〖四面楚歌〗[sìmiànchǔgē]
be surrounded by the enemy on four sides; be in dire straits
〖四平八稳〗[sìpíngbāwěn]
steady and sure; not to take a single risk
〖四舍五入〗[sìshěwǔrù]
omitting decimal fractions smaller than 0.5 and counting all others, including 0.5, as 1
〖四声〗(名)[sìshēng]
the four tones
〖四体不勤,五谷不分〗
[sìtǐbùqín, wǔgǔbùfēn]
can neither do physical work nor distinguish rice from wheat
〖四通八达〗[sìtōngbādá]
having communications with places far and near
〖四野〗[sìyě]
the surrounding country; a vast expanse of open ground
〖四月〗(名)[sìyuè]
April
〖四肢〗(名)[sìzhī]
limbs; arms and legs
〖四周〗(名)[sìzhōu]
all sides; vicinity; widely

寺(名)[sì]
temple
〖寺庙〗(名)[sìmiào]
temple

似(动)[sì]
seem; look like
　另见 shì
〖似乎〗(副)[sìhū]
apparently; as if; seem

S

〖似是而非〗[sìshì'érfēi]
appear what it is really not; specious (e.g. reasoning)

伺[sì]
〖伺机〗[sìjī]
await an opportunity

饲[sì]
〖饲料〗(名)[sìliào]
animal feed; fodder
〖饲养〗(动)[sìyǎng]
raise (animals)

肆(数)[sì]
four
〖肆无忌惮〗[sìwújìdàn]
unscrupulously; unprincipled
〖肆意〗(副)[sìyì]
wantonly

sōng

松(名、形、动)[sōng]
①pine ②loose ③loosen; relax
〖松弛〗(形)[sōngchí]
loose; relax; slacken
〖松紧带〗(名)[sōngjǐndài]
[条 tiáo] rubber band
〖松劲〗[sōngjìn]
relax one's efforts
〖松快〗(形)[sōngkuai]
feel relieved; in a relaxed mood
〖松气〗[sōngqì]
relax
〖松软〗(形)[sōngruǎn]
soft
〖松散〗(形)[sōngsǎn]
loose
〖松树〗(名)[sōngshù][棵 kē]
pine tree
〖松懈〗(形、动)[sōngxiè]
slacken; relax

sǒng

怂[sǒng]
〖怂恿〗(动)[sǒngyǒng]
instigate; abet; strongly encourage

耸(动)[sǒng]
rise (shoot); high up
〖耸立〗(动)[sǒnglì]
rise straight up; tower (e.g. to the skies)
〖耸人听闻〗[sǒngréntīngwén]
sensational

sòng

送(动)[sòng]
①send; see (sb.) off; ②present; offer
〖送别〗(动)[sòngbié]
send off
〖送礼〗[sònglǐ]
send gifts; make presents
〖送命〗[sòngmìng]
lose one's life worthlessly
〖送气〗[sòngqì]
aspirate; aspiration
〖送行〗(动)[sòngxíng]
see off

颂(动)[sòng]
praise; chant
〖颂词〗(名)[sòngcí]
eulogy; panegyric
〖颂歌〗(名)[sònggē]
song of praise
〖颂扬〗(动)[sòngyáng]
sing the praises of

sōu

搜(动)[sōu]
search; ransack
〖搜捕〗(动)[sōubǔ]
search and arrest
〖搜查〗(动)[sōuchá]
search; raid(e.g. house)
〖搜刮〗(动)[sōuguā]
loot; take away by force; plunder
〖搜集〗(动)[sōují]
collect; gather
〖搜罗〗(动)[sōuluó]
gather; collect; assemble
〖搜索〗(动)[sōusuǒ]
search; hunt for; comb for
〖搜寻〗(动)[sōuxún]
seek; search

嗖(象声)[sōu]
onomatopoeia(whistling sound)

馊(形)[sōu]
(food) spoiled; bad

艘(量)[sōu]
a measure word(for ships)

sū

苏[sū]
〖苏打〗(名)[sūdá]
soda
〖苏区〗(名)[sūqū]
a short form for the Soviet District during the Second Civil War period in the history of Chinese revolution
〖苏维埃〗(名)[Sūwéi'āi]
Soviet
〖苏醒〗(动)[sūxǐng]
wake up; come round; revive

酥(形)[sū]
crisp

sú

俗(形)[sú]
vulgar; common
〖俗话〗(名)[súhuà]
common saying; proverb
〖俗名〗(名)[súmíng]
common name; colloquial term
〖俗语〗(名)[súyǔ]
proverb; popular saying
〖俗字〗(名)[súzì]
popular form of a character

sù

诉(动)[sù]
tell; narrate
〖诉苦〗[sùkǔ]
pour out grievances
〖诉说〗(动)[sùshuō]
narrate; state(e.g. wish, feel-

ings)
〖诉讼〗(名)[sùsòng]
lawsuit
〖诉诸武力〗[sùzhūwǔlì]
recourse to force; resort to force

肃[sù]
〖肃反〗[sùfǎn]
(short form for) cleaning out counterrevolutionaries; the suppression of counterrevolutionaries
〖肃静〗(形)[sùjìng]
solemnly silent
〖肃立〗(动)[sùlì]
stand solemnly; stand at attention
〖肃清〗(动)[sùqīng]
clear away; liquidate; clean up; mop up
〖肃然〗(形)[sùrán]
respectful

素(形)[sù]
①white ②simple; unadorned
〖素材〗(名)[sùcái]
unprocessed materials
〖素菜〗(名)[sùcài]
vegetarian dish
〖素常〗(名)[sùcháng]
usual
〖素来〗(副)[sùlái]
usually; heretofore
〖素描〗(名)[sùmiáo]
sketch
〖素养〗(名)[sùyǎng]
cultivation of learning; cultivated manners
〖素质〗(名)[sùzhì]
innate quality or property

速[sù]
〖速成〗(动)[sùchéng]
get ... done by quick method
〖速成班〗(名)[sùchéngbān]
crash course; accelerated course
〖速冻〗(动、形)[sùdòng]
quick-frozen (food)
〖速度〗(名)[sùdù]
speed; tempo; rate; pace
〖速记〗(动、名)[sùjì]
shorthand; stenography
〖速溶咖啡〗[sùróngkāfēi]
instant coffee
〖速效药〗[sùxiàoyào]
quick acting medicine
〖速写〗(名)[sùxiě]
sketch
〖速战速决〗[sùzhànsùjué]
prompt action and quick decision; quickly decided battle

宿[sù]
〖宿命论〗(名)[sùmìnglùn]
fatalism
〖宿舍〗(名)[sùshè]
dormitory
〖宿营〗(动)[sùyíng]
encamp
〖宿营地〗(名)[sùyíngdì]
camping-site
〖宿愿〗(名)[sùyuàn]

long cherished wish

塑(动)[sù]
sculpt; make clay figures
〖塑料〗(名)[sùliào]
plastics
〖塑像〗(名)[sùxiàng]
statue; (plastic, clay) figure
〖塑造〗(动)[sùzào]
sculpt; create; portray

簌[sù]
〖簌簌〗(象声)[sùsù]
onomatopoeia (for tears dropping or whistling wind)

suān

酸(名、形)[suān]
sour; acid
〖酸味〗(名)[suānwèi]
sour in taste
〖酸性〗(名)[suānxìng]
acidity

suàn

蒜(名)[suàn]
〔头 tóu、瓣 bànr〕garlic

算(动)[suàn]
count
〖算计〗(动)[suànji]
calculate; consider; plan
〖算了〗(动)[suànle]
forget (about) it; drop it; leave it
〖算盘〗(名)[suànpan]
abacus
〖算是〗(副)[suànshì]
after all
〖算术〗(名)[suànshù]
arithmetic
〖算术级数〗[suànshùjíshù]
arithmetical progression
〖算数〗[suànshù]
count; take as final; be taken seriously; mean what one says
〖算账〗[suànzhàng]
ask for bill to pay; reckon accounts; settle accounts

suī

虽(连)[suī]
although
〖虽然〗(连)[suīrán]
though; although
〖虽说〗(连)[suīshuō]
although; though

suí

随(动)[suí]
follow; accompany
〖随笔〗(名)[suíbǐ]
a form of informal or familiar essay; casual literary notes
〖随便〗(形)[suíbiàn]
please yourself; as one wishes; casual; informal
〖随波逐流〗[suíbōzhúliú]
drift with the tide; follow the current; go with the stream
〖随处〗(副)[suíchù]
in all places; everywhere
〖随从〗(动、名)[suícóng]

accompany; member of the retinue
〖随地〗(副)[suídì]
anywhere; everywhere; at random
〖随和〗(形)[suíhe]
easygoing; easy to get along with
〖随后〗(副)[suíhòu]
later on; soon after
〖随机〗[suíjī]
random
〖随机应变〗[suíjīyìngbiàn]
do as the circumstances dictate; adapt oneself to circumstances
〖随即〗(副)[suíjí]
immediately
〖随叫随到〗[suíjiàosuídào]
available on hand; at one's beck and call
〖随口〗(副)[suíkǒu]
(promise) freely; without consideration;without hesitation
〖随身〗[suíshēn]
carry something (always) on body
〖随身行李〗[suíshēnxíngli]
personal luggage
〖随声听〗(名)[suíshēntīng]
walkman
〖随声附和〗[suíshēngfùhè]
agree to what other people say; yes-man; blindly echo
〖随时〗(副)[suíshí]
any time ; anytime one likes; at all times
〖随时随地〗[suíshísuídì]
at all times and all places; any time and anywhere
〖随手〗(副)[suíshǒu]
ready at hand; convenient
〖随同〗(动)[suítóng]
accompany
〖随心所欲〗[suíxīnsuǒyù]
as one pleases; as the heart desires
〖随行人员〗[suíxíng rényuán]
entourage; member of one's suite; party
〖随意〗(形)[suíyì]
as one pleases; at one's convenience; at will
〖随员〗(名)[suíyuán]
assistant; member of the staff; attache

suì

岁 (量)[suì]
year; age
〖岁数〗(名)[suìshù]
a person's age
〖岁月〗(名)[suìyuè]
times and seasons; time and tide

遂 (动)[suì]
succeed
〖遂心〗[suìxīn]
be as one like it; fulfil one's desire

碎 (形)[suì]
broken; fragmentary

隧 [suì]
〖隧道〗(名)[suìdào]〔条 tiáo〕

tunnel; underground passage

穗(名)[suì]
ear (of grain); ear of wheat

sūn

孙(名)[sūn]
grandson
〖孙女〗(名)[sūnnǚ]
granddaughter
〖孙子〗(名)[sūnzi]
grandson

sǔn

损(动)[sǔn]
damage; harm; impair; spoil
〖损害〗(动)[sǔnhài]
harm; damage; spoil; impair; injure; hurt
〖损耗〗(动、名)[sǔnhào]
lose; wear out; loss
〖损坏〗(动)[sǔnhuài]
break; damage
〖损人利己〗[sǔnrénlìjǐ]
injure others for the sake of one's own advantage; profiting at others' expense
〖损伤〗(动)[sǔnshāng]
hurt; injure; damage
〖损失〗(动、名)[sǔnshī]
lose; loss

笋(名)[sǔn]
bamboo shoot

suō

唆 [suō]
〖唆使〗(动)[suōshǐ]
incite

缩(动)[suō]
shrink; condense
〖缩短〗(动)[suōduǎn]
shorten
〖缩减〗(动)[suōjiǎn]
reduce; decrease; cut; shrink
〖缩手缩脚〗[suōshǒusuōjiǎo]
handicapped and passive; timid in a restrained manner; diffident
〖缩微〗(动)[suōwēi]
micro; micrify
〖缩小〗(动)[suōxiǎo]
shrink; reduce
〖缩写〗(名、动)[suōxiě]
abbreviation; abbreviate ... to ...; shorten
〖缩影〗(名)[suōyǐng]
miniature; epitome

suǒ

所(量、助)[suǒ]
① a measure word for building ② by
〖所属〗(动)[suǒshǔ]
army units or staff under one's command; attached to; be affiliated to
〖所谓〗(形)[suǒwèi]
so-called
〖所向披靡〗[suǒxiàngpīmǐ]
ever triumphant; ever victorious
〖所向无敌〗[suǒxiàngwúdí]

all-conquering; invincible; invincible wherever it goes
〖所以〗(连)[suǒyǐ]
therefore; so
〖所以然〗[suǒyǐrán]
the whys and wherefores; reason
〖所有〗(动)[suǒyǒu]
all one's possessions; own; belong to
〖所有权〗(名)[suǒyǒuquán]
ownership
〖所有制〗(名)[suǒyǒuzhì]
ownership
〖所在〗(动、名)[suǒzài]
a place
〖所在地〗(名)[suǒzàidì]
seat (e.g. government); the whereabouts
〖所作所为〗[suǒzuòsuǒwéi]
all one's actions; one's deeds; what one does

索[suǒ]

〖索赔〗[suǒpéi]
claim indemnity
〖索取〗(动)[suǒqǔ]
extort; ask for
〖索性〗(副)[suǒxìng]
simply ...; flatly; even; might as well
〖索引〗(名)[suǒyǐn]
an index (title index, author index, etc.)

琐[suǒ]

〖琐事〗(名)[suǒshì]
trifles; chores
〖琐碎〗(形)[suǒsuì]
petty; fragmentary; tedious; trivial
〖琐细〗(形)[suǒxì]
trivial trifling

锁(名、动)[suǒ]〔把 bǎ〕

a lock; lock up
〖锁链〗(名)[suǒliàn]〔条 tiáo〕
(iron) chain; fetters

tā

他(代)[tā]
he
〖他们〗(代)[tāmen]
they (m. or f.—for persons)
〖他人〗(代)[tārén]
the other; other person or persons

它(代)[tā]
it
〖它们〗(代)[tāmen]
they (neuter—not for person)

她(代)[tā]
she
〖她们〗(代)[tāmen]
they (for f.)

塌(动)[tā]
cave in; fall in; collapse
〖塌方〗[tā fāng]
cave-in; rock-fall
〖塌陷〗(动)[tāxiàn]
cave in; sink downward; fall in; give way (under pressure)

踏[tā]
另见 tà
〖踏实〗(形)[tāshi]
in a thorough going manner; on a firm footing

tǎ

塔(名)[tǎ][座 zuò]
pagoda

tà

踏(动)[tà]
tread; stamp on; trample
另见 tā
〖踏步〗(动)[tàbù]
mark time

tāi

胎(名)[tāi]

①embryo ②tyre
〖胎儿〗(名)[tāi'ér]
embryo
〖胎记〗(名)[tāijì]
birthmark
〖胎教〗(名)[tāijiào]
prenatal education
〖胎盘〗(名)[tāipán]
placenta

tái

台(名、量)[tái]
① a flat raised surface (e.g. platform, stage) ② dais; podium ③ a measure word (e.g. for machine)
〖台灯〗(名)[táidēng]〔盏 zhǎn〕
table lamp
〖台风〗(名)[táifēng]
typhoon
〖台阶〗(名)[táijiē]
step(of a staircase)
〖台子〗(名)[táizi]
table

抬(动)[tái]
carry; lift up; raise
〖抬举〗(动)[táiju]
think highly of sb. and praise or promote him
〖抬头〗(动)[táitóu]
① raise one's head ② gain ground

tài

太(副)[tài]
too; over; excessively
〖太极拳〗(名)[tàijíquán]
Tai Chi boxing; Tai Chi Chuan—one kind of the traditional Chinese callisthenics (for physical training)
〖太空〗(名)[tàikōng]
outer space; sky; firmament
〖太平〗(形)[tàipíng]
peaceful
〖太平门〗(名)[tàipíngmén]
emergency exit; safety exit
〖太平天国运动〗
[TàipíngTiānguóYùndòng]
the Movement of the Taiping Heavenly kingdom
〖太平洋〗(名)[Tàipíngyáng]
the Pacific Ocean
〖太阳〗(名)[tàiyáng]
the sun
〖太阳能〗(名)[tàiyángnéng]
solar energy
〖太阳系〗(名)[tàiyángxì]
solar system

态[tài]
〖态度〗(名)[tàidu]
attitude; approach; position; manner
〖态势〗(名)[tàishì]
state; situation; posture

泰[tài]
〖泰然〗(形)[tàirán]
calm;cool; collected; composed

tān

坍(动)[tān]

collapse
〖坍塌〗(动)[tāntā]
collapse; crumble; fall down

贪(动)[tān]
be greedy for; covet
〖贪得无厌〗[tāndéwúyàn]
covetous for gain; avaricious; insatiable greed
〖贪多必失〗[tānduōbìshī]
grasp all, lose all
〖贪官污吏〗[tānguānwūlì]
corrupt officials
〖贪婪〗(形)[tānlán]
voracious; rapacious; greedy for; covetous
〖贪生怕死〗[tānshēngpàsǐ]
coward; poltroon; afraid of death; cling to life notwithstanding dishonour
〖贪天之功〗[tāntiānzhīgōng]
credit other people's meritorious service to oneself; arrogate credit to oneself
〖贪图〗(动)[tāntú]
covet; desire eagerly; hanker after (e.g. a life of ease)
〖贪污〗(动)[tānwū]
corrupt; embezzle; corruption and graft
〖贪赃枉法〗[tānzāngwǎngfǎ]
take bribes and bend the law; pervert justice for a bribe

摊(动)[tān]
① set up; put on display ② share; divide up; share out
〖摊牌〗[tānpái]
have a show down; put the cards on the table
〖摊子〗(名)[tānzi]
booth; stall

瘫(动)[tān]
paralyze
〖瘫痪〗(动)[tānhuàn]
paralyze

tán

坛[tán]
〖坛坛罐罐〗[tántánguànguàn]
pots and pans; household goods
〖坛子〗(名)[tánzi]〔个 gè〕
earthenware jars

昙[tán]
〖昙花一现〗[tánhuāyīxiàn]
vanish as soon as it appears; a flash in the pan

谈(动)[tán]
talk
〖谈话〗[tánhuà]
speak; talk; converse
〖谈论〗(动)[tánlùn]
discuss; talk about
〖谈判〗(动)[tánpàn]
negotiate; conference
〖谈笑风生〗
[tánxiàofēngshēng]
light hearted and interesting (in talking)
〖谈心〗[tánxīn]

frank and serious talk; have a heart-to-heart talk

弹(动)[tán]
①spring; bounce ②flick; fillip ③play(e.g. piano)
另见 dàn
〖弹劾〗(动)[tánhé]
impeach
〖弹簧〗(名)[tánhuáng]
spring (metal)
〖弹力〗(名)[tánlì]
elasticity
〖弹性〗(名)[tánxìng]
elasticity
〖弹性工作制〗[tánxìng gōngzuòzhì]
flexible job system
〖弹性限度〗[tánxìngxiàndù]
limit of elasticity

T

痰(名)[tán]
phlegm; spit
〖痰盂〗(名)[tányú][个 gè]
spittoon

潭(名)[tán]
pool; pond

檀[tán]
〖檀香〗(名)[tánxiāng]
sandal wood

tǎn

忐[tǎn]
〖忐忑不安〗[tǎntèbù'ān]
feeling uneasy; restless

坦[tǎn]
〖坦白〗(动)[tǎnbái]
confess; make a clean breast of
〖坦克〗(名)[tǎnkè][辆 liàng]
(mil.) tank
〖坦然〗(形)[tǎnrán]
calm; cool (e.g. headed); composedly
〖坦率〗(形)[tǎnshuài]
open; straightforward; frank

袒[tǎn]
〖袒护〗(动)[tǎnhù]
be partial to; screen (e.g. sb. from blame)

毯[tǎn]
〖毯子〗(名)[tǎnzi]
blanket (e.g. woolen blanket)

tàn

叹(动)[tàn]
sigh
〖叹词〗(名)[tàncí]
(gram.) interjection
〖叹气〗[tànqì]
give a sigh; sigh over...
〖叹息〗(动)[tànxī]
sigh; sigh audibly

炭(名)[tàn]
charcoal

探(动)[tàn]

pry out; ferret out; investigate; find out
〖探测〗(动)[tàncè]
prospect; explore; probe into
〖探亲〗[tànqīn]
visit relatives (usu. parents, wife or husband)
〖探索〗(动)[tànsuǒ]
explore; probe into
〖探讨〗(动)[tàntǎo]
study; investigate; look into
〖探听〗(动)[tàntīng]
find out; make inquiries; pry
〖探望〗(动)[tànwàng]
visit
〖探险〗[tànxiǎn]
go on an adventure; explore
〖探询〗(动)[tànxún]
make inquiries; find out
〖探照灯〗(名)[tànzhàodēng]
search-light

碳(名)[tàn]
carbon
〖碳水化合物〗[tànshuǐhuàhéwù]
carbohydrate
〖碳酸〗(名)[tànsuān]
carbonic acid

tāng

汤(名)[tāng]
soup; broth
〖汤匙〗(名)[tāngchí]
spoon
〖汤药〗(名)[tāngyào]
concocted medicinal herbs; concoctions (medicinal herbs)

táng

堂[táng]
〖堂皇〗(形)[tánghuáng]
majestic; grand; magnificent; pomp

搪(动)[táng]
stop up; block
〖搪瓷〗(名)[tángcí]
enamel
〖搪塞〗(动)[tángsè]
perform one's duty perfunctorily

糖(名)[táng]
① sugar ② sweets; candy
〖糖果〗(名)[tángguǒ]
sweets; candies
〖糖衣炮弹〗[tángyīpàodàn]
sugar-coated bullets

螳[táng]
〖螳臂当车〗[tángbìdāngchē]
(lit.) a mantis tries to stop a carriage with its legs; (fig.) overrate one's own strength
〖螳螂〗(名)[tángláng]〔只 zhī〕
mantis

tǎng

倘(连)[tǎng]
if; supposing that
〖倘若〗(连)[tǎngruò]
if

躺(动)[tǎng]
lie down
〖躺椅〗(名)[tǎngyǐ]
deck chair

tàng

烫(动、形)[tàng]
scald; heat up; scalding; hot
〖烫伤〗(名)[tàngshāng]
scald

趟(量)[tàng]
a measure word(e.g. one trip)

tāo

掏(动)[tāo]
take out; pull out; reach for

滔[tāo]
〖滔滔〗(形)[tāotāo]
overflowing; exuberant; incessantly
〖滔天〗(形)[tāotiān]
① rolling; billowy (e.g. waves) ② heinous; towering(e.g. crimes)

táo

逃(动)[táo]
flee; escape; run away
〖逃避〗(动)[táobì]
evade; shun; shirk
〖逃兵〗(名)[táobīng]
deserter
〖逃窜〗(动)[táocuàn]
flee; run away
〖逃荒〗[táohuāng]
flee from famine area
〖逃难〗[táonàn]
flee for one's life; seek refuge
〖逃跑〗(动)[táopǎo]
① run away; flee ② desert
〖逃生〗(动)[táoshēng]
escape with one's life; flee for life
〖逃脱〗(动)[táotuō]
succeed in escaping
〖逃亡〗(动)[táowáng]
seek safety in flight; flee from home or country
〖逃之夭夭〗[táozhīyāoyāo]
make a getaway; take to one's heels; run away

桃(名)[táo]
peach
〖桃花〗(名)[táohuā]〔朵 duǒ〕
peach blossom
〖桃子〗(名)[táozi]〔个 gè〕
peach

陶[táo]
〖陶器〗(名)[táoqì]
pottery; earthenware; porcelain
〖陶冶〗(动)[táoyě]
① mould ② influence through contact
〖陶醉〗(动)[táozuì]
become intoxicated with; be infatuated with; be indulged in

淘(动)[táo]

①rinse; wash; clean out ②eliminate

〖淘气〗(形)[táoqì]
naughty; mischievous

〖淘汰〗(动)[táotài]
eliminate; sift out

tǎo

讨(动)[tǎo]
① beg ② ask for seek for ③ take punitive action

〖讨伐〗(动)[tǎofá]
take punitive action against

〖讨饭〗[tǎofàn]
beg; go begging

〖讨好〗(动)[tǎohǎo]
curry favour with; ingratiate; flatter; fawn on

〖讨价还价〗[tǎojiàhuánjià]
bargaining; haggle (e.g. about terms)

〖讨教〗(动)[tǎojiào]
seek advice from; consult

〖讨论〗(动)[tǎolùn]
discuss; talk over

〖讨嫌〗(动、形)[tǎoxián]
① excite dislike ② detest; detestable; disgusting; irritating

〖讨厌〗(动、形)[tǎoyàn]
①be disgusted at; detestable ②be annoyed about; be sick of

tào

套(动、量)[tào]
①put (nooses) around; slip over; harness; hitch ②apply ③a measure word, set (for furniture, method, etc.)

〖套购〗(动)[tàogòu]
illegally transact

〖套汇〗[tàohuì]
arbitrage

〖套用〗(动)[tàoyòng]
apply mechanically

〖套种〗(动)[tàozhòng]
intercropping; interplanting

tè

特[tè]

〖特别〗(形)[tèbié]
special; exceptional; particular

〖特产〗(名)[tèchǎn]
local products; special products (peculiar to a particular place or region)

〖特长〗(名)[tècháng]
speciality; special aptitudes; strong points

〖特等〗(名)[tèděng]
specially high grade or class; deluxe quality; top class or highest class

〖特地〗(副)[tèdì]
specially; purposely; on purpose

〖特点〗(名)[tèdiǎn]
distinguishing characteristic; special features or traits; salient features

〖特定〗(形)[tèdìng]
specific; peculiar; particular; designated

T

〖特技〗(名)[tèjì]
① special techniques; special skill ② trick photography (cinema)
〖特刊〗(名)[tèkān]
special issue
〖特快列车〗[tèkuàilièchē]
express train; express
〖特快专递〗[tèkuàizhuāndì]
special delivery; express mail service (EMS)
〖特困户〗(名)[tèkùnhù]
destitute household
〖特命全权大使〗
[tèmìngquánquándàshǐ]
ambassador extraordinary and plenipotentiary
〖特权〗(名)[tèquán]
prerogatives; privileges; special right
〖特色〗(名)[tèsè]
characteristics; distinctive feature
〖特赦〗(动)[tèshè]
amnesty; pardon by special decree
〖特使〗(名)[tèshǐ]
special envoy
〖特殊〗(形)[tèshū]
special; particular; extraordinary; exceptional; specific
〖特殊化〗(动)[tèshūhuà]
hanker after special privileges; specialization; specialize
〖特殊性〗(名)[tèshūxìng]
particularity; speciality; specific characteristics
〖特务〗(名)[tèwu]
secret agent; spy
〖特效〗(名)[tèxiào]
(medicine) specificity; specific
〖特写〗(名)[tèxiě][篇 piān]
① feature; special article ② close-up (cinema)
〖特性〗(名)[tèxìng]
speciality; feature; character
〖特邀〗(动)[tèyāo]
specially invite
〖特异功能〗[tèyìgōngnéng]
extraordinary powers; extrasensory perception
〖特意〗(副)[tèyì]
purposely; on purpose
〖特约〗(动)[tèyuē]
by special invitation or appointment; specially invite or appoint
〖特征〗(名)[tèzhēng]
specific feature; characteristic
〖特种〗(名)[tèzhǒng]
special (e.g. kind, brand, troops)

téng

疼(动)[téng]
① pain ② love
〖疼爱〗(动)[téng'ài]
love dearly
〖疼痛〗(形)[téngtòng]
painful

腾(动)[téng]

① mount; ascend ② make place for; empty...for

〖腾空〗(动)[téngkōng]
soar to the skies

誊(动)[téng]
make a fair copy; copy up (e.g. notes)

〖誊清〗(动)[téngqīng]
make a fair copy; copy up (notes)

〖誊写〗(动)[téngxiě]
copy up

tī

剔(动)[tī]
① scrape ② pick (e.g. pick one's teeth)

〖剔除〗(动)[tīchú]
reject (e.g. the feudal dross); get rid of what is bad or undesirable

梯(名)[tī]
① ladder ② stairs

〖梯田〗(名)[tītián]
terraced fields

〖梯形〗(名)[tīxíng]
trapezoid

〖梯子〗(名)[tīzi]
ladder

踢(动)[tī]
kick

tí

提(动)[tí]
① carry ② lift; raise; elevate ③ mention; put forward
另见 dī

〖提案〗(名)[tí'àn]
motion; proposition; resolution

〖提拔〗(动)[tíbá]
promote (e.g. rank or position)

〖提倡〗(动)[tíchàng]
advocate; encourage; promote; initiate

〖提成〗(名)[tíchéng]
royalties

〖提法〗(名)[tífa]
formulation; presentation; wording; version

〖提纲〗(名)[tígāng]
outline; thesis; general sketch

〖提纲挈领〗[tígāngqièlǐng]
give an outline; put forward the main points

〖提高〗(动)[tígāo]
improve; raise; heighten; enhance

〖提供〗(动)[tígōng]
present; provide; offer; render

〖提交〗(动)[tíjiāo]
hand over; submit; deliver

〖提炼〗(动)[tíliàn]
purify; refine; sift

〖提名〗[tímíng]
nominate; nomination

〖提前〗(动)[tíqián]
ahead of schedule

〖提琴〗(名)[tíqín]〔把 bǎ〕
cello; double-bass; violin;

T

viola
〖提取〗(动)[tíqǔ]
① take delivery of ② take out; extract
〖提审〗(动)[tíshěn]
bring up for trial; bring (a criminal) before the court
〖提升〗(动)[tíshēng]
promote (in rank or position)
〖提示〗(动)[tíshì]
point out; draw (sb.'s) attention (to sth.)
〖提问〗(动)[tíwèn]
ask questions
〖提心吊胆〗[tíxīndiàodǎn]
sick with fear or terror
〖提醒〗(动)[tíxǐng]
bring to mind; remind; alert (sb.) to
〖提要〗(名)[tíyào]
brief summary; chief points
〖提议〗(动、名)[tíyì]
propose; put forward; recommend; bring up (e.g. a proposal); proposal
〖提早〗(动)[tízǎo]
(do sth.) earlier than usual; bring forward

啼(动)[tí]
cry; weep; whimper
〖啼哭〗(动)[tíkū]
cry; weep
〖啼笑皆非〗[tíxiàojiēfēi]
one can neither cry nor laugh

题(动、名)[tí]
subject; topic; theme
〖题材〗(名)[tícái]
subject matter; subject
〖题词〗(名)[tící]
① instructive; encouraging or complimentary remarks ② inscription
〖题解〗(名)[tíjiě]
explanation
〖题名〗(名)[tímíng]
inscription
〖题目〗(名)[tímù]
title; topic
〖题字〗(名)[tízì]
inscription

蹄[tí]
〖蹄子〗(名)[tízi][只 zhī]
hoof

tǐ

体[tǐ]
〖体裁〗(名)[tǐcái]
form or style of writing
〖体操〗(名)[tǐcāo]
gymnastic exercises; gymnastics
〖体格〗(名)[tǐgé]
physical constitution (of person)
〖体会〗(动、名)[tǐhuì]
① appreciation; understand; realize ② size up (a situation)
〖体积〗(名)[tǐjī]
volume
〖体力〗(名)[tǐlì]
① physical strength ② manual

(labour)
〖体力劳动〗[tǐlìláodòng]
physical labour; manual work
〖体例〗(名)[tǐlì]
form; style
〖体谅〗(动)[tǐliàng]
make allowance for; excuse
〖体面〗(形)[tǐmiàn]
① honourable; dignified; prestigious ② good-looking
〖体贴〗(动)[tǐtiē]
be considerate of (others); be thoughtful
〖体统〗(名)[tǐtǒng]
propriety; decorum
〖体温〗(名)[tǐwēn]
(bodily) temperature
〖体无完肤〗[tǐwúwánfū]
① the body is covered with wounds all over ② be refuted down to the last point; smashed to smithereens
〖体系〗(名)[tǐxì]
system
〖体现〗(动)[tǐxiàn]
find expression in...; embody...in; manifest
〖体验〗(动)[tǐyàn]
experience; go through
〖体育〗(名)[tǐyù]
physical culture
〖体育场〗(名)[tǐyùchǎng]
stadium
〖体育馆〗(名)[tǐyùguǎn]
gymnasium
〖体制〗(名)[tǐzhì]
system; system of organisation
〖体质〗(名)[tǐzhì]
physical constitution
〖体重〗(名)[tǐzhòng]
weight (of a person)

tì

替(动、介)[tì]
substitute; on behalf of; in place of; instead of
〖替代〗(动)[tìdài]
substitute; change; replace
〖替换〗(动)[tìhuàn]
change; exchange; replace (sb.)
〖替罪羊〗(名)[tìzuìyáng]
scapegoat

tiān

天(名)[tiān]
① the sky ② season ③ weather ④ day (period of twenty-four hours)
〖天安门〗(名)[Tiān'ānmén]
Tien An Men
〖天才〗(名)[tiāncái]
genius
〖天窗〗(名)[tiānchuāng]
skylight
〖天地〗(名)[tiāndì]
the universe; heaven and earth
〖天翻地覆〗[tiānfāndìfù]
the sky and earth turning upside down; earth-shaking (changes)
〖天赋〗(名)[tiānfù]
natural ability; gift; talent
〖天花板〗(名)[tiānhuābǎn]
ceiling
〖天花乱坠〗[tiānhuāluànzhuì]

speak in superlatives; laud sth. to the skies; extravagantly laud
〖天经地义〗[tiānjīngdìyì]
(lit.)natural law and earth's way; (fig.)it stands to reason; universally accepted principle; unalterable principles; by nature
〖天空〗(名)[tiānkōng]
the sky
〖天罗地网〗[tiānluódìwǎng]
dragnet; nets above and snares below; escapeproof net
〖天南地北〗[tiānnándìběi]
far apart; poles apart
〖天平〗(名)[tiānpíng]
(weighing) scales
〖天气〗(名)[tiānqì]
weather
〖天气预报〗[tiānqìyùbào]
weather forecast
〖天堑〗(名)[tiānqiàn]
natural barrier; a deep chasm
〖天桥〗(名)[tiānqiáo]
overpass
〖天然〗(形)[tiānrán]
natural (not artificial)
〖天然气〗(名)[tiānránqì]
natural gas
〖天色〗(名)[tiānsè]
time or weather of the day as judged by the colour of the sky
〖天生〗(形)[tiānshēng]
naturally; born to be
〖天堂〗(名)[tiāntáng]
paradise; heaven
〖天体〗(名)[tiāntǐ]
heavenly body; celestial body
〖天文〗(名)[tiānwén]
astronomy
〖天文台〗(名)[tiānwéntái]
observatory
〖天下〗(名)[tiānxià]
the whole world(country, place)
〖天下大乱〗[tiānxiàdàluàn]
there is great disorder under heaven; the whole world(country, place) is in great chaos
〖天险〗(名)[tiānxiǎn]
natural defence; natural fortifications
〖天线〗(名)[tiānxiàn]
antenna
〖天涯海角〗[tiānyáhǎijiǎo]
the end of the sky and the corners of the sea; the four corners of the earth; the remotest regions of the earth
〖天灾〗(名)[tiānzāi]
natural calamities; natural disasters; natural catastrophe
〖天灾人祸〗[tiānzāirénhuò]
natural and man-made calamities
〖天真〗(形)[tiānzhēn]
naive; innocent
〖天诛地灭〗[tiānzhūdìmiè]
be executed by heaven and destroyed by earth; absolutely and utterly destroyed
〖天资〗(名)[tiānzī]
talent; (a man of) natural endowment

添(动)[tiān]
add; increase
〖添补〗(动)[tiānbǔ]
supplement; make up; replenish
〖添枝加叶〗[tiānzhījiāyè]
deliberately embellish the facts
〖添置〗(动)[tiānzhì]
buy more (e.g. furniture)

tián

田(名)[tián]
farm
〖田地〗(名)[tiándì]
① farm land ② situation (usu. bad)
〖田埂〗(名)[tiángěng]
ridge (of the furrowed field)
〖田间管理〗[tiánjiānguǎnlǐ]
farm management
〖田径〗(名)[tiánjìng]
track and field
〖田野〗(名)[tiányě]
open country

恬[tián]
〖恬不知耻〗[tiánbùzhīchǐ]
shameless; past all sense of shame
〖恬静〗(形)[tiánjìng]
tranquil; calm

甜(形)[tián]
sweet
〖甜菜〗(名)[tiáncài]
sugar beet
〖甜美〗(形)[tiánměi]
① sweet ② sweet and comfortable
〖甜蜜〗(形)[tiánmì]
sweet; loving; comfortable
〖甜头〗(名)[tiántou]
① sweet taste ② benefit
〖甜言蜜语〗[tiányánmìyǔ]
(lit.) sweet words and honeyed phrases; honey-lipped; honeyed words

填(动)[tián]
① fill up (hole, ditch, etc.) ② fill in (form)
〖填表〗[tián biǎo]
fill in a blank form
〖填补〗(动)[tiánbǔ]
make up; replenish
〖填空〗[tiánkòng]
fill up the gap
〖填写〗(动)[tiánxiě]
fill in (a form)
〖填鸭式〗(名)[tiányāshì]
cramming; cram

tiǎn

舔(动)[tiǎn]
lick

tiāo

挑(动)[tiāo]
① carry with a pole on the shoulder ② choose; select; pick out
　另见 tiǎo

T

〖挑肥拣瘦〗[tiāoféijiǎnshòu]
(lit.)pick the fat or choose the lean; (fig.) choose whichever is to one's personal advantage
〖挑剔〗(动)[tiāotī]
be critical (toward); carp at (others)
〖挑选〗(动)[tiāoxuǎn]
choose; select
〖挑子〗(名)[tiāozi]
load

tiáo

条(名、量)[tiáo]
① strip; bar; slip ② a measure word (for long, thin things, e.g. carrying pole, river, snake, fish)
〖条件〗(名)[tiáojiàn]
conditions; terms
〖条件反射〗[tiáojiànfǎnshè]
conditioned reflex
〖条款〗(名)[tiáokuǎn]
clause (e.g. agreement)
〖条理〗(名)[tiáolǐ]
orderly; systematically
〖条例〗(名)[tiáolì]
regulations; statutes; ordinances
〖条目〗(名)[tiáomù]
articles; items
〖条文〗(名)[tiáowén]
article
〖条约〗(名)[tiáoyuē]
treaty; pact
〖条子〗(名)[tiáozi]
a slip of paper; a short note

调(动)[tiáo]
① blend; harmonize ② stir
另见 diào
〖调和〗(动、形)[tiáohé]
① mediate; reconcile; conciliate; reconcilable ② compromise
〖调剂〗(动)[tiáojì]
regulate; adjust; put right
〖调节〗(动)[tiáojié]
adjust; regulate
〖调解〗(动)[tiáojiě]
mediate; reconcile
〖调理〗(动)[tiáolǐ]
① look after ② recuperate
〖调皮〗(形)[tiáopí]
naughty; cheeky
〖调停〗(动)[tiáotíng]
mediate
〖调味〗[tiáowèi]
season; seasoning (spices)
〖调养〗(动)[tiáoyǎng]
recuperate
〖调整〗(动)[tiáozhěng]
readjust; reorganise

tiǎo

挑(动)[tiǎo]
① lift up; raise ② poke up (e.g. the fire) ③ stir up; incite
另见 tiāo
〖挑拨〗(动)[tiǎobō]
foment (disunity and dissention); stir up
〖挑拨离间〗[tiǎobōlíjiàn]

foment dissension; sow discord; poison the relations between; create dissension
〖挑动〗(动)[tiǎodòng]
instigate; provoke; stir up
〖挑花〗[tiǎohuā]
needle point (e.g. lace, embroidery)
〖挑起〗(动)[tiǎoqǐ]
instigate; stir up; provoke
〖挑唆〗(动)[tiǎosuō]
instigate; incite
〖挑衅〗(动)[tiǎoxìn]
provoke
〖挑战〗[tiǎozhàn]
challenge; issue a challenge; throw down the glove

tiào

眺(动)[tiào]
survey; gaze
〖眺望〗(动)[tiàowàng]
survey or look far into the distance

跳(动)[tiào]
①jump ②twitch; palpitate
〖跳板〗(名)[tiàobǎn]
spring board; diving board
〖跳槽〗[tiàocáo]
change one's profession; abandon one occupation in favour of another; job transfer
〖跳动〗(动)[tiàodòng]
jump about
〖跳高〗(名)[tiàogāo]
high jump
〖跳伞〗[tiàosǎn]
land by parachute; parachute
〖跳水〗(名)[tiàoshuǐ]
dive
〖跳舞〗[tiàowǔ]
dance
〖跳远〗(名)[tiàoyuǎn]
long jump
〖跳跃〗(动)[tiàoyuè]
jump; hop

tiē

贴(动)[tiē]
①paste up ②come close
〖贴金〗[tiējīn]
gild; beautify; embellish
〖贴切〗(形)[tiēqiè]
pertinent; very much to the point
〖贴心〗(形)[tiēxīn]
intimate (e.g. friend or talk)

tiě

铁(名)[tiě]
iron
〖铁板〗(名)[tiěbǎn][块 kuài]
iron plate
〖铁板一块〗[tiěbǎnyīkuài]
iron-plated; (fig.) a monolithic bloc; of one cut; invariable
〖铁饼〗(名)[tiěbǐng]
discus
〖铁道兵〗(名)[tiědàobīng]
railway corps
〖铁轨〗(名)[tiěguǐ]
the rails (of railway)
〖铁路〗(名)[tiělù]

railway

〖铁面无私〗[tiěmiànwúsī]
(a person of) unbending principles or firm integrity

〖铁锹〗(名)[tiěqiāo][把 bǎ]
shovel; spade

〖铁树开花〗[tiěshùkāihuā]
(lit.) an iron-tree blossoms; (fig.) an impossibility

〖铁水〗(名)[tiěshuǐ]
melted iron

〖铁丝〗(名)[tiěsī]
wire; steel wire

〖铁蹄〗(名)[tiětí]
iron heel

〖铁锨〗(名)[tiěxiān][把 bǎ]
spade; shovel

〖铁证〗(名)[tiězhèng]
iron-clad evidence; iron-clad proof

〖铁证如山〗[tiězhèngrúshān]
irrefutable proof; a mass of cast iron proof

tīng

厅(名)[tīng]
① hall ② a department in a big organisation (e.g.in a ministry) ③ a department or bureau under provincial government

听(动)[tīng]
① hear; listen ② obey

〖听从〗(动)[tīngcóng]
obey

〖听而不闻〗[tīng'érbùwén]
pay no attention; turn a deaf ear to

〖听候〗(动)[tīnghòu]
wait (for decision, etc.); be prepared for; pending (e.g. further instructions)

〖听话〗(形)[tīnghuà]
obedient; be docile

〖听见〗(动)[tīngjiàn]
hear

〖听讲〗(动)[tīngjiǎng]
attend lectures

〖听觉〗(名)[tīngjué]
sense of hearing

〖听力〗(名)[tīnglì]
hearing; perception of sound

〖听其自然〗[tīngqízìrán]
let matters take their own course; let things drift

〖听取〗(动)[tīngqǔ]
listen to; hear (opinion)

〖听任〗(动)[tīngrèn]
let sb. have his own way

〖听说〗[tīngshuō]
it is said that; be told that

〖听写〗(动)[tīngxiě]
dictate; dictation

〖听信〗(动)[tīngxìn]
lend oneself to; listen to and believe

〖听诊器〗(名)[tīngzhěnqì]
stethoscope

〖听之任之〗[tīngzhīrènzhī]
let matters drift; allow (sb.) to continue; let sb. have his own way

〖听众〗(名)[tīngzhòng]
audience

tíng

亭[tíng]
〖亭子〗(名)[tíngzi]〔个 gè〕
pavilion

庭[tíng]
〖庭院〗(名)[tíngyuàn]
courtyard

停(动)[tíng]
① stop; halt; discontinue ② park(e.g. a car)
〖停泊〗(动)[tíngbó]
(of ship) lie at anchor
〖停车〗[tíngchē]
① stop a vehicle ② parking
〖停当〗(形)[tíngdang]
all set; all arranged
〖停电〗[tíngdiàn]
power cut; power failure
〖停顿〗(动)[tíngdùn]
be at a standstill
〖停工〗[tínggōng]
stop work
〖停火〗[tínghuǒ]
cease fire
〖停刊〗[tíngkān]
stop publication.
〖停留〗(动)[tíngliú]
① stop over (e.g. during journey) ② remain (stagnant); stand still
〖停业〗[tíngyè]
suspend business; close down
〖停战〗[tíngzhàn]
armistice; truce; cessation of hostilities
〖停止〗(动)[tíngzhǐ]
stop; halt
〖停滞〗(动)[tíngzhì]
stand still; cease; be tied up; hold back
〖停滞不前〗[tíngzhìbùqián]
be at a standstill; remain stagnant; cease to make progress; remain at the same stage of

tǐng

挺(动、副)[tǐng]
① stand erect; stick up ② thrust out; stick out ③ hold out; make it; manage ④ very; quite
〖挺拔〗(形)[tǐngbá]
① straight and towering ② firm and powerful
〖挺进〗(动)[tǐngjìn]
push forward; make a deep thrust into (e.g. enemy position); advance
〖挺立〗(动)[tǐnglì]
stand erect; straighten up
〖挺身而出〗[tǐngshēn'érchū]
step forward courageously; come out boldly

铤[tǐng]
〖铤而走险〗[tǐng'érzǒuxiǎn]
risk danger in desperation

tōng

通(形、动)[tōng]
① through; go through ② be we-

T

ll versed in; understand ③ common; general; ordinary ④ all; whole
〖通报〗(动、名)[tōngbào]
notification for general information; circular
〖通病〗(名)[tōngbìng]
① common failing ② common illness
〖通常〗(形)[tōngcháng]
usual; ordinary; generally
〖通畅〗(形)[tōngchàng]
① fluent; ② advance unimpeded
〖通车〗[tōngchē]
be open to traffic
〖通称〗(动)[tōngchēng]
generally known as
〖通道〗(名)[tōngdào][条 tiáo]
thoroughfare
〖通敌〗[tōngdí]
conspire with the enemy
〖通电〗(动、名)[tōngdiàn]
① make electric connection ② circular telegram; open telegram
〖通风〗[tōngfēng]
① airy; well ventilated ② provide (sb.) with information; reveal; disclose
〖通告〗(动、名)[tōnggào]
notify the public; official public notice
〖通观全局〗[tōngguānquánjú]
take an overall view of the situation
〖通过〗(动)[tōngguò]
① pass through ② pass (a resolution, etc.); approve
〖通航〗(动)[tōngháng]
be open to navigation
〖通红〗(形)[tōnghóng]
burning red; glowing red
〖通货〗(名)[tōnghuò]
currency
〖通货膨胀〗[tōnghuòpéngzhàng]
inflation (e.g. financial)
〖通缉〗(动)[tōngjī]
issue a wanted notice; order the arrest of sb.
〖通令〗(动、名)[tōnglìng]
issue an order (e.g. to the whole country); an order
〖通明〗(形)[tōngmíng]
lit up; brightly lit; ablaze with light
〖通盘〗(副)[tōngpán]
all round
〖通情达理〗[tōngqíngdálǐ]
be reasonable; be sensible
〖通融〗(动)[tōngróng]
be accommodating or flexible
〖通商〗[tōngshāng]
trade with (e.g. other country)
〖通史〗(名)[tōngshǐ]
general history; comprehensive history
〖通顺〗(形)[tōngshùn]
fluent; flowing (e.g. writing)
〖通俗〗(形)[tōngsú]
popular; simple (e.g. language)
〖通俗化〗(动)[tōngsúhuà]
popularize; popularization
〖通通〗(副)[tōngtōng]
all; altogether; entirely
〖通统〗(副)[tōngtǒng]
all; altogether; entirely

〖通宵〗(名)[tōngxiāo]
all night; through the night
〖通晓〗(动)[tōngxiǎo]
be well versed in; understand thoroughly
〖通信〗[tōngxìn]
correspond
〖通信兵〗(名)[tōngxìnbīng]
signal corps
〖通行〗(动)[tōngxíng]
① be current (e.g. language, customs) ② be open to traffic
〖通讯〗(名)[tōngxùn]
communications
〖通讯处〗(名)[tōngxùnchù]
address
〖通讯社〗(名)[tōngxùnshè]
news agency
〖通讯员〗(名)[tōngxùnyuán]
correspondent
〖通用〗(动)[tōngyòng]
be current; apply universally
〖通知〗(动、名)[tōngzhī]
notify; inform; notice

tóng

同(形、介、连)[tóng]
same; similar; with; and; together
〖同班〗[tóngbān]
in the same class (e.g. school)
〖同伴〗(名)[tóngbàn]
companion; mate
〖同胞〗(名)[tóngbāo]
compatriot; fellow-countryman
〖同病相怜〗
[tóngbìngxiānglián]
fellow sufferers sympathize with one another; those who have the same complaint sympathize with each other
〖同仇敌忾〗[tóngchóudíkài]
fight shoulder to shoulder with; bear common hatred for the enemy
〖同床异梦〗
[tóngchuángyìmèng]
sleep in the same bed but dream different dreams
〖同等〗(形)[tóngděng]
equivalent; the same level or standard
〖同等学历〗[tóngděngxuélì]
have the same educational level
〖同甘共苦〗[tónggāngòngkǔ]
share joys and sorrows; share weal and woe
〖同感〗(名)[tónggǎn]
common feelings; same feelings
〖同工同酬〗
[tónggōngtóngchóu]
equal pay for equal work
〖同归于尽〗[tóngguīyújìn]
both sides are doomed; end in common ruin
〖同行〗(名)[tóngháng]
person of same profession
〖同伙〗(名)[tónghuǒ]
copartner
〖同流合污〗[tóngliúhéwū]
join in the evil-doings
〖同盟〗(名)[tóngméng]
alliance; ally
〖同盟军〗(名)[tóngméngjūn]
allied forces; allies

〖同情〗(动)[tóngqíng]
sympathize; sympathy
〖同时〗(名、副)[tóngshí]
at the same time; simultaneity
〖同事〗(名)[tóngshì]
colleague
〖同位素〗(名)[tóngwèisù]
isotope
〖同位语〗(名)[tóngwèiyǔ]
appositive
〖同乡〗(名)[tóngxiāng]
person of the same village, country or province; fellow-townsmen
〖同心同德〗[tóngxīntóngdé]
with one heart and one mind; unite (for the same cause)
〖同心协力〗[tóngxīnxiélì]
unite in a concerted effort
〖同心圆〗(名)[tóngxīnyuán]
concentric circles
〖同性〗(名)[tóngxìng]
①same sex ②of similar quality
〖同学〗(名)[tóngxué]
schoolmate
〖同样〗(形)[tóngyàng]
same; likewise
〖同一性〗(名)[tóngyīxìng]
identity
〖同义词〗(名)[tóngyìcí]
synonyms
〖同意〗(动)[tóngyì]
agree; approve
〖同音词〗(名)[tóngyīncí]
homonym
〖同志〗(名)[tóngzhì]
comrade
〖同舟共济〗[tóngzhōugòngjì]
come together rain or shine; be together through thick and thin; be in the same boat; help each other in distress

铜(名)[tóng]
copper
〖铜墙铁壁〗[tóngqiángtiěbì]
wall of bronze; bastion of iron

童[tóng]
〖童工〗(名)[tónggōng]
child labourer
〖童话〗(名)[tónghuà]
fairy tales
〖童年〗(名)[tóngnián]
childhood

tǒng

统[tǒng]
〖统称〗(动)[tǒngchēng]
generally known as; be generally named
〖统筹〗(动)[tǒngchóu]
plan as a whole
〖统筹兼顾〗[tǒngchóujiāngù]
overall planning and all-round considerations
〖统共〗(副)[tǒnggòng]
altogether; all counted
〖统购统销〗[tǒnggòutǒngxiāo]
planned purchase and marketing by the state
〖统计〗(动)[tǒngjì]
(compile) statistics
〖统帅〗(名、动)[tǒngshuài]
commander

〖统率〗(动)[tǒngshuài]
command
〖统统〗(副)[tǒngtǒng]
entirely; all; altogether
〖统一〗(动)[tǒngyī]
unify; coordinate; achieve unity
〖统一体〗(名)[tǒngyītǐ]
entity
〖统一战线〗[tǒngyīzhànxiàn]
united front
〖统治〗(动)[tǒngzhì]
rule; dominate
〖统治阶级〗[tǒngzhìjiējí]
ruling class

捅(动)[tǒng]
poke; stir up

桶(名、量)[tǒng][只 zhī]
① pail; bucket ② a measure word(e.g. a bucket of)

筒(名)[tǒng]
a hard tube-shaped container
〖筒子〗(名)[tǒngzi][个 gè]
a hard tube-shaped container

tòng

痛(动、副)[tòng]
① pain; ache ② bitterly ③ thoroughly
〖痛斥〗(动)[tòngchì]
thoroughly refute; bitterly denounce; rebut severely
〖痛处〗(名)[tòngchù]
sensitive spot; tender subject; the quick
〖痛改前非〗[tònggǎiqiánfēi]
reform earnestly one's misdeeds; mend one's ways
〖痛感〗(动)[tònggǎn]
feel keenly
〖痛恨〗(动)[tònghèn]
hate bitterly
〖痛哭〗(动)[tòngkū]
cry bitterly
〖痛哭流涕〗[tòngkūliútì]
cry and shed bitter tears
〖痛苦〗(形)[tòngkǔ]
painful; bitter
〖痛快〗(形)[tòngkuài]
① to one's heart's content ② outspoken; straight forward; thrilled with gladness
〖痛心〗(形)[tòngxīn]
heart rending; heart stricken
〖痛心疾首〗[tòngxīnjíshǒu]
with deep hatred
〖痛痒〗(名)[tòngyǎng]
pain and itch; concern; well-being

tōu

偷(动)[tōu]
steal; thieve
〖偷盗〗(动)[tōudào]
steal; rob
〖偷工减料〗[tōugōngjiǎnliào]
cheat in work and cut down material; do shoddy work and use inferior materials; jerry-built

T

〖偷懒〗[tōulǎn]
idle; negligent
〖偷梁换柱〗[tōuliánghuànzhù]
stealing the beams and pillars and replacing them with rotten timbers; resort to fraudulence
〖偷窃〗(动)[tōuqiè]
steal; rob
〖偷偷〗(副)[tōutōu]
stealthily; secretly
〖偷偷摸摸〗(形)[tōutōumōmō]
stealthy; quietly and secretly
〖偷袭〗(动)[tōuxí]
make a surprise attack; raid

tóu

头(名、量、尾)[tóu]
① head ② a measure word (e.g. for farm animal) ③ a suffix
〖头等〗(名)[tóuděng]
first class; paramount; prime (e.g. importance)
〖头发〗(名)[tóufa]〔根 gēn〕
hair on human head
〖头号〗(名)[tóuhào]
the biggest; No.1
〖头巾〗(名)[tóujīn]〔条 tiáo〕
headscarf
〖头颅〗(名)[tóulú]
skull
〖头目〗(名)[tóumù]
head; boss; chieftain; chief
〖头脑〗(名)[tóunǎo]
head; brains; the human mind
〖头破血流〗[tóupòxuèliú]
be badly battered
〖头痛〗[tóutòng]
headache
〖头头是道〗[tóutóushìdào]
clear and convincing; systematically and methodically
〖头衔〗(名)[tóuxián]
rank; title
〖头绪〗(名)[tóuxù]
in order; (in good) working order
〖头子〗(名)[tóuzi]
chief; boss; head

投(动)[tóu]
① throw; hurl; cast ② jump into; throw (oneself) into ③ submit; send in; deliver
〖投奔〗(动)[tóubèn]
go to join...; fly to...for support
〖投产〗(动)[tóuchǎn]
put into production; begin production
〖投诚〗(动)[tóuchéng]
come over to brightness; surrender to the people
〖投弹〗[tóudàn]
hand-grenade throwing
〖投敌〗[tóudí]
surrender to enemy
〖投递〗(动)[tóudì]
deliver
〖投稿〗[tóugǎo]
submit manuscripts (for publication)
〖投合〗(动)[tóuhé]
① be suitable to; suit; cater ② cater for the taste
〖投机〗(形、动)[tóujī]
① speculate; opportunist ②

T

harmonious; agreeing; suiting
〖投机倒把〗[tóujīdǎobǎ]
speculate; profiteering
〖投机取巧〗[tóujīqǔqiǎo]
gain something by fraud
〖投靠〗(动)[tóukào]
become retainer of; throw oneself into the arms of
〖投票〗[tóupiào]
cast vote
〖投入〗(动)[tóurù]
plunge; throw(oneself) into
〖投身〗(动)[tóushēn]
plunge into; participate in; throw oneself into
〖投降〗(动)[tóuxiáng]
surrender; capitulate
〖投影〗(名)[tóuyǐng]
projection
〖投掷〗(动)[tóuzhì]
throw; cast
〖投资〗(名)[tóuzī]
investment
〖投资环境〗[tóuzīhuánjìng]
environment for investment
〖投资者〗(名)[tóuzīzhě]
investor

tòu

透(动、形)[tòu]
pass through; penetrate; penerated
〖透彻〗(形)[tòuchè]
thorough; profound; penetrating; incisive
〖透风〗[tòufēng]
well ventilated
〖透镜〗(名)[tòujìng]
lens
〖透亮〗(形)[tòuliàng]
transparent; clear
〖透露〗(动)[tòulù]
reveal; disclose; bring to light
〖透明〗(形)[tòumíng]
transparent
〖透明度〗(名)[tòumíngdù]
openness; transparency
〖透辟〗(形)[tòupì]
deep; thorough; profound
〖透视〗(动)[tòushì]
have an X-ray examination
〖透支〗(动)[tòuzhī]
overdraw; make an overdraft

tū

凸(形)[tū]
convex

秃(形)[tū]
①bald; devoid of hair ②a tree without leaf or branch; bare

突[tū]
〖突变〗(动)[tūbiàn]
change suddenly; a sudden change takes place; a sudden leap takes place
〖突出〗(动、形)[tūchū]
be outstanding; striking
〖突飞猛进〗[tūfēiměngjìn]
advance by leaps and bounds
〖突击〗(动)[tūjī]
① make surprise attack ② rush (work)

〖突击队〗(名)[tūjīduì]
storm troops; shock brigade; assault force
〖突破〗(动)[tūpò]
make a breakthrough; breach (e.g. enemy's line)
〖突起〗(动)[tūqǐ]
suddenly arise; bulge
〖突然〗(形)[tūrán]
sudden; abrupt
〖突如其来〗[tūrúqílái]
suddenly; abruptly
〖突围〗[tūwéi]
break through encirclement

tú

图(名、动)[tú]

①picture; chart; illustration; any kind of drawing ②seek after; hope for
〖图案〗(名)[tú'àn]
design; pattern
〖图表〗(名)[túbiǎo]
chart; graph; diagram; blueprint
〖图钉〗(名)[túdīng]
thumbtacks
〖图画〗(名)[túhuà]〔张 zhāng〕
painting; drawing
〖图解〗(名)[tújiě]
illustration; graph
〖图景〗(名)[tújǐng]
prospects
〖图谋〗(动)[túmóu]
plot (e.g. a conspiracy)
〖图片〗(名)[túpiàn]〔张 zhāng〕
picture
〖图书〗(名)[túshū]
books in general
〖图书馆〗(名)[túshūguǎn]
library
〖图像〗(名)[túxiàng]
painted picture; portrait; graph
〖图形〗(名)[túxíng]
sketch figure; graph; diagram
〖图样〗(名)[túyàng]
a sketch
〖图章〗(名)[túzhāng]〔枚 méi〕
(official or personal) seal; stamp
〖图纸〗(名)[túzhǐ]〔张 zhāng〕
design; blue-print

徒[tú]

〖徒步〗(动)[túbù]
on foot
〖徒弟〗(名)[túdì]
apprentice; disciple
〖徒劳〗(形、动)[túláo]
futile; of no avail; fruitless (labour); try in vain
〖徒然〗(副)[túrán]
in vain
〖徒手〗(形)[túshǒu]
barehanded
〖徒刑〗(名)[túxíng]
legal sentence (e.g. life sentence)
〖徒子徒孙〗[túzǐtúsūn]
(derog.) disciples and followers

途[tú]

〖途径〗(名)[tújìng]
path; way
〖途中〗(名)[túzhōng]
on the way

涂(动)[tú]
① apply; rub on; smear ② erase; cross out
〖涂改〗(动)[túgǎi]
alter; make correction
〖涂抹〗(动)[túmǒ]
smear over
〖涂脂抹粉〗[túzhīmǒfěn]
(lit.) apply rouge and powder; (fig.) prettify; whitewash

屠[tú]
〖屠刀〗(名)[túdāo]〔把 bǎ〕
butcher's knife
〖屠杀〗(动)[túshā]
kill; massacre; slaugther
〖屠宰〗(动)[túzǎi]
slaughter (killing of animals, esp. for food)

tǔ

土(名)[tǔ]
① earth; soil ② land ③ native; local
〖土崩瓦解〗[tǔbēngwǎjiě]
disintegrate and collapse; crumble and perish; fall apart
〖土产〗(名)[tǔchǎn]
local products
〖土地〗(名)[tǔdì]
land
〖土地改革〗[tǔdìgǎigé]
land reform
〖土地革命战争〗
[TǔdìGémìngZhànzhēng]
the War of the Agrarian Revolution
〖土豆〗(名)[tǔdòu]
potato
〖土法上马〗[tǔfǎshàngmǎ]
employ indigenous methods
〖土匪〗(名)[tǔfěi]
bandit
〖土改〗(名)[tǔgǎi]
land reform
〖土豪劣绅〗[tǔháolièshēn]
local tyrants and evil gentry; local bullies and bad gentry
〖土木工程〗[tǔmùgōngchéng]
civil engineering
〖土壤〗(名)[tǔrǎng]
soil
〖土生土长〗[tǔshēngtǔzhǎng]
indigenous; locally born and brought up
〖土星〗(名)[tǔxīng]〔颗 kē〕
Saturn
〖土洋结合〗[tǔyángjiéhé]
simultaneous employment of modern and indigenous methods (of production)
〖土质〗(名)[tǔzhì]
properties of soil

吐(动)[tǔ]
spit out
另见 tù
〖吐故纳新〗[tǔgùnàxīn]
get rid of the stale and take in

T

the fresh
〖吐露〗(动)[tǔlù]
disclose; reveal

tù

吐(动)[tù]
throw up; vomit
另见 tǔ

兔(名)[tù]
hare
〖兔死狐悲〗[tùsǐhúbēi]
the fox mourns over the death of the hare; like mourns over the death of like
〖兔子〗(名)[tùzi]〔只 zhī〕
hare; rabbit

tuān

T

湍[tuān]
〖湍急〗(形)[tuānjí]
(of river) flowing rapidly
〖湍流〗(名)[tuānliú]
a swift flow (stream, river, etc.)

tuán

团(名、动、量)[tuán]
①a roundish mass; a ball ②body; organization; delegation ③ regiment ④ a measure word (for round things, e.g. a ball of knitting wool)
〖团拜〗(动)[tuánbài]
mass greetings; exchange greetings at a get-together held on New Year's Day or in Spring Festival
〖团伙〗(名)[tuánhuǒ]
band; gang
〖团结〗(动)[tuánjié]
unite
〖团结批评团结〗
[tuánjiépīpíngtuánjié]
unity criticism unity
〖团聚〗(动)[tuánjù]
have a reunion; rally
〖团体〗(名)[tuántǐ]
body; group; organization
〖团体操〗(名)[tuántǐcāo]
group calisthenics
〖团员〗(名)[tuányuán]
①member of a delegation②league member (member of the Communist Youth League of China)
〖团圆〗(动)[tuányuán]
have a family reunion
〖团长〗(名)[tuánzhǎng]
① regimental commander ② head of a delegation

tuī

推(动)[tuī]
①push ②shift; evade ③infer
〖推波助澜〗[tuībōzhùlán]
(lit.) help intensify the billows and waves; fan the fire; add fuel to the fire (usu. negative)
〖推测〗(动)[tuīcè]
infer; speculate;draw an inference; fathom out
〖推陈出新〗[tuīchénchūxīn]

weed through the old to let the new grow; the new emerging out of the old
〖推迟〗(动)[tuīchí]
postpone; put back
〖推辞〗(动)[tuīcí]
reject; decline (e.g. invitation, offer, etc.)
〖推倒〗(动)[tuīdǎo]
overthrow; push down
〖推动〗(动)[tuīdòng]
spur... onto action; push forward; propel; promote
〖推断〗(动)[tuīduàn]
infer; draw an inference; deduce
〖推翻〗(动)[tuīfān]
overthrow
〖推广〗(动)[tuīguǎng]
popularize; spread; extend; promote
〖推荐〗(动)[tuījiàn]
recommend
〖推进〗(动)[tuījìn]
propel; advance; push (ahead)
〖推举〗(动)[tuījǔ]
nominate; recommend
〖推理〗(名、动)[tuīlǐ]
inference; deduction; deduce; infer
〖推论〗(名、动)[tuīlùn]
inference; reasoning; infer; conclude; deduce
〖推敲〗(动)[tuīqiāo]
weigh and consider; fathom out; work out in detail
〖推却〗(动)[tuīquè]
reject; shirk (e.g. responsibility)
〖推让〗(动)[tuīràng]
courteously decline in favour of another
〖推算〗(动)[tuīsuàn]
calculate; deduce; work out
〖推土机〗(名)[tuītǔjī]
bulldozer
〖推托〗(动)[tuītuō]
make an excuse; find a pretext for
〖推脱〗(动)[tuītuō]
shirk
〖推委〗(动)[tuīwěi]
shift (e.g. responsibility); evade by excuse
〖推想〗(动、名)[tuīxiǎng]
reason out; speculate; conjecture; infer; inference; calculation
〖推销〗(动)[tuīxiāo]
peddle; promote the sale of...
〖推卸〗(动)[tuīxiè]
evade; shove off (e.g. duty); shirk
〖推心置腹〗[tuīxīnzhìfù]
deal honestly and sincerely with others
〖推行〗(动)[tuīxíng]
promote; carry through
〖推选〗(动)[tuīxuǎn]
choose; elect
〖推移〗(动)[tuīyí]
progress (rapidly); (as time) goes on
〖推子〗(名)[tuīzi]〔把 bǎ〕
hair clippers

tuí

颓 [tuí]

〖颓败〗(形)[tuíbài]
decadent
〖颓废〗(形)[tuífèi]
decadent dispirited
〖颓丧〗(形)[tuísàng]
drooping; decadent; disconcerted
〖颓唐〗(形)[tuítáng]
dispirited; disconsolate; decadent

tuǐ

腿 (名)[tuǐ]〔条 tiáo〕
① leg; thigh (of the body) ② legs of furniture
〖腿脚〗(名)[tuǐjiǎo]
steps (e.g. firm, weak)

T

tuì

退 (动)[tuì]
① retreat; fall back ② return (e.g. goods, etc.) ③ resign; withdraw; retire
〖退步〗(动、名)[tuìbù]
retrograde; degenerate; fall behind; retrogression; degeneration
〖退潮〗[tuìcháo]
ebb tide
〖退出〗(动)[tuìchū]
withdraw from
〖退化〗(动)[tuìhuà]
fall behind in development; become decadent
〖退还〗(动)[tuìhuán]
send back; return; reject
〖退回〗(动)[tuìhuí]
return; send back
〖退路〗(名)[tuìlù]
① a way out ② room for retreat
〖退却〗(动)[tuìquè]
① step back; retreat ② back down
〖退让〗(动)[tuìràng]
make concessions to; make compromise
〖退色〗[tuìsè]
fade in colour
〖退烧〗[tuìshāo]
reduce fever
〖退缩〗(动)[tuìsuō]
shrink back
〖退伍〗[tuìwǔ]
be demobilised
〖退席〗(动)[tuìxí]
① leave meeting or dinner party half way ② walk out (e.g. in protest)
〖退休〗(动)[tuìxiū]
retire (stop work in old age)
〖退休金〗(名)[tuìxiūjīn]
pension; retirement pay
〖退学〗(动)[tuìxué]
leave school; discontinue one's schooling
〖退职〗(动)[tuìzhí]
resign or be discharged from office; quit working

蜕 [tuì]

〖蜕变〗(动)[tuìbiàn]
degenerate

〖蜕化〗(动)[tuìhuà]
degenerate
〖蜕化变质〗[tuìhuàbiànzhì]
degenerate; degeneration

tūn

吞(动)[tūn]
swallow
〖吞并〗(动)[tūnbìng]
annex; annexation
〖吞没〗(动)[tūnmò]
swallow up; gobble up; devour
〖吞噬〗(动)[tūnshì]
gobble up; eat up in large mouthfuls
〖吞吐量〗(名)[tūntǔliàng]
loading and unloading capacity
〖吞吞吐吐〗[tūntūntǔtǔ]
mince words; mutter and mumble; hum and haw

tún

屯(动)[tún]
pile up; accumulate; hoard
〖屯田〗(名)[túntián]
station soldiers on borders making them raise their own food (archaic)

囤(动)[tún]
hoard; stock up
另见 dùn
〖囤积〗(动)[túnjī]
hoard; stockpile (of goods for sale at a higher price)
〖囤积居奇〗[túnjījūqí]
hoarding and speculation

臀(名)[tún]
buttocks; bottom

tuō

托(动、名)[tuō]
① carry on the palm; support with hands ② entrust (sth. to sb.) ③ something that supports (e.g. tray, receptacle)
〖托词〗(名)[tuōcí]
pretext; excuse
〖托儿所〗(名)[tuō'érsuǒ]
nursery
〖托福〗[tuō fú]
thanks to
〖托付〗(动)[tuōfù]
entrust
〖托管〗(动)[tuōguǎn]
put under trusteeship
〖托运〗(动)[tuōyùn]
send by freight or in the goods van (of a train)

拖(动)[tuō]
① drag; pull ② prolong; delay
〖拖把〗(名)[tuōbǎ]
mop
〖拖车〗(名)[tuōchē]〔辆 liàng〕
trailer
〖拖拉〗(形)[tuōlā]
slack; procrastinating
〖拖拉机〗(名)[tuōlājī]〔台 tái〕
tractor
〖拖泥带水〗[tuōnídàishuǐ]
(lit.) be dragged through the mud; (fig.) messy matter
〖拖鞋〗(名)[tuōxié]

〔双 shuāng〕slippers
〖拖延〗(动)[tuōyán]
procrastinate; delay

脱(动)[tuō]

①peel; fall out (e.g. skin, hair, paint) ②take off (e.g. shoes)
〖脱产〗[tuōchǎn]
relieve of production or other work (to undertake fresh responsibilities)
〖脱产进修〗[tuōchǎnjìnxiū]
be released from work to further one's studies
〖脱产学习〗[tuōchǎnxuéxí]
take leave of absence to study
〖脱节〗[tuōjié]
out of keeping with; lack of coordination; out of gear
〖脱口而出〗[tuōkǒu'érchū]
speak without any consideration; speak rashly
〖脱离〗(动)[tuōlí]
separate from; detach from; divorce from; keep aloof from; isolate...from; alienate from
〖脱粒机〗(名)[tuōlìjī]〔台 tái〕
thresher
〖脱落〗(动)[tuōluò]
drop; fall
〖脱毛〗[tuōmáo]
moult
〖脱身〗[tuōshēn]
get away; disengagement
〖脱胎换骨〗[tuōtāihuàngǔ]
make a thoroughgoing change; completely remoulded
〖脱险〗[tuōxiǎn]
escape from danger
〖脱销〗(动)[tuōxiāo]
run out of supplies; out of stock; sold out

tuó

驮(动)[tuó]

carry on back

驼[tuó]

〖驼背〗(名)[tuóbèi]
hunchback

鸵[tuó]

〖鸵鸟〗(名)[tuóniǎo]〔只 zhī〕
ostrich

tuǒ

妥(形)[tuǒ]

good; well arranged; sound; ready
〖妥当〗(形)[tuǒdang]
well thought-out; sound; good; solid; safe
〖妥善〗(形)[tuǒshàn]
well thought-out; proper
〖妥帖〗(形)[tuǒtiē]
proper; appropriate
〖妥协〗(动)[tuǒxié]
compromise

椭[tuǒ]

〖椭圆〗(形、名)[tuǒyuán]
oval shaped; ellipse; oval

tuò

拓 [tuò]

〖拓荒〗[tuòhuāng]
reclaim waste-land

〖拓荒者〗(名)[tuòhuāngzhě]
pioneer; pathbreaker; trail-blazer

〖拓宽〗(动)[tuòkuān]
widen; broaden

唾 (动)[tuò]
spit

〖唾骂〗(动)[tuòmà]
abuse; rebuke coarsely

〖唾沫〗(名)[tuòmo]
spittle

〖唾弃〗(动)[tuòqì]
cast aside; renounce; repudiate

〖唾手可得〗[tuòshǒukědé]
extremely easy to obtain

〖唾液〗(名)[tuòyè]
saliva

wā

挖(动)[wā]
dig
〖挖掘〗(动)[wājué]
① dig out; excavate; tap (e.g. potentialities)
〖挖空心思〗[wākōngxīnsī]
rack one's brains; think hard
〖挖苦〗(动)[wāku]
ridicule; hurt others by sarcastic remarks
〖挖潜〗[wāqián]
tap potential
〖挖墙脚〗[wāqiángjiǎo]
subvert; undermine the foundation
〖挖土机〗(名)[wātǔjī]〔台 tái〕
excavator; dredge

洼(形)[wā]
low; hollow; depressed

蛙(名)[wā]〔只 zhī〕
frog
〖蛙泳〗(名)[wāyǒng]
breast stroke

wá

娃(名)[wá]
baby
〖娃娃〗(名)[wáwa]〔个 gè〕
① baby ② doll
〖娃娃鱼〗(名)[wáwayú]
giant salamander

wǎ

瓦(名)[wǎ]
tile
〖瓦工〗(名)[wǎgōng]
bricklayer
〖瓦解〗(动)[wǎjiě]
break up; disintegrate; cause to collapse; undermine
〖瓦斯〗(名)[wǎsī]
gas
〖瓦特〗(量)[wǎtè]

a measure word, watt (unit of electrical power)

wà

袜(名)[wà]
socks; stockings
〖袜子〗(名)[wàzi]〔双 shuāng〕
socks; stockings

wāi

歪(形)[wāi]
① not straight; crooked; awry; slanted ② immoral; indecent; crooked
〖歪风邪气〗[wāifēngxiéqì]
gust of evil winds; evil trends
〖歪曲〗(动)[wāiqū]
distort; misrepresent; twist
〖歪歪扭扭〗(形)
[wāiwāiniǔniǔ]
twisting; twisted

wài

外(名)[wài]
outside; external
〖外边〗(名)[wàibian]
the outside
〖外表〗(名)[wàibiǎo]
appearance; surface; outward show
〖外宾〗(名)[wàibīn]
foreign guest
〖外部〗(名)[wàibù]
outside part; outside; exterior; surface
〖外地〗(名)[wàidì]
places other than one's own; other area; other place
〖外观〗(名)[wàiguān]
appearance; external
〖外国〗(名)[wàiguó]
foreign country
〖外行〗(名、形)[wàiháng]
out of one's normal line; inexperienced
〖外号〗(名)[wàihào]
nickname
〖外汇〗(名)[wàihuì]
foreign currency; foreign exchange
〖外汇储备〗[wàihuìchǔbèi]
foreign exchange reserves
〖外汇牌价〗[wàihuìpáijià]
list of exchange rate quotations
〖外籍〗(名)[wàijí]
foreign nationality
〖外交〗(名)[wàijiāo]
diplomacy
〖外交关系〗[wàijiāoguānxi]
diplomatic relations
〖外交路线〗[wàijiāolùxiàn]
diplomatic line
〖外交使团〗[wàijiāoshǐtuán]
diplomatic corps; diplomatic mission
〖外交特权〗[wàijiāotèquán]
diplomatic immunity
〖外界〗(名)[wàijiè]
outside world
〖外科〗(名)[wàikē]
surgery; surgical department
〖外壳〗(名)[wàiké]
shell; crust

〖外来词〗(名)[wàiláicí]
borrowed words (from other languages)
〖外力〗(名)[wàilì]
external force
〖外流〗(动)[wàiliú]
outflow
〖外贸〗(名)[wàimào]
foreign trade
〖外貌〗(名)[wàimào]
looks; external appearance; exterior aspect
〖外面〗(名)[wàimiàn]
outside; exterior
〖外强中干〗
[wàiqiángzhōnggān]
strong in appearance but weak inside; outwardly strong, inwardly weak
〖外侨〗(名)[wàiqiáo]
foreign nationals; immigrants
〖外勤〗(名)[wàiqín]
field(outside) work
〖外伤〗(名)[wàishāng]
trauma
〖外甥〗(名)[wàisheng]
nephew(sister's son)
〖外甥女〗(名)[wàishengnǚ]
niece(sister's daughter)
〖外事〗(名)[wàishì]
foreign affairs
〖外孙女〗(名)[wàisūnnǚ]
daughter's daughter
〖外孙子〗(名)[wàisūnzi]
daughter's son
〖外套〗(名)[wàitào]〔件 jiàn〕
overcoat; outer garment
〖外头〗(名)[wàitou]
the outside
〖外围〗(名)[wàiwéi]
outer circles; periphery; outerring (e.g. organization)
〖外位语〗(名)[wàiwèiyǔ]
extra-positional word
〖外文〗(名)[wàiwén]
foreign language
〖外项〗(名)[wàixiàng]
(math.) extremes
〖外向型〗[wàixiàngxíng]
exportoriented
〖外向型企业〗
[wàixiàngxíngqǐyè]
exportoriented enterprise
〖外衣〗(名)[wàiyī]〔件 jiàn〕
① coat; overcoat ② camouflage; (under) the cloak of
〖外因〗(名)[wàiyīn]
external causes
〖外语〗(名)[wàiyǔ]
foreign language
〖外援〗(名)[wàiyuán]
foreign aid
〖外债〗(名)[wàizhài]
foreign debts, foreign loans
〖外祖父〗(名)[wàizǔfù]
maternal grandfather
〖外祖母〗(名)[wàizǔmǔ]
maternal grandmother

wān

弯(形、动)[wān]
bent; bend
〖弯路〗(名)[wānlù]

twists and turns along the road; zigzags; detour; tortuous road

〖弯曲〗(形)[wānqū]

bent; curving

wán

丸(名、量)[wán]

①pill; small ball ②a measure word, (e.g. a pill of medicine)

〖丸药〗(名)[wányào]

(med.)pills; tablets

完(动)[wán]

finish; complete

〖完备〗(形)[wánbèi]

complete; well provided; perfect; comprehensive

〖完毕〗(动)[wánbì]

come to an end; be finished; be completed

〖完成〗(动)[wánchéng]

complete; fulfil; accomplish

〖完工〗[wángōng]

complete work

〖完好〗(形)[wánhǎo]

not cracked; in good condition

〖完结〗(动)[wánjié]

end; be closed; conclude

〖完美〗(形)[wánměi]

fine and complete; beautiful (e.g. work of art); perfect

〖完美无缺〗[wánměiwúquē]

without defect and omission; faultless; perfect

〖完全〗(形)[wánquán]

complete; full; absolutely

〖完善〗(形)[wánshàn]

perfect; excellent

〖完整〗(形)[wánzhěng]

① intact and complete; not broken ② comprehensive③ integrity

玩(动)[wán]

① play; have fun with ② play with(tricks, etc.)

〖玩忽职守〗[wánhūzhíshǒu]

neglect one's duty

〖玩火自焚〗[wánhuǒzìfén]

he who plays with fire gets burned

〖玩具〗(名)[wánjù]

toy

〖玩弄〗(动)[wánnòng]

①play with; flirt with ②practise tricks and deceptions

〖玩耍〗(动)[wánshuǎ]

play; have fun with

〖玩笑〗(名)[wánxiào]

joke; jest

顽[wán]

〖顽敌〗(名)[wándí]

diehard enemy

〖顽固〗(形)[wángù]

stubborn; obstinate

〖顽固不化〗[wángùbùhuà]

incorrigible; headstrong; diehard

〖顽抗〗(动)[wánkàng]

resist stubbornly

〖顽皮〗(形)[wánpí]

naughty; cheeky; mischievous

〖顽强〗(形)[wánqiáng]

indomitable; staunch; tenacious

wǎn

挽(动)[wǎn]
①pull②retrieve; save
〖挽歌〗(名)[wǎngē]
elegy; dirge
〖挽回〗(动)[wǎnhuí]
retrieve (a situation, etc.); avert; save (e.g. a situation)
〖挽救〗(动)[wǎnjiù]
save; avert; rescue; redeem
〖挽留〗(动)[wǎnliú]
persuade or ask sb. to stay

婉[wǎn]
〖婉言谢绝〗[wǎnyánxièjué]
refuse politely; refuse (an offer) tactfully and mildly
〖婉转〗(形)[wǎnzhuǎn]
① in a tactful way;politely ② sweet and charming (e.g. singing)

晚(名、形)[wǎn]
①evening ②late; later
〖晚饭〗(名)[wǎnfàn]
supper; evening meal
〖晚会〗(名)[wǎnhuì]
(evening) gathering; evening party
〖晚婚〗(名)[wǎnhūn]
late marriage
〖晚节〗(名)[wǎnjié]
man's integrity in his old age; one's revolutionary integrity in one's later years
〖晚年〗(名)[wǎnnián]
old age
〖晚期〗(名)[wǎnqī]
late period; late stage
〖晚上〗(名)[wǎnshang]
evening; night
〖晚霞〗(名)[wǎnxiá]
sunset glow; colourful sky at sunset

碗(名)[wǎn]〔个 gè〕
bowl

wàn

万(数)[wàn]
ten thousand
〖万变不离其宗〗
[wànbiànbùlíqízōng]
no matter what changes he has made, he has not departed from his basic position
〖万恶〗(形)[wàn'è]
completely atrocious; thoroughly wicked;diabolical; evil
〖万分〗(形)[wànfēn]
exceedingly; very; extremely
〖万古长青〗[wàngǔchángqīng]
be evergreen; ever new; flourish forever
〖万花筒〗(名)[wànhuātǒng]
kaleidoscope
〖万金油〗(名)[wànjīnyóu]
Jack of all trades
〖万里长城〗[WànlǐChángchéng]
the Great Wall
〖万里长征〗[wànlǐchángzhēng]
① a long march of ten thousand

"li" ② the Long March
〖万马奔腾〗[wànmǎbēnténg]
ten thousand horses gallop forward; surging forward
〖万能〗(形)[wànnéng]
allpowerful; universal; all-purpose
〖万能胶〗(名)[wànnéngjiāo]
all-purpose adhesive
〖万能钥匙〗[wànnéngyàoshi]
master key
〖万千〗(形)[wànqiān]
innumerable
〖万事大吉〗[wànshìdàjí]
everything will be fine; everything goes off without a hitch
〖万事通〗(名)[wànshìtōng]
know-all
〖万寿无疆〗[wànshòuwújiāng]
long live; a long life to
〖万水千山〗[wànshuǐqiānshān]
(lit.)ten thousand mountains and rivers; ten thousand crags and torrents; (fig.)a long and arduous journey
〖万岁〗[wànsuì]
long live
〖万万〗(副)[wànwàn]
absolutely; never
〖万无一失〗[wànwúyīshī]
not a chance of an error; absolutely certain
〖万物〗(名)[wànwù]
all things
〖万幸〗(形)[wànxìng]
unusually lucky
〖万一〗(副)[wànyī]
in case; in the event of
〖万用表〗(名)[wànyòngbiǎo]
multimeter
〖万有引力〗[wànyǒuyǐnlì]
the force of gravity
〖万众一心〗[wànzhòngyīxīn]
all of one heart and one mind; united like one man
〖万紫千红〗[wànzǐqiānhóng]
a profusion of colour; innumerable flowers of purple and red

腕[wàn]

〖腕子〗(名)[wànzi]
the wrist

wāng

汪[wāng]

〖汪洋〗(名)[wāngyáng]
a vast expanse of water
〖汪洋大海〗[wāngyángdàhǎi]
a vast ocean; a boundless ocean

wáng

亡(动)[wáng]

① flee; escape ② subjugate; subdue ③ die; perish ④ destroy
〖亡国〗[wángguó]
national subjugation; ruin of a country; national disaster
〖亡命之徒〗[wángmìngzhītú]
desperado; wild ruffian
〖亡羊补牢〗[wángyángbǔláo]
(lit.)mend the fold after losing the sheep; (fig.)not too late to take precautions for the future

王(名)[wáng]
①king ②head; chief ③best or strongest of its kind
〖王国〗(名)[wángguó]
kingdom
〖王牌〗(名)[wángpái]
trump card

wǎng

网(名)[wǎng]
net; network
〖网兜〗(名)[wǎngdōu][个 gè]
reticule; string bag
〖网罗〗(动)[wǎngluó]
gather; seek and collect
〖网络〗(名)[wǎngluò]
network
〖网球〗(名)[wǎngqiú]
tennis

枉[wǎng]
〖枉费心机〗[wǎngfèixīnjī]
rack one's brains in vain; waste one's efforts
〖枉然〗(形)[wǎngrán]
in vain

往(动)[wǎng]
①go ②head toward; leave for; ③toward
〖往常〗(名)[wǎngcháng]
usually; as usual
〖往返〗(动、名)[wǎngfǎn]
go and come back; back-and-forth
〖往来〗(动、名)[wǎnglái]
①go and come back ②have dealings with each other; (friendly) intercourse
〖往来账户〗[wǎngláizhànghù]
current account; running account
〖往年〗(名)[wǎngnián]
former years; previous years
〖往日〗(名)[wǎngrì]
former days; past
〖往事〗(名)[wǎngshì]
things of the past
〖往往〗(副)[wǎngwǎng]
often; usually

wàng

妄[wàng]
〖妄图〗(动)[wàngtú]
try in vain to; make a vain attempt
〖妄想〗(动、名)[wàngxiǎng]
indulge in vain hopes; try in vain; vain attempt
〖妄自菲薄〗[wàngzìfěibó]
underestimate one's achievements; belittle; demean oneself; have an inferiority complex
〖妄自尊大〗[wàngzìzūndà]
conceited; sense of superiority; be overbearing

忘(动)[wàng]
forget
〖忘本〗[wàngběn]
forget one's class origin; forget one's bitter past
〖忘掉〗(动)[wàngdiào]
forget

〖忘恩负义〗[wàng'ēnfùyì]
be ungrateful; devoid of all gratitude
〖忘乎所以〗[wànghūsuǒyǐ]
so happy or excited that one forgets oneself; walk on air; beside oneself
〖忘记〗(动)[wàngjì]
forget
〖忘却〗(动)[wàngquè]
forget
〖忘我〗(形)[wàngwǒ]
selfless

旺(形)[wàng]
prosperous; vigorous
〖旺季〗(名)[wàngjì]
flourishing or prosperous season; busy season; peak period
〖旺盛〗(形)[wàngshèng]
flourishing; energetic; vigorous

望(动)[wàng]
①look; glance②visit; inspect ③hope; expect; wish
〖望尘莫及〗[wàngchénmòjí]
(lit.)unable to see the dust of the rider ahead; (fig.)lag a long way behind; unequal to
〖望而生畏〗[wàng'érshēngwèi]
be filled with fear at the sight of(e.g. person)
〖望风披靡〗[wàngfēngpīmǐ]
flee pell-mell; flee helter-skelter
〖望文生义〗[wàngwénshēngyì]
interpret the meaning of a word or sentence superficially
〖望眼欲穿〗[wàngyǎnyùchuān]
gaze anxiously till one's eyes are overstrained; look forward expectantly to
〖望洋兴叹〗[wàngyángxīngtàn]
(lit.)gaze at the ocean and complain of its infinitude; (fig.)willing but lacking the power to do it
〖望远镜〗(名)[wàngyuǎnjìng]
telescope; field glasses

wēi

危(形)[wēi]
①dangerous; harmful ②dying
〖危害〗(动)[wēihài]
harm; endanger; damage
〖危害性〗(名)[wēihàixìng]
harmfulness
〖危机〗(名)[wēijī]
crisis
〖危急〗(形)[wēijí]
urgent; critical; in peril; at stake
〖危惧〗(动)[wēijù]
be in fear
〖危难〗(名)[wēinàn]
danger and disaster; at stake
〖危亡〗(名)[wēiwáng]
(the fate of a nation is) at stake; in imminent danger of being conquered
〖危险〗(形)[wēixiǎn]
dangerous
〖危险性〗(名)[wēixiǎnxìng]

W

dangerousness
〖危言耸听〗[wēiyánsǒngtīng]
a provocative statement attracts attention
〖危在旦夕〗[wēizàidànxī]
death is expected at any moment; in imminent danger of death

威 [wēi]
〖威风〗(名、形)[wēifēng]
dignity; majesty; grandeur; prestige; grand; splendid; majestic
〖威风凛凛〗[wēifēnglǐnlǐn]
awful air; with great dignity
〖威吓〗(动)[wēihè]
threaten; terrify by threats; intimidate
〖威力〗(名)[wēilì]
might; power; force
〖威慑〗(动)[wēishè]
threaten with force; deterrent
〖威望〗(名)[wēiwàng]
high prestige; high reputation
〖威武〗(形)[wēiwǔ]
power and grandeur; dominant; powerful
〖威武雄壮〗
[wēiwǔxióngzhuàng]
power and grandeur
〖威胁〗(动)[wēixié]
threaten; menace; coerce; intimidate
〖威信〗(名)[wēixìn]
prestige; credit; high repute; dignity
〖威信扫地〗[wēixìnsǎodì]
with one's dignity in the dust; forfeited prestige; be thoroughly discredited
〖威严〗(形)[wēiyán]
dignified; august; commanding

逶 [wēi]
〖逶迤〗(形)[wēiyí]
winding; meandering

微 (形)[wēi]
①small; tiny ②fine; delicate
〖微波〗(名)[wēibō]
microwave
〖微波炉〗(名)[wēibōlú]
microwave oven
〖微薄〗(形)[wēibó]
meagre; feeble
〖微不足道〗[wēibùzúdào]
not worth mentioning; insignificant; trivial
〖微乎其微〗[wēihūqíwēi]
very small; very little
〖微积分〗(名)[wēijīfēn]
(math.) differential and integral calculus
〖微粒〗(名)[wēilì]
minute particle
〖微妙〗(形)[wēimiào]
delicate; subtle; tenuous
〖微弱〗(形)[wēiruò]
weak; feeble; meagre
〖微生物〗(名)[wēishēngwù]
microbe
〖微微〗(形)[wēiwēi]
a little; feeble; slight

〖微细〗(形)[wēixì]
very small; fine; very thin
〖微小〗(形)[wēixiǎo]
very small; little; tiny
〖微笑〗(动)[wēixiào]
smile
〖微型〗(名)[wēixíng]
miniature; midget
〖微型计算机〗
[wēixíngjìsuànjī]
microcomputer
〖微型汽车〗[wēixíngqìchē]
minicar
〖微型小说〗[wēixíngxiǎoshuō]
mini novel; open-page novel

巍 [wēi]
〖巍峨〗(形)[wēi'é]
very high (e.g. mountain or building)
〖巍然〗(副)[wēirán]
stand firmly and majestically

wéi

为 (动、介)[wéi]
① do ② take as ③ become; make ④ by; for
另见 wèi
〖为非作歹〗[wéifēizuòdǎi]
evil doings
〖为难〗(动)[wéinán]
①embarrass ②put obstacles in the way; make things hard (for sb.)
〖为人〗(动)[wéirén]
behaviour; manner in dealing with others
〖为首〗[wéishǒu]
headed by; led by
〖为…所…〗[wéi…suǒ…]
by
〖为所欲为〗[wéisuǒyùwéi]
do whatever one likes; do as one pleases

违 (动)[wéi]
disobey; defy; violate
〖违背〗(动)[wéibèi]
violate; act contrary to; run counter to
〖违法〗[wéifǎ]
break the law
〖违法乱纪〗[wéifǎluànjì]
breach of law and discipline; break laws and violate discipline
〖违反〗(动)[wéifǎn]
go against; infringe; violate
〖违抗〗(动)[wéikàng]
defy and reject

围 (动)[wéi]
surround; circle
〖围脖儿〗(名)[wéibór]〔条 tiáo〕
muffler; scarf
〖围攻〗(动)[wéigōng]
attack and encirclement; attack from all sides; converging attack
〖围歼〗(动)[wéijiān]
encircle and wipe out
〖围剿〗(动)[wéijiǎo]
launch a campaign of encir-

clement and annihilation; encircle and suppress
〖围巾〗(名)[wéijīn]〔条 tiáo〕
muffler; scarf
〖围困〗(动)[wéikùn]
besiege; confine
〖围棋〗(名)[wéiqí]
Go (game similar to chess)
〖围绕〗(动)[wéirào]
surround; encircle; revolve around

桅[wéi]
〖桅杆〗(名)[wéigān]
ship's mast

唯[wéi]
另见 wěi
〖唯生产力论〗(名)
[wéishēngchǎnlìlùn]
the theory that productive forces decide everything
〖唯武器论〗(名)[wéiwǔqìlùn]
the theory that weapons decide everything
〖唯物辩证法〗
[wéiwùbiànzhèngfǎ]
dialectical materialism
〖唯物论〗(名)[wéiwùlùn]
materialism
〖唯物主义〗(名)[wéiwùzhǔyì]
materialism
〖唯心论〗(名)[wéixīnlùn]
idealism
〖唯心主义〗(名)[wéixīnzhǔyì]
idealism

惟(副)[wéi]
only
〖惟独〗(副)[wéidú]
only; solely; alone
〖惟恐〗(动)[wéikǒng]
only fear; for fear
〖惟利是图〗[wéilìshìtú]
make profit as one's only aim; profit grabbing; engage in unscrupulous profiteering
〖惟妙惟肖〗[wéimiàowéixiào]
life-like; strikingly true to life
〖惟命是听〗[wéimìngshìtīng]
at one's beck and call; very obedient
〖惟我独尊〗[wéiwǒdúzūn]
overlordship; behaving like an overlord
〖惟一〗(形)[wéiyī]
sole; only; single
〖惟有〗(连)[wéiyǒu]
except; only

维[wéi]
〖维持〗(动)[wéichí]
maintain; keep; preserve
〖维护〗(动)[wéihù]
uphold; safeguard
〖维纶〗(名)[wéilún]
vinylon
〖维生素〗(名)[wéishēngsù]
vitamin
〖维修〗(动)[wéixiū]
maintain; maintenance (e.g. of machinery)

wěi

伟[wěi]

〖伟大〗(形)[wěidà]
great
〖伟绩〗(名)[wěijī]
meritorious service; deeds; great service

伪(形)[wěi]
①false; forged ②puppet (e.g. regime)
〖伪币〗(名)[wěibì]
bogus money; counterfeit money; forged bank note
〖伪君子〗(名)[wěijūnzǐ]
hypocrite
〖伪善〗(形)[wěishàn]
hypocritical
〖伪造〗(动)[wěizào]
fabricate; counterfeit; bogus
〖伪证〗(名)[wěizhèng]
false testimony; perjury
〖伪装〗(动、名)[wěizhuāng]
conceal; disguise; camouflage

尾(名)[wěi]
①tail ②end ③minor parts
〖尾巴〗(名)[wěiba]
①tail; end part ②vestige
〖尾声〗(名)[wěishēng]
the last echo; last act of some disappearing movement; end
〖尾随〗(动)[wěisuí]
follow; tail after; shadow

纬(名)[wěi]
latitude
〖纬度〗(名)[wěidù]
degree of latitude

委[wěi]
〖委靡〗(形)[wěimǐ]
look blue; low in spirits; be depressed
〖委靡不振〗[wěimǐbùzhèn]
be low in spirits; dispirited
〖委派〗(动)[wěipài]
appoint
〖委曲求全〗[wěiqūqiúquán]
suffer wrong for the sake of achieving one's final purpose; make compromises to achieve one's final aim
〖委屈〗(动)[wěiqu]
suffer from injustice; be wrongly accused
〖委托〗(动)[wěituō]
entrust; appoint; put in charge; consign
〖委员〗(名)[wěiyuán]
committee member
〖委员会〗(名)[wěiyuánhuì]
committee; commission; council; board
〖委员长〗(名)[wěiyuánzhǎng]
chairman of a committee

娓[wěi]
〖娓娓动听〗[wěiwěidòngtīng]
be pleasing to the ear

萎[wěi]
〖萎靡〗(形)[wěimǐ]
low in spirits; down-hearted; dejected
〖萎缩〗(动)[wěisuō]
①shrivel; wither ②diminish

唯[wěi]
另见 wéi
〖唯唯诺诺〗(形)
[wěiwěinuònuò]
slavishly; meanly submissive; servile

wèi

卫[wèi]
〖卫兵〗(名)[wèibīng]
guards
〖卫道士〗(名)[wèidàoshì]
apologist
〖卫生〗(名、形)[wèishēng]
hygiene
〖卫生间〗(名)[wèishēngjiān]
toilet
〖卫生设备〗[wèishēngshèbèi]
sanitation facility
〖卫生所〗(名)[wèishēngsuǒ]
clinic
〖卫生员〗(名)[wèishēngyuán]
medical personnel
〖卫生院〗(名)[wèishēngyuàn]
public health centre
〖卫生站〗(名)[wèishēngzhàn]
clinic; health station
〖卫戍〗(动)[wèishù]
guard; garrison
〖卫星〗(名)[wèixīng][颗 kē]
satellite
〖卫星城市〗[wèixīngchéngshì]
satellite city
〖卫星云图〗[wèixīngyúntú]
satellite cloud picture

为(介)[wèi]
for; for the sake of
另见 wéi
〖为…而…〗[wèi…ér…]
for; for the sake of
〖为何〗[wèihé]
why
〖为虎作伥〗[wèihǔzuòchāng]
act as a jackal to a tiger; act as a cat's paw; accomplice; lackey
〖为了〗(介)[wèile]
for; so as to; with a view to
〖为…起见〗[wèi…qǐjiàn]
for the sake of
〖为什么〗[wèishénme]
why

未(副)[wèi]
not; not yet
〖未必〗(副)[wèibì]
not sure; not necessarily so; perhaps not; not necessarily
〖未曾〗(副)[wèicéng]
never; not yet; unprecedented
〖未尝〗(副)[wèicháng]
① never; there is no ② used in double negative to express the positive
〖未来〗(名)[wèilái]
future; the time to come
〖未免〗(副)[wèimiǎn]
can't say that it isn't; really is
〖未遂〗[wèisuì]
not realized; not fulfilled; not attained
〖未知数〗(名)[wèizhīshù]
an unknown quantity or number

位(名、量)[wèi]
① seat; position ② status or situation ③a measure word, for person
〖位于〗(动)[wèiyú]
situate
〖位置〗(名)[wèizhi]
position
〖位子〗(名)[wèizi]
seat; post

味(名、量)[wèi]
①taste; flavour ② smell ③ interest ④ one medicine or prescription (using in Chinese traditional herbs)
〖味道〗(名)[wèidào]
① taste (of food); smell ② interest (e.g. in reading or conversation)
〖味精〗(名)[wèijīng]
monosodium glutamate
〖味同嚼蜡〗[wèitóngjiáolà]
it tastes no better than tallow

畏(动)[wèi]
fear
〖畏惧〗(动)[wèijù]
fear
〖畏首畏尾〗[wèishǒuwèiwěi]
be over-cautious; be frightened all over
〖畏缩〗(动)[wèisuō]
flinch; recoil in fear
〖畏罪〗[wèizuì]
fear punishment for one's crime

胃(名)[wèi]
stomach
〖胃病〗(名)[wèibìng]
stomach upset
〖胃口〗(名)[wèikǒu]
appetite

谓[wèi]
〖谓语〗(名)[wèiyǔ]
(gram.) predicate

喂(动)[wèi]
feed; bring up
〖喂养〗(动)[wèiyǎng]
feed

蔚[wèi]
〖蔚蓝〗(形)[wèilán]
sky-blue; azure
〖蔚然成风〗[wèiránchéngfēng]
become a common practice which prevails

慰[wèi]
〖慰劳〗(动)[wèiláo]
extend (one's) best wishes to; express regards and concern for
〖慰问〗(动)[wèiwèn]
visit and extend solicitude to; express regards and concern for

wēn

温(形、动)[wēn]
① lukewarm; warm; warm up ② temperate ③ review; revise
〖温饱〗(名)[wēnbǎo]

W

warmly clothed and well-fed
〖温饱问题〗[wēnbǎowèntí]
the problem of supplying adequate food and clothing for the population
〖温床〗(名)[wēnchuáng]
hotbed
〖温带〗(名)[wēndài]
temperate zone
〖温度〗(名)[wēndù]
temperature
〖温度计〗(名)[wēndùjì]
thermometor
〖温和〗(形)[wēnhé]
mild; gentle; moderate
〖温暖〗(形)[wēnnuǎn]
warm
〖温情〗(名)[wēnqíng]
warm feeling
〖温泉〗(名)[wēnquán]
hot spring
〖温柔〗(形)[wēnróu]
gentle; meek; pleasingly affectionate
〖温室〗(名)[wēnshì]
hothouse; greenhouse
〖温室效应〗[wēnshìxiàoyìng]
green house effect
〖温习〗(动)[wēnxí]
review (e.g. lessons)

wén

文(名、形)[wén]
① writing ② civilised ③ gentle
〖文不对题〗[wénbùduìtí]
go off the subject; wide of the mark
〖文采〗(名)[wéncǎi]
beauty of style of writing; literary embellishment
〖文牍主义〗(名)[wéndúzhǔyì]
red-tape; red-tapeism; a kind of working style in which one embeds oneself in documents; bureaucratism
〖文风〗(名)[wénfēng]
literary fashion; style of writing
〖文工团〗(名)[wéngōngtuán]
art troupe; ensemble
〖文过饰非〗[wénguòshìfēi]
gloss over one's fault; cover up one's error by excuses
〖文豪〗(名)[wénháo]
a famous writer
〖文化〗(名)[wénhuà]
culture
〖文化程度〗[wénhuàchéngdù]
educational level
〖文化宫〗(名)[wénhuàgōng]
cultural palace
〖文化市场〗[wénhuàshìchǎng]
cultural products market
〖文化素养〗[wénhuàsùyǎng]
artistic appreciation
〖文化遗产〗[wénhuàyíchǎn]
cultural heritage
〖文集〗(名)[wénjí]
a writer's works
〖文件〗(名)[wénjiàn]
document; programme
〖文件柜〗(名)[wénjiànguì]
filing cabinet
〖文件夹〗(名)[wénjiànjiā]
file

〖文教〗(名)[wénjiào]
culture and education
〖文具〗(名)[wénjù]
stationery
〖文科〗(名)[wénkē]
arts department
〖文盲〗(名)[wénmáng]
illiterate; illiteracy
〖文明〗(形、名)[wénmíng]
civilization; civilized
〖文明单位〗[wénmíngdānwèi]
model unit; advanced unit
〖文明生产〗
[wénmíngshēngchǎn]
carry out production strictly in accordance with rules and regulations; civilized production
〖文凭〗(名)[wénpíng]
certificate; diploma
〖文人〗(名)[wénrén]
man of letters; writer
〖文人相轻〗[wénrénxiāngqīng]
scholars scorn each other
〖文书〗(名)[wénshū]
secretary
〖文坛〗(名)[wéntán]
literary world or circles
〖文体〗(名)[wéntǐ]
literary style
〖文物〗(名)[wénwù]
historical relics
〖文献〗(名)[wénxiàn]
literary or historical data; historical document
〖文选〗(名)[wénxuǎn]
selected works
〖文学〗(名)[wénxué]
literature
〖文学家〗(名)[wénxuéjiā]
writers; man of letters
〖文学史〗(名)[wénxuéshǐ]
history of literature
〖文雅〗(形)[wényǎ]
refined; elegant
〖文言〗(名)[wényán]
classical literary language
〖文艺〗(名)[wényì]
literature and arts
〖文艺理论〗[wényìlǐlùn]
theory of literature and art
〖文艺批评〗[wényìpīpíng]
literary and art criticism
〖文娱〗(名)[wényú]
recreation
〖文章〗(名)[wénzhāng]
literary composition; essay; article
〖文质彬彬〗[wénzhìbīnbīn]
with elegant manners; gentle; temperate; refined
〖文字〗(名)[wénzì]
written language; character; words
〖文字改革〗[wénzìgǎigé]
reform of written language

纹(名)[wén]
① stripes; lines; streaks ② ripples (e.g. on the water)
〖纹丝不动〗[wénsībùdòng]
not a wrinkle was touched; untouched

闻(动)[wén]

①hear ②smell; scent
〖闻风而动〗[wénfēng'érdòng]
go into action as soon as one gets wind of sth.
〖闻风丧胆〗[wénfēngsàngdǎn]
lose courage at hearing it
〖闻名〗[wénmíng]
famous; well-known
〖闻所未闻〗[wénsuǒwèiwén]
unprecedented; never even heard of

蚊 (名)[wén]
mosquito
〖蚊香〗(名)[wénxiāng]
mosquito-repellent incense
〖蚊帐〗(名)[wénzhàng]
mosquito net
〖蚊子〗(名)[wénzi][个 gè]
mosquito

wěn

吻 (动)[wěn]
kiss
〖吻合〗(动)[wěnhé]
agree; in conformity with

紊 [wěn]
〖紊乱〗(形)[wěnluàn]
disorderly; confused

稳 (形)[wěn]
stable; steady; safe; firm
〖稳步〗[wěnbù]
by steady steps; steadily
〖稳产高产〗[wěnchǎngāochǎn]
stable and high yields
〖稳当〗(形)[wěndang]
safe and sure
〖稳定〗(动)[wěndìng]
stabilize; stable
〖稳定性〗(名)[wěndìngxìng]
stability
〖稳固〗(形)[wěngù]
strong (e.g. foundation); solid; stable
〖稳健〗(形)[wěnjiàn]
solid; steady; firm
〖稳妥〗(形)[wěntuǒ]
safe and reliable
〖稳扎稳打〗[wěnzhāwěndǎ]
go ahead steadily and strike sure blows; wage steady and sure struggles
〖稳重〗(形)[wěnzhòng]
steady; not flighty

wèn

问 (动)[wèn]
①question; ask; inquire ② ask about one's health ③ examine
〖问长问短〗[wènchángwènduǎn]
ask all sorts of questions; bombard (sb.) with questions
〖问答〗(名)[wèndá]
questions and answers
〖问寒问暖〗[wènhánwènnuǎn]
ask after one's needs; express concern for
〖问好〗[wènhǎo]
give (one's) regards to
〖问号〗(名)[wènhào]
question mark

〖问候〗(动)[wènhòu]
greet; give (one's) regards to
〖问世〗(动)[wènshì]
be presented to the public (e.g. the publication of books)
〖问题〗(名)[wèntí]
question; problem
〖问讯处〗(名)[wènxùnchù]
inquiry office; information desk

wèng

瓮(名)[wèng]
jar
〖瓮中之鳖〗[wèngzhōngzhībiē]
(lit.) a turtle in a jar; (fig.) a sure catch

wō

窝(名、动、量)[wō]
① nest; lair ② a hollow part of place ③ give shelter to ④ bend ⑤ a measure word, nest, lair (for bees, birds, etc.)
〖窝藏〗(动)[wōcáng]
shelter; conceal booty or hide a fugitive from justice; harbour
〖窝工〗[wōgōng]
hold up of work (due to poor planning or arrangement)
〖窝棚〗(名)[wōpeng]
a mat shed
〖窝头〗(名)[wōtóu]〔个 gè〕
corn bread

蜗[wō]
〖蜗牛〗(名)[wōniú]〔只 zhī〕
snail

wǒ

我(代)[wǒ]
I
〖我们〗(代)[wǒmen]
we

wò

卧(动)[wò]
lie down
〖卧倒〗(动)[wòdǎo]
lie down; lie on (one's) stomach
〖卧铺〗(名)[wòpù]
berth
〖卧室〗(名)[wòshì]
bedroom
〖卧薪尝胆〗[wòxīnchángdǎn]
(lit.) sleep on woodpile and taste gall; (fig.) endure hardship to achieve one's purpose

握(动)[wò]
grasp; take by the hand; wield
〖握手〗[wòshǒu]
shake hands

斡[wò]
〖斡旋〗(动)[wòxuán]
bring around (e.g. disputing parties); mediate

wū

乌[wū]
〖乌合之众〗[wūhézhīzhòng]

W

mob; a disorderly band; a motley crowd
〖乌黑〗(形)[wūhēi]
jet black
〖乌纱帽〗(名)[wūshāmào]
(lit.) the headgear of an official; (fig.) official post
〖乌托邦〗(名)[wūtuōbāng]
utopia
〖乌鸦〗(名)[wūyā]〔只 zhī〕
crow
〖乌烟瘴气〗[wūyānzhàngqì]
vicious practices; create a foul atmosphere
〖乌云〗(名)[wūyún]
dark clouds

污[wū]
〖污点〗(名)[wūdiǎn]
① stain (on clothing) ② stain on character
〖污垢〗(名)[wūgòu]
dirt; filth; stain
〖污秽〗(形)[wūhuì]
disreputable (conduct); filthy
〖污泥浊水〗[wūnízhuóshuǐ]
mud and filthy water
〖污染〗(动)[wūrǎn]
pollute
〖污辱〗(动)[wūrǔ]
stain; insult
〖污水〗(名)[wūshuǐ]
filthy water

呜(象声)[wū]
onomatopoeia (whistling sound)
〖呜咽〗(动)[wūyè]
sob

诬[wū]
〖诬告〗(动)[wūgào]
accuse falsely
〖诬赖〗(动)[wūlài]
make false charges against
〖诬蔑〗(动)[wūmiè]
vilify; smear; slander
〖诬陷〗(动)[wūxiàn]
implicate falsely; injure by false accusation

屋(名)[wū] house; room
〖屋子〗(名)[wūzi]〔间 jiān〕
room; household

wú

无(动)[wú]
have nothing
〖无比〗(形)[wúbǐ]
matchless; without comparison; unparalleled
〖无边无际〗[wúbiānwújì]
boundless
〖无产阶级〗(名)[wúchǎnjiējí]
proletariat
〖无产阶级专政〗[wúchǎnjiējízhuānzhèng]
dictatorship of the proletariat
〖无产者〗(名)[wúchǎnzhě]
proletarian
〖无常〗[wúcháng]
① variable changeable; ② impermanence
〖无偿〗[wúcháng]

gratis; free of charge
〖无耻〗(形)[wúchǐ]
shameless; unscrupulous
〖无耻谰言〗[wúchǐlányán]
brazen lie; shameless slanders
〖无从〗(副)[wúcóng]
having no way (to do something)
〖无党派人士〗
[wúdǎngpàirénshì]
public figure without party affiliation; nonparty personage
〖无敌〗[wúdí]
matchless; unmatched
〖无的放矢〗[wúdìfàngshǐ]
shoot at random; aimless and fruitless
〖无动于衷〗[wúdòngyúzhōng]
aloof and indifferent; untouched
〖无恶不作〗[wú'èbùzuò]
commit all manner of crimes; be as wicked as possible
〖无法无天〗[wúfǎwútiān]
lawless; reckless; unruly
〖无妨〗[wúfáng]
it's no harm to do
〖无非〗(副)[wúfēi]
it's only; nothing but
〖无缝钢管〗[wúfènggāngguǎn]
seamless steel tube
〖无辜〗(名)[wúgū]
innocent; innocence
〖无故〗[wúgù]
for no reason
〖无关〗(动)[wúguān]
has nothing to do with
〖无国籍〗[wúguójí]
stateless
〖无害〗[wúhài]
harmless
〖无机化学〗[wújīhuàxué]
inorganic chemistry
〖无机物〗(名)[wújīwù]
inorganic matter
〖无稽之谈〗[wújīzhītán]
baseless gossip
〖无济于事〗[wújìyúshì]
of no help; of no avail
〖无价之宝〗[wújiàzhībǎo]
priceless treasure
〖无坚不摧〗[wújiānbùcuī]
all-conquering; invincible
〖无精打采〗[wújīngdǎcǎi]
in low spirits; crestfallen
〖无可非议〗[wúkěfēiyì]
above reproach; unimpeachable
〖无可奉告〗[wúkěfènggào]
no comment; have nothing to say
〖无可奈何〗[wúkěnàihé]
helplessness; unable to do anything
〖无可争辩〗[wúkězhēngbiàn]
indisputable
〖无孔不入〗[wúkǒngbùrù]
lose no chance; poke into every nook and corner; all pervasive
〖无愧〗(动)[wúkuì]
be worthy of
〖无赖〗(名)[wúlài]
knavish; roguish; rascal
〖无理取闹〗[wúlǐqǔnào]
unreasonable quarrelling; unprovoked quarrel; mischief-making
〖无聊〗(形)[wúliáo]
nonsense; ennui; boring; te-

W

dious
〖无论〗(连)[wúlùn]
no matter; whatever; however
〖无论如何〗[wúlùnrúhé]
no matter what; in spite of all; in any case
〖无名〗[wúmíng]
anonymous; nameless
〖无奈〗[wúnài]
① have no alternative but... ② but
〖无能〗(形)[wúnéng]
incapable; impotent
〖无能为力〗[wúnéngwéilì]
powerless; incapable; can do nothing about it
〖无奇不有〗[wúqíbùyǒu]
strange things of every description
〖无情〗(形)[wúqíng]
merciless; heartless; ruthless
〖无穷〗(形)[wúqióng]
endless; infinite
〖无穷无尽〗[wúqióngwújìn]
inexhaustible
〖无人〗[wúrén]
unmanned; self-service
〖无人售票公共汽车〗[wúrénshòupiàogōnggòngqìchē]
conductorless bus
〖无色〗[wúsè]
colourless
〖无商不活〗[wúshāngbùhuó]
there will be no economic revitalization without the development of a commodity economy
〖无上〗(形)[wúshàng]
highest
〖无神论〗(名)[wúshénlùn]
atheism
〖无声无臭〗[wúshēngwúxiù]
soundless and odourless
〖无时无刻〗[wúshíwúkè]
at any moment; all the time
〖无事生非〗[wúshìshēngfēi]
make trouble out of nothing; make much ado about nothing
〖无视〗(动)[wúshì]
disregard
〖无数〗(形)[wúshù]
innumerable; countless; no end of
〖无私〗(形)[wúsī]
selfless
〖无所不为〗[wúsuǒbùwéi]
stop at nothing
〖无所不用其极〗
[wúsuǒbùyòngqíjí]
employ the meanest of tricks; go to every extreme
〖无所事事〗[wúsuǒshìshì]
idle; loafing
〖无所适从〗[wúsuǒshìcóng]
do not know where to turn
〖无所谓〗[wúsuǒwèi]
① it does not matter if...; not care a fig for ② cannot be taken as; cannot be regarded as
〖无所作为〗[wúsuǒzuòwéi]
not aspiring; have no high ideals
〖无条件〗[wútiáojiàn]
unconditional
〖无往不胜〗[wúwǎngbùshèng]
invincible; all-conquering
〖无微不至〗[wúwēibùzhì]

W

lavish every care
〖无味〗[wúwèi]
tasteless; flat; drab
〖无畏〗(形)[wúwèi]
fearless; daring; bold
〖无息〗[wúxī]
interest-free
〖无隙可乘〗[wúxìkěchéng]
no crack to get in by; watertight (e.g. plan)
〖无限〗(形)[wúxiàn]
infinite; boundless
〖无线电〗(名)[wúxiàndiàn]
wireless; radio
〖无效〗[wúxiào]
invalid; null and void; ineffective
〖无懈可击〗[wúxièkějī]
invulnerable; perfect
〖无心〗[wúxīn]
① without any intention ② have no mind to
〖无形〗[wúxíng]
invisible; intangible
〖无形贸易〗[wúxíngmàoyì]
invisible trade
〖无形资产〗[wúxíngzīchǎn]
incorporeal property
〖无形中〗[wúxíngzhōng]
invisibly
〖无臭〗[wú xiù]
odourless
〖无烟煤〗(名)[wúyānméi]
anthracite; smokeless coal
〖无依无靠〗[wúyīwúkào]
have no dependents and no one to depend upon; be alone in the world
〖无疑〗(形)[wúyí]
doubtless
〖无以复加〗[wúyǐfùjiā]
in the extreme; can add no more
〖无意〗[wúyì]
unintentional
〖无影无踪〗[wúyǐngwúzōng]
not a trace left; untraceable
〖无用〗[wúyòng]
useless
〖无与伦比〗[wúyǔlúnbǐ]
matchless; beyond comparison
〖无缘无故〗[wúyuánwúgù]
without any reason
〖无政府主义〗(名)[wúzhèngfǔzhǔyì]
anarchism
〖无知〗(形)[wúzhī]
ignorant; lacking knowledge
〖无中生有〗[wúzhōngshēngyǒu]
unfounded; groundless; sheer fabrication; fabricate rumours out of thin air
〖无主句〗(名)[wúzhǔjù]
sentence with no subject
〖无足轻重〗[wúzúqīngzhòng]
of little importance; insignificant

wǔ

五(数)[wǔ] five
〖五保户〗(名)[wǔbǎohù]
families with five guarantees (the aged, infirm, old widows and widowers and orphans) are taken care of by the people's commune in five ways i.e. food,

W

clothing, medical care, housing and burial expenses
〖五彩〗(名)[wǔcǎi]
multicolours; colourful
〖五彩缤纷〗[wǔcǎibīnfēn]
full of colours; multicoloured
〖五谷〗(名)[wǔgǔ]
grain
〖五官〗(名)[wǔguān]
five sense organs
〖五光十色〗[wǔguāngshísè]
what a great variety; kaleidoscopic
〖五湖四海〗[wǔhúsìhǎi]
all corners of the country
〖五花八门〗[wǔhuābāmén]
kaleidoscopic; manifold; a motley variety of
〖五讲四美〗[wǔjiǎngsìměi]
five stresses and four beautifications—stress on decorum, on manners, on hygiene, on discipline and on moral; beautification of the mind, of the language, of the behaviour and of the environment
〖五金〗(名)[wǔjīn]
the five metals (gold, silver, copper, iron and pewter)
〖五岳〗[wǔyuè]
the Five Mountains, namely, Taishan Mountain (泰山) in Shandong, Hengshan Mountain (衡山) in Hunan, Huashan Mountain (华山) in Shanxi, Hengshan Mountain (恒山) in Shanxi and Songshan Mountain (嵩山) in Henan
〖五四青年节〗
[WǔSìQīngniánjié]
May 4 Youth Day
〖五体投地〗[wǔtǐtóudì]
kneel at the feet of; on all fours before
〖五线谱〗(名)[wǔxiànpǔ]
musical notation; score
〖五星红旗〗[wǔxīnghóngqí]
the Five-star Red Flag
〖五颜六色〗[wǔyánliùsè]
colourful; full of various colours
〖五一国际劳动节〗
[WǔYīGuójìLáodòngjié]
May 1, International Labour Day
〖五月〗(名)[wǔyuè]
May
〖五脏〗(名)[wǔzàng]
the five internal organs (the heart, liver, spleen, lungs and kidney)

午[wǔ]
〖午饭〗(名)[wǔfàn]
lunch
〖午睡〗(名)[wǔshuì]
nap after lunch; siesta
〖午夜〗(名)[wǔyè]
midnight

武(名)[wǔ]
①military ②chivalrous
〖武断〗(形)[wǔduàn]
arbitrary
〖武官〗(名)[wǔguān]
military attache

〖武力〗(名)[wǔlì]
force of arms; military force
〖武器〗(名)[wǔqì]
weapon
〖武术〗(名)[wǔshù]
(Chinese traditional) martial art
〖武装〗(名、动)[wǔzhuāng]
arms; arm

侮 [wǔ]
〖侮辱〗(动、名)[wǔrǔ]
humiliate; humiliation; insult

捂 (动)[wǔ]
cover up

舞(名、动)[wǔ]
dance
〖舞弊〗(动)[wǔbì]
juggle with the law; indulge in malpractices; irregularity
〖舞蹈〗(名)[wǔdǎo]
dance
〖舞剧〗(名)[wǔjù]
dance drama
〖舞台〗(名)[wǔtái]
stage; scene
〖舞厅〗(名)[wǔtīng]
ballroom; dance hall

wù

勿 (副)[wù]
must not

戊 [wù]
〖戊戌变法〗[WùxūBiànfǎ]
the Bourgeois Reform Movement of 1898

务 (动)[wù]
undertake; do
〖务必〗(副)[wùbì]
must; should
〖务农〗[wùnóng]
take farming as profession
〖务实〗[wùshí]
practical; down to earth
〖务虚〗[wùxū]
discuss principles; discuss ideological guidelines

物 (名)[wù]
① things; goods ② content
〖物产〗(名)[wùchǎn]
produce or manufactured products
〖物极必反〗[wùjíbìfǎn] when a thing reaches its limit, it turns round; a thing turns into its opposite if pushed too far
〖物价〗(名)[wùjià]
price
〖物理〗(名)[wùlǐ]
physics
〖物理性质〗[wùlǐxìngzhì]
physical property
〖物力〗(名)[wùlì]
economic or material strength; material resources
〖物品〗(名)[wùpǐn]
articles; goods
〖物色〗(动)[wùsè]

look for; select
〖物体〗(名)[wùtǐ]
form and state of matter; substance; things
〖物业〗(名)[wùyè]
property; real estate
〖物以类聚〗[wùyǐlèijù]
birds of a feather flock together
〖物证〗(名)[wùzhèng]
material evidence
〖物质〗(名)[wùzhì]
material; matter
〖物质不灭定律〗[wùzhìbùmièdìnglǜ]
law of conservation of matter
〖物质刺激〗[wùzhìcìjī]
material incentive
〖物质鼓励〗[wùzhìgǔlì]
material reward
〖物资〗(名)[wùzī]
goods; materials; commodity

误(动)[wù]
miss
〖误差〗(名)[wùchā]
error
〖误导〗(动)[wùdǎo]
mislead
〖误点〗[wù diǎn]
late for
〖误会〗(动、名)[wùhuì]
misunderstand; misunderstanding; misconception
〖误解〗(动、名)[wùjiě]
misinterpret; misinterpretation; misunderstanding
〖误区〗(名)[wùqū]
longstanding mistaken ideas or concepts
〖误事〗[wùshì]
spoil an affair or a thing

雾(名)[wù]
fog

xī

夕[xī]
〖夕阳〗(名)[xīyáng]
the setting sun

西(名)[xī]
west
〖西边〗(名)[xībian]
west side
〖西餐〗(名)[xīcān]
European food
〖西方〗(名)[xīfāng]
① the west ② the western world
〖西服〗(名)[xīfú]
〔套 tào、件 jiàn〕western style dress
〖西瓜〗(名)[xīguā]〔个 gè〕
watermelon
〖西红柿〗(名)[xīhóngshì]
〔个 gè〕tomato
〖西医〗(名)[xīyī]
① doctor of western medicine ② western medicine

吸(动)[xī]
① suck; draw in; absorb ② appeal; attract
〖吸毒〗[xīdú]
drug taking; drug abuse
〖吸取〗(动)[xīqǔ]
① assimilate; draw ② accept
〖吸收〗(动)[xīshōu]
① absorb; take in; assimilate ② draw in; admit into
〖吸烟〗[xīyān]
smoke (e.g. cigarette or pipe); smoking
〖吸引〗(动)[xīyǐn]
attract; pin down; be drawn into
〖吸引力〗(名)[xīyǐnlì]
force of attraction; gravitation

希(动)[xī]
hope
〖希罕〗(形、动)[xīhan]
rare; uncommon; appreciate sth.

for its rareness

〖希奇〗(形)[xīqí]
rare and curious

〖希望〗(动、名)[xīwàng]
aspire; hope

〖希望工程〗[xīwànggōngchéng]
Project Hope — a programme to collect funds to support education in poor areas

昔(名)[xī]
the past

〖昔日〗(名)[xīrì]
former days; early days

牺[xī]

〖牺牲〗(动)[xīshēng]
sacrifice

〖牺牲品〗(名)[xīshēngpǐn]
victim; prey; scapegoat

息[xī]

〖息息相关〗[xīxīxiāngguān]
vitally interrelated; be linked with each other closely

X

奚[xī]

〖奚落〗(动)[xīluò]
ridicule; rail at; make sarcastic remarks

惜(动)[xī]
hold sth. dear; treasure; love and care

〖惜别〗(动)[xībié]
be reluctant to part with sb.

稀(形)[xī]
rare; few; dilute; thin(e.g. thinly populated); sparse

〖稀薄〗(形)[xībó]
thin and diluted; rarefied

〖稀少〗(形)[xīshǎo]
rare; few; sparse

〖稀有〗(形)[xīyǒu]
rare

〖稀有金属〗[xīyǒujīnshǔ]
rare metals

〖稀有元素〗[xīyǒuyuánsù]
rare (chemical) element

溪(名)[xī]
brook; stream

熙[xī]

〖熙熙攘攘〗(形)[xīxīrǎngrǎng]
hustle and bustle about; busy coming and going (of crowds)

熄(动)[xī]
extinguish; die out; go out

〖熄灭〗(动)[xīmiè]
extinguish; put out; die out

膝(名)[xī]
knee

〖膝盖〗(名)[xīgài]
kneecap

嬉[xī]

〖嬉笑〗(动)[xīxiào]
laugh merrily

xí

习[xí]
〖习惯〗(名、动)[xíguàn]
habits; usual practice; be used to; be accustomed to
〖习惯势力〗[xíguànshìlì]
the force of habit
〖习气〗(名)[xíqì]
bad habit; temperament or working style which is disapproved of
〖习性〗(名)[xíxìng]
temperament or characteristics cultivated under specific natural or social conditions
〖习以为常〗[xíyǐwéicháng]
become accustomed to; be used to

席(名、量)[xí]
①mat ②table of (guests); seat; place ③a measure word for banquet
〖席卷〗(动)[xíjuǎn]
sweep through; engulf; rage over
〖席位〗(名)[xíwèi]
place or seating during dinner, meeting or assembly; seat (membership of international organizations and parliament, etc.)
〖席子〗(名)[xízi]
mat

袭(动)[xí]
raid
〖袭击〗(动)[xíjī]
surprise assault on; make a surprise attack; raid

媳(名)[xí]
daughter-in-law
〖媳妇〗(名)[xífu]
①daughter-in-law ②wife; married woman

檄[xí]
〖檄文〗(名)[xíwén]
official public declaration for a campaign; summons to war

xǐ

洗(动)[xǐ]
①wash; clean ②develop (e.g. film)
〖洗涤〗(动)[xǐdí]
wash; cleanse
〖洗涤剂〗(名)[xǐdíjì]
detergent
〖洗礼〗(名)[xǐlǐ]
baptism; the cleansing flames (of war)
〖洗刷〗(动)[xǐshuā]
①wash and brush ②wash away; be cleared of; cleanse
〖洗衣店〗(名)[xǐyīdiàn]
laundry
〖洗衣机〗(名)[xǐyījī]
washing machine
〖洗澡〗[xǐzǎo]
take a bath

铣(动)[xǐ]
mill

〖铣床〗(名)[xǐchuáng]〔台 tái〕
milling machine
〖铣工〗(名)[xǐgōng]
milling machine operator; miller

喜(动、名)[xǐ]
① enjoy; delight; be pleased with; happiness ② love; like; prefer
〖喜爱〗(动)[xǐ'ài]
love; like; be fond of
〖喜报〗(名)[xǐbào]
happy news; good tidings; glad tidings
〖喜出望外〗[xǐchūwàngwài]
joy beyond all expectations; in pleased surprise
〖喜好〗(动)[xǐhào]
love; like; be fond of
〖喜欢〗(动)[xǐhuan]
①like; be partial to ②delight; enjoy
〖喜酒〗(名)[xǐjiǔ]
①wine drunk at a wedding feast ② wedding feast
〖喜剧〗(名)[xǐjù]〔出 chū〕
comedy

〖喜气洋洋〗[xǐqìyángyáng]
overwhelmed with joy; outburst of joy; effusion of joy
〖喜鹊〗(名)[xǐquè]〔只 zhī〕
magpie
〖喜色〗(名)[xǐsè]
a jovial countenance
〖喜事〗(名)[xǐshì]
①a happy event; a joyous occasion ②marriage
〖喜闻乐见〗[xǐwénlèjiàn]
love to see and hear; be preferred
〖喜笑颜开〗[xǐxiàoyánkāi]
beaming with smiles
〖喜形于色〗[xǐxíngyúsè]
happy expression on one's face
〖喜讯〗(名)[xǐxùn]
happy news; pleasant news; good news
〖喜悦〗(形)[xǐyuè]
happy; joyful; delightful

xì

戏(名)[xì]〔出 chū〕
theatrical shows; play; the theatre
〖戏法〗(名)[xìfǎ]
conjuring; tricks
〖戏剧〗(名)[xìjù]
drama; play; opera
〖戏剧性〗(名)[xìjùxìng]
dramatic; dramatization
〖戏弄〗(动)[xìnòng]
mock; tease; make fun of
〖戏曲〗(名)[xìqǔ]
theatrical performance
〖戏院〗(名)[xìyuàn]
theatre

系(名、动)[xì]
①strain ②department ③system ④fasten
〖系列〗(名)[xìliè]
serial; series; set
〖系数〗(名)[xìshù]

coefficient
〖系统〗(名、形)[xìtǒng]
system; systematic
〖系统工程〗
[xìtǒnggōngchéng]
systems engineering
〖系统性〗(名)[xìtǒngxìng]
systematization

细(形)[xì]
①thin; slender ②small ③fine; delicate; polished ④careful
〖细胞〗(名)[xìbāo]
cell
〖细节〗(名)[xìjié]
details
〖细菌〗(名)[xìjūn]
bacteria; germ
〖细粮〗(名)[xìliáng]
refined grain (e.g. flour, rice)
〖细密〗(形)[xìmì]
① fine; delicate ② careful; thoroughgoing
〖细腻〗(形)[xìnì]
dainty; fine; detailed
〖细水长流〗[xìshuǐchángliú]
(lit.) a small but steady stream; (fig.) continiously do sth. bit by bit; plan on a long-term basis
〖细微〗(形)[xìwēi]
small; minute
〖细小〗(形)[xìxiǎo]
small; trivial; unimportant; minute
〖细心〗(形)[xìxīn]
careful; patient; meticulous
〖细致〗(形)[xìzhì]
meticulous; fine; delicate; dainty; polished

xiā

虾(名)[xiā]〔只 zhī〕
prawn; shrimp; lobster
〖虾米〗(名)[xiāmi]
dried shrimp
〖虾仁儿〗(名)[xiārénr]
shelled shrimp meat

瞎(动、形、副)[xiā]
① become blind ② blind
③ blindly
〖瞎指挥〗[xiāzhǐhuī]
issue confused orders; mess things up by giving wrong orders
〖瞎子〗(名)[xiāzi]
blind person

xiá

匣(名)[xiá]
box
〖匣子〗(名)[xiázi]〔个 gè〕
box

峡(名)[xiá]
gorge; sharp ravine
〖峡谷〗(名)[xiágǔ]
gorge; sharp ravine

狭(形)[xiá]
narrow
〖狭隘〗(形)[xiá'ài]

①narrow; small②narrow-minded; illiberal
〖狭路相逢〗[xiálùxiāngféng]
(the two enemies) meet in a narrow path (and are ready to have it out with each other)
〖狭小〗(形)[xiáxiǎo]
narrow
〖狭义〗(名)[xiáyì]
in the narrow or strict sense of the word
〖狭窄〗(形)[xiázhǎi]
①narrow ②narrow-minded

霞(名)[xiá]
rosy cloud; roseate cloud

xià

下(名、动、量)[xià]
① underneath; under; below; next② go down; descend; dismount③ fall(e.g.rain, snow)④ put in⑤ a measure word, times
〖下班〗[xiàbān]
go off duty; be off duty
〖下边〗(名)[xiàbian]
the underneath; the following

〖下不为例〗[xiàbùwéilì]
should not take such an action next time
〖下策〗(名)[xiàcè]
ill-advised policy; an unwise policy
〖下层〗(名)[xiàcéng]
lower strata; lower level; subordinate level
〖下厂〗[xià chǎng]
go out to the factory
〖下场〗(名)[xiàchǎng]
①end; fate; shameful end of person's career ② exit (of actors or players)
〖下达〗(动)[xiàdá]
(policy or document, etc.) be made known to the lower levels; be conveyed to the lower levels
〖下地〗[xiàdì]
① go to work in the field② get up from bed (usu. referring to an invalid)
〖下风〗[xiàfēng]
① leeward, ② disadvantageous position
〖下岗〗[xiàgǎng]
① come or go off sentry duty ② be laid off; be unemployed
〖下工夫〗[xià gōngfu]
exert great effort; devote time and effort
〖下海〗[xiàhǎi]
quit one's job to engage in commercial activities; turn one's profession to doing business
〖下级〗(名)[xiàjí]
subordinate; lower levels
〖下降〗(动)[xiàjiàng]
① descend ② reduce; go down; decrease; decline
〖下脚料〗(名)[xiàjiǎoliào]
remnant; scraps
〖下课〗[xiàkè]
the class is over
〖下来〗[xiàlái]
come down; descend; dismount
〖下里巴人〗[xiàlǐbārén]

the "Song of the Rustic Poor", popular literature and art (参阅"阳春白雪")

〖下列〗(名)[xiàliè]
the following

〖下令〗[xiàlìng]
issue a decree or order; give instruction

〖下流〗(名、形)[xiàliú]
① lower reaches of river; downstream ② despicable; scurrilous; vulgar

〖下落〗(名)[xiàluò]
whereabouts

〖下马〗[xiàmǎ]
(lit.) dismount; get off the horse; (fig.) the laying off of an important project

〖下马看花〗[xiàmǎkànhuā]
(lit.) dismount and look at flowers; (fig.) on-the-spot investigation

〖下马威〗(名)[xiàmǎwēi]
instant severity; display (one's) might immediately

〖下面〗(名)[xiàmian]
① below; the next part; the following ② lower level

〖下坡路〗(名)[xiàpōlù]
on the decline; declining; getting worse

〖下情〗(名)[xiàqíng]
feelings of common people and sub rdinates; conditions at the lower levels

〖下去〗[xiàqù]
go down; descend

〖下身〗(名)[xiàshēn]
① the lower part of body ② trousers

〖下手〗[xiàshǒu]
① start doing sth. ② an assistant

〖下台〗[xià tái]
① exit (of actors or players) ② be relieved of office; step down; removed from power ③ get out of embarrassing situation

〖下头〗(名)[xiàtou]
① underneath ② subordinates; lower level

〖下文〗(名)[xiàwén]
① the next part; the following ② the continuation or the end of sth.

〖下午〗(名)[xiàwǔ]
afternoon

〖下乡〗[xiàxiāng]
go to the countryside

〖下旬〗(名)[xiàxún]
the last ten days of a month

〖下游〗(名)[xiàyóu]
lower reaches of river; lower river valley; downstream

〖下中农〗(名)[xiàzhōngnóng]
lower-middle peasant—the term lower-middle peasant refers to original class status, not present economic position

吓(动)[xià]
frighten; scare

〖吓唬〗(动)[xiàhu]
frighten; threaten

夏(名)[xià]

summer
〖夏管〗(名)[xiàguǎn]
summer farming management
〖夏季〗(名)[xiàjì]
summer; the summer season
〖夏收〗(名)[xiàshōu]
summer harvest
〖夏天〗(名)[xiàtiān]
summer; summer days
〖夏种〗(名)[xiàzhòng]
summer planting

xiān

先(名、副)[xiān]
① place ahead ② time before ③ first
〖先辈〗(名)[xiānbèi]
the elder generation; forefathers
〖先导〗(名)[xiāndǎo]
pioneer; guide; precursor
〖先发制人〗[xiānfāzhìrén]
take the advantage or initiative by starting to attack first; gain mastery by striking first
〖先锋〗(名)[xiānfēng]
pioneer; vanguard
〖先锋队〗(名)[xiānfēngduì]
vanguard
〖先后〗(名、副)[xiānhòu]
① first and last; in order of precedence ② successively; one after the other
〖先见之明〗[xiānjiànzhīmíng]
foresight; able to predict; prescience
〖先进〗(形)[xiānjìn]
outstanding; advanced; progressive
〖先决条件〗[xiānjué tiáojiàn]
precondition; prerequisite
〖先例〗(名)[xiānlì]
precedent
〖先烈〗(名)[xiānliè]
martyr
〖先前〗(名)[xiānqián]
previous; in earlier times; former
〖先遣〗(名)[xiānqiǎn]
advance units
〖先遣队〗(名)[xiānqiǎnduì]
vanguard; advance detachment
〖先驱〗(名)[xiānqū]
forerunner; pioneer; vanguard
〖先入为主〗[xiānrùwéizhǔ]
first impressions are firmly entrenched; formulate preconeived ideas
〖先生〗(名)[xiānsheng]
① teacher ② gentleman; sir; mister
〖先天〗(名)[xiāntiān]
congenital; inborn; innate; inherent
〖先验论〗(名)[xiānyànlùn]
apriorism
〖先斩后奏〗[xiānzhǎnhòuzòu]
act first and report afterwards

纤[xiān]
〖纤维〗(名)[xiānwéi]
fibre; filament
〖纤细〗(形)[xiānxì]

slender; thin

掀(动)[xiān]
① raise; lift up ② expose; reveal ③ cause; create; launch; bring about

鲜(形)[xiān]
① fresh ② tasty; delicious ③ clear-cut(e.g. stand)
〖鲜红〗(形)[xiānhóng]
bright red
〖鲜花〗(名)[xiānhuā]
〔朵 duǒ、束 shù〕fresh flower
〖鲜美〗(形)[xiānměi]
good and fresh (in taste)
〖鲜明〗(形)[xiānmíng]
crystal clear; clear-cut; vivid
〖鲜血〗(名)[xiānxuè]
fresh blood
〖鲜艳〗(形)[xiānyàn]
bright; colourful; splendour
〖鲜艳夺目〗[xiānyànduómù]
splendour blinding the eye

xián

闲(形)[xián]
leisurely; unoccupied
〖闲话〗(名)[xiánhuà]
gossip; chitchat
〖闲逛〗(动)[xiánguàng]
take a stroll; saunter; loiter
〖闲聊〗(动)[xiánliáo]
talk at random; palaver; tattle; idle talk; chat
〖闲情逸致〗[xiánqíngyìzhì]
carefree
〖闲人免进〗[xiánrénmiǎnjìn]
no admittance except on business; admittance to staff only
〖闲散〗(名、形)[xiánsǎn]
free and leisure; idle; unused

弦(名)[xián]
① string ② chord

咸(形)[xián]
salty; salted
〖咸菜〗(名)[xiáncài]
salted (preserved) vegetable

衔(动、名)[xián]
① hold in the mouth ② rank; title
〖衔接〗(动)[xiánjiē]
connect up; link

嫌(动)[xián]
① suspect ② disapprove; dislike; prejudiced against
〖嫌恶〗(动)[xiánwù]
be sick of; dislike; detest
〖嫌疑〗(名)[xiányí]
suspicion
〖嫌疑犯〗(名)[xiányífàn]
suspect

xiǎn

显(动)[xiǎn]
show; appear; display
〖显得〗(动)[xiǎnde]
appear to be

〖显而易见〗[xiǎn'éryìjiàn]
clearly show; obvious; evident
〖显赫〗(形)[xiǎnhè]
resplendent; impressive; powerful; eminent
〖显露〗(动)[xiǎnlù]
reveal; become manifest
〖显然〗(形)[xiǎnrán]
clearly; evidently; obviously; apparently
〖显示〗(动)[xiǎnshì]
show; reveal; display; demonstrate
〖显微镜〗(名)[xiǎnwēijìng]
[架 jià] microscope
〖显现〗(动)[xiǎnxiàn]
appear; reveal
〖显像管〗(名)[xiǎnxiàngguǎn]
kinescope; picture tube
〖显眼〗(形)[xiǎnyǎn]
attractive; striking; arresting
〖显要〗(形)[xiǎnyào]
① a high and powerful (position) ② high ranking and powerful; prominent
〖显著〗(形)[xiǎnzhù]
remarkable; conspicuous; noteworthy; outstanding

险(形)[xiǎn]
dangerous
〖险恶〗(形)[xiǎn'è]
wicked; treacherous; sinister; pernicious; dangerous; precarious
〖险峻〗(形)[xiǎnjùn]
steep; precipitous
〖险些〗(副)[xiǎnxiē]
nearly; almost
〖险要〗(形)[xiǎnyào]
strategic points; strong natural defence position
〖险阻〗(形)[xiǎnzǔ]
difficult to cross; danger

xiàn

县(名)[xiàn]
county
〖县委〗(名)[xiànwěi]
county party committee

现(动)[xiàn]
present; appear; reveal
〖现场〗(名)[xiànchǎng]
on-the-spot
〖现场报道〗[xiànchǎngbàodào]
on-the-scene report
〖现场办公〗
[xiànchǎngbàngōng]
work on the spot; go to work in a unit with piled up problems to find ways to solve them
〖现成〗(形)[xiànchéng]
ready-made; off the peg
〖现成饭〗(名)[xiànchéngfàn]
① food ready for the table ② unearned gain
〖现代〗(名)[xiàndài]
modern age; contemporary era; modern
〖现代化〗(动)[xiàndàihuà]
modernize
〖现货〗(名)[xiànhuò]

X

merchandise on hand; spot stocks
〖现货交易〗[xiànhuòjiāoyì]
spot transaction; over-the-counter trading
〖现金〗(名)[xiànjīn]
cash; money in coin or notes
〖现款〗(名)[xiànkuǎn]
cash
〖现身说法〗[xiànshēnshuōfǎ]
persuade (sb.) by taking oneself as an example
〖现实〗(名、形)[xiànshí]
reality; realistic; practical; actual
〖现实性〗(名)[xiànshíxìng]
reality
〖现实主义〗(名)[xiànshízhǔyì]
realism
〖现象〗(名)[xiànxiàng]
〔种 zhǒng〕phenomenon
〖现行〗(形)[xiànxíng]
current; active; present
〖现在〗(名)[xiànzài]
nowadays; at present; now
〖现状〗(名)[xiànzhuàng]
present conditions; existing state of; status quo

限(动)[xiàn]
limit; set limit to; define
〖限定〗(动)[xiàndìng]
limit; set limit to; definite
〖限度〗(名)[xiàndù]
limits; extent
〖限额〗(名)[xiàn'é]
quota; ration; norm
〖限量〗(动)[xiànliàng]
limited capacity; fixed quantity
〖限期〗(名、动)[xiànqī]
within a set time; within a definite time
〖限于〗(动)[xiànyú]
confine to; restrict to; be bound to; be limited to
〖限制〗(动)[xiànzhì]
limit; restrict; be restrained; constrain

线(名)[xiàn]
①thread ②line; route ③a ray of
〖线路〗(名)[xiànlù]
line of communication; circuit
〖线圈〗(名)[xiànquān]
coil
〖线索〗(名)[xiànsuǒ]
clue; line of (story;) hint; indication
〖线条〗(名)[xiàntiáo]
the line in drawing; contour
〖线装书〗(名)[xiànzhuāngshū]
thread-bound Chinese book

宪[xiàn]
〖宪兵〗(名)[xiànbīng]
military police; gendarme
〖宪法〗(名)[xiànfǎ]
constitution (law)
〖宪章〗(名)[xiànzhāng]
charter

陷(动)[xiàn]
①sink into; fall into ②make

false accusation ③ find oneself in; get bogged down in
〖陷害〗(动)[xiànhài]
frame up; make false accusation
〖陷阱〗(名)[xiànjǐng]
trap; pitfall
〖陷落〗(动)[xiànluò]
sink into; sink down; fall
〖陷入〗(动)[xiànrù]
fall into; sink into; get bogged down in; be beset with

馅 [xiàn]
〖馅儿〗(名)[xiànr]
stuffing (of pastry)

羡 [xiàn]
〖羡慕〗(动)[xiànmù]
adore; admire

献 (动)[xiàn]
① present; give; offer ② pay; contribute
〖献策〗[xiàncè]
present a plan or strategy; submit schemes for
〖献词〗(名)[xiàncí]
greeting message (e.g. New Year message)
〖献花〗[xiànhuā]
present bouquets or flowers
〖献计〗[xiànjì]
suggest ways and means; offer plans (for)
〖献礼〗[xiànlǐ]
a contribution; make contributions
〖献媚〗(动)[xiànmèi]
curry favour; fawn upon
〖献身〗[xiànshēn]
devote oneself to; dedicate oneself to

xiāng

乡 (名)[xiāng]
① countryside; village ② native place; home town
〖乡村〗(名)[xiāngcūn]
village; countryside
〖乡亲〗(名)[xiāngqīn]
fellow citizen of the same district; villager
〖乡土〗(名)[xiāngtǔ]
native place or district
〖乡下〗(名)[xiāngxià]
the countryside; village

相 [xiāng]
另见 xiàng
〖相比〗(动)[xiāngbǐ]
compare with each other; contrast
〖相差〗(动)[xiāngchà]
differ; deviate
〖相称〗(形)[xiāngchèn]
fit; correspond; match; well-balanced; worthy
〖相乘〗(动)[xiāngchéng]
multiply by; multiplication of
〖相持〗(动)[xiāngchí]
(both parties) will not give in; be locked in a fight; stalemate; refuse to yield
〖相斥〗(动)[xiāngchì]

reprehend each other; mutually repel

〖相除〗(动)[xiāngchú]
divide by

〖相处〗(动)[xiāngchǔ]
live or work together

〖相传〗(动)[xiāngchuán]
pass from one to another or from place to place; pass on; be handed down

〖相当〗(动、形、副)[xiāngdāng]
① ...equal... ② appropriate; fairly ③ in a certain degree; to a certain extent

〖相等〗(动)[xiāngděng]
be equal to; equivalent

〖相对〗(动、形)[xiāngduì]
① opposite ② relative; comparative

〖相对真理〗[xiāngduìzhēnlǐ]
relative truth

〖相反〗(形)[xiāngfǎn]
contrary to;counter;opposite; converse

〖相反相成〗
[xiāngfǎnxiāngchéng]
things that oppose each other also complement each other

〖相仿〗(形)[xiāngfǎng]
alike; similar; analogous

〖相逢〗(动)[xiāngféng]
meet; come face to face with

〖相符〗(动)[xiāngfú]
agree with; correspond with

〖相辅相成〗
[xiāngfǔxiāngchéng]
complement each other

〖相干〗(动)[xiānggān]
have to do with; relate to; concern

〖相关〗(动)[xiāngguān]
have something to do with; be relevant to; be related to

〖相互〗(形)[xiānghù]
mutual; reciprocal; interrelation

〖相互作用〗[xiānghùzuòyòng]
mutual action

〖相继〗(动)[xiāngjì]
follow one another; successive

〖相加〗(动)[xiāngjiā]
add together

〖相减〗(动)[xiāngjiǎn]
subtract from

〖相交〗(动)[xiāngjiāo]
① (lines) cross each other; intersec ② make friends with each other

〖相接〗(动)[xiāngjiē]
connect with; meet

〖相切〗(动)[xiāngqiē]
(math.) contact

〖相识〗(动)[xiāngshí]
be acquainted with; know each other

〖相思〗(名)[xiāngsī]
yearning between lovers; love-sickness

〖相似〗(形)[xiāngsì]
similar; analogous; resemble each other

〖相提并论〗[xiāngtíbìnglùn]
mention in the same breath; regard in same category; put sth. on a par with

〖相同〗(形)[xiāngtóng]

be alike; be the same
〖相信〗(动)[xiāngxìn]
believe; have faith in; trust; confident
〖相形见绌〗[xiāngxíngjiànchù]
be inferior by comparison; appear deficient in comparison; lose by comparison
〖相依为命〗[xiāngyīwéimìng]
share life together; depend on each other
〖相应〗(动、形)[xiāngyìng]
correspond; proper; accordingly; corresponding

香(形)[xiāng]
fragrant; nice-smelling; aromatic
〖香肠〗(名)[xiāngcháng]
sausage
〖香花〗(名)[xiānghuā]
fragrant flowers
〖香蕉〗(名)[xiāngjiāo]
banana
〖香料〗(名)[xiāngliào]
condiment; spice; perfume
〖香喷喷〗(形)[xiāngpēnpēn]
rich in fragrance; fragrant
〖香水〗(名)[xiāngshuǐ]
perfume
〖香甜〗(形)[xiāngtián]
sweet and nicesmelling
〖香烟〗(名)[xiāngyān]
〔盒 hé、枝 zhī〕cigarette
〖香皂〗(名)[xiāngzào]
〔块 kuài〕toilet soap

箱(名)[xiāng]
trunk; box; case
〖箱子〗(名)[xiāngzi]〔个 gè〕
trunk; box; case

镶(动)[xiāng]
inset with; inlay; fill

xiáng

详(形)[xiáng]
in detail; detailed; comprehensive
〖详尽〗(形)[xiángjìn]
with complete detail; in full detail
〖详情〗(名)[xiángqíng]
details; minutest details
〖详细〗(形)[xiángxì]
detailed; at length

降(动)[xiáng]
① surrender ② give in; yield; subdue
另见 jiàng
〖降服〗(动)[xiángfú]
subdue; overpower; put down
〖降龙伏虎〗[xiánglóngfúhǔ]
(lit.) subdue the dragon and the tiger; (fig.) very powerful

xiǎng

享(动)[xiǎng]
enjoy
〖享乐〗(动)[xiǎnglè]
enjoy material comforts; seek pleasure; indulge in luxuries
〖享受〗(动)[xiǎngshòu]

enjoy (e. g. ease and comforts, rights)

〖享有〗(动)[xiǎngyǒu]

possess; have in possession of

响(动、形)[xiǎng]

① sound; ring; echo; respond ② loud

〖响彻云霄〗[xiǎngchèyúnxiāo]

resound through the skies; echoing to the skies

〖响动〗(名)[xiǎngdòng]

noise of movement; sound

〖响亮〗(形)[xiǎngliàng]

loud and clear; resounding

〖响声〗(名)[xiǎngshēng]

a sound

〖响应〗(动)[xiǎngyìng]

respond; answer (the call of)

想(动、助动)[xiǎng]

① think ② suppose ③ want to; would like to

〖想必〗(副)[xiǎngbì]

surely; likely

〖想不到〗[xiǎngbudào]

never thought of; unexpectedly

〖想不开〗[xiǎngbukāi]

take things too hard; keep on worrying; be upset

〖想当然〗[xiǎngdāngrán]

take for granted; jump to conclusion without proof; assumption

〖想得到〗[xiǎngdedào]

expect; foresee; think of

〖想得开〗[xiǎngdekāi]

make light of worries; take things easy

〖想法〗(名)[xiǎngfǎ]

ideas; thinking

〖想见〗(动)[xiǎngjiàn]

conclude from assumption; imagine

〖想来〗(副)[xiǎnglái]

possibly; probably

〖想念〗(动)[xiǎngniàn]

miss; cherish the memory of; yearn

〖想入非非〗[xiǎngrùfēifēi]

fantastic ideas; wishful thinking; indulge in dreams of...

〖想像〗(动)[xiǎngxiàng]

imagine

〖想像力〗(名)[xiǎngxiànglì]

imagination; fancy; conception

xiàng

向(动、介)[xiàng]

①face; turn towards ②side with; favour ③ toward; to

〖向导〗(名)[xiàngdǎo]

guide; person who shows others the way

〖向来〗(副)[xiànglái]

usually; so far

〖向前看〗[xiàngqiánkàn]

be forward-looking; be optimistic about one's future

〖向钱看〗[xiàngqiánkàn]

turn one's eyes towards money; worship mammon

〖向上〗[xiàngshàng]

upward

〖向上爬〗[xiàngshàngpá]
be intent on personal advancement (e.g. a social climber)
〖向往〗(动)[xiàngwǎng]
aspire to; long for; be filled with a desire for
〖向心力〗(名)[xiàngxīnlì]
centripetal force
〖向阳〗[xiàngyáng]
facing the sun
〖向着〗(动)[xiàngzhe]
face; turn towards

项(名、量)[xiàng]
①(math.) the neck ②a sum; term ③a measure word, item, etc.
〖项链〗(名)[xiàngliàn]〔条 tiáo〕
necklace
〖项目〗(名)[xiàngmù]
article; clause; item; project; course

巷(名)[xiàng]
alley-way; alley; lane
〖巷战〗(名)[xiàngzhàn]
street fight ing; house-to-house fighting

相(名)[xiàng]
① appearance; looks ② minister
另见 xiāng
〖相机行事〗[xiàngjīxíngshì]
watch for right time for action
〖相貌〗(名)[xiàngmào]
appearance; looks
〖相片儿〗(名)[xiàngpiānr]
〔张 zhāng〕photograph
〖相声〗(名)[xiàngsheng]
cross talk; comic dialogue

象(名、动)[xiàng]
①elephant ②resemble; look like; symbolize
〖象棋〗(名)[xiàngqí]〔盘 pán〕
chess
〖象声词〗(名)[xiàngshēngcí]
onomatopoeia
〖象形文字〗[xiàngxíngwénzì]
hieroglyph; pictograph
〖象牙〗(名)[xiàngyá]
ivory; elephant tusk
〖象征〗(名、动)[xiàngzhēng]
symbol; token; symbolize; signify

像(名、动)[xiàng]
① portrait; statue; figure ② resemble; like
〖像样儿〗[xiàngyàngr]
decent; pretty good; proper; passable

橡[xiàng]
〖橡胶〗(名)[xiàngjiāo]
rubber; caoutchouc
〖橡皮〗(名)[xiàngpí]〔块 kuài〕
rubber

xiāo

削(动)[xiāo]
①cut; sharpen ②peel
另见 xuē

骁 [xiāo]

〖骁勇〗(形)[xiāoyǒng]
valiant; brave

逍 [xiāo]

〖逍遥〗(形)[xiāoyáo]
leisurely; unhurried; wander about at leisure
〖逍遥法外〗[xiāoyáofǎwài]
(criminal) be at large

消 (动)[xiāo]

①disappear; vanish; melt② extinguish; extinct; diminish
〖消沉〗(形)[xiāochén]
down-hearted
〖消除〗(动)[xiāochú]
eliminate; remove; abolish; do away with
〖消毒〗[xiāodú]
disinfection; sterilization
〖消防〗(动)[xiāofáng]
put out fire; fight fire
〖消防车〗(名)[xiāofángchē]
fire engine; fire truck
〖消防队〗(名)[xiāofángduì]
fire brigade
〖消费〗(动)[xiāofèi]
consume; spend
〖消费品〗(名)[xiāofèipǐn]
consumer goods
〖消耗〗(动)[xiāohào]
deplete; diminish; eat up; exhaust; drain; wear down; consume
〖消化〗(动)[xiāohuà]
digest; absorb
〖消化不良〗[xiāohuàbùliáng]
indigestion; dyspepsia
〖消极〗(形)[xiāojí]
passive; dispirited; negative
〖消灭〗(动)[xiāomiè]
eradicate; wipe out; destroy; abolish; exterminate
〖消磨〗(动)[xiāomó]
①waste away; wear off ②while away; pass away (e.g. time)
〖消遣〗(动)[xiāoqiǎn]
spend spare time pleasantly
〖消融〗(动)[xiāoróng]
melt
〖消散〗(动)[xiāosàn]
disperse; diffuse
〖消失〗(动)[xiāoshī]
vanish; disappear; fade away
〖消逝〗(动)[xiāoshì]
wither away; vanish
〖消瘦〗(动)[xiāoshòu]
emaciate
〖消亡〗(动)[xiāowáng]
perish; wither away; die out
〖消息〗(名)[xiāoxi]
① news; news report; information
〖消炎〗[xiāoyán]
decrease swelling; decrease inflammation

萧 [xiāo]

〖萧瑟〗(形)[xiāosè]
disconsolate; gloomy; dull
〖萧条〗(形)[xiāotiáo]
①very dull; languish; lonely
②depression; slack; slump

硝(名)[xiāo]
saltpeter; niter
〖硝酸〗(名)[xiāosuān]
nitric acid
〖硝烟〗(名)[xiāoyān]
smoke of gunpowder

销(动)[xiāo]
①melt (metals) ②end; close; cancel ③sell
〖销毁〗(动)[xiāohuǐ]
destroy; ruin
〖销声匿迹〗[xiāoshēngnìjì]
draw in one's horns
〖销售〗(动)[xiāoshòu]
sell; sale
〖销售部〗(名)[xiāoshòubù]
marketing department

潇[xiāo]
〖潇洒〗(形)[xiāosǎ]
elegant and unconventional

xiǎo

小(形)[xiǎo]
①little; small ②young

〖小本经营〗[xiǎoběnjīngyíng]
business with a small capital; do business in a small way
〖小便〗(名、动)[xiǎbiàn]
urine; urinate
〖小吃〗(名)[xiǎochī]
snacks
〖小丑〗(名)[xiǎochǒu]
clown
〖小道消息〗[xiǎodàoxiāoxi]
hearsay; grapevine
〖小动作〗(名)[xiǎodòngzuò]
petty and mean action; dirty tricks
〖小恩小惠〗[xiǎo'ēnxiǎohuì]
paltry charity; sops; a small economic bait
〖小儿科〗(名)[xiǎo'érkē]
division of pediatrics
〖小费〗(名)[xiǎofèi]
tip; gratuity; service charge
〖小鬼〗(名)[xiǎoguǐ]
little devil; little ones; kiddy
〖小孩儿〗(名)[xiǎoháir]
child
〖小伙子〗(名)[xiǎohuǒzi]
young fellow; young man
〖小节〗(名)[xiǎojié]
minor points of conduct
〖小金库〗(名)[xiǎojīnkù]
unauthorized departmental coffer
〖小康〗(名、形)[xiǎokāng]
well-to-do; comfortably off; fairly well-off
〖小麦〗(名)[xiǎomài]
wheat
〖小卖部〗(名)[xiǎomàibù]
buffet
〖小米〗(名)[xiǎomǐ][粒 lì]
millet
〖小脑〗(名)[xiǎonǎo]
cerebellum
〖小农经济〗[xiǎonóngjīngjì]
small-scale peasant farming; small-scale peasant economy
〖小品文〗(名)[xiǎopǐnwén]
short essay; sketch

〖小气〗(形)[xiǎoqi]
① pettiness; mean ② narrow-minded
〖小巧玲珑〗[xiǎoqiǎolínglóng]
pretty; cleverly made; cute
〖小商品〗(名)[xiǎoshāngpǐn]
small-scale commodity; petty commodities
〖小生产〗(名)[xiǎoshēngchǎn]
small-scale production
〖小时〗(名)[xiǎoshí]
hour
〖小手工业者〗(名)
[xiǎoshǒugōngyèzhě]
small handicraftsman
〖小数〗(名)[xiǎoshù]
(math.) decimal
〖小数点〗(名)[xiǎoshùdiǎn]
decimal point
〖小说〗(名)[xiǎoshuō]
〔本 běn〕novel
〖小私有者〗(名)
[xiǎosīyǒuzhě]
petty proprietor; small holder
〖小苏打〗(名)[xiǎosūdá]
sodium bicarbonate; bicarbonate of soda
〖小题大作〗[xiǎotídàzuò]
make a fuss about a trifling matter; make a mountain out of a mole hill
〖小偷〗(名)[xiǎotōu]
thief; pilferer
〖小巫见大巫〗
[xiǎowūjiàn dàwū]
be dwarfed; pale into insignificance in comparison with
〖小写〗(名、动)[xiǎoxiě]
small letter
〖小心〗(动、形)[xiǎoxīn]
take care; careful
〖小心翼翼〗[xiǎoxīnyìyì]
extremely careful
〖小型〗(名)[xiǎoxíng]
small type; small scale
〖小学〗(名)[xiǎoxué]
primary school; elementary school
〖小于〗(动)[xiǎoyú]
be smaller than
〖小篆〗(名)[xiǎozhuàn]
style of writing Chinese characters popular in Chin and Han Dynasties
〖小资产阶级〗(名)
[xiǎozīchǎnjiējí]
petty-bourgeoisie
〖小组〗(名)[xiǎozǔ]
team; section; group

晓(名、动)[xiǎo]
①dawn; daybreak ②know; understand
〖晓得〗(动)[xiǎode]
know; understand

xiào

肖[xiào]
〖肖像〗(名)[xiàoxiàng]
〔张 zhāng〕portrait

校(名)[xiào]
school; college; academy
另见 jiào
〖校风〗(名)[xiàofēng]

X

school spirit
〖校规〗(名)[xiàoguī]
school regulations
〖校庆〗(名)[xiàoqìng]
school anniversary
〖校舍〗(名)[xiàoshè]
school building
〖校友〗(名)[xiàoyǒu]
alumnus(male); alumna(female)
〖校园〗(名)[xiàoyuán]
school campus
〖校长〗(名)[xiàozhǎng]
head of a school (e.g. president, principal, director)

笑(动)[xiào]
laugh; smile
〖笑柄〗(名)[xiàobǐng]
laughing-stock
〖笑话〗(名、动)[xiàohuà]
joke; laugh at
〖笑里藏刀〗[xiàolǐcángdāo]
murderous intent behind one's smile; cover the dagger with a smile
〖笑脸〗(名)[xiàoliǎn]
〔张 zhāng〕smiling face
〖笑眯眯〗(形)[xiàomīmī]
smiling
〖笑容〗(名)[xiàoróng]
a happy, smiling expression
〖笑嘻嘻〗(形)[xiàoxīxī]
smile happily
〖笑逐颜开〗[xiàozhúyánkāi]
beam with smiles; beaming covered with smiles

效(名、动)[xiào]
①effect ②follow the example ③work in the service of; serve the ends of
〖效果〗(名)[xiàoguǒ]
effect result
〖效法〗(动)[xiàofǎ]
pattern on; follow the example; imitate; learn from
〖效劳〗(动)[xiàoláo]
be in the service of; serve the ends of; work for
〖效力〗(动、名)[xiàolì]
①efficacy ②render one's services to
〖效率〗(名)[xiàolǜ]
efficiency
〖效能〗(名)[xiàonéng]
efficacy; function; capacity
〖效益〗(名)[xiàoyì]
efficacy; benefit
〖效益工资〗[xiàoyìgōngzī]
wages based on economic performance; efficiency related wages
〖效用〗(名)[xiàoyòng]
effect; result; function

xiē

些(量)[xiē]
a measure word, some, few, a few, etc.

歇(动)[xiē]
①rest ②stop
〖歇后语〗(名)[xiēhòuyǔ]
a popular phrase with its lat-

ter part (usu. implication) understood or not spoken
〖歇脚〗[xiējiǎo]
stop for rest after a walk
〖歇斯底里〗(名)[xiēsīdǐlǐ]
hysteria

蝎(名)[xiē]
scorpion
〖蝎子〗(名)[xiēzi]〔只 zhī〕
scorpion

xié

协[xié]
〖协定〗(名)[xiédìng]
agreement; convention
〖协会〗(名)[xiéhuì]
association; league
〖协力〗(动)[xiélì]
pull together; cooperate
〖协商〗(动)[xiéshāng]
consult and discuss with each other
〖协调〗(动)[xiétiáo]
adjust to each other; readjust; coordinate
〖协同〗(动)[xiétóng]
work together; cooperate
〖协议〗(名)[xiéyì]
agreement
〖协助〗(动)[xiézhù]
provide help to; assist; help; support; aid
〖协奏曲〗(名)[xiézòuqǔ]
concerto
〖协作〗(动)[xiézuò]
cooperate

邪(形)[xié]
vicious; evil; wicked; crooked
〖邪路〗(名)[xiélù]〔条 tiáo〕
immoral or illegal doings; crooked means
〖邪气〗(名)[xiéqì]
sinister trend; noxious influence of

胁[xié]
〖胁从〗(名)[xiécóng]
person forced into wrong doing; accomplice under duress; those who are coerced into joining
〖胁迫〗(动)[xiépò]
coerce; intimidate; compel; force

挟[xié]
〖挟持〗(动)[xiéchí]
force to do one's bidding; force others to submit to one's will; be under duress

偕[xié]
〖偕同〗(动)[xiétóng]
accompany with; together with

斜(形)[xié]
slanting; inclining; sloping; oblique
〖斜边〗(名)[xiébiān]〔条 tiáo〕
hypotenuse
〖斜面〗(名)[xiémiàn]
inclined plane

X

〖斜线〗(名)[xiéxiàn]〔条 tiáo〕
oblique line

谐 [xié]
〖谐和〗(形)[xiéhé]
agreeable; harmonious

携(动)[xié]
carry; bring
〖携带〗(动)[xiédài]
carry; take with; bring
〖携手〗[xiéshǒu]
hand in hand; side by side

鞋(名)[xié]〔双 shuāng〕
shoes
〖鞋带儿〗(名)[xiédàir]〔根 gēn〕
shoe-lace; shoe-string
〖鞋油〗(名)[xiéyóu]〔盒 hé〕
shoe cream; shoe polish

xiě

写(动)[xiě]
write; portray
〖写生〗(名、动)[xiěshēng]
sketch; a branch of painting; portraying living things; pai-nt; portray;
〖写照〗(名)[xiězhào]
portrayal; description; sketch
〖写作〗(名、动)[xiězuò]
essay-writing; write (essay, story, novel, etc.)

血(名)[xiě] blood
另见 xuè
〖血淋淋〗(形)[xiělīnlīn]
bloodshed; bleeding

xiè

泄(动)[xiè]
① drain ② let out; disclose; betray ③ vent
〖泄劲〗[xiè jìn]
lose one's confidence and relax one's efforts
〖泄漏〗(动)[xièlòu]
betray; leak out; broach; dis-close
〖泄密〗[xièmì]
betray one's secret; disclose a secret; broach a secret
〖泄气〗[xièqì]
lose one's spirit; disappoint-ing

卸(动)[xiè]
discharge; unload

谢(动)[xiè]
①thank; express one's thanks ② make an apology ③wither
〖谢绝〗(动)[xièjué]
decline in polite terms
〖谢幕〗[xiè mù]
(performers appear on stage) thank audience for curtain calls
〖谢谢〗(动)[xièxie]
thank; express one's thanks
〖谢意〗(名)[xièyì]
gratitude

懈 [xiè]

〖懈怠〗(形)[xièdài]
slack; sluggish; indolent; idle

xīn

心(名)[xīn]
①heart ②centre
〖心爱〗(动)[xīn'ài]
love; favour; hold ... dear
〖心安理得〗[xīn'ānlǐdé]
have an easy conscience; one's conscience is void of offence; feel at ease
〖心不在焉〗[xīnbùzàiyān]
absent-minded; preoccupied; with one's mind wandering; inattentive
〖心肠〗(名)[xīncháng]
①intention; heart ②mood
〖心潮〗(名)[xīncháo]
state of mind; emotion
〖心潮澎湃〗[xīncháopéngpài]
be full of excitement
〖心得〗(名)[xīndé]
personal insight; individual understanding or experiences
〖心烦〗(形)[xīnfán]
annoyed; vexed
〖心服口服〗[xīnfúkǒufú]
utterly convinced; submit willingly
〖心腹〗(名)[xīnfù]
henchman; trusted fellows; confidant
〖心腹之患〗[xīnfùzhīhuàn]
a disease in one's very vitals; a thorn in sb.'s side
〖心甘情愿〗[xīngānqíngyuàn]
willingly; content oneself with
〖心花怒放〗[xīnhuānùfàng]
one's heart bursts into bloom
〖心怀鬼胎〗[xīnhuáiguǐtāi]
with misgivings in one's heart; have evil intention
〖心慌〗(形)[xīnhuāng]
mentally confused; nervous; palpitate
〖心慌意乱〗[xīnhuāngyìluàn]
mentally confused
〖心机〗(名)[xīnjī]
expedient; resource; plot
〖心急如火〗[xīnjírúhuǒ]
with a confused and worried mind; on tenterhooks
〖心惊胆战〗[xīnjīngdǎnzhàn]
be deeply alarmed; tremble with fright
〖心惊肉跳〗[xīnjīngròutiào]
shudder with fear
〖心坎〗(名)[xīnkǎn]
chest; bosom; the bottom of one's heart
〖心理〗(名)[xīnlǐ]
psychology
〖心理测验〗[xīnlǐcèyàn]
mental test; psychometry
〖心理年龄〗[xīnlǐniánlíng]
mental age
〖心理战〗[xīnlǐzhàn]
psychological warfare
〖心理障碍〗[xīnlǐzhàng'ài]
psychogenic disorder
〖心里〗(名)[xīnli]
in one's heart; mind
〖心灵〗(名)[xīnlíng]

①clever in mind ②mentality; heart; spirit

〖心灵手巧〗[xīnlíngshǒuqiǎo]
clever in mind and skillful in hand

〖心领神会〗[xīnlǐngshénhuì]
appreciate thoroughly; understand fully

〖心乱如麻〗[xīnluànrúmá]
mind confused like entangled hemp

〖心满意足〗[xīnmǎnyìzú]
satisfy; satisfaction; content

〖心明眼亮〗[xīnmíngyǎnliàng]
see and think clearly; clear minds and sharp eyesight

〖心目〗(名)[xīnmù]
(in) one's mind; (in) the eyes

〖心平气和〗[xīnpíngqìhé]
be in a calm mood; in one's sober senses

〖心情〗(名)[xīnqíng]
feeling; emotion; state of mind

〖心如刀割〗[xīnrúdāogē]
heart-rending

〖心神不定〗[xīnshénbùdìng]
agitated; in a state of discomposure; wandering in thought

〖心事〗(名)[xīnshì]
things that weigh on one's mind; worries in mind; cares

〖心思〗(名)[xīnsi]
thinking; motive; mood

〖心疼〗(动)[xīnténg]
①love; be fond of ②be reluctant to part with

〖心头〗(名)[xīntóu]
heart

〖心心相印〗[xīnxīnxiāngyìn]
see eye to eye with; in mutual understanding; share the feelings of

〖心胸〗(名)[xīnxiōng]
①breadth of mind ②ambition

〖心虚〗(形)[xīnxū]
① afraid of being found out ② lack of confidence

〖心血〗(名)[xīnxuè]
heartfelt labour; energy; effort

〖心血来潮〗[xīnxuèláicháo]
suddenly hit upon an idea

〖心眼儿〗(名)[xīnyǎnr]
①bottom of heart ②intention

〖心意〗(名)[xīnyì]
intention; purpose; good will

〖心愿〗(名)[xīnyuàn]
desire; wish; hope

〖心悦诚服〗[xīnyuèchéngfú]
submit willingly; gladly and wholeheartedly

〖心脏〗(名)[xīnzàng]
heart

〖心脏病〗(名)[xīnzàngbìng]
heart trouble; heart disease

〖心照不宣〗[xīnzhàobùxuān]
tacit understanding; tacit agreement

〖心直口快〗[xīnzhíkǒukuài]
open-hearted and out-spoken; wear one's heart on one's sleeve

〖心中有数〗[xīnzhōngyǒushù]
understand the situation; be concerned and know what to do next

辛 [xīn]

〚辛亥革命〛[XīnhàiGémìng]
the (Bourgeois Democratic) Revolution of 1911
〚辛苦〛(形)[xīnkǔ]
hard; exhausting; with much toil; industrious
〚辛劳〛(形)[xīnláo]
painstaking; laborious; industrious
〚辛勤〛(形)[xīnqín]
diligent; laborious; industrious
〚辛酸〛(形)[xīnsuān]
sad; tearful

欣 [xīn]

〚欣然〛(形)[xīnrán]
readily; gladly
〚欣赏〛(动)[xīnshǎng]
take pleasure in; appreciate; enjoy
〚欣慰〛(形)[xīnwèi]
be glad and at ease
〚欣喜若狂〛[xīnxǐruòkuáng]
leap with joy; go wild with joy; rejoice
〚欣欣向荣〛[xīnxīnxiàngróng]
growing prosperity; thriving; flourishing

新 (形)[xīn]

new; recently
〚新陈代谢〛[xīnchéndàixiè]
the transition from the old order of things to the new; metabolism; the new displacing the old; the old being superseded by the new
〚新华社〛(名)[Xīnhuáshè]
Hsinhua News Agency
〚新纪元〛[xīnjìyuán]
new epoch; new era
〚新老交替〛[xīnlǎojiāotì]
succession of the older generation by the younger generation; replacement of the old by the new
〚新民主主义〛[xīnmínzhǔzhǔyì]
new-democratism
〚新民主主义革命〛[xīnmínzhǔzhǔyìgémìng]
new democratic revolution
〚新年〛(名)[xīnnián]
New Year
〚新奇〛(形)[xīnqí]
novel; interesting; strange; surprising
〚新人新事〛[xīnrénxīnshì]
new people and new things; new personalities and new deeds
〚新生〛(名)[xīnshēng]
① newborn (e. g. force, things)
② new students
〚新生事物〛[xīnshēngshìwù]
new emerging things; newborn things
〚新式〛(名)[xīnshì]
new type; modern type; new style
〚新四军〛(名)[Xīnsìjūn]
the New Fourth Army
〚新闻〛(名)[xīnwén]
press; news
〚新闻公报〛[xīnwéngōngbào]
press communique

〖新鲜〗(形)[xīnxiān]
fresh
〖新兴〗(形)[xīnxīng]
new rising; new emerging; newly established; new born
〖新型〗(名)[xīnxíng]
new type; new pattern; new mould
〖新颖〗(形)[xīnyǐng]
novel (e.g. ideas); new
〖新殖民主义〗[xīnzhímínzhǔyì]
neo-colonialism

薪(名)[xīn]
① salary ② firewood
〖薪水〗(名)[xīnshui]
salary; pay

xìn

信(名、动)[xìn]〔封 fēng〕
① letter ② belief; faith; believe; have confidence in ③ credit
〖信贷〗(名)[xìndài]
credit
〖信封〗(名)[xìnfēng]〔个 gè〕
envelope
〖信服〗(动)[xìnfú]
believe and be convinced
〖信号〗(名)[xìnhào]
signal
〖信件〗(名)[xìnjiàn]
general term for letters and other printed matter
〖信口开河〗[xìnkǒukāihé]
talk drivel; talk at random; say whatever comes to one's mind
〖信赖〗(动)[xìnlài]
trust; rely on
〖信念〗(名)[xìnniàn]
faith; belief; creed
〖信任〗(动、名)[xìnrèn]
trust; place confidence in; have confidence in; faith
〖信使〗(名)[xìnshǐ]
messenger; courier; emissary
〖信手拈来〗[xìnshǒuniānlái]
pick up sth. easily and casually
〖信守〗(动)[xìnshǒu]
observe honestly; keep one's words or promise
〖信筒〗(名)[xìntǒng]
pillar box
〖信徒〗(名)[xìntú]
disciple; follower; adherent
〖信托〗(动)[xìntuō]
trust; entrust
〖信息〗(名)[xìnxī]
information; message; news
〖信息爆炸〗[xìnxībàozhà]
information explosion
〖信息高速公路〗
[xìnxīgāosùgōnglù]
information expressway
〖信息业〗(名)[xìnxīyè]
information service
〖信箱〗(名)[xìnxiāng]
post box
〖信心〗(名)[xìnxīn]
confidence; conviction; belief
〖信仰〗(动、名)[xìnyǎng]
belief; creed; faith; worship
〖信义〗(名)[xìnyì]
faith; honesty
〖信用〗(名)[xìnyòng]

①trustworthiness ②credit
〖信用卡〗(名)[xìnyòngkǎ]
credit card
〖信用社〗(名)[xìnyòngshè]
credit cooperative
〖信纸〗(名)[xìnzhǐ]
〔张 zhāng〕letter paper

xīng

兴(动)[xīng]
① grow prosperous; thrive ② prevail ③ establish; build ④ rise
另见 xìng
〖兴办〗(动)[xīngbàn]
establish; build
〖兴奋〗(形)[xīngfèn]
excited; elated
〖兴风作浪〗[xīngfēngzuòlàng]
stir up trouble; incite and create trouble; fan the flames of disorder
〖兴建〗(动)[xīngjiàn]
build
〖兴隆〗[xīnglóng]
prosperous, thriving, flourishing, brisk
〖兴起〗(动)[xīngqǐ]
spring up; establish; start; rise; arise
〖兴盛〗(形)[xīngshèng]
prosperous; flourishing
〖兴师动众〗[xīngshīdòngzhòng]
(usu.derog.)mobilise a lot of people to do something
〖兴衰〗(名)[xīngshuāi]
the rise and fall
〖兴亡〗(名)[xīngwáng]
the rise and fall
〖兴旺〗(形)[xīngwàng]
be vigorous and flourishing; prosperous; thriving
〖兴修〗(动)[xīngxiū]
build; renovate
〖兴许〗[xīngxǔ]
perhaps, maybe

星(名)[xīng]〔颗 kē〕
star
〖星火〗(名)[xīnghuǒ]
spark
〖星火燎原〗[xīnghuǒliáoyuán]
a single spark can start a prairie fire
〖星罗棋布〗[xīngluóqíbù]
scattered about like the pieces on a chess-board; dotted around like stars in the sky; scattered about in every direction
〖星期〗(名)[xīngqī]
week
〖星期二〗(名)[xīngqī'èr]
Tuesday
〖星期六〗(名)[xīngqīliù]
Saturday
〖星期日〗(名)[xīngqīrì]
Sunday
〖星期三〗(名)[xīngqīsān]
Wednesday
〖星期四〗(名)[xīngqīsì]
Thursday
〖星期五〗(名)[xīngqīwǔ]
Friday
〖星期一〗(名)[xīngqīyī]

Monday
〖星系〗(名)[xīngxì]
galaxy
〖星云〗(名)[xīngyún]
nebula
〖星座〗(名)[xīngzuò]
constellation

猩 [xīng]
〖猩红热〗(名)[xīnghóngrè]
scarlet fever
〖猩猩〗(名)[xīngxing]〔只 zhī〕
chimpanzee

腥(形)[xīng]
smelling of fish;rancid;stinking

xíng

刑(名)[xíng]
corporal punishment; punishment
〖刑罚〗(名)[xíngfá]
punishment
〖刑事〗(名)[xíngshì]
matters pertaining to crimes and law (e.g. criminal case, criminal code)
〖刑事犯〗(名)[xíngshìfàn]
criminal

行(动、形)[xíng]
①walk; go ②act; move; do; practise; proceed ③able; competent ④all right; (that) will do
另见 háng

〖行程〗(名)[xíngchéng]
route or distance of travel; itinerary
〖行动〗(动、名)[xíngdòng]
①walk; go; move ②act; do ③deed; action; operation
〖行贿〗[xínghuì]
bribe; corruption
〖行将〗(副)[xíngjiāng]
on the verge of; be going to; soon
〖行径〗(名)[xíngjìng]
(usu.derog.)action;conduct; behaviour
〖行军〗[xíngjūn]
march
〖行李〗(名)[xíngli]
baggage; luggage
〖行人〗(名)[xíngrén]
walker; pedestrian
〖行使〗(动)[xíngshǐ]
exercise; carry out; perform
〖行驶〗(动)[xíngshǐ]
sail; drive
〖行书〗(名)[xíngshū]
cursive script
〖行为〗(名)[xíngwéi]
action; behavior; conduct; deed
〖行星〗(名)[xíngxīng]〔颗 kē〕
planet
〖行凶〗[xíngxiōng]
commit assault or murder
〖行政〗(名)[xíngzhèng]
administration
〖行之有效〗[xíngzhīyǒuxiào]
come into effect; produce results

X

〖行装〗(名)[xíngzhuāng]
clothes and bedding needed for travel
〖行踪〗(名)[xíngzōng]
person's whereabouts

形(名)[xíng]
① shape ② material form ③ appearance
〖形成〗(动)[xíngchéng]
take shape; become; form
〖形而上学〗(名)
[xíng'ér shàngxué]
metaphysics
〖形迹可疑〗[xíngjìkěyí]
suspicious behavior or conduct
〖形容〗(动)[xíngróng]
describe; express by words or looks; modify
〖形容词〗(名)[xíngróngcí]
adjective
〖形式〗(名)[xíngshì]
pattern; form
〖形式主义〗(名)[xíngshìzhǔyì]
formalist method; formalism
〖形势〗(名)[xíngshì]
① geographical outlay ② situation; conditions; circumstances; state of affairs
〖形势逼人〗[xíngshìbīrén]
reality is a compelling force; the situation is pressing
〖形态〗(名)[xíngtài]
① outlook ② form; shape
〖形体〗[xíngtǐ]
① shape (of a person's body), physique body; ② form and structure
〖形象〗(名、形)[xíngxiàng]
image; figure; form
〖形象化〗(动)[xíngxiànghuà]
vivify; picturize; pictorialize
〖形形色色〗(形)[xíngxíng sèsè]
of all shades; of various forms; of all kinds
〖形影不离〗[xíngyǐngbùlí]
(two people) inseparable; follow each other like form and shadow
〖形状〗(名)[xíngzhuàng]
shape; form

型(名)[xíng]
type; pattern; model

xǐng

醒(动)[xǐng]
① awake; wake up ② sober up ③ come to realize
〖醒目〗(形)[xǐngmù]
refreshing to the eye; attractive looking; attract attention
〖醒悟〗(动)[xǐngwù]
come to realize; awaken

xìng

兴[xìng]
另见 xīng
〖兴高采烈〗[xìnggāocǎiliè]
exhilaration; in high spirits; jubilant
〖兴趣〗(名)[xìngqù]
interest

〖兴味〗(名)[xìngwèi]
keen interest
〖兴致〗(名)[xìngzhì]
interest; mood to enjoy
〖兴致勃勃〗[xìngzhìbóbó]
in high spirits

杏(名)[xìng][个 gè]
apricot
〖杏黄〗(形)[xìnghuáng]
apricot yellow

幸[xìng]
〖幸而〗(副)[xìng'ér]
luckily; fortunately
〖幸福〗(形、名)[xìngfú]
happy; fortunate; happiness
〖幸好〗(副)[xìnghǎo]
luckily; fortunately
〖幸亏〗(副)[xìngkuī]
fortunately; luckily; thanks to
〖幸免〗(动)[xìngmiǎn]
escape through good luck; narrow escape
〖幸运〗(形)[xìngyùn]
lucky
〖幸灾乐祸〗[xìngzāilèhuò]
gloat over disaster of other; take pleasure in the calamity of others; be glad when other people are in difficulties

性(名、尾)[xìng]
①nature ②sex ③a suffix
〖性别〗(名)[xìngbié]
sex (male or female)
〖性格〗(名)[xìnggé]
character; temperament; quality; nature
〖性急〗(形)[xìngjí]
impatient; impetuous; quick-tempered
〖性命〗(名)[xìngmìng]
life
〖性能〗(名)[xìngnéng]
properties; function; performance; working capacity
〖性情〗(名)[xìngqíng]
temperament; character; nature
〖性质〗(名)[xìngzhì]
properties; essence; character; nature; quality
〖性状〗(名)[xìngzhuàng]
nature and appearance; characteristics

姓(名、动)[xìng]
surname; (one's) surname is...
〖姓名〗(名)[xìngmíng]
forename and surname

xiōng

凶(形)[xiōng]
①evil, ill; bad ②wicked; brutal; ferocious
〖凶暴〗(形)[xiōngbào]
cruel; brutal
〖凶残〗(形)[xiōngcán]
ferocious; brutal; ruthless; savage
〖凶恶〗(形)[xiōng'è]
ferocious; cruel; vicious; brutal

〖凶狠〗(形)[xiōnghěn]
brutal; cruel
〖凶猛〗(形)[xiōngměng]
ferocious; fierce
〖凶手〗(名)[xiōngshǒu]
murderer
〖凶险〗(形)[xiōngxiǎn]
extremely hazardous; dangerous
〖凶相毕露〗[xiōngxiàngbìlù]
reveal the atrocious features; bare one's fangs

兄(名)[xiōng]
elder brother
〖兄弟〗(名)[xiōngdì]
brothers

汹[xiōng]
〖汹涌澎湃〗
[xiōngyǒngpéngpài]
rise in a surging tide; rise in tempestuous waves; surge forward

胸(名)[xiōng]
bosom; breast
〖胸怀〗(名、动)[xiōnghuái]
① chest; bosom ② mind; outlook; heart; show concern for
〖胸怀祖国〗[xiōnghuáizǔguó]
keep the interests of the country at heart; have one's motherland at heart
〖胸襟〗(名)[xiōngjīn]
breadth of mind; breadth of vision
〖胸膛〗(名)[xiōngtáng]
chest
〖胸有成竹〗[xiōngyǒuchéngzhú]
have a preconceived idea before doing sth.
〖胸中无数〗[xiōngzhōngwúshù]
not sure of (oneself); have no figures in one's head
〖胸中有数〗[xiōngzhōngyǒushù]
have a head for figures

xióng

雄(形)[xióng]
① male ② heroic; valiant; bold; brave ③ strong; superior
〖雄辩〗(名、形)[xióngbiàn]
persuasive argument; cloquent; incontrovertibly
〖雄厚〗(形)[xiónghòu]
tremendous; solid
〖雄健〗(形)[xióngjiàn]
strong; robust; healthy and mighty
〖雄赳赳〗(形)[xióngjiūjiū]
strong; strong and valiant
〖雄师〗(名)[xióngshī]
strong and mighty army
〖雄伟〗(形)[xióngwěi]
great; stately; magnificent; splendid; grand
〖雄文〗(名)[xióngwén]
excellent writings; powerful works
〖雄心〗(名)[xióngxīn]
ambition; lofty aspiration; high aims
〖雄心壮志〗[xióngxīnzhuàngzhì]

lofty aspirations and high aims; a high aspiring mind
〖雄鹰〗(名)[xióngyīng]
[只 zhī] strong and brave eagle
〖雄壮〗(形)[xióngzhuàng]
full of grandeur; stalwart; magnificent; majestic

熊(名)[xióng][只 zhī]
bear
〖熊猫〗(名)[xióngmāo]
[只 zhī]panda
〖熊市〗(名)[xióngshì]
bear market (referring to the decline of prices at the stock market)
〖熊熊〗(形)[xióngxióng]
flaming; raging(e.g. flame)

xiū

休(动)[xiū]
① cease; give up ② rest; retire
〖休会〗[xiūhuì]
adjourn (meeting); stand adjourned; recess
〖休假〗[xiūjià]
on holiday; on leave
〖休克〗(名、动)[xiūkè]
shock; have a shock
〖休戚相关〗[xiūqīxiāngguān]
be bound together (in a common cause); be of close concern to each other; a feeling of solidarity
〖休戚与共〗[xiūqīyǔgòng]
share the same fate; share common weal and woe with
〖休息〗(动)[xiūxi]
rest; relax; repose
〖休想〗(动)[xiūxiǎng]
do not think; never expect
〖休学〗[xiūxué]
drop out of school; give up schooling
〖休养〗(动)[xiūyǎng]
① rest;recuperate; convalesce ② rehabilitation
〖休战〗[xiūzhàn]
truce; ceasefire; armistice
〖休整〗(动)[xiūzhěng]
rest and reorganize; rest and consolidation
〖休止〗(动)[xiūzhǐ]
stop; cease

修(动)[xiū]
① repair; mend; put right ② modify; revise ③ build
〖修辞〗(名)[xiūcí]
rhetoric; the skill of using words effectively
〖修订〗(动)[xiūdìng]
revise; re-edit
〖修复〗(动)[xiūfù]
renovate; restore
〖修改〗(动)[xiūgǎi]
modify; revise; correct; amend
〖修建〗(动)[xiūjiàn]
build; erect
〖修旧利废〗[xiūjiùlìfèi]
repair old things and make use of waste materials
〖修理〗(动)[xiūlǐ]
repair; mend; put right
〖修配〗(动)[xiūpèi]

overhaul; repair and restore to good working order
〖修缮〗(动)[xiūshàn]
repair (buildings)
〖修饰〗(动)[xiūshì]
① make up; beautify ② adorn; decorate; embellish ③ polish (e.g. an article); improve on
〖修养〗(动)[xiūyǎng]
① learning or skill of art and literature ② cultivate
〖修造〗(动)[xiūzào]
build; construct
〖修整〗(动)[xiūzhěng]
keep in good condition; cut even; level (e. g. ground)
〖修正〗(动)[xiūzhèng]
revise; amend; correct
〖修正主义〗(名)[xiūzhèngzhǔyì]
revisionism
〖修筑〗(动)[xiūzhù]
build

羞(形)[xiū]
① shy; bashful ② shameful
〖羞耻〗(形、名)[xiūchǐ]
shameful; ashamed; shame
〖羞答答〗(形)[xiūdādā]
bashful; shy; timid
〖羞愧〗(形)[xiūkuì]
feel ashamed; shame; disgrace

xiǔ

朽(形)[xiǔ]
rotten; decayed
〖朽木〗(名)[xiǔmù]
decayed wood; rotten wood

xiù

秀(形、动)[xiù]
① beautiful; delicate ② burst into; put forth
〖秀丽〗(形)[xiùlì]
delicate; graceful; beautiful (landscape)
〖秀气〗(形)[xiùqi]
refined; delicate; elegant; exquisite

袖(名)[xiù]
sleeve
〖袖手旁观〗[xiùshǒupángguān]
look on with folded arms; stand by with indifference
〖袖章〗(名)[xiùzhāng]
armband; insignia
〖袖珍〗(形)[xiùzhēn]
pocket (edition); small-format (edition); pocket-sized
〖袖子〗(名)[xiùzi][只 zhī]
sleeve

绣(动)[xiù]
embroider
〖绣花〗[xiùhuā]
embroidery; cover with embroidery; doing embroidery

锈(名、动)[xiù]
rust; get rusty

嗅(动)[xiù]
smell
〖嗅觉〗(名)[xiùjué]

sense of smell

xū

须(助动)[xū]
must; have to
〖须知〗(动)[xūzhī]
must bear in mind; must know

虚(形)[xū]
① vacant; empty ② visionary; vague ③ false; sham; fictitious; hypocritical ④ modest ⑤ weak; feeble
〖虚报〗(动)[xūbào]
give a false report
〖虚词〗(名)[xūcí]
grammatical particle; functional word and form word
〖虚构〗(动、名)[xūgòu]
imagine; imagination; invent (e. g. story); fabricate; fiction; invention; fabrication
〖虚假〗(形)[xūjiǎ]
false; sham; unreal; fictitious
〖虚惊〗(动、名)[xūjīng]
cause a false alarm; get alarmed for nothing
〖虚夸〗(动)[xūkuā]
boast; exaggerate
〖虚名〗(名)[xūmíng]
a reputation without the facts to support it; undeserved reputation; unwarranted reputation
〖虚荣〗(形)[xūróng]
vanity; vain glory
〖虚弱〗(形)[xūruò]
feeble; weak
〖虚设〗(动)[xūshè]
nominal; in name; symbolic; titular
〖虚实〗(名)[xūshí]
① hollow and solid; truth and deceit ② true condition
〖虚数〗(名)[xūshù]
imaginary number; imaginary quantity
〖虚脱〗(名、动)[xūtuō]
physical collapse from general debility
〖虚伪〗(形)[xūwěi]
hypocritical; false
〖虚无主义〗(名)[xūwúzhǔyì]
nihilism
〖虚线〗(名)[xūxiàn][条 tiáo]
dotted line
〖虚心〗(形)[xūxīn]
modest; ready to take advice; open-minded
〖虚张声势〗[xūzhāngshēngshì]
make pompous but empty show of (power and influence)

需(动)[xū] need
〖需求〗(名)[xūqiú]
demand; requirement
〖需要〗(动、名)[xūyào]
need; necessary

xú

徐 [xú]
〖徐徐〗(副)[xúxú]
slowly

xǔ

许(动)[xǔ]

X

allow; permit
〖许多〗(形)[xǔduō]
a great many; a lot of; numerous; plenty of
〖许久〗(名)[xǔjiǔ]
a long time; such a long time
〖许可〗(动)[xǔkě]
permit; consent; approve
〖许可证〗(名)[xǔkězhèng]
licence; permit
〖许诺〗(动)[xǔnuò]
promise; give one's word
〖许愿〗[xǔyuàn]
make promise

栩 [xǔ]
〖栩栩如生〗[xǔxǔrúshēng]
like real life; lively; vivid

xù

旭 [xù]
〖旭日〗(名)[xùrì]
the morning sun; the rising sun
〖旭日东升〗[xùrìdōngshēng]
the morning sun rises in the eastern sky; the rising sun in the eastern sky

序(名)[xù]
① order; sequence ② prelude; preface; introduction
〖序幕〗(名)[xùmù]
① prologue; prelude ② the beginning of sth. important
〖序曲〗(名)[xùqǔ]
prelude; overture
〖序数〗(名)[xùshù]
ordinal number
〖序言〗(名)[xùyán]
introduction; preface; foreword

叙(动)[xù]
narrate
〖叙事诗〗(名)[xùshìshī]
〔首 shǒu〕epic poetry
〖叙述〗(动)[xùshù]
describe; narrate; state; exposition
〖叙说〗(动)[xùshuō]
narrate; relate; recount

畜(名)[xù]
animal
另见 chù
〖畜产〗(名)[xùchǎn]
livestock product
〖畜牧〗(名)[xùmù]
livestock breeding; animal husbandry

酗 [xù]
〖酗酒〗(动)[xùjiǔ]
become drunk and violent; hard drinking

绪 [xù]
〖绪论〗(名)[xùlùn]
introduction; preliminary remarks; preface

絮(名)[xù]
a tassel-like cluster
〖絮叨〗(形、动)[xùdāo]

unending and tedious talk; chatter

蓄(动)[xù]
save; hoard up; keep for a long time; store
〖蓄电池〗(名)[xùdiànchí]
storage battery; accumulator; storage cell
〖蓄洪〗[xùhóng]
flood storage; water retention
〖蓄谋〗(动)[xùmóu]
conceive a plot in secret; harbour a long-intended conspiracy
〖蓄意〗(动)[xùyì]
be calculated; deliberate

xuān

宣(动)[xuān]
declare; publish; advertise; propagate
〖宣布〗(动)[xuānbù]
declare; announce; proclaim
〖宣称〗(动)[xuānchēng]
make known; declare; announce
〖宣传〗(动、名)[xuānchuán]
propagate; advertise; publicize; propaganda; publicity
〖宣传画〗(名)[xuānchuánhuà]
〔张 zhāng〕propaganda picture
〖宣读〗(动)[xuāndú]
read out
〖宣告〗(动)[xuāngào]
proclaim; declare; make an announcement
〖宣讲〗(动)[xuānjiǎng]
explain (e.g. policy, document)
〖宣判〗(动)[xuānpàn]
give decision in a case; pass sentence; pass judgement
〖宣誓〗[xuānshì]
swear; take an oath
〖宣言〗(名)[xuānyán]
declaration; manifesto
〖宣扬〗(动)[xuānyáng]
advocate; advertise; praise; play up
〖宣战〗[xuānzhàn]
declare war; declaration of war

喧[xuān]
〖喧宾夺主〗[xuānbīnduózhǔ]
(lit.) the guest takes precedence over the host; (fig.) minor takes precedence over a major issue
〖喧哗〗(动)[xuānhuá]
be noisy; tumultuous; clamour
〖喧嚣〗(动)[xuānxiāo]
clamour; disturbingly noisy; bluster

xuán

玄(形)[xuán]
profound; mysterious; subtle
〖玄虚〗(名)[xuánxū]
trick; mystery; abstrusencss

悬(动)[xuán]
①hang; suspend ②think of
〖悬案〗(名)[xuán'àn]
①unsettled legal case ②undecided question

〖悬而未决〗[xuán'érwèijué]
pending; waiting for decision; not yet decided; outstanding
〖悬挂〗(动)[xuánguà]
hang up; suspend
〖悬空〗(动)[xuánkōng]
in the air; dangle; without basis
〖悬念〗(动)[xuánniàn]
constantly think of (person in absence); keep sb. in suspense
〖悬殊〗(形)[xuánshū]
wide disparity; wide gap between; inequalities in ...
〖悬崖〗(名)[xuányá]
cliff; precipice
〖悬崖绝壁〗[xuányájuébì]
overhanging cliff; precipice
〖悬崖勒马〗[xuányálèmǎ]
(lit.) rein in one's horse on the brink of a precipice; (fig.) ward off disaster at the critical moment; stop doing sth. before it is too late

旋 [xuán]
另见 xuàn
〖旋律〗(名)[xuánlǜ]
melody; rhythm; tunefulness; cadence
〖旋涡〗(名)[xuánwō]
a whirlpool; an eddy; vortex
〖旋转〗(动)[xuánzhuǎn]
revolve; spin; rotate

xuǎn

选(动)[xuǎn]
①select; choose ②elect
〖选拔〗(动)[xuǎnbá]
select; choose; recommend
〖选集〗(名)[xuǎnjí]
selected works
〖选辑〗(动)[xuǎnjí]
compile; edit; editing
〖选举〗(动、名)[xuǎnjǔ]
elect; vote; election
〖选举权〗(名)[xuǎnjǔquán]
the right to vote (or elect)
〖选民〗(名)[xuǎnmín]
voter; elector
〖选派〗(动)[xuǎnpài]
select and appoint
〖选票〗(名)[xuǎnpiào]
ballot paper; ballot
〖选手〗(名)[xuǎnshǒu]
chosen men; player (of sport, contest); contestant; competiter
〖选修〗(动)[xuǎnxiū]
take an optional subject
〖选择〗(动)[xuǎnzé]
pick and choose; make the choice; take one's preference
〖选种〗[xuǎnzhǒng]
seed selection

癣(名)[xuǎn]
general term for various skin diseases (e.g. pityriasis, favus)

xuàn

炫 [xuàn]
〖炫耀〗(动)[xuànyào]
make a display; show off; boast;

cut a dash

绚 [xuàn]
〖绚烂〗(形)[xuànlàn]
flashing; brilliant with lighting and colours
〖绚丽〗(形)[xuànlì]
brilliant with colours

旋 (动)[xuàn]
rotate; whirl
另见 xuán
〖旋床〗(名)[xuànchuáng]
lathe; turning machine
〖旋风〗(名)[xuànfēng]
〔阵 zhèn〕whirlwind

渲 [xuàn]
〖渲染〗(动)[xuànrǎn]
① add touches (of colour) ② play up; exaggerate

xuē

削 [xuē]
另见 xiāo
〖削减〗(动)[xuējiǎn]
cut down; reduce
〖削弱〗(动)[xuēruò]
weaken; impair; curtail
〖削足适履〗[xuēzúshìlǚ]
cut the feet to fit the shoes

靴 (名)[xuē]
boot
〖靴子〗(名)[xuēzi]〔双 shuāng〕
boots

xué

穴 (名)[xué]
① cave; hole ② acupuncture points
〖穴位〗(名)[xuéwèi]〔个 gè〕
certain points of human body containing vital arteries; acupuncture points

学 (动)[xué]
① learn; study ② imitate
〖学报〗(名)[xuébào]
academic periodical (e. g. college periodical)
〖学潮〗(名)[xuécháo]
tide of student movement
〖学费〗(名)[xuéfèi]
school fees; tuition
〖学分制〗(名)[xuéfēnzhì]
the credit system
〖学风〗(名)[xuéfēng]
style of study
〖学工〗[xuégōng]
learn industrial production; learn from workers
〖学籍〗(名)[xuéjí]
record of registration as qualifications for studying in schools or colleges
〖学军〗[xuéjūn]
learn military affairs; learn from soldiers (P.L.A.)
〖学科〗(名)[xuékē]
①subjects in school or college ② branch of earning such as physics, chemistry, etc.
〖学历〗(名)[xuélì]

curriculum vitae; record of schooling
〖学龄〗(名)[xuélíng]
school age
〖学龄儿童〗[xuélíngértóng]
children of school age
〖学名〗(名)[xuémíng]
scientific name
〖学年〗(名)[xuénián]
academic year
〖学农〗[xuénóng]
learn agricultural production; learn from peasants
〖学派〗(名)[xuépài]
school of thought; schools
〖学期〗(名)[xuéqī]
semester; academic term
〖学生〗(名)[xuésheng]
student; pupil
〖学生证〗(名)[xuéshengzhèng]
student's identity card
〖学时〗(名)[xuéshí]
hours of study
〖学识〗(名)[xuéshí]
knowledge; learning
〖学术〗(名)[xuéshù]
academic knowledge
〖学说〗(名)[xuéshuō]
theory; teachings; doctrine
〖学徒工〗(名)[xuétúgōng]
apprentice
〖学位〗(名)[xuéwèi]
academic degree
〖学文〗[xuéwén]
learn book knowledge; learn literary knowledge
〖学问〗(名)[xuéwèn]
learning; knowledge
〖学习〗(动)[xuéxí]
learn; study
〖学习班〗(名)[xuéxíbān]
study group; study class
〖学校〗(名)[xuéxiào]
school
〖学业〗(名)[xuéyè]
studies; lessons and school assignments
〖学员〗(名)[xuéyuán]
trainee; participant of training cause or institution as different from regular student; student (e. g. worker-peasant-soldier student)
〖学院〗(名)[xuéyuàn]〔所 suǒ〕
academy; institute; college
〖学者〗(名)[xuézhě]
scholar
〖学制〗(名)[xuézhì]
educational system; school system; arrangements for schooling

xuě

雪(名、动)[xuě]
①snow ②avenge
〖雪白〗(形)[xuěbái]
snow-white
〖雪崩〗(名)[xuěbēng]
snow-slide; avalanche
〖雪耻〗[xuěchǐ]
wipe out shame; avenge on
〖雪花〗(名)[xuěhuā]
snow-flakes
〖雪茄〗(名)[xuějiā]〔支 zhī〕
cigar

〖雪亮〗(形)[xuěliàng]
bright as snow
〖雪橇〗(名)[xuěqiāo]
sledge
〖雪球〗(名)[xuěqiú]
snowball
〖雪人〗(名)[xuěrén]
snowman
〖雪山〗(名)[xuěshān]〔座 zuò〕
snow-covered mountain
〖雪中送炭〗
[xuězhōngsòngtàn] (lit.)offer fuel in snowy weather; (fig.)timely assistance

xuè

血(名)[xuè]
blood
另见 xiě
〖血管〗(名)[xuèguǎn]〔条 tiáo〕
blood vessel
〖血海深仇〗[xuèhǎishēnchóu]
huge debt in blood; immense and deep-seated hatred
〖血汗〗(名)[xuèhàn]
sweat and blood; hard toil
〖血红〗(形)[xuèhóng]
bloodred(colour)
〖血迹〗(名)[xuèjī]
blood-stain
〖血口喷人〗[xuèkǒupēnrén]
make unfounded and scurrilous attacks upon others
〖血泪〗(名)[xuèlèi]
blood and tears
〖血泪斑斑〗[xuèlèibānbān]
stained with blood and tears
〖血泊〗(名)[xuèpō]
bloodbath
〖血球〗(名)[xuèqiú]
blood cell; blood corpuscle
〖血肉〗(名)[xuèròu]
flesh and blood
〖血肉相连〗[xuèròuxiānglián]
flesh and blood relationship; be related by flesh and blood; have close ties with
〖血统〗(名)[xuètǒng]
blood heritage
〖血腥〗(形)[xuèxīng]
bloody; bloodstained; sanguinary
〖血型〗(名)[xuèxíng]
blood group; blood type
〖血压〗(名)[xuèyā]
blood pressure
〖血压计〗(名)[xuèyājì]
sphygmomanometer
〖血液〗(名)[xuèyè]
blood
〖血缘〗(名)[xuèyuán]
blood relationship; consanguinity
〖血债〗(名)[xuèzhài]
debt in blood; blood-debt
〖血战〗(动)[xuèzhàn]
fight to the finish; a war to the finish; fight to the last drop of one's blood

xūn

勋[xūn]
〖勋章〗(名)[xūnzhāng]〔枚 méi〕
decoration; medal

熏(动)[xūn]
be stained; be imbued with; be nurtured by; be smoked
〖熏染〗(动)[xūnrǎn]
(usually derog.)have slow but deep-going influence over sb.
〖熏肉〗(名)[xūnròu]
smoked meat
〖熏陶〗(动)[xūntáo]
have gradual good influence over sb.; thinking or learning from people or environment constantly contacted; be nurtured by

xún

旬(名)[xún]
ten-day period; duration of ten years

寻(动)[xún]
find; seek; look for
〖寻常〗(形)[xúncháng]
ordinary; usual
〖寻觅〗(动)[xúnmì]
look for; search; find
〖寻求〗(动)[xúnqiú]
seek; look for
〖寻找〗(动)[xúnzhǎo]
look for; find; search; hunt for

驯(动)[xún]
tame; subdue
〖驯服〗(动、形)[xúnfú]
tame; make obey; obedient; subdued; docile

巡(动)[xún]
patrol; go on circuit and inspect
〖巡回〗(动)[xúnhuí]
go on circuit; make the circuit of
〖巡回医疗〗[xúnhuíyīliáo]
mobile medical service
〖巡警〗(名)[xúnjǐng]
policeman on patrol
〖巡逻〗(动)[xúnluó]
patrol
〖巡视〗(动)[xúnshì]
make one's rounds of; supervise; inspect
〖巡洋舰〗(名)[xúnyángjiàn]
〔艘 sōu〕a cruiser

询[xún]
〖询问〗(动)[xúnwèn]
inquire; ask

循[xún]
〖循规蹈矩〗[xúnguīdǎojǔ]
stick to convention; observe due decorum; follow the custom or law
〖循环〗(动)[xúnhuán]
move in cycles; circulate; recur
〖循环赛〗(名)[xúnhuánsài]
round robin
〖循环小数〗[xúnhuánxiǎoshù]
recurrent decimal
〖循序渐进〗[xúnxùjiànjìn]
progress step by step; advance by regular steps; develop by

gradations; follow in proper sequence and make steady progress

〖循循善诱〗[xúnxúnshànyòu]
lead one gradually into good practices

xùn

训(动)[xùn]
train; order; command; teach

〖训斥〗(动)[xùnchì]
scold; rebuke; reprimand

〖训练〗(动)[xùnliàn]
train; drill

讯(名)[xùn]
news; intelligence

〖讯问〗(动)[xùnwèn]
① try at court ② inquire after information

迅[xùn]

〖迅猛〗(形)[xùnměng]
fast; rapid; swift and violent

〖迅速〗(形)[xùnsù]
speedy; fast

逊[xùn]

〖逊色〗(形)[xùnsè]
inferior by comparison; compare unfavourably

殉(动)[xùn]
die for; lay down one's life for

〖殉难〗[xùnnàn]
die for one's country or just cause

〖殉葬〗(动)[xùnzàng]
be buried alive with the dead

〖殉葬品〗(名)[xùnzàngpǐn]
a funerary object; a sacrificial object

〖殉职〗[xùnzhí]
die a martyr at one's post

yā

压(动)[yā]

① bear down on;exert pressure on ② oppress;hold ... back; suppress; repress; hold down; prevail over; subdue

〖压倒〗(动)[yādǎo]
prevail over; overwhelm; overcome; overpower

〖压服〗(动)[yāfú]
domineer; vanquish; subdue; coerce into submission; suppress; overwhelm

〖压力〗(名)[yālì]
pressure; force of pressure

〖压力锅〗(名)[yālìguō]
pressure cooker

〖压路机〗(名)[yālùjī]
road roller; roller

〖压迫〗(动)[yāpò]
① subdue; oppress ② press hard on; bear down upon

〖压迫者〗(名)[yāpòzhě]
oppressor

〖压岁钱〗(名)[yāsuìqián]
money given to children as a lunar New Year gift

〖压缩〗(动)[yāsuō]
① compress; compact ② reduce; cut down

〖压抑〗(动)[yāyì]
suppress; keep down; be constricted; hold ... back

〖压韵〗[yā yùn] rhyme

〖压榨〗(动)[yāzhà]
① squash; squeeze; bleed ② oppress and exploit; fleece

〖压制〗(动)[yāzhì]
suppress; stifle; smother; hold down; muzzle; clamp down

呀(叹)[yā]

int. Ah!

另见 ya

押(动)[yā]

① mortgage; deposit ② detain in custody
〖押金〗(名)[yājīn]
deposit; cash pledge; security
〖押送〗(动)[yāsòng]
turn sb. over; send under escort

鸦 [yā]
〖鸦片战争〗[YāpiànZhànzhēng]
the Opium War
〖鸦雀无声〗[yāquèwúshēng]
dead silent

鸭 (名)[yā]
duck
〖鸭子〗(名)[yāzi]〔只 zhī〕
duck

yá

牙 (名)[yá]
a tooth
〖牙齿〗(名)[yáchǐ]
tooth
〖牙床〗(名)[yáchuáng]
① jaw; alveolus ② ivory-inlaid bed
〖牙雕〗(名)[yádiāo]
ivory carving
〖牙膏〗(名)[yágāo]
toothpaste; dental cream
〖牙科〗(名)[yákē]
dentistry
〖牙签儿〗(名)[yáqiānr]
toothpick
〖牙刷〗(名)[yáshuā]〔把 bǎ〕
toothbrush

芽 (名)[yá]
sprout; shoot; bud

蚜 (名)[yá]
aphis
〖蚜虫〗(名)[yáchóng]
aphis

yǎ

哑 (动、形)[yǎ]
dumb; mute
〖哑巴〗(名)[yǎba]
dumb; a dumb person
〖哑口无言〗[yǎkǒuwúyán]
dumb-founded

雅 [yǎ]
〖雅观〗(形)[yǎguān]
nice looking; nice appearance
〖雅俗共赏〗[yǎsúgòngshǎng]
(literally and artistic works) enjoyed by the socalled scholars and the common people alike (arch.)
〖雅致〗(形)[yǎzhì]
refined; elegant; beautiful

yà

亚 [yà]
〖亚军〗(名)[yàjūn]
runner-up; winner of second prize in contests
〖亚热带〗(名)[yàrèdài]
subtropics
〖亚运会〗(名)[Yàyùnhuì]
Asian Games

〖亚洲〗(名)[Yàzhōu]
Asia

ya

呀(助)[ya]
a particle, Oh!
另见 yā

yān

咽(名)[yān]
the throat
另见 yàn
〖咽喉〗(名)[yānhóu]
① throat ② vital communication line

烟(名)[yān]
① smoke ② tobacco; cigarette
〖烟草〗(名)[yāncǎo]
tobacco
〖烟囱〗(名)[yāncōng]
chimney
〖烟袋〗(名)[yāndài]
tobacco pipe
〖烟斗〗(名)[yāndǒu]
tobacco pipe
〖烟灰〗(名)[yānhuī]
cigarette ashes
〖烟灰缸〗(名)[yānhuīgāng]
ash tray
〖烟火〗(名)[yānhuo]
fireworks
〖烟煤〗(名)[yānméi]
soft coal; bituminous coal
〖烟幕〗(名)[yānmù]
① smokescreen ② smoke; smoke cloud
〖烟幕弹〗(名)[yānmùdàn]
① smoke-bomb ② smokescreen
〖烟丝〗(名)[yānsī]
pipe tobacco
〖烟筒〗(名)[yāntong]
stove pipe; chimney
〖烟雾〗(名)[yānwù]
mist; haze
〖烟消云散〗[yānxiāoyúnsàn]
vanish without a trace; disappear in a flash
〖烟叶〗(名)[yānyè]
tobacco leaf
〖烟嘴儿〗(名)[yānzuǐr]
cigarette holder

阉[yān]
〖阉割〗(动)[yāngē]
castrate; emasculate; cut sth. out of (e.g. an article)

淹(动)[yān]
drown; soak
〖淹没〗(动)[yānmò]
drown thoroughly (in water); submerge; immerse

yán

延(动)[yán]
① prolong; lengthen ② postpone; put off; delay ③ invite (e.g. a teacher)
〖延长〗(动)[yáncháng]
prolong; lengthen
〖延长线〗(名)[yánchángxiàn]
prolonged line; prolongation

Y

of a line
〖延迟〗(动)[yánchí]
postpone; delay
〖延搁〗(动)[yángē]
postpone; delay; hold over
〖延缓〗(动)[yánhuǎn]
postpone; be postponed; retard; delay
〖延期〗[yánqī]
postpone; put off
〖延伸〗(动)[yánshēn]
extend; spread to; stretch
〖延续〗(动)[yánxù]
continue
〖延展性〗(名)[yánzhǎnxìng]
ductility; extensibility

严(形)[yán]
①rigid; exact; strait ②strict ③harsh; stern; severe; serious; solemn
〖严打〗(动,名)[yándǎ]
crack down on; punish severely
〖严冬〗(名)[yándōng]
severe winter
〖严防〗(动)[yánfáng]
be on sharp guard against; take strict precautions against; maintain high vigilance
〖严格〗(形、动)[yángé]
strict; exact; be strict with
〖严寒〗(形)[yánhán]
severely cold
〖严紧〗(形)[yánjǐn]
rigid; carefully guarded; tightly organized
〖严谨〗(形)[yánjǐn]
conscientious and careful; strict and cautious
〖严禁〗(动)[yánjìn]
strictly forbid; strict prohibition
〖严峻〗(形)[yánjùn]
severe; vigorous; stern
〖严酷〗(形)[yánkù]
① stern; strict; severe ② cruel; ruthless; unrelenting
〖严厉〗(形)[yánlì]
harsh; severe; stern
〖严密〗(形)[yánmì]
closeknit; tight; close
〖严明〗(形)[yánmíng]
stern and impartial; strict and just
〖严实〗(形)[yánshi]
close; tight
〖严守〗(动)[yánshǒu]
strictly observe; strictly abide by; maintain strictly
〖严肃〗(形)[yánsù]
strict; earnest; conscientious; serious; stern
〖严阵以待〗[yánzhènyǐdài]
stand ready in battle array; remain in combat readiness
〖严整〗(形)[yánzhěng]
orderly; neat; well-disciplined
〖严正〗(形)[yánzhèng]
solemn; impartial; strict; serious
〖严重〗(形)[yánzhòng]
severe; serious; stern; grave

言(名、动)[yán]

① speech; words ② say; talk; tell
〖言不由衷〗[yánbùyóuzhōng]
one's words belie his mind insincere in one's words hypocritical
〖言传身教〗[yánchuánshēnjiào]
teach sb. by words and influence him by deed
〖言过其实〗[yánguòqíshí]
exaggerate; bombast
〖言简意赅〗[yánjiǎnyìgāi]
what one says is precise and to the point
〖言论〗(名)[yánlùn]
speech; public opinion
〖言听计从〗[yántīngjìcóng]
readily listen to one's advice; readily accept
〖言外之意〗[yánwàizhīyì]
insinuation; implication; meaning between lines
〖言行〗(名)[yánxíng]
words and deeds
〖言行不一〗[yánxíngbùyī]
say one thing and do another; one's words and deed are at complete variance; one's acts belie one's words
〖言语〗(名)[yányǔ]
spoken language; words
〖言者无罪,闻者足戒〗
[yánzhě wúzuì, wénzhězújiè]
blame not the speaker but be warned by his words

岩(名)[yán]

rock; cliff
〖岩石〗(名)[yánshí]
rock

炎(形、名)[yán]

① hot ② inflammation; flame
〖炎热〗(形)[yánrè]
blazing hot; sweltering

沿(动、名、介)[yán]

① follow (e.g. sb.'s example) ② edge; border ③ along
〖沿革〗(名)[yángé]
course of development and changes
〖沿海〗(名)[yánhǎi]
along the coast; in-shore; offshore
〖沿海地区〗[yánhǎidìqū]
coastal region; coastland
〖沿途〗(名)[yántú]
along the road; on the way
〖沿袭〗(动)[yánxí]
follow the old conventions
〖沿用〗(动)[yányòng]
continue to use
〖沿着〗(介)[yánzhe]
along

研(动)[yán]

① grind; grind up ② study; discuss; investigate; research
〖研究〗(动)[yánjiū]
research; study
〖研究生〗(名)[yánjiūshēng]
graduate student; postgraduate

〖研究所〗(名)[yánjiūsuǒ]
research institute
〖研究员〗(名)[yánjiūyuán]
research fellow
〖研讨〗(动)[yántǎo]
study and discuss
〖研讨会〗(名)[yántǎohuì]
workshop; seminar; symposium

盐(名)[yán]
salt
〖盐碱地〗(名)[yánjiǎndì]
saline and alkaline land
〖盐酸〗(名)[yánsuān]
hydrochloric acid

筵[yán]
〖筵席〗(名)[yánxí]
a banquet; full dinner; feast

颜(名)[yán]
① facial appearance; countenance ② colour
〖颜料〗(名)[yánliào]
dyestuff
〖颜色〗(名)[yánsè]
①colour ②countenance; facial expression

yǎn

奄[yǎn]
〖奄奄一息〗[yǎnyǎnyīxī]
scarcely a breath left; on the point of dying; at one's last gasp

俨[yǎn]
〖俨然〗(形)[yǎnrán]
① impressive; solemn ② look like ③ orderly

掩(动)[yǎn]
① cover up ② close ③ waylay; ambush
〖掩蔽〗(动)[yǎnbì]
cover up; shelter
〖掩藏〗(动)[yǎncáng]
hide; lie concealed
〖掩耳盗铃〗[yǎn'ěrdàolíng]
(lit.) stuff one's ears when stealing a bell; (fig.) self-deceit
〖掩盖〗(动)[yǎngài]
cover up; conceal; hide
〖掩护〗(动)[yǎnhù]
provide cover; under cover of; camouflage
〖掩埋〗(动)[yǎnmái]
bury
〖掩饰〗(动)[yǎnshì]
cover up; conceal; mask; under the cloak of
〖掩体〗(名)[yǎntǐ]
emplacement; pill-box; blindage; dug-out

眼(名、量)[yǎn]〔只 zhī〕
① the eye ② hole ③ a measure word (e.g. a well)
〖眼高手低〗[yǎngāoshǒudī]
have high aim but no real ability

〖眼光〗(名)[yǎnguāng]
① vision; eyesight; insight ② judgement
〖眼红〗(形)[yǎnhóng]
① envious; jealous; repine at (e.g. other's prosperity) ② angry look
〖眼花缭乱〗[yǎnhuāliáoluàn]
dazzling
〖眼界〗(名)[yǎnjiè]
field of vision; range of experience
〖眼睛〗(名)[yǎnjing]〔只 zhī〕
eye
〖眼镜〗(名)[yǎnjìng]〔副 fù〕
spectacles; glasses
〖眼看〗(动、副)[yǎnkàn]
① at once; immediately ② let things slide; give way ③ see ... with one's own eyes
〖眼科〗(名)[yǎnkē]
ophthalmic department; ophthalmology
〖眼泪〗(名)[yǎnlèi]
tears
〖眼力〗(名)[yǎnlì]
① vision ② power of discrimination
〖眼明手快〗[yǎnmíngshǒukuài]
quick of eye and deft of hand
〖眼前〗(名)[yǎnqián]
in the present moment; immediate; under one's nose
〖眼球〗(名)[yǎnqiú]
eyeball
〖眼色〗(名)[yǎnsè]
look; glance
〖眼神〗(名)[yǎnshén]
look; expression in one's eyes
〖眼生〗(形)[yǎnshēng]
looking unfamiliar
〖眼熟〗(形)[yǎnshú]
familiar-looking
〖眼中钉〗(名)[yǎnzhōngdīng]
a thorn in the flesh; an eyesore; a thorn in one's side

演 (动)[yǎn]
① evolve; develop ② deliver a speech ③ (math.) operate ④ perform; act
〖演变〗(动)[yǎnbiàn]
evolve; develop; evolution
〖演唱〗(动)[yǎnchàng]
sing for the audience
〖演出〗(动、名)[yǎnchū]
present; perform; put on performance; play; show
〖演技〗(名)[yǎnjì]
acting skill; virtuosity; acting
〖演示〗(动)[yǎnshì]
demonstrate; show
〖演说〗(动、名)[yǎnshuō]
deliver a speech; lecture
〖演算〗(动)[yǎnsuàn]
do exercise in mathematics; operate
〖演习〗(动)[yǎnxí]
exercise; manoeuvre
〖演义〗(名)[yǎnyì]
historical novel
〖演绎〗(动)[yǎnyì]

deduce
〖演员〗(名)[yǎnyuán]
actor; performer
〖演奏〗(动)[yǎnzòu]
play or perform on musical instrument

yàn

厌(动)[yàn]
①be tired of ②loathe; dislike
〖厌烦〗(动)[yànfán]
feel annoyed; be tired of
〖厌倦〗(动)[yànjuàn]
be weary of; fatigued; grow tired of
〖厌恶〗(动)[yànwù]
detest; loathe; hate; dislike
〖厌战〗[yànzhàn]
be loath to continue fighting battles; war-weariness; battle fatigue

咽(动)[yàn]
swallow
另见 yān

艳(形)[yàn]
beautiful; resplendent; attractive
〖艳丽〗(形)[yànlì]
beautiful; attractive; gorgeous

唁[yàn]
〖唁电〗(名)[yàndiàn]
message of condolence

宴(名)[yàn]
banquet; feast
〖宴会〗(名)[yànhuì]
dinner party; banquet
〖宴请〗(动)[yànqǐng]
invite to dinner; give a dinner

验(动)[yàn]
inspect; examine
〖验收〗(动)[yànshōu]
check before reception

谚[yàn]
〖谚语〗(名)[yànyǔ]
proverb; idiom; saying

雁(名)[yàn]〔只 zhī〕
wild goose

燕(名)[yàn]
swallow
〖燕子〗(名)[yànzi]〔只 zhī〕
swallow (bird)

yāng

秧(名)[yāng]
①seedlings ②young fry
〖秧歌〗(名)[yāngge]
Yangko dance; Yangko opera; song accompanied by dance
〖秧苗〗(名)[yāngmiáo]
〔株 zhū〕seedling of any plant nursery (e.g. rice seedling)
〖秧田〗(名)[yāngtián]
〔块 kuài〕paddy field; a field

where rice seedlings are raised

yáng

扬(动)[yáng]
①raise;lift ②throw up ③flutter; soar ④praise
〖扬长避短〗[yángchángbìduǎn]
make the best use of the advantages and bypass the disadvantages; develop the strong points and avoid the weak ones
〖扬长而去〗[yángcháng'érqù]
shake the sleeves and go away haughtily
〖扬场〗[yángcháng]
winnow
〖扬眉吐气〗[yángméitǔqì]
be elated;feel proud;hold one's head high
〖扬弃〗(动)[yángqì]
discard; abandon
〖扬水站〗(名)[yángshuǐzhàn]
water-raising station
〖扬言〗(动)[yángyán]
clamour; make known; claim; announce openly

羊(名)[yáng]〔只 zhī〕
sheep; goat
〖羊肠小道〗
[yángchángxiǎodào]
small winding path
〖羊羔〗(名)[yánggāo]〔只 zhī〕
lamb; kid
〖羊倌儿〗(名)[yángguānr]
shepherd
〖羊毛〗(名)[yángmáo]
sheep's wool
〖羊毛出在羊身上〗
[yángmáochūzàiyángshēn shàng]
after all,the wool still comes from the sheep's back;after all, it is the consumer who pays; in the long run, whatever you're given, you pay for it
〖羊肉〗(名)[yángròu]
mutton

阳(名)[yáng]
① sun ② anode
〖阳春白雪〗[yángchūnbáixuě]
"The Spring Snow"—a song of the 3rd Cent.B.C.which was on a higher level than the "下里巴人"("Song of the Rustic Poor")
〖阳奉阴违〗[yángfèngyīnwéi]
(lit.) outwardly compliant but inwardly unsubmissive; (fig.) feign compliance; comply in public but oppose in private
〖阳光〗(名)[yángguāng]
sunshine; sunlight
〖阳极〗(名)[yángjí]
anode
〖阳历〗(名)[yánglì]
solar calendar
〖阳平〗(名)[yángpíng]
the second tone of a Chinese character
〖阳台〗(名)[yángtái]
balcony
〖阳性〗(名)[yángxìng]
① the male sex; masculinity②

positive

杨(名)[yáng]
aspen
〖杨树〗(名)[yángshù]〔棵 kē〕
aspen tree

洋(名、形)[yáng]
①seas; oceans②foreign③modern
〖洋奴哲学〗[yángnúzhéxué]
philosophy of servility to things foreign; philosophy of servile dependence on foreigners for everything
〖洋为中用〗
[yángwéizhōngyòng]
make foreign things serve China
〖洋洋得意〗[yángyángdéyì]
beside oneself with glee; become wild with joy
〖洋溢〗(动)[yángyì]
be full of; fill with

yǎng

仰(动)[yǎng]
①face upward; look up②admire ③hope; rely on
〖仰慕〗(动)[yǎngmù]
admire and respect
〖仰望〗(动)[yǎngwàng]
①look up②look up to
〖仰泳〗(名)[yǎngyǒng]
back stroke (in swimming)
〖仰仗〗(动)[yǎngzhàng]
rely on; depend on

养(动)[yǎng]
①keep②raise; feed ③give birth ④cultivate; bring up ⑤care for
〖养病〗[yǎngbìng]
convalesce; recuperate from illness through rest and medical treatment
〖养分〗(名)[yǎngfèn]
nutritive value of (food)
〖养活〗(动)[yǎnghuo]
①give birth②feed; raise
〖养精蓄锐〗[yǎngjīngxùruì]
build up one's strength; conserve strength and store up energy
〖养老保险〗[yǎnglǎobǎoxiǎn]
endowment insurance
〖养老金〗(名)[yǎnglǎojīn]
old-age pension
〖养料〗(名)[yǎngliào]
nutrition; nourishment
〖养伤〗[yǎngshāng]
on leave to recuperate from one's wounds
〖养神〗[yǎngshén]
refresh one's spirit by keeping quiet (for a while)
〖养育〗(动)[yǎngyù]
bring up; foster
〖养尊处优〗[yǎngzūnchǔyōu]
revel in a high position and indulge in comfort

氧(名)[yǎng]
oxygen
〖氧化〗(动)[yǎnghuà]

oxidize
〖氧化物〗(名)[yǎnghuàwù]
oxides

痒 (动)[yǎng]
itch

yàng

样 (名、量)[yàng]
① pattern; model; kind; form; shape; sample ② manner; figure; feature
〖样板〗(名)[yàngbǎn]
① templets ② model
〖样品〗(名)[yàngpǐn]
sample; specimen
〖样式〗(名)[yàngshì]
style; form; pattern
〖样子〗(名)[yàngzi]
① pattern; sample; shape ② manner; figure; feature

yāo

夭 [yāo]
〖夭折〗(动)[yāozhé]
die young; early death

妖 (名)[yāo]
evil spirit
〖妖风〗(名)[yāofēng]〔股 gǔ〕
evil winds; evil blast; vicious blast
〖妖魔鬼怪〗[yāomóguǐguài]
monsters of every description; demons and ghosts; demons and monsters
〖妖娆〗(形)[yāoráo]
charming

要 [yāo]
另见 yào
〖要求〗(动、名)[yāoqiú]
demand; ask; request
〖要挟〗(动)[yāoxié]
coerce; extort

腰 (名)[yāo]
waist
〖腰带〗(名)[yāodài]
belt; girdle

邀 (动)[yāo]
invite
〖邀请〗(动、名)[yāoqǐng]
invite; invitation

yáo

窑 (名)[yáo]
① kiln ② cave dwelling ③ mine pit
〖窑洞〗(名)[yáodòng]〔个 gè〕
cave residence; cave dwelling

谣 (名)[yáo]
① folk song; nursery rhymes ② rumour
〖谣传〗(动、名)[yáochuán]
rumour; hearsay; misinform
〖谣言〗(名)[yáoyán]
rumour

摇 (动)[yáo]

shake; quake; flutter; wag

〖摇摆〗(动)[yáobǎi]

stagger; move to and fro; vacillate; waver

〖摇动〗(动)[yáodòng]

shake; wave; swing

〖摇晃〗(动)[yáohuàng]

tremble; flutter; sway

〖摇篮〗(名)[yáolán]

cradle

〖摇旗呐喊〗[yáoqínàhǎn]

wave the flag and shout; functioning as followers or supporters; clamour

〖摇手〗[yáoshǒu]

make a hand motion showing disapproval

〖摇头〗[yáotóu]

shake one's head

〖摇尾乞怜〗[yáowěiqǐlián]

wag the tail and flatter; fawn on

〖摇摇欲坠〗[yáoyáoyùzhuì]

totter; shaky; crumble

遥(形)[yáo]

far away; remote

〖遥感〗[yáogǎn]

remote sensing

〖遥控〗(动)[yáokòng]

remote control

〖遥控开关〗[yáokòngkāiguān]

teleswitch

〖遥相呼应〗[yáoxiānghūyìng]

action in cooperation with each other across a great distance

〖遥遥〗(形)[yáoyáo]

faraway; remote

〖遥远〗(形)[yáoyuǎn]

faraway; long (journey, etc.); remote

yǎo

杳[yǎo]

〖杳无音信〗[yǎowúyīnxìn]

no tidings have been heard for a long time; no news has been received from sb. for a long time

咬(动)[yǎo]

①clench (teeth); bite ②fix

〖咬文嚼字〗[yǎowénjiáozì]

pedantry; mince words in speech or writing; talk pedantically

〖咬牙切齿〗[yǎoyáqièchǐ]

gnash one's teeth and show deep-seated hatred; bare one's fangs and show one's inveterate hatred

舀(动)[yǎo]

ladle up

yào

药(名)[yào]

medicine

〖药材〗(名)[yàocái]

medical herbs; medicinal crops

〖药厂〗(名)[yàochǎng]

pharmaceutical factory

〖药方〗(名)[yàofāng]

prescription; medical recipe

〖药房〗(名)[yàofáng]

pharmacy; drugstore; dispensary
〖药费〗(名)[yàofèi]
fees for medicine; medical fees
〖药膏〗(名)[yàogāo]
medical ointment
〖药棉〗(名)[yàomián]
antiseptic cotton
〖药片〗(名)[yàopiàn]
tablet of medicine
〖药品〗(名)[yàopǐn]
medicine
〖药水〗(名)[yàoshuǐ]〔瓶 píng〕
liquid medicine
〖药丸〗(名)[yàowán]
pill (medicine)

要(动、助动)[yào]
① want; need to; desire ② ask; request ③ going to ④ must; should; need
另见 yāo
〖要不〗(连)[yàobù]
otherwise; if not
〖要不得〗[yàobude]
intolerable; unacceptable; no good
〖要不是〗(连)[yàobùshì]
had it not been for...;but for ...
〖要道〗(名)[yàodào]
strategic pass; main route; main line
〖要地〗(名)[yàodì]
important place; strategic position; key area
〖要点〗(名)[yàodiǎn]
main point; essentials
〖要饭〗[yàofàn]
beg for food; go begging
〖要害〗(名)[yàohài]
① vital part of body ② key point; vital issue; the quick of the matter ③ vital area of defence; key military point
〖要紧〗(形)[yàojǐn]
important
〖要领〗(名)[yàolǐng]
main themes; main point; essential element
〖要么〗(连)[yàome]
or; else
〖要命〗[yào mìng]
① fatal ② extremely; exceedingly
〖要强〗(形)[yàoqiáng]
want to forge ahead; unwilling to lag behind
〖要塞〗(名)[yàosài]
strnghold; fortress
〖要是〗(连)[yàoshi]
if
〖要素〗(名)[yàosù]
vital factor; essential element

钥[yào]
〖钥匙〗(名)[yàoshi]〔把 bǎ〕
key

耀[yào]
〖耀武扬威〗[yàowǔyángwēi]
make a big show of one's powers; swashbuckling

〖耀眼〗(形)[yàoyǎn]
dazzling

yē

椰[yē]
〖椰子〗(名)[yēzi]
coconut

噎(动)[yē]
choke down

yé

爷(名)[yé]
grandfather
〖爷爷〗(名)[yéye]
grandfather; grandpa

yě

也(副)[yě]
also; too; as well as; besides
〖也罢〗(助)[yěbà]
①might as well; all right②let it be
〖…也好,…也好〗
[…yěhǎo, …yěhǎo]
either ...or; no matter ...
〖也许〗(副)[yěxǔ]
perhaps

冶(动)[yě]
〖冶金〗[yějīn]
metallurgical
〖冶炼〗(动)[yěliàn]
forge; smelt

野(形)[yě]
①wild②uncivilized; savage; uncivil
〖野菜〗(名)[yěcài]
wild vegetable
〖野地〗(名)[yědì]
open country; wilderness
〖野蛮〗(形)[yěmán]
uncivilized; brute; savage; barbarous
〖野兽〗(名)[yěshòu]
beast; wild animal
〖野外〗(名)[yěwài]
open field
〖野心〗(名)[yěxīn]
vaulting ambition; covetous desire; aggressive designs
〖野心家〗(名)[yěxīnjiā]
careerist; social climber
〖野营〗(动)[yěyíng]
encamp
〖野战军〗(名)[yězhànjūn]
field army

yè

业(名)[yè]
①work; business; profession; occupation② enterprise; undertaking③property; possessions
〖业绩〗(名)[yèjì]
outstanding accomplishment; great achievement
〖业务〗(名)[yèwù]
vocational work; specialized; profession; occupation
〖业务知识〗[yèwùzhīshi]
professional knowledge

〖业务学习〗[yèwùxuéxí]
vocational study
〖业已〗(副)[yèyǐ]
already
〖业余〗(形)[yèyú]
① sparetime; off-duty hour; after working hours ② amateur
〖业主〗(名)[yèzhǔ]
owner; proprieter

叶(名)[yè]
leaf
〖叶公好龙〗[Yègōnghàolóng]
(lit.) Lord Yeh is fond of dragons (the proverbial Lord Yeh who claimed to be fond of dragons but in fact was mortally afraid of them); (fig.) insincere love for things
〖叶子〗(名)[yèzi]
leaf

页(名、量)[yè]
① page ② a measure word, page

夜(名)[yè]
night
〖夜间〗(名)[yèjiān]
during the night
〖夜市〗(名)[yèshì]
night fair; night market
〖夜晚〗(名)[yèwǎn]
evening; night
〖夜宵〗(名)[yèxiāo]
night snack
〖夜校〗(名)[yèxiào]
evening school or class
〖夜以继日〗[yèyǐjìrì]
day and night
〖夜总会〗(名)[yèzǒnghuì]
nightclub

液(名)[yè]
liquid; fluid
〖液化石油气〗[yèhuàshíyóuqì]
liquefied petroleum gas (LPG)
〖液态〗(名)[yètài]
fluid state
〖液体〗(名)[yètǐ]
liquid; fluid
〖液压〗(名)[yèyā]
fluid pressure

谒[yè]
〖谒见〗(动)[yèjiàn]
be honoured with an interview (with a person in higher position)

腋(名)[yè]
armpit
〖腋下〗(名)[yèxià]
under the armpit

yī

一(数、副)[yī]
① a; one; one of ...; each ② placed before a verb to express a quick or brief action (e.g. no sooner than, as soon as)
〖一把手〗(名)[yībǎshǒu]
① good hand; able man ② head;

chief; CEO
〖一败涂地〗[yībàitúdì]
a thorough defeat; a total loss; complete fiasco
〖一般〗(形)[yībān]
① alike; just as ② general; ordinary; usual
〖一半〗[yībàn]
half
〖一辈子〗[yībèizi]
lifetime; all one's life
〖一本正经〗[yīběnzhèngjīng]
serious; grave (mostly sarcastic)
〖一笔勾销〗[yībǐgōuxiāo]
wipe out all the gains; write off at one stroke
〖一笔抹杀〗[yībǐmǒshā]
obliterate; be written off at one stroke; completely deny
〖一边〗(名)[yībiān]
① side; edge; end ② by the side; beside; aside
〖一边…一边…〗
[yībiān…yībiān…]
...as...; while; at the same time
〖一并〗(副)[yībìng]
together; along with
〖一不怕苦,二不怕死〗
[yībù pàkǔ, èrbùpàsǐ]
fear neither hardship nor death
〖一不做,二不休〗
[yībùzuò, èrbùxiū]
once it is started, go through with it; a thing once begun will not be put off until done
〖一步一个脚印儿〗
[yībùyīgè jiǎoyìnr]
(lit.) one step leaves one footmark; (fig.) do things in a down-to-earth manner
〖一草一木〗[yīcǎoyīmù]
every grass and every tree (referring to every bit of property)
〖一场空〗[yīchǎng kōng]
come to naught; come to nothing
〖一唱一和〗[yīchàngyīhè]
sing a duet; sing the same tune; chime in with; echo each other
〖一尘不染〗[yīchénbùrǎn]
not to be stained with a particle of dust; pure-minded
〖一成不变〗[yīchéngbùbiàn]
changeless; unchangable; invariable; unalterable
〖一筹莫展〗[yīchóumòzhǎn]
could do nothing with it
〖一触即发〗[yīchùjífā]
to an explosive point; touch-and-go
〖一次〗[yīcì]
once
〖一蹴而就〗[yīcùérjiù]
accomplish in one move
〖一代〗(名)[yīdài]
one generation; of one age
〖一带〗(名)[yīdài]
area; surroundings
〖一旦〗(副)[yīdàn]
once; whenever; as soon as; one day
〖一刀两断〗[yīdāoliǎngduàn]
break with ... once for all; make a clear break with

〖一刀切〗[yīdāoqiē]
impose uniformity
〖一道〗(副)[yīdào]
together; together with
〖一得之功〗[yīdézhīgōng]
occasional successes
〖一点儿〗[yīdiǎnr]
just a little; a small amount; just a tiny bit
〖一点论〗(名)[yīdiǎnlùn]
one point theory; theory of one point
〖一定〗(形、副)[yīdìng]
certain; definite; bound to; certainly; definitely; firmly
〖一度〗[yīdù]
once; for a time
〖一发千钧〗[yīfàqiānjūn]
a thousand piculs suspended by a single hair; hang by a thread; an impending situation
〖一帆风顺〗[yīfānfēngshùn]
smooth sailing; have a favourable wind throughout the voyage; all plain sailing
〖一方面…一方面…〗
[yīfāng miàn… yīfāngmiàn…]
on the one hand... on the other hand
〖一分为二〗[yīfēnwéi'èr]
one divides into two; divide one into two
〖一概〗(副)[yīgài]
all; without exception; altogether
〖一概而论〗[yīgài'érlùn]
lump people or things under one head; lump together
〖一干二净〗[yīgān'èrjìng]
lock, stock and barrel; root and branch; altogether
〖一个劲儿〗[yīgejìnr]
with one effort; make one vigorous effort; stubbornly; with complete devotion
〖一共〗(副)[yīgòng]
altogether; in total; in all; wholly; entirely
〖一股脑儿〗[yīgǔnǎor]
complete abandonment of; altogether; the whole lot
〖一鼓作气〗[yīgǔzuòqì]
make one vigorous effort; with one effort
〖一贯〗(形)[yīguàn]
consistent; invariable; all along; always
〖一国两制〗[yīguóliǎngzhì]
principle of "one country, two systems"; one nation, two systems
〖一哄而散〗[yīhòng'érsàn]
disperse in a rush
〖一会儿〗(名)[yīhuìr]
in a while; at one time; in a short moment
〖一伙〗[yīhuǒ]
a group of; a gang of; a band of; a bunch of
〖一技之长〗[yījìzhīcháng]
a single skill;capable of one specific job;useful in some kind of work
〖一见如故〗[yījiànrúgù]
like fast friends at the first meeting

〖一箭双雕〗[yījiànshuāngdiāo]
kill two birds with one stone; achieve two things at one stroke
〖一经〗(副)[yījīng]
as soon as ...; immediately after; whereupon
〖一…就…〗[yī…jiù…]
no sooner ... than ...; as soon as ...
〖一举两得〗[yījǔliǎngdé]
kill two birds with one stone; achieve two things at one stroke; double gain
〖一蹶不振〗[yījuébùzhèn]
total collapse; accelerating downfall
〖一孔之见〗[yīkǒngzhījiàn]
one-sided view; partial view
〖一口气〗[yīkǒuqì]
in one breath; at one go
〖一块儿〗(名、副)[yīkuàir]
①together ②at the same place
〖一来…二来…〗
[yīlái…èrlái…]
on the one hand ... on the other hand; firstly ... secondly ...
〖一劳永逸〗[yīláoyǒngyì]
solution that holds good for all time; once and for all
〖一连〗(副)[yīlián]
serially; successively; on end; continuously
〖一连串〗(形)[yīliánchuàn]
serial; a series of; a succession of; a whole string of
〖一路平安〗[yīlùpíng'ān]
a pleasant journey; a good journey; a safe journey; bon voyage
〖一律〗(形、副)[yīlǜ]
undiscriminatingly; without exception; all; without distinction
〖一落千丈〗[yīluòqiānzhàng]
(lit.) drop 10,000 feet in one fall; (fig.) sudden decline; disastrous drop
〖一马当先〗[yīmǎdāngxiān]
taking the lead; be in the van of others
〖一脉相承〗[yīmàixiāngchéng]
be imbued with the same spirit; run in a single line
〖一毛不拔〗[yīmáobùbá]
very sparing in spending money; miserly
〖一面…一面…〗
[yīmiàn…yīmiàn…]
...as...; while; on the one hand...; on the other hand
〖一鸣惊人〗[yīmíngjīngrén]
achieve overnight success
〖一目了然〗[yīmùliǎorán]
understand fully at a glance
〖一年半载〗[yīniánbànzǎi]
round about a year
〖一年到头〗[yīniándàotóu]
all the year round; in season and out of season
〖一盘散沙〗[yīpánsǎnshā]
a heap of loose sand; disunited; disunion
〖一旁〗(名)[yīpáng]
by the side of
〖一片〗[yīpiàn]
①sheet; a sheet of ②a stretch

Y

of; a vast expanse; everywhere

〖一齐〗(副)[yīqí]
together; all at once

〖一起〗(名、副)[yīqǐ]
① together; together with; jointly ② at the same time; simultaneously

〖一气呵成〗[yīqìhēchéng]
complete sth. at a stretch

〖一钱不值〗[yīqiánbùzhí]
not worth a rap; completely insignificant

〖一窍不通〗[yīqiàobùtōng]
be utterly ignorant of; know nothing of

〖一切〗(形、代)[yīqiè]
all; everything; every kind of; whole; entire

〖一清二楚〗[yīqīng'èrchǔ]
perfectly clear; as clear as daylight

〖一丘之貉〗[yīqiūzhīhé]
jackals of the same lair; birds of a feather

〖一去不复返〗[yīqùbùfùfǎn]
once gone, never to return; be gone forever

〖一穷二白〗[yīqióng'èrbái]
poverty and blankness; backward both economically and culturally

〖一日千里〗[yīrìqiānlǐ]
a thousand li a day; at a tremendous pace

〖一如既往〗[yīrújìwǎng]
be as usual

〖一扫而光〗[yīsǎo'érguāng]
make a clean sweep of; a clean sweep

〖一生〗(名)[yīshēng]
all one's life; life time; in one's whole life

〖一声不响〗[yīshēngbùxiǎng]
keep silent; say nothing at all; keep one's mouth tight shut

〖一时〗(名)[yīshí]
momentary; at a given moment; for the time being; for a while

〖一事无成〗[yīshìwúchéng]
nothing accomplished; achieve nothing

〖一视同仁〗[yīshìtóngrén]
be treated the same; treat equally without discrimination

〖一手〗(名、副)[yīshǒu]
① skill ② trick ③ by oneself

〖一手包办〗[yīshǒubāobàn]
control exclusively; be stage-managed by

〖一手遮天〗[yīshǒuzhētiān]
(lit.) shut out the heavens with one palm; (fig.) attempt to hoodwink public opinion

〖一丝不苟〗[yīsībùgǒu]
in all seriousness

〖一丝一毫〗[yīsīyīháo]
the slightest; the least; a shred of...

〖一塌糊涂〗[yītāhútú]
in a great mess; in the worst state; in utter disorder

〖一天到晚〗[yītiāndàowǎn]
from morning to night; all day long

〖一条龙〗[yītiáolóng]
one continuous line; a coordi-

nated process; a connected sequence

〖一条心〗[yītiáoxīn]
be of one mind with; all of one mind

〖一同〗(副)[yītóng]
together; together with

〖一团和气〗[yītuánhéqì]
unprincipled peace; maintain unprincipled good terms

〖一碗水端平〗[yīwǎnshuǐduānpíng]
(lit.)hold a cup of water level; (fig.)be fair and just in handling matters

〖一网打尽〗[yīwǎngdǎjìn]
all captured at once; catch all in a dragnet

〖一往无前〗[yīwǎngwúqián]
go ahead boldly; go straight with an indomitable spirit; go right on; indomitable

〖一味〗(副)[yīwèi]
obsessively; persistently; doggedly

〖一无是处〗[yīwúshìchù]
nothing is right; without a sin-gle virtue; not a single merit

〖一无所有〗[yīwúsuǒyǒu]
have nothing at all; penniless; destitute

〖一五一十〗[yīwǔyīshí]
the way of counting; (fig.) in good order and with nothing missing

〖一系列〗[yīxìliè]
a train of (e.g. events); a series of; a number of; a great deal of

〖一下〗(副)[yīxià]
①once; one time ②all at once; suddenly

〖一向〗(副)[yīxiàng]
consistently; always

〖一小撮〗[yīxiǎocuō]
a handful of; a small number of; a bunch of

〖一些〗[yīxiē]
some; a little; a few; several

〖一心〗(副)[yīxīn]
set one's mind on; heart and soul; with one heart and one mind

〖一心为公〗[yīxīnwèigōng]
be heart and soul devoted to public interests; whole-hearted devotion to the public interests

〖一心一意〗[yīxīnyīyì]
with all one's heart and mind; heart and soul

〖一星半点〗[yīxīngbàndiǎn]
a little; a few; a bit of

〖一行〗(名)[yīxíng]
company; party; suite

〖一言不发〗[yīyánbùfā]
keep silent; say nothing; keep one's mouth tight shut

〖一言堂〗(名)[yīyántáng]
rule by the voice of one man alone; the practice of "what I say counts"

〖一言一行〗[yīyányīxíng]
each word and deed; every word and action

〖一言以蔽之〗[yīyányǐbìzhī]

in a word; in short; in a nutshell
〖一样〗(形)[yīyàng]
same; of one size; like
〖一一〗(副)[yīyī]
one by one
〖一意孤行〗[yīyìgūxíng]
have everything one's own way; act arbitrarily; act in disregard of other people's opinions
〖一语道破〗[yīyǔdàopò]
pinpoint; hit upon the truth
〖一元化〗(动)[yīyuánhuà]
unify
〖一元化领导〗[yīyuánhuàlǐngdǎo]
unified leadership; centralized leadership
〖一月〗(名)[yīyuè]
January
〖一再〗(副)[yīzài]
again and again; once and again; repeatedly; many times
〖一张一弛〗[yīzhāngyīchí]
tense and relax alternatively
〖一朝一夕〗[yīzhāoyīxī]
overnight; a short duration of time
〖一针见血〗[yīzhēnjiànxiě]
hit the nail on the head; make a pointed remark; put one's finger on one's weak spot
〖一针一线〗[yīzhēnyīxiàn]
a single needle or a piece of thread
〖一阵子〗[yīzhènzi]
for a short time
〖一整套〗[yī zhěngtào]
a whole set of; the whole range of
〖一知半解〗[yīzhībànjiě]
scant knowledge; the scantiness of knowledge; half-baked knowledge
〖一直〗(副)[yīzhí]
all the time; all the while; always
〖一纸空文〗[yīzhǐkōngwén]
a mere scrap of paper; empty words on a sheet of paper
〖一致〗(形)[yīzhì]
unanimous; unified; identical
〖一字不漏〗[yīzìbùlòu]
not omit a single word

伊[yī]

〖伊斯兰教〗(名)[Yīsīlánjiào]
Islam

衣(名)[yī]

clothes; coat; dress
〖衣钵〗(名)[yībō]
mantle; legacy (of ideology, technology and learning, etc.)
〖衣服〗(名)[yīfu]〔件 jiàn〕
clothes; dress
〖衣裳〗(名)[yīshang]〔件 jiàn〕
(coll.) clothes; dress
〖衣食住行〗[yīshízhùxíng]
clothing, food, lodging, and means of travel
〖衣着〗(名)[yīzhuó]
what one wears; clothing

医(名、动)[yī]
① medical science; ② doctor③ cure; heal; give medical treatment
〖医疗〗(名)[yīliáo]
medical care; medical treatment
〖医疗队〗(名)[yīliáoduì]
medical team
〖医生〗(名)[yīshēng]
doctor; physician; surgeon
〖医术〗(名)[yīshù]
medical art; medical skill
〖医务〗(名)[yīwù]
medical service
〖医学〗(名)[yīxué]
medical science
〖医学院〗(名)[yīxuéyuàn]
college of medicine
〖医院〗(名)[yīyuàn]
hospital
〖医治〗(动)[yīzhì]
cure; treat; give medical treatment; heal

依(动、介)[yī]
① depend on; rely on ② obey; follow; adhere to③ according to; in the light of
〖依次〗(副)[yīcì]
in proper order; in turn; in order of
〖依存〗(动)[yīcún]
interdepend; depend upon sb. or sth. (for existence); (mutual) dependence for existence
〖依附〗(动)[yīfù]
rely on; depend on; become an appendage to; attach to
〖依旧〗(副)[yījiù]
as it used to be; still as usual
〖依据〗(动、名)[yījù]
base on; adhere to; rest on; basis
〖依靠〗(动)[yīkào]
rely on; depend on; rest on
〖依赖〗(动)[yīlài]
rely on; place total reliance on; depend on
〖依然〗(副)[yīrán]
still; yet
〖依依不舍〗[yīyībùshě]
unwilling to part with; reluctance to part from
〖依照〗(介)[yīzhào]
according to; adhere to; as; in the light of

yí

仪[yí]
〖仪表〗(名)[yíbiǎo]
① person's appearance ② instrument
〖仪器〗(名)[yíqì]
instrument
〖仪式〗(名)[yíshì]
form of ceremony
〖仪仗队〗(名)[yízhàngduì]
guard of honour

姨(名)[yí]
① maternal aunt ② wife's sister
〖姨父〗(名)[yífu]

maternal aunt's husband
〖姨母〗(名)[yímǔ]
maternal aunt

移(动)[yí]

①move;remove ②change;transfer
〖移动〗(动)[yídòng]
move; shift; change of place
〖移动电话〗[yídòngdiànhuà]
portable phone
〖移风易俗〗[yífēngyìsú]
change existing habits and customs; transform established traditions and practices
〖移交〗(动)[yíjiāo]
turn over; hand over
〖移民〗[yímín]
immigrate; immigrant; emigrant; emigrate; settler
〖移山倒海〗[yíshāndǎohǎi]
remove mountains and drain seas (refers to man's mighty strength in conquering nature)
〖移植〗(动)[yízhí]
transplant; graft

遗[yí]

〖遗产〗(名)[yíchǎn]
heritage; inheritance; legacy
〖遗臭万年〗[yíchòuwànnián]
leave a bad name for thousands of years to come;everlasting shame; leave a bad name forever
〖遗传〗(动)[yíchuán]
inherit; heridity; inheritance; transmit; carry over
〖遗憾〗(形)[yíhàn]
sorry; regretful; regretted; regrettable
〖遗迹〗(名)[yíjì]
vestiges; remnants; relics; trace
〖遗留〗(动)[yíliú]
leave; leave behind; hand down
〖遗漏〗(动、名)[yílòu]
omit; miss; omission
〖遗弃〗(动)[yíqì]
desert; abandon
〖遗容〗(名)[yíróng]
① portrait of a respectable person who is dead ② countenance of a deceased person
〖遗失〗(动)[yíshī]
lose; miss
〖遗书〗(名)[yíshū]
① dying testament ② writings of a deceased author
〖遗体〗(名)[yítǐ]
the body of a respectable person who is dead; remains
〖遗忘〗(动)[yíwàng]
forget
〖遗像〗(名)[yíxiàng]
portrait of a respectable person who is dead
〖遗志〗(名)[yízhì]
person's last will
〖遗嘱〗(名)[yízhǔ]
person's last will; dying words
〖遗著〗(名)[yízhù]
writings of a dead author

疑[yí]

〖疑案〗(名)[yí'àn]

① a disputed case at court ② an unsolved question
〖疑惑〗(动)[yíhuò]
doubt
〖疑虑〗(动、名)[yílǜ]
worry; trouble; concern
〖疑难〗(形)[yínán]
difficult
〖疑问〗(名)[yíwèn]
problem; question; doubt
〖疑问句〗(名)[yíwènjù]
interrogative sentence
〖疑心〗(动、名)[yíxīn]
doubt; suspicion
〖疑义〗(名)[yíyì]
doubtful point

yǐ

乙(名)[yǐ]
number two in decimal cycle; second

已(副)[yǐ]
already
〖已经〗(副)[yǐjīng]
already
〖已知数〗(名)[yǐzhīshù]
known number

以(介)[yǐ]
with; in the form of; use...as...
〖以便〗(连)[yǐbiàn]
in order to; so that; so as to
〖以点带面〗[yǐdiǎndàimiàn]
use the experience of one point to lead the whole area
〖以讹传讹〗[yǐ é chuán é]
incorrectly relay an erroneous message (so that it becomes increasingly distorted)
〖以攻为守〗[yǐgōngwéishǒu]
use attack as a method of defence; defend by way of attacking
〖以后〗(名)[yǐhòu]
later on; afterwards
〖以及〗(连)[yǐjí]
and; as well as
〖以己度人〗[yǐjǐduórén]
measure other's corn by one's own bushel
〖…以来〗[…yǐlái]
since
〖以礼相待〗[yǐlǐxiāngdài]
treat sb. with due respect
〖以理服人〗[yǐlǐfúrén]
persuade through reasoning; convince people by reasoning
〖以邻为壑〗[yǐlínwéihè]
use the neighbour's field as an outlet for his overflow; dump rubbish in the neighbour's yard
〖以卵击石〗[yǐluǎnjīshí]
(lit.) throw an egg at a stone; (fig.) grossly overestimate one's own strength
〖以貌取人〗[yǐmàoqǔrén]
judge people solely by their appearance
〖以免〗(连)[yǐmiǎn]
lest; in order to prevent
〖以内〗(名)[yǐnèi]
including; within; within the limit of ...
〖以前〗(名)[yǐqián]

before; previous; former; prior to; in the past
〖以求〗[yǐqiú]
in order to, in an attempt to
〖以权谋私〗[yǐquánmóusī]
abuse one's power for personal gains
〖以商养文〗[yǐshāngyǎngwén]
support cultural activities with profits from a business
〖以上〗(名)[yǐshàng]
① above; above-mentioned ② upwards; more than
〖以身试法〗[yǐshēnshìfǎ]
defy the law; challenge the law personally
〖以身殉职〗[yǐshēnxùnzhí]
die a martyr at one's post
〖以身作则〗[yǐshēnzuòzé]
make oneself serve as an example to others; set an example with one's own conduct
〖以外〗(名)[yǐwài]
beyond; excluding; outside
〖以往〗(名)[yǐwǎng]
the past; bygone days
〖以为〗(动)[yǐwéi]
think; consider; take it for granted that; presume
〖以…为…〗[yǐ…wéi…]
with ... as; regard ... as; take ... for
〖以下〗(名)[yǐxià]
below; what follows
〖以眼还眼,以牙还牙〗
[yǐyǎn huányǎn, yǐyáhuányá]
an eye for an eye, a tooth for a tooth
〖以一当十〗[yǐyīdàngshí]
pit one against ten
〖以逸待劳〗[yǐyìdàiláo]
wait at one's ease for the fatigued enemy
〖以至〗(连)[yǐzhì]
to such an extent that ...; go so far as to ...
〖以致〗(连)[yǐzhì]
with the result that; resulting in
〖以资〗[yǐzī]
as a means of

迤[yǐ]
〖迤逦〗(形)[yǐlǐ]
wind; circle about

倚(动)[yǐ]
lean on; depend on; rely on
〖倚靠〗(动)[yǐkào]
depend on; rely on
〖倚赖〗(动)[yǐlài]
solely rely on; place reliance on
〖倚仗〗(动)[yǐzhàng]
rely on; hang on sb's coat-tails

椅(名)[yǐ]
chair
〖椅子〗(名)[yǐzi]〔把 bǎ〕
chair

yì

亿(数)[yì]

a hundred million
〖亿万〗(数)[yìwàn]
hundreds of millions

义(名)[yì]
① just ② duty; obligation ③ feelings ④ meaning
〖义不容辞〗[yìbùróngcí]
act from a strong sense of duty; bounden duty; inescapable duty
〖义愤〗(名)[yìfèn]
righteous indignation
〖义愤填膺〗[yìfèntiányīng]
be filled with righteous indignation
〖义和团运动〗[Yìhétuán Yùndòng]
the Yi Ho Tuan Movement
〖义卖〗(名)[yìmài]
sale of goods for charity or other worthy causes; charity bazaar
〖义务〗(名)[yìwù]
voluntary duty; voluntary service; responsibility; obligation
〖义务兵役制〗[yìwù bīngyìzhì]
system of general military service; compulsory service system
〖义务教育〗[yìwùjiàoyù]
compulsory education
〖义务劳动〗[yìwùláodòng]
voluntary labour
〖义演〗(名)[yìyǎn]
benefit performance
〖义正词严〗[yìzhèngcíyán]
just and severe terms

艺[yì]
〖艺人〗(名)[yìrén]
professional player (artist, acrobat, etc.)
〖艺术〗(名)[yìshù]
① art ② skill
〖艺术标准〗[yìshù biāozhǔn]
artistic criteria
〖艺术家〗(名)[yìshùjiā]
artist
〖艺术品〗(名)[yìshùpǐn]
works of art; arts and crafts
〖艺术性〗(名)[yìshùxìng]
artistic level; artistry
〖艺术字〗(名)[yìshùzì]
characters in a fancy style
〖艺苑〗(名)[yìyuàn]
the realm of art and literature; art and literary circles

忆(动)[yì]
recall; think over
〖忆苦思甜〗[yìkǔsītián]
recall one's past sufferings and think over present happiness; contrast past bitterness with present happiness

议(动)[yì]
discuss
〖议案〗(名)[yì'àn]
proposal; bill
〖议程〗(名)[yìchéng]
agenda
〖议定书〗(名)[yìdìngshū]

protocol
〖议会〗(名)[yìhuì]
parliament
〖议价〗(名)[yìjià]
negotiated price
〖议论〗(动、名)[yìlùn]
discuss; discussion
〖议论文〗(名)[yìlùnwén]
argumentative writing; argumentation
〖议事日程〗[yìshìrìchéng]
agenda
〖议题〗(名)[yìtí]
a subject of discussion
〖议员〗(名)[yìyuán]
member of a legislative assembly
〖议院〗(名)[yìyuàn]
legislative assembly; parliament; congress

屹[yì]
〖屹立〗(动)[yìlì]
stand rock-firm;stand firmly; stand mighty

亦(副)[yì]
as well as; and; also; too
〖亦步亦趋〗[yìbùyìqū]
follow in one's steps; ape sb. at every step
〖亦工亦农〗[yìgōngyìnóng]
take part both in industry and agriculture

异[yì]
〖异常〗(形)[yìcháng]
extraordinary; unusual; abnormal; exceptional
〖异乎寻常〗[yìhūxúncháng]
extraordinary and immense; unusual; extraordinary
〖异己〗(名)[yìjǐ]
those not of one's ilk; dissidents; alien (e.g.element)
〖异口同声〗[yìkǒutóngshēng]
cry out in one voice; with one voice; with one accord
〖异曲同工〗[yìqǔtónggōng]
play the same tune on different instruments; the same result achieved by different methods
〖异体字〗(名)[yìtǐzì]
different forms of a same character or letter
〖异想天开〗[yìxiǎngtiānkāi]
wishful thinking; fanciful ideas; wild hopes
〖异性〗(名)[yìxìng]
①opposite sex ②different qualities (of matter);different in properties
〖异议〗(名)[yìyì]
disagreement; objection; dissension; dissent

抑[yì]
〖抑扬顿挫〗[yìyángdùncuò]
rising and falling of tones; rhythmical
〖抑制〗(动)[yìzhì]
restrain; repress

呓[yì]

〖呓语〗(名)[yìyǔ]
nonsensical talk; ravings; ranting; crazy talk

译(动)[yì]
translate; interpret
〖译文〗(名)[yìwén]
translation
〖译员〗(名)[yìyuán]
interpreter
〖译者〗(名)[yìzhě]
translator
〖译制片〗(名)[yìzhìpiàn]
dubbed film

易(形)[yì]
easy; simple
〖易拉罐〗(名)[yìlāguàn]
easy-open tin; pop-top can; pop can
〖易燃〗(动)[yìrán]
easy to kindle; inflammability; combustible
〖易燃品〗(名)[yìránpǐn]
anything inflammable
〖易如反掌〗[yìrúfǎnzhǎng]
as easy as turning one's palm
〖易于〗(动)[yìyú]
easily; be apt to ...

Y

疫[yì]
〖疫苗〗(名)[yìmiáo]
vaccine

益(名)[yì]
benefit; profit; advantage
〖益处〗(名)[yìchù]
benefit; advantage

意[yì]
〖意见〗(名)[yìjiàn]
opinion; idea; suggestion; view
〖意境〗(名)[yìjìng]
mood and atmosphere (e.g. artistic and literary works)
〖意料〗(动)[yìliào]
expect; conjecture
〖意气〗(名)[yìqì]
① spirit; enthusiasm ② impulse; momentary
〖意气风发〗[yìqìfēngfā]
boundless enthusiasm; heroism in full display
〖意识〗(名、动)[yìshí]
consciousness; ideology; outlook; realize; be conscious of; be aware of
〖意识形态〗[yìshíxíngtài]
ideology; ideological form
〖意思〗(名)[yìsi]
meaning; opinion
〖意图〗(名)[yìtú]
intention; purpose
〖意外〗(名)[yìwài]
① beyond expectation ② unexpected accident; unforeseen
〖意味〗(名)[yìwèi]
meaning; purport; implication
〖意味着〗(动)[yìwèizhe]
mean; suggest; imply; signify
〖意向书〗(名)[yìxiàngshū]
statement of intention; letter of intent

〖意义〗(名)[yìyì]
meaning; significance; purport
〖意译〗(动)[yìyì]
liberal translation; free translation
〖意愿〗(名)[yìyuàn]
will and wishes; desire; aspirations
〖意志〗(名)[yìzhì]
will; ambition; purpose

肄[yì]
〖肄业〗(动)[yìyè]
study (referring to students studying in school or who have left school before graduation)

毅[yì]
〖毅力〗(名)[yìlì]
stamina; fortitude; will power
〖毅然〗(副)[yìrán]
courageously; determinedly

臆[yì]
〖臆测〗(动)[yìcè]
conjecture; make baseless assumption
〖臆断〗(动)[yìduàn]
make arbitrary decision; guess; make groundless conclusion
〖臆造〗(动)[yìzào]
concoct; conjecture; imagine

翼(名)[yì]
wing; flank

yīn

因(名、连)[yīn]
①cause; reason ②according to; on account of ③because; for; thanks to
〖因材施教〗[yīncáishījiào]
teach in accordance with different aptitudes
〖因此〗(连)[yīncǐ]
therefore; so that; hence; thus
〖因地制宜〗[yīndìzhìyí]
take such measures as are suitable to local conditions; adapt the working method to local conditions
〖因而〗(连)[yīn'ér]
therefore; because of
〖因果〗(名)[yīnguǒ]
the causes and effects
〖因陋就简〗[yīnlòujiùjiǎn]
make do with whatever is available; make use of the available conditions
〖因人设事〗[yīnrénshèshì]
create a job to accommodate a person
〖因式〗(名)[yīnshì]
factor
〖因式分解〗[yīnshìfēnjiě]
factoring; resolutions into factors
〖因势利导〗[yīnshìlìdǎo]
guide it along its course of development; guide ... in the light of its general trend
〖因素〗(名)[yīnsù]
factor; element

Y

〖因为〗(连)[yīnwèi]
because; as; for; due to
〖因袭〗(动)[yīnxí]
inherit; follow (e.g. the old rules)
〖因循守旧〗[yīnxúnshǒujiù]
follow the beaten track
〖因噎废食〗[yīnyēfèishí]
give up eating for fear of choking; (fig.) be put off easily

阴(形)[yīn]
① dark; gloomy ② insidious; sinister; vicious
〖阴暗〗(形)[yīn'àn]
dark; dull; gloomy; dim
〖阴极〗(名)[yīnjí]
cathode; negative pole
〖阴历〗(名)[yīnlì]
the lunar year; the lunar calendar
〖阴凉〗(形)[yīnliáng]
cool
〖阴谋〗(名、动)[yīnmóu]
ill-intended scheme; sinister plot;conspiracy;conspire;intrigue against
〖阴谋家〗(名)[yīnmóujiā]
conspirator; plotter; schemer
〖阴平〗(名)[yīnpíng]
the even tone or the first tone (of Chinese characters)
〖阴天〗(名)[yīntiān]
overcast; a cloudy day
〖阴险〗(形)[yīnxiǎn]
insidious; sinister; vicious; malicious
〖阴性〗(名)[yīnxìng]
feminine character; feminine gender; negative
〖阴影〗(名)[yīnyǐng]
shadow

荫[yīn]
〖荫蔽〗(动)[yīnbì]
bring under protection;covert; conceal; hidden

音(名)[yīn]
① sound; voice; tone; tune ② news; tidings
〖音节〗(名)[yīnjié]
syllable; key or pitch in music
〖音量〗(名)[yīnliàng]
volume of sound
〖音素〗(名)[yīnsù]
phoneme
〖音响〗(名)[yīnxiǎng]
sound; acoustics
〖音响设备〗[yīnxiǎngshèbèi]
stereo set
〖音像〗(名)[yīnxiàng]
audio and video
〖音信〗(名)[yīnxìn]
news; tidings
〖音译〗(动)[yīnyì]
transliterate by sound
〖音乐〗(名)[yīnyuè]
music
〖音乐会〗(名)[yīnyuèhuì]
concert

殷[yīn]

〚殷切〛(形)[yīnqiè]
earnest; sincere; ardent
〚殷勤〛(形)[yīnqín]
attentive; solicitous; obliging; affable

yín

银(名)[yín]
silver
〚银白〛(形)[yínbái]
silver white; silvery
〚银根〛(名)[yíngēn]
money market; money
〚银行〛(名)[yínháng]
bank
〚银河〛(名)[yínhé]
the Milky Way; the Galaxy
〚银灰〛(形)[yínhuī]
silver grey
〚银幕〛(名)[yínmù]
screen
〚银团贷款〛[yíntuándàikuǎn]
syndicated loan

yǐn

引(动)[yǐn]
① draw ② guide; lead; conduct ③ cause; lead to; attract
〚引导〛(动)[yǐndǎo]
guide; lead; conduct; usher
〚引渡〛(动)[yǐndù]
extradite; deliver
〚引而不发〛[yǐn'érbùfā]
draw the bow without shooting; get ready for action
〚引号〛(名)[yǐnhào]
quotation mark
〚引进〛(动)[yǐnjìn]
introduce; import; usher in
〚引经据典〛[yǐnjīngjùdiǎn]
quote classical works; quote authoritative works
〚引狼入室〛[yǐnlángrùshì]
bring a wolf into the house; let wolves into the house
〚引力〛(名)[yǐnlì]
attraction; gravitation
〚引起〛(动)[yǐnqǐ]
arouse; give rise to; draw; lead to; cause
〚引桥〛(名)[yǐnqiáo]
approach span of a bridge
〚引人入胜〛[yǐnrénrùshèng]
interesting and absorbing; attractive; fascinating
〚引人注目〛[yǐnrénzhùmù]
attract one's attention; draw one's attention; conspicuous
〚引申〛(动)[yǐnshēn]
extend ... to; figuratively apply; amplification
〚引文〛(名)[yǐnwén]
quotations from other writings
〚引言〛(名)[yǐnyán]
introduction; preface
〚引以为戒〛[yǐnyǐwéijiè]
take warning; serve as a grave warning
〚引用〛(动)[yǐnyòng]
quote; cite
〚引诱〛(动)[yǐnyòu]
lure; seduce; tempt; entice; allure
〚引证〛(动)[yǐnzhèng]

quote from; cite

〖引子〗(名)[yǐnzi]

introduction; brief introduction to a book; opening song in opera

饮(动)[yǐn]

drink (e.g. water)

〖饮料〗(名)[yǐnliào]

drink

〖饮食〗(名)[yǐnshí]

food and drink; food

〖饮水思源〗[yǐnshuǐsīyuán]

when drinking the water think of its source

〖饮鸩止渴〗[yǐnzhènzhǐkě]

(lit.) drink poisoned wine to quench thirst; (fig.) temporary relief which results in disaster

隐[yǐn]

〖隐蔽〗(动)[yǐnbì]

cover up; hide; take cover; conceal

〖隐藏〗(动)[yǐncáng]

conceal; hide; cover up

〖隐患〗(名)[yǐnhuàn]

hidden danger; latent trouble

〖隐晦〗(形)[yǐnhuì]

insidious; vague

〖隐瞒〗(动)[yǐnmán]

conceal; cover up

〖隐痛〗(名)[yǐntòng]

untold bitterness

〖隐约〗(形)[yǐnyuē]

indistinctly visible or audible

瘾(名)[yǐn]

habit; addiction; hobby; craving

yìn

印(动、名)[yìn]

① print; publish ② seal; mark

〖印度洋〗(名)[Yìndùyáng]

Indian Ocean

〖印发〗(动)[yìnfā]

print and publish; issue

〖印染〗(动)[yìnrǎn]

print and dye

〖印刷〗(动)[yìnshuā]

print

〖印刷品〗(名)[yìnshuāpǐn]

printed matter

〖印刷体〗(名)[yìnshuātǐ]

writing in printing form

〖印象〗(名)[yìnxiàng]

impression

〖印证〗(动)[yìnzhèng]

corroborate

yīng

应(动、助动)[yīng]

① answer; promise ② should; need

另见 yìng

〖应当〗(助动)[yīngdāng]

must; should; ought

〖应该〗(助动)[yīnggāi]

should; need; ought

〖应届〗(名)[yīngjiè]

graduating (e.g. students, class)

Y

英[yīng]

〖英俊〗(形)[yīngjùn]
brilliant and handsome
〖英明〗(形)[yīngmíng]
wise; brilliant; far-seeing
〖英雄〗(名)[yīngxióng]
hero
〖英勇〗(形)[yīngyǒng]
brave; valiant; heroic; courageous
〖英姿〗(名)[yīngzī]
heroic figure; bright and brave; valiant and fine looking

婴[yīng]

〖婴儿〗(名)[yīng'ér]
infant; baby

鹰(名)[yīng]〔只 zhī〕
eagle; falcon
〖鹰犬〗(名)[yīngquǎn]
① falcon and hound ② obsequious lackey

yíng

迎(动)[yíng]
①face; meet ②welcome; receive
〖迎风招展〗
[yíngfēngzhāozhǎn]
wave in the wind
〖迎合〗(动)[yínghé]
cater to; fawn upon; accommodation to serve the purposes of
〖迎接〗(动)[yíngjiē]
meet; welcome; receive
〖迎面〗[yíngmiàn]
meet face to face
〖迎刃而解〗[yíngrèn'érjiě]
(lit.) splits off as if meets the edge of knife; (fig.) once the main problem is grasped, all the other problems can easily be solved
〖迎头痛击〗[yíngtóutòngjī]
deal head-on blows; deal a telling blow
〖迎新〗[yíngxīn]
welcome the new comers

荧[yíng]

〖荧光屏〗(名)[yíngguāngpíng]
fluorescent screen

盈[yíng]

〖盈亏〗(名)[yíngkuī]
① waxing and waning (of the moon) ②profit and loss
〖盈余〗(动、名)[yíngyú]
surplus; profit

营(名)[yíng]
① battalion ② management; business
〖营房〗(名)[yíngfáng]
barracks; quarters
〖营救〗(动)[yíngjiù]
save; rescue; go to the rescue of
〖营垒〗(名)[yínglěi]
camp
〖营私舞弊〗[yíngsīwǔbì]
malpractices; embezzlement
〖营养〗(名)[yíngyǎng]

nourishment; nutrition
〖营业〗(动)[yíngyè]
do business; trade; commercial enterprise; buying and selling
〖营长〗(名)[yíngzhǎng]
battalion commander

赢(动)[yíng]
win; gain; score; obtain
〖赢得〗(动)[yíngdé]
win over; gain; score

yǐng

影(名)[yǐng]
shadow
〖影片〗(名)[yǐngpiàn]〔部 bù〕
cinema; film
〖影评〗(名)[yǐngpíng]
movie review; comment on films
〖影射〗(动)[yǐngshè]
insinuate; hint at (sth. else); innuendo
〖影响〗(名、动)[yǐngxiǎng]
have an effect on; affect; influence; impact
〖影印〗(动)[yǐngyìn]
photoprint; photostat
〖影子〗(名)[yǐngzi]
shadow

yìng

应(动)[yìng]
① answer; respond ② promise; comply with ③ deal with
另见 yīng
〖应承〗(动)[yìngchéng]
promise; comply with
〖应酬〗(动)[yìngchou]
engage in social activities; have social intercourse
〖应付〗(动)[yìngfù]
cope with; deal with; temporize; contend with; manage
〖应接不暇〗[yìngjiēbùxiá]
too busy to attend to; have no time to tend to
〖应聘〗[yìngpìn]
accept an offer of employment
〖应声虫〗(名)[yìngshēngchóng]
echoer; mouthpiece; yes-man
〖应邀〗[yìngyāo]
in response to an invitation; answer the invitation of; at the invitation of
〖应用〗(动)[yìngyòng]
apply; put to use
〖应用文〗(名)[yìngyòngwén]
practical writings (such as letters, notices, invitations, etc.)
〖应运而生〗[yìngyùn'érshēng]
arise at the historic moment; emerge as the times require
〖应战〗[yìngzhàn]
① accept battle; accept combat; engage ... in battle ② accept a challenge
〖应征〗[yìngzhēng]
① enlist; join the army ② essay-writing in response to the editor's arrangements

硬(形、副)[yìng]
① hard ② unyielding ③ delib-

erately; wilfully; arbitrarily
〖硬币〗(名)[yìngbì]
hard currency; specie; coin
〖硬度〗(名)[yìngdù]
hardness
〖硬功夫〗(名)[yìnggōngfu]
great efficiency; masterly skill
〖硬骨头〗(名)[yìnggǔtou]
spirit of unyielding integrity; steel-willed person
〖硬化〗(动)[yìnghuà]
sclerotize; cementate; vulcanize; hardening; stiffening
〖硬席〗(名)[yìngxí]
hard seat; wooden seat
〖硬仗〗(名)[yìngzhàng]
fierce battle; desperate combat; stiff fight

yō

哟(叹)[yō]
int. Oh!

yōng

拥[yōng]
〖拥抱〗(动)[yōngbào]
embrace; hug; fold in one's arms
〖拥护〗(动)[yōnghù]
support; stand for; uphold
〖拥挤〗(形)[yōngjǐ]
crowded; packed; pressed together
〖拥军优属〗[yōngjūnyōushǔ]
support the army and give preferential treatment to the families of the armymen
〖拥有〗(动)[yōngyǒu]
retain; possess; take possession of; have
〖拥政爱民〗[yōngzhèng'àimín]
support the government and cherish the people

庸[yōng]
〖庸俗〗(形)[yōngsú]
vulgar; philistine
〖庸俗化〗(动)[yōngsúhuà]
vulgarization; debase

臃[yōng]
〖臃肿〗(形)[yōngzhǒng]
① swollen ② heavily padded; burdensome ③ overstaffed and overlapping (e.g. organization)

yǒng

永(副)[yǒng]
ever; forever; for good; permanent; eternal
〖永别〗(动)[yǒngbié]
parting forever
〖永垂不朽〗[yǒngchuíbùxiǔ]
eternal glory to; immortal; live forever in the hearts of; win immortality
〖永恒〗(形)[yǒnghéng]
eternal; everlasting
〖永久〗(形)[yǒngjiǔ]
perpetual; everlasting; forever
〖永久性〗(名)[yǒngjiǔxìng]
eternity; perpetuity
〖永生〗(名、动)[yǒngshēng]

eternal life
〖永远〗(副)[yǒngyuǎn]
always; forever; eternally; perpetual; everlasting

甬 [yǒng]
〖甬道〗(名)[yǒngdào]〔条 tiáo〕
gallery; passageway; hallway; covered corridor

勇 (形)[yǒng]
brave; valiant; courageous; bold
〖勇敢〗(形)[yǒnggǎn]
bold; courageous; brave
〖勇猛〗(形)[yǒngměng]
valiant; militant; fearless
〖勇气〗(名)[yǒngqì]
courage; dauntless spirit
〖勇士〗(名)[yǒngshì]
brave man; hero; valiant fighter
〖勇往直前〗[yǒngwǎngzhíqián]
dauntless march; stride bravely forward; advance courageously
〖勇于〗(动)[yǒngyú]
dare to; have the courage to

涌 (动)[yǒng]
gush forth; push forward
〖涌现〗(动)[yǒngxiàn]
come to the fore; come forward in great numbers

踊 [yǒng]
〖踊跃〗(形)[yǒngyuè]
① jumping joyfully ② eagerly; enthusiastically

yòng

用 (动)[yòng]
① use; exert; employ; apply; make use of; resort to ② need
〖用不着〗[yòngbuzháo]
there is no need to; needless
〖用处〗(名)[yòngchu]
use; application; function
〖用得着〗[yòngdezháo]
of use; needful; necessary
〖用非所学〗[yòngfēisuǒxué]
fail to apply what one has learned; be engaged in an occupation not related to one's training
〖用功〗[yònggōng]
study hard; work hard
〖用户〗(名)[yònghù]
consumer; user
〖用劲〗[yòngjìn]
exert; with all one's energy; make great effort
〖用具〗(名)[yòngjù]
appliance; instrument; tool
〖用力〗[yònglì]
exert one's strength; devote greater efforts
〖用品〗(名)[yòngpǐn]
usable things (matters); necessities
〖用途〗(名)[yòngtú]
use; application
〖用心〗[yòngxīn]
① with concentration; set

one's mind upon ② intention; purpose

〖用以〗(动)[yòngyǐ]
serve as; in order to; for

〖用意〗(名)[yòngyì]
intention; purpose; meaning; attempt

〖用语〗(名)[yòngyǔ]
phrases; phraseology; terms

yōu

优(形)[yōu]
excellent; superior; fine; outstanding

〖优待〗(动、名)[yōudài]
give preferential treatment; lenient treatment

〖优点〗(名)[yōudiǎn]
merit; strong point; advantage; virtue

〖优等〗(形)[yōuděng]
special grade; excellent grade

〖优厚〗(形)[yōuhòu]
(of treatment) favourable; generous; good

〖优化〗(动)[yōuhuà]
optimize; rationalize

〖优惠〗(形)[yōuhuì]
preferential; favourable

〖优良〗(形)[yōuliáng]
excellent; good; fine

〖优美〗(形)[yōuměi]
elegant; beautiful; graceful

〖优柔寡断〗[yōuróuguǎduàn]
incapable of taking strong decision; weak-kneed; be in two minds; indecisive

〖优胜〗(形)[yōushèng]
outstanding; superior

〖优势〗(名)[yōushì]
have the upper hand; dominant position; superiority

〖优先〗(形)[yōuxiān]
priority; precedence; preference

〖优秀〗(形)[yōuxiù]
excellent; outstanding; brilliant; splendid

〖优选法〗(名)[yōuxuǎnfǎ]
optimum seeking method

〖优异〗(形)[yōuyì]
excellent; outstanding

〖优越〗(形)[yōuyuè]
superior; advantageous

〖优越性〗(名)[yōuyuèxìng]
superiority; advantage; supremacy

〖优质〗(名)[yōuzhì]
good quality; excellent quality

〖优质服务〗[yōuzhìfúwù]
first-rate service

〖优质钢〗(名)[yōuzhìgāng]
high-grade steel; quality steel

忧[yōu]

〖忧愁〗(形)[yōuchóu]
sorrowful; worried; anxious; sad

〖忧虑〗(动)[yōulǜ]
worry; concern; be anxious

〖忧伤〗(形)[yōushāng]
sad; grieved; sorrowful

〖忧心忡忡〗[yōuxīnchōngchōng]
gloomy; grieved; look dismal and unhappy
〖忧郁〗(形)[yōuyù]
melancholy; sad; depressed

幽[yōu]
〖幽静〗(形)[yōujìng]
quiet; tranquil; secluded
〖幽灵〗(名)[yōulíng]
spirit; phantom; apparition; spectre; ghost
〖幽默〗(形)[yōumò]
humourous
〖幽雅〗(形)[yōuyǎ]
tranquil and enjoyable; quiet and in good taste

悠[yōu]
〖悠久〗(形)[yōujiǔ]
long enduring; long-standing
〖悠闲〗(形)[yōuxián]
carefree; free; leisurely
〖悠扬〗(形)[yōuyáng]
(melody) floating; rhythmical

yóu

尤(副)[yóu]
extraordinarily; particularly; especially
〖尤其〗(副)[yóuqí]
extraordinary; especially; particularly

由(介)[yóu]
①by; for ②from; thus; hence ③from ... to ... ④because of; thanks to; due to
〖由表及里〗[yóubiǎojílǐ]
from the outside to the inside; proceed from the exterior to the interior; from outward appearance to inner essence
〖由不得〗[yóubude]
cannot help ...
〖由此及彼〗[yóucǐjíbǐ]
proceed from one to the other; proceed from one point to another
〖由点到面〗[yóudiǎndàomiàn]
develop from isolated point into a whole area
〖由来〗(名)[yóulái]
① origin of occurrence ② reason; cause
〖由近及远〗[yóujìnjíyuǎn]
from the close-by examples to those far off
〖由浅入深〗[yóuqiǎnrùshēn]
from the shallower to the deeper; proceed from the simple to the more complex; from the superficial to the deep
〖由于〗(介)[yóuyú]
because of; thanks to; owing to; due to
〖由衷〗(形)[yóuzhōng]
from the heart; from the bottom of one's heart

邮(动)[yóu]
post

〖邮包〗(名)[yóubāo]〔个 gè〕
postal parcel
〖邮递员〗(名)[yóudìyuán]
postman
〖邮电局〗(名)[yóudiànjú]
post office
〖邮费〗(名)[yóufèi]
postage; postal charges
〖邮购〗[yóugòu]
buy by mail order
〖邮件〗(名)[yóujiàn]
letters and parcels; postal matter
〖邮票〗(名)[yóupiào]
〔张 zhāng〕post stamp
〖邮筒〗(名)[yóutǒng]
pillar box
〖邮箱〗(名)[yóuxiāng]
post box
〖邮政〗(名)[yóuzhèng]
postal service
〖邮政编码〗[yóuzhèngbiānmǎ]
postcode; zip code
〖邮政储蓄〗[yóuzhèngchǔxù]
postal savings account

犹[yóu]

〖犹如〗(动)[yóurú]
as if; like
〖犹豫〗(形)[yóuyù]
hesitate; uncertain
〖犹豫不决〗[yóuyùbùjué]
indecisive; hesitate to act; not able to make up one's mind; shilly-shally; vacillate

油(名、动)[yóu]

①oil; fat ②varnish; paint
〖油泵〗(名)[yóubèng]〔台 tái〕
oil pump
〖油画〗(名)[yóuhuà]〔幅 fú〕
oil painting
〖油井〗(名)[yóujǐng]〔口 kǒu〕
oil well
〖油料〗(名)[yóuliào]
oil-yielding material
〖油料作物〗[yóuliàozuòwù]
oil-bearing crops
〖油腻〗(形)[yóunì]
greasy; oily (food)
〖油漆〗(名)[yóuqī]
varnish; oil paint
〖油水〗(名)[yóushui]
①oil or fat in meal
②perquisite
〖油田〗(名)[yóutián]
oil-field
〖油汪汪〗(形)[yóuwāngwāng]
very shiny; oily
〖油印〗(动)[yóuyìn]
mimeograph
〖油毡〗(名)[yóuzhān]
asphaltic rug; linoleum

游(动)[yóu]

① swim ② tour; travel; roam ③ float; drift ④play
〖游船〗(名)[yóuchuán]〔只 zhī〕
yacht; motor-boat
〖游逛〗(动)[yóuguàng]
wander; roam; take a stroll
〖游击〗(名)[yóujī]
guerrilla; wage guerrilla warfare

Y

〖游击队〗(名)[yóujīduì]
guerrillas; partisans
〖游击战〗(名)[yóujīzhàn]
guerrilla warfare
〖游记〗(名)[yóujì]
travels; a travel sketch; travelogue
〖游客〗(名)[yóukè]
tourist; traveller; sight-seer
〖游览〗(动)[yóulǎn]
tour; go sight-seeing
〖游离〗(动)[yóulí]
① ionize ② isolate; drift
〖游人〗(名)[yóurén]
traveller; tourist
〖游手好闲〗[yóushǒuhàoxián]
loaf; idle
〖游玩〗(动)[yóuwán]
play; amuse (oneself)
〖游戏〗(名)[yóuxì]
(play) game
〖游行〗(动、名)[yóuxíng]
parade; demonstration; march
〖游弋〗(动)[yóuyì]
cruise
〖游艺〗(名)[yóuyì]
pastime; amusement
〖游泳〗(名、动)[yóuyǒng]
swim
〖游泳池〗(名)[yóuyǒngchí]
swimming pool
〖游园〗[yóuyuán]
take part in (grand) garden party; gala party

yǒu

友(名)[yǒu]
friend
〖友爱〗(动)[yǒu'ài]
befriend; amiable
〖友邦〗(名)[yǒubāng]
friendly country
〖友好〗(形)[yǒuhǎo]
friendly; goodwill; amiable; cordial
〖友情〗(名)[yǒuqíng]
friendship; cordial feelings
〖友人〗(名)[yǒurén]
friend
〖友谊〗(名)[yǒuyì]
friendship
〖友谊第一,比赛第二〗
[yǒuyìdì yī, bǐsàidì'èr]
friendship first, competition second

有(动)[yǒu]
① have; there is ② appear; present; take place ③ possess; own
〖有备无患〗[yǒubèiwúhuàn]
preparedness averts peril; preparedness prevents calamity
〖有待〗(动)[yǒudài]
wait for; have still to be; remain to be seen
〖有的〗(代)[yǒude]
some; certain
〖有的是〗[yǒudeshì]
a lot of; many; be abundant in
〖有的放矢〗[yǒudìfàngshǐ]
shoot the arrow at the target; with a definite object in view
〖有点儿〗[yǒudiǎnr]

a few; a little
〖有关〗(动)[yǒuguān]
relative; relevant; concerned; have ... to do with
〖有过之而无不及〗
[yǒuguò zhī'érwúbùjí]
(usu. derog.) go farther than
〖有害〗[yǒuhài]
harmful; pernicious; detrimental; do harm to; impair; damage
〖有机〗(形)[yǒujī]
organic
〖有机肥料〗[yǒujī féiliào]
organic fertilizer
〖有机化学〗[yǒujī huàxué]
organic chemistry
〖有机物〗(名)[yǒujīwù]
organic matter
〖有奖销售〗
[yǒujiǎngxiāoshòu]
comeback premium; offer a premium with the sale of an item
〖有口皆碑〗[yǒukǒujiēbēi]
be praised by all; universal praise
〖有赖〗(动)[yǒulài]
depend on; rely on; place hope upon; rest with
〖有理〗[yǒulǐ]
reasonable; be in the right; with good reason; on just ground
〖有力〗(形)[yǒulì]
weighty; convincing; powerful; effective
〖有利〗(形)[yǒulì]
favourable; with advantage; advantageous
〖有名〗[yǒumíng]
famous; wellknown; renowned
〖有名无实〗[yǒumíngwúshí]
titular; in name but not in reality; symbolic; merely nominal
〖有目共睹〗[yǒumùgòngdǔ]
obvious to all; clear to all
〖有气无力〗[yǒuqìwúlì]
lifeless; feebly
〖有趣〗(形)[yǒuqù]
interesting; amusing; pleasant
〖有色金属〗[yǒusèjīnshǔ]
non-ferrous metals
〖有生力量〗[yǒushēnglìliàng]
effective strength; effectives
〖有声有色〗[yǒushēngyǒusè]
vivid; alive; full of sound and colour
〖有时〗[yǒushí]
sometimes; at times; occasionally; now and then; from time to time
〖有始有终〗[yǒushǐyǒuzhōng]
finish what is started; do sth. well from beginning to end; prosecute to the end
〖有恃无恐〗[yǒushìwúkǒng]
have sth. secure to rely on; be emboldened by the support of ...
〖有数〗[yǒushù]
① know what's what ② a limited number; a few; not much
〖有说有笑〗[yǒushuōyǒuxiào]
talking and joking
〖有条不紊〗[yǒutiáobùwěn]
systematic; in perfect order; orderly; (everything) in good

order

〖有条有理〗[yǒutiáoyǒulǐ]
methodical; well-organized and clearly stated

〖有为〗(形)[yǒuwéi]
promising; capable

〖有隙可乘〗[yǒuxìkěchéng]
a possibility to take advantage of a chance for ...; there is a crack to wedge oneself into

〖有限〗(形)[yǒuxiàn]
limited; restricted

〖有限公司〗[yǒuxiàngōngsī]
limited company; limited liability company

〖有线电视〗[yǒuxiàndiànshì]
cable television; cable TV

〖有线广播〗[yǒuxiànguǎngbō]
wire broadcasting; wired broadcasting

〖有效〗[yǒuxiào]
① efficient; effective ② valid; remain in effect; in force

〖有些〗[yǒuxiē]
① some; a part of; a bit of ② there is a few; have a little; several

〖有血有肉〗[yǒuxuèyǒuròu]
vivid; life-like (referring to an article, story, etc. with vivid description and rich content)

〖有心〗[yǒuxīn]
① having the intention to; set one's mind to ② deliberately; purposely

〖有形〗[yǒuxíng]
tangible; visible; material

〖有形贸易〗[yǒuxíngmàoyì]
visible trade

〖有形资产〗[yǒuxíngzīchǎn]
tangible assets

〖有益〗[yǒuyì]
beneficial; useful; helpful; good for

〖有意〗[yǒuyì]
want to; have a mind; intentionally; purposely; deliberately

〖有意识〗[yǒuyìshi]
consciously; deliberately

〖有意思〗[yǒuyìsi]
① significant; meaningful ② interesting

〖有用〗[yǒuyòng]
useful; suitable; serviceable

〖有则改之,无则加勉〗[yǒuzé gǎizhī, wúzéjiāmiǎn]
correct mistakes if you have committed them and guard against them if you have not

〖有增无减〗[yǒuzēngwújiǎn]
never reduce but increase

〖有朝一日〗[yǒuzhāoyīrì]
some day; there will be a day

〖有着〗(动)[yǒuzhe]
there is; have; possess

〖有志者事竟成〗[yǒuzhìzhě shìjìngchéng]
where there is a will there is a way; strong will leads to success

yòu

又(副)[yòu]
① again ② and; both; also ③ in

addition to; more ④ moreover; further
〖又及〗[yòují]
postscript (PS)

右(名、形)[yòu]
①right; right side ②rightist (ideas, way of thinking, etc.)
〖右边〗(名)[yòubian]
the right side; right hand side
〖右派〗(名)[yòupài]
rightist
〖右倾〗(名)[yòuqīng]
right deviation; right opportunist tendencies
〖右倾机会主义〗[yòuqīngjīhuìzhǔyì]
right opportunism
〖右翼〗(名)[yòuyì]
right-wing; right flank

幼(形)[yòu]
① young; infantile ② naive; childish
〖幼儿〗(名)[yòu'ér]
young child; baby; infant
〖幼儿园〗(名)[yòu'éryuán]
kindergarten
〖幼苗〗(名)[yòumiáo]
sprout; young shoot
〖幼小〗(形)[yòuxiǎo]
infantile; young
〖幼稚〗(形)[yòuzhì]
childish; naive; immature; infantile

诱(动)[yòu]
①lure; entice; seduce ②guide; induce
〖诱导〗(动)[yòudǎo]
guide and instruct; deduce; induce
〖诱饵〗(名)[yòu'ěr]
bait; entice
〖诱惑〗(动)[yòuhuò]
①lure; induce; incite ②fascinate
〖诱骗〗(动)[yòupiàn]
lure; entice; inveigle ... into the trap

yū

迂[yū]
〖迂回〗(动、形)[yūhuí]
go round; walk round; roundabout; tortuous; circuitous

淤(动)[yū]
silt; block up; be clogged up
〖淤积〗(动)[yūjī]
form sediment; accumulation of mud
〖淤塞〗(动)[yūsè]
silt; block up; be clogged up; full of sediment
〖淤血〗(名)[yūxuè]
blood clot; extravasated blood

yú

于(介)[yú]
①to ②at; in ③with ④from
〖于是〗(连)[yúshì]
therefore; hence; also; then; accordingly; consequently

余(动、形)[yú]
remain; leave over; leftover; surplus
〖余地〗(名)[yúdì]
room (for); extra space (for); (enough) place (for); margin
〖余毒〗(名)[yúdú]
pernicious vestiges; left-over poison
〖余额〗(名)[yú'é]
① available sum unused ② vacancies not taken up
〖余粮〗(名)[yúliáng]
grain surplus
〖余孽〗(名)[yúniè]
left-over evils; remaining evils
〖余数〗(名)[yúshù]
left-over number; remainder after subtraction
〖余味〗(名)[yúwèi]
remaining taste; after-taste
〖余暇〗(名)[yúxiá]
leisure; spare time

鱼(名)[yú]〔条 tiáo〕
fish
〖鱼雷〗(名)[yúléi]
torpedo
〖鱼雷快艇〗[yúléikuàitǐng]
〔艘 sōu〕propeller torpedo boat
〖鱼米之乡〗[yúmǐzhīxiāng]
region teeming with fish and rice; district where fish and rice are abundant
〖鱼目混珠〗[yúmùhùnzhū]
(lit.) pass fish eyes for pearls; (fig.) mix the genuine with the fictitious

娱[yú]
〖娱乐〗(动、名)[yúlè]
amuse; pass time; recreation; entertainment

渔(名)[yú]
① fishery ② fishing for (profit)
〖渔利〗(动)[yúlì]
fish for profits at others' expense; seek gains out of strife
〖渔民〗(名)[yúmín]
fisherman
〖渔业〗(名)[yúyè]
fishery

愉[yú]
〖愉快〗(形)[yúkuài]
happy; merry; pleasant; delightful

逾(动)[yú]
exceed; go beyond
〖逾期〗[yúqī]
passed time limit; overdue
〖逾越〗(动)[yúyuè]
go beyond; exceed

愚(形)[yú]
foolish; dull-witted
〖愚笨〗(形)[yúbèn]
dull-witted; silly; blockhead

〖愚蠢〗(形)[yúchǔn]
blockhead; foolish; stupid
〖愚公移山〗[Yúgōngyíshān]
The Foolish Old Man Who Removed the Mountains (the story of how an old man removed the mountains)
〖愚昧〗(形)[yúmèi]
ignorant
〖愚弄〗(动)[yúnòng]
dupe; fool; deceive

舆[yú]
〖舆论〗(名)[yúlùn]
public opinion
〖舆论导向〗[yúlùndǎoxiàng]
direction toward which people are guided in thinking
〖舆论工具〗[yúlùngōngjù]
mass media

yǔ

与(介、连)[yǔ]
①with; together with ②and
〖与其…不如…〗[yǔqí…bùrú…]
rather ... than ...; more ... than ...; prefer ... to ...
〖与人为善〗[yǔrénwéishàn]
aim at helping others; with good intentions toward others
〖与日俱增〗[yǔrìjùzēng]
increase with each passing day; multiply daily; grow with time
〖与世隔绝〗[yǔshìgéjué]
seclude from the world

予(动)[yǔ]
give
〖予以〗(动)[yǔyǐ]
give

宇[yǔ]
〖宇宙〗(名)[yǔzhòu]
cosmos; universe; heaven and earth
〖宇宙观〗(名)[yǔzhòuguān]
world outlook

羽[yǔ]
〖羽毛〗(名)[yǔmáo]
feather; fledge
〖羽毛球〗(名)[yǔmáoqiú]
badminton

雨(名)[yǔ]
rain
〖雨过天晴〗[yǔguòtiānqíng]
sunny spell after rain; difficult period gives way to bright future
〖雨后春笋〗[yǔhòuchūnsǔn]
(spring up like) bamboo shoots after spring rain
〖雨季〗(名)[yǔjì]
rainy season
〖雨具〗(名)[yǔjù]
things used as protection against rain (raincoat, umbrella, etc.)
〖雨量〗(名)[yǔliàng]
rainfall; precipitation
〖雨露〗(名)[yǔlù]
rain and dew
〖雨伞〗(名)[yǔsǎn]〔把 bǎ〕

umbrella
〖雨鞋〗(名)[yǔxié]
〔双 shuāng〕rain shoes
〖雨衣〗(名)[yǔyī]〔件 jiàn〕
raincoat

语(名、动)[yǔ]

①language; words ②idiom; saying ③say; speak
〖语病〗(名)[yǔbìng]
mistakes in use of words; a rhetorical error
〖语调〗(名)[yǔdiào]
intonation
〖语法〗(名)[yǔfǎ]
grammar
〖语汇〗(名)[yǔhuì]
vocabulary
〖语句〗(名)[yǔjù]
sentence
〖语录〗(名)[yǔlù]
quotation
〖语气〗(名)[yǔqì]
tone of one's words
〖语气词〗(名)[yǔqìcí]
modal particle
〖语文〗(名)[yǔwén]
language and its written forms
〖语无伦次〗[yǔwúlúncì]
ramble in one's statement
〖语言〗(名)[yǔyán]
language
〖语言规范化〗
[yǔyánguīfànhuà]
standardization of language
〖语音〗(名)[yǔyīn]
phonetics
〖语重心长〗[yǔzhòngxīncháng]
in all earnestness; meaningfully; sincere advice of which each word carries weight
〖语助词〗(名)[yǔzhùcí]
particle

yù

玉(名)[yù]〔块 kuài〕

jade; gem
〖玉雕〗(名)[yùdiāo]
jade carving
〖玉米〗(名)[yùmǐ]
maize; corn

育(动)[yù]

①give birth; ②breed; cultivate; bring up
〖育苗〗[yùmiáo]
cultivate sprout; cultivate seedling
〖育种〗[yùzhǒng]
breeding of seeds

浴[yù]

〖浴室〗(名)[yùshì]
bathroom
〖浴血奋战〗[yùxuèfènzhàn]
bloodshed fight; fierce battle

预[yù]

〖预报〗(动)[yùbào]
forecast (e.g. weather forecast)
〖预备〗(动)[yùbèi]
prepare; get ready; arrange for

〖预订〗(动)[yùdìng]
place an order for; book; subscribe
〖预定〗(动)[yùdìng]
prearrange; preconcert; predefine; predetermine
〖预防〗(动)[yùfáng]
prevent; provide against; guard against
〖预防为主〗[yùfángwéizhǔ]
put prevention first
〖预感〗(动、名)[yùgǎn]
have premonitions of; presage
〖预告〗(动、名)[yùgào]
predict; foretell; forecast; presage; prediction
〖预计〗(动)[yùjì]
expect envisage; reckon in advance
〖预见〗(名、动)[yùjiàn]
foresee; prediction; foresight
〖预料〗(动)[yùliào]
predict; expect; foresee; anticipate
〖预期〗(形)[yùqī]
expect; anticipate
〖预赛〗(名)[yùsài]
preliminary contest
〖预示〗(动)[yùshì]
presage; portend; predict; foretell
〖预算〗(名、动)[yùsuàn]
budget
〖预习〗(动)[yùxí]
prepare lessons
〖预先〗(形)[yùxiān]
preliminary; pre; in advance; beforehand
〖预想〗(动)[yùxiǎng]
expect; anticipate; previously formulate; contemplate
〖预言〗(名、动)[yùyán]
predict; presage; foretell; prophesy
〖预演〗(动)[yùyǎn]
rehearsal; rehearse
〖预约〗(动)[yùyuē]
pre-engage; make an appointment ... beforehand
〖预展〗(动)[yùzhǎn]
exhibit in advance
〖预兆〗(名)[yùzhào]
omen; augur; presage; foreshadow

欲[yù]

〖欲盖弥彰〗[yùgàimízhāng]
the more one tries to hide, the more one is exposed; the more concealed, the more conspicuous
〖欲望〗(名)[yùwàng]
desire; longing; hankering

遇(动)[yù]

meet
〖遇到〗(动)[yùdào]
meet; meet with; encounter; run into (e.g. difficulties)
〖遇害〗[yùhài]
be murdered; be killed
〖遇见〗(动)[yùjiàn]
meet; encounter
〖遇救〗[yùjiù]

be rescued
〖遇难〗[yùnàn]
die in an accident or as a result of persecution
〖遇险〗[yùxiǎn]
meet with danger

寓[yù]
〖寓所〗(名)[yùsuǒ]
residence; place of residence
〖寓言〗(名)[yùyán]
fable; parable

愈(动、副)[yù]
① recover from an illness ② the more ... the more; more and more
〖愈合〗(动)[yùhé]
heal up
〖愈加〗(副)[yùjiā]
increasingly; all the more
〖愈…愈…〗[yù…yù…]
the more ... the more ...

yuān

渊[yuān]
〖渊博〗(形)[yuānbó]
profound (e.g. knowl edge); broad (e.g. erudition)
〖渊深〗(形)[yuānshēn]
deep (e.g. learning)

Y

冤(名、动)[yuān]
① injustice; false charge; unfairness; wrong ② enmity; hatred
〖冤仇〗(名)[yuānchóu]
enmity; hatred
〖冤屈〗(动)[yuānqū]
be wronged
〖冤枉〗(动、形)[yuānwang]
① be falsely accused; be wronged ② unfair; injustice; false charge

yuán

元(量)[yuán]
a measure word, Yuan (unit of money in China)
〖元旦〗(名)[Yuándàn]
New Year's Day
〖元件〗(名)[yuánjiàn]
parts; accessories (of machine, meter, radio set, etc.)
〖元老〗(名)[yuánlǎo]
veteran
〖元首〗(名)[yuánshǒu]
head of state
〖元帅〗(名)[yuánshuài]
marshal
〖元素〗(名)[yuánsù]
(chemical) element
〖元素符号〗[yuánsùfúhào]
(chemical) element symbol
〖元素周期表〗[yuánsùzhōuqībiǎo]
the periodic table (of chemical elements)
〖元音〗(名)[yuányīn]
vowel
〖元月〗(名)[yuányuè]
January

园(名)[yuán]
garden

〖园地〗(名)[yuándì]
a general term for vegetable plot, fruit orchard, flower garden, etc.
〖园林〗(名)[yuánlín]
park garden; landscape garden
〖园田化〗(动)[yuántiánhuà]
meticulously cultivate field
〖园艺〗(名)[yuányì]
art of gardening; horticulture
〖园子〗(名)[yuánzi]
vegetable patch; vegetable plot

员(尾)[yuán]
suffix (person)
〖员工〗(名)[yuángōng]
staff members and workers

原(形)[yuán]
①primitive; primeval; original②crude (e.g. oil); raw (e.g. materials)
〖原产地〗(名)[yuánchǎndì]
country of origin
〖原封不动〗[yuánfēngbùdòng]
be kept intact; remain unchanged; in its original state; untouched
〖原稿〗(名)[yuángǎo]
original; original manuscript; original copy
〖原告〗(名)[yuángào]
plaintiff; accuser
〖原籍〗(名)[yuánjí]
native home; native place
〖原来〗(形、副)[yuánlái]
①at first; at the beginning; originally②it turns out that ...; as a matter of fact
〖原理〗(名)[yuánlǐ]
principle; fundamental theory; axiom
〖原谅〗(动)[yuánliàng]
pardon; excuse
〖原料〗(名)[yuánliào]
raw materials
〖原始〗(形)[yuánshǐ]
①primitive; virgin; primeval; primordial②original; initial; firsthand
〖原始社会〗[yuánshǐshèhuì]
primitive society
〖原先〗(形)[yuánxiān]
original; at first
〖原形毕露〗[yuánxíngbìlù]
(derog.) reveal one's true nature; show one's true colours
〖原野〗(名)[yuányě]
open country
〖原因〗(名)[yuányīn]
cause; reason; grounds
〖原油〗(名)[yuányóu]
crude oil
〖原原本本〗(形)[yuányuánběnběn]
from the beginning to the end
〖原则〗(名)[yuánzé]
principle; fundamental rule
〖原则性〗(名)[yuánzéxìng]
of principle; highly principled
〖原著〗(名)[yuánzhù]
original; original copy
〖原子〗(名)[yuánzǐ]

atom
〖原子弹〗(名)[yuánzǐdàn]
atom bomb
〖原子反应堆〗
[yuánzǐfǎnyìngduī]
atomic reactor
〖原子核〗(名)[yuánzǐhé]
atomic nucleus
〖原子结构〗[yuánzǐjiégòu]
atom structure
〖原子量〗(名)[yuánzǐliàng]
atomic weight
〖原子能〗(名)[yuánzǐnéng]
atomic energy
〖原子序数〗[yuánzǐxùshù]
atomic number

圆 (名、形)[yuán]
① circle ② money unit (Yuan) ③ round; smooth; circular
〖圆规〗(名)[yuánguī]
compasses
〖圆滑〗(形)[yuánhuá]
oily; cunning; slippery
〖圆满〗(形)[yuánmǎn]
satisfactory; complete; perfect; round off
〖圆圈〗(名)[yuánquān]
circle; ring
〖圆心〗(名)[yuánxīn]
centre of a circle
〖圆形〗(名)[yuánxíng]
circular; round
〖圆周〗(名)[yuánzhōu]
circumference
〖圆周率〗(名)[yuánzhōulǜ]
Pi (π); the ratio of circumference to diameter
〖圆珠笔〗(名)[yuánzhūbǐ]
〔枝 zhī〕ball-pen
〖圆柱〗(名)[yuánzhù]
cylinder; column; pillar
〖圆锥〗(名)[yuánzhuī]
cone

援 (动)[yuán]
① support; help; assist; aid ② quote; cite
〖援救〗(动)[yuánjiù]
rescue; extricate from danger; save
〖援军〗(名)[yuánjūn]
rescue troops; reinforcement
〖援引〗(动)[yuányǐn]
quote; cite
〖援助〗(动、名)[yuánzhù]
help; assist; support; aid

缘 [yuán]
〖缘故〗(名)[yuángù]
reason; cause

猿 (名)[yuán]
ape
〖猿人〗(名)[yuánrén]
anthropoid ape; ape man

源 (名)[yuán]
source; fountain
〖源泉〗(名)[yuánquán]
spring; fountain; source
〖源源〗(副)[yuányuán]

continuously; uninterruptedly

yuǎn

远(形)[yuǎn]
far; long; remote; distant; far away
〖远大〗(形)[yuǎndà]
far-reaching; great; broad; long-range
〖远方〗(名)[yuǎnfāng]
distant; remote
〖远见〗(名)[yuǎnjiàn]
far-sighted view; far-sightedness; foresight
〖远近〗(名)[yuǎnjìn]
distance
〖远景〗(名)[yuǎnjǐng]
distant prospect; outlook; long-range prospective
〖远期〗(名)[yuǎnqī]
forward; at a specified future date
〖远洋〗(名)[yuǎnyáng]
the distant seas; ocean-going (e.g. vessel)
〖远征〗(动)[yuǎnzhēng]
① expedition; military expedition ② long march
〖远走高飞〗[yuǎnzǒuggāofēi]
go away to a distant place

yuàn

怨(名、动)[yuàn]
① hatred; grudge ② blame; resent
〖怨不得〗[yuànbude]
cannot blame; not to be blamed
〖怨恨〗(名、动)[yuànhèn]
hatred; grudge; hate; bear resentment against
〖怨气〗(名)[yuànqì]
grudge; resentment; complaint
〖怨声载道〗[yuànshēngzàidào]
voices of discontent are heard everywhere
〖怨天尤人〗[yuàntiānyóurén]
blame Heaven and others; blame all and sundry
〖怨言〗(名)[yuànyán]
grumble; repining; complaints

院(名)[yuàn]
① court ② courtyard ③ institution
〖院子〗(名)[yuànzi]
courtyard

愿(助动)[yuàn]
wish; would like
〖愿望〗(名)[yuànwàng]
wish; desire; aspiration; hope; expectation
〖愿意〗(助动)[yuànyì]
① be willing; be ready ② want; like; desire

yuē

约(动)[yuē]
① make an appointment ② invite ③ keep in control; bind; restrain
〖约定俗成〗[yuēdìngsúchéng]

recognition (of customs or terminology, etc.) is resulted from common practice
〖约分〗[yuēfēn]
common denomination
〖约会〗(动、名)[yuēhuì]
appointment; engagement; rendezvous
〖约请〗(动)[yuēqǐng]
invite
〖约束〗(动、名)[yuēshù]
restrain; control; bind; confine
〖约数〗(名)[yuēshù]
① approximate number ② divider

yuè

月 (名)[yuè]
① the moon ② month
〖月初〗(名)[yuèchū]
the beginning of a month
〖月底〗(名)[yuèdǐ]
the end of a month
〖月份〗(名)[yuèfèn]
month as a period of time
〖月份牌〗(名)[yuèfènpái]
monthly calendar
〖月光〗(名)[yuèguāng]
moonlight
〖月经〗(名)[yuèjīng]
menstruation; menses
〖月亮〗(名)[yuèliàng]
the moon
〖月票〗(名)[yuèpiào]
〔张 zhāng〕monthly ticket
〖月球〗(名)[yuèqiú]
the moon
〖月色〗(名)[yuèsè]
moonlight
〖月食〗(名)[yuèshí]
eclipse of the moon
〖月中〗(名)[yuèzhōng]
the middle of a month

乐(名)[yuè]
music
另见 lè
〖乐队〗(名)[yuèduì]
orchestra; band
〖乐理〗(名)[yuèlǐ]
musical theory
〖乐谱〗(名)[yuèpǔ]
musical score; score sheets
〖乐器〗(名)[yuèqì]
musical instrument
〖乐曲〗(名)[yuèqǔ]
melody; musical composition
〖乐团〗(名)[yuètuán]
musical troupe

岳[yuè]
〖岳父〗(名)[yuèfù]
father-in-law (wife's father)
〖岳母〗(名)[yuèmǔ]
mother-in-law (wife's mother)

悦[yuè]
〖悦耳〗(形)[yuè'ěr]
pleasant to the ear; please the ear
〖悦目〗(形)[yuèmù]
pleasant to the eye; please the eye

阅(动)[yuè]
see; read; go over
〖阅兵〗[yuèbīng]
review troops; a military review
〖阅读〗(动)[yuèdú]
read
〖阅览〗(动)[yuèlǎn]
read
〖阅览室〗(名)[yuèlǎnshì]
reading room

跃(动)[yuè]
jump
〖跃进〗(动)[yuèjìn]
make progress by leaps and bounds; make a leap; leap forward
〖跃跃欲试〗[yuèyuèyùshì]
anxious to try; itch to have a go

越(动、副)[yuè]
① exceed; surpass; cross ② deviate from; departure from (rules, principles, etc.) ③ more and more; all the more
〖越发〗(副)[yuèfā]
more and more; increasingly
〖越轨〗[yuè guǐ]
beyond bounds; derail; deviate; departure from (rules, principles, etc.)
〖越过〗(动)[yuèguò]
surpass; pass over; cross; pass by
〖越境〗[yuèjìng]
illegally cross over a boundary
〖越来越…〗(副)[yuèláiyuè…]
more and more; ever more; all the more; increasingly
〖越野〗[yuèyě]
cross-country
〖越狱〗[yuèyù]
escape from prison;break prison
〖越…越…〗[yuè…yuè…]
the more ... the more ...

yūn

晕(动)[yūn]
faint; dizzy
另见 yùn
〖晕头转向〗
[yūntóuzhuànxiàng]
muddle-headed; dizzy

yún

云(名)[yún]
clouds
〖云彩〗(名)[yúncai]
clouds
〖云层〗(名)[yúncéng]
cloud layer
〖云集〗(动)[yúnjí]
gather together
〖云消雾散〗[yúnxiāowùsàn]
the sky has cleared up; clear up; disappear; vanish without a trace

匀(形、动)[yún]
① even; well-divided; well-balanced ② share; divide; smooth out; even up

〖匀称〗(形)[yúnchèn]
well-balanced; well-proportioned

〖匀净〗(形)[yúnjing]
well-balanced; well-proportioned

〖匀速运动〗[yúnsùyùndòng]
uniform motion

〖匀速转动〗[yúnsùzhuàndòng]
uniform rotation

〖匀整〗(形)[yúnzhěng]
well-proportioned and orderly

yǔn

允(动)[yǔn]
allow; permit; promise; approve; give consent

〖允许〗(动)[yǔnxǔ]
promise; permit; give permission; allow

yùn

孕(名)[yùn]
pregnancy

〖孕妇〗(名)[yùnfù]
pregnant woman

〖孕育〗(动)[yùnyù]
be pregnant with; breed; carry within itself

运(动)[yùn]
① transport ② apply; utilize; put to use

〖运筹学〗(名)[yùnchóuxué]
operations research

〖运动〗(动、名)[yùndòng]
① move; be in motion ② sports; athletics ③ campaign; movement

〖运动服〗(名)[yùndòngfú]
〔件 jiàn〕sports clothes

〖运动会〗(名)[yùndònghuì]
athletics meeting; sports meeting; games

〖运动员〗(名)[yùndòngyuán]
athlete

〖运动战〗(名)[yùndòngzhàn]
mobile warfare

〖运费〗(名)[yùnfèi]
freight; carriage; transportation expenses

〖运河〗(名)[yùnhé]〔条 tiáo〕
canal

〖运气〗(名)[yùnqi]
luck; fortune

〖运输〗(动)[yùnshū]
transport

〖运送〗(动)[yùnsòng]
send; deliver; transport

〖运算〗(动)[yùnsuàn]
(math.) operate

〖运行〗(动)[yùnxíng]
circulate; revolve

〖运行机制〗[yùnxíngjīzhì]
operating mechanism; operational mechanism

〖运用〗(动)[yùnyòng]
apply; put to use; utilize

〖运载〗(动)[yùnzài]
carry; deliver

〖运载火箭〗[yùnzàihuǒjiàn]
carrier rocket

〖运转〗(动)[yùnzhuǎn]
revolve

晕(动)[yùn]
feel giddy; be dizzy
另见 yūn
〖晕车〗[yùnchē]
carsick
〖晕船〗[yùnchuán]
seasick

酝[yùn]
〖酝酿〗(动)[yùnniàng]
brew; foment; ferment

韵(名)[yùn]
tone; rhyme; "yun" — final of a syllable
〖韵母〗(名)[yùnmǔ]
"yun", final part of a syllable

蕴[yùn]
〖蕴藏〗(动)[yùncáng]
hoard; hide

熨(动)[yùn]
press; iron (e.g. clothes)
〖熨斗〗(名)[yùndǒu]
iron (for pressing clothes)

zā

扎(动)[zā]
tie;bind; fasten
另见 zhā

zá

杂(形、动)[zá]
①miscellaneous; mixed; assorted②mix; blend
〖杂感〗(名)[zágǎn]〔篇 piān〕
fleeting impression; random thoughts
〖杂记〗(名)[zájì]〔篇 piān〕
①random note ②miscellanies
〖杂技〗(名)[zájì]
acrobatics
〖杂交〗(动)[zájiāo]
crossbreed;hybridize
〖杂粮〗(名)[záliáng]
coarse cereals; miscellaneous grain crops (e.g.maize, millet, etc.)
〖杂乱〗(形)[záluàn]
disorderly; disarranged; confused
〖杂乱无章〗[záluànwúzhāng]
out of order; untidy; in a mess
〖杂七杂八〗[záqīzábā]
bits of everything; bitty
〖杂文〗(名)[záwén]〔篇 piān〕
short essays; essay; satirical essay
〖杂务〗(名)[záwù]
odd job; miscellaneous business
〖杂音〗(名)[záyīn]
interference (e.g.radio); confused noise
〖杂志〗(名)[zázhì]〔本 běn〕
magazine; periodical
〖杂质〗(名)[zázhì]
impurity; pollution

砸(动)[zá]
bash; smash
〖砸碎〗(动)[zásuì]

break; smash to pieces

zāi

灾(名)[zāi]
disaster; calamity
〖灾害〗(名)[zāihài]
(natural) disaster; calamity
〖灾荒〗(名)[zāihuāng]
famine
〖灾祸〗(名)[zāihuò]
disaster; calamity; sufferings; catastrophic consequences
〖灾难〗(名)[zāinàn]
[场 chǎng] misfortune; catastrophe
〖灾情〗(名)[zāiqíng]
extent of a famine or natural disaster
〖灾区〗(名)[zāiqū]
disaster area
〖灾殃〗(名)[zāiyāng]
natural disaster; misfortune; catastrophe

栽(动)[zāi]
①plant; cultivate; foster ②shift (the blame on to); plant ... on sb.
〖栽培〗(动)[zāipéi]
① plant and cultivate ② educate; train; foster; cultivate

zǎi

载(名)[zǎi]
①year ②on record
另见 zài

宰(动)[zǎi]
kill; slaughter
〖宰割〗(动)[zǎigē]
① cut up ② trample underfoot; oppress and exploit

zài

再(副)[zài]
①again; once more; time and again; repeatedly ② further; more ③continuously ④then
〖再版〗(动)[zàibǎn]
reprint; republish; second edition
〖再度〗(副)[zàidù]
once more; again; once again
〖再见〗(动)[zàijiàn]
see you again; goodbye
〖再接再厉〗[zàijiēzàilì]
make unremitting efforts; make sustained and redoubled efforts
〖再三〗(副)[zàisān]
repeatedly; again and again; time and again
〖再生产〗[zàishēngchǎn]
reproduce
〖再说〗(动、连)[zàishuō]
① see to sth. later; attend to sth. later ② furthermore
〖再现〗(动)[zàixiàn]
reappear

在(动、副、介)[zài]
①be; exist; be present ②lie in; rest with; depend on ③ amo-

ng; at; in; on; over; amidst
〖在场〗(动)[zàichǎng]
in the presence; on the spot; be present
〖在乎〗(动)[zàihu]
① be particular about; mindful of; care about ② lie in; rest in; depend on
〖在…看来〗[zài…kànlái]
from the point of view of ...; as ... sees it
〖在…里〗[zài…lǐ]
inside; in
〖在…内〗[zài…nèi]
included; in; among
〖在…上〗[zài…shàng]
above; over; on; up
〖在世〗(动)[zàishì]
alive; live
〖在望〗(动)[zàiwàng]
be within reach; within sight
〖在…下〗[zài…xià]
below; under; underneath; beneath
〖在意〗(动)[zàiyì]
be particular about; mindful of; care about; mind
〖在于〗(动)[zàiyú]
① lie in; rest with ② depend on
〖在职〗(动)[zàizhí]
be in office; at one's post; at work
〖在职培训〗[zàizhípéixùn]
on-the-job training; in-service training
〖在职期间〗[zàizhíqījiān]
during one's tenure of office
〖在…中〗[zài…zhōng]
in; among; in the midst of
〖在座〗(动)[zàizuò]
be present at; in the presence of

载(动)[zài]
carry; convey; transport
另见 zǎi
〖载歌载舞〗[zàigēzàiwǔ]
singing and dancing
〖载重〗[zàizhòng]
the load; loading capacity

zán

咱(代)[zán]
I; me
〖咱们〗(代)[zánmen]
we; us

zǎn

攒(动)[zǎn]
save; accumulate

zàn

暂(副)[zàn]
temporarily; for a short time
〖暂且〗(副)[zànqiě]
for the time being; for the moment; for the present
〖暂时〗(形)[zànshí]
temporary; provisional; not permanent
〖暂行〗(形)[zànxíng]
provisional; interim; transitional

赞(动)[zàn]

approve; admire; praise

〖赞不绝口〗[zànbùjuékǒu]
praise (sb. or sth.) unceasingly

〖赞成〗(动)[zànchéng]
approve; assent; favour; agree; second

〖赞歌〗(名)[zàngē][首 shǒu]
song of praise; ode

〖赞美〗(动)[zànměi]
admire; praise

〖赞赏〗(动)[zànshǎng]
appreciate; praise

〖赞叹〗(动)[zàntàn]
praise highly; admire

〖赞同〗(动)[zàntóng]
assent; agree; second; favour

〖赞许〗(动)[zànxǔ]
approve; commendation

〖赞扬〗(动)[zànyáng]
extol; praise; speak favourably of

〖赞助〗(动)[zànzhù]
support; aid; assistance

zāng

脏(形)[zāng]
dirty; filthy

zàng

葬(动)[zàng]
bury

〖葬礼〗(名)[zànglǐ]
funeral ceremony; obsequies

〖葬送〗(动)[zàngsòng]
bring ... to ruin; ruin

zāo

遭(动、量)[zāo]
① meet with (calamity, death, etc.); suffer (e.g. setbacks); sustain ② a measure word (for time, occasion, circle, ring, etc.)

〖遭到〗(动)[zāodào]
meet with; come under; sustain

〖遭受〗(动)[zāoshòu]
suffer; endure; undergo

〖遭殃〗[zāoyāng]
suffer a catastrophe; meet with disaster; run into calamity; suffer

〖遭遇〗(动、名)[zāoyù]
① meet with (disaster, difficulties, etc.); come under; encounter ② (bitter) experience; (hard) lot

糟(形)[zāo]
① disordered; in chaos and ruin
② decayed; ruined; rotten

〖糟糕〗(形)[zāogāo]
in a terrible mess; too bad; bad luck

〖糟粕〗(名)[zāopò]
slag; scum; dregs; waste matter; dross

〖糟蹋〗(动)[zāotà]
① spoil; waste; misuse ② disgrace; trample; ravage

záo

凿(动)[záo]

Z

cut a hole; chisel

zǎo

早(形)[zǎo]
early
〖早操〗(名)[zǎocāo]
morning exercise
〖早晨〗(名)[zǎochén]
morning
〖早点〗(名)[zǎodiǎn]
a light breakfast
〖早饭〗(名)[zǎofàn]〔顿 dùn〕
breakfast
〖早期〗(名)[zǎoqī]
earlier period; early stage
〖早日〗(副)[zǎorì]
soon; earlier
〖早上〗(名)[zǎoshang]
morning
〖早熟〗(形)[zǎoshú]
early ripening; precocity; premature
〖早晚〗(名、副)[zǎowǎn]
① morning and evening ② sooner or later
〖早先〗(名)[zǎoxiān]
in former times; formerly
〖早已〗(副)[zǎoyǐ]
already
〖早早儿〗(副)[zǎozǎor]
make haste; lose no time

枣(名)[zǎo]
date
〖枣儿〗(名)[zǎor]〔个 gè〕
date
〖枣红〗(形)[zǎohóng]
reddish-brown; date-red

zào

灶(名)[zào]
kitchen-range; oven

造(动)[zào]
① form; make; create; manufacture; cause ② bring up; train
〖造成〗(动)[zàochéng]
form; make; manufacture; cause (e.g. difficulties)
〖造反〗[zàofǎn]
rebel against; revolt; rebellion
〖造福〗(动)[zàofú]
bring benefit to; benefit
〖造价〗(名)[zàojià]
construction costs
〖造就〗(动)[zàojiù]
train; bring up; cultivate
〖造句〗[zàojù]
(gram.) make a sentence
〖造林〗[zàolín]
afforest; afforestation
〖造型〗(名)[zàoxíng]
plastic design; plastic (e. g. arts)
〖造谣〗[zàoyáo]
start a rumour; rumour mongering
〖造谣惑众〗[zàoyáohuòzhòng]
spread rumours to deceive people
〖造诣〗(名)[zàoyì]
literary or artistic attainments

〖造作〗(形)[zàozuo]
pretentious; affected; artificial; laboured

zé

则(连、量)[zé]
① but; however ② then; only ③ a measure word, item

责(名、动)[zé]
① responsibility; duty ② entrust; enjoin ③ reproach; rebuke; blame ④ reprimand; censure
〖责备〗(动)[zébèi]
reproach; blame; censure
〖责成〗(动)[zéchéng]
enjoin; entrust
〖责怪〗(动)[zéguài]
reprimand; blame
〖责难〗(动)[zénàn]
censure; rebuke
〖责任〗(名)[zérèn]
responsibility; duty; obligation
〖责任心〗(名)[zérènxīn]
sense of responsibility
〖责问〗(动)[zéwèn]
take (sb.) to task
〖责无旁贷〗[zéwúpángdài]
bounden duty; an inescapable duty

zéi

贼(名)[zéi]
thief
〖贼喊捉贼〗[zéihǎnzhuōzéi]
(lit.) a robber cries "stop thief"; (fig.) cover oneself up by shouting with the crowd

zěn

怎(代)[zěn]
how? why?
〖怎么〗(代)[zěnme]
① what? ② how? why?
〖怎么办〗[zěnmebàn]
what is to be done?
〖怎么样〗(代)[zěnmeyàng]
what about? how?
〖怎么着〗(代)[zěnmezhe]
how about? how?
〖怎样〗(代)[zěnyàng]
how? why?

zēng

增(动)[zēng]
add; multiply; strengthen; increase; enlarge; grow
〖增产〗[zēngchǎn]
increase production
〖增产节约〗[zēngchǎn jiéyuē]
increase production and practise economy
〖增光〗[zēngguāng]
add to the glory
〖增加〗(动)[zēngjiā]
increase; add; enhance; enlarge; grow
〖增进〗(动)[zēngjìn]
increase; promote; develop; heighten; enhance
〖增强〗(动)[zēngqiáng]
strengthen; multiply; intensify

〖增添〗(动)[zēngtiān]
add; replenish
〖增援〗(动)[zēngyuán]
reinforce
〖增长〗(动)[zēngzhǎng]
enhance; grow; increase
〖增值〗[zēngzhí]
rise (increase) in value; accretion; appreciation; increment
〖增值税〗(名)[zēngzhíshuì]
value-added tax; increment value duty

憎[zēng]
〖憎恨〗(动)[zēnghèn]
hate; detest
〖憎恶〗(动)[zēngwù]
detest; hate; be disgusted at

zèng

赠(动)[zèng]
present; offer (e.g. gift)
〖赠送〗(动)[zèngsòng]
give a present to; grant; present
〖赠言〗(名)[zèngyán]
parting advice
〖赠阅〗(动)[zèngyuè]
give sb. ... to read

zhā

扎(动)[zhā]
① prick; puncture ② settle down
另见 zā

〖扎根〗[zhāgēn]
take root; settle down
〖扎实〗(形)[zhāshi]
solid; in a down-to-earth way; sturdy

渣(名)[zhā]
① refuse; scum; dregs; dross ② dirt; small bits of left-over
〖渣滓〗(名)[zhāzǐ]
dregs; scum; refuse; dross; waste

zhá

札[zhá]
〖札记〗(名)[zhájì]〔篇 piān〕
notes or comments

轧(动)[zhá]
roll (e.g. steel)
〖轧钢〗[zhágāng]
steel-rolling

闸(名、动)[zhá]
sluice gate; lockgate; lock
〖闸门〗(名)[zhámén]
lockgate; lock; sluice gate

炸(动)[zhá]
fry
另见 zhà

铡(动)[zhá]
cut with a guillotine
〖铡刀〗(名)[zhádāo]

guillotine (for cutting fodder, etc.)

zhǎ

眨(动)[zhǎ]
wink; blink
〖眨眼〗[zhǎyǎn]
① blink ② in the twinkling of an eye

zhà

乍(副)[zhà]
① newly; just ② suddenly

诈(动)[zhà]
① cheat; deceive; trick into; blackmail ② pretend; feint
〖诈骗〗(动)[zhàpiàn]
deceive; swindle; defraud

炸(动)[zhà]
explode; bomb; blow up; blast
另见 zhá
〖炸弹〗(名)[zhàdàn]〔枚 méi〕
bomb
〖炸药〗(名)[zhàyào]
explosives; dynamite

栅[zhà]
〖栅栏〗(名)[zhàlan]
balustrade; fence

榨(动)[zhà]
squeeze out; extract; press out
〖榨取〗(动)[zhàqǔ]
① obtain by pressing; drain; extract ② exploit; exact

zhāi

摘(动)[zhāi]
① pick; pluck ② excerpt ③ borrow from
〖摘抄〗(动)[zhāichāo]
copy sth. selectively
〖摘录〗(动)[zhāilù]
record excerpts; make an extract; excerpt
〖摘要〗(名)[zhāiyào]
digest; make an extract; summary; abstract
〖摘引〗(动)[zhāiyǐn]
quote

zhái

择(动)[zhái]
select

zhǎi

窄(形)[zhǎi]
① narrow ② narrow-minded

zhài

债(名)[zhài]〔笔 bǐ〕
debt
〖债券〗(名)[zhàiquàn]
bond; debenture
〖债台高筑〗[zhàitáigāozhù]
run heavily into debt; deep in debt
〖债务〗(名)[zhàiwù]
debt

〖债务人〗(名)[zhàiwùrén]
debtor
〖债主〗(名)[zhàizhǔ]
creditor

寨(名)[zhài]
①stockade; stronghold; camp ② village
〖寨子〗(名)[zhàizi]
village or stronghold with fence or walled defence

zhān

沾(动)[zhān]
①wet ②tinge; stain; be touched with ③benefit by
〖沾光〗[zhānguāng]
get an advantage; benefit by
〖沾染〗(动)[zhānrǎn]
be affected with; be contaminated with (e. g. bad habits); be stained with (e. g. the blood of)
〖沾沾自喜〗[zhānzhānzìxǐ]
complacent; self satisfied

粘(动)[zhān]
paste up; stick on; affix to
另见 nián

瞻[zhān]
〖瞻前顾后〗[zhānqiángùhòu]
(lit.)peer ahead and look behind; (fig.)①think over carefully ② be over-cautious and indecisive
〖瞻望〗(动)[zhānwàng]
look forward; look ahead
〖瞻仰〗(动)[zhānyǎng]
admire; look up to

zhǎn

斩(动)[zhǎn]
cut; chop off
〖斩草除根〗[zhǎncǎochúgēn]
uproot; pull up weeds by the root; eliminate the cause of
〖斩钉截铁〗[zhǎndīngjiétiě]
resolute; determined; adamant; in a clearcut way
〖斩客〗[zhǎnkè]
make profits higher than the stipulated margin; price gouging; gouge excessive profits

盏(量)[zhǎn]
a measure word (e. g. a lamp, a cup)

展(动)[zhǎn]
① open; unfold; launch ② delay; extend; postpone ③ exhibit; be on display; put on display
〖展出〗(动)[zhǎnchū]
exhibit; be on display; put on display
〖展开〗(动)[zhǎnkāi]
① open up; expand ② launch; unfold; develop; spread out
〖展览〗(动、名)[zhǎnlǎn]
exhibit; be on display; exhibition

〖展览会〗(名)[zhǎnlǎnhuì]
exhibition
〖展示〗(动)[zhǎnshì]
show; display
〖展望〗(动)[zhǎnwàng]
forecast; look forward; prospect
〖展现〗(动)[zhǎnxiàn]
unfold; open and spread out; lay open to view

崭[zhǎn]
〖崭新〗(形)[zhǎnxīn]
brand new

辗[zhǎn]
〖辗转〗(动)[zhǎnzhuǎn]
mill around; turn over and over again; toss and turn

zhàn

占(动)[zhàn]
①occupy; possess ②prevail ③account for; constitute; make up
〖占据〗(动)[zhànjù]
occupy; take over; hold
〖占领〗(动)[zhànlǐng]
occupy; seize
〖占有〗(动)[zhànyǒu]
possess; own; hold

战(动、名)[zhàn]
①war; battle; struggle; fight; combat ②tremble; quiver
〖战败〗(动)[zhànbài]
①be defeated; lose the battle ②beat; overcome (the enemy); over-power
〖战报〗(名)[zhànbào]〔份 fèn〕
war communique
〖战备〗(名)[zhànbèi]
preparation against war; get prepared against war
〖战场〗(名)[zhànchǎng]
battle field; field of operations (war)
〖战斗〗(动、名)[zhàndòu]
①battle; fight ②combat; struggle
〖战斗力〗(名)[zhàndòulì]
fighting strength; fighting capacity
〖战斗性〗(名)[zhàndòuxìng]
fighting spirit; militancy; combativeness
〖战犯〗(名)[zhànfàn]
war criminal
〖战俘〗(名)[zhànfú]
prisoner-of-war; captive
〖战歌〗(名)[zhàngē]〔首 shǒu〕
war song; battle march
〖战鼓〗(名)[zhàngǔ]
war drum
〖战果〗(名)[zhànguǒ]
outcome of battle; results
〖战壕〗(名)[zhànháo]〔条 tiáo〕
dugout; trenches
〖战火〗(名)[zhànhuǒ]
flames of war
〖战机〗(名)[zhànjī]
(good) combat opportunity; the right time to strike
〖战绩〗(名)[zhànjī]

Z

military success
〖战局〗(名)[zhànjú]
war situation
〖战栗〗(动)[zhànlì]
shudder; shiver
〖战略〗(名)[zhànlüè]
strategy
〖战旗〗(名)[zhànqí]〔面 miàn〕
the colours; flag of an army
〖战胜〗(动)[zhànshèng]
defeat (the enemy); triumph over; be victorious
〖战士〗(名)[zhànshì]
soldier; fighter
〖战术〗(名)[zhànshù]
tactics
〖战天斗地〗[zhàntiāndòudì]
(lit.) fight against heaven and earth; (fig.) combat all forces of nature
〖战无不胜〗[zhànwúbùshèng]
invincible; ever-victorious
〖战线〗(名)[zhànxiàn]
〔条 tiáo〕(mil.) front
〖战役〗(名)[zhànyì]
campaign; battle
〖战友〗(名)[zhànyǒu]
comrade-in-arms
〖战战兢兢〗(形)
[zhànzhàn jīngjīng]
quaking with terror; tremble with fright; very cautious
〖战争〗(名)[zhànzhēng]
war; warfare

Z

站(动、名)[zhàn]
① stand ② stop; cease; stand still ③ station; stop (e. g. bus) ④ service centre; station
〖站队〗[zhànduì]
fall in; line up; take up one's position; take sides
〖站岗〗[zhàngǎng]
keep guard; stand sentry
〖站票〗(名)[zhànpiào]
ticket for standing room; ticket without an assigned seat
〖站台〗(名)[zhàntái]
platform (usu. railway)
〖站住〗(动)[zhànzhù]
① stop; stand still; stay ② hold water; stand up

蘸(动)[zhàn]
dip

zhāng

张(动、量)[zhāng]
① open up; stretch ② expand; exaggerate ③ a measure word, for table, paper, picture, etc.
〖张冠李戴〗[zhāngguānlǐdài]
(lit.) Li is putting on Chang's hat; (fig.) the cap is on the wrong head; mistake one thing for another
〖张皇失措〗[zhānghuángshīcuò]
be scared out of one's wits; be frightened and at a loss for what to do
〖张口结舌〗[zhāngkǒujiéshé]
stare open-mouthed; gape with astonishment
〖张罗〗(动)[zhāngluo]

① make arrangements ② try to find sth. for certain needs
〖张贴〗(动)[zhāngtiē]
put up (a notice, poster, etc.)
〖张望〗(动)[zhāngwàng]
look about; look around
〖张牙舞爪〗[zhāngyáwǔzhǎo]
show one's claws; bare one's teeth; rampant and overbearing

章(名、量)[zhāng]
① chapter ② seal ③ a measure word-chapter
〖章程〗(名)[zhāngchéng]
rules and regulations; charter
〖章节〗(名)[zhāngjié]
chapter; section

樟[zhāng]
the camphor tree
〖樟脑〗(名)[zhāngnǎo]
camphor

zhǎng

长(动、形、尾)[zhǎng]
①grow ②increase; heighten ③elder; older ④suffix (e.g. leader, head, chief)
另见 cháng
〖长进〗(动)[zhǎngjìn]
progress
〖长势〗(名)[zhǎngshì]
growing

涨(动)[zhǎng]
rise; go upward; soar; grow
另见 zhàng
〖涨潮〗[zhǎngcháo]
floodtide; rising tide

掌(动、名)[zhǎng]
① control; handle; in charge of ② palm (of hand); paw; hoof
〖掌舵〗[zhǎngduò]
helm; be at the helm
〖掌管〗(动)[zhǎngguǎn]
in charge of; handle; control
〖掌权〗[zhǎngquán]
be in power; take power
〖掌声〗(名)[zhǎngshēng]
applause; clapping; the sound of clapping
〖掌握〗(动)[zhǎngwò]
grasp; gain control of; possess; master

zhàng

丈(动、量)[zhàng]
① measure; survey ② a length (approx. 3 metres)
〖丈夫〗(名)[zhàngfu]
husband
〖丈量〗(动)[zhàngliáng]
survey (land); measure

帐(名)[zhàng]
camp; tent
〖帐篷〗(名)[zhàngpeng]
tent
〖帐子〗(名)[zhàngzi]〔顶 dǐng〕
mosquito net

账[zhàng]

①account ②debt
〖账目〗(名)[zhàngmù]
account

胀(动)[zhàng]
swell (up)

涨(动)[zhàng]
① swell; expand; inflate ② exceed
另见 zhǎng

障[zhàng]
〖障碍〗(名、动)[zhàng'ài]
obstruct; stand in the way; hinder; barrier; obstruction; obstacle

zhāo

招(动)[zhāo]
① call; beckon ② recruit; enrol; enlist ③ provoke; incite; incur; attract
〖招兵买马〗[zhāobīngmǎimǎ]
hire men and buy horses; enlist followers
〖招待〗(动)[zhāodài]
receive; entertain; give a reception to
〖招待会〗(名)[zhāodàihuì]
reception
〖招待所〗(名)[zhāodàisuǒ]
reception centre; guest house
〖招呼〗(动)[zhāohu]
① call; hail ② greet;wave to (sb.) ③ tell; inform ④ attend to; look after
〖招架〗(动)[zhāojià]
defend; ward off; resist
〖招领〗(动)[zhāolǐng]
notice for owner to claim lost things
〖招募〗(动)[zhāomù]
enlist; recruit
〖招牌〗(名)[zhāopai]
signboard; shop sign
〖招聘〗(动)[zhāopìn]
invite applications for a job; give public notice of a vacancy to be filled
〖招聘广告〗[zhāopìnguǎnggào]
employment advertisement; wanted
〖招惹〗(动)[zhāorě]
provoke; incur; arouse
〖招商〗[zhāoshāng]
solicit business; attract investment; business invitation
〖招生〗[zhāoshēng]
enrolling students
〖招收〗(动)[zhāoshōu]
enrol
〖招手〗[zhāoshǒu]
beckon; wave to
〖招降纳叛〗[zhāoxiángnàpàn]
recruit turncoats and accept renegades
〖招摇撞骗〗
[zhāoyáozhuàng piàn]
use the name or authority of others to swindle; bluff and deceive
〖招展〗(动)[zhāozhǎn]
wave; flutter

〖招致〗(动)[zhāozhì]
① enrol; accept; take in ② cause; give rise to; result in

昭[zhāo]

〖昭然若揭〗[zhāoránruòjiē]
clear as daylight; everything above board

着[zhāo]

另见 zháo zhe zhuó

〖着儿〗(名)[zhāor]
① a move (in chess) ② trick

朝[zhāo]

另见 cháo

〖朝不虑夕〗[zhāobùlǜxī]
(lit.) in the morning one doesn't worry what will happen in the evening; short-sighted

〖朝令夕改〗[zhāolìngxīgǎi]
issue an order in the morning and rescind it in the evening; fickle (in policy, feelings, etc.); changeable

〖朝气〗(名)[zhāoqì]
vigour; ardour; vitality; animation

〖朝气蓬勃〗[zhāoqìpéngbó]
full of vigour and vitality

〖朝三暮四〗[zhāosānmùsì]
changeable; shift and veer; play fast and loose; blow hot and cold

〖朝夕〗(名)[zhāoxī]
① every day; morning and evening ② a short time

〖朝霞〗(名)[zhāoxiá]
rays and clouds in the morning sun

〖朝阳〗(名)[zhāoyáng]
morning sun; rising sun

zháo

着(动)[zháo]

① touch; hit ② catch (e. g. cold)

另见 zhāo zhe zhuó

〖着慌〗[zháohuāng]
arouse fear; panic

〖着火〗[zháohuǒ]
catch fire

〖着急〗[zháojí]
anxious; worried

〖着凉〗[zháoliáng]
catch cold

zhǎo

爪[zhǎo]

〖爪牙〗(名)[zhǎoyá]
cat's-paw; accomplice; lackey; henchman

找(动)[zhǎo]

look for; find; seek

〖找钱〗[zhǎoqián]
give (one his) change; small change

〖找寻〗(动)[zhǎoxún]
look for; seek for; search for; hunt for

沼[zhǎo]

〖沼气〗(名)[zhǎoqì]
methane gas; marsh-gas
〖沼泽〗(名)[zhǎozé]
marsh; swamp; bog; quagmire

zhào

召(动)[zhào]
①call; beckon ②assemble; convene
〖召唤〗(动)[zhàohuàn]
call
〖召回〗(动)[zhàohuí]
recall; call back
〖召集〗(动)[zhàojí]
call up; convene; assemble; summon; gather
〖召见〗(动)[zhàojiàn]
summon; send for
〖召开〗(动)[zhàokāi]
call (e.g. a meeting); hold; summon

兆(数)[zhào]
trillion (archaic); million
〖兆周〗(量)[zhàozhōu]
megacycle

照(动、介)[zhào]
① shine; illuminate; mirror ② take (a photograph) ③ know; understand ④ according to; in the light of; in accordance with
〖照办〗(动)[zhàobàn]
do as one is told
〖照本宣科〗[zhàoběnxuānkē]
echo what the book says
〖照常〗[zhàocháng]
as usual; function as usual
〖照顾〗(动)[zhàogù]
① consider ② give due consideration to; take care of; look after
〖照管〗(动)[zhàoguǎn]
take charge of; look after; take care of
〖照会〗(动、名)[zhàohuì]
send a note to ...; note (diplomatic)
〖照旧〗[zhàojiù]
as usual
〖照例〗(副)[zhàolì]
according to the rules; as usual
〖照料〗(动)[zhàoliào]
take care of
〖照猫画虎〗[zhàomāohuàhǔ]
(lit.) draw a tiger after the model of a cat; (fig.) copy; copycat
〖照明〗(动)[zhàomíng]
illuminate; light (up)
〖照片〗(名)[zhàopiàn]
〔张 zhāng〕photograph; photo; picture
〖照相〗[zhàoxiàng]
take photograph; photographing
〖照相馆〗(名)[zhàoxiàngguǎn]
photo studio; graphics studio
〖照相机〗(名)[zhàoxiàngjī]
〔架 jià〕camera
〖照样〗[zhàoyàng]
① in the same way; likewise ② as usual
〖照耀〗(动)[zhàoyào]
shine; illuminate

〖照应〗(动)[zhàoying]
look after; take care of; give consideration
〖照章〗[zhàozhāng]
as required; in accordance with rules and regulations

罩(名、动)[zhào]
shade; cover

肇[zhào]
〖肇事〗[zhàoshì]
cause an accident; make trouble

zhē

折(动)[zhē]
toss and turn
另见 zhé shé
〖折腾〗(动)[zhēteng]
① do sth. repeatedly ② bother; toss; worry

遮(动)[zhē]
① cover ② block off; conceal
〖遮蔽〗(动)[zhēbì]
shade; cover; block off
〖遮盖〗(动)[zhēgài]
cover up; overcast; conceal
〖遮羞布〗(名)[zhēxiūbù]
fig-leaf
〖遮掩〗(动)[zhēyǎn]
① cover; overcast ② conceal; hide

zhé

折(动)[zhé]
① break ② lose ③ bend; fold ④ turn over; turn back ⑤ give a discount ⑥ exchange; depreciation; convert into
另见 zhē shé
〖折叠〗(动)[zhédié]
fold
〖折合〗(动)[zhéhé]
convert into; be worth; amount to
〖折扣〗(名)[zhékòu]
discount
〖折磨〗(动)[zhémó]
torture; grind down; undergo an ordeal; bother
〖折射〗(动)[zhéshè]
refract; refraction
〖折衷〗(动)[zhézhōng]
compromise; eclecticism
〖折衷主义〗(名)
[zhézhōngzhǔ yì]
eclecticism

哲[zhé]
〖哲学〗(名)[zhéxué]
philosophy

zhě

者(尾)[zhě]
suffix, referring to a person as "er" in "reader", etc.

褶[zhě]
〖褶子〗(名)[zhězi]
pleat

zhè

这(代)[zhè]
this
〖这个〗(代)[zhège]
this
〖这会儿〗(名)[zhèhuìr]
at this moment
〖这里〗(代)[zhèlǐ]
here
〖这么〗(代)[zhème]
such; so
〖这儿〗(代)[zhèr]
here
〖这些〗(代)[zhèxiē]
these
〖这样〗(代)[zhèyàng]
such; in this way; thus

zhe

着(尾)[zhe]
suffix
另见 zhāo zháo zhuó

zhēn

针(名)[zhēn]〔根 gēn〕
① needle ② injection ③ acupuncture
〖针刺麻醉〗[zhēncìmázuì]
acupuncture anaesthesia
〖针对〗(动)[zhēnduì]
direct towards; point at; in point of; in light of
〖针对性〗(名)[zhēnduìxìng]
to the point; with a clear aim in mind
〖针锋相对〗[zhēnfēngxiāngduì]
tit for tat
〖针灸〗(名、动)[zhēnjiǔ]
acupuncture and moxibustion
〖针织品〗(名)[zhēnzhīpǐn]
knitted goods; knitwear; hosiery

侦[zhēn]
〖侦察〗(动)[zhēnchá]
scout; reconnoitre; reconnaissance
〖侦察兵〗(名)[zhēnchábīng]
scout
〖侦探〗(动、名)[zhēntàn]
detect; spy; detective; secret service agent

珍[zhēn]
〖珍藏〗(动)[zhēncáng]
treasure
〖珍贵〗(形)[zhēnguì]
valuable; precious
〖珍视〗(动)[zhēnshì]
cherish; treasure; prize
〖珍惜〗(动)[zhēnxī]
love dearly; treasure and value; value highly
〖珍重〗(动)[zhēnzhòng]
take good care; hold dear
〖珍珠〗(名)[zhēnzhū]〔颗 kē〕
pearl

真(形)[zhēn]
real; genuine; real; true; actual
〖真才实学〗[zhēncáishíxué]

real ability and learning; genuine talent
〖真诚〗(形)[zhēnchéng]
honest; earnest; sincere; truly
〖真空〗(名)[zhēnkōng]
vacuum
〖真理〗(名)[zhēnlǐ]
truth
〖真面目〗[zhēnmiànmù]
true feature; true colours
〖真凭实据〗[zhēnpíngshíjù]
factual evidence; indisputable evidence
〖真切〗(形)[zhēnqiè]
realistic; distinct
〖真情〗(名)[zhēnqíng]
①reality; actual state; real situation ②real emotion or feelings
〖真实〗(形)[zhēnshí]
real; true; actual
〖真相〗(名)[zhēnxiàng]
truth; true state; real facts
〖真相大白〗[zhēnxiàngdàbái]
the actual state of affairs has been made clear
〖真正〗(形)[zhēnzhèng]
real; genuine
〖真挚〗(形)[zhēnzhì]
sincere; cordial; genuine

斟[zhēn]
〖斟酌〗(动)[zhēnzhuó]
weigh and consider; deliberate; think over

甄[zhēn]
〖甄别〗(动)[zhēnbié]
screen; determine the true nature of a case

zhěn

诊(动)[zhěn]
diagnose; consult; examine
〖诊断〗(名、动)[zhěnduàn]
diagnosis; diagnose
〖诊疗〗(动)[zhěnliáo]
consult and give medical treatment
〖诊治〗(动)[zhěnzhì]
treat; cure; heal

枕(动)[zhěn]
pillow; rest head on (e. g. pillow)
〖枕巾〗(名)[zhěnjīn]〔条 tiáo〕
pillow cover
〖枕木〗(名)[zhěnmù]
sleeper; rails
〖枕头〗(名)[zhěntou]〔个 gè〕
pillow

zhèn

阵(名、量)[zhèn]
① battle field; position ② a measure word, for wind, rain, applause
〖阵地〗(名)[zhèndì]
position; battle field; front
〖阵地战〗(名)[zhèndìzhàn]
〔场 chǎng〕positional warfare
〖阵脚〗(名)[zhènjiǎo]
forefront (mostly figurative)

〖阵容〗(名)[zhènróng]
line-up; battle array
〖阵势〗(名)[zhènshì]
① battle array; disposition of forces ② situation
〖阵线〗(名)[zhènxiàn]
battle front; front
〖阵营〗(名)[zhènyíng]
camp
〖阵雨〗(名)[zhènyǔ]
shower

振(动)[zhèn]
① oscillate ② pluck up; inspire
〖振动〗(动)[zhèndòng]
oscillate; vibrate
〖振奋〗(动)[zhènfèn]
inspire; stimulate; enliven; animate
〖振兴〗(动)[zhènxīng]
invigorate; rejuvenate; vitalize
〖振兴中华〗[zhènxīngzhōnghuá]
rejuvenating China; achieve China's rejuvenation
〖振振有辞〗[zhènzhènyǒucí]
say plausibly; high-sounding
〖振作〗(动)[zhènzuò]
pull oneself together; inspire; hearten; encourage

震(动)[zhèn]
① shock; shake ② be alarmed
〖震荡〗(动)[zhèndàng]
shake; tremor; oscillate
〖震动〗(动)[zhèndòng]
① tremor; vibrate; shock ② alarm
〖震撼〗(动)[zhènhàn]
shake; shock
〖震惊〗(动)[zhènjīng]
shock; alarm

镇(名)[zhèn]
town
〖镇定〗(形)[zhèndìng]
(remain) calm; calm down; (keep) cool; steady
〖镇静〗(形)[zhènjìng]
sedative; mollified; calm; steady
〖镇压〗(动)[zhènyā]
repress; suppress; put down; quell

zhēng

争(动)[zhēng]
① fight for; contend for; seize; strive for ② quarrel; contest; dispute
〖争霸〗(动)[zhēngbà]
seek hegemony; strive for hegemony
〖争辩〗(动)[zhēngbiàn]
argue; debate; refute
〖争吵〗(动)[zhēngchǎo]
quarrel; squabble
〖争端〗(名)[zhēngduān]
point of contention; cause of dispute
〖争夺〗(动)[zhēngduó]
strive for; seize; fight for; scramble for; contend for

〖争分夺秒〗[zhēngfēnduómiǎo]
(lit.) seize every minute and every second; (fig.) race against time
〖争光〗[zhēngguāng]
win honour
〖争论〗(动、名)[zhēnglùn]
argue; debate; controversy
〖争气〗[zhēngqì]
try to be a credit to; strive to live up to; work hard to win honour for
〖争取〗(动)[zhēngqǔ]
①win over; obtain ②strive for
〖争权夺利〗[zhēngquánduólì]
struggle for power and wealth
〖争先〗[zhēngxiān]
contend for first place; compete to be the first
〖争先恐后〗
[zhēngxiānkǒnghòu]
struggle to be at forefront and not willing to lag behind
〖争议〗(动、名)[zhēngyì]
argue; dispute; debate; controversy
〖争执〗(动)[zhēngzhí]
dispute with; contend; be at odds with

征(动)[zhēng]

①capture; attack ②draft; recruit ③levy (e. g. taxes) ④consult; ask for; request; solicit; seek
〖征兵〗[zhēngbīng]
conscription; recruit; draft
〖征服〗(动)[zhēngfú]
conquer; overcome
〖征购〗(动)[zhēnggòu]
requisition; purchase by the state
〖征候〗(名)[zhēnghòu]
omen; symptoms of a disease; sign
〖征集〗(动)[zhēngjí]
collect; gather
〖征求〗(动)[zhēngqiú]
consult; ask for (opinion); solicit
〖征收〗(动)[zhēngshōu]
levy and collect; impose (a duty) on
〖征途〗(名)[zhēngtú]
underway (of a long journey)
〖征象〗(名)[zhēngxiàng]
symbol; symptom
〖征用〗(动)[zhēngyòng]
requisition; expropriation

挣[zhēng]

〖挣脱〗(动)[zhēngtuō]
struggle to free oneself; shake off; get rid of
〖挣扎〗(动)[zhēngzhá]
struggle desperately; flounder desperately

峥[zhēng]

〖峥嵘〗(形)[zhēngróng]
①steep; sheer ②outstanding; prominent; eminent

狰[zhēng]

〖狰狞〗(形)[zhēngníng]
hideous; ferocious; vile; vicious

症[zhēng]
另见 zhèng
〖症结〗(名)[zhēngjié]
keypoint; knotty problem

睁(动)[zhēng]
open (e.g. eyes)

蒸(动)[zhēng]
①steam②evaporate
〖蒸发〗(动)[zhēngfā]
evaporate
〖蒸馏水〗(名)[zhēngliúshuǐ]
distilled water
〖蒸汽机〗(名)[zhēngqìjī]
steam engine
〖蒸蒸日上〗
[zhēngzhēngrìshàng]
ever more flourishing; become more prosperous; more thriving with each passing day

zhěng

拯[zhěng]
〖拯救〗(动)[zhěngjiù]
save; rescue

整(形、动)[zhěng]
①whole; total; entire; complete; overall ②orderly ③pack; put in order; arrange; get ready; reorganize④check over; rectify
〖整编〗(动)[zhěngbiān]
reorganize
〖整党〗[zhěngdǎng]
consolidation of the party; party consolidation
〖整顿〗(动)[zhěngdùn]
reorganize; readjust; rectify; straighten; put ... in good order
〖整风〗[zhěngfēng]
rectification of style of work; rectify incorrect styles of work
〖整改〗(动)[zhěnggǎi]
rectify
〖整个〗(形)[zhěnggè]
whole; total; entire
〖整洁〗(形)[zhěngjié]
neat and tidy
〖整理〗(动)[zhěnglǐ]
regulate; put things in order; rehabilitate; adjust
〖整流〗[zhěngliú]
current regulator
〖整流器〗[zhěngliúqì]
(electr.) rectifier; commutator
〖整齐〗(形)[zhěngqí]
uniform; in good order; tidy
〖整数〗(名)[zhěngshù]
(math.) whole number; integer
〖整体〗(名)[zhěngtǐ]
the whole; as a whole; integration; entity
〖整修〗(动)[zhěngxiū]
repair; put in order
〖整训〗(动)[zhěngxùn]

train and consolidate
〖整整〗(形)[zhěngzhěng]
exactly; whole

zhèng

正(形、动、副)[zhèng]
① straight ② positive ③ upright; honest ④ put right ⑤ chief; main (contrasted with vice, deputy)
〖正比〗(名)[zhèngbǐ]
(math.) direct ratio
〖正常〗(形)[zhèngcháng]
normal
〖正常化〗(动)[zhèngchánghuà]
normalize; render normal; bring back to normal
〖正当〗[zhèngdāng]
at a time when; just when; when; while
〖正当〗(形)[zhèngdàng]
proper; legitimate; rightful; due
〖正电〗(名)[zhèngdiàn]
positive electricity
〖正方体〗(名)[zhèngfāngtǐ]
(math.) cube
〖正方形〗(名)[zhèngfāngxíng]
(math.) square
〖正告〗(动)[zhènggào]
inform in all seriousness; solemnly inform; serve notice on
〖正规〗(形)[zhèngguī]
regular
〖正规军〗(名)[zhèngguījūn]
regular army; regular forces
〖正轨〗(名)[zhèngguǐ]
the right track
〖正好〗(形、副)[zhènghǎo]
① fit; suitable ② just; just all right ③ a good chance
〖正号〗(名)[zhènghào]
positive sign
〖正经〗(形)[zhèngjing]
① decent; honest ② real; proper
〖正面〗(名)[zhèngmiàn]
① front; frontal; frontage ② positive side; in a positive way
〖正面人物〗[zhèngmiànrénwù]
positive character
〖正派〗(形)[zhèngpài]
upright; honest; decent
〖正气〗(名)[zhèngqì]
uprightness; integrity; probity; open and above-board
〖正巧〗(副)[zhèngqiǎo]
by (a happy) chance; by coincidence
〖正确〗(形)[zhèngquè]
correct; right
〖正式〗(形)[zhèngshì]
official; recorded; formal; full
〖正视〗(动)[zhèngshì]
envisage; face squarely
〖正数〗(名)[zhèngshù]
positive number
〖正统〗(名)[zhèngtǒng]
orthodox
〖正文〗(名)[zhèngwén]
the main text
〖正义〗(形、名)[zhèngyì]
just; justice; righteous; right

〖正义战争〗[zhèngyìzhànzhēng]
just war
〖正音〗[zhèngyīn]
correct pronunciation
〖正在〗(副)[zhèngzài]
in the process of; in the act of
〖正直〗(形)[zhèngzhí]
just; upright; fair-minded; honest

证(名)[zhèng]
certificate; evidence; proof
〖证件〗(名)[zhèngjiàn]
papers; certificates
〖证据〗(名)[zhèngjù]
evidence; proof
〖证明〗(动、名)[zhèngmíng]
①prove; confirm; testify; proof ②certificate
〖证券〗(名)[zhèngquàn]
securities; stock
〖证券交易所〗[zhèngquànjiāoyìsuǒ]
stock exchange
〖证实〗(动)[zhèngshí]
confirm; corroborate; verify; testify
〖证书〗(名)[zhèngshū]
[张 zhāng]certificate; testimonial

郑[zhèng]
〖郑重〗(形)[zhèngzhòng]
serious; solemn

政(名)[zhèng]
government; politics
〖政变〗(名)[zhèngbiàn]
coup; coup d'etat
〖政策〗(名)[zhèngcè]
policy
〖政党〗(名)[zhèngdǎng]
political party
〖政敌〗[zhèngdí]
political opponent
〖政法〗[zhèngfǎ]
politics and law
〖政府〗(名)[zhèngfǔ]
government
〖政纲〗[zhènggāng]
political programme; platform
〖政绩〗[zhèngjī]
achievements in one's official career
〖政见〗[zhèngjiàn]
political view
〖政局〗(名)[zhèngjú]
political situation; political scene
〖政客〗(名)[zhèngkè]
(derog.)politician; political hack
〖政令〗[zhènglìng]
government decree (或 order)
〖政论〗(名)[zhènglùn]
political comment
〖政权〗(名)[zhèngquán]
political power
〖政体〗(名)[zhèngtǐ]
political constitution; system of government; form of government
〖政委〗(名)[zhèngwěi]
political commissar
〖政治〗(名)[zhèngzhì]

politics
〖政治避难〗[zhèngzhìbìnàn]
political asylum; political refuge
〖政治标准〗[zhèngzhìbiāozhǔn]
political criterion
〖政治家〗(名)[zhèngzhìjiā]
statesman;politician
〖政治经济学〗[zhèngzhìjīngjìxué]
political economy
〖政治路线〗[zhèngzhìlùxiàn]
political line
〖政治面貌〗[zhèngzhìmiànmào]
political affiliation or background
〖政治骗子〗[zhèngzhìpiànzi]
political swindler
〖政治性〗(名)[zhèngzhìxìng]
political character

症(名)[zhèng]
illness; disease
另见 zhēng
〖症状〗(名)[zhèngzhuàng]
symptom

zhī

之(代、助)[zhī]
① it; his; her; them ② used as an abstract pronoun ③ possessive part,"of" ④ a preposition of position placed before the noun
〖之后〗[zhīhòu]
behind; after; later
〖…之际〗[…zhījì]
while ...; just as
〖…之间〗[…zhījiān]
in the midst of; between
〖…之类〗[…zhīlèi]
such; alike
〖…之流〗[…zhīliú]
such as; … and his like; … and his ilk
〖…之内〗[…zhīnèi]
inside; within
〖…之前〗[…zhīqián]
before; prior to ...
〖…之外〗[…zhīwài]
besides; apart from
〖…之一〗[…zhīyī]
one of ...
〖…之中〗[…zhīzhōng]
in the midst of; among

支(动、量)[zhī]
① raise; lift; erect ② support; sustain ③ send away; dominate; control ⑤ pay ④ a measure word, for song, candle, organization, etc.
〖支部〗(名)[zhībù]
branch of an organization
〖支撑〗(动)[zhīchēng]
prop up; support; sustain
〖支持〗(动)[zhīchí]
support; hold up; sustain; back
〖支出〗(动)[zhīchū]
pay out; disburse; expenditure
〖支付〗(动)[zhīfù]
pay; payment
〖支解〗(动)[zhījiě]

dismember
〖支离破碎〗[zhīlípòsuì]
shattered; splintered; split
〖支流〗(名)[zhīliú]
①tributary ②subsidiary trend; secondary stream
〖支配〗(动)[zhīpèi]
control; dominate; manipulate
〖支票〗(名)[zhīpiào]〔张 zhāng〕
cheque
〖支书〗(名)[zhīshū]
secretary (of a party branch)
〖支吾〗(动、形)[zhīwú]
quibble; stall
〖支援〗(动)[zhīyuán]
support; aid; hold up; help; back
〖支柱〗(名)[zhīzhù]
mainstay; brace; pillar
〖支柱产业〗[zhīzhùchǎnyè]
support industry

只(量)[zhī]
a measure word (referring to one of a pair of things such as shoe, sock, ear, hand, etc.)
另见 zhǐ

汁(名)[zhī]
juice

芝[zhī]
〖芝麻〗(名)[zhīma]〔粒 lì〕

sesame

枝(名、量)[zhī]
① branch of a tree ② a measure word, for pistol, pen, candle, etc.
〖枝节〗(名)[zhījié]
side issue; minor issue; minor problem

知(动)[zhī]
know; be aware of
〖知道〗(动)[zhīdào]
know; be aware of
〖知己知彼〗[zhījǐzhībǐ]
know the enemy and know yourself
〖知觉〗(名)[zhījué]
consciousness
〖知名〗[zhīmíng]
famous; well-known; celebrated
〖知难而进〗[zhīnán'érjìn]
push on in spite of difficulties; advance despite difficulties
〖知趣〗[zhīqù]
know how to act on different occasions; tactful
〖知识〗(名)[zhīshi]
knowledge
〖知识产权〗[zhīshichǎnquán]
intellectual property right
〖知识分子〗[zhīshifènzǐ]
intellectuals; intelligentsia
〖知识青年〗[zhīshiqīngnián]
educated youth
〖知无不言,言无不尽〗
[zhīwú bùyán, yánwúbùjìn]
say all you know and say it without reserve
〖知心〗[zhīxīn]

①intimate ②intimate friend; close friend; bosom friend

织(动)[zhī]
knit; weave
〖织补〗(动)[zhībǔ]
knit up

脂[zhī]
〖脂肪〗(名)[zhīfáng]
fat; grease

蜘[zhī]
〖蜘蛛〗(名)[zhīzhū]〔只 zhī〕
spider

zhí

执(动)[zhí]
①hold; take ②execute; preside ③persist in; stick to; adhere to ④carry out; perform
〖执笔〗(动)[zhíbǐ]
write down by
〖执法〗(动)[zhífǎ]
enforce the law; execute the law
〖执迷不悟〗[zhímíbùwù]
persist in error; refuse to come to one's senses; refuse to mend one's way
〖执行〗(动)[zhíxíng]
carry out; perform; put into effect; execute
〖执照〗(名)[zhízhào]
〔张 zhāng〕certificate; lience
〖执政〗(动)[zhízhèng]
govern; be in power; rule

直(形、动、副)[zhí]
①straight ②vertical ③righteous; honest ④straightforward ⑤straighten ⑥unceasingly ⑦simply
〖直达〗(动)[zhídá]
through (train); through-traffic
〖直到〗(动)[zhídào]
until; till; up to
〖直观〗(名)[zhíguān]
intuition; visual (e.g. aids)
〖直角〗(名)[zhíjiǎo]
(math.) right angle
〖直接〗(形)[zhíjiē]
direct; immediate
〖直截了当〗[zhíjiéliǎodàng]
outspoken; straight; bluntly
〖直径〗(名)[zhíjìng]
diameter
〖直流电〗(名)[zhíliúdiàn]
direct-current electricity (D.C.)
〖直升飞机〗[zhíshēngfēijī]
helicopter
〖直属〗(动)[zhíshǔ]
(departments) directly under…
〖直率〗(形)[zhíshuài]
frank; straightforward; plain spoken; outright
〖直爽〗(形)[zhíshuǎng]
straight-forward; outspoken; frank
〖直系亲属〗[zhíxìqīnshǔ]
lineal relative

〖直辖〗(动)[zhíxiá]
directly under the central authorities; direct jurisdiction
〖直辖市〗(名)[zhíxiáshì]
municipality directly under the central authorities
〖直线〗(名)[zhíxiàn]〔条 tiáo〕
straight line
〖直言不讳〗[zhíyánbùhuì]
speak without reservation; mince no words
〖直译〗(动)[zhíyì]
literal translation; word for word translation

侄(名)[zhí]
nephew
〖侄女〗(名)[zhínǚ]
niece (brother's daughter)
〖侄子〗(名)[zhízi]
nephew (brother's son)

值(名、动)[zhí]
① value ② cost; be worth; merit; deserve
〖值班〗[zhíbān]
be on duty
〖值得〗(动)[zhídé]
be worth; merit; deserve
〖值钱〗[zhíqián]
valuable
〖值勤〗(动)[zhíqín]
be on duty; do guard duty
〖值日〗(动)[zhírì]
be on duty (for the day)

职(名)[zhí]
① duty ② position; post
〖职别〗(名)[zhíbié]
profession; occupation
〖职工〗(名)[zhígōng]
staff and workers
〖职能〗(名)[zhínéng]
function
〖职权〗(名)[zhíquán]
positions and powers
〖职位〗(名)[zhíwèi]
position; post
〖职务〗(名)[zhíwù]
position; post
〖职业〗(名)[zhíyè]
occupation; profession; vocation
〖职业病〗(名)[zhíyèbìng]
occupational disease
〖职业介绍所〗
[zhíyèjièshàosuǒ]
employment service agency; job centre
〖职业学校〗[zhíyèxuéxiào]
vocational school
〖职员〗(名)[zhíyuán]
staff; office worker
〖职责〗(名)[zhízé]
responsibility; duty

植(动)[zhí]
plant; grow; cultivate
〖植物〗(名)[zhíwù]
plants; botany; flora

殖[zhí]
〖殖民地〗(名)[zhímíndì]
colony

〖殖民主义〗(名)[zhímínzhǔyì]
colonialism

zhǐ

止(动、副)[zhǐ]
① stop; cease ② check; hold back; allay ③ merely; only
〖止步〗[zhǐbù]
stop; halt
〖止境〗(名)[zhǐjìng]
limit; boundary
〖止痛〗[zhǐtòng]
analgesic; allay pains; pain killing
〖止血〗[zhǐxuè]
stanch; stop bleeding

只(副)[zhǐ]
merely; only
另见 zhī
〖只得〗(副)[zhǐdé]
have to; cannot but; have no choice but to ...
〖只顾〗(副)[zhǐgù]
merely; just; be preoccupied only with ...
〖只管〗(副)[zhǐguǎn]
① go ahead; by all means ② just; merely; be concerned only with...
〖只好〗(副)[zhǐhǎo]
could not but; cannot help but
〖只见树木,不见森林〗[zhǐjiànshùmù, bùjiànsēnlín]
seeing the trees but not the forest; fail to see the wood for the trees
〖只是〗(副、连)[zhǐshì]
① only; simply ② but
〖只许州官放火,不许百姓点灯〗[zhǐxǔzhōuguānfànghuǒ, bùxǔ bǎixìngdiǎndēng]
(lit.) the magistrates were allowed to burn down houses, but the common people were forbidden even to light lamps; (fig.) the powerful can do what they want, the weak are not allowed to do anything
〖只要〗(连)[zhǐyào]
so long as; if only; provided that; on condition that
〖只有〗(连)[zhǐyǒu]
only (by); can only be ...; only in this way; only thus; not otherwise
〖只争朝夕〗[zhǐzhēngzhāoxī]
seize the day, seize the hour; seize the time

纸(名)[zhǐ]〔张 zhāng〕
paper
〖纸币〗(名)[zhǐbì]
bank note; paper currency
〖纸浆〗(名)[zhǐjiāng]
paper pulp; pulp
〖纸上谈兵〗[zhǐshàngtánbīng]
empty talk; armchair strategy; fight only on paper
〖纸张〗(名)[zhǐzhāng]
paper

指(名、动)[zhǐ]
① finger ② point at; mean; po-

int out ③ depend on; rely on
〖指标〗(名)[zhǐbiāo]
quota; aim; target
〖指出〗(动)[zhǐchū]
point out; indicate
〖指导〗(动)[zhǐdǎo]
instruct; guide; direct; lead
〖指导员〗(名)[zhǐdǎoyuán]
political instructor
〖指点〗(动)[zhǐdiǎn]
instruct; point; show; indicate
〖指定〗(动)[zhǐdìng]
appoint; assign; name; charge with
〖指挥〗(动、名)[zhǐhuī]
command; conduct; direct
〖指挥棒〗(名)[zhǐhuībàng]
〔根 gēn〕baton; club
〖指挥部〗(名)[zhǐhuībù]
headquarters; command post
〖指挥员〗(名)[zhǐhuīyuán]
commander; commanding officer
〖指甲〗(名)[zhǐjia]
nail
〖指教〗(动)[zhǐjiào]
instruct; teach; comment; advise
〖指令〗(名)[zhǐlìng]
instruction; order; command; mandatory
〖指名〗[zhǐmíng]
point out sb.'s name; mention ... by name
〖指明〗(动)[zhǐmíng]
clearly demonstrate; clearly point out
〖指南〗(名)[zhǐnán]
guide; compass
〖指南针〗(名)[zhǐnánzhēn]
compass
〖指日可待〗[zhǐrìkědài]
the day is not far off; just round the corner
〖指桑骂槐〗[zhǐsāngmàhuái]
(lit.) revile the locust while pointing to the mulberry; (fig.) curse one thing while pointing at another; make oblique accusations
〖指使〗(动)[zhǐshǐ]
instigate; incite
〖指示〗(名、动)[zhǐshì]
① indicate ② instruct; directive
〖指手画脚〗[zhǐshǒuhuàjiǎo]
order (others) about with wild gestures; carp and cavil
〖指数〗(名)[zhǐshù]
index
〖指头〗(名)[zhǐtou]〔个 gè〕
finger
〖指望〗(动)[zhǐwàng]
① look forward to; expect ② pin one's hopes on; count on
〖指引〗(动)[zhǐyǐn]
guide; conduct; lead
〖指责〗(动)[zhǐzé]
censure; blame; denounce; charge; accuse
〖指战员〗(名)[zhǐzhànyuán]
commander and fighter
〖指针〗(名)[zhǐzhēn]
guidance; direction
〖指正〗(动)[zhǐzhèng]
correct

趾 (名)[zhǐ]
toe
〖趾高气扬〗[zhǐgāoqìyáng]
give oneself airs and swagger about; breed pride and arrogance; cocky

zhì

至 (动)[zhì]
approach; reach; be until
〖至多〗(副)[zhìduō]
at most
〖至高无上〗[zhìgāowúshàng]
most lofty; supreme; paramount
〖至今〗[zhìjīn]
up to now; until now; hitherto
〖至少〗(副)[zhìshǎo]
at least; minimum
〖至于〗(连、副)[zhìyú]
as for; as to; concerning; with regard to

志 (名)[zhì]
will; ambition
〖志气〗(名)[zhìqì]
will; ambition; noble aspirations; lofty ideals
〖志趣〗(名)[zhìqù]
will and interest; aspirations
〖志士〗(名)[zhìshì]
people with lofty ideals; honest patriot
〖志同道合〗[zhìtóngdàohé]
cherish the same ideals and follow the same path; two minds with but a single thought
〖志向〗(名)[zhìxiàng]
aspiration
〖志愿〗(名)[zhìyuàn]
①will; desire; wish ②of one's own free will; voluntary

制 (动)[zhì]
①produce; make; create ②draw up; map out; work out ③restrain; subdue; tame; censure
〖制裁〗(动)[zhìcái]
impose sanction on; be dealt with according to law
〖制定〗(动)[zhìdìng]
enact; lay down; regulate; work out; adopt; devise
〖制动〗(动)[zhìdòng]
brake
〖制度〗(名)[zhìdù]
system; rule; principle; institution
〖制服〗(名)[zhìfú]〔件 jiàn〕
uniform
〖制服〗(动)[zhìfú]
subdue; conquer
〖制胜〗(动)[zhìshèng]
come out victorious; gain mastery over
〖制图〗[zhìtú]
make charts or blueprints
〖制约〗(动)[zhìyuē]
restrain
〖制造〗(动)[zhìzào]
①produce; make; manufacture ②fabricate (e.g. rumours); create (e.g. tension); foment (dissension, split, etc.)
〖制止〗(动)[zhìzhǐ]

stop; check; restrain; prevent
〖制作〗(动)[zhìzuò]
create; manufacture; form

质(名)[zhì]
①substance ②nature; character ③quality; qualitative
〖质变〗(名)[zhìbiàn]
qualitative change
〖质地〗(名)[zhìdì]
natural constitution and quality (of materials)
〖质量〗(名)[zhìliàng]
quality
〖质量第一,顾客至上〗[zhìliàngdìyī, gùkèzhìshàng]
quality first and treating the customers as supremacy
〖质量管理〗[zhìliàngguǎnlǐ]
quality control
〖质问〗(动)[zhìwèn]
query; interrogate; question; take (sb.) to task
〖质子〗(名)[zhìzǐ]
proton

治(动)[zhì]
①govern; administer; tame; manage; put under control ②cure; heal; treat ③punish
〖治安〗(名)[zhì'ān]
public security; public order
〖治本〗[zhìběn]
give fundamental treatment
〖治标〗[zhìbiāo]
alleviate symptoms (of disease or social illness)
〖治病救人〗[zhìbìngjiùrén]
cure the sickness to save the patient
〖治理〗(动)[zhìlǐ]
①govern; run; manage ②harness; tame; bring under control
〖治疗〗(动)[zhìliáo]
remedy; cure; treat; heal
〖治丧〗[zhìsāng]
funeral service; mourning service
〖治山〗[zhìshān]
transform mountains
〖治水〗[zhìshuǐ]
tame a river
〖治外法权〗[zhìwàifǎquán]
extraterritoriality

桎[zhì]
〖桎梏〗(名)[zhìgù]
shackles; yoke

致(动)[zhì]
①pay (e.g. respects); send (e.g. letter, congratulation, etc.); salute; extend (e.g. greetings) ②concentrate on; devote oneself to ③cause
〖致词〗[zhìcí]
make a speech; address
〖致敬〗(动)[zhìjìng]
salute
〖致力〗(动)[zhìlì]
devote oneself to; make efforts in; concentrate effort on
〖致命〗(形)[zhìmìng]
fatal; vital; lethal; mortal

〖致使〗(动)[zhìshǐ]
cause; bring about
〖致谢〗(动)[zhìxiè]
extend thanks to
〖致意〗(动)[zhìyì]
send one's regards; give one's compliments to; extend greetings

秩[zhì]
〖秩序〗(名)[zhìxù]
order

掷(动)[zhì]
throw; cast

窒[zhì]
〖窒息〗(动)[zhìxī]
stifle; smother; suffocate; choke

智(名)[zhì]
wisdom; intelligence; wit
〖智慧〗(名)[zhìhuì]
wisdom
〖智力〗(名)[zhìlì]
intelligence
〖智力测验〗[zhìlìcèyàn]
IQ test
〖智力投资〗[zhìlìtóuzī]
investment in intellectual development
〖智谋〗(名)[zhìmóu]
wisdom; strategy; wit
〖智取〗(动)[zhìqǔ]
outwit; take by strategy
〖智商〗(名)[zhìshāng]
intelligence quotient (IQ)
〖智育〗(名)[zhìyù]
education to develop intellectually

置(动)[zhì]
① place; put ② set aside ③ purchase; buy
〖置办〗(动)[zhìbàn]
buy
〖置换〗(动)[zhìhuàn]
displace; replace; substitute
〖置若罔闻〗[zhìruòwǎngwén]
ignore completely; take no notice of; turn a deaf ear
〖置身〗(动)[zhìshēn]
place oneself in; put oneself in
〖置于〗(动)[zhìyú]
put in; place in
〖置之不理〗[zhìzhībùlǐ]
ignore; pay no attention to; leave alone
〖置之度外〗[zhìzhīdùwài]
ignore; not take into acount; disregard

zhōng

中(名)[zhōng]
① centre; middle ② inside; among; in
另见 zhòng
〖中波〗(名)[zhōngbō]
medium wave
〖中餐〗(名)[zhōngcān]
chinese meal
〖中草药〗(名)[zhōngcǎoyào]
traditional Chinese medicinal

herbs

〖中等〗(形)[zhōngděng]
average; moderate; medium

〖中点〗(名)[zhōngdiǎn]
middle point

〖中断〗(动)[zhōngduàn]
break off; interrupt; come to a stop; disrupt

〖中国共产党〗
[ZhōngguóGòngchǎndǎng]
the Communist Party of China

〖中国共产党中央委员会〗
[ZhōngguóGòngchǎndǎng ZhōngyāngWěiyuánhuì]
the Central Committee of the Communist Party of China

〖中国共产党中央政治局〗
[ZhōngguóGòngchǎndǎng ZhōngyāngZhèngzhìjú]
the Political Bureau of the Central Committee of the Communist Party of China

〖中国共产主义青年团〗
[ZhōngguóGòngchǎnzhǔyì Qīngniántuán]
the Communist Youth League of China

〖中国工农红军〗
[ZhōngguóGōngNóngHóngjūn]
the Chinese Workers' and Peasants' Red Army

〖中国红十字会〗
[ZhōngguóHóngshízìhuì]
the Red Cross Society of China

〖中国人民解放军〗
[ZhōngguóRénmínJiěfàngjūn]
the Chinese People's Liberation Army

〖中国人民政治协商会议〗
[ZhōngguóRénmínZhèngzhì XiéshāngHuìyì]
the Chinese People's Political Consultative Conference

〖中国人民志愿军〗
[ZhōngguóRénmínZhìyuànjūn]
the Chinese People's Volunteers

〖中国少年先锋队〗
[ZhōngguóShàoniánXiānfēng duì]
the Young Pioneers of China

〖中和〗(动)[zhōnghé]
neutralize

〖中华民族〗[ZhōnghuáMínzú]
the Chinese nation

〖中华全国妇女联合会〗
[ZhōnghuáQuánguóFùnǚLián héhuì]
the All-China Women's Federation

〖中华全国总工会〗
[ZhōnghuáQuánguóZǒnggōng huì]
the All-China Federation of Trade Unions

〖中华人民共和国〗
[ZhōnghuáRénmínGònghéguó]
the People's Republic of China

〖中级〗(形)[zhōngjí]
intermediate; middle rank; secondary

〖中坚〗(名)[zhōngjiān]
centre; pillar; backbone; mainstay; nucleus of

〖中间〗(名)[zhōngjiān]
① the inside; the middle; among

② in the middle; half way; in the process
〖中间派〗(名)[zhōngjiānpài]
middle-of-the-roaders; middle section
〖中立〗(动)[zhōnglì]
neutrality; neutral; standing in the middle; neither on one side nor the other
〖中立国〗(名)[zhōnglìguó]
neutral country
〖中立化〗(动)[zhōnglìhuà]
neutralize
〖中流砥柱〗[zhōngliúdǐzhù]
pillar; rock; mainstay
〖中年〗(名)[zhōngnián]
middle-age
〖中农〗(名)[zhōngnóng]
middle peasant (the term middle peasants refers to original class status, not present economic position)
〖中篇小说〗
[zhōngpiānxiǎoshuō]
novella; novelette
〖中秋节〗[Zhōngqiūjié]
Mid-Autumn Festival
〖中山装〗(名)
[zhōngshānzhuāng]
man's jacket with closed collar
〖中世纪〗(名)[zhōngshìjì]
the Middle Ages; medieval
〖中式服装〗[zhōngshìfúzhuāng]
old style Chinese suit
〖中枢〗(名)[zhōngshū]
axis
〖中途〗(名)[zhōngtú]
midway
〖中文〗(名)[Zhōngwén]
Chinese language
〖中午〗(名)[zhōngwǔ]
midday; noon
〖中西医结合〗
[zhōngxīyījiéhé]
combination of both modern and traditional Chinese medical treatment
〖中线〗(名)[zhōngxiàn]
(math.) median (of the triangle); line from apex of triangle to middle of base
〖中心〗(名)[zhōngxīn]
centre; core; heart; key; central
〖中性〗(名)[zhōngxìng]
neutral character; neutrality
〖中学〗(名)[zhōngxué][所 suǒ]
middle school; secondary school
〖中旬〗(名)[zhōngxún]
the second ten days of a month; mid-month
〖中央〗(名)[zhōngyāng]
① centre ② central leading organ (e. g. central committee)
〖中央集权〗[zhōngyāngjíquán]
centralization; centralization of authority
〖中央委员〗
[zhōngyāngwěiyuán]
member of the central committee
〖中药〗(名)[zhōngyào]
traditional Chinese medicine
〖中叶〗(名)[zhōngyè]
middle period (e. g. dynasty, century)

Z

〖中医〗(名)[zhōngyī]
doctor of the traditional Chinese school of medicine; traditional Chinese medical science
〖中游〗(名)[zhōngyóu]
middle reaches (of a river)
〖中原〗(名)[Zhōngyuán]
the Central Plain of China
〖中子〗(名)[zhōngzǐ]
neutron

忠(名)[zhōng]
loyalty; faithfulness; devotion
〖忠诚〗(形、动)[zhōngchéng]
loyal; faithful; truthful; be staunch; be loyal; be devoted
〖忠告〗(名、动)[zhōnggào]
counsel; admonish; advise; earnest advice
〖忠实〗(形)[zhōngshí]
loyal; faithful; devoted; staunch
〖忠心〗(名)[zhōngxīn]
loyalty; faithfulness; devotion
〖忠心耿耿〗[zhōngxīngěnggěng]
infinitely loyal; loyal and devoted; most faithful and true
〖忠言逆耳〗[zhōngyánnì'ěr]
honest advice is hard to take; sincere advice jars on the ear
〖忠于〗(动)[zhōngyú]
be true to; be loyal to; be faithful to

终[zhōng]
〖终点〗(名)[zhōngdiǎn]
terminal (point)
〖终端〗(名)[zhōngduān]
terminal
〖终归〗(副)[zhōngguī]
after all; in the end; be bound to;
〖终结〗(动)[zhōngjié]
wind up; end up
〖终究〗(副)[zhōngjiū]
after all; in the end; finally
〖终了〗(动)[zhōngliǎo]
be over; be finished; end up
〖终年〗(名)[zhōngnián]
whole year round
〖终日〗(名)[zhōngrì]
all day long
〖终身〗(名)[zhōngshēn]
whole life long; life-time
〖终生〗(名)[zhōngshēng]
whole life long; life-time
〖终于〗(副)[zhōngyú]
in the end; finally; after all
〖终止〗(动)[zhōngzhǐ]
stop; cease; put an end to; conclude; close

衷[zhōng]
〖衷心〗(形)[zhōngxīn]
heartfelt; wholehearted; sincere; from the bottom of one's heart

钟(名)[zhōng][座 zuò]
① bell ② clock ③ hour (o'clock); time of the day
〖钟表〗(名)[zhōngbiǎo]

general word for clock; watch
〖钟点工〗(名)[zhōngdiǎngōng]
daily help; daily woman; time-worker
〖钟头〗(名)[zhōngtóu][个 gè]
hour

zhǒng

肿 (动)[zhǒng]
be swollen
〖肿瘤〗(名)[zhǒngliú]
tumour

种 (名、量)[zhǒng]
① seed ② race; racial ③a measure word, kind, sort, variety, species
另见 zhòng
〖种类〗(名)[zhǒnglèi]
class; kind; variety; species
〖种子〗(名)[zhǒngzi]
seed
〖种族〗(名)[zhǒngzú]
race; racial
〖种族歧视〗[zhǒngzúqíshì]
racial discrimination
〖种族主义〗(名)
[zhǒngzúzhǔyì]
racialism; racism

zhòng

中 (动)[zhòng]
① hit (e. g. target) ② be touched
另见 zhōng
〖中毒〗[zhòngdú]
be poisoned
〖中肯〗(形)[zhòngkěn]
sincere and to the point (e. g. advice)
〖中伤〗(动)[zhòngshāng]
cast slanderous remarks; hurt with damaging remarks
〖中暑〗[zhòngshǔ]
sunstroke; heat stroke

众 (形)[zhòng]
numerous; many
〖众多〗(形)[zhòngduō]
numerous
〖众口难调〗
[zhòngkǒunántiáo]
it is difficult to cater for all tastes
〖众叛亲离〗[zhòngpànqīnlí]
opposed by the masses and deserted by one's followers; be deserted by one's followers
〖众人拾柴火焰高〗
[zhòngrénshícháihuǒyàngāo]
(lit.) the fire burns high when everybody adds wood to it; (fig.) great things may be done by mass effort
〖众矢之的〗[zhòngshǐzhīdì]
under attack on all sides
〖众说纷纭〗[zhòngshuōfēnyún]
many different opinions
〖众所周知〗[zhòngsuǒzhōuzhī]
as all know; it is known to all
〖众志成城〗
[zhòngzhìchéngchéng]
a united people is like a strong city fortification; unity is

strength

重 (形)[zhòng]
① heavy; weighty ② serious ③ deep; profound (e.g. feelings)
另见 chóng
〖重兵〗(名)[zhòngbīng]
strong forces
〖重大〗(形)[zhòngdà]
important; great; vital; major
〖重担〗(名)[zhòngdàn]
heavy burden; heavy loads; heavy responsibility
〖重地〗(名)[zhòngdì]
vital centres
〖重点〗(名)[zhòngdiǎn]
focal point; emphasis; main point; key-point
〖重读〗(动)[zhòngdú]
(pron.) stress
〖重工业〗(名)[zhònggōngyè]
heavy industry
〖重活〗(名)[zhònghuó]
heavy work
〖重力〗(名)[zhònglì]
gravitation; gravity
〖重量〗(名)[zhòngliàng]
weight
〖重任〗(名)[zhòngrèn]
a task of importance; prime task; a task of great significance
〖重视〗(动)[zhòngshì]
pay great attention to; take ... seriously; attach importance to

〖重心〗(名)[zhòngxīn]
centre of gravity
〖重型〗(名)[zhòngxíng]
heavy type; heavy (e.g. machine building, equipment, etc.)
〖重要〗(形)[zhòngyào]
important; significant; essential; major
〖重音〗(名)[zhòngyīn]
stress
〖重用〗(动)[zhòngyòng]
put sb. in important position
〖重于泰山〗[zhòngyútàishān]
be weightier than Mount Tai; be of great significance

种 (动)[zhòng]
plant; sow; cultivate
另见 zhǒng
〖种地〗[zhòngdì]
do farm work
〖种痘〗[zhòngdòu]
vaccinate; vaccination
〖种瓜得瓜,种豆得豆〗
[zhòngguādéguā, zhòngdòudédòu]
plant melons and get melons, sow beans and get beans; reap what one has sown; as you make your bed, so you shall lie on it
〖种植〗(动)[zhòngzhí]
plant; sow

zhōu

舟 (名)[zhōu]
boat

周 (名、形、量)[zhōu]
① circle; circuit; circumfer-

ence ② week ③ complete; thorough; careful ④ a measure word (for week, circle, etc.)
〖周报〗(名)[zhōubào]
weekly
〖周长〗(名)[zhōucháng]
perimeter; circumference
〖周到〗(形)[zhōudào]
thoughtful; considerate
〖周而复始〗[zhōu'érfùshǐ]
go round and begin again
〖周刊〗(名)[zhōukān]
weekly magazine
〖周密〗(形)[zhōumì]
careful; thorough; well-considered
〖周年〗(名)[zhōunián]
anniversary
〖周期〗(名)[zhōuqī]
period
〖周期表〗(名)[zhōuqībiǎo]
periodic chart; periodic table
〖周期性〗(名)[zhōuqīxìng]
periodicity; cyclical character
〖周岁〗(名)[zhōusuì]
age; years of age
〖周围〗(名)[zhōuwéi]
circumference; surroundings
〖周详〗(形)[zhōuxiáng]
detailed and complete
〖周旋〗(动)[zhōuxuán]
treat; deal with; tackle
〖周游〗(动)[zhōuyóu]
tour
〖周折〗(名)[zhōuzhé]
twists and turns; tortuous course
〖周转〗(动)[zhōuzhuǎn]
① revolve; turn over; circulate ② turn round

洲 (名)[zhōu]
continent
〖洲际导弹〗[zhōujìdǎodàn]
intercontinental missile

粥 (名)[zhōu]
gruel; conjee; porridge

zhóu

轴 (名、量)[zhóu]
① axis; axle ② a measure word (for thread)
〖轴承〗(名)[zhóuchéng]
bearing; axle bearing; shaft bearing
〖轴心〗(名)[zhóuxīn]
centre of axis; axial centre

zhǒu

肘 (名)[zhǒu]
the elbow

zhòu

咒 (动)[zhòu]
curse; abuse
〖咒骂〗(动)[zhòumà]
curse; abuse; vilify

昼 (名)[zhòu]
daytime

〖昼夜〗(名)[zhòuyè]
day and night; round the clock

皱 (动)[zhòu]
wrinkle; crease; knit
〖皱纹〗(名)[zhòuwén]
line; wrinkle; crease

骤 (形)[zhòu]
sudden; unexpected
〖骤然〗(副)[zhòurán]
suddenly; unexpectedly

zhū

朱[zhū]
〖朱红〗(形)[zhūhóng]
vermilion; scarlet

珠 (名)[zhū]
① a pearl ② a bead
〖珠宝〗(名)[zhūbǎo]
pearls and jewels; jewelry
〖珠宝店〗(名)[zhūbǎodiàn]
a jeweller's
〖珠算〗(名)[zhūsuàn]
abacus; using an abacus
〖珠子〗(名)[zhūzi]〔颗 kē〕
bead

株 (量)[zhū]
a measure word (for trees)

诸[zhū]
〖诸侯〗(名)[zhūhóu]
the feudal princes
〖诸如〗(动)[zhūrú]
like; such as
〖诸如此类〗[zhūrúcǐlèi]
so on and so forth; things like this; all such things
〖诸位〗(代)[zhūwèi]
polite form of addressing a group of people

猪 (名)[zhū]〔头 tóu〕
pig
〖猪排〗(名)[zhūpái]
pork chop
〖猪皮〗(名)[zhūpí]
pigskin; hogskin
〖猪肉〗(名)[zhūròu]
pork

蛛[zhū]
spider
〖蛛丝马迹〗[zhūsīmǎjì]
(lit.) spider's web and horse's footprint; (fig.) traces; clues; hints

zhú

竹 (名)[zhú]
bamboo
〖竹竿〗(名)[zhúgān]〔根 gēn〕
bamboo pole
〖竹笋〗(名)[zhúsǔn]
bamboo shoot
〖竹子〗(名)[zhúzi]
bamboo

逐 (动)[zhú]

① chase; pursue ② drive out; expel
〖逐步〗(副)[zhúbù]
little by little; gradually; bit by bit; step by step
〖逐个〗(副)[zhúgè]
one by one
〖逐渐〗(副)[zhújiàn]
gradually; step by step
〖逐年〗(副)[zhúnián]
year by year; with each passing year
〖逐一〗(副)[zhúyī]
one by one
〖逐字逐句〗[zhúzìzhújù]
word for word; literal; literally

zhǔ

主(名)[zhǔ]
host; possessor; owner; master
〖主办〗(动)[zhǔbàn]
sponsor; be responsible for; be in charge of
〖主编〗(名、动)[zhǔbiān]
editor in chief; edit
〖主持〗(动)[zhǔchí]
①manage; direct; preside over; conduct; sponsor ② uphold; stand for
〖主次〗(名)[zhǔcì]
primary and secondary (e.g. imporance)
〖主导〗(名、形)[zhǔdǎo]
leading (factor, role, etc.); dominant (e.g. ideas, thought, etc.)
〖主动〗(形)[zhǔdòng]
initiative
〖主攻〗(动)[zhǔgōng]
main attack; assault the main target; the main direction for attack
〖主观〗(名、形)[zhǔguān]
subjective; subjectivity
〖主观能动性〗[zhǔguānnéngdòngxìng]
subjective initiative
〖主观世界〗[zhǔguānshìjiè]
subjective world
〖主观唯心主义〗[zhǔguānwéixīnzhǔyì]
subjective idealism
〖主观性〗(名)[zhǔguānxìng]
subjectivity
〖主观主义〗(名)[zhǔguānzhǔyì]
subjectivism
〖主管〗(动)[zhǔguǎn]
be responsible for; be in charge of
〖主将〗(名)[zhǔjiàng]
commanding general
〖主角〗(名)[zhǔjué]
leading actor or actress; main role; title-role
〖主力〗(名)[zhǔlì]
main forces
〖主力军〗(名)[zhǔlìjūn]
the main force; principal force
〖主流〗(名)[zhǔliú]
mainstream; main current; main trend
〖主谋〗(名)[zhǔmóu]
chief instigator
〖主权〗(名)[zhǔquán]

sovereignty
〖主人〗(名)[zhǔrén]
① host; master of the house ② master ③ owner; proprietor; possessor
〖主人翁〗(名)[zhǔrénwēng]
① master (of one's own house, country, etc.) ② hero (in story, novel, etc.)
〖主任〗(名)[zhǔrèn]
chairman; director
〖主食〗(名)[zhǔshí]
staple food
〖主使〗(动)[zhǔshǐ]
instigate
〖主题〗(名)[zhǔtí]
main theme; chief subject
〖主体〗(名)[zhǔtǐ]
mainstay; main boby; essential part
〖主席〗(名)[zhǔxí]
chairman
〖主席台〗(名)[zhǔxítái]
platform; rostrum
〖主演〗(动)[zhǔyǎn]
be the main performer
〖主要〗(形)[zhǔyào]
main; principal; essential; leading; important; major; key
〖主意〗(名)[zhǔyi]
opinion; decision; idea
〖主语〗(名)[zhǔyǔ]
(gram.) subject
〖主宰〗(动)[zhǔzǎi]
dominate; master; control; dictate
〖主张〗(名、动)[zhǔzhāng]
proposal; opinion; assertion; maintain; advocate; hold
〖主子〗(名)[zhǔzi]
boss; master; wirepuller

煮(动)[zhǔ]
cook; boil

嘱[zhǔ]
〖嘱咐〗(动)[zhǔfù]
bid; enjoin; direct; instruct
〖嘱托〗(动)[zhǔtuō]
entrust; require (sb. to do sth.)

zhù

助(动)[zhù]
help; assist; aid
〖助词〗(名)[zhùcí]
particle
〖助动词〗(名)[zhùdòngcí]
auxiliary verb
〖助理〗(名)[zhùlǐ]
assistant; helper
〖助燃〗[zhùrán]
helping to combust; combustion supporting
〖助人为乐〗[zhùrénwéilè]
take pleasure in helping others; ready to help others
〖助手〗(名)[zhùshǒu]
helping hands; assistant; helper
〖助兴〗[zhùxìng]
join in merry-making
〖助学金〗(名)[zhùxuéjīn]
student subsidies; student grant

〖助威〗[zhùwēi]
give oral or moral support; cheer sb. up
〖助长〗(动)[zhùzhǎng]
indulge; give a loose rein to

住(动)[zhù]

① live; reside; inbabit; lodge ② stop; cease
〖住房〗(名)[zhùfáng]
housing; living quarters
〖住房公积金〗[zhùfánggōngjījīn]
collective housing funds
〖住户〗(名)[zhùhù]
inhabitant
〖住口〗[zhùkǒu]
shut up; keep (one's) mouth shut
〖住手〗[zhùshǒu]
Stop! Hands off!
〖住宿〗(动)[zhùsù]
stay for the night
〖住宅〗(名)[zhùzhái]
residence; house; dwelling
〖住宅小区〗[zhùzháixiǎoqū]
residential complex; residential area
〖住址〗(名)[zhùzhǐ]
address

贮(动)[zhù]

store up; keep; reserve
〖贮藏〗(动)[zhùcáng]
hoard; save
〖贮存〗(动)[zhùcún]
stock; store up

注(动)[zhù]

① instil; inject ② concentrate; draw attention; take notice of ③ give explanation; notes
〖注册〗[zhùcè]
enroll; register
〖注定〗(动)[zhùdìng]
be doomed to (failure); be bound to
〖注解〗(动、名)[zhùjiě]
explain; explanation; notes
〖注目〗(动)[zhùmù]
focus attention; bring to one's notice
〖注入〗(动)[zhùrù]
instil; imbue; inject
〖注射〗(动)[zhùshè]
inject; injection
〖注视〗(动)[zhùshì]
watch attentively; watch with concern
〖注释〗(动、名)[zhùshì]
explain; explanation; notes
〖注销〗(动)[zhùxiāo]
write off; cancel
〖注意〗(动)[zhùyì]
pay attention to; be attentive; take notice of
〖注意力〗(名)[zhùyìlì]
attention
〖注音〗[zhùyīn]
phonetic annotation
〖注重〗(动)[zhùzhòng]
attach attention to; pay great attention to; claim one's attention; lay stress on

驻 (动)[zhù]
encamp; be stationed
〖驻地〗(名)[zhùdì]
station; garrison
〖驻防〗(动)[zhùfáng]
garrison
〖驻军〗(名)[zhùjūn]
station troops
〖驻守〗(动)[zhùshǒu]
defend with stationed troops; garrison
〖驻扎〗(动)[zhùzhā]
encamp; garrison

柱 (名)[zhù]
pillar
〖柱石〗(名)[zhùshí]
stone pillar (usu. fig.); mainstay
〖柱子〗(名)[zhùzi]〔根 gēn〕
pillar

祝 (动)[zhù]
offer (one's) compliments to; wish; greet; congratulate
〖祝词〗(名)[zhùcí]
text of a felicitation; congratulations
〖祝福〗(动)[zhùfú]
bless; wish; blessing
〖祝贺〗(动、名)[zhùhè]
congratulate; greet; congratulation

〖祝酒〗[zhùjiǔ]
toast; drink a toast
〖祝寿〗(动)[zhùshòu]
congratulate on one's birthday (for an aged person)
〖祝愿〗(动、名)[zhùyuàn]
wish; good wishes

著 (动)[zhù]
compose; write
〖著称〗(动)[zhùchēng]
be noted for; be known for
〖著名〗(形)[zhùmíng]
famous; well-known; celebrated
〖著作〗(名)[zhùzuò]
works; writings

蛀 (动)[zhù]
eat into
〖蛀虫〗(名)[zhùchóng]
moth; (insect) borer

铸 (动)[zhù]
cast (e.g. metals)
〖铸工〗(名)[zhùgōng]
foundry worker
〖铸件〗(名)[zhùjiàn]
casting; cast
〖铸造〗(动)[zhùzào]
cast; foundry

zhuā

抓 (动)[zhuā]
① clutch; grab ② scratch ③ catch; arrest ④ grasp at; seize on
〖抓耳挠腮〗[zhuā'ěrnáosāi]
twisting ears and beards (e.g. anxiously or joyously)
〖抓差〗[zhuāchāi]
draft sb. for a particular task; press sb. into service

〖抓工夫〗[zhuāgōngfu]
make good use of one's time; findtime (to do sth.)
〖抓紧〗(动)[zhuājǐn]
take a firm hold on; attend most closely to; grasp firmly

zhuān

专(形)[zhuān]
① attentive; wholehearted ② special; professional ③ arbitrary; high-handed
〖专案〗(名)[zhuān'àn]
special case
〖专长〗(名)[zhuāncháng]
professional ability; technical skill; speciality; specialized skill; be particularly good at
〖专车〗(名)[zhuānchē]
special train
〖专程〗(副)[zhuānchéng]
be on a special trip to
〖专横跋扈〗[zhuānhèngbáhù]
arbitrary; tyrannical; despotic; ride roughshod over
〖专机〗(名)[zhuānjī]
special plane
〖专家〗(名)[zhuānjiā]
specialist; expert
〖专刊〗(名)[zhuānkān]
special issue
〖专科学校〗[zhuānkēxuéxiào]
technical college; vocational school
〖专栏〗(名)[zhuānlán]
(newspaper) column; special column
〖专利〗(名)[zhuānlì]
patent
〖专利品〗(名)[zhuānlìpǐn]
patented article
〖专门〗(形)[zhuānmén]
specialized; special
〖专区〗(名)[zhuānqū]
special administrative district; administrative region; sub-provincial region
〖专题〗(名)[zhuāntí]
special theme
〖专心〗(形)[zhuānxīn]
wholehearted; attentive
〖专心致志〗[zhuānxīnzhìzhì]
devote oneself to; set one's heart on; wholehearted and exclusive
〖专业〗(名)[zhuānyè]
special line; speciality; profession
〖专业队伍〗[zhuānyèduìwǔ]
professional contingent
〖专业户〗(名)[zhuānyèhù]
specialized househlod—rural household engaging in only one kind of agricultural production
〖专用〗(动)[zhuānyòng]
(reserved) for special use
〖专政〗(名、动)[zhuānzhèng]
dictatorship; exercise dictatorship over; dictate
〖专职〗(名)[zhuānzhí]
post taken by appointed people
〖专制〗(名、动)[zhuānzhì]
tyrannize; autocratic; despot-

ic

砖 (名)[zhuān]〔块 kuài〕
brick

zhuǎn

转 (动)[zhuǎn]
① change or alter direction; turn ② send; transfer; pass on; deliver; hand over
另见 zhuàn
〖转变〗(动、名)[zhuǎnbiàn]
change into; be transformed; remould; change; transformation; alternation
〖转播〗(动)[zhuǎnbō]
relay
〖转产〗[zhuǎnchǎn]
switch to the manufacture of other products
〖转车〗[zhuǎnchē]
change train or bus halfway
〖转达〗(动)[zhuǎndá]
convey
〖转动〗(动)[zhuǎndòng]
revolve; rotate; turn about
〖转化〗(动)[zhuǎnhuà]
transform into; change into; invert; turn into; transmute
〖转换〗(动)[zhuǎnhuàn]
change; transform
〖转机〗(名)[zhuǎnjī]
a change for the better; favourable turn
〖转嫁〗(动)[zhuǎnjià]
shift...to; divert from; transfer
〖转交〗(动)[zhuǎnjiāo]
hand over; forward through; deliver through; onward transmission
〖转口贸易〗[zhuǎnkǒumàoyì]
transit (entrepot) trade
〖转念〗(动)[zhuǎnniàn]
be on second thoughts
〖转让〗(动)[zhuǎnràng]
make over; convey; transfer; alienate
〖转身〗[zhuǎnshēn]
turn round
〖转述〗(动)[zhuǎnshù]
convey (e.g. opinion); transmit
〖转瞬之间〗[zhuǎnshùnzhījiān]
in a twinkling; in the twinkling of an eye; in no time; on the instant
〖转弯〗[zhuǎnwān]
turn a corner
〖转弯抹角〗[zhuǎnwānmòjiǎo]
beat about the bush; in a roundabout way; oblique
〖转危为安〗[zhuǎnwēiwéi'ān]
carry over the crisis; be past danger
〖转学〗[zhuǎnxué]
transfer to another school
〖转眼〗(动、副)[zhuǎnyǎn]
in the twinkling of an eye
〖转业〗[zhuǎnyè]
change one's occupation or profession; switch to another type of enterprise; shift one's occupation
〖转移〗(动)[zhuǎnyí]

Z

shift; divert from; switch; move from; transfer
〖转运〗(动)[zhuǎnyùn]
transport; forward
〖转载〗(动)[zhuǎnzǎi]
reprint; reproduce
〖转战〗(动)[zhuǎnzhàn]
fight from place to place
〖转折〗(动、名)[zhuǎnzhé]
change course; turn (e.g. direction); take a turn
〖转折点〗(名)[zhuǎnzhédiǎn]
turning point
〖转正〗[zhuǎnzhèng]
(of a temporary worker) become a regular worker; pass the probationary period to become a permanent employee with fixed salary grade

zhuàn

传 (名)[zhuàn]
biography
另见 chuán
〖传记〗(名)[zhuànjì]
biography
〖传略〗(名)[zhuànlüè]
(short) biography

转 (动)[zhuàn]
turn round; revolve; rotate; roll
另见 zhuǎn
〖转动〗(动)[zhuàndòng]
revolve; rotate; turn round
〖转炉〗(名)[zhuànlú]
converter
〖转向〗[zhuànxiàng]
diversion; change direction; lose one's bearings

赚 (动)[zhuàn]
earn; gain; reap; make (money)

zhuāng

庄 (名)[zhuāng]
village
〖庄稼〗(名)[zhuāngjia]
crops
〖庄严〗(形)[zhuāngyán]
solemn; magnificent; grand; dignified
〖庄园〗(名)[zhuāngyuán]
manor; estate
〖庄重〗(形)[zhuāngzhòng]
solemn; serious

桩 (名、量)[zhuāng]
① a pile driven into the ground ② a measure word (for occurrence)
〖桩子〗(名)[zhuāngzi][根 gēn]
stake; pile

装 (动)[zhuāng]
① load; stuff; fill ② pretend; disguise ③ dress up ④ install; fix up
〖装扮〗(动)[zhuāngbàn]
dress oneself up as; deck out as; guise; make up
〖装备〗(动、名)[zhuāngbèi]

equip; furnish with; install; fit out; equipment; installation
〖装订〗(动)[zhuāngdìng]
bind (e.g. a book)
〖装潢〗(动、名)[zhuānghuáng]
furnish and decorate; furnishing and decorations
〖装甲兵〗(名)[zhuāngjiǎbīng]
armoured corps
〖装配〗(动)[zhuāngpèi]
assemble; install
〖装腔作势〗
[zhuāngqiāngzuòshì]
strike a pose; give oneself airs; have a pretentious manner
〖装饰〗(动、名)[zhuāngshì]
decorate; embellish; bedeck; adorn; decoration
〖装饰品〗(名)[zhuāngshìpǐn]
decorations; adornment; garnish
〖装束〗(动、名)[zhuāngshù]
attire; dress up
〖装卸〗(动)[zhuāngxiè]
loading and unloading
〖装载〗(动)[zhuāngzài]
transport; carry (from one place to another)
〖装置〗(动、名)[zhuāngzhì]
install; furnish with; equip with; installation; device

zhuàng

壮 (形、动)[zhuàng]
① robust; strong; stout; dauntless ② great; grand
〖壮大〗(动)[zhuàngdà]
become big and lusty; strengthen; grow in strength; expand
〖壮观〗(形)[zhuàngguān]
grandeur; grand and impressive sight
〖壮举〗(名)[zhuàngjǔ]
a great undertaking; heroic undertaking
〖壮阔〗(形)[zhuàngkuò]
grand and expansive
〖壮丽〗(形)[zhuànglì]
grand-looking; magnificent
〖壮烈〗(形)[zhuàngliè]
courageous; heroic
〖壮年〗(名)[zhuàngnián]
in one's prime; middle age
〖壮志〗(名)[zhuàngzhì]
lofty ambition; great aspiration
〖壮志凌云〗[zhuàngzhìlíngyún]
soaring determination

状 (名)[zhuàng]
① form ② condition; state of affairs
〖状况〗(名)[zhuàngkuàng]
conditions; general aspects
〖状态〗(名)[zhuàngtài]
manner or appearance; condition or state of things
〖状语〗(名)[zhuàngyǔ]
adverbial adjunct

撞 (动)[zhuàng]
collide; strike with force; knock; clash

zhuī

追 (动)[zhuī]
catch up; chase after; pursue
〖追查〗(动)[zhuīchá]
investigate; inquire; search into; find out
〖追悼〗(动)[zhuīdào]
grieve for person's death; memorial
〖追肥〗[zhuīféi]
additional fertilizer; additional manure
〖追赶〗(动)[zhuīgǎn]
chase after; run after; race with
〖追击〗(动)[zhuījī]
pursue; pursuit
〖追究〗(动)[zhuījiū]
search into; find out; carry on an inquiry
〖追求〗(动)[zhuīqiú]
seek after; pursuit of
〖追认〗(动)[zhuīrèn]
subsequent confirmation; confer posthumously
〖追溯〗(动)[zhuīsù]
trace back; investigate into the origins of
〖追随〗(动)[zhuīsuí]
follow; go after; tail behind
〖追问〗(动)[zhuīwèn]
cross-examine; get to the roots of things
〖追逐〗(动)[zhuīzhú]
chase after; pursue
〖追踪〗(动)[zhuīzōng]
pursue

锥 (名、动)[zhuī]
a drill; drill
〖锥子〗(名)[zhuīzi]〔把 bǎ〕
an awl; a drill

zhuì

坠 (动)[zhuì]
① fall ② hang; bend (e.g. under weight)
〖坠毁〗(动)[zhuìhuǐ]
crash
〖坠落〗(动)[zhuìluò]
crash; fall
〖坠入〗(动)[zhuìrù]
fall into

zhūn

谆[zhūn]
〖谆谆〗(形)[zhūnzhūn]
earnest; untiringly; unwearied

zhǔn

准 (形、动、名)[zhǔn]
① allow; permit ② exact; accurate; precise ③ accepted standards; guiding principle ④ sure; certainty
〖准备〗(动、名)[zhǔnbèi]
prepare; pave the way for; be ready; preparation; preparedness; readiness
〖准确〗(形)[zhǔnquè]
accurate; exact; precise
〖准绳〗(名)[zhǔnshéng]
criteria for; accepted standards

〖准时〗(形)[zhǔnshí]
punctual; on time
〖准许〗(动)[zhǔnxǔ]
permit; allow; consent; approve of
〖准予〗(动)[zhǔnyǔ]
give permission to
〖准则〗(名)[zhǔnzé]
guiding principle; code; accepted standards

zhuō

拙 (形)[zhuō]
stupid; dull; clumsy
〖拙笨〗(形)[zhuōbèn]
clumsy; awkward
〖拙劣〗(形)[zhuōliè]
clumsy; inferior; deficient

卓[zhuō]
〖卓见〗(名)[zhuōjiàn]
highly commendable idea; distinguished opinion
〖卓绝〗(形)[zhuōjué]
extremely; unsurpassed; exceedingly; outstanding
〖卓有成效〗
[zhuōyǒuchéngxiào]
very effective
〖卓越〗(形)[zhuōyuè]
outstanding; brilliant; distinguished
〖卓著〗(形)[zhuōzhù]
eminent; well-known; outstanding

捉 (动)[zhuō]
catch; capture; seize; arrest
〖捉摸〗(动)[zhuōmō]
conjecture; guess
〖捉弄〗(动)[zhuōnòng]
play trick upon sb.

桌 (名)[zhuō]
table; desk
〖桌布〗(名)[zhuōbù]〔块 kuài〕
table-cloth
〖桌面儿上〗[zhuōmiànrshang]
on the table
〖桌子〗(名)[zhuōzi]〔张 zhāng〕
table; desk

zhuó

灼[zhuó]
〖灼热〗(形)[zhuórè]
scalding hot

茁[zhuó]
〖茁壮〗(形)[zhuózhuàng]
sturdy; healthy and strong

浊 (形)[zhuó]
muddy; turbid
〖浊音〗(名)[zhuóyīn]
voiced consonant

酌 (动)[zhuó]
weigh and consider; consider
〖酌量〗(动)[zhuóliáng]
deal with on the merits of each case; appropriately
〖酌情〗[zhuóqíng]
according to circumstances; on

the merits of each case

啄 (动)[zhuó]
peck
〖啄木鸟〗(名)[zhuómùniǎo]
〔只 zhī〕woodpecker

琢 (动)[zhuó]
chisel; grind
另见 zuó
〖琢磨〗(动)[zhuómó]
① chisel (e.g. jade) ② polish by slow painstaking work ③ think hard; chew over
另见 zuómo

着 (动)[zhuó]
① put on; dress ② touch ③ begin; set to
另见 zhāo zháo zhe
〖着陆〗[zhuólù]
land; landing
〖着落〗(名)[zhuóluò]
① whereabouts ② a satisfactory result or settlement
〖着手〗(动)[zhuóshǒu]
begin; set to; get down to; carry out
〖着想〗(动)[zhuóxiǎng]
bear ... in mind; consider the interest of; think of
〖着眼〗(动)[zhuóyǎn]
fix one's attention on; have... in mind
〖着重〗(动)[zhuózhòng]
make a special effort to; stress; centre on; concentrate on
〖着重号〗(名)[zhuózhònghào]
emphasis mark (in writing)

zī

孜[zī]
〖孜孜不倦〗[zīzībùjuàn]
persevering; indefatigable; industrious; tireless; diligently

咨[zī]
〖咨文〗(名)[zīwén]
message (a formal official communication)
〖咨询〗(动)[zīxún]
seek advice; consult; seek the counsel of; consult
〖咨询服务〗[zīxúnfúwù]
consultant (consulting) service

姿[zī]
〖姿势〗(名)[zīshì]
gesture; gesticulation; posture
〖姿态〗(名)[zītài]
① gesture; one's bearing or carriage; form ② attitude

资[zī]
〖资本〗(名)[zīběn]
capital
〖资本家〗(名)[zīběnjiā]
capitalist
〖资本主义〗(名)[zīběnzhǔyì]
capitalism

〚资财〛[zīcái]
capital and goods; assets
〚资产〛(名)[zīchǎn]
assets; property; estate
〚资产阶级〛(名)[zīchǎnjiējí]
bourgeoisie
〚资产阶级分子〛
[zīchǎnjiējífènzǐ]
bourgeois element
〚资方〛[zīfāng]
those representing capital; capital
〚资格〛(名)[zīgé]
qualifications; have the right to; be qualified to
〚资金〛(名)[zījīn]
funds; capital
〚资历〛(名)[zīlì]
work record; qualifications and previous experience
〚资料〛(名)[zīliào]
① materials for some specific use ② data
〚资望〛[zīwàng]
seniority and prestige
〚资源〛(名)[zīyuán]
resources
〚资质〛[zīzhì]
natural endowments; intelligence
〚资助〛(动)[zīzhù]
subsidize; assist financially; give financial backing to

滋 (动)[zī]
sprout; spring up; flourish; grow
〚滋润〛(形、动)[zīrùn]
moist; moisten
〚滋生〛(动)[zīshēng]
multiply; sprout; spring up
〚滋味〛(名)[zīwèi]
taste; flavour
〚滋长〛(动)[zīzhǎng]
grow; spring up

zǐ

子 (名、尾)[zǐ]
① son ② seed ③ suffix (attached to a noun)
〚子弹〛(名)[zǐdàn][发 fā]
bullet; shell
〚子弟〛(名)[zǐdì]
① son; younger brother; nephew ② general term for young generations
〚子弟兵〛(名)[zǐdìbīng]
troops who are the sons and brothers of the people
〚子宫〛(名)[zǐgōng]
womb
〚子女〛(名)[zǐnǚ]
sons and daughters
〚子孙〛(名)[zǐsūn]
① children and grand-children; sons and grandsons ② descendents; future generation
〚子音〛(名)[zǐyīn]
consonants

仔[zǐ]
〚仔细〛(形)[zǐxì]
careful; attentive; cautious; prudent

紫 (形)[zǐ]
violet
〖紫红〗(形)[zǐhóng]
purple
〖紫外线〗(名)[zǐwàixiàn]
ultraviolet rays

zì

自(代、介、副)[zì]
①self; oneself ②from; since ③naturally; spontaneously
〖自白〗(名)[zìbái]
confession; make a clean breast of
〖自暴自弃〗[zìbàozìqì]
throw oneself away; abandon oneself to despair;give oneself up to vice
〖自卑〗(形)[zìbēi]
inferiority; self-abased
〖自吹自擂〗[zìchuīzìléi]
brag and boast; blow one's own trumpet; self-praise
〖自从〗(介)[zìcóng]
from; since
〖自大〗(形)[zìdà]
self-important; arrogant; conceited
〖自动〗(形)[zìdòng]
automatic
〖自动化〗(动)[zìdònghuà]
automate; automation; automatize
〖自发〗(动)[zìfā]
spontaneous (e.g. trend, force, struggle, etc.)
〖自费〗(名)[zìfèi]
at one's own expense
〖自封〗(动)[zìfēng]
self-appointed; proclaim oneself; self-styled
〖自负〗(形)[zìfù]
① conceited; proud ② sole responsibility for (e.g. one's own profits or losses)
〖自高自大〗[zìgāozìdà]
full of vainglory; conceit; be disgustingly self-satisfied; arrogance
〖自告奋勇〗[zìgàofènyǒng]
volunteer one's service for; willingly take the responsibility upon oneself
〖自供状〗(名)[zìgòngzhuàng]
self-confession
〖自顾不暇〗[zìgùbùxiá]
unable even to fend for oneself
〖自豪〗(形)[zìháo]
pride; proud of
〖自己〗(代)[zìjǐ]
oneself; one's own
〖自己人〗[zìjǐrén]
one of us
〖自给〗(动)[zìjǐ]
be self-supporting; self-sufficiency; be self-reliant
〖自给自足〗[zìjǐzìzú]
self-reliant; self-sufficiency; able to support oneself
〖自居〗(动)[zìjū]
style oneself; claim to be ; consider oneself to be
〖自觉〗(形)[zìjué]
self-conscious; awakened; aware

〖自觉性〗(名)[zìjuéxìng]
self-awakening; consiousness; awareness
〖自觉自愿〗[zìjuézìyuàn]
voluntary and conscious; of one's own accord; willing; be ready to
〖自绝〗(动)[zìjué]
alienate oneself from
〖自夸〗(动)[zìkuā]
boast; talk big; plume oneself
〖自来水〗(名)[zìláishuǐ]
tap water; pipe water
〖自力更生〗[zìlìgēngshēng]
rely on one's own efforts; self-reliance; self-reliant
〖自立〗(动)[zìlì]
support oneself; rely on oneself
〖自流〗(动)[zìliú]
①be left to take its own course ②drift along; let things slide
〖自留地〗(名)[zìliúdì]
private plots; plots for private use
〖自满〗(形)[zìmǎn]
complacent; self-satisfied; conceited
〖自命不凡〗[zìmìngbùfán]
think of oneself as superior being; pride oneself on being out of the ordinary
〖自欺欺人〗[zìqīqīrén]
try to deceive others only to end in deceiving oneself; deceive oneself and others; sheer hypocrisy
〖自然〗(名、形、副)[zìrán]
①nature ②natural; naturally; spontaneously
〖自然辩证法〗
[zìránbiànzhèngfǎ]
natural dialectics
〖自然规律〗[zìránguīlǜ]
natural laws; law of nature
〖自然科学〗[zìránkēxué]
natural sciences
〖自然主义〗(名)[zìránzhǔyì]
naturalism
〖自燃〗[zìrán]
spontaneous combustion; self-ignite
〖自如〗(形)[zìrú]
skilfully (e.g. apply); freely
〖自杀〗(动)[zìshā]
commit suicide
〖自身〗(名)[zìshēn]
oneself
〖自食其果〗[zìshíqíguǒ]
reap what one has sown; be made to pay for one's evil doing; court self-destruction
〖自食其力〗[zìshíqílì]
earn one's own living; live on one's own toil; self-supporting
〖自首〗(动)[zìshǒu]
give oneself up to (law); make confession
〖自私〗(形)[zìsī]
selfish; egotistic
〖自私自利〗[zìsīzìlì]
selfish; selfishness
〖自投罗网〗[zìtóuluówǎng]
fall into a trap through one's own fault; fall into one's own

snare
〖自卫〗(动)[zìwèi]
defend oneself; self-defence
〖自卫战争〗[zìwèi zhànzhēng]
war of self-defence
〖自我〗(代)[zìwǒ]
oneself
〖自我批评〗[zìwǒpīpíng]
self-criticism
〖自习〗(动)[zìxí]
review one's lessons
〖自信〗(动)[zìxìn]
believe in oneself; self-confidence
〖自行〗(副)[zìxíng]
① by oneself; of one's own accord; ② spontaneously
〖自行车〗(名)[zìxíngchē]
〔辆 liàng〕bicycle
〖自修〗(动)[zìxiū]
study on one's own
〖自诩〗(动)[zìxǔ]
brag and boast; self-important
〖自学〗(动)[zìxué]
study by oneself
〖自学成才〗[zìxuéchéngcái]
become educated through independent study
〖自学考试〗[zìxuékǎoshì]
examination for the selftaught
〖自以为是〗[zìyǐwéishì]
consider oneself always in the right; be cocksure
〖自由〗(名、形)[zìyóu]
freedom; liberty
〖自由竞争〗[zìyóujìngzhēng]
free competition
〖自由落体〗[zìyóuluòtǐ]
free falling body
〖自由体操〗[zìyóutǐcāo]
free exercises; floor exercises
〖自由王国〗[zìyóuwángguó]
the realm of freedom
〖自由泳〗(名)[zìyóuyǒng]
free style
〖自由职业者〗[zìyóuzhíyèzhě]
professionals; professional men
〖自由主义〗(名)[zìyóuzhǔyì]
liberalism
〖自圆其说〗[zìyuánqíshuō]
make out a good case; justify oneself; justify one's argument
〖自愿〗(动)[zìyuàn]
be of one's own free will; on one's own initiative; voluntarily; willingly
〖自在〗(形)[zìzài]
① carefree; without the least worry ② comfortable; pleasant
〖自知之明〗[zìzhīzhīmíng]
know oneself
〖自治〗(动)[zìzhì]
exercise autonomy; autonomous rule
〖自治区〗(名)[zìzhìqū]
autonomous region
〖自治权〗(名)[zìzhìquán]
autonomy
〖自治县〗(名)[zìzhìxiàn]
autonomous county
〖自治州〗(名)[zìzhìzhōu]
autonomous district
〖自主〗(动)[zìzhǔ]

be independent; be one's own master

〖自主权〗(名)[zìzhǔquán]
autonomy; decision making power

〖自助〗(动)[zìzhù]
self-service; do-it-yourself

〖自助餐〗(名)[zìzhùcān]
buffet

〖自转〗(动)[zìzhuǎn]
rotate

〖自传〗(名)[zìzhuàn]
autobiography

〖自尊心〗(名)[zìzūnxīn]
self-respect

〖自作聪明〗[zìzuòcōngmíng]
fancy oneself clever; consider oneself to be clever

字(名)[zì]
character

〖字典〗(名)[zìdiǎn]
〔本 běn、部 bù〕dictionary

〖字迹〗(名)[zìjì]
one's handwriting

〖字据〗(名)[zìjù]
a written receipt

〖字里行间〗[zìlǐhángjiān]
between the lines

〖字面〗(名)[zìmiàn]
the literal sense (of the word)

〖字母〗(名)[zìmǔ]
letters of the alphabet

〖字幕〗(名)[zìmù]
captions; subtitle

〖字体〗(名)[zìtǐ]
the form of a written character; type

〖字帖〗(名)[zìtiè]〔本 běn〕
copy-book; reproductions of the works of master calligraphers

zōng

宗(量)[zōng]
a measure word (for a large sum of money, goods, etc.)

〖宗教〗(名)[zōngjiào]
religion

〖宗派〗(名)[zōngpài]
faction; sectarian; group; sect

〖宗派主义〗(名)[zōngpàizhǔyì]
factionalism; sectarianism

〖宗旨〗(名)[zōngzhǐ]
purpose; aim; intention; object

〖宗族〗(名)[zōngzú]
clan; tribe

综[zōng]

〖综合〗(动)[zōnghé]
① sum up ② integrate; synthesize; multiple; comprehensive

踪(名)[zōng]
trace; footprint

〖踪迹〗(名)[zōngjì]
trace; footprint; track; vestige

〖踪影〗(名)[zōngyǐng]
trace; sight

zǒng

总(动、形、副)[zǒng]
①collect; gather; assemble; add together ②general; main; chief③total; in all; overall; gross amount ④at any rate; in a word; anyway; anyhow
〖总得〗(助动)[zǒngděi]
have to; must
〖总动员〗[zǒngdòngyuán]
general mobilization; mobilize all
〖总额〗(名)[zǒng'é]
grand total; total sum; total
〖总而言之〗[zǒng'éryánzhī]
in a word; in short; put it briefly
〖总纲〗(名)[zǒnggāng]
general programme
〖总共〗(副)[zǒnggòng]
altogether; in all; in sum; gross amount; in its entirety
〖总归〗(副)[zǒngguī]
in the end; anyway; anyhow
〖总和〗(名)[zǒnghé]
the sum and substance of
〖总计〗(动)[zǒngjì]
amount to; add up; total
〖总结〗(动、名)[zǒngjié]
sum up; summary
〖总括〗(动)[zǒngkuò]
sum up; put in a nutshell
〖总理〗(名)[zǒnglǐ]
premier; prime minster
〖总量〗(名)[zǒngliàng]
the grand total
〖总是〗(副)[zǒngshì]
always; generally
〖总数〗(名)[zǒngshù]
total amount; sum total
〖总算〗(副)[zǒngsuàn]
①finally ②at least
〖总体〗(名)[zǒngtǐ]
sum total; totality
〖总统〗(名)[zǒngtǒng]
president
〖总务〗(名)[zǒngwù]
general affairs
〖总则〗(名)[zǒngzé]
general rules; general provisions
〖总之〗(连)[zǒngzhī]
in short; in a word; at any rate

zòng

纵(名、动)[zòng]
①vertical; from north to south ②leap forward or upwards
〖纵队〗(名)[zòngduì]
(mil.) column; brigade
〖纵横〗(动)[zònghéng]
① vertically and horizontally; perpendicular and horizontal; ② length and breadth
〖纵横交错〗[zònghéngjiāocuò]
crisscross; crosswise
〖纵虎归山〗[zònghǔguīshān]
(lit.) allow a tiger back to the mountain; (fig.) allow the enemy or bad element to escape
〖纵情〗(副)[zòngqíng]
indulge one's passions; indulge oneself
〖纵然〗(连)[zòngrán]

even if

〖纵容〗(动)[zòngróng]
connive at; be indulgent; tolerate; pamper

〖纵身〗(动)[zòngshēn]
leap forward or upwards

〖纵深〗(名)[zòngshēn]
deep and penetrating; in depth

〖纵使〗(连)[zòngshǐ]
even if

zǒu

走(动)[zǒu]
①walk; move; go ②leave; depart

〖走动〗(动)[zǒudòng]
walk around; move about

〖走狗〗(名)[zǒugǒu]
lackey; running dog; stooge

〖走过场〗[zǒu guòchǎng]
make sth. a sham; reduced to mere formality

〖走红〗[zǒuhóng]
be in the luck; become popular; make a hit

〖走后门〗[zǒuhòumén]
a backdoor deal; through the "back door"

〖走火〗[zǒuhuǒ]
① fire accidentally ② short-circuited

〖走廊〗(名)[zǒuláng]
corridor;passageway

〖走漏〗(动)[zǒulòu]
leak out; let out (a secret)

〖走路〗[zǒulù]
walk

〖走马看花〗[zǒumǎkànhuā]
(lit.) look at the flowers while on horseback; (fig.) take a hurried glance; glance over sth.

〖走投无路〗[zǒutóuwúlù]
find oneself cornered; go down a blind alley; come to an impasse

〖走向〗(动、名)[zǒuxiàng]
① head towards; walk towards ② alignment

〖走穴〗[zǒuxué]
(of an actor, singer, etc.) take one's show on the road

〖走样〗[zǒuyàng]
change in shape

〖走私〗[zǒusī]
smuggle

〖走卒〗(名)[zǒuzú]
cat's paw; stooge; lackey

zòu

奏(动)[zòu]
①play music ②prove effective

〖奏效〗[zòu xiào]
show results; prove effective

〖奏乐〗[zòuyuè]
play music; strike up

揍(动)[zòu]
hit; beat; strike

zū

租(动、名)[zū]
lease; rent; taxes

〖租界〗(名)[zūjiè]
concession; foreign settlement; leased territory

〖租借〗(动)[zūjiè]
lease
〖租赁〗(动)[zūlìn]
rent; lease; hire

zú

足(名、形)[zú]
① foot ② enough; full; sufficient; ample
〖足够〗(动)[zúgòu]
be sufficient; adequate; ample
〖足迹〗(名)[zújī]
trace; footprints
〖足球〗(名)[zúqiú][个 gè]
football
〖足以〗(副)[zúyǐ]
enough to...

zǔ

诅[zǔ]
〖诅咒〗(动)[zǔzhòu]
curse; abuse

阻[zǔ]
〖阻碍〗(动、名)[zǔ'ài]
stand in the way; obstruct; hinder
〖阻挡〗(动)[zǔdǎng]
block; hold back; stop
〖阻击〗(动)[zǔjī]
intercept; hold off and attack (e.g. the enemy)
〖阻拦〗(动)[zǔlán]
hinder; obstruct; stop
〖阻力〗(名)[zǔlì]
resistance
〖阻挠〗(动)[zǔnáo]
hamper; hinder; check
〖阻塞〗(动)[zǔsè]
block; obstruct
〖阻止〗(动)[zǔzhǐ]
prevent; obstruct; stop; hold up; check; hinder

组(名)[zǔ]
a group; section; unit
〖组成〗(动)[zǔchéng]
constitute; be composed of; make up; consist of
〖组合〗(动、名)[zǔhé]
① be composed of; make up ② (math.) combinations
〖组合家具〗[zǔhéjiājù]
unit furniture; assembled furniture
〖组合音响〗[zǔhéyīnxiǎng]
music centre; stereo set
〖组织〗(动、名)[zǔzhī]
organize; organization
〖组织路线〗[zǔzhīlùxiàn]
organizational line
〖组织性〗(名)[zǔzhīxìng]
sense of organization
〖组装〗(动)[zǔzhuāng]
assemble sth. with imported assembly parts (opposite of being completely manufactured in country of origin)

祖[zǔ]
〖祖父〗(名)[zǔfù]
grandfather
〖祖国〗(名)[zǔguó]
motherland

〖祖母〗(名)[zǔmǔ]
grandmother
〖祖先〗(名)[zǔxiān]
forefather; forebear; ancestor
〖祖宗〗(名)[zǔzōng]
ancestry; ancestor
〖祖祖辈辈〗[zǔzǔbèibèi]
for generations

zuān

钻(动)[zuān]
drill; bore; go through; worm through
另见 zuàn
〖钻空子〗[zuānkòngzi]
avail oneself of loopholes
〖钻探〗(动)[zuāntàn]
drill; bore
〖钻研〗(动)[zuānyán]
make an intensive study of

zuàn

钻(名)[zuàn]
auger; drill; bit
另见 zuān
〖钻床〗(名)[zuànchuáng]
driller; drilling machine
〖钻机〗(名)[zuànjī]
drilling machine; boring machine
〖钻石〗(名)[zuànshí]
diamond
〖钻头〗(名)[zuàntóu]
drill; boring head

攥(动)[zuàn]
clasp; clutch; clench

zuǐ

嘴(名)[zuǐ]〔张 zhāng〕
mouth
〖嘴巴〗(名)[zuǐba]
mouth
〖嘴唇〗(名)[zuǐchún]
lip
〖嘴脸〗(名)[zuǐliǎn]
(derog.) face; physiognomy

zuì

最(副)[zuì]
①most; best; to the highest degree ②least
〖最初〗(名)[zuìchū]
at first; at the very beginning; original; initial
〖最好〗(副)[zuìhǎo]
①best of all ②had better
〖最后〗(名)[zuìhòu]
final; the last; eventual; ultimate
〖最后通牒〗[zuìhòutōngdié]
ultimatum
〖最惠国待遇〗[zuìhuìguódàiyù]
most-favoured-nation treatment
〖最近〗(名)[zuìjìn]
recently; of late; lately

罪(名)[zuì]
offence; crime; guilt
〖罪大恶极〗[zuìdà'èjí]
most heinous crimes; be guilty of terrible crimes
〖罪恶〗(名)[zuì'è]
evil; sin; wickedness; crime

〖罪恶滔天〗[zuì'ètāotiān]
monstrous crimes
〖罪犯〗(名)[zuìfàn]
criminal; convict
〖罪过〗(名)[zuìguò]
crime; sin; wrong
〖罪魁祸首〗[zuìkuíhuòshǒu]
chief criminal; arch-criminal
〖罪名〗(名)[zuìmíng]
criminal charge
〖罪孽〗(名)[zuìniè]
sin; crime; evil; iniquity
〖罪行〗(名)[zuìxíng]
criminal act; vicious act
〖罪证〗(名)[zuìzhèng]
evidence of crimes
〖罪状〗(名)[zuìzhuàng]
crime; guilt; charge

醉(动)[zuì]
be drunk
〖醉心〗(动)[zuìxīn]
be preoccupied with; be fascinated with; be infatuated with; be obsessed with; be drunk with
〖醉醺醺〗(形)[zuìxūnxūn]
tipsy; fuddled (drunk)

zūn

尊[zūn]
〖尊称〗(名)[zūnchēng]
term of respect; respectful appellation
〖尊崇〗(动)[zūnchóng]
hold in high esteem; honour; respect
〖尊贵〗(形)[zūnguì]
respectable; honourable
〖尊敬〗(动)[zūnjìng]
respect; esteem; revere
〖尊严〗(名)[zūnyán]
dignity
〖尊重〗(动)[zūnzhòng]
hold in esteem; respect

遵[zūn]
〖遵从〗(动)[zūncóng]
obey; follow
〖遵命〗[zūnmìng]
in compliance with the order
〖遵守〗(动)[zūnshǒu]
observe; adhere to; abide by
〖遵循〗(动)[zūnxún]
follow; abide by; comply with; act in accordance with
〖遵义会议〗[ZūnyìHuìyì]
Tsunyi Meeting (the enlarged meeting of the Political Bureau of the Central Commitee of the Communist Party of China which was convened in Tsunyi, Kweichow, in January 1935)
〖遵照〗(动)[zūnzhào]
adhere to; conform to; according to; comply with

zuó

昨[zuó]
〖昨天〗(名)[zuótiān]
yesterday

琢[zuó]
另见 zhuó

〖琢磨〗(动)[zuómo]
ponder deeply over sth.; mull sth. over; think carefully
另见 zhuómó

zuǒ

左(名、形)[zuǒ]
left
〖左边〗(名)[zuǒbian]
left side
〖左顾右盼〗[zuǒgùyòupàn]
peep right and left at each step; with one's heart in one's mouth
〖左面〗(名)[zuǒmiàn]
left side
〖左派〗(名)[zuǒpài]
leftist
〖左倾〗(名)[zuǒqīng]
"Left" deviation
〖左倾机会主义〗[zuǒqīngjīhuìzhǔyì]
"left" opportunism
〖左说右说〗[zuǒshuōyòushuō]
say sth. over and over again
〖左思右想〗[zuǒsīyòuxiǎng]
think of this and that; turn over in the mind; rack one's brains; keep thinking
〖左一趟右一趟〗[zuǒyītàngyòuyītàng]
many a time; over and over again
〖左翼〗(名)[zuǒyì]
left wing; left flank
〖左右〗(名、动)[zuǒyòu]
① both sides; the left and the right ② about; approximately ③ dominate; hold (sb.) under one's thumb; control
〖左右逢源〗[zuǒyòuféngyuán]
win advantage from both sides

zuò

作(动)[zuò]
① make ② write; compose; work at ③ take sth. as
〖作罢〗(动)[zuòbà]
give up; dismiss
〖作弊〗[zuòbì]
practise fraud; indulge in corrupt practices
〖作对〗(动)[zuòduì]
set against; be opposed to
〖作废〗(动)[zuòfèi]
declare invalid; make null and void
〖作风〗(名)[zuòfēng]
style of work; working style
〖作梗〗(动)[zuògěng]
obstruct; impede; hamper; hinder
〖作怪〗(动)[zuòguài]
make trouble; play tricks; be a nuisance; do mischief
〖作家〗(名)[zuòjiā]
writer; author
〖作茧自缚〗[zuòjiǎnzìfù]
(lit.) weave a cocoon and get imprisoned in it; (fig.) be caught in one's own trap
〖作客〗[zuòkè]
be a guest
〖作料〗(名)[zuòliao]
ingredient; condiment

〖作难〗(动)[zuònán]
put obstacles in the way; make it difficult for....
〖作陪〗(动)[zuòpéi]
keep company
〖作品〗(名)[zuòpǐn]
a literary or artistic work; composition
〖作曲〗[zuòqǔ]
compose; musical composition
〖作曲家〗(名)[zuòqǔjiā]
composer
〖作祟〗(动)[zuòsuì]
cause trouble; make mischief; play tricks
〖作威作福〗[zuòwēizuòfú]
abuse one's power tyrannically; ride roughshod over; play the tyrant
〖作为〗(动、名)[zuòwéi]
①behaviour ② accomplishments; achievements; make contributions; make achievements ③ regard as; serve as
〖作文〗(名)[zuòwén]
composition; essay; article
〖作息〗(动)[zuòxī]
work and rest
〖作业〗(名)[zuòyè]
① work ② homework
〖作用〗(名、动)[zuòyòng]
① function; result; consequence ② work; produce effect; act; function
〖作用点〗(名)[zuòyòngdiǎn]
point of action
〖作用力〗(名)[zuòyònglì]
force of action; mechanism of action
〖作战〗(动)[zuòzhàn]
fight; make war; operations; fighting
〖作者〗(名)[zuòzhě]
author

坐(动)[zuò]
① sit ② go by; ride in (car, boat, airplane, etc.)
〖坐标〗(名)[zuòbiāo]
coordinates
〖坐标轴〗(名)[zuòbiāozhóu]
coordinate axis
〖坐井观天〗[zuòjǐngguāntiān]
(lit.) see the sky from the bottom of a well; (fig.) take a narrow view of things
〖坐牢〗[zuòláo]
be put in prison; be imprisoned; be sent to jail
〖坐立不安〗[zuòlìbù'ān]
restless; on pins and needles
〖坐落〗(动)[zuòluò]
situate; locate
〖坐山观虎斗〗
[zuòshānguānhǔdòu]
(lit.) sit on top of the mountain to watch the tigers fight; (fig.) see both sides jump on each other and not get involved in it
〖坐视〗(动)[zuòshì]
look on with indifference; sit by and watch
〖坐卧不宁〗[zuòwòbùníng]
unable to sit down or sleep at ease; be uneasy in one's sitting

and sleeping

〖坐享其成〗[zuòxiǎngqíchéng]
sit around waiting to share the victory or success of others with folded arms

座(量)[zuò]

a measure word (for mountain, bridge, tall building, reservoir, etc.)

〖座次〗(名)[zuòcì]
order of seats

〖座谈〗(动)[zuòtán]
have a discussion meeting

〖座谈会〗(名)[zuòtánhuì]
forum; symposium; discussion meeting

〖座位〗(名)[zuòwèi]
seat

〖座无虚席〗[zuòwúxūxí]
no empty seat

〖座右铭〗(名)[zuòyòumíng]
motto; maxim

〖座子〗(名)[zuòzi]
① rack; stand (e.g. of a clock) ② seat (of bicycle, etc.)

做(动)[zuò]

① do; work; undertake ② make ③ write

〖做伴〗[zuòbàn]
keep sb. company

〖做法〗(名)[zuòfǎ]
way of making things; ways and means; tactics

〖做工〗[zuògōng]
do (manual) work

〖做客〗[zuòkè]
be guest

〖做梦〗[zuòmèng]
dream

〖做贼心虚〗[zuòzéixīnxū]
have a guilty conscience like a thief

〖做主〗[zuòzhǔ]
decide (things) for oneself; take (matters) into one's own hand

〖做作〗(形)[zuòzuo]
unnatural; pretentious; affected

计量单位简表
Weights and Measures

	市制及进位法 Chinese System	折合公制 Metric Value	折合英美制 British and U.S. Value
长度 Length	1分(10厘)		
	1寸(10分)	3.3333 厘米(cm.)	1.3123 吋(in.)
	1尺(10寸)	0.3333 米(m.)	1.0936 呎(ft.)
	1丈(10尺)	3.3333 米(m.)	3.6454 码(yd.)
	1里(150丈)	0.5000 公里(km.) 0.2700 浬(nautical mile)	0.3107 哩(mi.)
面积和地积 Area	1平方尺(100平方寸)	0.1111 平方米(sq.m.)	1.1960 平方呎(sq.ft.)
	1平方丈(100平方尺)	11.1111 平方米(sq.m.)	
	1平方里(22500平方丈)	0.2500 平方公里(sq.km.)	0.0965 平方哩(sq.mi.)
	1分(6平方丈)		
	1亩(10分)	6.6667 公亩(a.) 0.0667 公顷(ha.)	0.1644 畂(a.)
	1顷(100亩)	6.6667 公顷(ha.)	

	市制及进位法 Chinese System	折合公制 Metric Value	折合英美制 British and U.S. Value
体积和容量 Physical volume and capacity	1立方尺(1000立方寸)	0.0370 立方米(cubic m.)	1.3078 立方呎(cubic ft.)
	1 立方丈(1000 立方尺)	37.0370 立方米(cubic m.)	
	1 合	100 毫升(ml.)	
	1 升(10 合)	1 升(l.)	1.7598 品脱(英)(pt.) 0.2200 加仑(英)(gal.)
	1 斗(10 升)	10 升(l.)	
	1 石(10 斗)	100 升(l.)	2.7498 蒲式耳(英)(bu.)
重量 Weight	1钱	5克(g.)	
	1两(10 钱)	50 克(g.)	1.7637 盎司(常衡) 1.7637 oz.(Avoirdupois)
	1 斤(10 两)	0.5000 公斤(kg.)	1.1023 磅(常衡) 1.1023 lb.(Avoirdupois)
	1 担(100 斤)	0.5000 公担(q.)	

化 学 元 素 表

Chemical Elements

原子序数 Atomic Number	元素名称 Names of Elements		符 号 Symbols	英文名称 English Names
1	氢	qīng	H	hydrogen
2	氦	hài	He	helium
3	锂	lǐ	Li	lithium
4	铍	pí	Be	beryllium
5	硼	péng	B	boron
6	碳	tàn	C	cabon
7	氮	dàn	N	nitrogen
8	氧	yǎng	O	oxygen
9	氟	fú	F	fluorine
10	氖	nǎi	Ne	neon
11	钠	nà	Na	sodium
12	镁	měi	Mg	magnesium
13	铝	lǚ	Al	aluminium
14	硅	guī	Si	silicon
15	磷	lín	P	phosphorus
16	硫	liú	S	sulfur
17	氯	lǜ	Cl	chiorine
18	氩	yà	Ar	argon
19	钾	jiǎ	K	potassium
20	钙	gài	Ca	calcium
21	钪	kàng	Sc	scandium
22	钛	tài	Ti	titanium
23	钒	fán	V	vanadium
24	铬	gè	Cr	chromium
25	锰	měng	Mn	manganese
26	铁	tiě	Fe	iron

原子序数 Atomic Number	元素名称 Names of Elements		符号 Symbols	英文名称 English Names
27	钴	gǔ	Co	cobalt
28	镍	niè	Ni	nickel
29	铜	tóng	Cu	copper
30	锌	xīn	Zn	zinc
31	镓	jiā	Ga	gallium
32	锗	zhě	Ge	germanium
33	砷	shēn	As	arsenic
34	硒	xī	Se	selenium
35	溴	xiù	Br	bromine
36	氪	kè	Kr	krypton
37	铷	rú	Rb	rubium
38	锶	sī	Sr	strontium
39	钇	yǐ	Y	yttrium
40	锆	gào	Zr	zirconium
41	铌	nì	Nb	niobium
42	钼	mù	Mo	molybdenum
43	锝	dé	Tc	technetium
44	钌	liǎo	Ru	ruthenium
45	铑	lǎo	Rh	rhodium
46	钯	bǎ	Pd	palladium
47	银	yín	Ag	silver
48	镉	gé	Cd	cadmium
49	铟	yīn	In	indium
50	锡	xī	Sn	tin
51	锑	tī	Sb	antimony
52	碲	dì	Te	tellruium
53	碘	diǎn	I	iodine
54	氙	xiān	Xe	xenon
55	铯	sè	Cs	cesium

原子序数 Atomic Number	元素名称 Names of Elements		符号 Symbols	英文名称 English Names
56	钡	bèi	Ba	barium
57	镧	lán	La	lanthanum
58	铈	shì	Ce	cerium
59	镨	pǔ	Pr	Praseodymium
60	钕	nǚ	Nd	neodymium
61	钷	pǒ	Pm	promethium
62	钐	shān	Sm	smarium
63	铕	yǒu	Eu	europium
64	钆	gá	Gd	gadolinium
65	铽	tè	Tb	terbium
66	镝	dì	Dy	dysprosium
67	钬	huǒ	Ho	holmium
68	铒	ěr	Er	erbium
69	铥	diū	Tm	thulium
70	镱	yì	Yb	ytterbium
71	镥	lǔ	Lu	lutecium
72	铪	hā	Hf	hafnium
73	钽	tǎn	Ta	tantalum
74	钨	wū	W	tungsten
75	铼	lái	Re	rhenium
76	锇	é	Os	osmium
77	铱	yī	Ir	iridium
78	铂	bó	Pt	platinum
79	金	jīn	Au	gold
80	汞	gǒng	Hg	mercury
81	铊	tā	Tl	thallium
82	铅	qiān	Pb	lead
83	铋	bì	Bi	bismuth
84	钋	pō	Po	polonium

原子序数 Atomic Number	元素名称 Names of Elements		符号 Symbols	英文名称 English Names
85	砹	ài	At	astatine
86	氡	dōng	Rn	radon
87	钫	fāng	Fr	fracium
88	镭	léi	Ra	radium
89	锕	ā	Ac	actinium
90	钍	tǔ	Th	thorium
91	镤	pú	Pa	protactinium
92	铀	yóu	U	uranium
93	镎	ná	Np	neptunium
94	钚	bù	Pu	plutonium
95	镅	méi	Am	americium
96	锔	jú	Cm	curium
97	锫	péi	Bk	berkelium
98	锎	kāi	Cf	californium
99	锿	āi	Es	einstenium
100	镄	fèi	Fm	fermium
101	钔	mén	Md	mendelevium
102	锘	nuò	No	nobelium
103	铹	láo	Lr	lawrencium